Random House Webster's Pocket Japanese Dictionary

Second Edition

Japanese • English
English • Japanese

D0028091

RANDOM HOUSE
NEW YORK

This book was originally published as the *Random House Japanese Dictionary* in 1996. Adapted from the *Random House Japanese-English English-Japanese Dictionary*, compiled by Seigo Nakao, published in 1995. Copyright © 1995 by Random House, Inc

This book is available for special purchases in bulk by organizations and institutions, not for resale, at special discounts. Please direct your inquiries to the Random House Special Sales Department, toll-free 888-591-1200 or fax 212-572-4961.

Please address inquiries about electronic licensing of this division's products, for use on a network or in software or on CD-ROM, to the Subsidiary Rights Department, Random House Reference & Information Publishing, fax 212-940-7370.

Typeset and Printed in the United States of America.

Visit the Random House Reference & Information Publishing Web site at www.randomwords.com

First Edition
0 9 8 7 6 5 4
ISBN: 0-679-77373-8

New York   Toronto   London   Sydney   Auckland

Guide to the Dictionary

Main Features

The *Random House Japanese Dictionary* is primarily intended for two types of English-speaking users: those who have no knowledge of Japanese and those who already have some knowledge of the language but still need a dictionary in which all Japanese words and phrases are explained from the standpoint of English and in English grammatical terms. It should also prove indispensable to anyone who needs a bilingual dictionary that presents the basic vocabulary of both languages in an accessible, easy to use format.

Since the Japanese written forms of Japanese words are given after the romanized form on first mention within an entry, the dictionary will also serve as an aid to those who are learning to read and write the language. Because the romanized forms always appear first, the user does not have to know the Japanese writing system to look up a word or pinpoint a definition.

Arrangement and Content of Entries

In both sections of the dictionary, Japanese to English and English to Japanese, **main entries** are in strict letter-by-letter alphabetical order, ignoring punctuation and parentheses except when doing so would violate common sense. (A special case is the many Japanese adjectives that are followed by the syllable **na** or **no** in parentheses: alphabetization stops before the parenthesis when listing these as entries.)

In both sections, **main entries** are in boldface type. Many entries in both sections contain **subentries,** which are also in boldface type. These subentries, which consist of idioms, common expressions, compounds, phrases, and example sentences, increase the usefulness of the dictionary, and they were included to the extent permitted by space limitations.

Japanese–English Section

In this section, the boldfaced Japanese **main entry** in **rōmaji** (roman letters) is followed (in most cases) by an italicized **part-of-speech** label and then by the Japanese written form of the entry word or phrase, either in **kana** (the Japanese phonetic script), **kanji** (Chinese characters), or a mixture of kanji and kana, following common Japanese usage. These are followed by English equivalents or definitions and, in some cases, by boldfaced **subentries** (idioms, phrases, etc.).

When an entry has two or more distinct meanings or can be used, from the point of view of English grammar, as more than one part of speech, its English equivalents are numbered. However, English equivalents that are closely related in meaning are separated by semicolons rather than being numbered, and in any case there is never more than one sequence of numbers: if numbers have been used to separate parts of speech, then any distinctions of meaning within those divisions are merely separated by semicolons.

Examples:

ippuku, *n.* 一服 1. puff (tobacco). 2. one dose; one portion.

ippō 一方 1. *n.* one side; the other party. 2. *adv.* on the other hand.

ireru, *vb.* 入れる 1. put in(to); let in. 2. send someone to. 3. comply with; accept. 4. make (tea, coffee).

In cases like the second example above, where parts of speech are separated by numbers, the part-of-speech labels are given after the numbers rather than immediately following the main-entry word or phrase.

When a Japanese main-entry word is borrowed from a foreign language other than Chinese, the source language is indicated in parentheses before the English equivalent(s). The original word in the source language is also given, in italics, when it would be difficult to guess from its Japanese pronunciation. Example: **buranko,** *n.* (Pg. *balanço*) swing.

English–Japanese Section

In this section, the boldfaced English **main entry** is followed by an italicized **part-of-speech** label, then the entry's Japanese equivalents. All Japanese equivalents for main entries are given in both **rōmaji** and Japanese writing (**kanji** and/or **kana**). However, in the case of boldfaced English **subentries**, the Japanese written form is omitted if part of it would repeat Japanese writing that has already appeared elsewhere in the entry. For example, in the entry for **domestic**, the Japanese written forms for the subentries

domestic flight (kokunaisen) and **domestic car** (kokusansha) are not shown because the kanji corresponding to the syllables **kokunai** and **kokusan** (which convey the root meanings of two different senses of "domestic") were given earlier in the entry.

When an English entry has two or more distinct meanings, their Japanese equivalents are numbered. When the separate meanings are closely related, they are separated by semicolons rather than being numbered. In either case, the Japanese equivalents of the separate meanings are often followed by English glosses in parentheses to identify the sense that is being translated by the Japanese.

Examples:

brink, *n.* 1. fuchi 縁; hashi 端 (edge). 2. setogiwa 瀬戸際 (verge).

hair, *n.* kami(noke) 髪(の毛) (head hair); ke 毛 (body hair, fur).

When the sense that is being translated is considered self-evident, a parenthesized gloss is not given. When only the last of a group of Japanese equivalents has a parenthesized gloss, the gloss refers to all Japanese equivalents to its left until either another gloss or another definition number is encountered. In the following example, the entry for **accord,** the Japanese words **itchi** and **chōwa** both mean "harmony."

accord, 1. *n.* itchi 一致; chōwa 調和 (harmony); kyōtei 協定 (agreement), **of one's own accord** jihatsu-teki ni 自発的に. 2. *vb.* itchi suru 一致する; chōwa suru 調和する.

Lastly, when an English main entry can be used as more than one part of speech (as in the above example), the Japanese equivalents are numbered, with part-of-speech labels following the numbers rather than the boldfaced entry itself. In entries of this type, distinctions of meaning are separated by semicolons rather than being numbered.

Romanization of Japanese

The system of romanization used in this dictionary is a modified form of the widely used Hepburn system. The only significant modification is the use of an apostrophe to indicate a break between certain double letters.

The apostrophe is widely used in the Hepburn system to indicate a break between "n" and a following vowel or the glide "y." In this dictionary, the use of the apostrophe is extended to certain double letters such as "nn" and "uu," where an apostrophe is inserted between the letters (n'n and u'u) to indicate that there is a break between them and they are not pronounced as a single letter.

For a table of the basic syllables of Japanese as spelled in the Hepburn system and as represented in the two types of kana scripts, hiragana and katakana, see pages xii–xiii.

Pronunciation

Vowels

Japanese has five basic vowels, usually referred to as short vowels, which are romanized as **a, i, u, e,** and **o**. These are pronounced approximately like the "a" in "father," the "ee" in "feet," the "oo" in "mood," the "e" in "met," and the "o" in "fort," respectively. They are all pronounced in a relatively short, clipped manner in contrast to the so-called long vowels, which are produced by drawing out the sounds of the short vowels to approximately twice their normal length. In the Hepburn system, the long vowels corresponding to **a, u,** and **o** are written by placing a macron over those letters, producing **ā, ū,** and **ō.** The Hepburn system writes the long vowels for **i** and **e** in two ways: in words borrowed from languages other than Chinese, they are written with a macron as **ī** and **ē;** otherwise they are written as **ii** and **ei,** respectively. (The actual pronunciation of **ē,** or **ei,** varies considerably: some speakers pronounce it as an elongation of the short vowel **e,** others as a sequence of the short vowels **e** and **i.**)

Other vowel combinations, aside from the long vowels **ii** and **ei,** are pronounced as sequences of the two vowels, though sometimes with a glide between them. Such vowel combinations as **ai, au, oi,** and **ue** often sound like "eye," "ow" (as in "cow"), "oy" (as in "boy"), and "we" (as in "wet") to the ears of English speakers. The contrast between **ai** and **ae** is important. The former ends in a sound like the "ee" of "feet" and the latter in a sound like the "e" of "met."

The vowel **u** in the syllable **su** tends to be pronounced very faintly or not at all (so that the syllable sounds like **s**) before some consonants, as in **sukoshi** ("a little bit"), and at the end of some words, as in the polite copula **desu** and the polite verb suffix **-masu.** These examples are often pronounced "skoshi," "des," and "mas."

The vowel **i** also has a tendency to be pronounced very faintly or even whispered in certain contexts, especially in the syllable **shi,** but also in the syllables **chi, hi, ki,** and **pi.** This muting of the **i** sound most commonly occurs when **shi, chi, hi, ki,** or **pi** precedes any of the following consonants: **ch, f, h, k, p, s, sh, t,** or **ts.** For example, **shikata** (way, method) is often pronounced "shkata," and **hito** (person, human being) is often pronounced in a way that sounds like "hto" or "shto" to most English speakers. However, Japanese speakers hear the **i**, as it is whispered rather than dropped entirely. These pronunciation patterns are widespread, but they are seldom indicated in dictionaries and textbooks. They are best learned by observing the speech of native speakers.

Consonants

Most Japanese consonants are pronounced more or less the way the same letters would be pronounced in English. However, there are some important differences.

1. The combination **ch** is always pronounced as in "chair," never as in "character" or "charade."
2. The letter **g** is always pronounced as in "gift" or "get," never as in "ginger" or "generation."
3. The **ts** of the syllable **tsu** corresponds to nothing in English. It sounds rather like the "ts" of "footsore"; however, it is really a single consonant, and it always begins the syllable in which it occurs.
4. The **f** of the syllable **fu** often sounds more like an "h" than like an English "f." (It is produced more by narrowing the gap between the upper and lower lips rather than by bringing the upper teeth close to the lower lip as in English.) A glance at the table of Japanese syllables on page xii will reveal that **fu** belongs to the **h** row.
5. The Japanese **r** is not at all like the retroflex American "r," in which the tongue is rolled back, then forward. Instead it is produced by flapping the tip of the tongue downward from just behind the upper front teeth. It often sounds very much like an "l" to English speakers. Aside from this, Japanese has no "l" sound, and the **r** is used in pronouncing foreign loanwords that contain the letter "l."
6. The letter **y** that appears after some consonants is a glide between the consonant and the following vowel rather than a vowel as it sometimes is in English. Thus **tōkyō** (the name of the city), which is often pronounced in English as three syllables (to-ky-o), is actually two syllables in Japanese (**tō** and **kyō**).
7. The Japanese **n** has two pronunciations. One is at the beginning of the syllables **na, ni, nu, ne,** and **no,** where it is pronounced like the English "n." The other is the so-called syllabic **n.** This is a nasalized "n," sometimes described as always coming at the end of a syllable. However, the nasalized "n" is counted as a syllable by itself, so that the word **kin** (gold) consists of two syllables (**ki** and **n**). The word **nan** (what) contains both types of **n.** When the syllabic **n** comes before a vowel (or the glide **y**) within a word, it is important to distinguish it from the syllable-beginning type. In speech, there is a break

between this **n** and the following vowel. In the Hepburn system, it is often marked with an apostrophe, as in **kan'en** (hepatitis), and this dictionary follows that practice.

Double Consonants

When a word contains double consonants, for example, the two "p's" in **kippu** (ticket), the two are pronounced separately with a break between them rather than as a single consonant. In this case, the two "p's" are pronounced like those in "hip pocket" and not like those in "hippie." In the same way, the two "k's" of **gakkō** (school) are pronounced like the "kc" of "bookcase" and not the "k" of "bookies." Other such consonant pairs are **ss, tt,** and **nn.** In this dictionary, the two "n's" of **nn** are separated by an apostrophe, as in **kan'nen** (idea, sense), since the first of the pair is the syllabic **n.**

The consonant combination "tch," as in **itchi** (accord), also has a break between the "t" and the "ch," being pronounced like the "tch" in "hatcheck" and not like that in "hatchet."

Accent

The Japanese accent pattern is fundamentally different from the English one, in which accented syllables are stressed more heavily than unaccented ones. The Japanese accent pattern is often described as flat, meaning that every syllable is stressed equally. Japanese does have an accent, which consists of a change in pitch on certain syllables, and this change in pitch can be used to differentiate between two words that are otherwise pronounced the same, as **háshi** (chopsticks) and **hashí** (bridge). However, such distinctions are not as crucial as they would be in English, where a misunderstanding might arise if a particular syllable is not stressed. A general guideline for the Japanese accent is to avoid putting a heavy stress on any syllable. Even without a proper pitch accent, meanings can be understood from context. On the other hand, if a speaker does put a strong stress accent on any syllables, the words will sound foreign to most Japanese ears.

Pronunciation of Foreign Words

Loanwords from English which have pronunciations similar to the original English word and which retain the original meaning have been omitted from this dictionary. This section describes the basics of pronouncing such loanwords.

As can be seen from the table on pages xii–xiii, the typical Japanese syllable consists of either a vowel alone or a consonant (or consonant plus glide) followed by a vowel. Aside from the doubling of certain consonants and the frequent appearance of syllabic **n** before other consonants, Japanese has few consonant clusters, especially compared to English and some other European languages. As a result, when a loanword from English (as pronounced in English) contains a succession of consonants, its pronunciation in Japanese often requires a vowel between the consonants. This pronunciation is of course reflected when such words are romanized. For example, pronunciation of the word "illustration" in Japanese requires insertion of a vowel between "s" and "t" and between "t" and "r," resulting in **irasutorēshon.**

Japanese also has few vowel sounds compared to English, and one Japanese vowel often has to do the work of several English ones. The Japanese **a** is used to represent the English short "u," as in the example above, and the Japanese long **ā** is often used for both the short English "a" of "fast" and the rather different vowel sound of "first."

Japanese does not have a "v" sound, and English "v" becomes "b" in borrowed words. For example, "vest" and "best" are both pronounced (and romanized) as **besuto.** Although there is no "v" in rōmaji, the constant influx of foreign words into Japanese is so great that many consonant sounds that were previously nonexistent are being gradually added to both spoken Japanese and the rōmaji alphabet. For example, **ti** and **tī** are now commonly used for such borrowed words as **tisshū** (tissue) and **aisu-tī** (iced tea). Since modern Japanese originally lacked the "f" sound of English, some earlier loanwords using this sound were given an approximate pronunciation, as in the case of **kōhī** for "coffee." More recently, however, such syllables as **fa, fi, fe,** and **fo** have gained currency, especially among younger people.

Word Division, Special Marks

Spacing and Hyphens

In the Japanese writing system, the language is written without spacing between words. There are punctuation marks, such as commas, brackets for quotations, and the equivalent of a period at the end of a sentence. Otherwise, however, the characters within a sentence are spaced equally, with divisions between one thought unit and another being recognized in terms of inflectional endings, case markers, and function words, much as they would be in speech. The use of **kanji,** or Chinese characters, which are seen as sense units, also aids in the process of comprehension.

When writing Japanese in romanization, without the visual aid of kanji, it is obvious that the words need to be divided by spaces as they would be in European languages. The tendency of Japanese to build words into longer units by compounding and the addition of prefixes and suffixes sometimes makes it difficult to do the dividing without separating elements that really go together logically. In this dictionary, longer Japanese sense units have been divided into smaller units by spacing except when it was felt that doing so might obscure the overall sense. When spacing was ruled out, hyphens were often used to show the divisions within the compound word.

Aside from such commonsense (and admittedly subjective) decisions, a number of general rules have been followed.

1. When introducing a word of the type that is never used alone but always forms part of another word, e.g., **sū-** (several), a hyphen is used to indicate that it would begin (or end) another word. However, in examples of use, the hyphen is omitted, as in **sūshūkan** (several weeks).

2. Hyphens are used to link doubled words, as in **moshi-moshi** (hello).

3. When a word consists of more than seven syllables, it is divided with hyphens to aid in comprehension and pronunciation, as in **teiki-kankōbutsu** (journal, periodical).

4. The suffix **-teki** (or **-teki na**), which is used to form adjectives from certain nouns, is always hyphenated.

5. Compounds of two or more foreign loanwords are usually hyphenated, as are compounds of a Japanese word and a foreign loanword. Examples: **kurisumasu-pātī** (Christmas party); **ha-burashi** (toothbrush, from Japanese **ha,** or tooth, and English "brush").

Ellipses

Ellipses indicate that some word or phrase (as a subject, object, indirect object, etc.) must be added in order to complete the thought: for example, **... ni hitteki suru** (correspond to), in which a noun needs to be supplied before the **ni** (as after English "to").

Parentheses

Throughout the dictionary, parentheses are used in Japanese words and phrases to indicate parts of the word or phrase that could be omitted without changing the meaning. Examples: **irasshai(mase)** (Welcome!); **kitchiri (to)** (exactly).

A special use of parentheses is for the words **na** and **no** following certain types of adjectives or noun modifiers: for example, **akiraka (na)** (obvious). The **na** or **no** is used only

when the adjective appears before a noun as its modifier, not
when it appears in the predicate as a complement.

The Japanese Writing System

Japanese is written using three different basic scripts: **kanji**
(Chinese characters), **hiragana,** and **katakana,** the latter
being two distinct types of the Japanese phonetic script
known as **kana.** The basic vocabulary of Japanese, of which
Chinese loanwords are an integral part, is written in a
mixture of kanji and hiragana. In contemporary Japanese,
katakana is most commonly used to write loanwords from
languages other than Chinese and to write foreign personal
and place names; however, it is also sometimes used to write
Japanese words for some special reason such as emphasis.

When **kanji** are used to write uninflected words such as
nouns, they often represent the whole word. In the case of
inflected words such as verbs and adjectives, the kanji, when
used, represent the stem of the word, with inflectional
endings being written in **hiragana.** Function words,
including the particles that are used to indicate case, are
always written in hiragana. Certain other very common
words are now often written in hiragana even when kanji
exist for them. For example, **watashi** (the pronoun "I") can
be written either in hiragana as わたし or in kanji as 私. The
choice is a matter of usage. This dictionary gives the kanji for
a Japanese word (if kanji exist) whenever the word is more
frequently written in kanji than in hiragana in such
publications as newspapers and magazines.

The **hiragana** and **katakana** scripts are shown in the
table on pages xii–xiii, along with their pronunciations,
shown in **rōmaji.** Each of the scripts has 46 basic **kana**
characters, each of which represents one syllable. These are
combined to express more complex syllables such as **bya,**
gya, and **kya,** making a total of more than one hundred
syllables. In the hiragana script, long vowels are represented
by combining two hiragana characters, as in **tanoshii** 楽しい
(enjoyable, pleasant), where the kana for **shi** (し) is followed
by that for **i** (い) to form the long vowel **ii.** In katakana, on
the other hand, long vowels are represented by a dash (ー)
placed after a kana containing a short vowel, as in both
syllables of **kōhī** (coffee), which is written コーヒー.

Table of Japanese Syllables in Rōmaji, Hiragana, and Katakana

1) R = rōmaji; H = hiragana; K = katakana
2) An asterisk (*) marks those syllables that, to a speaker of English, appear to have beginning consonants that do not match those of the other syllables in the same row. They do not appear inconsistent from the standpoint of Japanese, which originally lacked such sounds as "si," "ti," "tu," etc.
3) The syllables shown in parentheses are essentially used in Japanese only in words borrowed from other languages.

	RHK	RHK	RHK	RHK	RHK
	a あ ア	i いイ	u うウ	e えエ	o おオ
k+vowel	ka かカ	ki きキ	ku くク	ke けケ	ko こコ
s	sa さサ	*shi しシ	su すス	se せセ	so そソ
t	ta たタ	*chi ちチ	*tsu つツ	te てテ	to とト
n	na なナ	ni にニ	nu ぬヌ	ne ねネ	no のノ
h	ha はハ	hi ひヒ	*fu ふフ	he へヘ	ho ほホ
m	ma まマ	mi みミ	mu むム	me めメ	mo もモ
y	ya やヤ		yu ゆユ		yo よヨ
r	ra らラ	ri りリ	ru るル	re れレ	ro ろロ
w	wa わワ				wo をヲ
n'	n' んン				
g	ga がガ	gi ぎギ	gu ぐグ	ge げゲ	go ごゴ
z	za ざザ	*ji じジ	zu ずズ	ze ぜゼ	zo ぞゾ
d	da だダ	*ji ぢヂ	*zu づヅ	de でデ	do どド
b	ba ばバ	bi びビ	bu ぶブ	be べベ	bo ぼボ
p	pa ぱパ	pi ぴピ	pu ぷプ	pe ぺペ	po ぽポ
ky	kya きゃキャ		kyu きゅキュ		kyo きょキョ
sh	sha しゃシャ	shi しシ	shu しゅシュ	(she)(しぇ)(シェ)	sho しょショ
ch	cha ちゃチャ	chi ちチ	chu ちゅチュ	(che)(ちぇ)(チェ)	cho ちょチョ
ny	nya にゃニャ		nyu にゅニュ		nyo にょニョ
hy	hya ひゃヒャ		hyu ひゅヒュ		hyo ひょヒョ
my	mya みゃミャ		myu みゅミュ		myo みょミョ
ry	rya りゃリャ		ryu りゅリュ		ryo りょリョ

Table of Japanese Syllables in Rōmaji, Hiragana, and Katakana

	R H K	R H K	R H K	R H K	R H K
gy	gya ぎゃ ギャ		gyu ぎゅ ギュ		gyo ぎょ ギョ
j	ja じゃ ジャ	ji じ ジ	ju じゅ ジュ	(je) (じぇ) (ジェ)	jo じょ ジョ
by	bya びゃ ビャ		byu びゅ ビュ		byo びょ ビョ
py	pya ぴゃ ピャ		pyu ぴゅ ピュ		pyo ぴょ ピョ

4) Katakana characters for words borrowed from foreign languages. Owing to their frequent use in words from other languages, the syllables "ti," "tu," "di," and "du" have become common both in writing and in speech. However, "va," "vi," "ve," and "vo" exist only in writing. These sounds are naturally expressed only in katakana, not in hiragana. Not shown in the table but also gaining currency are the combinations テュ and デュ, which are used in writing the "tu" and "du" of such words as "tuner" and "duet," respectively. If transcribed into the Hepburn system, they would have to be represented as "tyu" and "dyu."

t		ti テイ	tu トゥ	
d		di デイ	du ドゥ	
f	fa ファ	fi フィ		fe フェ	fo フォ
v	va ヴァ	vi ヴィ		ve ヴェ	vo ヴォ

5) Long vowels.

	ā ああ	ī いい	ū うう	ē ええ	ō おお
	アー	イー	ウー	エー	オー
	あー	いー	うー	えー	おう
					おー

Abbreviations

Source Languages of Loanwords

(D.) Dutch; (E.) English; (F.) French; (G.) German;
(It.) Italian; (Pg.) Portuguese; (Sp.) Spanish;
(Skt.) Sanskrit.

Parts of Speech

adj. adjective
adv. adverb
art. article
aux. vb. auxiliary verb
conj. conjunction
interj. interjection
n. noun
parti. particle
prep. preposition
pron. pronoun
vb. verb

A

abara(bone), *n.* 肋(骨) rib.

abareru, *vb.* 暴れる become violent.

abekku, *n.* アベック (F. *avec*) a couple (on a date).

abekobe (na, no), *adj.* あべこべ (な、の) opposite; topsy-turvy.

abiru, *vb.* 浴びる take a bath or shower; bask in sunlight; abundantly receive (praise or criticism).

abunai, *adj.* 危ない dangerous; risky; doubtful; life-threatening.

abura, *n.* 油 oil.

abura, *n.* 脂 fat.

aburu, *vb.* あぶる roast; broil.

achira あちら 1. *pron.* that; that person, thing, or place. 2. *adv.* over there; abroad.

achi(ra)kochi(ra) ni, *adv.* あち(ら)こち(ら) に here and there; in various places; back and forth.

adana, *n.* あだ名 nickname.

adokenai, *adj.* あどけない innocent; artless.

aegu, *vb.* あえぐ gasp; groan; suffer.

aemono, *n.* 和え物 vegetables or seafood dressed with vinegar, miso, or mashed tofu.

aete, *adv.* 敢えて positively; bravely; purposely.

afureru, *vb.* あふれる overflow.

afurika, *n.* アフリカ (E.) Africa.

agameru, *vb.* 崇める worship; adore.

agari 上がり 1. *n.* ascent; increase. 2. *n.* earnings; income. 3. *adj.* completed or ended; prepared; ready; **Sushi itchō agari.** Sushi coming up!

agaru, *vb.* 上がる 1. climb; go up; (price) rise. 2. enter (a house or room). 3. eat; drink. 4. improve. 5. stop (rain or snow). 6. become shy.

agemono, *n.* 揚げ物 deep-fried food.

ago, *n.* あご chin; jaw.

agura o kaku, *vb.* あぐらを かく sit cross-legged.

ahiru, *n.* あひる duck; **minikui ahiru no ko** ugly duckling.

ahō, *n.* 阿呆 fool; silly person.

ai, *n.* 愛 love.

ai, *n.* 藍 indigo; **ai'iro** deep violet blue.

aibō, *n.* 相棒 associate; partner; buddy.

aibu, *n.* 愛撫 caress.

aichaku, *n.* 愛着 affection; attachment.

aida, *n.* 間 interval; time; distance; relationship; **... no aida ni** between; during; while.

aihansuru, *adj.* 相反する conflicting; contradictory.

aijin, *n.* 愛人 love; lover; mistress; the other woman.

aijō, *n.* 愛情 love; affection.

aikagi, *n.* 合鍵 spare key; master key; passkey.

aikawarazu, *adv.* 相変らず as usual; as ... as ever.

aiko あいこ 1. *n.* tie (in sports). 2. *adj.* even; quits.

aikoku, *n.* 愛国 love of one's country.

aikyō, *n.* 愛敬 charm.

aima, *n.* 合間 interval; spare time.

aimai (na), *adj.* あいまい (な) ambiguous; vague; unsure.

ainiku, *adj., adv.* あいにく unfortunate(ly); disappointing(ly); **Oainiku(sama).** That's too bad!

ainori suru, *vb.* 相乗りする share a vehicle (esp. a cab) with others; ride together.

airashii, *adj.* 愛らしい (person or animal) amiable; captivating.

airon, *n.* アイロン (E.) iron; **airon o kakeru** press.

aisatsu, *n.* 挨拶 greeting; salutation.

aishadō, *n.* アイシャドー (E.) eye shadow.

aishō, *n.* 愛称 pet name.

aishō, *n.* 相性 affinity; compatibility.

aiso, aisō, *n.* 愛想 sociability; friendliness; cheerfulness; **aiso ga ii** friendly; **aiso ga tsukiru** be disgusted or disappointed.

aisu-kurīmu, *n.* アイスクリーム (E.) ice cream.

aisu-kyandē, *n.* アイスキャンデー (E.) ice cream on a stick; popsicle.

aita, *adj.* 開いた open.

aita, *adj.* 空いた unoccupied; vacant.

aite, *n.* 相手 1. partner; associate; **aite o/ni suru** keep company with; deal with a person sincerely; **aite**

ni shinai ignore a person. 2. rival; opponent.

aitsu, *n.* あいつ that damn person.

aitsugu, *adj.* 相次ぐ continuous; successive.

aizu, *n.* 合図 sign; signal.

aizuchi, *n.* 相槌 nod of assent.

aji, *n.* あじ horse mackerel.

aji, *n.* 味 taste; flavor.

ajia, *n.* アジア (E.) Asia.

ajisai, *n.* あじさい hydrangea.

aka 赤 1. *n.* red; crimson; scarlet. 2. *adj.* total; stark.

aka no tanin perfect stranger.

akachan, *n.* 赤ちゃん baby (affectionate usage).

akademikku (na), *adj.* アカデミック (な) (E.) academic.

akadenwa, *n.* 赤電話 public phone.

akaji, *n.* 赤字 deficit.

akaku naru, *vb.* 赤くなる blush (with embarrassment, shame, or drink).

akari, *n.* 灯 light; **akari o tsukeru** turn on the light.

akarui, *adj.* 明るい bright; lively.

akashingō, *n.* 赤信号 red (traffic) light.

akasu, *vb.* 明かす 1. disclose; reveal. 2. sit up the whole night.

-ake 明け the end of a thing or event; **tsuyuake** the end of the rainy season.

akegata, *n.* 明け方 daybreak.

akeru, *vb.* 開ける 1. open. 2. unwrap. 3. turn over (pages). 4. pierce; make a hole.

akeru, *vb.* 空ける empty; make room for.

aki, *n.* 秋 autumn; fall.

aki, *n.* 空き vacancy.

akinai, *n.* 商い trade; business.

akinau, *vb.* 商う trade in.

akiraka (na), *adj.* 明らか(な) obvious.

akirame, *n.* あきらめ resignation; abandonment.

akirameru, *vb.* あきらめる resign oneself to; yield to.

akireru, *vb.* あきれる be astounded; be disgusted.

akiru, *vb.* 飽きる get tired of.

akitarinai, *adj.* 飽き足りない insufficient; unsatisfying.

akiya, *n.* 空き家 vacant house; house to rent.

akka suru, *vb.* 悪化する go from bad to worse.

akke ni torareru, *vb.* あっけにとられる be taken aback; be flabbergasted; be dumbfounded.

akogareru, *vb.* 憧れる long for; yearn after.

aku, *n.* 悪 evil; vice.

aku, *vb.* 空く become vacant; become unused; **te ga aku** become free.

aku, *vb.* 開く open; start.

akubi, *n.* あくび yawn.

akui, *n.* 悪意 malice; ill will.

akuma, *n.* 悪魔 devil; demon; Satan; devilish person.

akumade(mo), *adv.* 飽くまで(も) to the utmost; to the end.

akumu, *n.* 悪夢 nightmare.

akunin, *n.* 悪人 wicked person; villain.

akusei (no), *adj.* 悪性 (の) malignant.

akuseku suru, *vb.* あくせくする fuss about; fidget; work in a restless manner; work constantly.

akuseru, *n.* アクセル (E.) accelerator.

akushitsu (na, no), *adj.* 悪質 (な、の) nasty; bad; of poor quality.

akushu, *n.* 握手 handshake.

akushū, *n.* 悪臭 bad smell.

akushumi, *n.* 悪趣味 poor taste.

ama, *n.* 海女 fisherwoman; female pearl diver.

ama, *n.* 尼 nun.

amadare, *n.* 雨垂れ raindrop.

amadera, *n.* 尼寺 nunnery.

amado, *n.* 雨戸 rain shutter.

amaeru, *vb.* 甘える depend on other people's goodwill; behave disrespectfully.

amagasa, *n.* 雨傘 umbrella.

amagumo, *n.* 雨雲 rain cloud.

amai, *adj.* 甘い 1. sweet. 2. indulgent.

amaku miru, *vb.* 甘く見る slight; underestimate.

amami, *n.* 甘味 sweetness.

amamizu, *n.* 雨水 rainwater.

amanattō, *n.* 甘納豆 sugared red bean.

amanogawa, *n.* 天の川 Milky Way.

amanojaku, *n.* あまのじゃく perverse person; stubborn person.

amari, *n.* 余り rest; surplus.

amari, *adv.* 余り 1. very much; excessively; more than. 2. **... no amari** as a result of.

amarimono, *n.* 余り物 leftovers.

amari ni (mo), *adv.* 余りに(も) excessively.

amaru, *vb.* 余る be left (over); remain.

amayakasu, *vb.* 甘やかす spoil (a person); indulge.

amazake, *n.* 甘酒 sweet sake.

ame, n. 雨 rain; rainfall.

ame, n. あめ candy; sweet.

amerika(gasshūkoku), n. アメリカ(合衆国) the United States.

amerikajin, n. アメリカ人 American (person).

amerika no, adj. アメリカの American (thing).

amidana, n. 網棚 rack (luggage).

amimono, n. 編み物 knitting.

amu, vb. 編む knit.

an, n. 案 idea; plan; proposal; **an o dasu** make a proposal; **meian** good idea.

an, n. あん sweet bean paste.

ana, n. 穴 hole; opening; crevice; cavity.

anadoru, vb. 侮る look down upon; slight; underestimate.

anago, n. 穴子 sea eel.

anata, pron. あなた you; darling (used by a woman to her husband or boyfriend).

anchoku (na) adj. 安直 (な) easy; cheap.

ando suru, vb. 安堵する feel relaxed; feel relieved.

ane, n. 姉 older sister.

angai, adv. 案外 unexpectedly; surprisingly.

angō, n. 暗号 code.

ani, n. 兄 older brother.

anime, animēshon, n. アニメ, アニメーション (E.) animated cartoon; animation.

aniyome, n. 兄嫁 older brother's wife.

anji, n. 暗示 hint; suggestion; insinuation.

anjiru, vb. 暗じる worry about; be concerned with.

anka (na), adj. 安価 (な) inexpensive.

ankēto, n. アンケート (F. enquête) questionnaire.

anki, n. 暗記 memorization.

ankoku, n. 暗黒 darkness.

anma, n. あんま masseur; masseuse; massage.

anmari あんまり 1. adj. irrational; cruel. 2. adv. unusually; extremely; very (much).

anmoku (no), adj. 暗黙 (の) implicit; tacit.

an'na, adj. あんな (derogatory) that; that sort; such; **An'na yatsu.** That creep!

an'nai, n. 案内 information; guidance; invitation; introduction.

an'naisho, n. 案内所 information booth.

an'naisho, n. 案内書 handbook; guidebook.

an'nai suru, vb. 案内する guide; show; introduce.

an'na ni, adv. あんなに such; so much; that much.

ano, adj. あの that; those; **ano hi** on that day; **ano koro** in those days.

ano ne, interj. あのね Well! Look!

ano yo, n. あの世 afterworld.

ano yō (na), adj. あの様な that kind of.

anpi, n. 安否 safety.

anraku (na), adj. 安楽 (な) cozy; comfortable.

anrakushi, n. 安楽死 mercy killing.

ansanburu, n. アンサンブル (F. ensemble) harmony; balance.

ansatsu, n. 暗殺 assassination.

ansatsusha, n. 暗殺者 assassin.

anshin, *n.* 安心 peace of mind; relief; **anshin dekiru** reliable.

anshōbangō, *n.* 暗証番号 code number.

antei, *n.* 安定 stability.

an'yo, *n.* あんよ baby's toddle.

anzan, *n.* 安産 easy delivery (of a baby).

anzan, *n.* 暗算 mental calculation.

anzen, *n.* 安全 safety; security.

anzen (na), *adj.* 安全 (な) safe; secure.

anzen-beruto, *n.* 安全ベルト seat belt.

anzen-pin, *n.* 安全ピン safety pin.

anzu, *n.* 杏 apricot.

ao, *n.* 青 blue; green.

aogu, *vb.* 仰ぐ look up; look up to; ask for (advice); depend on.

aogu, *vb.* 扇ぐ fan; instigate.

aoi, *adj.* 青い blue; green; unripe; inexperienced.

aojashin, *n.* 青写真 blueprint.

aojiroi, *adj.* 青白い pale.

aomono, *n.* 青物 vegetable.

aomuke ni, *adv.* 仰向けに on one's back.

aonisai, *n.* 青二才 greenhorn.

aonori, *n.* 青海苔 (dried) green seaweed.

aoshingō, *n.* 青信号 green light.

apāto, *n.* アパート (E.) apartment (for rent).

appaku suru, *vb.* 圧迫する suppress; oppress.

appare (na), *adj.* あっぱれ (な) admirable; **Appare.** Splendid! Good job!

appu, *n.* アップ (E. *up*) upswept hairdo; closeup.

appu suru, *vb.* アップする (E. *up*) lift; raise; improve.

ara, *interj.* あら Oh!

ara-arashii, *adj.* 荒々しい rough; violent; impudent.

arabia, *n.* アラビア (E.) Arabia.

arai, *adj.* 荒い violent; rough; rude.

arakajime, *adv.* あらかじめ beforehand.

aramashi, *n.* あらまし outline; story line; plot.

arankagiri no, *adj.* 有らん限りの utmost.

arare, *n.* あられ 1. hail. 2. rice cracker.

arashi, *n.* 嵐 storm.

arasou, *vb.* 争う fight; dispute; compete.

arasuji, *n.* 荒筋 story line; plot.

aratamaru, *vb.* 改まる 1. be renewed. 2. (person) become formal.

aratameru, *vb.* 改める change; renovate; correct.

aratamete, *adv.* 改めて again; anew; another time.

arata (na), *adj.* 新らた (な) new; fresh.

arau, *vb.* 洗う wash.

arawa (na), *adj.* あらわ (な) open; uncovered.

arawareru, *vb.* 現われる appear; show up.

arawasu, *vb.* 表わす signify; represent; express.

arawasu, *vb.* 著わす write; publish.

arayuru, *adj.* あらゆる all; every possible.

are, *pron.* あれ that.

are(k)kiri, *adv.* あれ(っ)きり since then.

arekore, *pron.* あれこれ this and that; every possible thing.

areru, *vb.* 荒れる deteriorate;

decline; become uncontrollable.

arerugī, n. アレルギー (G. *Allergie*) allergy.

ari, n. 蟻 ant.

ariamaru, vb. 有り余る be abundant; have more than necessary.

ariari to, adv. ありありと vividly; clearly.

ariawase, n. 有り合わせ anything on hand; something available.

arifureta, adj. ありふれた ordinary; banal.

arigatai, adj. 有難い grateful; welcome; appreciative.

arigata-meiwaku, n. 有難迷惑 misplaced or unwanted kindness.

arigatō, interj. 有難う Thank you! **Dōmo arigatō gozaimasu.** Thank you very much.

arika, n. 在りか whereabouts.

arikitari (na, no), adj. ありきたり (な、の) commonplace; conventional.

arinomama ni, adv. ありのままに as it is; frankly; honestly.

arisama, n. 有り様 state; circumstance.

arisō (na), adj. ありそう (な) likely; probable; believable.

arittake (no), adj. ありったけ (の) all; utmost.

aru, adj. 或る a; an; a certain; some; **aru hi** one day; **aru hito** someone; a certain person; **mukashi mukashi aru tokoro ni ...** Once upon a time, there lived ...

aru, vb. ある 1. have; there is (are); exist; be located. 2.

happen; take place. 3. experience; **-ta koto ga aru** have experienced; **mita koto ga aru** have seen before.

arubaito, n. アルバイト (G. *Arbeit*) part-time job; moonlighting.

aruchū, n. アル中 alcoholic; alcoholism.

aruiwa あるいは 1. conj. or. 2. adv. perhaps; maybe.

arukōru, n. アルコール (E.) alcohol; liquor.

arukōru-chūdoku, n. アルコール中毒 alcoholic; alcoholism.

aruku, vb. 歩く walk.

arumi-hoiru, n. アルミホイル (E.) aluminum foil.

arumi(niumu), n. アルミ (ニウム) (E.) aluminum.

arumi-sasshi, n. アルミサッシ (E.) aluminum window frame.

asa 朝 1. n. morning. 2. adv. in the morning.

asa, n. 麻 hemp; linen.

asagao, n. 朝顔 1. morning glory. 2. urinal.

asagohan, n. 朝御飯 breakfast.

asahi, n. 朝日 morning sun; rising sun.

asai, adj. 浅い shallow; short (days); inexperienced.

asameshimae, adj. 朝飯前 easy.

asaru, vb. 漁る rummage; forage; search for.

asatte, n., adv. あさって、明後日 the day after tomorrow.

ase, n. 汗 sweat; perspiration; **ase ga deru/ase o kaku** to sweat; perspire.

asemo, n. あせも prickly heat.

aseru, vb. 焦る get impatient; be in a hurry; be anxious and eager.

aseru, vb. 褪せる fade; discolor.

ashi, n. 足 1. foot; leg; foot of an animal. 2. transportation. 3. **ashi o arau** quit; **ashi ga deru** overspend.

ashidematoi, n. 足手まとい burden; nuisance.

ashidome, n. 足止め delay; stalemate; **ashidome o kū** be delayed; be held up.

ashika, n. あしか sea lion.

ashikake, adv. 足掛け approximately; **ashikake ninen** approximately two years.

ashikarazu 悪しからず I don't mean to be impolite; Don't take it badly.

ashikubi, n. 足首 ankle.

ashimoto, n. 足元 step; **Ashimoto ni ki o tsukete.** Watch your step.

ashioto, n. 足音 footstep.

ashirau, vb. あしらう deal with indifferently (lightly, badly).

ashita, n., adv. 明日 tomorrow.

asobaseru, vb. 遊ばせる leave idle; let play.

asobi, n. 遊び 1. play; game; diversion; relaxation. 2. playing around; dissipation. 3. having a good time. 4. visit; **Asobi ni kite kudasai.** Please come to see me.

asobihanbun de/ni, adv. 遊び半分で／に playfully; insincerely.

asobu, vb. 遊ぶ 1. play; enjoy; philander. 2. be idle; be left unused. 3. be unemployed.

asoko, n., adv. あそこ (on) that spot; there; over there.

assari (to), adv. あっさり (と) simply; lightly; easily.

assari shita, adj. あっさりした simple; light; easy.

asu, n., adv. 明日 tomorrow.

ataeru, vb. 与える give; award; cause.

atafuta suru, vb. あたふた する be in a hurry; be in a fluster.

atai, n. 価 value; price.

atakamo, conj. あたかも as if.

atama, n. 頭 1. head; face; hair. 2. brain; intelligence. 3. beginning.

atamadekkachi (na, no), adj. 頭でっかち (な、の) 1. top-heavy. 2. quixotic.

atamakin, n. 頭金 down payment.

atarashii, adj. 新しい fresh; new; latest.

atarashisa, n. 新しさ freshness; novelty.

atari 辺り 1. n. neighborhood; area. 2. adv. around.

atari, n. 当たり hit; success; (lottery) winning.

-atari 当たり per; **hitori atari** per person; **kokumin hitori atari** per capita.

atarihazure, n. 当たり外れ hit or miss.

atarikuji, n. 当たりくじ winning number.

atarimae (no), adj. 当たり前 (の) right; reasonable; natural.

atarisawari no nai, adj. 当たり障りのない innocuous; safe.

ataru, vb. 当たる 1. hit. 2. guess correctly.

ataru, vb. あたる 1. become sick from food poisoning. 2.

treat badly; take it out on.

atatakai, *adj.* 暖かい、温かい 1. mild; warm. 2. warmhearted; happy.

atatamaru, *vb.* 暖まる、温まる get warm.

atatameru, *vb.* 暖める、温める heat up; warm up.

ate, *n.* 当て expectation.

ate ga hazureru, *vb.* 当てが外れる be disappointed.

atehamaru, *vb.* 当てはまる fit; apply to.

atena, *n.* 宛名 address; addressee.

ate ni naranai, *adj.* 当てにならない unreliable.

ate ni suru, *vb.* 当てにする count on; depend upon; trust.

ateru, *vb.* 当てる 1. hit. 2. touch (by hand). 3. guess correctly. 4. expose (to the sun). 5. win (lottery or prize).

ateru, *vb.* あてる allocate.

ateru, *vb.* 宛てる address (mail).

ato 後 1. *adj.* another (with a number). 2. *prep.* after; behind.

ato, *n.* 後 1. the rear. 2. the rest. 3. successor; descendant.

ato, *n.* 跡 1. track; trace. 2. ruins.

atoaji, *n.* 後味 aftertaste.

ato de, *adv.* 後で later.

atokata, *n.* 跡形 trace.

atokatazuke o suru, *vb.* 後片付けをする clean up a place after using it.

atomawashi ni suru, *vb.* 後回しにする postpone.

atorie, *n.* アトリエ (F. *atelier*) studio.

atotsugi, *n.* 跡継ぎ heir; inheritor; successor.

atsui, *adj.* 熱い hot (food or

material); passionate.

atsui, *adj.* 暑い hot (weather).

atsui, *adj.* 厚い thick.

atsukamashii, *adj.* 厚かましい impudent; brazen.

atsukau, *vb.* 扱う treat; deal with; deal in; transact.

atsumari, *n.* 集まり meeting; collection.

atsumaru, *vb.* 集まる get together; meet; assemble.

atsumeru, *vb.* 集める collect; attract; summon.

atsuryoku, *n.* 圧力 pressure.

atto iu ma ni, *adv.* あっという間に in an instant.

atto iwaseru, *vb.* あっと言わせる take by surprise.

attō suru, *vb.* 圧倒する overwhelm; overpower.

attō-teki (na), *adj.* 圧倒的 (な) overwhelming.

au, *vb.* 会う see (a person); meet.

au, *vb.* 遭う be involved in (an accident); get caught in.

au, *vb.* 合う fit; suit; match; agree with.

awa, *n.* 泡 bubble; foam.

awabi, *n.* あわび abalone.

aware, *n.* 哀れ pity; misery.

awaremu, *vb.* 哀れむ feel pity for; feel sympathetic.

awaseru, *vb.* 合わせる 1. put together; combine. 2. harmonize; adjust. 3. add up (calculation).

awaseru, *vb.* 会わせる introduce people to each other.

awatemono, *n.* あわて者 hasty person.

awateru, *vb.* あわてる be hasty; get confused; be in a panic.

ayafuya (na), *adj.* あやふや (な) indecisive; vague; unreliable.

ayamachi, *n.* 過ち fault; error; mistake; blunder.

ayamaru, *vb.* 誤る err; make a mistake.

ayamaru, *vb.* 謝る apologize.

ayamatte, *adv.* 誤って by mistake; by accident.

ayame, *n.* あやめ iris (plant).

ayashii, *adj.* 怪しい suspicious; dubious; unreliable.

ayashimu, *vb.* 怪しむ suspect; doubt.

ayasu, *vb.* あやす 1. humor (a baby). 2. amuse; coax.

ayatsuru, *vb.* 操る manipulate; maneuver; handle; control.

ayumi, *n.* 歩み 1. walking; step. 2. history; record.

ayumi-yoru, *vb.* 歩み寄る 1. walk up to. 2. compromise.

aza, *n.* あざ birthmark; bruise; black eye.

azakeru, *vb.* 嘲る ridicule; mock; scoff.

azarashi, *n.* あざらし seal (sea animal).

azayaka (na), *adj.* 鮮か (な) 1. colorful; bright; vivid. 2. impressive; beautiful.

azen to suru, *vb.* 唖然とする be dumbfounded.

azukaru, *vb.* 預かる keep; take care of; be in charge of.

azukaru, *vb.* 与かる participate; share; be concerned with.

azukeru, *vb.* 預ける deposit; leave in charge of; check (coat or baggage).

azuki, *n.* 小豆 red bean.

azumaya, *n.* 東屋 bower; arbor.

B

ba, *n.* 場 place; spot; space; occasion.

ba'ai, *n.* 場合 1. case; occasion. 2. circumstance.

bachi, *n.* 罰 punishment; retribution; judgment.

bachiatari (na, no), *adj.* 罰当たり (な、の) spiteful; sinful; cursed.

bachigai (na), *adj.* 場違い (な) out of place.

bai, *n.* 倍 a double amount; **bai ni naru** to double.

-bai 倍 1. -fold; times; **sanbai** three times. 2. see **-hai.**

baibai, *n.* 売買 buying and selling.

baibai-keiyaku, *n.* 売買契約 sales contract.

baidoku, *n.* 梅毒 syphilis.

baika, *n.* 買価 purchase price.

baikai suru, *vb.* 媒介する carry (germs); mediate.

baikin, *n.* ばい菌 germ; bacteria.

baikingu, *n.* バイキング (E. Viking) smorgasbord; buffet-style restaurant meal.

baiku, *n.* バイク (E.) motorbike; motorcycle.

baikyaku suru, *vb.* 売却する sell.

baishaku, *n.* 媒酌 matchmaking.

baishin, *n.* 陪審 jury.

baishō, *n.* 賠償 compensation; reparation.

baishū suru, *vb.* 買収する purchase; bribe.

baishunfu, *n.* 売春婦 prostitute.

baiten, *n.* 売店 stall; booth;

kiosk; stand.

baito, n. バイト (G. *Arbeit*) part-time job.

baiu, n. 梅雨 rainy season (June and the first half of July).

baizō suru, vb. 倍増する double.

baka, n. 馬鹿 1. stupid person. 2. stupidity; absurdity. 3. **baka ni suru** ridicule; look down on. 4. **baka o miru** make a fool of oneself; **baka o iu** talk nonsense.

bakabakashii, adj. 馬鹿馬鹿しい ridiculous; stupid; nonsensical.

-bakari ばかり 1. about; **itsukabakari** for about five days. 2. just; **ima tsuitabakari** have just arrived. 3. only; **shigotobakari shiteiru** do nothing but work. 4. almost; **nakanbakari** almost crying.

bakasawagi, n. 馬鹿騒ぎ frolicking; revelry; merrymaking.

bakayarō, interj. 馬鹿野郎 You fool! Jerk!

bakemono, n. 化物 ghost; phantom; monster.

bakkin, n. 罰金 penalty; fine.

bakku, n. バック (E.) back; background.

bakku-mirā, n. バックミラー (E.) rearview mirror.

bakku-nanbā, n. バックナンバー (E.) back number; back issue.

bakuchi, n. 博打 gambling.

bakudai (na), adj. 莫大 (な) enormous; immense; vast.

bakudan, n. 爆弾 bomb;

genshi-bakudan atomic bomb; **chūseishibakudan** neutron bomb; **jigenbakudan** time bomb.

bakugeki, n. 爆撃 bombing; bombardment.

bakugeki suru, vb. 爆撃する bomb; bombard.

bakuha, n. 爆破 blast (with explosives).

bakuha suru, vb. 爆破する blow up; explode.

bakuhatsu, n. 爆発 explosion; eruption.

bakuhatsu suru, vb. 爆発する explode; erupt.

bakuhatsu-teki (na), adj. 爆発的 (な) characterized by an explosive increase in (popularity); faddish; voguish.

bakushō, n. 爆笑 burst of laughter.

bakuzen to shita, adj. 漠然とした ambiguous; uncertain; vague.

bamen, n. 場面 scene.

ban, n. 晩 evening; night.

ban, n. 番 1. watch (guard); **ban o suru** take care of. 2. turn; number; **kimi no ban** your turn; **ichiban** number 1.

-banare 離れ quitting; stopping (a habit); loss of interest; **chichi-banare** weaning (a baby); **katsujibanare** lose interest in reading.

bancha, n. 番茶 lowest quality green tea.

banchi, n. 番地 house number; street number.

bando, n. バンド (E.) band; belt.

bane, n. ばね spring (elastic).

bangō, n. 番号 number; **bangō o utsu** give a

number to.

bangōjun ni, *adv.* 番号順に in numerical order.

bangumi, *n.* 番組 TV or radio program.

banji, *n.* 万事 everything; all; **Banji kyūsu da.** It's all over (for me).

banken, *n.* 番犬 watchdog.

bankoku-hakurankai, *n.* 万国博覧会 international exposition.

-banme (no) 番目 (の) suffix used with a number to form an ordinal; **yonbanme no mondai** the fourth question.

banmeshi, *n.* 晩飯 dinner; supper.

ban'nin, *n.* 番人 guard; watchman; keeper.

ban'nō (na, no), *adj.* 万能 (な、の) almighty; all-around.

bansan, *n.* 晩さん formal dinner; **bansankai** dinner party; banquet.

banshaku, *n.* 晩酌 drink with dinner.

bansō, *n.* 伴奏 accompaniment (music).

bansōkō, *n.* 絆創膏 medical plaster; Band-Aid.

banzai, *interj.* 万歳 Hurrah!

banzen (no), *adj.* 万全 (の) thorough; sure; unerring; infallible.

bappon-teki (na), *adj.* 抜本的 (な) drastic; radical.

bara, *n.* ばら rose.

barabara ni naru, *vb.* ばらばらになる be scattered; be disassembled or broken into pieces; be separated from one another.

bara de, *adv.* ばらで separately; loose; not bound together or put in a package.

barakku, *n.* バラック (E.) barracks; shanty.

baramaku, *vb.* ばらまく scatter; strew; throw.

baransu no toreta, *adj.* バランスのとれた well-balanced.

barasu, *vb.* ばらす 1. expose (a secret). 2. disassemble. 3. kill.

barē, bare'e, *n.* バレー、バレエ (F.) ballet.

barē(bōru), *n.* バレー(ボール) (E.) volleyball.

bareru, *vb.* ばれる find out (a secret); reveal; leak.

bariki, *n.* 馬力 horsepower; stamina; power; strength.

bāsan, *n.* 婆さん old woman; old wife; grandmother.

basho, *n.* 場所 1. place; location; space; seat. 2. position. 3. sumo tournament.

bassoku, *n.* 罰則 penal regulations.

bassui, *n.* 抜すい excerpt; extract.

bassuru, *vb.* 罰する discipline; punish; penalize.

basu tei, *n.* バス停 (E.) bus stop.

bata-bata suru, *vb.* ばたばたする clatter; bustle about; be frantic.

bāten, *n.* バーテン (E.) bartender.

bateru, *vb.* ばてる get exhausted; get worn out.

batsu, *n.* 罰 discipline; punishment; penalty.

batsu, *n.* 閥 faction; circle; clique; group.

batsugun (na, no), *adj.* 抜群 (な、の) outstanding; fabulous.

batta, *n.* ばった grasshopper.

battari, *adv.* ばったり (fall)

with a thud; abruptly; accidentally; unexpectedly.

batteki suru, vb. 抜的する promote; single out.

bebī-kā, n. ベビーカー (E.) baby carriage; stroller.

beigo, n. 米語 American English.

beigun, n. 米軍 U.S. armed forces.

beikoku, n. 米国 the United States.

-bekarazu, interj. べからず (imperative use) it is prohibited to...; **Hairubekarazu.** Do not enter!

-beki, parti. べき should; must; **aubeki** 会うべき should or must meet.

bekkan, n. 別館 annex.

bekkō, n. べっ甲 tortoiseshell.

bekkyo, n. 別居 separation (of family members or a couple).

bekkyo suru, vb. 別居する live separately.

ben, n. 便 1. convenience. 2. transportation service. 3. feces.

-ben 弁 dialect; **nagoyaben** Nagoya dialect.

benchi, n. ベンチ (E.) bench.

bengi, n. 便宜 convenience; assistance; **bengi o hakaru** assist; help.

bengo, n. 弁護 defense.

bengoshi, n. 弁護士 lawyer.

bengo suru, vb. 弁護する defend; plead.

beni, n. 紅 red; rouge; lipstick.

beniya, n. ベニヤ (E.) veneer.

benjo, n. 便所 bathroom; rest room; toilet.

benkai, n. 弁解 excuse; rationalization; justification.

benkai suru, vb. 弁解する excuse; rationalize; justify.

benki, n. 便器 toilet; urinal.

benkyō, n. 勉強 study.

benkyō (o) suru, vb. 勉強 (を) する 1. study; learn. 2. give a discount.

benmei suru, vb. 弁明する defend oneself.

benpi, n. 便秘 constipation.

benri, n. 便利 convenience; handiness; usefulness.

benri (na), adj. 便利 (な) convenient; handy; useful.

benshō, n. 弁償 compensation; restitution.

benshō suru, vb. 弁償する compensate; restitute.

bentō, n. 弁当 box lunch.

beppin, n. べっぴん good-looking woman.

bera-bera (to), adv. べらべ ら (と) volubly; talkatively.

berugī, n. ベルギー (E.) Belgium.

besshi, n. 別紙 attached sheet of paper (form).

besshitsu, n. 別室 another room; separate room.

bessō, n. 別荘 summer house; villa; cottage.

bēsu, n. ベース (E.) foundation; base.

bēsu, n. ベース (E.) bass (singer); double bass (instrument).

besuto, n. ベスト (E.) the best; **besuto o tsukusu** do one's best.

beta-beta, adv. べたべた all over; thickly; stickily.

beta-beta suru, vb. べたべ たする be sticky; be clammy; cling to a person (lover).

betonamu, n. ベトナム (E.) Vietnam.

betsu (no), adj. 別 (の) separate; different; another;

other; extra.

betsu-betsu ni, *adv.* 別々に separately.

betsubin de, *adv.* 別便で under separate cover (mailing).

betsujin, *n.* 別人 different person; some other person.

betsumondai, *n.* 別問題 different issue; another matter.

betsu ni, *adv.* 別に particularly.

betsuri, *n.* 別離 separation.

betto ni, *adv.* 別途に separately.

bi, *n.* 美 beauty.

bichiku, *n.* 備蓄 emergency storage; **sekiyubichiku** emergency oil storage.

bidanshi, *n.* 美男子 good-looking man.

bien, *n.* 鼻炎 rhinitis.

bifuteki, *n.* ビフテキ (E.) beefsteak.

bigaku, *n.* 美学 esthetics.

bijin, *n.* 美人 beautiful woman; **bijin-kontesuto** beauty contest.

bijinesu-hoteru, *n.* ビジネスホテル (E. *business hotel*) inexpensive (Western-style) hotel.

bijutsu, *n.* 美術 art; the fine arts.

bijutsuhin, *n.* 美術品 work of art.

bijutsuka, *n.* 美術家 artist; painter.

bijutsukan, *n.* 美術館 art museum; gallery.

bijutsuten, *n.* 美術展 art exhibition.

-biki see **-hiki.**

bikkuri saseru, *vb.* びっくりさせる surprise; shock.

bikkuri suru, *vb.* びっくりする be surprised; be shocked.

bikō suru, *vb.* 尾行する follow; chase; shadow.

biku-biku suru, *vb.* びくびくする feel nervous; be afraid; tremble.

biku to mo shinai, *adj.* びくともしない composed; secure; stable.

bimyō (na), *adj.* 微妙 (な) subtle; delicate; ticklish.

bin, *n.* 瓶 bottle; jar; decanter.

-bin 便 1. flight; transportation. 2. mail; **kōkūbin** airmail.

binbō, *n.* 貧乏 poverty; destituion; poor person.

binbō (na), *adj.* 貧乏 (な) poor; destitute.

binbōyusuri, *n.* 貧乏ゆすり nervous habit; fidgeting.

binetsu, *n.* 微熱 slight fever.

biniru, *n.* ビニール (E.) vinyl.

binjō suru, *vb.* 便乗する 1. get a ride in a vehicle. 2. take advantage of. 3. follow the example of others.

binkan (na), *adj.* 敏感 (な) sensitive; delicate.

binsen, *n.* 便箋 stationery (writing paper).

bira, *n.* ビラ (E.) handbill.

biri, *n.* びり the last; the bottom.

birōdo, *n.* ビロード (Pg. *vellude*) velvet.

biru, *n.* ビル (E.) building.

bīru, *n.* ビール(E.) beer; **kan-bīru** canned beer; **nama-bīru** draft beer; **kurobīru** stout (black beer).

bīrusu, *n.* ビールス (G.) virus.

bishin, *n.* 微震 mild earthquake.

bishonure ni naru, *vb.* びしょぬれになる get drenched

to the skin.

bisuketto, n. ビスケット (E.) biscuit; cookie; cracker.

bi-teki (na), adj. 美的 (な) aesthetic.

biten, n. 美点 good point; merit.

bitoku, n. 美徳 virtue.

biwa, n. びわ loquat.

biyōin, n. 美容院 beauty parlor; beauty shop.

biyōshi, n. 美容師 hairdresser; beautician.

biyōtaisō, n. 美容体操 exercise to improve one's appearance.

bō, n. 棒 stick; pole; club; bar.

bochi, n. 墓地 cemetery; graveyard; churchyard.

bōchō suru, vb. 膨張する swell; expand.

bōdai na, adj. 膨大な huge; enormous; gigantic.

bōdan, n. 防弾 bulletproof; **bōdan-chokki** bulletproof vest; **bōdan-garasu** bulletproof glass.

bodī biru, n. ボディービル (E.) bodybuilding.

bodī-chekku, n. ボディーチェック (E. body check) body search; frisk.

bōdō, n. 暴動 riot; fight; scuffle.

bōei, n. 防衛 defense.

bōei suru, vb. 防衛する defend; protect.

bōeki, n. 貿易 international trade or commerce.

bōekimasatsu, n. 貿易摩擦 friction in international trade and business.

bōenkyō, n. 望遠鏡 telescope.

bōen-renzu, n. 望遠レンズ telephoto lens.

bōfū, n. 暴風 windstorm; **bōfū-keihō** windstorm

warning.

bōfura, n. ぼうふら mosquito larva.

bōfu'u, n. 暴風雨 storm; rainstorm.

bōfuzai, n. 防腐剤 food preservative.

bōgai, n. 妨害 interference; intrusion; disturbance; obstacle.

bōhan, n. 防犯 prevention of crime.

bōi, n. ボーイ (E. boy) waiter; busboy; bellboy.

boin, n. 拇印 thumbprint.

boin, n. 母音 vowel. **hanboin** semivowel.

bōka, n. 防火 fireproofing; fire prevention.

bōkansha, n. 傍観者 onlooker; bystander; spectator.

bōkan suru, vb. 傍観する be an onlooker.

bokashi, n. ぼかし shading; blurring; dimness.

bokasu, vb. ぼかす shade; blur; dim; obscure.

bōken, n. 冒険 adventure; venture; quest.

bokeru, vb. ぼける 1. become senile. 2. blur; fade.

boki, n. 簿記 bookkeeping.

bokin(undō), n. 募金(運動) fundraising (campaign).

bokki suru, vb. 勃起する have an erection.

bokō, n. 母校 one's alma mater.

bōkō, n. 膀胱 bladder.

bōkō, n. 暴行 violence; assault; rape.

bokoku, n. 母国 mother country; native land.

bokokugo, n. 母国語 mother tongue; native language.

boku, n. 僕 I (used by males).

bokujō, *n.* 牧場 stock farm; ranch; pasture.

bokushi, *n.* 牧師 (Christianity) pastor; minister; clergyman.

bōkyo, *n.* 暴挙 violence.

bōmei, *n.* 亡命 defection; fleeing from one's country.

bōmei suru, *vb.* 亡命する defect; seek refuge; go into exile.

bon, *n.* 盆 tray.

bon, *n.* 盆 Buddhist summer festival to worship one's ancestors.

-bon see **-hon.**

bonchi, *n.* 盆地 basin (land).

bōnenkai, *n.* 忘年会 end-of-year party or celebration.

bonjin, *n.* 凡人 ordinary person.

bonkura, *n.* ぼんくら blockhead.

bon'netto, *n.* ボンネット (E.) bonnet; car hood.

bonsai, *n.* 盆栽 bonsai; miniature tree(s) or plant(s) in a pot or a tray.

bon'yari shita (shiteiru), *adj.* ぼんやりした (している) 1. absent-minded; inattentive. 2. dim; vague; hazy.

bon'yari suru, *vb.* ぼんやりする 1. be absent-minded; be inattentive. 2. be idle.

bonyū, *n.* 母乳 mother's milk.

bō'on, *n.* 防音 soundproofing; **bō'onsōchi** soundproof device or system.

boppatsu, *n.* 勃発 outbreak.

bōraku, *n.* 暴落 sharp fall in value (currency, stocks).

bōrei, *n.* 亡霊 ghost; spirit.

bōringu, *n.* ボーリング (E.) 1. bowling. 2. drilling.

boro, *n.* ぼろ 1. rag; worn-out thing. 2. hidden fault.

boro-boro (no), *adj.* ぼろぼろ (の) ragged; worn-out.

bōru, *n.* ボール (E.) 1. ball. 2. bowl.

bōrubako, *n.* ボール箱 cardboard box.

bōrugami, *n.* ボール紙 cardboard.

bōru-pen, *n.* ボールペン (E.) ballpoint pen.

bōryoku, *n.* 暴力 brutality; violence.

bōryokudan, *n.* 暴力団 gang of hoodlums;

bōryokudan'in gangster.

bōryoku-teki (na), *adj.* 暴力的 (な) brutal; violent.

bōsan, *n.* 坊さん Buddhist priest or monk.

boseiai, *n.* 母性愛 maternal love.

boseihon'nō, *n.* 母性本能 maternal instinct.

boseki, *n.* 墓石 tombstone; gravestone.

boshi, *n.* 母子 mother and her child(ren).

bōshi, *n.* 帽子 hat; cap; **bōshi o kaburu** wear a hat or cap.

bōshi, *n.* 防止 prevention.

boshikatei, *n.* 母子家庭 single-mother family.

bōshitsu, *n.* 防湿 protection against moisture or dampness.

boshūkōkoku, *n.* 募集広告 want ad.

boshū suru, *vb.* 募集する recruit; place a want ad; look for workers or students.

bōshūzai, *n.* 防臭剤 deodorizer.

bōsōzoku, *n.* 暴走族 gang of motorcyclists or hot rodders.

bossuru, *vb.* 没する 1. sink (ship). 2. set (sun). 3. die.

bōsui, n. 防水 waterproofing; **bōsuitokei** waterproof watch.

bōtakatobi, n. 棒高跳 pole vault.

botamochi, n. ぼた餅 rice cake covered with sweetened bean paste.

botan, n. 牡丹 peony.

botan, n. ボタン (E.) button.

botchan, n. 坊っちゃん boy; young man; unworldly man; young master; other person's son.

botsu-botsu ぼつぼつ 1. n. dots; spots. 2. adv. gradually; little by little.

botsunyū suru, vb. 没入する be absorbed in; be immersed in.

boya, n. ぼや small fire.

bōya, n. 坊や boy; son.

boya-boya suru, vb. ぼやぼやする be inattentive; be slow to react; dawdle.

boyaku, vb. ぼやく complain; grumble.

bōzen to naru/suru, vb. 茫然となる／する be dumbfounded or petrified.

bōzu, n. 坊主 1. Buddhist priest or monk. 2. boy.

buaisō (na), adj. 無愛想 (な) unfriendly; aloof; curt.

buatsui, adj. 分厚い thick; bulky.

bubun, n. 部分 part (of).

bubun-teki (na), adj. 部分的 (な) partial.

buchikowasu, vb. ぶち壊す destroy; break; ruin.

buchimakeru, vb. ぶちまける disclose; let out.

buchō, n. 部長 section or department head.

budō, n. 武道 the way of the samurai.

budō, n. 葡萄 grape.

~~**budōshu,** n. 葡萄酒 wine.~~

buenryo (na), adj. 無遠慮 (な) impolite; rude; outspoken; unreserved.

bugaisha, n. 部外者 outsider.

bugaku, n. 舞楽 dance and music of ancient Japan.

bugei, n. 武芸 martial arts.

buin, n. 部員 member.

buitiāru, n. ブイティーアール (E.) VTR; videotape recorder; VCR.

buji, n. 無事 safety; peace; health; good condition.

buji ni, adv. 無事に safely; peacefully; well; without problem.

bujoku suru, vb. 侮辱する insult; humiliate; disgrace.

buka, n. 部下 subordinate staff member(s); junior officer(s).

bukakkō (na), adj. 不格好 (な) unshapely; ugly; crude.

buke, n. 武家 samurai family or member.

buki, n. 武器 weapon; arms.

bukimi (na), adj. 不気味 (な) uncanny; weird; eerie.

bukiyō (na), adj. 不器用 (な) clumsy; inept; unskillful.

bukka, n. 物価 price.

bukkirabō (na), adj. ぶっきらぼう (な) curt; blunt; unfriendly.

bukkyō, n. 仏教 Buddhism.

bukotsu (na), adj. 武骨 (な) unsophisticated; clumsy; rough; ill-mannered.

bumon, n. 部門 category; class; division; section; field.

bun, n. 文 sentence; composition.

bun, n. 分 1. one's share; **Watashi no bun wa ikura.** How much is my share of the bill? 2. quantity. 3. one's social status; **bun o**

wakimaeru recognize or accept one's social status. 4. means. 5. state of affairs.

-bun see **-fun**.

bunan (na), *adj.* 無難 (な) safe; acceptable; tolerable.

bunbōgu, *n.* 文房具 stationery; writing materials.

bunchin, *n.* 文鎮 paperweight.

bungaku, *n.* 文学 literature; **koten (chūsei, gendai, gaikoku) bungaku** classical (medieval, modern, foreign) literature.

bungakubu, *n.* 文学部 Department of Literature.

bungakushi, *n.* 文学士 Bachelor of Arts.

bungei, *n.* 文芸 literature; art and literature.

bungyō, *n.* 分業 division of labor.

bunjin, *n.* 文人 writer; man or woman of letters.

bunjō, *n.* 分譲 subdivision; lot; **bunjō-manshon** condominium.

bunka, *n.* 文化 culture.

bunkai suru, *vb.* 分解する take apart; disassemble; disintegrate; fall apart.

bunkasai, *n.* 文化祭 cultural festival.

bunka-teki (na), *adj.* 文化的 (な) cultural; cultured; civilized; sophisticated.

bunkatsubarai, *n.* 分割払い payment on the installment plan.

bunkatsu suru, *vb.* 分割する divide; split.

bunkazai, *n.* 文化財 cultural product; cultural asset.

bunkiten, *n.* 分岐点 crossroads; juncture; watershed; **jinsei no bunkiten** a turning point

in one's life.

bunko(bon), *n.* 文庫(本) pocket (-size) book.

bunkō, *n.* 分校 branch school.

bunmei, *n.* 文明 civilization.

bunmeiteki (na), *n.* 文明的 (な) civilized; cultured; enlightened.

bunmen, *n.* 文面 content (of a written text).

bunmyaku, *n.* 文脈 context.

bunpai, *n.* 分配 distribution; division.

bunpai suru, *vb.* 分配する distribute; divide.

bunpitsu, *n.* 分泌 secretion.

bunpō, *n.* 文法 grammar.

bunpō-ka/-gakusha, *n.* 文法家/〜学者 grammarian.

bunpu, *n.* 分布 distribution.

bunraku, *n.* 文楽 traditional Japanese puppet theater.

bunretsu, *n.* 分裂 division; split; separation.

bunri, *n.* 分離 separation.

bunrui, *n.* 分類 classification; categorization.

bunryō, *n.* 分量 quantity; volume; amount.

bunsan suru, *vb.* 分散する disperse; scatter; split.

bunseki, *n.* 分析 analysis; **seishin-bunseki** psychoanalysis; **seishin-bunseki-gakusha** psychoanalyst.

bunseki suru, *vb.* 分析する analyze.

bunshi, *n.* 分詞 participle; **genzai-bunshi** present participle; **kako-bunshi** past participle.

bunshi, *n.* 分子 1. group; sect. 2. molecule. 3. numerator.

bunsho, *n.* 文書 document; written material.

bunshō, *n.* 文章 sentence;

composition; writing.

bunshū, n. 文集 anthology.

bunsū, n. 分数 fraction.

buntai, n. 文体 literary style.

buntan, n. 分担 one's share; allotment; assignment.

buntsū, n. 文通 correspondence by mail.

buntsū suru, vb. 文通する correspond by mail.

bun'ya, n. 分野 field; area; sphere; **kenkyūbun'ya** field of study.

buppin, n. 物品 article; thing; goods; commodities.

bura-bura suru, vb. ぶらぶらする 1. swing (one's legs). 2. swing (in the air). 3. spend time idly; stroll idly. 4. be unemployed.

burajā, n. ブラジャー (F. brassière) brassiere.

burajiru, n. ブラジル (E.) Brazil.

buranko, n. ブランコ (Pg. balanço) swing.

burasagaru, vb. ぶら下がる hang down (from).

burasageru, vb. ぶら下げる suspend.

burashi, n. ブラシ (E.) brush; **ha-burashi** toothbrush.

buratsuku, vb. ぶらつく loiter.

burei (na), adj. 無礼 (な) rude; impolite; insolent.

-buri ぶり way; attitude; manner; **hanashiburi** the way one talks.

burikaesu, vb. ぶり返す come back; return.

buriki, n. ブリキ (D. blik) tinplate.

-buri ni ぶりに after an interval or absence; **ichinenburi ni** after a year's absence.

-buru ぶる pretend; feign; ii

ko-buru pretend to be a good person.

buryoku, n. 武力 military power; force.

buryoku-kainyū/-kanshō, n. 武力介入／〜干渉 armed intervention.

busahō, n. 不作法 bad manners; rudeness; impoliteness.

busahō (na), adj. 不作法 (な) ill-mannered; rude; impolite.

busaiku (na), adj. 不細工 (な) unattractive; uncouth; clumsy.

bushi, n. 武士 warrior; samurai.

bushidō, n. 武士道 the way of the samurai.

bushitsuke (na), adj. 不躾 (な) ill-mannered; rude; impolite.

bushō (na), adj. 不精 (な) lazy; inactive; **fudebushō** poor correspondent.

bussō (na), adj. 物騒 (な) dangerous; unsafe; threatening.

busu, n. ぶす ugly woman; hag.

busū, n. 部数 number of copies.

busui (na), adj. 不粋 (な) unsophisticated; inelegant; clumsy.

buta, n. 豚 1. pig; swine. 2. despicable person.

butai, n. 舞台 1. stage. 2. setting; scene.

butaniku, n. 豚肉 pork.

butsubutsu iu, vb. ぶつぶつ言う grumble; complain.

butsudan, n. 仏壇 Buddhist altar.

butsukaru, vb. ぶつかる crash; collide with; run into; meet with; fall on.

butsuri(gaku), n. 物理 (学)

physics.

butsurigakusha, *n.* 物理学者 physicist.

butsuzō, *n.* 仏像 Buddhist image or statue.

buttai, *n.* 物体 object; body (in physics).

buttōshi (ni/de), *adv.* ぶっ通しに(に、で) without end; at a stretch.

buyōjin (na), *adj.* 不用心 (な) careless; indiscreet.

buzoku, *n.* 部族 tribe.

byō, *n.* 秒 second (time); **ichibyō** one second.

byō, *n.* 鋲 tack; rivet.

byōdō, *n.* 平等 equality.

byōdō (na, no), *adj.* 平等 (な、の) equal; **byōdō no kenri** equal rights.

byōgen, *n.* 病原 cause of illness, sickness, or disease.

byōin, *n.* 病院 hospital.

byōki, *n.* 病気 illness; sickness; disease; **byōki ni naru/kakaru** fall ill; **byōki ga naoru** recover from an illness.

byōnin, *n.* 病人 sick person; invalid.

byōsha suru, *vb.* 描写する describe.

byōshin, *n.* 秒針 second hand (of a clock).

byōshitsu, *n.* 病室 hospital room; sickroom.

byō-teki (na), *adj.* 病的 (な) sick; morbid; abnormal; repulsive.

C

cha, *n.* 茶 tea.

chadō, *n.* 茶道 tea ceremony.

chagashi, *n.* 茶菓子 teacake.

chāhan, *n.* チャーハン fried rice with vegetables and meat.

chairo (na, no), *adj., n.* 茶色 (な、の) brown (color).

chakasu, *vb.* 茶化す ridicule; make fun of.

chakkari shiteiru, *adj.* ちゃっかりしている nimble; adroit; shrewd.

chakkō suru, *vb.* 着工する start (enterprise, construction).

chakku, *n.* チャック zipper; fastener.

-chaku 着 1. arrival; order of arrival (in a race); **narita-chaku no hikōki** an airplane arriving at Narita; **ni-chaku** finishing second. 2. number suffix indicating

a counter for clothes; **sebiro ni-chaku** two suits.

chaku-chaku (to), *adv.* 着々と steadily.

chakujitsu ni, *adv.* 着実に securely; reliably; steadily.

chakunin suru, *vb.* 着任する be appointed to a position; arrive at one's new post or office.

chakuriku, *n.* 着陸 landing (aircraft, etc.).

chakuriku suru, *vb.* 着陸する land.

chakuseki, *n.* 着席 taking a seat; sitting down.

chakuseki suru, *vb.* 着席する take a seat; sit down.

chame (na), *adj.* 茶目 (な) mischievous (in positive sense); playful.

-chan ちゃん (used after a person's given name to express intimacy and affection): **Toshi-chan;**

(also used as a diminutive for children and pets): **neko-chan** (for a cat).

chanbara, *n.* ちゃんばら sword fighting.

chankonabe, *n.* ちゃんこ鍋 special meal for sumo wrestlers.

chanoma, *n.* 茶の間 family room.

chanpon, *n.* ちゃんぽん mixture of different things; jumble.

chanto, *adv.* ちゃんと exactly; properly; neatly; clearly; respectably; without fail; fully.

chanto shita, *adj.* ちゃんとした respectable; neat; proper; well-established; **chanto shita hito** a respectable person.

charanporan (na), *adj.* ちゃらんぽらん unreliable; irresponsible.

charenji suru, *vb.* チャレンジする (E.) challenge; try; venture.

chasaji, *n.* 茶さじ teaspoon.

chātā-bin, *n.* チャーター便 (E.) chartered flight (bus, boat).

chawan, *n.* 茶碗 teacup; rice bowl.

chawanmushi, *n.* 茶碗蒸し steamed egg curd with meat and vegetables.

chazuke, *n.* 茶漬け green tea poured over a bowl of steamed rice.

che, *interj.* チェ Shucks! Damn!

chekku (no), *adj., n.* チェック (の) check; checkered.

chi, *n.* 地 ground; earth; place; location.

chi, *n.* 血 blood; **chi ga deru** bleed.

chian, *n.* 治安 safety; public

order.

chi(-chi)banare suru, *vb.* 乳離れする be weaned; become independent.

chibetto, *n.* チベット (E.) Tibet.

chibi, *n.* ちび (derogatory) short person; kid.

chibusa, *n.* 乳房 female breast.

chichi, *n.* 乳 milk; mother's milk.

chichi, *n.* 父 father; pioneer; originator.

chichūkai, *n.* 地中海 the Mediterranean.

chidarake (na, no), *adj.* 血だらけ (な、の)covered in blood.

chidoriashi, *n.* 千鳥足 a reeling movement (from intoxication).

chie, *n.* 知恵 wisdom; intelligence; idea.

chieokure (no), *adj.* 知恵遅れ (の) mentally retarded.

chifusu, *n.* チフス (G. *Typhus*) typhus; typhoid.

chigai, *n.* 違い difference.

chigainai 違いない 1. *adj.* sure; **ame ni chigainai** sure to rain. 2. (used postpositively as an *aux. vb.*) must; should; **Sō ni chigainai** It must be so.

chigau 違う 1. *vb.* differ. 2. *adj.* different; wrong.

chigireru, *vb.* ちぎれる tear off; come off.

chigiru, *vb.* ちぎる tear into pieces.

chiguhagu (na, no), *adj.* ちぐはぐ (な、の) mismatched; odd; unbalanced; inconsistent.

chiheisen, *n.* 地平線 horizon.

chihō, *n.* 痴呆 mental retardation; mentally

retarded person.

chihō, *n.* 地方 district; region; countryside.

chi'i, *n.* 地位 rank; status; position; status; **josei no shakai-teki chi'i** women's social status.

chi'iki, *n.* 地域 district; region; area; zone.

chiisai, *adj.* 小さい 1. small; little; young. 2. trivial; petty. 3. low (sound).

chiisaku naru, *vb.* 小さくなる 1. dwindle; diminish. 2. cringe; be afraid of. 3. become too small for (clothing).

chiji, *n.* 知事 prefectural governor.

chijimeru, *vb.* 縮める shorten; reduce; lessen; abridge.

chijimu, *vb.* 縮む shrink; become short; cringe.

chijin, *n.* 知人 acquaintance; friend.

chijō (de, ni), *adv.* 地上 (で、に) above ground; on earth; on land; on the surface of the earth.

chika, *n.* 地下 underground.

chikagai, *n.* 地下街 underground shopping mall.

chikagoro, *adv.* 近頃 recently.

chikai 近い 1. *adj.* near; close (to); intimate; nearsighted (myopic). 2. *adv.* almost.

chikai, *n.* 誓い vow; pledge.

chikajika, *adv.* 近々 soon; before long.

chikaku (de, ni, o), *adv.* 近く (で、に、を) 1. (space) in the neighborhood (of); close to; near; around. 2. (time) almost; before long.

chikaku (no), *adj.* 近く (の) nearby; **chikaku no**

resutoran a nearby restaurant.

chikamichi, *n.* 近道 shortcut.

chikan, *n.* 痴漢 sexual pervert.

chikara, *n.* 力 1. force; power; energy; ability; talent; skill; **eigo no chikara** skill in English. 2. help; influence.

chikaraippai (ni), *adv.* 力一杯 (に) with all one's might; to one's utmost ability.

chikaramochi, *n.* 力持ち a powerful or strong person.

chikara ni naru, *vb.* 力になる 1. *vb.* help; support. 2. *adj.* helpful.

chikara o awaseru, *vb.* 力を合わせる cooperate.

chikara o tsukeru, *vb.* 力をつける make progress; become competent; encourage.

chikarashigoto, *n.* 力仕事 manual labor; blue-collar job.

chikarazuyoi, *adj.* 力強い powerful; encouraging; reassuring.

chikashitsu, *n.* 地下室 basement.

chikatetsu, *n.* 地下鉄 subway.

chikau, *vb.* 誓う vow; pledge; swear.

chikayoru, *vb.* 近寄る approach; come up to; go up to.

chikazukeru, *vb.* 近付ける 1. introduce a person to another. 2. draw (something) near to (a thing or person).

chikazuku, *vb.* 近付く approach; come up to; go up to; seek to become acquainted.

chikin-katsu, *n.* チキンカツ (E.) chicken cutlet.

chikoku suru, *vb.* 遅刻する be late (for); be behind time.

chiku, *n.* 地区 district; area; region; zone.

chikubi, *n.* 乳首 nipple; teat.

chiku-chiku suru, *vb.* ちくちくする be prickly; prickle; tingle.

chikushō, *n.* 畜生 beast; brute; repulsive person or thing; **Chikushō!** Damn it (you, him, her)! Beast!

chikyū, *n.* 地球 the Earth; the globe.

chikyūgi, *n.* 地球儀 globe.

chimame, *n.* 血豆 blood blister.

chimamire (na, no), *adj.* 血まみれ (な、の) covered with blood.

chimanako-de/-ninatte, *adv.* 血眼で／〜になって in a panic; frantically; desperately.

chimata, *n.* 巷 general public; society; street; **chimata no koe** public opinion.

chimei, *n.* 地名 place name.

chimei (na, no), *adj.* 知名 (な、の) famous; well-known.

chimei-teki (na), *adj.* 致命的 (な) fatal.

chin- 珍 rare; unique; bizarre; absurd; **chinmi** unique food; **chinji** bizarre incident; **chinsetsu** absurd opinion.

-chin 賃 wage; pay; rent; fare; **temachin** wage; pay; **yachin** house rent.

chin'age, *n.* 賃上げ wage increase.

chinami ni, *adv.* 因みに in passing; incidentally.

chinamu, *vb.* 因む derive from; be related to.

chin'atsu suru, *vb.* 鎮圧する control (a revolt).

chinbotsu suru, *vb.* 沈没する sink.

chinchikurin (na, no), *adj.* ちんちくりん (な、の) strange; unmatched; very short.

chinchin, *n.* ちんちん penis.

chinetsu, *n.* 地熱 geothermal heat; **chinetsu-hatsudensho** geothermal power plant.

chingin, *n.* 賃金 wage; pay; salary.

chinmoku, *n.* 沈黙 silence.

chinō, *n.* 知能 intelligence; intellect.

chinomigo, *n.* 乳呑児 nursing baby.

chinōshisū, *n.* 知能指数 IQ (intelligence quotient).

chinō tesuto, *n.* 知能テスト IQ test.

chinpanjī, *n.* チンパンジー (E.) chimpanzee.

chinpira, *n.* ちんぴら rowdy; punk; hoodlum.

chinpo(ko), *n.* ちんぽ(こ) (vulgar use) penis.

chinpu (na), *adj.* 陳腐 (な) banal; vulgar; insipid.

chinpunkanpun (na), *adj.* ちんぷんかんぷん (な) incomprehensible; unintelligible.

chinretsu, *n.* 陳列 display.

chinretsu suru, *vb.* 陳列する display; exhibit.

chintsūzai, *n.* 沈痛剤 painkiller.

chippoke na, *adj.* ちっぽけな tiny; small; petty.

chira-chira suru, *vb.* ちらちらする flicker.

chirari to, *adv.* ちらりと at a glance; in a moment;

chirari to miru glimpse;
chirari to kiku overhear.
chirashi, n. 散らし handbill;
flier.
chirashizushi, n. 散らし寿
司 a box of sushi rice topped
with raw fish.
chirasu, vb. 散らす scatter;
sprinkle.
chiratsuku, vb. ちらつく fall
(rain, snow); flicker; haunt
(image).
chiri, n. 塵 dust; litter.
chiri, n. 地理 geography.
chiri, n. チリ (E.) Chile.
chirigami, n. 塵紙 toilet
paper.
chirijiri(-barabara) ni, adv.
ちりぢり(ばらばら)に in all
directions; in pieces
(broken); separated (from
each other).
chirimen, n. 縮緬 crepe
(textile).
chiritori, n. 塵取 dustpan.
chiru, vb. 散る fall; scatter;
disperse; **ki ga chiru** be
distracted.
chiryō, n. 治療 medical
treatment.
chisei, n. 知性 intelligence.
chishiki, n. 知識 knowledge;
learning.
chishikijin, n. 知識人
intellectual; learned person.
chishima(rettō), n. 千島(列
島) the Kurile Islands.
chissoku, n. 窒息
suffocation.
chisuji, n. 血筋 bloodline;
lineage.
chitai, n. 地帯 zone; area;
district.
chi-teki (na), adj. 知的 (な)
intellectual.
chiten, n. 地点 spot; place;
point.
chitsu, n. 膣 vagina.
chitsujo, n. 秩序 order.

chittomo, adv. ちっとも not
at all.
chiyahoya suru, vb. ちやほ
やする pamper; extol.
chizu, n. 地図 map.
-cho 著 book by;
Tanizakicho book by
Tanizaki.
chō, n. 腸 intestine; bowel;
daichō large intestine;
shōchō small intestine.
chō, n. 兆 trillion.
chō- 超 ultra-; super-; over-;
chō-jin-teki (na)
superhuman; **chō-man'in**
overcrowded.
-chō 町 town; district;
pontochō Ponto district.
-chō 庁 agency
(government); **bōeichō**
Defense Agency.
chōbo, n. 帳簿 account
book.
chochiku, n. 貯蓄 saving.
chōchin, n. 提灯 lantern.
chōchō, chōcho, n. 蝶々
butterfly; **chōchōsan**
Madame Butterfly.
chōdai, vb. ちょうだい give
me (request).
-chōdai ちょうだい please
... (request); **hanashite-
chōdai** tell me please.
chōdai suru, vb. ちょうだい
する 1. receive. 2. eat;
drink.
chōdo, adv. 丁度 exactly.
chōeki, n. 懲役 penal
servitude.
chōhōkei, n. 長方形
rectangle; oblong.
chōhonnin, n. 張本人
ringleader; instigator;
provocateur.
choi-choi, adv. ちょいちょ
い frequently.
chōin suru, vb. 調印する
sign a treaty or contract.
chōja, n. 長者 millionaire.

chōjikan, adv. 長時間 for long hours.

chōjin-teki (na), adj. 超人的 (な) superhuman.

chōjo, n. 長女 eldest daughter.

chōjō, n. 頂上 top; summit; pinnacle.

chōju, n. 長寿 longevity.

chōka, n. 超過 excess; **yunyū-chōka** excess of imports.

chōkan, n. 朝刊 morning newspaper.

chōkan, n. 長官 chief; director.

chōkeshi ni suru, vb. 帳消しにする cancel; wipe out.

chōki, n. 長期 long period of time; **chōkikeikaku** long-range plan; **chōkiyohō** long-range forecast.

chokin, n. 貯金 savings.

chokkai o dasu, vb. ちょっかいを出す meddle in; interfere with.

chokkaku, n. 直角 right angle; **chokkaku-sankakkei** right triangle.

chokkei, n. 直径 diameter.

chokkei, n. 直系 direct scion of a family; direct disciple.

chokketsu, n. 直結 direct connection.

chokki, n. チョッキ vest.

chokkō, n. 直行 nonstop or direct transportation; **chokkōbin** nonstop flight.

chokkō suru, vb. 直行する go directly.

choko, n. ちょこ sake cup.

chōkō, n. 兆候 symptom; sign; harbinger.

chōkoku, n. 彫刻 sculpture; carving.

chōkokuka, n. 彫刻家 sculptor.

choku-choku, adv. ちょく

ちょく frequently.

chokugo ni, adv. 直後に immediately after or behind.

chokumen suru, vb. 直面する 1. face; confront with. 2. be involved in.

chokusen, n. 直線 straight line.

chokusetsu (ni), adv. 直接 (に) directly.

chokushanikkō, n. 直射日光 direct sunlight.

chokushin suru, vb. 直進する go straight.

chokutsū (no), adj. 直通 (の) nonstop; direct; **chokutsū-basu** nonstop bus; **chokutsū-denwa** direct call.

chokuyaku, n. 直訳 literal translation.

chokuyunyū, n. 直輸入 direct import.

chokuzen (ni), adv. 直前 (に) just before.

chōkyori, n. 長距離 long distance; **chōkyoridenwa** long-distance call.

chōmei, n. 町名 town name; street name.

chōmei, n. 長命 long life.

chōmen, n. 帳面 notebook.

chōmin, n. 町民 townspeople.

chōmiryō, n. 調味料 seasoning.

chōnan, n. 長男 eldest son.

chō-nekutai, n. 蝶ネクタイ bow tie.

chongiru, vb. ちょん切る chop off.

chonmage, n. ちょんまげ topknot (hair style for a samurai or sumo wrestler).

chōnōryoku, n. 超能力 supernatural power.

chōrei, n. 朝礼 morning assembly.

chōri, n. 調理 cooking.

chōritsu (no), *adj.* 町立 (の) municipal.

choromakasu, *vb.* ちょろまかす pocket; filch; deceive.

chōsa, *n.* 調査 investigation; survey; analysis.

chosakuken, *n.* 著作権 copyright; **chosakuken-shingai** infringement of a copyright.

chōsei, *n.* 調整 adjustment.

chōsen, *n.* 挑戦 challenge.

chōsetsu, *n.* 調節 adjustment; tuning.

chosha, *n.* 著者 writer.

chōshi, *n.* 調子 1. condition (health, thing); **chōshi ga ii** in good condition; harmonious. 2. tune; **chōshi o awaseru** in tune; tune oneself to one's surroundings.

chōshin, *n.* 長針 long hand (watch, clock).

chōshin (no), *adj.* 長身 (の) tall.

chōshizen (no), *adj.* 超自然 (の) supernatural.

chōsho, *n.* 長所 merit; strong point.

chōshoku, *n.* 朝食 breakfast.

chōshū, *n.* 聴衆 audience.

chōten, *n.* 頂点 pinnacle; climax; top.

chotto, *adv.* ちょっと 1. a little. 2. just a moment. 3. not a bit; not very; not easily.

chotto, *interj.* ちょっと Hey you!

chōwa, *n.* 調和 harmony; balance.

chōzei, *n.* 町税 town tax.

chozō suru, *vb.* 貯蔵する store up.

chū, *n.* 注 annotation; note.

chū, *n.* 中 medium; average.

-chū 中 in the middle of; in the process of; during; in;

among; **denwachū** (in the middle of speaking) on the phone.

chūbei, *n.* 中米 Central America.

chūburarin (na, no), *adj.* 宙 ぶらりん (な、の) pending.

chūdan suru, *vb.* 中断する discontinue; interrupt; stop.

chūdoku, *n.* 中毒 poisoning; addiction; **fuguchūdoku** blowfish poisoning; **mayaku-chūdoku** drug addiction.

chūdoku(sha), *n.* 中毒(者) addict.

chūgakkō, chūgaku, *n.* 中学校、中学 junior high school.

chūgakusei, *n.* 中学生 junior high school student.

chūgen, *n.* 中元 gift traditionally given in midsummer.

chūgen suru, *vb.* 忠言する admonish; warn.

chūgoku, *n.* 中国 1. China. 2. western part of Honshū (Hiroshima area).

chūgurai (na, no), *adj.* 中位 (な、の) medium-size.

chūi, *n.* 注意 attention; caution; advice.

chūihō, *n.* 注意報 weather warning.

chūi jinbutsu, *n.* 注意人物 person of questionable personality, background, or behavior.

chūi suru, *vb.* 注意する pay attention to; take care of; be careful of.

chūjien, *n.* 中耳炎 middle ear infection.

chūjitsu (na), *adj.* 忠実 (な) faithful; devoted.

chūjun (ni), *adv.* 中旬 (に) around the middle of a month.

chūkagai, n. 中華街 Chinatown.

chūkajinmin-kyōwakoku, n. 中華人民共和国 People's Republic of China.

chūkan, n. 中間 middle; midway.

chūkanabe, n. 中華鍋 wok.

chūkanshiken, n. 中間試験 midterm exam.

chūkaryōri, n. 中華料理 Chinese food.

chūkei, n. 中継 broadcasting; **terebi-chūkei** TV broadcasting.

chūkintō, n. 中近東 the Near and Middle East.

chūkohin, n. 中古品 secondhand goods.

chūkoku, n. 忠告 advice; admonition.

chūkosha, n. 中古車 used car.

chūkyū, n. 中級 intermediate level; **nihongochūkyū** intermediate Japanese.

chūmoku, n. 注目 attention.

chūmon, n. 注文 order; request.

chūmon suru, vb. 注文する order; request.

chūnen (no), adj. 中年 (の) middle-aged.

chū ni, adv. 宙に in the air.

chūō, n. 中央 center; middle.

chūō, n. 中欧 Central Europe.

chūritsu (no), adj. 中立 (の) neutral.

chūryū(kaikyū), n. 中流(階級) the middle class.

chūsai, n. 仲裁 arbitration; mediation.

chūsei, n. 忠誠 loyalty; allegiance.

chūsei, n. 中世 the Middle Ages; medieval period.

chūsei, n. 中性 neuter.

chūseisenzai, n. 中性洗剤 neutral detergent.

chūseishi, n. 中性子 neutron; **chūseishi-bakudan** neutron bomb.

chūsen, n. 抽選 lot; drawing; raffle.

chūsha, n. 注射 injection; shot.

chūsha, n. 駐車 parking.

chūshahan, n. 駐車違反 parking violation.

chūshajō, n. 駐車場 parking lot.

chūshakinshi, n. 駐車禁止 No Parking.

chūsha suru, vb. 駐車する park a car.

chūshin, n. 中心 center; core; focus.

chūshinten, n. 中心点 central (focal) point.

chūshi suru, vb. 中止する suspend; cancel; stop.

chūshoku, n. 昼食 lunch.

chūshōmeishi, n. 抽象名詞 abstract noun.

chūshō-teki (na), adj. 抽象的 (な) abstract; vague.

chūtai suru, chūtotaigaku suru, vb. 中退する, 中途退学する drop out of school; quit school.

chūtō, n. 中東 the Middle East.

chūto de, adv. 中途で midway; halfway.

chūtohanpa (na, no), adj. 中途半端 (な、の) 1. incomplete; fragmentary. 2. halfhearted.

chūwa suru, vb. 中和する neutralize.

chūya, n. 昼夜 night and day; around the clock.

chūzetsu, n. 中絶 1. interruption; discontinuation; suspension. 2. abortion.

D

dābī, n. ダービー (E. *derby*) horse race.

dabokushō, n. 打撲傷 bruise.

dabudabu (no), adj. だぶだぶ (の) baggy.

daburu, adj. ダブル (E.) double; double-breasted.

daburu, vb. ダブる (E. *double*) overlap; duplicate.

daeki, n. 唾液 saliva.

daen(kei), n. 楕円(形) oval.

dageki, n. 打撃 shock; impact.

dai, n. 大 large size.

dai, n. 代 1. generation. 2. reign. 3. lifetime. 4. a certain age; **gojūdai no hito** a person in his or her fifties.

dai, n. 題 title; topic.

dai, n. 台 1. stand; base. 2. a certain amount of space, time, or money.

dai- 第 (ordinal number indicator) **dai-ichi** first place.

dai- 大 1. big; serious; **daimondai** big problem. 2. very (much); **dai-suki to** like very much.

-dai 代 cost; price; **basudai** bus fare; **shokujidai** cost of meal.

daiben, n. 大便 feces; bowel movement.

daibu(n), adv. 大分 considerably; quite.

daibubun, n. 大部分 major part; majority.

daibutsu, n. 大仏 large statue of Buddha.

daichō, n. 大腸 large intestine.

daidokoro, n. 台所 kitchen.

daietto suru, vb. ダイエットする (E.) go on a diet.

daigaku, n. 大学 college; university; **kokuritsu (shiritsu, shūritsu, joshi) daigaku** national (private, state, women's) college or university.

daigakuin, n. 大学院 graduate school.

daigakunyūshi, n. 大学入試 college or university entrance examination.

daigakusei, n. 大学生 college or university student.

daihyō, n. 代表 delegate; representative; representation.

daihyō-teki (na), adj. 代表的 (な) representative; exemplary.

dai-ichi (no), adj. 第一 (の)the most; the best; first.

dai-ichiji-sekaitaisen, n. 第一次世界大戦 World War I.

daiji (na), adj. 大事 (な) important; precious; **(O)daiji ni.** Take care!

daijōbu, adj. 大丈夫 all right; safe; fine; **Daijōbu.** I am (it is) all right.

daikibo (na, no), adj. 大規模 (な、の) large-scale.

daikin, n. 代金 cost; price; charge.

daikon, n. 大根 large white winter radish.

daimeishi, n. 代名詞 pronoun.

dainashi ni suru, vb. 台無しにする mar; ruin.

dai-niji-sekaitaisen, n. 第二次世界大戦 World War II.

dairi, n. 代理 agent; proxy; substitute; surrogate; **ryokō-dairiten** travel agency.

dairiseki, n. 大理石 marble.

daisotsu, n. 大卒 college or university graduate.

daitai, adv. 大体 mostly; almost; approximately.

daitan (na), adj. 大胆 (な) bold; brave.

daitasū, n. 大多数 majority.

daitōryō, n. 大統領 (nation's) president; **fukudaitōryō** vice president.

daiya, n. ダイヤ (E.) diagram; train schedule.

daiya(mondo), n. ダイヤ(モンド) (E.) diamond.

daiyaku, n. 代役 substitute; understudy.

daizu, n. 大豆 soybean.

dajare, n. 駄洒落 corny joke; **dajare o tobasu** tell a corny joke.

dakara, adv. だから therefore; so.

dake, parti. だけ only; simply; **anata dake** only you; **miru dake no tame ni** just looking.

dakedo, conj. だけど although; but.

daketsu suru, vb. 打決する reach agreement; settle (a matter).

daku, vb. 抱く hold; embrace; hug.

dakyō suru, vb. 妥協する compromise.

damaru, vb. 黙る keep silent.

damasu, vb. だます deceive; cheat.

dame (na), adj. だめ (な) 1. bad; wrong. 2. useless; impossible. 3. necessary; **ikanakutewa dame** necessary to go.

dan, n. 段 1. stair; step; **dan o agaru** climb steps. 2. (learning or martial art) level; grade; **karate sandan**

3rd grade in karate.

dan, n. 壇 platform.

-dan 団 group; party; **kishadan** press group.

danbō, n. 暖房 heating.

danbōru, n. 段ボール cardboard.

danbō-setsubi, n. 暖房設備 heating equipment or system.

danchi, n. 団地 public housing or apartment complex.

danchō, n. 団長 group leader.

dan-dan, adv. 段々 gradually.

dandori, n. 段取り preparation; arrangement; direction.

dangen suru, vb. 断言する allege; assert; declare.

dango, n. 団子 dumpling.

dani, n. だに 1. tick (insect). 2. scoundrel; scum.

danji, n. 男児 male; boy.

danjiki, n. 断食 fast.

danjite, adv. 断じて 1. (with a negative) definitely not; absolutely not. 2. never.

danjo, n. 男女 both sexes.

dankai, n. 段階 stage (development); step.

danketsu suru, vb. 団結する unite; consolidate.

dankotaru, adj. 断固たる resolved; determined.

danmen, n. 断面 aspect; section.

dan'nasan, n. 旦那さん male customer; husband; master.

dan'netsu, n. 断熱 insulation.

danpan, n. 談判 negotiation.

danraku, n. 段落 paragraph.

danryoku(sei), n. 弾力(性) elasticity; flexibility.

dansei, n. 男性 male

(person).

dansei-teki (na), adj. 男性的 (な) masculine.

danshi, n. 男子 boy; male.

dansu, n. ダンス (E.) dance.

dantai, n. 団体 group; organization; **shōhisha dantai** consumer group.

dantei, n. 断定 conclusion; affirmation.

dantei suru, vb. 断定する conclude.

dan'yū, n. 男優 actor.

danzen, adv. 断然 by far; prominently.

danzoku-teki (na), adj. 断続的 (な) intermittent.

-darake (no) だらけ (の) full of; **hitodarake** full of people.

daraku, n. 堕落 depravity; corruption.

darashinai, adj. だらしない sloppy; disorganized; undisciplined.

dare, pron. 誰 who.

dare demo, pron. 誰でも anyone; **Dare demo ii.** Anyone will do.

darehitori, pron. 誰ひとり (with a negative) no one; **Darehitori konakatta.** No one came.

dareka, pron. 誰か someone.

dare ni, pron. 誰に (to) whom.

dare no, pron. 誰の whose.

darō aux. vb. だろう may; will probably; **kuru darō** will probably come.

darui, adj. だるい lethargic; sluggish; dull.

dashi, n. 出し soup stock.

dashin suru, vb. 打診する sound out (a person).

dashinuke ni, adv. 出し抜けに suddenly; abruptly.

dassen, n. 脱線 derailment; digression.

dasshutsu suru, vb. 脱出する escape; flee.

dasshūzai, n. 脱臭剤 deodorizer.

dassuru, vb. 脱する extricate oneself from (crisis, problem).

dasu, vb. 出す 1. put forth; produce; issue. 2. draw out; take out. 3. generate. 4. show. 5. mail. 6. hand in. 7. serve (meal).

-dasu 出す start; **hashiri-dasu** start running.

dāsu, n. ダース (E.) dozen.

-date (no) 建て -storied (building); **nikaidate no** two-storied.

date otoko, n. 伊達男 dandy.

datō (na), adj. 妥当 (な) right; appropriate; reasonable.

datō suru, vb. 打倒する defeat; win.

de, parti. で 1. (space) at; in; on; **tōkyō de** in Tokyo. 2. (time) in; **gofun de** in five minutes. 3. (means) by; in; on; **inki de** in ink; **denwa de** on the phone. 4. (age) at. 5. (price) at; for. 6. (made) from; of. 7. (cause) because of. 8. per.

deai, n. 出会い encounter; meeting.

dearuku, vb. 出歩く walk around; stroll.

deashi, n. 出足 1. start; **deashi ga ii** good start. 2. turnout.

deau, vb. 出会う encounter; meet.

deban, n. 出番 one's turn.

debu, n. でぶ (derogatory) fat person.

debushō, n. 出不精 homebody; stay-at-home.

debyū, n. デビュー (F.)

debut.

dedokoro, *n.* 出所 source; origin.

defure, *n.* デフレ (E.) deflation.

deguchi, *n.* 出口 exit.

deiri, *n.* 出入り comings and goings.

deka, *n.* でか (derogatory) policeman; detective.

dekai, *adj.* でかい big; huge.

dekakeru, *vb.* 出掛ける go out; leave.

dekasegi, *n.* 出稼ぎ working temporarily away from home (migrant, seasonal labor).

dekashita, *interj.* でかした Great! Good job! Well done!

deki, *n.* 出来 1. result; product; quality; **deki ga ii** good result (product, quality). 2. ability.

dekiagaru, *vb.* 出来上がる be completed; be ready.

dekibae, *n.* 出来栄え result; outcome.

dekigokoro, *n.* 出来心 impulse; **dekigokoro de** impulsively; thoughtlessly.

dekigoto, *n.* 出来事 occurrence; event.

dekimono, *n.* 出来物 boil; polyp; ulcer.

dekireba, *adv.* 出来れば if possible.

dekiru, *vb.* 出来る 1. be able (to); excel (in); be capable (of). 2. be ready; be finished. 3. be established; be built. 4. be made; be produced.

dekiru-dake/-kagiri, *adv.* 出来るだけ/～限り as (much, many, soon) as possible; to the best of one's ability.

dekiru(koto)nara, *adv.* 出来る(こと)なら if possible.

dekitate (no hoya-hoya), *adj.* 出来立て (のほやほや) freshly made; brand-new.

dekoboko (na, no), *adj.* でこぼこ (な、の) uneven or bumpy (surface).

dema, *n.* デマ (G. *Demagogie*) unsupported rumor; **dema o nagasu** spread a rumor.

demae, *n.* 出前 (food) delivery service; catering service.

demakase ni, *adv.* 出任せに irresponsibly; haphazardly.

demo, *n.* デモ (E.) demonstration.

demo, *conj.* でも however; but.

demo でも 1. *adj.* any; **dare demo** anyone; **Nan demo ii.** Anything will do. 2. *adv.* even; at least; as well; **Boku demo dekiru.** Even I can do that.

demukaeru, *vb.* 出迎える meet or pick someone up (at an airport, etc.); salute; welcome.

denaosu, *vb.* 出直す come back later; start again.

den'atsu, *n.* 電圧 voltage.

denchi, *n.* 電池 battery.

dengen, *n.* 電源 electric power source.

dengon, *n.* 伝言 message.

denka, *n.* 殿下 title bestowed on imperial family members.

denki, *n.* 伝記 biography.

denki, *n.* 電気 electricity; **denkigama (denkimōfu, denkisentakuki, denkisōjiki)** electric rice cooker (blanket, washing machine, vacuum cleaner).

denkiseihin, *n.* 電気製品 electrical appliance; equipment.

denkyū, n. 電球 electric bulb.

denpa, n. 電波 radio wave.

denpō, n. 電報 telegram; **denpō o utsu** send a telegram.

denpun, n. でんぷん starch.

denryoku, n. 電力 electric power.

denryoku-gaisha/-kaisha, n. 電力会社 electric power company.

denryū, n. 電流 electric current.

densen, n. 電線 electric wire; telephone line; cable.

densenbyō, n. 伝染病 infectious or contagious disease.

densetsu, n. 伝説 legend.

densha, n. 電車 train.

denshi, n. 電子 electron.

denshikeisanki, n. 電子計算機 computer.

denshi kōgaku, n. 電子工学 electronics.

denshi-renji, n. 電子レンジ microwave oven.

dentaku, n. 電卓 calculator.

dentatsu, n. 伝達 communication; transmission; message; report.

dentō, n. 電灯 electric light.

dentō, n. 伝統 tradition; heritage.

dentō-teki (na), adj. 伝統的 (な) traditional.

denwa, n. 電話 telephone; **aka-/kōshū-denwa** public phone; **itazuradenwa** crank call; **kokusaidenwa** international call; **machigaidenwa** wrong number; **denwa o kakeru/suru** make a phone call.

denwabangō, n. 電話番号 telephone number.

denwachō, n. 電話帳 telephone directory.

denwakyoku, n. 電話局 telephone company or office.

deru, vb. 出る 1. come out; go out; leave; graduate from. 2. attend; participate. 3. appear. 4. be published.

deshabari, n. 出しゃばり nosy person.

deshabaru, vb. 出しゃばる poke one's nose into.

deshi, n. 弟子 disciple; follower; apprentice.

deshō, aux. vb. でしょう 1. will. 2. probably. 3. I think that; I am afraid that; it seems that. 4. Don't you think that ... ?

detarame (na, no), adj. でたらめ (な、の) nonsensical; absurd; irresponsible; random.

dēta-shori, n. データ処理 (E.) data processing.

detchiageru, vb. でっち上げる fake (a story or rumor); fabricate.

dewa, interj. では Now ...; Well ...; Then ...

-do 度 1. degree (temperature, angle, latitude, altitude); **sesshi jūdo** ten degrees Celsius. 2. time (frequency); **sando** three times. 3. proof (alcohol).

dō, n. 銅 copper.

dō, n. 胴 torso; trunk (body).

dō, adv. どう 1. would you like; **Kōhī wa dō.** Would you like coffee? 2. what; what about; **Sore o dō omoimasu ka.** What do you think of that? 3. how; how about; **Ryokō wa dō deshita ka.** How was your trip? 4. **Dō itashimashite.**

My pleasure.

doai, *n.* 度合い degree; extent; intensity.

dobokukōji, *n.* 土木工事 construction project.

dōbutsu, *n.* 動物 animal.

dōbutsuen, *n.* 動物園 zoo.

dochaku (no), *adj.* 土着 (の) aboriginal; indigenous; native.

dochira どちら 1. *pron.* who; which. 2. *adj.* which; what. 3. *adv.* where.

dochira ka, *n.* どちらか one of the two; either ... or ...

dochira mo, *n.* どちらも 1. both. 2. neither of the two; **Dochira mo yokunai.** Neither of them is good.

dodai, *n.* 土台 foundation; basis.

Dō demo ii. どうでもいい It does not matter.

dōdō-taru/-toshita/-toshiteiru, *adj.* 堂々たる／〜とした／〜としている stately; imposing.

dōfū suru, *vb.* 同封する enclose in an envelope).

dogimagi suru, *vb.* どぎまぎする feel embarrassed; be abashed.

dōgu, *n.* 道具 appliance; utensil; tool.

dōhan suru, *vb.* 同伴する go together; accompany.

dohyō, *n.* 土俵 sumo ring.

dōi, *n.* 同意 agreement; consent.

dōigo, *n.* 同意語 synonym.

dōin suru, *vb.* 動員する mobilize.

dōi suru, *vb.* 同意する agree; consent.

doitsu, *n.* ドイツ (G. *Deutschland*) Germany.

dōitsu (no), *adj.* 同一 (の) same; alike; equal.

dō iu どう言う 1. *adj.* what

sort of; **dō iu hon** what sort of book. 2. *adv.* **dō iu wake de** why; **dō iu fu ni** how.

dōjidai (no), *adj.* 同時代 (の) coeval; contemporary.

dōji ni, *adv.* 同時に simultaneously.

dōji tsūyaku, *n.* 同時通訳 simultaneous interpretation; simultaneous interpreter.

dōjō, *n.* 道場 place for practice or tournament (martial arts).

dōjō, *n.* 同情 sympathy; pity.

dōjō suru, *vb.* 同情する sympathize; feel pity for.

dōka どうか (used in combination with a *vb.*) 1. (asking) please; be so kind as to; **Dōka tetsudatte kudasai.** Please help me. 2. (expressing a hope or wish) **Dōka ki o tsukete kudasai.** Please take care of yourself. 3. whether (or not); **Iku ka dōka wakaranai.** I'm not sure whether I'll go. 4. disagreement; doubt; **dōka to omou** think questionable.

dōkan suru, *vb.* 同感する have the same opinion; have the same feeling (as another).

dokasu, *vb.* どかす remove (a thing out of one's way).

dōka shiteiru, *vb.* どうかしている be out of one's mind; be out of sorts.

dōke, *n.* 道化 clown; buffoon.

doki, *n.* 土器 earthenware.

dōki, *n.* 動機 motive.

doki-doki suru, *vb.* どきどきする feel nervous; have heart palpitations.

doko (ni), *adv.* どこ (に)

where.

dōkōkai, n. 同好会 circle; league; clique.

-dokoroka どころか 1. in addition; as well as; **kodomo-dokoroka otona mo** adults as well as children. 2. conversely; on the contrary.

dōkō suru, vb. 同行する accompany; go with someone.

doku, n. 毒 poison.

doku, vb. どく step aside; make way for (someone).

dokudan-teki (na), adj. 独断的 (な) arbitrary; dogmatic.

dokuji (na, no), adj. 独自 (な、の) unique; original.

dokuritsu suru, vb. 独立する become independent.

dokusen, n. 独占 monopoly.

dokusha, n. 読者 reader.

dokushin (no), adj. 独身 (の) celibate; single; unmarried.

dokusho, n. 読書 reading.

dokusō-teki (na), adj. 独創的 (な) creative; original; unique.

dokutoku (na, no), adj. 独特 (な、の) unique; characteristic; original.

dōkutsu, n. 洞窟 grotto; cave.

dokyō, n. 度胸 courage; audacity; **dokyō ga aru** be courageous.

dōkyo, n. 同居 cohabitation; living together.

dōkyūsei, n. 同級生 classmate.

dō medaru, n. 銅メダル bronze medal.

dōmei, n. 同盟 alliance; league; union.

dō mite mo, udv. どう見ても definitely; indubitably.

dōmo, adv. どうも 1. very much; terribly; **Dōmo arigatō.** Thank you very much. 2. somehow; somewhat. 3. probably. **Dōmo dame darō.** It probably won't (work, happen).

domoru, vb. 吃る stammer; stutter.

dōmyaku, n. 動脈 artery.

donabe, n. 土鍋 earthenware pot.

donaru, vb. どなる yell at; shout.

donata, pron. どなた who.

donburi, n. 丼 bowl (for noodles, rice); meal served in such a bowl.

donchansawagi, n. どんちゃん騒ぎ uproarious merrymaking; revelry.

don-don どんどん 1. n. beating sound; tom-tom. 2. adv. progressively; rapidly.

donguri, n. どんぐり acorn.

dōnika, adv. どうにか somehow; barely.

donkan (na), adj. 鈍感 (な) insensitive.

don'na, adj. どんな what kind of; what.

don'na ni, adv. どんなに however hard; how; **don'na ni hataraite mo** however hard I work.

dono, adj. どの 1. which; what. 2. every; any.

dono hen (ni), adv. どの辺 (に) where.

dono-kurai/-gurai, adv. どの位 how long (many, much, often).

dono yō na, adj どの様な what kind of.

dono yō ni, adv. どの様に how; in what way.

donzoko, n. どん底 depths.

dōon'igigo, n. 同音異義語.

homonym.

dōraku, *n.* 道楽 1. hobby. 2. dissipation.

dore, *pron.* どれ which; what.

dore dake, *adv.* どれだけ how many; how much.

dorei, *n.* 奴隷 slave.

dore-kurai/-gurai, *adv.* どれ位 how far (long, many, much).

-dōri 通り street;
aoyamadōri Aoyama Street.

dōri, *n.* 道理 right; reason;
dōri ni kanau do the right thing.

dōri de, *adv.* 道理で (it is) no wonder.

doro, *n.* 泥 mud.

dōro, *n.* 道路 road.

dorobō, *n.* 泥棒 thief.

doru, *n.* ドル (E.) dollar.

dōrui (no), *adj.* 同類 (の) of the same kind.

dōryō, *n.* 同僚 pal; colleague; coworker.

doryoku, *n.* 努力 effort.

dōsa, *n.* 動作 movement.

dosakusa, *n.* どさくさ confusion.

dōsan, *n.* 動産 personal property.

dōse, *adv.* どうせ at best; anyway; as supposed.

dōsei, *n.* 同姓 same surname.

dōsei, *n.* 同棲 cohabitation (unmarried couple).

dōseiai, *n.* 同性愛 homosexuality; lesbianism.

dōseidōmei, *n.* 同姓同名 same family and given names.

dōshi, *n.* 動詞 verb.

dōshi 同士 1. *n.* peer; member; comrade. 2. *pron.* each other.

doshi-doshi, *adv.* どしどし quantitatively; frequently.

dō shita, *pron., adj.* どうした what; **Dō shita no.** What happened?

dō shite, *adv.* どうして why; how.

dō shite mo, *adv.* どうしても by any means.

dōshitsu (no), *adj.* 同質の of the same quality.

dō shiyō mo nai, *adj.* どうしようもない helpless; impossible.

dōshu (no), *adj.* 同種 (の) of the same type or kind.

dosoku de, *adv.* 土足で with one's shoes on.

dossari (to), *adv.* どっさり (と) abundantly.

dotabata, *n.* どたばた confusion; noise.

dōtai, *n.* 胴体 body; torso.

dotanba de, *adv.* 土壇場で at a crucial moment; at the last moment.

dotchi, *pron.* どっち which.

dotchi mo, *pron.* どっちも 1. both. 2. neither of the two.

dōtoku, *n.* 道徳 morality; moral; ethics;
kōshūdōtoku public morals.

dotto, *adv.* どっと in a torrent; suddenly.

dōwa, *n.* 童話 fairy tale.

dowasure suru, *vb.* 度忘れ する forget temporarily.

doya-doya (to), *adv.* どやど や (と) boisterously; noisily.

dō yara, *adv.* どうやら probably; somehow.

dō yatte, *adv.* どうやって how.

dōyō, *n.* 童謡 children's song.

dōyō (na, no), *adj.* 同様 (な、の) similar; same.

doyōbi, *n.* 土曜日 Saturday; **doyōbi ni** on Saturday.

dōyō suru, *vb.* 動揺する feel uneasy; get agitated; lose composure.

dōzen (no), *adj.* 同然の same; equal.

dōzo, *adv.* どうぞ please; **Dōzo kochira ni.** This way, please. **Dōzo yoroshiku.** Nice to meet you.

dōzō, *n.* 銅像 bronze statue.

dōzoku, *n.* 同族 same stock; same tribe.

E

e, *n.* 絵 painting; drawing.

e, *parti.* へ to; for; toward; **nihon e iku** go to Japan.

ē, *adv.* ええ yes.

e', ē, *interj.* えっ、えー 1. (utterance expressing surprise or doubt) Eh? What? 2. (hesitation) Well ...

eakon, *n.* エアコン (E.) air conditioner.

ebi, *n.* 海老 shrimp; prawn.

eda, *n.* 枝 bough; branch; twig.

egaku, *vb.* 描く 1. paint; draw. 2. portray; describe.

egao, *n.* 笑顔 smiling face.

ehagaki, *n.* 絵葉書 picture postcard.

ehon, *n.* 絵本 picture book.

elbun, *n.* 英文 English-language text.

eien, *n.* 永遠 eternity.

eien ni, *adv.* 永遠に eternally; forever.

eien no, *adj.* 永遠の eternal; infinite; undying.

eiga, *n.* 映画 movie; film; **eiga o miru** watch a movie.

eigakan, *n.* 映画館 movie theater; cinema.

eigo, *n.* 英語 English language.

eigyō, *n.* 営業 business.

eijishinbun, *n.* 英字新聞 English-language newspaper.

eijūsha, *n.* 永住者 permanent resident.

eijū suru, *vb.* 永住する make one's permanent home in.

eikaiwa, *n.* 英会話 English conversation.

eikō, *n.* 栄光 glory; eminence.

eikoku, *n.* 英国 England.

eikyō, *n.* 影響 influence; effect.

eikyū, *n.* 永久 eternity.

eikyū ni, *adv.* 永久に forever; permanently.

eimin, *n.* 永眠 death.

eiri, *n.* 営利 profit; lucre.

eiri no, *adj.* 絵入りの illustrated.

eisei, *n.* 衛生 hygiene; sanitation.

eisei, *n.* 衛星 satellite; **kishōeisei** weather satellite.

eiseihōsō, *n.* 衛星放送 satellite broadcast.

eisei-teki (na), *adj.* 衛生的 (な) hygienic; sanitary.

eiyō, *n.* 栄養 nutrition; nourishment.

eiyōshitchō, *n.* 栄養失調 malnutrition.

eiyū, *n.* 英雄 hero.

eizō, *n.* 映像 image; picture (screen).

eizoku-teki (na), *adj.* 永続的 (な) lasting; enduring.

eizu, *n.* エイズ (E.) AIDS.

eizu-kanja, *n.* エイズ患者

AIDS patient.

ejiki, *n.* えじき prey; victim.

ekaki, *n.* 絵かき painter (artist).

eki, *n.* 駅 railway station.

eki, *n.* 益 usefulness; benefit; profit.

eki, *n.* 液 liquid.

ekiben, *n.* 駅弁 box lunches sold at train stations.

ekibyō, *n.* 疫病 plague; epidemic.

ekichō, *n.* 駅長 railway stationmaster.

eki'in, *n.* 駅員 railway station employee.

ekijō no, *adj.* 液状の liquid.

ekishō, *n.* 液晶 liquid crystal.

ekitai, *n.* 液体 liquid.

ekkusu-sen, *n.* エックス線 (E.) X-ray.

ekohiiki suru, *vb.* えこひいきする be partial (to a person); favor.

ekubo, *n.* えくぼ dimple.

emono, *n.* 獲物 game (hunting); catch (fishing).

en, *n.* 円 1. Japanese yen. 2. circle.

en, *n.* 縁 1. relation; bond; kinship. 2. fate.

enbun, *n.* 塩分 salt or sodium content.

enchō suru, *vb.* 延長する extend; prolong.

endai (na), *adj.* 遠大 (な) far-reaching.

endaka, *n.* 円高 appreciation of the yen.

endan, *n.* 縁談 marriage proposal.

endōi, *adj.* 縁遠い dissociated; unrelated.

en-en (to), *adv.* 延々 (と) at great length (time).

engan, *n.* 沿岸 coast.

engawa, *n.* 縁側 veranda.

engei, *n.* 演芸 entertainment; performing art.

engeki, *n.* 演劇 drama; play.

engi, *n.* 演技 performance (stage).

engi, *n.* 縁起 luck.

engo suru, *vb.* 援護する protect; support.

engumi, *n.* 縁組み marriage.

enjiru, *vb.* 演じる act; perform; play.

enjo, *n.* 援助 support; aid; help; **shikin'enjo** financial aid.

enjo suru, *vb.* 援助する support; aid; help.

enkai, *n.* 宴会 party (celebration).

enkei (no), *adj.* 円形 (の) circular.

enki suru, *vb.* 延期する postpone.

enman (na), *adj.* 円満 (な) 1. harmonious; satisfying. 2. (person) contented.

enmusubi, *n.* 縁結び matchmaking.

enogu, *n.* 絵具 artist's paint; **abura-enogu** oil paint.

e no yō na, *adj.* 絵の様な picturesque.

enpitsu, *n.* 鉛筆 pencil.

enryo, *n.* 遠慮 hesitation; **enryo-naku** without hesitation or reserve.

enryobukai, *adj.* 遠慮深い shy; reserved.

enryo suru, *vb.* 遠慮する hesitate; refrain from; **tabako o enryo suru** refrain from smoking.

enshi, *n.* 遠視 farsightedness.

enshō, *n.* 炎症 inflammation.

enshū, *n.* 演習 1. exercise (study). 2. maneuver (military).

enshutsu, *n.* 演出 direction

(stage, movie).

ensō, *n.* 演奏 performance (music).

ensō-ka/-sha, *n.* 演奏家/〜者 performer (music).

ensōkai, *n.* 演奏会 recital; concert.

ensoku, *n.* 遠足 hiking; outing.

entotsu, *n.* 煙突 chimney.

en'yasu, *n.* 円安 depreciation of the yen.

enzetsu, *n.* 演説 speech.

erabu, *vb.* 選ぶ choose; elect.

erai, *adj.* 偉い 1. eminent (person). 2. awful.

eri, *n.* 襟 collar; lapel.

erigonomi suru, *vb.* 選り好みする be choosy.

erinuki no, *adj.* 選り抜きの select.

eriwakeru, *vb.* 選り分ける sort out.

ero, *n.* エロ (E.) eroticism.

ero(chikku na), *adj.* エロ (チックな) (E.) erotic.

esa, *n.* 餌 bait; animal feed.

eshaku suru, *vb.* 会釈する salute; bow.

etai no shirenai, *adj.* 得体の知れない questionable; untrustworthy; enigmatic.

etchi, *n.* エッチ lecherous person.

ēto, *interj.* え - と Well ...; Let me see.

F

faito, *n.* ファイト (E.) fight; guts.

fu, *n.* 府 prefecture; **kyōtofu** Kyoto Prefecture.

fū, *n.* 封 seal (envelope); **fū o suru** seal a letter; **fū o kiru** open a letter.

fū, *n.* 風 1. appearance; condition. 2. style; **wafū** Japanese style.

fuan (na), *adj.* 不安 (な) uneasy; anxious.

fuben (na), *adj.* 不便 (な) inconvenient.

fubi, *n.* 不備 inadequacy; lack.

fubin (na), *adj.* 不憫 (な) pitiable; poignant.

fubo, *n.* 父母 parents.

fubuki, *n.* 吹雪 blizzard.

fuchi, *n.* 縁 1. edge; brim; tip. 2. eyeglass frames.

fuchi no, fuji no, *adj.* 不治の incurable: **fuchi no yamai** incurable disease.

fuchō, *n.* 不調 slump; undesirable condition.

fuchō, *n.* 婦長 head nurse.

fūchō, *n.* 風潮 trend.

fuchūi, *n.* 不注意 carelessness; inattentiveness.

fuda, *n.* 札 1. label; tag; signboard. 2. game card. 3. paper talisman.

fudangi, *n.* 普段着 casual clothing.

fudan no, *adj.* 普段の usual; casual; everyday.

fude, *n.* 筆 brush for writing or painting.

fudebushō, *n.* 筆不精 poor correspondent.

fudemame, *n.* 筆まめ good correspondent.

fūdo, *n.* 風土 natural characteristics of an area; climate.

fudō (no), *adj.* 不動 (の) steadfast; firm.

fudōsan, *n.* 不動産 real estate.

fudōtoku (na), *adj.* 不道徳 (な) immoral.

fue, *n.* 笛 pipe (music); flute; whistle.

fueisei (na), *adj.* 不衛生 (な) unsanitary.

fueru, *vb.* 増える increase.

fūfu, *n.* 夫婦 married couple; **shinkonfūfu** newlyweds.

fūfugenka, *n.* 夫婦げんか married couple's quarrel.

fūgawari (na), *adj.* 風変わり (な) eccentric; odd.

fugi, *n.* 不義 adultery.

fugōkaku, *n.* 不合格 failure (test); **fugōkaku ni naru** fail (an examination).

fugōri (na), *adj.* 不合理 (な) absurd; irrational.

fugu, *n.* ふぐ blowfish; puffer.

fuhai suru, *vb.* 腐敗する 1. decompose; rot; decay. 2. become corrupt.

fuhei, *n.* 不平 complaint; dissatisfaction; **fuhei o iu** complain.

fuhen (no), *adj.* 不変 (の) constant; unchanging; eternal.

fuhinkō, *n.* 不品行 immorality; impropriety.

fuhitsuyō (na), *adj.* 不必要 (な) unnecessary.

fuhō (na, no), *adj.* 不法 (な、の) illegal.

fuhon'i (na), *adj.* 不本意 (な) unwilling; reluctant.

fui ni, *adv.* 不意に suddenly; unexpectedly.

fui ni naru, *vb.* ふいになる become useless; fail.

fui ni suru, *vb.* ふいにする miss (an opportunity); lose.

fūin suru, *vb.* 封印する affix a seal (to a letter).

fuirumu, *n.* see **firumu.**

fuitchi, *n.* 不一致 disharmony; disparity; incompatibility.

fuiuchi, *n.* 不意打ち surprise

attack; **fuiuchishiken** surprise exam.

fuji, *n.* 藤 wisteria.

fujichaku(riku), *n.* 不時着 (陸) emergency landing.

fujimi (no), *adj.* 不死身 (の) immortal; invulnerable.

fujin, *n.* 夫人 wife (of someone other than the speaker).

fujin, *n.* 婦人 woman; lady.

fujinka, *n.* 婦人科 gynecology.

fujinkeikan, *n.* 婦人警官 policewoman.

fuji no, *adj.* see **fuchi no.**

fujitsu (na, no), *adj.* 不実 (な、の) 1. unfaithful; insincere. 2. untrue.

fujiyū (na), *adj.* 不自由 (な) 1. inconvenient; uncomfortable. 2. impecunious. 3. physically handicapped.

fujobōkō, *n.* 婦女暴行 rape.

fujo(shi), *n.* 婦女(子) woman; women.

fujūbun (na), *adj.* 不十分 (な) insufficient.

fujun (na), *adj.* 不順 (な) changeable or unseasonable (weather).

fukai, *adj.* 深い 1. deep; profound. 2. dense. 3. intimate.

fukai (na), *adj.* 不快 uncomfortable; offensive.

fukaketsu (na, no), *adj.* 不可欠 (な、の) indispensable.

fukakujitsu (na), *adj.* 不確実 (な) uncertain; unreliable.

fukameru, *vb.* 深める 1. deepen. 2. elaborate.

fukanō (na), *adj.* 不可能 (な) impossible.

fukanzen (na), *adj.* 不完全 (な) incomplete; imperfect.

fukasa, *n.* 深さ depth.

fukasu, vb. 蒸かす steam (food).

fukasu, vb. 吹かす 1. exhale cigarette smoke. 2. rev up (engine).

fuke, n. ふけ dandruff; **fuketori-shanpū** dandruff shampoo.

fukei, n. 父兄 parents; guardians.

fūkei, n. 風景 view; scenery; landscape.

fukeiki (na), adj. 不景気 (な) 1. recessionary (economy). 2. glum; uninteresting.

fukeizai (na), adj. 不経済 (な) uneconomical.

fukenkō (na), adj. 不健康 (な) unhealthy.

fukeru, vb. 老ける age; lose youthful appearance.

fuketsu (na), adj. 不潔 (な) 1. unsanitary; filthy. 2. dirty (person); impure; immoral.

fukidasu, vb. 吹き出す 1. start to blow (wind); erupt; gush out. 2. burst into laughter.

fukidemono, n. 吹き出物 skin eruption; pimple; boil; acne.

fukigen (na), adj. 不機嫌 (な) morose; bad-tempered; sullen.

fukikakeru, vb. 吹き掛ける sprinkle; spray; blow.

fukikomu, vb. 吹き込む 1. blow into. 2. instruct; influence. 3. record (music).

fukin, n. 布巾 dish towel.

fukin, n. 付近 neighborhood; **kono fukin ni** in this neighborhood; **fukin no resutoran** neighborhood restaurant.

fukitaosu, vb. 吹き倒す

blow down.

fukitobu, vb. 吹き飛ぶ be blown away.

fukitoru, vb. 拭き取る wipe off; mop up.

fukitsu 不吉 1. n. ill omen. 2. adj. unlucky; ominous.

fukkatsu, n. 復活 revival; resurrection.

fukkatsusai, n. 復活祭 Easter.

fukki suru, vb. 復帰する make a comeback.

fukkura shita, adj. ふっくらした chubby; plump.

fukkyū suru, vb. 復旧する restore; resume service.

fukō, n. 不幸 1. unhappiness; ill fortune. 2. death.

fukōhei (na), adj. 不公平 (な) unfair; discriminatory; biased.

fuku, n. 福 good luck; fortune.

fuku, n. 服 clothing; clothes. **fuku o kiru** put on clothes; **fuku o kigaeru** change clothes; **fuku o nugu** undress.

fuku, vb. 吹く 1. blow (wind, breath); breathe. 2. whistle; play a wind instrument.

fuku, vb. 拭く wipe; mop; dry (dishes).

fuku- 副 vice-; **fukudaitōryō** vice president.

fukugyō, n. 副業 moonlighting; second job.

fukuji, n. 服地 fabric (cloth).

fukujū suru, vb. 服従する obey; submit.

fukumen, n. 覆面 mask; **fukumen-patokā** unmarked police car.

fukumeru, vb. 含める include.

fukumete, *prep.* 含めて including; **kyō o fukumete** including today.

fukurama-seru/-su, *vb.* ふくらませる／〜す 1. blow up; **fūsen o fukuramaseru** blow up a balloon. 2. fill; **yume de mune o fukuramaseru** fill one's heart with dreams.

fukuramu, *vb.* ふくらむ swell; bloat; enlarge.

fukureru, *vb.* ふくれる 1. swell; increase. 2. pout; sulk.

fukuro, *n.* 袋 bag; sack; pack.

fukusayō, *n.* 副作用 side effect.

fukusha, *n.* 複写 duplicate; reproduction; copy.

fukushaki, *n.* 複写機 copy machine.

fukushi, *n.* 福祉 welfare; **shakai-fukushi** social welfare.

fukushi, *n.* 副詞 adverb.

fukushū, *n.* 復讐 revenge.

fukushū, *n.* 復習 review of lessons.

fukusū, *n.* 複数 plural.

fukusū (no), *adj.* 複数 (の) plural; more than one.

fukuzatsu (na), *adj.* 複雑 (な) complex; complicated; difficult.

fukyō, *n.* 不況 depression (economic); recession.

fukyū suru, *vb.* 普及する become popular; prevail; become widespread.

fumajime (na), *adj.* 不真面目 (な) inattentive; lazy; insincere.

fuman, *n.* 不満 dissatisfaction; discontent; **fuman ga aru** feel dissatisfied; **fuman o iu** complain; grumble.

fumei (na, no), *adj.* 不明 (な、の) unidentified; unclear.

fumikiri, *n.* 踏み切り railroad crossing.

fuminshō, *n.* 不眠症 insomnia.

fumitsukeru, *vb.* 踏みつける trample; insult; victimize.

fumu, *vb.* 踏む 1. step on; tread on. 2. experience; go through; **butai o fumu** perform on the stage.

-fun, -(p)pun, -bun 分 minute; **i-ppun** one minute; **gofun kan** for five minutes.

funare (na), *adj.* 不慣れ (な) unfamiliar; unaccustomed; inexperienced.

fundoshi, *n.* ふんどし loincloth.

fune, *n.* 舟、船 ship; boat.

funiai (na, no), *adj.* 不似合い (な、の) unbecoming; unsuitable.

fun'iki, *n.* 雰囲気 ambiance; atmosphere; mood.

funinjō (na, no), *adj.* 不人情 (な、の) unsympathetic; heartless.

funinki (na), *adj.* 不人気 (な) unpopular.

funinshō (no), *adj.* 不妊症 (の) sterile.

funka, *n.* 噴火 volcanic eruption.

funmatsu, *n.* 粉末 powder.

funō, *n.* 不能 impossibility; impotence; sterility (male).

funō (na, no), *adj.* 不能 (な、の) impossible; impotent; sterile (male).

funshitsu suru, *vb.* 紛失する lose (have no longer).

funsō, *n.* 紛争 dispute; fight.

funsui, *n.* 噴水 fountain.

fura-fura suru, *vb.* ふらふらする 1. be shaky; be

unstable. 2. feel dizzy; stagger. 3. be irresolute. 4. be idle.

fura-fura to, *adv.* ふらふら と unthinkingly; impulsively.

furansu, *n.* フランス France.

furareru, *vb.* 振られる be spurned (romance).

furari to, *adv.* ふらりと without notice; casually; without planning (outing); **furari to bā ni tachiyoru** drop in at a bar.

furenzoku (na, no), *adj.* 不連続 (な、の) discontinuous.

fureru, *vb.* 触れる 1. touch; **kokoro ni fureru** touch one's heart. 2. be introduced to; experience; **nihonbunka ni fureru** be introduced to Japanese culture. 3. touch upon; refer to; **jibun no kako ni fureru** touch upon one's past. 4. infringe; violate; **hō ni fureru** violate the law.

furi, *n.* 振り 1. appearance; pretense; **shiranai furi o suru** feign ignorance. 2. choreography.

furi (na), *adj.* 不利 (な) disadvantageous; unfavorable.

furī (na, no), *adj.* フリー (な、の) (E.) free or unoccupied; freelance.

furiageru, *vb.* 振り上げる fling up; raise (hand, thing).

furidasu, *vb.* 降り出す start (raining, snowing).

furigana, *n.* 振り仮名 small kana placed to the side of or above kanji to show how they are pronounced.

furikae, *n.* 振り替え alternative; substitute; **furikae-daiya** alternative

train schedule; **furikae-kyūjitsu** compensatory holiday.

furikaeru, *vb.* 振り返る look back; turn around.

furikakaru, *vb.* 振りかかる befall.

furikakeru, *vb.* 振りかける sprinkle.

furikomu, *vb.* 振り込む transfer; pay (into an account).

furimaku, *vb.* 振りまく sprinkle; scatter; give lavishly.

furimuku, *vb.* 振り向く turn around.

furin, *n.* 不倫 adultery; immorality.

furisode, *n.* 振り袖 kimono with very long sleeves, worn by unmarried women.

furitsuzuku, *vb.* 降り続く continue to rain or snow.

furiyamu, *vb.* 降り止む stop raining or snowing.

furo, *n.* 風呂 [fuɾo] Japanese bath or bathtub; **furo ni hairu** take a bath; **furoya** public bathhouse.

furoshiki, *n.* 風呂敷 square of cloth used for wrapping.

furu, *vb.* 降る fall (rain, snow).

furu, *vb.* 振る 1. wave; shake; swing. 2. sprinkle. 3. wag (a tail). 4. change kanji into kana. 5. assign; **bangō o furu** assign a number. 6. reject someone's advances; **otoko o furu** reject a man's advances.

furubiru, *vb.* 古びる wear out; grow old or antiquated.

furudōgu, *n.* 古道具 used object (furniture, tools).

furueagaru, *vb.* 震え上がる shudder or shiver violently.

furueru, vb. 震える tremble; shake; shiver.

furugi, n. 古着 secondhand clothing.

furuhon, n. 古本 used book.

furui, adj. 古い 1. ancient; old. 2. used; worn-out; stale.

furui ni kakeru, vb. ふるいにかける sift; screen; select the best from among many.

furukusai, adj. 古臭い outdated or old-fashioned (thing, idea).

furumai, n. 振る舞い 1. behavior. 2. treat (of food and/or drink).

furumau, vb. 振る舞う 1. behave. 2. treat to food and/or drink.

furumono, n. 古物 curio; secondhand goods.

furusato, n. 故郷 hometown; homeland.

furu'u, vb. 振るう 1. wield (weapon); **katana o furu'u** wield a sword. 2. exert; **ude o furu'u** exercise one's ability or skill. 3. be powerful; be active.

furyō, n. 不良 1. delinquent. 2. poor condition; **eiyōfuryō** malnutrition.

furyōhin, n. 不良品 defective goods.

fūryoku, n. 風力 wind force.

fusa, n. 房 1. bunch; cluster. 2. tassel.

fusagaru, vb. 塞がる 1. be closed up; be clogged up. 2. be occupied.

fusagu, vb. 塞ぐ 1. fill up; cover up. 2. block (road). 3. take up (space).

fusai, n. 夫妻 married couple.

fusai, n. 負債 debt.

fusansei, n. 不賛成 disagreement; disapproval.

fūsa suru, vb. 封鎖する blockade.

fusawashii, adj. ふさわしい suitable; harmonious.

fusegu, vb. 防ぐ prevent; defend.

fusei, n. 不正 wrongdoing; unlawfulness; injustice; **fusei torihiki** dishonest dealings.

fūsen, n. 風船 balloon; **fūsen-gamu** bubblegum.

fusenmei (na), adj. 不鮮明 (な) unclear; blurred.

fuseru, vb. 伏せる 1. lay (an object) facedown. 2. lie down; take to one's bed due to illness. 3. cast down (eyes).

fushi, n. 節 1. knot (wood). 2. joint (human body). 3. melody.

fushiawase, n. 不幸せ unhappiness; misfortune.

fushigi (na, no), adj. 不思議 (な、の) 1. mysterious; magical. 2. strange; unintelligible.

fushimatsu, n. 不始末 misconduct; mismanagement; carelessness; **hi no fushimatsu** carelessness with fire.

fushin, n. 不振 1. slump; lapse; decline; **eigyōfushin** decline (business). 2. loss; **shokuyoku-fushin** loss of appetite.

fushin, n. 不審 suspicion; doubt; **fushin ni omou** suspect.

fushinsetsu (na), adj. 不親切 (な) unkind.

fushizen (na), adj. 不自然 (な) unnatural.

fushō, n. 負傷 injury; wound.

fushōchi, n. 不承知

disapproval; disagreement.

fushōjiki (na), *adj.* 不正直 (な) dishonest.

fushōka, *n.* 不消化 indigestion.

fushoku, *n.* 腐食 corrosion; rust.

fushō suru, *vb.* 負傷する be injured; be wounded.

fūshū, *n.* 風習 custom; tradition.

fusoku, busoku, *n.* 不足 shortage; lack; **mizubusoku** water shortage.

fūsoku, *n.* 風速 wind velocity.

fusu, *vb.* see **fuseru**.

fusuma, *n.* 襖 sliding door of paper on wood frame.

futa, *n.* 蓋 cover; cap (bottle); lid.

futago, *n.* 双子 twins.

futan, *n.* 負担 1. responsibility. 2. burden. 3. charge.

futari, *n.* 二人 two people.

futatabi, *adv.* 再び again.

futatōri, *n.* 二通り two methods or ways.

futatsu, *n.* 二つ two (things); two years old.

futegiwa, *n.* 不手際 mismanagement; failure; clumsiness.

futei (no), *adj.* 不定 (の) uncertain; unfixed; changeable; **jūshofutei no hito** a person with no permanent address.

futeishi, *n.* 不定詞 infinitive (grammar).

futekitō (na), *adj.* 不適当 (な) improper; inappropriate; unfit.

futekusareru, *vb.* ふてくされる pout, sulk.

futettei (na, no), *adj.* 不徹底 (な、の) partial or

inadequate; not thorough.

futo, *adv.* ふと accidentally; suddenly; casually.

futō (na, no), *adj.* 不当 (な、の) unjust; unfair.

fūtō, *n.* 封筒 envelope.

futodoki (na), *adj.* 不届き (な) unmannerly; disrespectful; insolent.

futoi, *adj.* 太い 1. thick. 2. boldface (letters). 3. deep (voice). 4. brazen; rude.

futōitsu (na, no), *adj.* 不統一 (な、の) 1. divided; disunited. 2. unharmonious.

futokoro, *n.* 懐 bosom; heart; **futokoro ga hiroi** benevolent; kindhearted.

futokoroguai, *n.* 懐具合 financial condition.

futokui (na), *adj.* 不得意 (な) not good at.

futon, *n.* 布団 futon; Japanese bedding; **futon o shiku** lay out bedding.

futoru, *vb.* 太る gain weight.

futotta, *adj.* 太った fat; plump.

futsū, *n.* 不通 interruption of traffic or telephone service.

futsū, *adv.* 普通 ordinarily; usually; generally.

futsū(no), *adj.* 普通 (の) 1. ordinary; usual; general. 2. average.

futsugō (na), *adj.* 不都合 (な) inconvenient; troublesome.

futsukayoi, *n.* 二日酔い hangover.

futtō suru, *vb.* 沸騰する boil (liquid).

fu'un na, *adj.* 不運な unfortunate.

fuwa-fuwa-shita/-suru, *adj.* ふわふわした／～する

fluffy; spongy.

fuyasu, vb. 増やす increase; raise.

fuyō (na, no), adj. 不用 (な、の) unused; useless; unnecessary.

fuyōi ni, adv. 不用意に carelessly; thoughtlessly.

fuyōjin (na), adj. 不用心 (な) careless; negligent.

fuyu, n. 冬 winter.

fuyukai (na), adj. 不愉快 (な) unpleasant.

fuyuyasumi, n. 冬休み winter break.

fuzai, n. 不在 absence; **anata no fuzaichū ni** during your absence.

fuzakeru, vb. ふざける 1. flirt. 2. fool around.

fūzoku, n. 風俗 manners and customs.

fuzoku (no), adj. 付属 (の) affiliated; attached.

fuzoroi (na, no), adj. 不揃い (な、の) uneven; irregular.

G

gabyō, n. 画鋲 thumbtack.

-gachi (na, no) がち (な、の) be inclined to; tend to; **yasumigachi** tend to be absent.

gachō, n. 鵞鳥 goose.

gai, n. 害 harm; damage; **gai ga aru** be harmful; **gai o ataeru** do harm; do damage.

-gai see **-kai, -kkai, gai.**

gaibu, n. 外部 exterior; outside. 1. exterior; outside. 2. others; outside world.

gaido, n. ガイド (E.) guide; guidebook.

gaihaku suru, vb. 外泊する spend the night away from home.

gaijin, n. 外人 foreigner.

gaikan, n. 外観 surface; exterior.

gaikan, n. 概観 overview; outline.

gaiken, n. 外見 appearance.

gaikō, n. 外交 diplomacy.

gaikōkan, n. 外交官 diplomat.

gaikōkankei, n. 外交関係 diplomatic relations.

gaikoku, n. 外国 foreign country.

gaikokugo, n. 外国語 foreign language.

gaikokujin, n. 外国人 foreigner.

gaikotsu, n. 骸骨 skeleton.

gaimen, n. 外面 appearance.

gaimu daijin, n. 外務大臣 foreign minister.

gaimushō, n. 外務省 Ministry of Foreign Affairs.

gainen, n. 概念 concept; idea.

gairai (no), adj. 外来 (の) from outside; foreign.

gairyaku, n. 概略 outline; summary.

gaisan, n. 概算 estimate.

gaisha, n. 外車 foreign car.

gaishoku, n. 外食 dining out.

gaishutsu suru, vb. 外出する go out.

gaitō, n. 街灯 street light.

gaitō, n. 街頭 street.

gaitō suru, vb. 該当する apply to; correspond to.

gaka, n. 画家 painter.

-gakari がかり (related to number of people or time) necessary manpower or time; **yonin-gakari (mikkagakari) no shigoto**

a job that requires four people (three days).

gake, n. 崖 cliff; precipice.

gaki, n. 餓鬼 brat; child.

gakka, n. 学科 1. subject of study. 2. department; **eibungakka** English Department.

gakkai, n. 学会 academic association; academic conference.

gakkari suru, vb. がっかりする be disappointed; be discouraged.

gakki, n. 楽器 musical instrument.

gakki, n. 学期 school term; semester; **ichigakki** first term.

gakkimatsu-shiken, n. 学期末試験 final examination.

gakkō, n. 学校 school.

gaku, n. 額 1. picture frame. 2. sum of money.

gaku, n. 学 learning; study; **gaku no aru hito** learned person.

gakubu, n. 学部 school; college; department; **hōgakubu** law school.

gakudan, n. 楽団 orchestra.

gakufu, n. 楽譜 sheet music.

gakugei, n. 学芸 arts and sciences.

gakuhi, n. 学費 tuition.

gakumen, n. 額面 face value.

gakumon, n. 学問 education; learning; study.

gakunen, n. 学年 1. school year. 2. grade.

gakureki, n. 学歴 educational background.

gakusei, n. 学生 student.

gakusha, n. 学者 scholar.

gakushigō, n. 学士号 bachelor's degree.

gakushū suru, vb. 学習する learn; study.

gakuya, n. 楽屋 backstage; dressing room.

gakuyōhin, n. 学用品 school supplies.

gama, n. see **kama.**

gaman suru, vb. 我慢する be patient; put up with; tolerate.

gamen, n. 画面 screen; picture (film, TV).

gametsui, adj. がめつい stingy.

gan, n. 雁 wild goose.

gan, n. 癌 cancer; **igan** stomach cancer.

ganbaru, vb. 頑張る persevere; do one's best.

ganbō, n. 願望 wish; longing.

ganjitsu, n. 元日 New Year's Day.

ganjō (na), adj. 頑丈 (な) sturdy; strong.

ganka, n. 眼科 ophthalmology.

ganko (na), adj. 頑固 (な) stubborn.

ganpeki, n. 岸壁 pier; wharf.

ganrai (wa), adv. 元来 (は) naturally; originally.

gansho, n. 願書 application form; **gansho o dasu** submit an application.

ganso, n. 元祖 originator; founder.

gantan, n. 元旦 New Year's Day.

gan to shite, adv. 頑として resolutely; persistently; stubbornly.

gappei suru, vb. 合併する incorporate; merge.

gara, n. 柄 1. design; pattern. 2. personality; one's nature; **gara ga warui** boorish. 3. physical build.

garakuta, n. がらくた junk.

garan to shita, adj. がらん

とした empty (space).

garari to, adv. がらりと 1. abruptly; 2. completely.

garasu-bin, n. ガラス瓶 glass bottle.

garō, n. 画廊 art gallery.

gasatsu (na), adj. がさつ (な) coarse; ill-mannered.

gashi suru, vb. 餓死する die of starvation.

gasorin-sutando, n. ガソリンスタンド (E. gasoline stand) gas station.

gasshō, n. 合唱 chorus.

gasshō-dan/-tai, n. 合唱団／〜隊 chorus group.

gasshuku, n. 合宿 training camp.

gassō, n. 合奏 ensemble (music).

gata-gata suru, vb. がたがたする 1. rattle; quake; tremble. 2. be rickety or shaky (structure).

-gatai 難い difficult to do; **chikayori-gatai** inaccessible.

gatchiri がっちり 1. adj. sturdy; firm. 2. adv. sturdily; firmly.

gawa, n. 側 side; **migigawa** the right-hand side.

gaya-gaya suru, vb. がやがやする make noise.

gayōshi, n. 画用紙 drawing paper.

gazō, n. 画像 picture (film, TV).

ge, n. 下 1. lower in quality or ranking; **ge no ge** lowest quality or ranking. 2. lower position. 3. latter part.

gedatsu suru, vb. 解脱する be emancipated from worldly cares (Buddhism).

gedokuzai, n. 解毒剤 antidote.

gehin (na), adj. 下品 (な) indecent; coarse; vulgar.

gei, n. 芸 1. art or craft; artistic skill or technique. 2. (animal) trick.

geijutsu, n. 芸術 art.

geijutsu-teki (na), adj. 芸術的 (な) artistic.

geimei, n. 芸名 stage name.

geinō, n. 芸能 entertainment; performance.

geisha, n. 芸者 geisha.

gejun, n. 下旬 last third of the month.

geka, n. 外科 surgery (medical specialty).

geki, n. 劇 play; drama.

gekihen, n. 激変 drastic change.

gekijō, n. 劇場 theater.

gekitotsu suru, vb. 激突する collide.

gekitsū, n. 激痛 acute pain.

gekkan(shi), n. 月刊(紙) monthly (magazine).

gekkei, n. 月経 menstruation.

gekkō, n. 月光 moonlight.

gekkyū, n. 月給 monthly salary.

gekkyūbi, n. 月給日 payday.

gen, n. 弦 (musical instrument) bow; string.

gen'an, n. 原案 original proposal or plan.

genba, n. 現場 site; scene; **kōji-genba** construction site.

genbaku, n. 原爆 atomic bomb.

genbun, n. 原文 original text.

genchi, n. 現地 location; **genchi-jikan** local time.

gendai (no), adj. 現代 (の) present-day; contemporary.

gendai-teki (na), adj. 現代的 (な) up-to-date; advanced; current.

gendo, n. 限度 limit;

restriction.

gendōryoku, n. 原動力 driving force.

gen'eki (no), adj. 現役 (の) active nonretired person.

gengakki, n. 弦楽器 stringed instrument.

gengaku suru, vb. 減額する cut (salary or price).

gengogaku, n. 言語学 linguistics; philology.

gengoshōgai, n. 言語障害 speech problem.

gen'in, n. 原因 cause.

genjiru, vb. 減じる decrease; deduct.

genjitsu, n. 現実 reality; fact.

genjitsu-teki (na), adj. 現実 的 (な) practical; realistic.

genjō, n. 現状 present condition.

genjū na, adj. 厳重な severe; strict.

genjūsho, n. 現住所 present address.

genka, n. 原価 original cost.

genkai, n. 限界 limit.

genkan, n. 玄関 vestibule, entranceway.

genki, n. 元気 health; energy; **genki ga aru** energetic; **genki o dasu** cheer up.

genki (na), adj. 元気 (な) healthy; fine; energetic; **(O)genki desu ka.** How are you? **Genki desu.** I am fine.

genkin, n. 現金 cash.

genkin (na), adj. 現金 (な) opportunistic; mercenary.

genko, genkotsu, n. げん こ、げんこつ fist.

genkō, n. 原稿 manuscript; draft.

genkōhan de, adv. 現行犯で in flagrante delicto; red-handed.

genkō (no), adj. 現行 (の) currently practiced or used; existing.

genkyū suru, vb. 言及する mention, refer to.

genmai, n. 玄米 brown rice.

genmitsu ni, adv. 厳密に strictly; exactly; closely.

gen ni, adv. 現に actually.

genpatsu, n. 原発 nuclear power.

genpon, n. 原本 original text or copy.

genri, n. 原理 principle.

genryō, n. 原料 raw material.

gensaku, n. 原作 original work (writing).

gensen suru, vb. 厳選する choose carefully.

genshi, n. 原子 atom.

genshibakudan, n. 原子爆 弾 atomic bomb.

genshiro, n. 原子炉 nuclear reactor.

genshiryoku-hatsudensho, n. 原子力発 電所 nuclear power plant.

genshi-teki (na), adj. 原始 的 (な) primitive.

genshō, n. 現象 phenomenon.

genshō, n. 減少 decrease.

genshō suru, vb. 減少する decrease; decline.

genshuku (na), adj. 厳粛 (な) solemn; serious.

genshu suru, vb. 厳守する observe strictly (regulations, promises, time).

gensoku, n. 原則 general rule; principle; **gensoku to shite** in principle.

gensuibaku, n. 原水爆 1. atomic bomb. 2. hydrogen bomb.

gentei suru, vb. 限定する limit; restrict.

genzai, n. 現在 present time.

genzaibunshi, *n.* 現在分詞 present participle.

genzai-kanryōkei, *n.* 現在完了形 present perfect tense.

genzai-shinkōkei, *n.* 現在進行形 present progressive tense.

genzon no, *adj.* 現存の living; existing.

genzon suru, *vb.* 現存する live; exist.

genzō suru, *vb.* 現像する develop (film).

geppu, *n.* げっぷ belch.

geppu, *n.* 月賦 monthly installment.

geri, *n.* 下痢 diarrhea.

gesha suru, *vb.* 下車する get off (vehicle).

geshuku, *n.* 下宿 lodgings; room and board.

geshuku-dai/-ryō, *n.* 下宿代／〜料 charges for room and board.

geshuku suru, *vb.* 下宿する rent a room.

gessha, *n.* 月謝 monthly tuition fee.

gesshū, *n.* 月収 monthly income.

gesuidō, *n.* 下水道 sewage system.

geta, *n.* 下駄 Japanese wooden clogs.

getsumatsu, *n.* 月末 end of the month.

getsuyōbi, *n.* 月曜日 Monday; **getsuyōbi ni** on Monday.

gezai, *n.* 下剤 laxative.

gian, *n.* 議案 proposal; bill (legislative); **gian o dasu** propose a bill.

gichō, *n.* 議長 chairperson.

gidai, *n.* 議題 agenda; discussion topics.

gi'in, *n.* 議員 member of the legislature; **kokkaigi'in**

Diet member.

gijutsu, *n.* 技術 1. skill; technique; **gijutsu ga aru** skilled. 2. technology.

gijutsu-teki (na), *adj.* 技術的 (な) technical.

gijutsu-teki ni, *adv.* 技術的に technically.

gikai, *n.* 議会 national assembly; Congress; Diet.

giketsu, *n.* 議決 (group) resolution; decision.

gikochinai, *adj.* ぎこちない stiff; clumsy.

gimon, *n.* 疑問 question; doubt; **gimon o idaku** have doubts.

gimu, *n.* 義務 obligation; duty; **gimu o hatasu** discharge one's duties.

gin, *n.* 銀 silver.

gin'iro, *n.* 銀色 silver (color).

ginga, *n.* 銀河 the Milky Way.

ginkō, *n.* 銀行 bank; **nihonginkō** Bank of Japan.

ginkōgōtō, *n.* 銀行強盗 bank robbery; bank robber.

ginkonshiki, *n.* 銀婚式 silver wedding anniversary.

ginō, *n.* 技能 technique; (technical) skill.

giri, *n.* 義理 moral debt; obligation; duty.

giri no, *adj.* 義理の related by marriage; **giri no chichi** father-in-law.

giron, *n.* 議論 discussion; controversy; argument; **giron no mato** subject of discussion (controversy, argument).

gishi, *n.* 技師 engineer.

gishiki, *n.* 儀式 ritual; ceremony; formality.

gishiki-teki (na), *adj.* 儀式的 (な) ritualistic; ceremonial; formal.

gisshiri (to), *adv.* ぎっしり

(と) tightly; **gisshiri (to) tsumeru** pack or fill tightly.

giwaku, n. 疑惑 suspicion; doubt.

gizen, n. 偽善 hypocrisy.

go 五 1. n. five; **gonin** five people. 2. adj. fifth;
gobanme the fifth.

go, n. 碁 Japanese board game played with black and white stones.

go, n. 語 language; word;
nihongo Japanese language.

gobu-gobu (no), adj. 五分五分 (の) fifty-fifty; even.

gocha-gocha suru, vb. ごちゃごちゃする be confused; be disorganized.

gochisō, n. 御馳走 delicacy.

gochisō suru, vb. 御馳走する treat someone to food or drink.

gōdō suru, vb. 合同する join; combine.

gogaku, n. 語学 1. language study. 2. study of a foreign language.

gogatsu, n. 五月 May.

gogatsu no sekku, n. 五月の節句 Boys' Day Festival (May 3).

gogo, n. 午後 afternoon;
p.m.; **gogo rokuji ni** at six p.m.

gogo ni, adv. 午後に in the afternoon.

gohan, n. 御飯 meal; cooked rice; **asa-(hiru-, ban-)gohan** breakfast (lunch, dinner).

gōhō-teki (na), adj. 合法的 (な) legal; lawful.

gōi, n. 合意 consent; agreement.

gōin ni, adv. 強引に high-handedly; pushily; by force.

gōi suru, vb. 合意する consent; agree.

gōjō (na), adj. 強情 (な) bullheaded; stubborn; unyielding.

goju, n., adj. 五十 fifty.

gojū no tō, n. 五重の塔 five-storied pagoda.

gokai suru, vb. 誤解する misunderstand; misconstrue.

gōkaku suru, vb. 合格する pass; succeed in (examination).

gōkan, n. 強姦 rape.

gōkanhan'nin, n. 強姦犯人 rapist.

gōkei, n. 合計 sum; total.

gōkei de, adv. 合計で in total.

gōkei suru, vb. 合計する add up.

gokiburi, n. ごきぶり cockroach.

goku, n. 語句 words and phrases.

goku, adv. 極く quite; extremely; very; **goku atarimae** quite natural or usual.

gokuhi (no), adj. 極秘 (の) top-secret; strictly confidential;
gokuhibunsho top-secret document.

gokuraku, n. 極楽 nirvana (Buddhism); blissful or ecstatic sensation.

gokurō(-sama/-san) 御苦労 (様) Thank you for your trouble.

goma, n. 胡麻 sesame.

gomakasu, vb. ごまかす 1. tell a lie; falsify; camouflage. 2. cheat. 3. steal money.

gōman (na), adj 傲慢 (な) insolent; arrogant.

goma o suru, vb. 胡麻をする flatter; fawn.

gomasuri, n. 胡麻すり flatterer; flattery.

gomen (nasai) 御免 (なさい) I am sorry; excuse me; pardon me.

gomi, n. ごみ garbage; rubbish; dust; waste.

gomibako, n. ごみ箱 garbage can; dustbin; wastebasket.

goraku, n. 娯楽 diversion; recreation; entertainment.

goran kudasai 御覧下さい Please look at...

gōrei, n. 号令 order; command; **gōrei o kakeru** to command.

gōrika, n. 合理化 1. streamlining. 2. rationalization

gōrika suru, vb. 合理化する 1. streamline. 2. rationalize.

gōri-teki (na), adj. 合理的 (な) practical; rational.

-goro 頃 1. sometime around (time); **ichigatsugoro** sometime around January; **ichijigoro** sometime around one o'clock. 2. toward.

gorotsuki, n. ごろつき rascal; ruffian.

gorufu, n. ゴルフ (E.) golf.

gosho, n. 御所 Imperial Palace.

gota-gota こたこた 1. n. trouble; chaos; **gota-gota o okosu** cause trouble. 2. adv. chaotically; haphazardly; **gota-gota naraberu** arrange haphazardly.

gota-gota suru, vb. ごたごたする be chaotic; be complicated; be crowded.

gōtō, n. 強盗 burglar; robber.

-goto ni 毎に every; each; **sanjikangoto ni** every three hours; **higoto ni** every day; **au hitogoto ni** every person I meet.

gottagaesu, vb. ごった返す be very crowded; be cluttered.

goza, n. ござ straw mat.

gozen, n. 午前 morning; a.m.; **gozenchū ni** in the morning; **gozen kuji ni** at nine a.m.

gozonji, vb. 御存知 know; **gozonji no yō ni** as you already know (honorific).

guai, n. 具合 1. condition; **karada no guai** physical condition. 2. convenience. 3. the way (to do something); **kon'na guai ni** in this way.

guchi, n. 愚痴 complaint.

gun, n. 郡 county.

gun, gunbu, n. 軍、軍部 military forces.

gunshū, n. 群衆 crowd.

guntai, n. 軍隊 military forces.

-gurai, see **-kurai.**

guratsuku, vb. ぐらつく jolt; shake.

gurīnsha, n. グリーン車 first-class car (train).

guru, n. ぐる accomplice; conspirator.

gururi to, adv. ぐるりと (turning) around.

gussuri (to), adv. ぐっすり (と) (sleep) soundly.

gūsū, n. 偶数 even number.

gutai-teki (na), adj. 具体的 (な) concrete (idea, plan); descriptive.

gūzen, n. 偶然 coincidence.

gūzen ni, adv. 偶然に coincidentally; accidentally.

guzu, n. 愚図 slowpoke.

guzutsuku, vb. 愚図つく be unsettled (weather).

gyakukōka, n. 逆効果 effect opposite to the one desired.

gyaku ni, adv. 逆に 1. on the contrary; antithetically.

2. the other way around; inside out.

gyaku (no), adj. 逆 (の) contrary; opposite; antithetical.

gyō, n. 行 line; **sangyōme** the third line (text).

gyōgi, n. 行儀 conduct; behavior; manners; **gyōgi yoku suru** behave oneself.

gyōgisahō, n. 行儀作法 etiquette; good manners.

gyogyō, n. 漁業 fishing industry.

gyōji, n. 行事 event; **nenjūgyōji** annual event.

gyōmu, n. 業務 business responsibilities.

gyōretsu, n. 行列 march;

parade; line of people or animals.

gyōsei, n. 行政 government administration.

gyōseki, n. 業績 accomplishments; results; performance (business).

gyosen, n. 漁船 fishing boat.

gyōten suru, vb. 仰天する be astounded.

gyotto suru, vb. ぎょっとする be startled.

gyū-gyūzume (no), adj. ぎゅうぎゅうづめ (の) jam-packed.

gyūniku, n. 牛肉 beef; **yunyū-gyūniku** imported beef.

gyūnyū, n. 牛乳 cow's milk.

H

ha, n. 歯 tooth.

ha, n. 派 group; sect; school.

ha, n. 葉 leaf; foliage.

ha, n. 刃 blade; edge of a knife.

haba, n. 幅 width.

habataku, vb. はばたく 1. fly; flap (wings). 2. embark on a venture.

habuku, vb. 省く 1. omit. 2. cut down (cost); save.

hachi, n. 八 eight.

hachi, n. 鉢 bowl; flowerpot.

hachi, n. 蜂 bee.

hachigatsu, n. 八月 August.

hachijū, n. 八十 eighty.

hachimitsu, n. 蜂蜜 honey.

hada, n. 肌 1. skin. 2. disposition (personality).

hadagi, n. 肌着 underwear.

hadaka (no), adj. 裸 (の) naked; uncovered.

hadashi (no), adj. 裸足 (の) barefoot.

hade (na), adj. 派手 (な) colorful; gaudy; loud.

hae, n. はえ fly (insect).

haeru, vb. 生える grow; sprout.

hagaki, n 葉書 postcard; **ehagaki** picture postcard; **hagaki o dasu** send a postcard.

hagasu, hagu, vb. 剥がす、剥ぐ 1. strip (the skin, etc.) from something. 2. reveal.

hage, n. 禿げ baldness.

hagemasu, vb. 励ます encourage; cheer up.

hagemu, vb. 励む be diligent; make an effort.

hageru, vb. 禿げる become bald.

hageru, vb. 剥げる come off; peel off.

hageshii, adj. 激しい 1. fierce; tempestuous. 2. crowded (traffic). 3. frequent (change).

haguki, n. 歯茎 gum (mouth).

hagureru, vb. はぐれる stray

or lose sight of one's
companions.

haguruma, *n.* 歯車 gear.

haha, *n.* 母 one's mother;
haha no hi Mother's Day.

hai, *adv.* はい 1. yes. 2. here
(roll call).

hai, *n.* 灰 ash.

hai, *n.* 肺 lung.

-hai, -bai, -ppai 杯 number
suffix indicating a counter
for a glass of; cup of; bowl
of; **kōhī ippai** a cup of
coffee.

haiboku, *n.* 敗北 defeat.

haibun suru, *vb.* 配分する
allot; distribute.

haichi suru, *vb.* 配置する 1.
arrange (furniture,
decoration). 2. place;
station.

haien, *n.* 肺炎 pneumonia.

haifu suru, *vb.* 配布する
hand out; distribute.

hai'iro, *n., adj.* 灰色 1. gray
(color). 2. dreary; gloomy.

haijo suru, *vb.* 排除する
eliminate; remove.

haikei 拝啓 Dear (salutation
in a letter).

haikei, *n.* 背景 background.

haiken suru, *vb.* 拝見する
read; see (formal).

haiku, *n.* 俳句 type of
Japanese poetry.

hairu, *vb.* 入る 1. enter; go
or come in. 2. join. 3.
obtain; get; **okane ga hairu**
receive money.

hairyo, *n.* 配慮 1.
consideration; attention. 2.
support.

haisen, *n.* 配線 wiring.

haisha, *n.* 歯医者 dentist.

haisui, *n.* 排水 drainage.

haitatsu, *n.* 配達 delivery
service; **shinbunhaitatsu**
newspaper delivery service.

haitatsu suru, *vb.* 配達する

deliver.

haiyā, *n.* ハイヤー (E. *hire*)
hired car and driver.

haiyū, *n.* 俳優 actor; actress.

haizara, *n.* 灰皿 ashtray.

haji, *n.* 恥 shame; disgrace;
haji o kaku disgrace
oneself; **Haji o shire!**
Shame on you!

hajimari, *n.* 始まり
beginning; opening (event).

hajimaru, *vb.* 始まる begin;
break out; open (event).

hajime, *n.* 初め 1. start;
beginning; earlier part
(time); **kotoshi-hajime**
earlier this year. 2. origin.

hajime kara, *adv.* 初めから
from the start.

hajimemashite 初めまして
How do you do?

hajime ni, *adv.* 初めに at the
start; first.

hajime no, *adj.* 初めの 1.
first. 2. former.

hajimete, *adv.* 初めて for
the first time.

hajime wa, *adv.* 初めは at
first.

hajiru, *vb.* 恥じる feel
shame.

hajishirazu (na, no), *adj.* 恥
知らず（な、の）shameless.

haka, *n.* 墓 gravestone;
graveyard; tomb.

hakadoru, *vb.* 捗る develop
further; make progress.

hakai suru, *vb.* 破壊する
destroy; devastate.

hakai-teki (na), *adj.* 破壊的
（な）destructive;
devastating.

hakama, *n.* 袴 traditional
men's trousers resembling
culottes.

hakari, *n.* 秤 scale (weight).

hakaru, *vb.* 量る weigh.

hakaru, *vb.* 計る time.

hakaru, *vb.* 図る、謀る plot;

attempt.

hakase, *n.* 博士 doctoral degree holder.

haken suru, *vb.* 派遣する send (a person); dispatch.

haki-haki shita, *adj.* はきはきした lively; clever.

hakike, *n.* 吐き気 nausea; **hakike ga suru** feel nauseated.

hakimono, *n.* 履物 shoes; footwear.

hakka, *n.* 薄荷 mint (herb).

hakken suru, *vb.* 発見する discover.

hakketsubyō, *n.* 白血病 leukemia.

hakkiri shita, *adj.* はっきりした clear; obvious; certain; definite.

hakki suru, *vb.* 発揮する exert or demonstrate (one's ability, skill).

hakkōsha, *n.* 発行者 issuer; publisher.

hakkō suru, *vb.* 発行する issue; publish.

hakkō suru, *vb.* 発酵する ferment.

hakkyō suru, *vb.* 発狂する go mad.

hako, *n.* 箱 box; case.

hakobu, *vb.* 運ぶ 1. convey; transport; carry. 2. make progress.

haku, *vb.* 履く wear (shoes or socks).

haku, *vb.* 掃く sweep.

haku, *vb.* 吐く 1. exhale. 2. vomit; spit. 3. puff.

-haku, -(p)paku 泊 overnight stay; **sanpakuryokō** three-night stay.

hakubutsukan, *n.* 博物館 museum (other than art).

hakuchō, *n.* 白鳥 swan.

hakugai suru, *vb.* 迫害する persecute; victimize.

hakuhatsu, *n.* 白髪 gray or white hair.

hakui, *n.* 白衣 white uniform.

hakujin, *n.* 白人 Caucasian.

hakujō, *n.* 白状 confession.

hakujō (na), *adj.* 薄情 (な) cruel; heartless; uncaring.

hakujō suru, *vb.* 白状する confess; admit (one's fault, crime).

hakurankai, *n.* 博覧会 exposition; exhibition.

hakuryoku ga aru, *adj.* 迫力がある dynamic; powerful; overwhelming.

hakushi, *n.* 白紙 blank paper.

hakushironbun, *n.* 博士論文 doctoral dissertation.

hakusho, *n.* 白書 white paper (official government report).

hakushu suru, *vb.* 拍手する applaud.

hama(be), *n.* 浜(辺) beach; seaside.

hamaguri, *n.* 蛤 clam.

hamaru, *vb.* はまる 1. fall into; be caught. 2. fit in or into.

hame, *n.* 羽目 unwelcome or unfortunate consequence.

hameru, *vb.* はめる 1. put a thing in the right place; fit; mold. 2. deceive; frame. 3. button; fasten; put on (gloves, watch).

hamidasu, *vb.* はみ出す stick out.

hamigaki, *n.* 歯磨き toothpaste.

hamono, *n.* 刃物 knife; cutting tool.

hamu, *n.* ハム (E.) ham.

han, *n.* 印 signature seal; stamp.

han, *n.* 半 half; **gojihan ni**

at five-thirty.

hana, *n.* 花 flower; **hana o ikeru** arrange flowers.

hanabi, *n.* 鼻 nose.

hanabi, *n.* 花火 fireworks.

hanagami, *n.* 鼻紙 facial tissue.

hanaji, *n.* 鼻血 nosebleed.

hanami, *n.* 花見 cherry blossom viewing party.

hanamizu, *n.* 鼻水 runny nose.

hanamuko, *n.* 花婿 bridegroom.

hanareru, *vb.* 離れる move away from; separate from; leave.

hanashi, *n.* 話 1. talk; speech. 2. tale; story. 3. news; rumor.

hanashiau, *vb.* 話し合う talk with; discuss; converse.

hanashikakeru, *vb.* 話しかける address; speak to.

hanasu, *vb.* 話す talk; speak; tell.

hanasu, *vb.* 離す set away from; separate.

hanasu, *vb.* 放す set free; loosen.

hanataba, *n.* 花束 bouquet (flowers).

hanaya, *n.* 花屋 florist.

hanayome, *n.* 花嫁 bride.

hanbai suru, *vb.* 販売する sell.

hanbun, *n.* 半分 half.

handan, *n.* 判断 conclusion; decision; judgment.

handō, *n.* 反動 reaction.

handoru, *n.* ハンドル (E.) 1. handle; knob. 2. steering wheel.

hane, *n.* 羽、羽根 feather; wing.

han'ei, *n.* 反映 reflection.

han'ei, *n.* 繁栄 prosperity.

hanekaeru, *vb.* 跳ね返る rebound.

hanenokeru, *vb.* はね除ける push away.

hanerareru, *vb.* はねられる 1. be run over or be hit (by a car). 2. be rejected; be turned down.

haneru, *vb.* はねる 1. run over or hit (with a car). 2. reject.

haneru, *vb.* 跳ねる 1. spring out; jump; hop; bound. 2. splash.

hangaku, *n.* 半額 fifty-percent discount.

han-han, *adv.* 半々、半半 fifty-fifty; half-and-half.

han'i, *n.* 範囲 extent; area; range.

han'igo, *n.* 反意語 antonym.

hanjō, *n.* 繁盛 success or prosperity (in business).

hankachi, *n.* ハンカチ (E.) handkerchief.

hankagai, *n.* 繁華街 busy shopping area.

hankan, *n.* 反感 ill feelings; animosity; repulsion; **hankan o idaku** have ill feelings.

hankei, *n.* 半径 radius.

hanketsu, *n.* 判決 judgment (court).

hankō, *n.* 犯行 crime.

hankō, *n.* 反抗 rebellion; defiance; resistance.

hankyō, *n.* 反響 1. echo; repercussion. 2. response; reaction.

hankyū, *n.* 半球 hemisphere; **kita (minami) hankyū** Northern (Southern) Hemisphere.

hanmei suru, *vb.* 判明する 1. prove to be. 2. become clear.

hanmen 反面 1. *n.* the other or opposite side. 2. *adv.* on the other hand.

han'nin, *n.* 犯人 criminal;

lawbreaker; offender.

han'nō, *n.* 反応 reaction; response.

hanpa (na), *adj.* 半端（な）1. insufficient; incomplete. 2. odd. 3. insincere.

hanpatsu suru, *vb.* 反発する 1. defy; resist. 2. repulse; rebound.

hansei, *n.* 反省 1. scrutiny; self-scrutiny. 2. regret.

hansha, *n.* 反射 reflection (of light, sound, heat).

hanshinhangi, *n.* 半信半疑 suspicion; doubt; disbelief.

hansode, *n.* 半袖 short-sleeves.

hantai, *n.* 反対 opposition; contrast; reverse.

hantai suru, *vb.* 反対する oppose; object.

hantei, *n.* 判定 judgment; decision.

hantō, *n.* 半島 peninsula.

hantsuki, *n.* 半月 half a month.

hanzai, *n.* 犯罪 crime.

hanzubon, *n* 半ズボン shorts.

haori, *n.* 羽織 short jacket worn over kimono.

happi, *n.* 法被 traditional Japanese work jacket.

happyō suru, *vb.* 発表する announce; publish; reveal.

hara, *n.* 腹 1. stomach; abdomen; **hara ga itai** have a stomachache. 2. true feelings.

harabau, *vb.* 腹ばう lie on one's stomach.

hara ga suku, *vb.* 腹が空く be hungry.

hara ga tatsu, *vb.* 腹が立つ become angry.

hara-hara suru, *vb.* はらはらする worry; feel apprehensive.

hara o tateru, *vb.* 腹を立て

る get angry; get upset.

harau, *vb.* 払う 1. pay (money, attention). 2. brush or sweep off.

hare, *n.* 晴れ fair or fine weather.

haregi, *n.* 晴れ着 one's best clothes.

haremono, *n.* 腫れ物 abscess; swelling; lump.

hareru, *vb.* 晴れる 1. clear up (weather). 2. be dispelled (suspicion).

hareru, *vb.* 腫れる swell up.

hari, *n.* 針 1. needle; pin. 2. hand (clock, watch, dial).

hari, *n.* 鍼 acupuncture.

harigami, *n.* 貼り紙、張り紙 public notice; advertisement; poster.

haritsumeru, *vb.* 張り詰める be tense; be anxious.

haru, *n.* 春 spring (season).

haru, *vb.* 貼る、張る paste; stick; attach.

haru, *vb.* 張る 1. stretch; spread. 2. become tense.

harubaru to, *adv.* はるばると (travel) from afar.

haruka (na, ni), *adj., adv.* 遥か（な、に）1. far away; way back; **haruka na mukashi ni** very long ago. 2. by far; much (greater); **haruka ni ōkii** much bigger.

haruyasumi, *n.* 春休み spring break or vacation.

hasamareru, *vb.* 挟まれる be caught in between; lie in between.

hasami, *n.* 鋏 scissors; claw (crab).

hasamu, *vb.* 挟む hold or place between; pinch.

hasan suru, *vb.* 破産する go bankrupt.

hashi, *n.* 箸 chopsticks.

hashi, *n.* 橋 bridge; **hashi o kakeru** build a bridge.

hashi, n. 端 edge; end; border.

hashigo, n. 梯子 ladder.

hashika, n. はしか measles; **hashika ni kakaru** get the measles.

hashira, n. 柱 pillar; post; column.

hashiru, vb. 走る run; rush.

hassan suru, vb. 発散する discharge; emanate; release.

hassei suru, vb. 発生する 1. break out; occur. 2. generate; breed.

hassha, n. 発射 firing (firearms); launching (rocket).

hassha, n. 発車 departure (train or bus); **hasshajikan** departure time.

hassō, n. 発想 1. idea; inspiration. 2. notion; concept.

hassō suru, vb. 発送する send off; ship; dispatch.

hasu, n. 蓮 lotus.

hata, n. 旗 banner; flag.

hatake, n. 畑 1. field (for cultivation). 2. field of expertise.

hatarakaseru, vb. 働かせる 1. activate; use; **atama o hatarakaseru** use one's brain. 2. put a person to work.

hataraku, vb. 働く 1. work. 2. function. 3. commit (crime).

hatashite, adv. 果たして 1. actually; as imagined. 2. really...?

hatasu, vb. 果たす accomplish; realize.

hate, n. 果て most remote point or part; tip; end.

hateshinai, adj. 果てしない endless.

hato, n. 鳩 dove; pigeon.

hatsu (no), adj. 初 (の) first.

-hatsu 発 leaving; **nyū-yōku-hatsu no hikōki** flight leaving New York.

hatsubai, n. 発売 sale.

hatsubai suru, vb. 発売する sell; put on the market.

hatsudensho, n. 発電所 power plant.

hatsugen suru, vb. 発言する make a statement.

hatsukoi, n. 初恋 first love.

hatsumei, n. 発明 invention.

hatsumimi, n. 初耳 first time one hears something.

hatsuon, n. 発音 pronunciation.

hatsuonkigō, n. 発音記号 phonetic symbol.

hattatsu suru, vb. 発達する progress; develop; grow.

hatten, n. 発展 development; prosperity.

hatto suru, vb. はっとする be startled.

hau, vb. 這う creep; crawl.

hayabike/hayabiki suru, vb. 早引け／早引きする leave early (from office, school).

hayai, adj. 速い speedy; fast; **hayai norimono** fast vehicle.

hayai, adj. 早い early; **hayai jikan** early hours.

hayaimonogachi (ni), adv. 早い者勝ち (に) on a first-come, first-served basis.

hayaku, adv. 速く speedily; fast; **hayaku hashiru** run fast.

hayaku, adv. 早く early; soon; **hayaku okiru** get up early.

hayakuchi, n. 早口 speaking quickly.

hayakute (mo), adv. 早くて (も) at the earliest.

hayameru, vb. 早める、速め

る speed up; hasten.

hayaoki, n. 早起き early rising.

hayaru, vb. はやる 1. become popular; come into fashion. 2. become successful; prosper.

hayasa, n. 速さ speed.

hayashi, n. 林 grove; woods.

-hazu 筈 1. should; ought; **kekkon suruhazu** due to get married. 2. must; **mitahazu** should have seen. 3. obviously; surely.

-hazu ga nai 筈がない 1. cannot be. 2. inconceivable; impossible.

hazukashii, adj. 恥ずかしい ashamed; embarrassed; shy.

hazukashigaru, vb. 恥ずかしがる feel ashamed, embarrassed, or shy.

hazumu, vb. 弾む 1. become lively; become animated. 2. accelerate. 3. bound.

hazureru, vb. 外れる 1. fail; lose; miss; **yosō ga hazureru** fail to meet one's expectations. 2. come off; be dislocated. 3. stray.

hazusu, vb. 外す 1. remove; take off. 2. miss. 3. go away.

hebi, n. 蛇 snake.

hei, n. 塀 fence; wall.

hei, n. 兵 army; soldiers.

heibon (na), adj. 平凡 (な) mediocre; commonplace; ordinary.

heigen, n. 平原 grassland; plain.

heijitsu, n. 平日 weekday(s).

heika, n. 陛下 Emperor; Your Majesty.

heiki (na), adj. 平気 (な) unconcerned; nonchalant.

heikin, n. 平均 average; **heikin shite** on the average.

heikō, n. 平行 parallel.

heikōsen, n. 平行線 parallel lines.

heikō suru, vb. 平行する 1. parallel. 2. take place or exist simultaneously.

heimen, n. 平面 flat surface.

heisa suru, vb. 閉鎖する close down.

heisa-teki (na), adj. 閉鎖的 (な) closed; exclusive.

heishi, heitai, n. 兵士、兵隊 soldier.

heiten, n. 閉店 closing (shop, office, etc.).

heiwa, n. 平和 peace; tranquillity.

heiya, n. 平野 vast flatland; plain.

hekomaseru, hekomasu, vb. 凹ませる／凹ます 1. make a dent or hollow in. 2. win over; beat.

hekomu, vb. 凹む become dented or hollow; sink.

hema, n. へま clumsiness; blunder.

hen, n. 偏 radical of a kanji character.

hen, n. 辺 side (geometry).

-hen 辺 neighborhood; surroundings; **konohen ni** in this neighborhood.

hen (na), adj. 変 (な) funny; strange; clumsy.

hendō, n. 変動 1. change. 2. commotion; uproar.

henji, n. 返事 answer; reply.

henjin, n. 変人 eccentric person.

henji o suru, vb. 返事をする answer; reply.

henka suru, vb. 変化する change; vary.

henkei, n. 変形 deformity; transformation.

henken, n. 偏見 prejudice; bigotry.

henkō, n. 変更 change;

alteration.

henkyaku suru, *vb.* 返却する return something borrowed.

hensai suru, *vb.* 返済する pay off; pay back.

hensei suru, *vb.* 編成する organize; constitute; form.

henshin, *n.* 変身 transformation; transmutation.

henshin, *n.* 変心 change of mind.

henshin, *n.* 返信 reply (mail).

henshoku suru, *vb.* 変色する fade; discolor.

henshū suru, *vb.* 編集する edit.

hensō suru, *vb.* 変装する disguise.

hentai, *n.* 変態 1. pervert; perversion. 2. metamorphosis (insect).

herasu, *vb.* 減らす lessen; decrease; reduce.

herikudaru, *vb.* へりくだる humble oneself.

heru, *vb.* 減る 1. decrease; lose; **taijū ga heru** lose weight. 2. wear out. 3. **hara ga heru** get hungry.

heso, *n.* へそ navel.

hesokuri, *vb.* へそくり secret savings.

heta (na), *adj.* 下手 (な) poor (at); inept; **nihongo ga heta** poor at Japanese.

heto-heto ni naru, *vb.* へとへとになる become exhausted.

heya, *n.* 部屋 1. room. 2. sumo barracks.

hi, *n.* 日 1. sun; sunlight; **hi no de** sunrise. 2. day; **aru hi** one day. 3. times; days. 4. daytime.

hi, *n.* 火 fire.

hi- 非 non-; in-; un-;

hikazeihin nontaxable item; **higōhō** illegal.

-hi 費 cost; expense; **shokuhi** food cost; **gakuhi** school expense.

hiatari ga ii, *adj.* 日当りがいい sunny; sunlit.

hibachi, *n.* 火鉢 hibachi; charcoal brazier.

hibi, *n.* ひび crack; chap (skin, lips).

hibiki, *n.* 響き echo; repercussion; sound.

hidari, *n.* 左 1. left; **hidarite** left hand; **hidarigawa ni** on the left side. 2. leftist.

hidari-gitcho/-kiki, *n.* 左ぎっちょ／～利き left-handed person.

hidoi, *adj.* ひどい 1. inhuman; cruel. 2. bad; absurd. 3. painful. 4. violent.

hidoku, *adv.* ひどく 1. very; badly. 2. hard; violently.

hieru, *vb.* 冷える 1. become chilly or cold. 2. cool.

hifu, *n.* 皮膚 skin.

higaeri, *n.* 日帰り day trip.

higai, *n.* 被害 damage; loss.

higaisha, *n.* 被害者 victim.

higashi, *n.* 東 east.

hige, *n.* 髭 whiskers.

higoro no, *adj.* 日頃の usual; everyday.

higure, *n.* 日暮れ nightfall; dusk.

hihan suru, *vb.* 批判する criticize.

hihyō, *n.* 批評 review; remark; criticism.

hihyōka, *n.* 批評家 reviewer; critic.

hi'iki, *n.* ひいき favoritism; partiality; patronage.

hi'iki suru, *vb.* ひいきする favor; be partial to; patronize.

hiji, *n.* 肘 elbow.

hijō, *n.* 非常 emergency.

hijōguchi, *n.* 非常口 emergency exit.

hijōkaidan, *n.* 非常階段 fire escape.

hijō na, *adj.* 非常な great; extreme; outstanding.

hijō ni, *adv.* 非常に very much; extremely; outstandingly.

hikaeme (na, no), *adj.* 控え目 (な、の) moderate; retiring.

hikaeru, *vb.* 控える 1. refrain from. 2. take notes. 3. be imminent (event).

hikaeshitsu, *n.* 控え室 waiting room.

hikagaku-teki (na), *adj.* 非科学的 (な) unscientific.

hikage, *n.* 日陰 shade.

hikaku suru, *vb.* 比較する compare.

hikaku-teki (ni), *adv.* 比較的 (に) comparatively.

hikan suru, *vb.* 悲観する be pessimistic; feel hopeless.

hikari, *n.* 光 light; ray; brilliance.

hikaru, *vb.* 光る 1. shine; glitter. 2. stand out.

hiketsu, *n.* 秘訣 knack; key to (success).

-hiki, -biki, -ppiki 匹 number suffix indicating counter for animals, fish, insects, etc.; **inu ippiki** one dog; **sakana gohiki** five fish.

hikiageru, *vb.* 引き上げる 1. withdraw. 2. raise.

hikidashi, *n.* 引き出し 1. drawer; chest of drawers. 2. (bank) withdrawal.

hikidasu, *vb.* 引き出す 1. draw out. 2. foster (talent).

hikihanasu, *vb.* 引き離す 1. separate. 2. surpass; outrun.

hikikae ni, *adv.* 引き換えに in exchange.

hikikaesu, *vb.* 引き返す go back; turn back.

hikikorosu, *vb.* ひき殺す kill by running over.

hikinige, *n.* ひき逃げ hit-and-run.

hikiniku, *n.* 挽き肉 ground meat.

hikiokosu, *vb.* 引き起こす cause (problem); trigger.

hikisaku, *vb.* 引き裂く tear off; separate.

hikitoru, *vb.* 引き取る 1. take over. 2. take charge of. 3. take back. 4. go back.

hikitsugu, *vb.* 引き継ぐ succeed to; take over.

hikiukeru, *vb.* 引き受ける take charge of; undertake.

hikiwatasu, *vb.* 引き渡す 1. hand over. 2. surrender.

hikizuru, *vb.* 引きずる drag.

hikkaku, *vb.* 引っ掻く scratch.

hikki suru, *vb.* 筆記する write down.

hikkosu, *vb.* 引っ越す move (household).

hikkurikaeru, *vb.* ひっくり返る 1. overturn; tip over. 2. collapse.

hikōki, *n.* 飛行機 airplane; **hikōki de** by airplane.

hiku, *vb.* 引く 1. attract; draw; pull. 2. subtract.

hiku, *vb.* ひく run over (with a vehicle); grind.

hiku, *vb.* 弾く play (a stringed instrument).

hikui, *adj.* 低い 1. low. 2. short (person).

hima, *n.* 暇 free time; time; **hima ga aru/nai** have time/have no time; **hima o tsubusu** kill time.

hima (na), *adj.* 暇 (な) 1. unoccupied; idle. 2.

(business) slow.

himan, n. 肥満 overweight; obesity.

himatsubushi, n. 暇つぶし killing (time).

himawari, n. ひまわり sunflower.

hime, n. 姫 princess.

himei, n. 悲鳴 scream; shriek; cry of distress.

himitsu, n. 秘密 secret; **himitsu o mamoru (morasu)** keep (reveal) secret.

himo, n. 紐 rope; cord; string.

hin, n. 品 gracefulness; refinement; elegance.

hina, n. ひな 1. chick; baby bird. 2. dolls representing courtiers.

hinan suru, vb. 非難する criticize; accuse; blame.

hinan suru, vb. 避難する evacuate; take refuge.

hinata, n. 日向 sunny place.

hinatabokko suru, vb. 日向ぼっこする bask in the sun.

hineru, vb. ひねる twist; wriggle; turn.

hiniku, n. 皮肉 sarcasm; cynicism; irony.

hinketsushō, n. 貧血症 anemia.

hinode, n. 日の出 sunrise.

hinomaru, n. 日の丸 Japanese flag.

hinpan ni, adv. 頻繁に frequently; continuously.

hinshitsu, n. 品質 quality of goods.

hinshitsukanri, n. 品質管理 quality control.

hinshu, n. 品種 type; kind; category.

hipparu, vb. 引っ張る pull; draw.

hiragana, n. 平仮名 Japanese syllabary for

native words.

hira-hira suru, vb. ひらひらする flutter; wave; flap.

hiraku, vb. 開く 1. open; unfold. 2. hold (meeting, show, party).

hirame, n. 平目 sole (fish).

hiratai, adj. 平たい 1. flat. 2. simple.

hire(niku), n. ヒレ(肉) (E.) fillet (meat).

hiri-hiri suru, vb. ひりひりする ache; (pain) smart.

hiritsu, n. 比率 ratio; percentage.

hirō, n. 疲労 fatigue.

hiroba, n. 広場 plaza; square.

hiro-biro to shita, adj. 広々とした spacious; expansive; vast.

hirōen, n. 披露宴 wedding reception.

hirogaru, vb. 広がる spread; extend; stretch.

hirogeru, vb. 広げる spread; unfold; widen.

hiroi, adj. 広い large; wide; spacious.

hiroiageru, vb. 拾い上げる pick up; select.

hiroku, adv. 広く extensively; widely.

hiromaru, vb. 広まる pervade; become widespread.

hiromeru, vb. 広める publicize; propagate; spread.

hirō suru, vb. 披露する introduce; show.

hirou, vb. 拾う 1. pick up. 2. find. 3. flag down (a taxi).

hiru, n. 昼 noon; afternoon; daytime.

hirugohan, n. 昼御飯 lunch.

hirune, n. 昼寝 nap; **hirune o suru** take a nap.

hiruyasumi, n. 昼休み lunch break.

hiryō, n. 肥料 fertilizer; **kagaku-hiryō** chemical fertilizer; **yūki-hiryō** organic fertilizer.

hisan (na), adj. 悲惨 (な) woeful; miserable; pitiable.

hisashiburi, n. 久し振り a long interval (time).

hisashiburi ni, adv. 久し振りに after a long interval (time).

hisho, n. 秘書 secretary.

hisoka ni, adv. 密かに secretly; behind the scenes.

hisshi ni, adv. 必死に desperately; frantically.

hissori ひっそり 1. adj. quiet; still; motionless. 2. adv. quietly; secretly.

hitai, n. 額 forehead.

hitei suru, vb. 否定する negate; deny.

hitei-teki (na), adj. 否定的 (な) negative.

hito 人 1. n. person; human being. 2. pron. others.

hito-bito, n. 人々 people.

hitogara, n. 人柄 personality

hitogoroshi, n. 人殺し killer; murderer.

hitoiki de/ni, adv. 一息で／～に in a single stretch.

hitokire, n. 一切れ one slice; one piece.

hitome, n. 一目 (one) glance; sight; **hitome aitai** want to get a look at; **hitomebore** love at first sight.

hitome de, adv. 一目で at first sight; at a glance.

hitomi, n. 瞳 pupil (eye).

hitonami (na, no), adj. 人並み (な、の) average; ordinary.

hitori, n. 一人 one person.

hitoriatari, adv. 一人当たり per person.

hitori de, adv. 一人で by or for oneself.

hitorigoto, n. 独り言 talking to oneself.

hitorikko, n. 一人っ子 only child.

hitosashi yubi, n. 人差し指 index finger.

hitoshii, adj. 等しい same; equal.

hitotsu 一つ 1. n. one. 2. n. one-year-old. 3. adj. same.

hitotsubu, n. 一粒 one grain; one drop.

hitotsuzutsu, adv. 一つずつ one by one (objects).

hitsū (na), adj. 悲痛 (な) poignant; sorrowful.

hitsuji, n. 羊 sheep.

hitsujuhin, n. 必需品 necessity; essential.

hitsuyō (na), adj. 必要 (な) necessary; indispensable; integral.

hittakuri, n. ひったくり purse-snatcher; **hittakuri ni au** have one's purse snatched.

hiya-hiya suru, vb. ひやひやする feel scared; feel nervous.

hiyakasu, vb. 冷やかす ridicule; mock; tease.

hiyake, n. 日焼け sunburn; suntan.

hiyasu, vb. 冷やす chill; cool.

hiyō, n. 費用 cost; expense.

hiyoko, n. ひよこ chick.

hiza, n. 膝 1. knee. 2. lap.

hizuke, n. 日付 date (calendar).

hō, n. 頬 cheek.

hō, n. 法 1. law. 2. method.

hō 方 1. n. direction; side; **migi no hō ni** on the right side. 2. conj. (better, bigger, closer, etc.) than; **Kochira no hō ga achira yori ii.**

This is better than that.

-ho, -(p)po 歩 step; **ippo** one step; **sanpo** three steps; **goho** five steps.

hōbi, *n.* 褒美 reward; **hōbi o ageru (morau)** give (receive) a reward.

hobo, *adv.* ほぼ almost; about.

hōchō, *n.* 包丁 kitchen knife.

hodo, *parti.* 程 1. about; **gonin hodo** about five people. 2. (comparison) not as ... as; **Kore wa are hodo yokunai.** This is not as good as that. 3. to a (... degree); **shinu hodo suki** love someone desperately.

hodō, *n.* 歩道 sidewalk.

hodoku, *vb.* 解く untie; loosen.

hoeru, *vb.* 吠える howl; bark.

hōfu (na), *adj.* 豊富 (な) abundant; full of.

hōgaku, *n.* 法学 law (study of).

hōgaku, *n.* 方角 route; direction.

hogaraka (na), *adj.* 朗らか (な) happy; cheerful.

hōgen, *n.* 方言 dialect.

hogo, *n.* 保護 protection; care; **shizenhogo** environmental protection.

hogo suru, *vb.* 保護する protect; guard; take care of.

hoho, *n.* 頬 cheek.

hōhō, *n.* 方法 method; way; means.

hohoemashii, *adj.* 微笑まし い heartwarming.

hohoemu, *vb.* 微笑む smile.

hoikuen, *n.* 保育園 day-care center; nursery school.

hojikuru, *vb.* ほじくる 1. dig around in. 2. pry into.

hōjin, *n.* 法人 corporation;

hōjin-zei corporate tax.

hojo, *n.* 補助 subsidy; aid; support.

hoka, *n.* 他、外 another person, object, or place.

hōka, *n.* 放火 arson.

hōkago (ni), *adv.* 放課後 (に) after school.

hoka ni 他に 1. *adv.* as well as; besides; **kono hoka ni** besides this. 2. *n.* anything or anyone else; **Hoka ni nani ka o-iri desu ka.** Do you need anything else?

hoka no, *adj.* 他の another; other; some or any other.

hokan suru, *vb.* 保管する keep a close watch over; take good care of.

hoka wa, *prep.* 他は other than; except.

hoken, *n.* 保険 insurance; **kokumin-kenkōhoken** national health insurance; **seimei hoken** life insurance.

hōki, *n.* 箒 broom.

hōki suru, *vb.* 放棄する give up; renounce.

hokkyoku, *n.* 北極 Arctic; North Pole.

hokkyokusei, *n.* 北極星 North Star; Polaris; polestar.

hokō, *n.* 歩行 walking.

hōkō, *n.* 方向 direction; **hōkō-kankaku** sense of direction.

hōkoku suru, *vb.* 報告する report.

hokori, *n.* 誇り pride; dignity; self-esteem.

hokori, *n.* 埃 dust.

hokoru, *vb.* 誇る take pride in.

hokōsha, *n.* 歩行者 pedestrian.

hokubei, *n.* 北米 North America.

hokuō, *n.* 北欧 northern

Europe.

hokuro, *n.* ほくろ mole (on the skin).

hokusei, *n.* 北西 northwest.

hokutō, *n.* 北東 northeast.

hokyō suru, *vb.* 補強する strengthen; reinforce.

hokyū suru, *vb.* 補給する supplement; supply; replenish.

homare, *n.* 誉れ honor; distinction.

hōmen, *n.* 方面 area; region; direction.

homeru, *vb.* 褒める、賞める praise; compliment; admire.

hōmon, *n.* 訪問 visit.

hōmu, *n.* ホーム (F. *plateforme*) platform (station).

hōmuru, *vb.* 葬る bury; suppress.

hōmushō, *n.* 法務省 Ministry of Justice.

hon, *n.* 本 book; **hon ni-satsu** two books.

-hon, -bon, -ppon 本 number suffix indicating a counter for long things (bottles, fingers, flowers, neckties, rope, etc.); **bara gohon** five roses.

honbako, *n.* 本箱 bookcase.

honbu, *n.* 本部 headquarters; main office.

hondana, *n.* 本棚 bookshelf.

hondo, *n.* 本土 mainland.

hone, *n.* 骨 1. bone. 2. rib (umbrella); frame (shoji screen). 3. difficulty.

hone o oru, *vb.* 骨を折る 1. break a bone. 2. toil; make an effort.

hongoku, *n.* 本国 native country.

honjitsu, *n.* 本日 this day; today.

honkaku-teki (na), *adj.* 本格的 (な) 1. authentic; real.

2. full-scale.

honki de, *adv.* 本気で seriously; earnestly.

honmono, *n.* 本物 real or genuine article.

hon'ne, *n.* 本音 true feelings.

hon'nin, *n.* 本人 person in question; himself or herself.

hon no, *adj.* ほんの mere; only; just.

hon'nō-teki ni, *adv.* 本能的 に instinctively.

honobono to shita, *adj.* ほ のぼのとした heartwarming.

hono'o, *n.* 炎 blaze; flame.

honrai (wa), *adv.* 本来 (は) originally; by nature.

honsha, *n.* 本社 head or main office.

honshin, *n.* 本心 true intentions; conscience.

honshitsu, *n.* 本質 true nature; essence; substance.

honshitsu-teki (na), *adj.* 本 質的 (な) essential; substantial.

honshū, *n.* 本州 Honshu (Japan's main island).

hontō (no), *adj.* 本当 (の) real; true; genuine.

hontō ni, *adv.* 本当に 1. really; truly; genuinely. 2. terribly; **Hontō ni sumimasen.** I am terribly sorry.

hontō wa, *adv.* 本当は in reality; to tell the truth.

hon'ya, *n.* 本屋 bookstore.

hon'yaku, *n.* 翻訳 translation.

honyūbin, *n.* 哺乳瓶 baby's bottle.

hō'ō, *n.* 法王 Pope.

horeru, *vb.* 惚れる fall in love; be attracted to.

hōritsu, *n.* 法律 law.

horobiru, *vb.* 滅びる perish;

be ruined.

horobosu, *vb.* 滅ぼす ruin; destroy.

horu, *vb.* 掘る dig.

horu, *vb.* 彫る engrave; carve; chisel.

hōseki, *n.* 宝石 precious; jewel.

hōshanō, *n.* 放射能 radioactivity.

hoshi, *n.* 星 star.

hōshi, *n.* 奉仕 service.

hoshii, *vb.* 欲しい want; yearn for.

hōshiki, *n.* 方式 1. methodology; method; formula. 2. style.

hōshin, *n.* 方針 policy; principle; direction.

hoshi uranai, *n.* 星占い astrology.

hoshō, *n.* 保証 warranty; guarantee; assurance.

hoshu-teki (na), *adj.* 保守的 (な) conservative.

hōsō, *n.* 放送 broadcast.

hōsō, *n.* 包装 wrapping.

hosoi, *adj.* 細い 1. thin; narrow; slim. 2. small; flimsy; **hosoi koe** small voice.

hōsōshi, *n.* 包装紙 wrapping paper.

hossa, *n.* 発作 attack; fit; **shinzō-hossa** heart attack; **hossa o okosu** have a fit (attack).

hossa-teki ni, *adv.* 発作的に fitfully; impulsively.

hosu, *vb.* 干す dry; air.

hōtai, *n.* 包帯 bandage.

hotategai, *n.* 帆立て貝 scallop.

hotchikisu, *n.* ホッチキス (E. *Hotchkiss* and Co.) stapler; staples.

hoteru, *n.* ホテル (E.) hotel.

hotoke, *n.* 仏 1. Buddha. 2. deceased person; **hotoke ni**

naru die.

hotondo, *adv.* ほとんど almost; nearly; **hotondo owatta** almost finished.

hotteoku, *vb.* ほっておく leave alone; let alone; neglect.

hotto suru, *vb.* ほっとする feel relieved; relax.

hozon, *n.* 保存 preservation.

hyakkajiten, *n.* 百科辞典 encyclopedia.

hyakkaten, *n.* 百貨店 department store.

hyaku, *n.* 百 hundred; **gohyaku** five hundred.

hyakuman, *n.* 百万 million.

hyakushō, *n.* 百姓 farmer.

hyō, *n.* 表 list; chart.

hyōban, *n.* 評判 1. reputation 2. popularity; **hyōban ga ii** popular. 3. rumor.

hyōgen, *n.* 表現 expression; **hyōgen no jiyū** freedom of expression.

hyōgen suru, *vb.* 表現する express; describe.

hyōhakuzai, *n.* 漂白剤 bleach.

hyōji suru, *vb.* 表示する indicate; express.

hyōjō, *n.* 表情 expression.

hyōjun, *n.* 標準 standard; average.

hyōjungo, *n.* 標準語 standard language.

hyōka, *n.* 評価 assessment; evaluation.

hyōkin (na), *adj.* ひょうきん (な) funny; comical.

hyōmen, *n.* 表面 surface; exterior.

hyōmen-teki (na), *adj.* 表面的 (な) superficial; shallow.

hyōronka, *n.* 評論家 critic; reviewer; commentator; analyst.

hyōshi, *n.* 表紙 cover (book,

magazine).
hyōshiki, n. 標識 sign (board).
hyotto, adv. ひょっと by chance; without planning or anticipation.

hyotto shitara, adv. ひょっとしたら 1. perhaps. 2. by some chance.
hyōzan, n. 氷山 iceberg; **hyōzan no ikkaku** tip of the iceberg.

I

i, n. 胃 stomach.
-i 位 rank; place (competition); **ichii** first place.
ibaru, vb. 威張る 1. be aloof; look down on. 2. brag about.
ibiki, n. いびき snoring.
ibo, n. いぼ wart.
ichi, n. 位置 position; location; situation.
ichi, n. 一 one; number one; beginning.
ichiba, n. 市場 market.
ichiban 一番 1. n. the first; the best. 2. adj. number one; first; best. 3. adv. most; best; **ichiban taisetsu** most precious.
ichibu(bun), n. 一部(分) part; section.
ichidan to, adv. 一段と better (worse, more, less, etc.) than usual (or before); especially; all the more; **ichidan to kirei** more beautiful than usual (or before).
ichido, adv. 一度 once; at one time; **ichido ni** all at once.
ichigatsu, n. 一月 January.
ichigo, n. 苺 strawberry.
ichi-ichi, adv. いちいち 1. one by one. 2. in every case. 3. in detail.
ichijirushii, adj. 著しい remarkable; conspicuous.
ichiji-teki ni, adv. 一時的に

temporarily; for the moment.
ichimai, n. 一枚 one sheet (paper); one slice.
ichimen, n. 一面 1. one side. 2. entire surface.
ichimonnashi (no), adj. 一文無し (の) penniless.
ichinen, n. 一年 one year; **ichinenkan** for one year; **ichinenjū** all year round.
ichinensei, n. 一年生 freshman; first grader.
ichinichi, n. 一日 one day; **ichinichijū** all day long.
ichininmae, n. 一人前 one serving
ichininmae (no), adj. 一人前 (の) grown-up; full-fledged.
-ichi no 一の (superlative indicator) first, best, etc.; **sekaiichi no kanemochi** the richest person in the world.
ichiren, n. 一連 series.
ichiryū (no), adj. 一流 (の) first-rate.
ichō, n. 銀杏 ginkgo (tree).
idai (na), adj. 偉大 (な) great; grand.
idaku, vb. 抱く 1. embrace; hold. 2. entertain (idea).
iden, n. 遺伝 heredity.
idenshi, n. 遺伝子 gene.
ido, n. 井戸 (water) well.
ido, n. 緯度 latitude.
idokoro, n. 居所 one's whereabouts or address.

idomu, *vb.* 挑む challenge.

idō suru, *vb.* 移動する move.

ie, *n.* 家 1. home; house. 2. family.

iede suru, *vb.* 家出する run away from home.

iedomo いえども 1. *conj.* although; however. 2. *adv.* even.

iegara, *n.* 家柄 one's lineage or family background.

iemoto, *n.* 家元 head or headquarters of a particular school of art.

ifuku, *n.* 衣服 clothing.

-igai 以外 except (for); other than.

igai ni, *adv.* 意外に unexpectedly.

igaku, *n.* 医学 medicine.

igan, *n.* 胃癌 stomach cancer.

igirisu, *n.* イギリス England.

igo, *n.* 囲碁 see **go**.

igo 以後 1. *prep.* after; since. 2. *adv.* from now on.

igokochi, *n.* 居心地 the way one feels in a particular ambience; **igokochi ga ii** cozy.

ihan, *n.* 違反 violation; illegality; offense; **chūshaihan** parking violation.

ihan suru, *vb.* 違反する break the law; commit an offense.

ihen, *n.* 異変 accident; calamity.

ihō (no), *adj.* 違法 (の) illegal.

ii, *adj.* 良い 1. good; fine. 2. appropriate; right. 3. beneficial.

ii いい 1. *adj.* enough. 2. *vb.* can do; may do; **kaette mo ii** can go back. 3. *vb.* would like to do; prefer.

iie, *interj.* いいえ No!

iikaeru, *vb.* 言い換える paraphrase.

ii kagen (na), *adj.* 好い加減 (な) 1. unreliable; unsubstantial. 2. proper.

iin, *n.* 医院 clinic; physician's office.

iin, *n.* 委員 committee member.

iinchō, *n.* 委員長 chairperson.

iinkai, *n.* 委員会 committee.

iitsukeru, *vb.* 言いつける 1. tell. 2. tell on; inform.

iitsutae, *n.* 言い伝え legend.

iiwake, *n.* 言い訳 excuse.

iiwake suru, *vb.* 言い訳する make excuses.

iiwatasu, *vb.* 言い渡す deliver (a sentence); order.

iji, *n.* 意地 1. stubbornness; **iji o haru** be stubborn. 2. pride. 3. courage.

iji, *n.* 維持 maintenance.

ijime, *n.* いじめ bullying; abuse.

ijimeru, *vb.* いじめる bully; abuse.

ijiru, *vb.* いじる handle; touch.

iji suru, *vb.* 維持する maintain.

ijiwaru (na, no), *adj.* 意地悪 (な、の) mean; nasty.

ijō 以上 1. *prep.* not less than. 2. *conj.* now that.

ijō (na), *adj.* 異常 (な) abnormal; bizarre.

ijū suru, *vb.* 移住する immigrate; emigrate.

ika, *n.* いか squid; cuttlefish.

ika 以下 1. *adj.* below; less than. 2. *n.* the following; the rest; others.

ikaga, *adv.* 如何 how; how about; would you like; **Ikaga desu ka.** How are you? How do you like it?

ikaiyō, *n.* 胃潰瘍 stomach ulcer.

ikan 遺憾 1. *n.* regret. 2. *adj.* regrettable.

ika ni, *adv.* いかに how.

ika ni mo, *adv.* いかにも really; indeed.

ikan nagara, *adv.* 遺憾ながら regrettably.

ikaru, *vb.* 怒る be angry; be furious.

ikasu, *vb.* 生かす 1. make the most of. 2. keep alive.

ikebana, *n.* 生け花 Japanese flower arrangement.

iken, *n.* 意見 opinion.

ikenai, *adj.* いけない 1. prohibited. 2. bad; unacceptable.

ikeru, *vb.* 生ける、活ける arrange (flowers).

iki, *n.* 息 breath; **iki o hikitoru** die.

iki, *n.* 行き going (outbound).

ikiatari-battari 行き当たりばったり 1. *n.* haphazardness. 2. *adj.* haphazard; aimless; random.

ikigai, *n.* 生き甲斐 reason for living.

iki-iki shita, *adj.* 生き生きした 1. vigorous; lively. 2. lifelike (description).

ikikaeru, *vb.* 生き返る revive; be resurrected.

ikimono, *n.* 生き物 living creature.

ikinari, *adv.* いきなり without notice; suddenly.

ikinokoru, *vb.* 生き残る survive.

ikinuki, *n.* 息抜き rest; break; diversion.

ikioi, *n.* 勢い power; energy.

iki o suru, *vb.* 息をする breathe.

ikiru, *vb.* 生きる live.

ikisaki, *n.* 行き先 destination.

ikita, *adj.* 生きた live.

ikizumari, *n.* 行き詰まり standstill; deadlock.

ikizumaru yō (na), *adj.* 息詰まるような 1. stifling; suffocating. 2. breathtaking; exciting.

ikka, *n.* 一家 family.

ikkai, *n.* 一階 first floor.

ikkai 一回 1. *n.* first time; first round. 2. *adv.* once.

ikki ni, *adv.* 一気に at a stretch; in one breath.

ikko, *n.* 一個 one item (a piece, slice, box, etc.).

ikkō, *n.* 一行 a party (of); group.

ikotsu, *n.* 遺骨 human remains; ashes.

iku, *vb.* 行く go; leave for; visit.

ikubun ka, *adv.* 幾分か to some extent; somehow; somewhat.

ikujinashi, *n., adj.* 意気地なし weak-willed (person).

ikuji no nai, *adj.* 意気地のない weak; spineless.

ikura, *n.* イクラ salmon roe.

ikura, *adv.* 幾ら How much?

ikura ka, *adv.* 幾らか somewhat; a little.

ikutsu, *adv.* 幾つ how many; how old.

ikutsu ka, *adj.* 幾つか some; several.

ikutsu mo, *adv.* 幾つも many.

ima, *n.* 居間 family room; living room.

ima 今 1. *n.* present moment. 2. *adv.* now.

ima demo, *adv.* 今でも even now; still.

imagoro wa, *adv.* 今頃は around this time; by now.

ima made, *adv.* 今迄 until

now.

ima no tokoro, adv. 今の所 up to now; so far.

ima sugu ni, adv. 今すぐに immediately; at once.

imi, n. 意味 meaning; sense; significance.

imo, n. 芋 sweet potato; taro; potato.

imōto, n. 妹 younger sister.

-inai ni 以内に (with)in: **go-fun-inai ni** (with)in five minutes.

inaka, n. 田舎 1. countryside; rural area. 2. hometown.

inchiki, n., adj. いんちき charlatan; phony; fake.

indo, n. インド India.

ine, n. 稲 rice plant.

inemuri, n. 居眠り catnap.

infure, n. インフレ (E.) inflation.

ingenmame, n. 隠元豆 string bean; green bean.

ininjō, n. 委任状 power of attorney.

inin suru, vb. 委任する authorize; commission.

inkan, n. 印鑑 signature seal.

inken (na), adj. 陰険 (な) cunning; sly; crafty.

inki (na), adj. 陰気 (な) gloomy; morose; depressing.

inkyo, n. 隠居 retiree; retirement.

inochi, n. 命 1. life. 2. most precious possession or person.

inori, n. 祈り prayer.

inoru, vb. 祈る pray.

inpo, n. インポ (E.) impotence.

inryoku, n. 引力 gravitation.

inryōsui, n. 飲料水 drinking water.

insatsu, n. 印刷 printing.

insatsubutsu, n. 印刷物 printed matter.

inshō, n. 印象 impression.

inshokubutsu, n. 飲食物 food and drink.

inshō-teki (na), adj. 印象的 (な) memorable; impressive.

inshu, n. 飲酒 drinking (liquor).

intai suru, vb. 引退する retire.

inu, n. 犬 dog.

in'yō suru, vb. 引用する quote; refer to.

iō, n. 硫黄 sulphur.

ippai 一杯 1. n. one cup (glass, spoonful, bowl). 2. n. alcoholic drink. 3. adj. full of.

ippan (no), adj. 一般 (の) common; general; usual.

ippan(-teki) ni, adv. 一般 (的) に commonly; generally; usually.

ippen 一遍 1. n. one time. 2. adv. once.

ippen de, adv. 一遍で the first time.

ippen ni, adv. 一遍に at the same time; all at once.

ippō 一方 1. n. one side; the other party. 2. adv. on the other hand; meanwhile.

ippon, n. 一本 one item (long thin object: bottle, necktie, pencil, rope, etc.).

ippō-teki (na), adj. 一方的 (な) one-sided; unilateral.

ippō tsūkō, n. 一方通行 one-way (street).

ippuku, n. 一服 1. puff (tobacco). 2. one dose; one portion.

ippuku suru, vb. 一服する 1. smoke. 2. take a break.

-irai 以来 since; **areirai** since then.

ira-ira suru, vb. いらいらする be testy or irritable; be impatient.

irai suru, vb. 依頼する ask; request; consign.

irasshai(mase), interj. いらっしゃい(ませ) Welcome!

ireba, n. 入れ歯 false tooth.

iremono, n. 入れ物 receptacle; box; case.

ireru, vb. 入れる 1. put in(to); let in. 3. send someone to. 3. comply with; accept. 4. make (tea, coffee).

irezumi, n. 入れ墨, 刺青 tattoo.

iriguchi, n. 入口 entrance.

iro, n. 色 color.

irogami, n. 色紙 colored origami paper.

iroha, n. いろは 1. Japanese syllable in poetic form. 2. the basics.

iro-iro (na, no), adj. 色々 (な、の) various; manifold.

iroke, n. 色気 sexiness.

irokichigai 色気違い 1. n. lecher; sex maniac. 2. adj. lecherous; lustful.

iro'otoko, n. 色男 attractive man; lady-killer.

iroppoi, adj. 色っぽい sexy.

iru, vb. 要る need; require.

iru, vb. いる、居る 1. be at; be present; exist; there is (are). 2. live in; stay at. 3. have; **koibito ga iru** have a lover, boyfriend, or girlfriend.

-iru, vb. いる be in the act of; **hanashiteiru** in the act of speaking.

iruka, n. いるか dolphin.

iryoku, n. 威力 power; authority.

isamashii, adj. 勇ましい 1. courageous, spirited; daring. 2. invigorating.

isan, n. 遺産 bequest; inheritance; heritage; legacy.

isasaka, adv. いささか a little; somewhat; to some extent.

ise'ebi, n. 伊勢えび small lobster.

isei, n. 異性 opposite sex.

iseki, n. 遺跡 remains; ruins.

isha, ishi, n. 医者、医師 physician.

ishi, n. 石 pebble; stone.

ishiki, n. 意識 awareness; consciousness; **ishiki ga nai** have no consciousness or awareness.

ishiki-teki ni, adv. 意識的に consciously; on purpose.

ishitsu (na, no), adj. 異質 (な、の) different (quality, nature).

isho, n. 遺書 will; testament.

ishō, n. 衣裳 clothing; costume.

isogashii, adj. 忙しい busy.

isogu, vb. 急ぐ hurry.

isoide, adv. 急いで in a hurry.

issai 一切 1. pron. everything. 2. pron. nothing (with negative). 3. adv. never; not at all (with negative).

issakujitsu, n., adv. 一昨日 day before yesterday.

issakunen, n. 一昨年 year before last.

issatsu, n. 一冊 one copy of a book.

issei ni, adv. 一斉に at the same time; all at once; all together.

isshō, n. 一生 lifetime.

isshō kenmei (ni), adv. 一生懸命 (に) with all one's might.

issho ni, adv. 一緒に together (with).

isshū, n. 一周 round; tour.

isshūkan 一週間 1. n. one week. 2. adv. for one week;

in a week.

isshun, *n.* 一瞬 moment; instant.

isshu no, *adj.* 一種の a kind of; a type of.

issō, *adv.* 一層 all the more; more ... than before.

isu, *n.* 椅子 1. chair; sofa. 2. post; position.

isuraeru, *n.* イスラエル Israel.

isuramukyō, *n.* イスラム教 Islam.

ita, *n.* 板 1. wooden board. 2. metal plate.

itachi, *n.* いたち weasel.

itadaki, *n.* 頂 mountaintop; peak.

itadakimasu 頂きます I am about to partake (civility exchanged before meal).

itadaku, *vb.* 頂く 1. receive. 2. eat; drink. 3. ask to do.

itai, *n.* 遺体 dead body.

itai, *adj.* 痛い painful; aching.

itamae, *n.* 板前 chef (Japanese cuisine).

itameru, *vb.* 炒める stir-fry; sauté.

itami, *n.* 痛み ache; pain.

itamidome, *n.* 痛み止め painkiller; analgesic.

itamu, *vb.* 痛む ache; feel pain; hurt.

itaria, *n.* イタリア Italy.

itaru, *vb.* 至る 1. lead to; reach. 2. result in.

itazura, *n.* いたずら prank; mischief.

iten suru, *vb.* 移転する move.

ito, *n.* 糸 string; thread.

itoko, *n.* いとこ cousin.

itsu, *adv.* いつ when; what time; **itsu made** until when.

itsuka, *n.* 五日 fifth day of

the month.

itsuka, *adv.* いつか 1. some day; in the future. 2. once; before.

itsumo, *adv.* いつも always; usually.

itsu no ma ni ka, *adv.* いつの間にか before one is aware.

ittai 一体 1. *n.* one body; a unit. 2. *adv.* how (what, who, etc.) on earth.

ittan, *adv.* 一旦 once; for a moment.

ittō, *n.* 一等 first place; gold award; first class.

iu, *vb.* 言う say; tell; speak.

iwa, *n.* 岩 rock.

iwashi, *n.* いわし sardine.

iwau, *vb.* 祝う celebrate; congratulate.

iya, *interj.* いや、嫌 No!

iya (na), *adj.* 嫌（な） disgusting; disturbing; uncomfortable.

iyagaru, *vb.* 嫌がる 1. dislike; resent. 2. hesitate (out of dislike).

iya-iya, *adv.* いやいや、嫌々 reluctantly.

iyasu, *vb.* 癒す 1. cure; heal. 2. quench (thirst).

iyo-iyo, *adv.* いよいよ 1. finally. 2. more and more.

izakaya, *n.* 居酒屋 small bar; tavern.

izen (ni), *adv.* 以前（に） (long time) ago; before.

izoku, *n.* 遺族 1. surviving family members. 2. the bereaved.

izumi, *n.* 泉 source; spring.

izure いずれ 1. *pron.* which. 2. *adv.* soon; someday. 3. *adv.* in the end.

izure mo, *pron.* いずれも all; every one of them.

J

jā, *interj.* じゃあ Well! Then!

jagaimo, *n.* じゃが芋 potato.

jaguchi, *n.* 蛇口 water faucet.

jakkan 若干 1. *adj.* a little; some. 2. *adv.* somehow; somewhat.

jakuten, *n.* 弱点 weak point; weakness.

jama suru, *vb.* 邪魔する hinder; interfere; disturb.

jan-jan, *adv.* じゃんじゃん abundantly; without hesitation.

jari, *n.* 砂利 gravel.

jettoki, *n.* ジェット機 (E.) jet plane.

ji, *n.* 字 character (letter); handwriting.

-ji 時 o'clock; time; **goji ni** at five o'clock.

jibiki, *n.* 字引き dictionary.

jibun, *n.* 自分 self; oneself; **jibun de** by oneself.

jibunkatte (na, no), *adj.* 自分勝手 (な、の) egoistic; selfish.

jidai, *n.* 時代 era; days; times.

jidaiokure (na, no), *adj.* 時代遅れ (な、の) old-fashioned; out-dated.

jidōhanbaiki, *n.* 自動販売機 vending machine.

jidō (no), *adj.* 自動 (の) automatic.

jidōsha, *n.* 自動車 car.

jidō-teki ni, *adv.* 自動的に automatically.

jieitai, *n.* 自衛隊 Self-Defense Forces.

jigazō, *n.* 自画像 self-portrait (painting).

jigen, *n.* 次元 dimension; level; **motto takai jigen** higher level.

jigenbakudan, *n.* 時限爆弾 time bomb.

jigoku, *n.* 地獄 hell; inferno; **iki-jigoku** living hell.

jigyō, *n.* 事業 business; enterprise.

jihatsu-teki ni, *adv.* 自発的に willingly; voluntarily; of one's own will.

jihi de, *adv.* 自費で at one's own expense.

jihyō, *n.* 辞表 written resignation; **jihyō o dasu** hand in a resignation.

ji'in, *n.* 寺院 temple (Buddhist).

jijii, *n.* じじい old man; grandfather.

jijitsu, *n.* 事実 fact; truth.

jijo, *n.* 次女 second daughter.

jijō, *n.* 事情 reason; situation; circumstances.

jikai ni, *adv.* 次回に next time.

jikaku suru, *vb.* 自覚する be aware of; be conscious of.

jikan, *n.* 時間 time; hour; class period; **jikan ga aru (nai)** have (no) time.

jika ni, *adv.* 直に directly.

jikasei (no), *adj.* 自家製 (の) homemade.

jiken, *n.* 事件 1. incident; happening. 2. criminal case.

jiki, *n.* 磁器 chinaware; porcelain.

jiki, *n.* 時期 time; season.

jiki, *n.* 時機 opportunity.

jiki ni, *adv.* 直に before long; soon.

jikka, *n.* 実家 one's parents' family (esp. on wife's side).

jikkan suru, *vb.* 実感する 1. feel keenly. 2. realize.

jikken, *n.* 実験 experiment.

jikkō suru, *vb.* 実行する carry out; realize;

implement.

jikkuri (to), adv. じっくり (と) thoroughly; over and over again; carefully.

jikkyō(hōsō), n. 実況(放送) live broadcast.

jiko, n. 事故 accident; **kōtsūjiko o okosu** cause a traffic accident.

jiko, n. 自己 self; oneself.

jiko chūshin-teki (na), adj. 自己中心的 (な) self-centered.

jikoku, n. 時刻 time; hour.

jikoshōkai, n. 自己紹介 self-introduction.

jiku, n. 軸 axle; axis; center.

jikyū, n. 時給 hourly wage; **jikyū godoru** five dollars per hour.

jikyūjisoku, n. 自給自足 self-sufficiency.

jime-jime shita, adj. じめじめした damp; humid; gloomy.

jimen, n. 地面 ground.

jimi (na), adj. 地味 (な) 1. subdued; inconspicuous. 2. unattractive.

jimoto (no), adj. 地元 (の) local; hometown.

jimuin, n. 事務員 clerk; office worker.

jimusho, n. 事務所 office.

jinan, n. 次男 second son.

jinbutsu, n. 人物 person; person of rank, note, or distinction.

jindō-teki na, adj. 人道的 (な) humanitarian; humane.

jinin suru, vb. 辞任する resign (from a position).

jinja, n. 神社 Shinto shrine.

jinkaku, n. 人格 personality; character.

jinken, n. 人権 human rights.

jinkō, n. 人口 population.

jinkō (no), adj. 人工 (の)

man-made; artificial.

jinkō-teki (na), adj. 人工的 (な) artificial; man-made.

jinmashin, n. じんましん hives; allergic skin rash.

jinmin, n. 人民 people; citizens.

jinmon suru, vb. 尋問する interrogate.

jinrui, n. 人類 human race.

jinruiai, n. 人類愛 philanthropy.

jinruigaku, n. 人類学 anthropology.

jinsei, n. 人生 human life.

jinshu, n. 人種 race (division of humankind).

jintai, n. 人体 human body.

jintsū, n. 陣痛 labor pains.

jinushi, n. 地主 landowner.

jinzai, n. 人材 talented (skilled, capable) person.

jinzō, n. 腎臓 kidney.

jīpan, n. ジーパン jeans.

jirasu, vb. 焦らす tantalize; tease.

jiriki de, adv. 自力で unassisted; without depending on others.

jiritsu suru, vb. 自立する become self-sufficient.

jisa, n. 時差 time difference.

jisa boke, n. 時差ぼけ jet lag.

jisan suru, vb. 持参する bring; take.

jisatsu suru, vb. 自殺する commit suicide.

jisei, n. 時制 tense (grammar).

jiseishin, n. 自制心 self-control.

jishaku, n. 磁石 magnet.

jishin, n. 地震 earthquake.

jishin, n. 自信 self-confidence.

jisho, n. 辞書 dictionary.

jishoku suru, vb. 辞職する resign (from a position).

jishu suru, vb. 自首する turn oneself in.

jishu-teki (na), adj. 自主的 (な) voluntary.

jisoku, n. 時速 speed.

jisonshin, n. 自尊心 self-esteem.

jissai ni, adv. 実際に in reality; in fact.

jisseki, n. 実績 accomplishment; achievement.

jisshitsu-teki (na), adj. 実質的 (な) substantive; practical.

jisuberi, n. 地滑り landslide.

jisui suru, vb. 自炊する cook for oneself.

jitabata suru, vb. じたばたする struggle.

jitai, n. 事態 situation; circumstance.

-jitai 自体 oneself; itself. **kono mondaijitai** the problem itself.

jitaku, n. 自宅 home or house.

jiten, n. 辞典 dictionary.

jitensha, n. 自転車 bicycle.

jitsubutsu, n. 実物 real thing; real person.

jitsuen, n. 実演 live performance; demonstration.

jitsugen suru, vb. 実現する materialize; realize; effect.

jitsu ni, adv. 実に really; indeed.

jitsu no, adj. 実の biological; real; **jitsu no haha** biological mother.

jitsuryoku, n. 実力 capability; proficiency.

jitsu wa, adv. 実は really; in fact.

jitsuyōhin, n. 実用品 useful or practical thing.

jitsuyō-teki (na), adj. 実用的 (な) useful; practical.

jitsuzai no, adj. 実在の existing; real.

jittai, n. 実体 fact; reality.

jitto, adv. じっと 1. without moving; still. 2. intently.

jiwa-jiwa (to), adv. じわじわ (と) slowly; gradually.

jiyū, n. 自由 liberty; freedom.

jiyū (na, no), adj. 自由 (な、の) unfettered; free.

jiyū ni, adv. 自由に freely; as one likes.

jizen, n. 慈善 charity.

jizen ni, adv. 事前に in advance; beforehand.

jizoku suru, vb. 持続する continue; maintain.

jo, n. 序 preface; foreword.

-jō 上 in terms of; **hito no kenkō-jō** in terms of one's health.

-jō 畳 (counter for tatami); **roku-jō** six tatami mats.

jōbu (na), adj. 丈夫 (な) healthy; hardy; strong.

jōdan, n. 冗談 joke; humor; **jōdan o iu** make a joke.

jōdan hanbun de/ni, adv. 冗談半分で／に half in jest.

jodōshi, n. 助動詞 auxiliary verb (grammar).

jōei, n. 上映 showing; screening (film).

jōen suru, vb. 上演する stage; perform.

jogai suru, vb. 除外する exclude; eliminate.

jogakkō, n. 女学校 girls' school.

jogakusei, n. 女学生 female student.

jōge 上下 1. up and down; top and bottom. 2. upper and lower status (ranking, part, position). 3. first and second volumes (of two).

jogen, n. 助言 advice; **jogen o ataeru** advise.

jōgi, *vb.* 定規 measure; ruler.

jōhatsu suru, *vb.* 蒸発する 1. evaporate. 2. disappear.

jōheki, *n.* 城壁 castle wall.

jōhin (na), *adj.* 上品 (な) elegant; graceful; refined.

jōhō, *n.* 情報 information; news.

joi, *n.* 女医 woman physician.

jōi (no), *adj.* 上位 (の) higher; highest.

jōin, *n.* 上院 Upper House; Senate.

jo-jo ni, *adv.* 徐々に gradually; step by step.

jōju, *n.* 成就 achievement; accomplishment; realization.

jōjun, *n.* 上旬 first third of a month.

jōken, *n.* 条件 requirement; condition; **... to iu jōken de** on condition that ... .

jōki, *n.* 蒸気 vapor; steam.

jōkigen (na), *adj.* 上機嫌 (な、の) good-humored; cheerful.

jokō suru, *vb.* 徐行する slow down.

jōkyaku, *n.* 乗客 passenger.

jōkyō, *n.* 状況 circumstance; state.

jokyōju, *n.* 助教授 assistant professor.

jokyoku, *n.* 序曲 overture; prelude.

jōkyū, *n.* 上級 advanced level; **nihongojōkyū** advanced Japanese.

jōmuin, *n.* 乗務員 crew member (plane, train, or ship).

jōmyaku, *n.* 静脈 vein (blood vessel).

jōnetsu-teki (na), *adj.* 情熱的 (な) enthusiastic; passionate.

jo'ō, *n.* 女王 queen.

jōren, *n.* 定連 regular customer (guest, visitor, etc.).

jōriku suru, *vb.* 上陸する 1. land. 2. hit (typhoon).

jōryū (no), *adj.* 上流 (の) upper-class.

josanpu, *n.* 助産婦 midwife.

josei, *n.* 女性 woman.

jōsei, *n.* 情勢 situation; circumstances.

jōsen suru, *vb.* 乗船する board (ship).

jōshaken, *n.* 乗車券 train or bus ticket.

jōsha suru, *vb.* 乗車する board (train, bus); get in (car).

joshi, *n.* 女子 girl; woman.

jōshi, *n.* 上司 superior (in a company).

jōshiki, *n.* 常識 common sense; conventional wisdom.

jōshitsu (na, no), *adj.* 上質 (な、の) of high quality.

jōshō suru, *vb.* 上昇する mount; rise.

joshu, *n.* 助手 assistant.

jōshūsha, *n.* 常習者 habitual user; addict.

josū, *n.* 序数 ordinal number.

jōtai, *n.* 状態 circumstances; state; condition.

jōtai, *n.* 上体 upper body; torso.

jōtatsu suru, *vb.* 上達する improve.

jōtō (na, no), *adj.* 上等 (な、の) excellent; very good.

jōyōsha, *n.* 乗用車 automobile.

jōyō suru, *vb.* 常用する use regularly; use constantly.

joyū, *n.* 女優 actress.

jōzai, *n.* 錠剤 tablet; pill (medicine).

jōzu (na), *adj.* 上手 (な)

good at; skilled; proficient.

jū, *n.* 十 ten.

jū, *n.* 銃 gun.

-jū 中 throughout;
ichinichijū all day long.

jūbun (na), *adj.* 十分 (な)
enough; ample.

jūdai, *n.* 十代 teens.

jūdai (na), *adj.* 重大 (な)
serious; important.

jūden suru, *vb.* 充電する
charge (battery).

judōtai, *n.* 受動体 passive
voice (grammar).

jūfuku/chōfuku suru, *vb.*
重複する overlap.

jūgatsu, *n.* 十月 October.

jugyō, *n.* 授業 class.

jugyōryō, *n.* 授業料 tuition.

jūi, *n.* 獣医 veterinarian.

jūichigatsu, *n.* 十一月
November.

jūjika, *n.* 十字架 cross;
crucifix.

jūjiro, *n.* 十字路 crossroads.

jūjitsu shita, *adj.* 充実した
fulfilling.

jūjun (na), *adj.* 従順 (な)
obedient.

juken suru, *vb.* 受験する
take an examination.

juku, *n.* 塾 cram school.

jukuren shita, *adj.* 熟練した
skilled; expert.

jukusu, *vb.* 熟す ripen;
mature.

jūkyo, *n.* 住居 residence;
house.

jukyū, *n.* 需給 supply and
demand.

jūman, *n.* 十万 (one)
hundred thousand;
nijūman two hundred
thousand.

jūmin, *n.* 住民 resident.

jumyō, *n.* 寿命 life span.

jun, *n.* 順 order; turn.

jun- 準 semi; second-best;
jun-kesshō semifinal.

jūnan (na), *adj.* 柔軟 (な)
flexible.

junban, *n.* 順番 one's turn;
order.

junbi, *n.* 準備 preparation.
junbi suru, *vb.* 準備する
prepare.

junchō (na), *adj.* 順調 (な)
smooth; no problem.

jun'i, *n.* 順位 ranking; place.

jūnigatsu, *n.* 十二月
December.

jūniji, *n.* 十二時 twelve
o'clock; **reizen (gogo)**.

jūniji, *n.* 十二時 twelve a.m. (p.m.).

junjo, *n.* 順序 order;
sequence.

junjō (na), *adj.* 純情 (な)
naive; unspoiled; pure.

junkan, *n.* 循環 circulation;
circular movement;
akujunkan vicious circle.

junketsu na (no), *adj.* 純潔
(な、の) pure; chaste;
innocent.

jun'nō suru, *vb.* 順応する
adapt to.

junrei, *n.* 巡礼 pilgrimage
(Buddhist).

junsa, *n.* 巡査 patrolman.

junsui (na, no), *adj.* 純粋
(な、の) pure; pure-
blooded; genuine.

jūoku, *n.* 十億 billion.

jūryō, *n.* 重量 weight.

jusei, *n.* 受精 fertilization;
insemination; **jinkō jusei**
artificial insemination.

jushin, *n.* 受信 reception
(TV, radio).

jushin, *n.* 受診 examination
by a physician.

jūshi suru, *vb.* 重視する
emphasize; give priority to.

jūsho, *n.* 住所 address.

jūshō, *n.* 重傷 serious injury.

jushō suru, *vb.* 受賞する
win an award.

jūtai, *n.* 重態 critical

condition.

jūtai, *n.* 渋滞 gridlock (traffic).

jūtaku, *n.* 住宅 residence; house.

jūtan, *n.* じゅうたん carpet; rug.

jūten, *n.* 重点 emphasis; stress; **jūten o oku**

emphasize.

jutsugo, *n.* 述語 predicate (grammar).

juwaki, *n.* 受話器 (telephone) receiver.

jūyō (na), *adj.* 重要 (な) 1. important. 2. prominent.

jūyō jinbutsu, *n.* 重要人物 VIP.

K

ka, *n.* 蚊 mosquito.

ka, *parti.* か 1. do (did, is, was, are, etc.) ... ?; **Oishii desu ka.** Does it taste good? 2. or; **are ka kore ka** this or that.

-ka 課 1. office section or department. 2. lesson.

-ka 科 1. academic department; **kokubunka** Department of Japanese Literature. 2. academic course. 3. medical department; medical specialty.

kaban, *n.* 鞄 bag; briefcase; suitcase.

kabau, *vb.* 庇う defend; protect; support.

kabe, *n.* 壁 wall.

kabi, *n.* かび mildew; mold.

kabin, *n.* 花瓶 vase.

kabocha, *n.* かぼちゃ pumpkin; squash.

kabu, *n.* かぶ turnip.

kabu, *n.* 株 1. stock. 2. stump.

kabuki, *n.* 歌舞伎 traditional Japanese drama.

kabureru, *vb.* かぶれる 1. be influenced. 2. develop a rash.

kaburu, *vb.* 被る 1. put something (on head). 2. be drenched with; be covered with.

kabushiki-gaisha, *n.* 株式会社 corporation.

kabuto, *n.* かぶと helmet.

kachi, *n.* 価値 value.

kachi, *n.* 勝ち win; victory.

kachō, *n.* 課長 section chief; manager.

kadai, *n.* 課題 1. topic. 2. problem; issue. 3. assignment.

kadan, *n.* 花壇 flower bed.

kado, *n.* 角 corner.

-ka dō ka かどうか whether (or not); **iku-ka dō ka kimerarenai** unable to decide whether or not to go.

kaeri, *n.* 帰り going back; coming back; return.

kaeru, *vb.* 帰る go back; come back; return.

kaeru, *vb.* 変える change; transform.

kaeru, *vb.* 替える、換える replace; exchange.

kaesu, *vb.* 返す 1. give back; return. 2. invert; reverse.

-kaesu 返す re-; back; **maki-kaesu** rewind.

kaette, *adv.* かえって 1. conversely; rather. 2. all the more.

kagaku, *n.* 科学 science.

kagaku, *n.* 化学 chemistry.

kagami, *n.* 鏡 mirror.

kagamu, *vb.* 屈む squat; crouch.

kagayaki, *n.* 輝き splendor; radiance; brilliance.

kagayaku, *vb.* 輝く shine; glitter; sparkle.

kage, *n.* 影 1. shadow. 2. silhouette.

kage, *n.* 陰 1. shade. 2. gloominess.

kage de, *adv.* 陰で behind one's back; behind the scenes.

kageguchi, *n.* 陰口 backbiting.

kageki, *n.* 歌劇 opera.

kagen, *n.* 加減 1. physical condition. 2. degree; **yu kagen** temperature of bath water.

kagen suru, *vb.* 加減する moderate; downgrade.

kagi, *n.* 鍵 1. key. 2. clue.

kagiranai, *vb.* 限らない not necessarily; not always.

kagiru, *vb.* 限る be limited to.

kago, *n.* 籠 basket; birdcage.

kagu, *n.* 家具 furniture.

kagu, *vb.* 嗅ぐ smell; sniff.

kahansū, *n.* 過半数 majority.

kai, *n.* 貝 seashell; shellfish.

kai, *n.* 会 1. meeting; conference. 2. party; gathering. 3. association.

-kai, -kkai 回 (counter) round; time; **jukkai** tenth round; ten times.

-kai, -kkai, -gai 階 counter for floors of a building; stairs; **nikai** second floor; **ikkai** first floor; **hachikai** eighth floor.

kaibō, *n.* 解剖 anatomy; autopsy.

kaibutsu, *n.* 怪物 monster.

kaichō, *n.* 会長 chairman; chairman of the board.

kaichō, *n.* 快調 good form

kaichū dentō, *n.* 懐中電燈 flashlight.

kaidan, *n.* 階段 steps; stairs.

kaifuku suru, *vb.* 回復する recover (from illness); improve.

kaigai 海外 1. *n.* foreign nations. 2. *adj., adv.* overseas.

kaigan, *n.* 海岸 coast, seashore; beach.

kaigara, *n.* 貝殻 seashell.

kaigi, *n.* 会議 meeting; conference; convention.

kaigun, *n.* 海軍 navy.

kaigyō suru, *vb.* 開業する open (business).

kaihatsu suru, *vb.* 開発する develop.

kaihi, *n.* 会費 membership fee.

kaihō suru, *vb.* 解放する emancipate; liberate; release.

kaihō suru, *vb.* 開放する open; leave open.

kaiin, *n.* 会員 member.

kaijo, *n.* 解除 lifting (of a ban); removal; cancellation.

kaijō, *n.* 会場 site of a gathering or event; venue.

kaijō, *adj.* 海上 marine.

kai-kaishiki, *n.* 開会式 opening ceremony.

kaikaku, *n.* 改革 reform.

kaikan, *n.* 会館 auditorium.

kaikatsu (na), *adj.* 快活 (な) lively; cheerful.

kaikei, *n.* 会計 1. account(s). 2. bill; check. 3. payment.

kaikeigaku, *n.* 会計学 accounting (discipline).

kaikeishi, *n.* 会計士 accountant; **kōnin-kaikeishi** Certified Public Accountant.

kaiken, *n.* 会見 1. meeting. 2. interview.

kaiko suru, *vb.* 解雇する dismiss; **ichiji-kaiko suru**

lay off.

kaikyō, *n.* 海峡 channel; strait.

kaikyō, *n.* 回教 Islam.

kaikyū, *n.* 階級 class; rank; caste.

kaimono, *n.* 買物 shopping.

kain, *n.* 下院 Lower House; House of Representatives (U.S.).

kairaku, *n.* 快楽 pleasure.

kairyō, *n.* 改良 improvement; reform.

kaisan suru, *vb.* 解散する dismiss (gathering, party, meeting); dissolve (Diet).

kaisatsuguchi, *n.* 改札口 turnstile; ticket gate.

kaisetsu suru, *vb.* 解説する explain; comment; interpret.

kaisha, *n.* 会社 corporation; company; office.

kaishaku suru, *vb.* 解釈する interpret; explain.

kaishū suru, *vb.* 回収する 1. recall. 2. collect (bills, loans).

kaisō, *n.* 海草 seaweed.

kaisō, *n.* 改装 renovation; remodeling.

kaisū, *n.* 回数 frequency; number of times.

kaisui, *n.* 海水 sea water.

kaisuiyoku, *n.* 海水浴 swimming in the ocean.

kaisui-yokujō, *n.* 海水浴場 bathing beach.

kaitaku suru, *vb.* 開拓する develop (wilderness); open up (new markets, etc.).

kaiten-doa, *n.* 回転ドア revolving door.

kaiten suru, *vb.* 回転する revolve; rotate.

kaiten suru, *vb.* 開店する open (business: restaurant, store, etc.) for the day; establish (business:

restaurant, store, etc.).

kaitō, *n.* 解答 answer; response; reply.

kaitsū suru, *vb.* 開通する go into service (highway, bridge, telephone, cable system).

kaiwa, *n.* 会話 conversation; **eikaiwa** English conversation.

kaizen, *n.* 改善 improvement.

kaji, *n.* 家事 household chores.

kaji, *n.* 火事 fire (conflagration).

kaji, *n.* 舵 helm; rudder.

kajiru, *vb.* かじる gnaw; crunch; bite.

kakaeru, *vb.* 抱える embrace; hold; employ (person).

kakaku, *n.* 価格 value; price.

kakari, *n.* 係 person in charge.

kakarichō, *n.* 係長 assistant section chief.

kakaru, *vb.* 罹る contract (an illness).

kakaru, *vb.* かかる 1. take (time); **gofun kakaru** take five minutes. 2. cost; **godoru kakaru** cost five dollars. 3. hang. 4. depend on. 5. consult (a doctor). 6. start moving.

kakato, *n.* 踵 heel (foot, shoe).

kakawarazu, *conj.* かかわらず in spite of; regardless of; although.

kakawaru, *vb.* 係る、関わる be connected with; be involved in.

kake, *n.* 賭け bet; gambling.

kakedasu, *vb.* 駆け出す start running; dash out.

kakegoe, *n.* 掛け声 shout;

cheer.

kakehanareru, *vb.* かけ離れる be far apart; be removed from.

kakei, *n.* 家系 lineage; genealogy.

kakei, *n.* 家計 household budget.

kakeibo, *n.* 家計簿 household accounts.

kakekin, *n.* 掛け金 1. premium (insurance). 2. (scheduled) payment.

kakeru, *vb.* 欠ける 1. lack. 2. break off.

kakeru, *vb.* 賭ける bet; gamble.

kakeru, *vb.* 掛ける 1. hang. 2. wear (glasses, necklace); cover. 3. sit down. 4. spend (time, money). 5. telephone. 6. keep in mind; care about.

kaki, *n.* かき oyster.

kaki, *n.* 柿 persimmon.

kakitome, *n.* 書留 registered mail.

kakitomeru, *vb.* 書き留める take notes; write down.

kakki, *n.* 活気 liveliness; activity.

kakko, *n.* かっこ parenthesis; bracket.

kakkō, *n.* 格好 1. form; appearance. 2. appropriateness; suitability.

kakko ii, *adj.* かっこいい attractive; good-looking.

kako, *n.* 過去 past.

kakobunshi, *n.* 過去分詞 past participle.

kakōhin, *n.* 加工品 processed goods (esp. food).

kakokanryōkei, *n.* 過去完了形 past perfect participle.

kakokei, *n.* 過去形 past tense.

kakomu, *vb.* 囲む circle; surround.

kaku, *n.* 核 core; nucleus; kernel.

kaku, *n.* 画 stroke (pen or brush) of kana or kanji.

kaku, *vb.* 書く write.

kaku, *vb.* 掻く scratch; scrape.

kaku- 各 each; **kakujin** each person.

kakuheiki, *n.* 核兵器 nuclear weapon.

kakubetsu (na, no), *adj.* 格別 (な、の) special; exceptional.

kakuchō suru, *vb.* 拡張する expand; enlarge; widen.

kakudo, *n.* 角度 angle.

kakueki(teisha), *n.* 各駅(停車) local train.

kakugo suru, *vb.* 覚悟する be prepared (for something unwelcome).

kakuho suru, *vb.* 確保する ensure.

kakuji no, *adj.* 各自の each; (one's) own.

kakujitsu (na), *adj.* 確実 (な) sure; guaranteed; reliable.

kakumei, *n.* 革命 revolution.

kakumei-teki (na), *adj.* 革命的 (な) revolutionary; innovative.

kakū no, *adj.* 架空の imaginary.

kakuri suru, *vb.* 隔離する isolate; quarantine.

kakusage, *n.* 格下げ demotion.

kakushin, *n.* 確信 confidence; conviction.

kakushin, *n.* 革新 reformation; innovation.

kakusu, *vb.* 隠す hide; cover up.

kakutei suru, *vb.* 確定する decide; conclude.

kakutoku suru, *vb.* 獲得する

る win; obtain.

kakyū, n. 下級 beginner's level; lower rank.

kama, gama, n. 釜 pot in which rice is cooked; **denkigama** electric rice cooker.

kamae, n. 構え (martial arts) posture.

kamau, vb. 構う care about; take care of; pay attention to.

kamawanai, vb. 構わない not mind; not care.

kame, n. 亀 tortoise; turtle.

kame, n. 瓶 earthenware jar.

kamen, n. 仮面 mask.

kami, n. 紙 paper.

kami, n. 神 god.

kami, n. 髪 hair (head).

kamikaze, n. 神風 1. divine wind. 2. name given to suicide pilots in World War II.

kaminari, n. 雷 lightning; thunder.

kamisori, n. 剃刀 razor.

kamo, n. 鴨 duck.

kamoku, n. 科目 course; subject (school).

kamome, n. かもめ seagull.

kamotsu, n. 貨物 freight.

kamu, vb. 噛む bite; chew.

kan, n. 缶 can.

kan, n. 勘 intuition; sixth sense.

-kan 間 for; during; **ichi-jikan han** for an hour and a half.

-kan 巻 volume (book).

kana, n. 仮名 Japanese syllabary (hiragana; katakana).

kanai, n. 家内 one's wife (humble).

kanamono, n. 金物 hardware.

kanarazu, adv. 必ず for certain; without fail.

kanarazushimo, adv. 必ずしも not necessarily; not always.

kanari, adv. かなり fairly; moderately.

kanashii, adj. 悲しい sad; sorrowful.

kanashimu, vb. 悲しむ feel sad; grieve; lament.

kanata 彼方 1. n. faraway place; yonder. 2. adv. faraway.

kanau, vb. 叶う (wish, dream) come true; be fulfilled.

kanawanai, vb. 適わない 1. be unable to endure. 2. be unable to compete with; be unable to best.

kanazuchi, n. 金槌 1. hammer. 2. person who cannot swim.

kanban, n. 看板 signboard (shop, movie theater).

kanbyō suru, vb. 看病する care for a sick person.

kanchigai, n. 勘違い misjudgment; misunderstanding.

kanchi suru, vb. 感知する discern; perceive.

kandai (na), adj. 寛大 (な) 1. understanding; lenient. 2. generous; broad-minded.

kandenchi, n. 乾電池 dry cell (battery).

kandō suru, vb. 感動する be touched; be moved.

kane, okane, n. 金、お金 money.

kane, n. 鐘 bell.

kanemochi, n. 金持ち rich person.

kanemōke, n. 金儲け money making.

kaneru, vb. 兼ねる serve multiple purposes (positions, functions, etc.) at the same time.

kanetsu suru, vb. 加熱する heat.

kangae, n. 考え idea; thought; view.

kangaechigai, n. 考え違い misunderstanding; misconception.

kangaekata, n. 考え方 viewpoint; way of thinking.

kangaenaosu, vb. 考え直す rethink; reconsider.

kangaeru, vb. 考える think; think up; consider.

kangei suru, vb. 歓迎する welcome.

kangeki suru, vb. 感激する be moved; be touched.

kangofu, n. 看護婦 nurse.

kango suru, vb. 看護する nurse.

kani, n. かに crab.

kanja, n. 患者 patient.

kanji, n. 漢字 Chinese characters used in Japanese writing.

kanji, n. 感じ impression; perception; feeling.

kanjin (na, no), adj. 肝心 (な、の) essential; most important; crucial.

kanjiru, vb. 感じる feel; sense.

kanjiyasui, adj. 感じやすい sensitive.

kanjō, n. 感情 feeling; emotion; sentiment.

kankaku, n. 感覚 sense; sensitivity; feeling.

kankaku, n. 間隔 interim; interval; pause; space.

kankei, n. 関係 relationship; relation; connection.

kankei-daimeishi, n. 関係代名詞 relative pronoun.

kankei ga aru (nai), vb. 関係がある (ない) be related (unrelated) to; have something (nothing) to do with.

kankiri, n. 缶切り can opener.

kankō, n. 観光 sightseeing; tourism.

kankōan'naisho, n. 観光案内所 tourist information office.

kankoku, n. 韓国 South Korea.

kankōkyaku, n. 観光客 sightseer; tourist.

kankyaku, n. 観客 audience; spectator.

kankyō, n. 環境 environment; surroundings.

kanmuri, n. 冠 crown.

kan'ningu, n. カンニング (E. cunning) cheating.

kanojo 彼女 1. pron. she; her. 2. n. girlfriend (used by males).

kanojo no, adj. 彼女の her; girlfriend's (used by males).

kanō (na), adj. 可能 (な) possible.

kanō na kagiri adv. 可能な限りto the extent possible.

kanōsei, n. 可能性 possibility.

kanō suru, vb. 化膿する fester.

kanpai, interj. 乾杯 Cheers! To your health! Bottoms up!

kanpōyaku, n. 漢方薬 traditional Chinese medicines.

kanran suru, vb. 観覧する watch (plays, sports, ballet, etc.)

kanren (no), adj. 関連 (の) related; associated.

kanri, n. 管理 supervision; administration; management.

kanryō suru, vb. 完了する finish; complete.

kansan suru, vb. 換算する exchange; convert.

kansatsu, *n.* 観察 observation.

kansei suru, *vb.* 完成する accomplish; complete; finish.

kansen, *n.* 感染 contagion; infection.

kansetsu, *n.* 関節 joint (knee, etc.).

kansetsu-teki (na), *adj.* 間接的 (な) indirect.

kansha suru, *vb.* 感謝する appreciate; feel grateful.

kanshi, *n.* 冠詞 article (grammar).

kanshin, *n.* 関心 concern; interest.

kanshin (na), *adj.* 感心 (な) impressive; admirable.

kanshin suru, *vb.* 感心する be impressed; admire.

kanshite, *prep.* 関して concerning; regarding.

kanshō, *n.* 干渉 interference; intervention.

kansō, *n.* 感想 opinion; impression.

kansōki, *n.* 乾燥機 dryer; clothes dryer.

kansoku, *n.* 観測 observation; survey.

kansō shiteiru/shita, *adj.* 乾燥している／〜した dry.

kansuru 関する 1. *vb.* be related to; concern. 2. *prep.* concerning; about.

kantan (na), *adj.* 簡単 (な) easy; simple; brief.

kantoku, *n.* 監督 director; superintendent; manager; **eiga-kantoku** film director.

kanyū suru, *vb.* 加入する join.

kanzei, *n.* 関税 (customs) duty; tariff.

kanzen (na), *adj.* 完全 (な) perfect; entire.

kanzen (ni), *adv.* 完全 (に) perfectly; entirely.

kanzō, *n.* 肝臓 liver.

kanzume, *n.* 缶詰 canned food.

kao, *n.* 顔 face; look; countenance; **kao o tsubusu** cause someone to lose face.

kaoiro, *n.* 顔色 complexion.

kaori, *n.* 香り、薫り fragrance; scent; smell; aroma.

kappatsu (na), *adj.* 活発 (な) active; vivacious.

kara (no), *adj.* 空 (の) empty; vacant.

-kara から 1. from; since; after. 2. starting at (time). 3. (in passive mode) by; (made) from; (made) of. 4. because; therefore; so.

kara'age, *n.* 空揚げ deep-fried food.

karada, *n.* 体 1. body. 2. health.

karai, *adj.* 辛い 1. bitter; hot (spicy); salty. 2. strict.

karakau, *vb.* からかう ridicule; jeer.

karamaru, *vb.* 絡まる become entangled in.

karashi, *n.* 辛子、芥子 mustard.

karasu, *n.* 烏 crow.

karate, *n.* 空手 karate.

kare 彼 1. *pron.* he; him. 2. *n.* boyfriend.

karē, *n.* カレー (E.) curry.

kare no, *adj.* 彼の his; boyfriend's.

karera, *pron.* 彼等 they.

kareru, *vb.* 枯れる wither.

kari ni, *conj.* 仮に if.

kari no, *adj.* 仮の tentative; temporary.

kariru, *vb.* 借りる 1. borrow; rent. 2. use (someone's telephone, rest room, etc.).

karōjite, *adv.* 辛うじて barely.

karōshi, *n.* 過労死 death from overwork.

karu, *vb.* 刈る reap; mow; cut (hair).

karui, *adj.* 軽い 1. light. 2. easy.

karuta, *n.* カルタ (Pg. *carta*) playing card(s).

kasa, *n.* 傘 umbrella.

kasai, *n.* 火災 fire.

kasanaru, *vb.* 重なる 1. be piled up. 2. be compounded. 3. occur at the same time.

kasaneru, *vb.* 重ねる 1. pile up. 2. repeat.

kasegu, *vb.* 稼ぐ earn.

kasei, *n.* 火星 Mars (planet).

kaseki, *n.* 化石 fossil.

kashi, *n.* 菓子 confection; cake.

kashi, *n.* 樫 oak.

kashi, *n.* 華氏 Fahrenheit.

kashi, *n.* 歌詞 lyrics.

kashikoi, *adj.* 賢い wise; clever; intelligent.

kashikomari-mashita, *interj.* かしこまりました1 understand. Yes, sir! (said by an inferior to a superior).

kashira, *n.* 頭 1. head. 2. chief; leader.

kashira moji, *n.* 頭文字 initial letter (of a word).

kashu, *n.* 歌手 singer.

kasō, *n.* 火葬 cremation.

kasoku, *n.* 加速 acceleration; **kasoku ga tsuku** accelerate.

kasu, *vb.* 貸す 1. lend; loan. 2. let someone use something.

kasuka (na), *adj.* 微か (な) faint; vague.

kasumu, *vb.* 霞 blur; be dim; be hazy.

kasurikizu, *n.* かすり傷 scratch; minor injury.

kasutera, *n.* カステラ (Pg. *Castella*) sponge cake.

kata, *n.* 肩 shoulder; **kata ga koru** have stiff shoulders.

kata, *n.* 型 form (martial arts, dance, etc.); posture; style.

kata, *n.* 形 model; type.

kata 方 1. how to; **tsukaikata** how to use. 2. person; **ano kata** that person.

katachi, *n.* 形 shape; form.

katai, *adj.* 固い 1. hard; firm; stiff. 2. upright; conscientious.

katakana, *n.* 片仮名 Japanese syllabary for foreign words.

kataki, *n.* 敵 enemy; rival.

kataki o utsu, *vb.* 敵を討つ revenge; avenge.

katakurushii, *adj.* 堅苦しい 1. rigid; stiff-mannered. 2. overly formal.

katamari, *n.* 固まり lump; mass.

katamaru, *vb.* 固まる 1. coagulate; harden. 2. group together.

katameru, *vb.* 固める 1. harden. 2. solidify. 3. strengthen.

katamuku, *vb.* 傾く 1. tilt; incline. 2. decline; go down.

katana, *n.* 刀 Japanese sword.

kataomoi, *n.* 片思い unrequited love.

kataru, *vb.* 語る talk; relate.

katate, *n.* 片手 one hand.

katatsumuri, *n.* かたつむり snail.

katazukeru, *vb.* 片付ける 1. tidy up; put things in order. 2. finish; settle. 3. get rid of.

katei, *n.* 家庭 home; household.

katei, *n.* 過程 process.

katei, *n.* 課程 course; curriculum.

katei, *n.* 仮定 supposition; hypothesis; conjecture.

katsu, *n.* カツ breaded, deep-fried cutlet; **tonkatsu** pork cutlet.

katsu, *vb.* 勝 win; defeat.

katsu, *adv., conj.* 且つ and; besides; in addition.

katsudō, *n.* 活動 activity.

katsugu, *vb.* 担ぐ 1. carry; shoulder. 2. trick; dupe.

katsuji, *n.* 活字 type (printing).

katsuo, *n.* 鰹 bonito.

katsura, *n.* かつら wig.

katsute, *adv.* かつて formerly; long ago.

katsuyaku suru, *vb.* 活躍する be active.

katsuyō suru, *vb.* 活用する make the most of.

katte, *n.* 勝手 1. selfishness. 2. one's personal concern; one's business; **watashi no katte** my business (none of your business).

katte (na), *adj.* 勝手 (な) 1. selfish. 2. arbitrary. 3. groundless.

katte ni, *adv.* 勝手に 1. selfishly. 2. voluntarily. 3. without permission.

katto naru, *vb.* かっとなる fly into a rage.

kau, *vb.* 買う 1. buy. 2. appreciate. 3. invite (a mishap).

kau, *vb.* 飼う keep (a pet); raise (cattle).

kawa, *n.* 皮 skin; leather; bark; rind.

kawa, *n.* 川 stream; river.

kawaigaru, *vb.* 可愛がる cherish; dote on.

kawairashii, *adj.* 可愛らしい lovely; cute.

kawaisō (na), *adj.* 可哀そう (な) pitiful; pitiable; poor.

kawaku, *vb.* 乾く become dry.

kawara, *n.* 瓦 roof tile.

kawari, *n.* 代わり 1. substitute. 2. second helping of food. 3. exchange; return; **sono kawari ni** in exchange or return for that.

kawariyasui, *adj.* 変わりやすい changeable; unstable.

kawaru, *vb.* 変わる change.

kawaru, *vb.* 代わる take the place of.

kawase, *n.* 為替 exchange (currency).

kawatta, *adj.* 変わった strange; different.

kayōbi, *n.* 火曜日 Tuesday.

kayou, *vb.* 通う commute; frequent.

kayui, *adj.* 痒い itchy.

kazan, *n.* 火山 volcano.

kazari, *n.* 飾り decoration; ornament.

kazaru, *vb.* 飾る decorate.

kaze, *n.* 風 breeze; wind; **kaze ga fuku** the wind blows.

kaze, *n.* 風邪 cold; **kaze o hiku** catch a cold.

kazoeru, *vb.* 数える count.

kazoku, *n.* 家族 family.

kazu, *n.* 数 number.

ke, *n.* 毛 1. hair. 2. fur; wool.

-ke 家 family; **Wadake** the Wada family.

kechi (na), *adj.* けち (な) 1. miserly. 2. stingy.

kega, *n.* 怪我 wound; injury.

kega o suru, *vb.* 怪我をする suffer an injury; get hurt.

kegawa, *n.* 毛皮 fur.

kei, *n.* 刑 criminal sentence; punishment.

keiba, *n.* 競馬 horse racing.

keibetsu suru, *vb.* 軽蔑する disdain; scorn.

keibi, *n.* 警備 guard; watch.

keibu, *n.* 警部 police inspector.

keiei suru, *vb.* 経営する manage; run (business).

keigen suru, *vb.* 軽減する reduce; alleviate.

keigo, *n.* 敬語 honorific language.

keigu 敬具 Yours truly; Yours sincerely.

keihō, *n.* 警報 warning; alarm.

keiji, *n.* 掲示 (written) notice; announcement.

keiji, *n.* 刑事 police detective.

keika, *n.* 経過 development; progress.

keikai suru, *vb.* 警戒する be cautious; watch out.

keikaku, *n.* 計画 project; plan; **keikaku o tateru** make a plan.

keikan, *n.* 警官 police officer.

keiken suru, *vb.* 経験する experience.

keiki, *n.* 景気 economic situation; business conditions.

keiko, *n.* 稽古 rehearsal; practice; training.

keikōtō, *n.* 蛍光灯 fluorescent light.

keimusho, *n.* 刑務所 prison.

keireki, *n.* 経歴 career history.

keiren, *n.* けいれん spasm; cramp.

keisan suru, *vb.* 計算する calculate; count.

keisatsu, *n.* 警察 the police.

keisatsusho, *n.* 警察署 police station.

keishiki, *n.* 形式 form; formality.

keitai, *n.* 形態 1. form; shape. 2. system.

keitai suru, *vb.* 携帯する carry.

keitai-yō (no), *adj.* 携帯用 (の) portable.

keito, *n.* 毛糸 woolen yarn.

keitō, *n.* 系統 system.

keiyaku, *n.* 契約 contract.

keiyakusho, *n.* 契約書 (written) contract.

keiyōshi, *n.* 形容詞 adjective.

keiyu (de), *adv.* 経由 (で) via; by way of.

keizai, *n.* 経済 economy.

keizaigaku, *n.* 経済学 economics.

keizai-teki (na), *adj.* 経済的 (な) economical.

keizoku suru, *vb.* 継続する continue.

keizu, *n.* 系図 lineage; genealogy.

kekka, *n.* 結果 result; consequence.

kekkaku, *n.* 結核 tuberculosis.

kekkan, *n.* 血管 blood vessel.

kekkō (na) 結構 (な) 1. *adj.* good. 2. *adj.* adequate; acceptable. 3. *adv.* rather; adequately.

kekkō desu 結構です No, thank you.

kekkonshiki, *n.* 結婚式 wedding.

kekkon suru, *vb.* 結婚する get married.

kekkyoku, *adv.* 結局 after all; eventually.

kemui, kemutai, *adj.* 煙い、煙たい 1. smoky. 2. ill at ease.

kemuri, *n.* 煙 smoke.

ken, *n.* 剣 sword.

ken, *n.* 券 ticket.

ken, *n.* 県 prefecture.

kenasu, *vb.* けなす slander; speak ill of; humiliate.

kenbikyō, *n.* 顕微鏡 microscope.

kenbutsu, *n.* 見物 sightseeing; watching (sporting event, etc.).

kenchikuka, *n.* 建築家 architect.

kenchō, *n.* 県庁 prefectural office.

kendō, *n.* 剣道 Japanese fencing with bamboo swords.

kengaku suru, *vb.* 見学する visit to observe.

ken'i, *n.* 権威 authority.

kenjū, *n.* 拳銃 handgun.

kenka, *n.* 喧嘩 fight; quarrel.

kenka suru, *vb.* 喧嘩する fight; quarrel.

kenketsu, *n.* 献血 blood donation.

kenkin, *n.* 献金 contribution (money); donation.

kenkō, *n.* 健康 health.

kenkyo, *n.* 謙虚 modesty.

kenkyū, *n.* 研究 study; research.

kenpō, *n.* 憲法 constitution (government).

kenri, *n.* 権利 right.

kensa, *n.* 検査 investigation; examination.

kensetsu, *n.* 建設 construction.

kenshū, *n.* 研修 training.

kenson, *n.* 謙遜 modesty.

kentō, *n.* 見当 assumption; speculation.

kentō suru, *vb.* 検討する 1. scrutinize. 2. consider.

keredo(mo) けれど(も) 1. *conj.* although; but. 2. *adv.* nevertheless.

keru, *vb.* 蹴る kick.

kesa, *n.*, *adv.* 今朝 this morning.

keshigomu, *n.* 消しゴム eraser.

keshi'in, *n.* 消し印 postmark.

keshikaran, *adj.* 怪しからん 1. ill-mannered; rude. 2. disgraceful.

keshiki, *n.* 景色 scenery; view.

keshō, *n.* 化粧 makeup.

keshōshitsu, *n.* 化粧室 dressing room; bathroom.

kessaku, *n.* 傑作 masterpiece.

kessei suru, *vb.* 結成する organize.

kesseki suru, *vb.* 欠席する be absent.

kessen, kesshō, *n.* 決戦、決勝 deciding match.

kesshin, *n.* 決心 decision; determination.

kesshite, *adv.* 決して never.

kesshō, *n.* 結晶 crystal.

kesu, *vb.* 消す 1. wipe out. 2. turn off. 3. extinguish.

ketsuatsu, *n.* 血圧 blood pressure.

ketsueki, *n.* 血液 blood.

ketsuron, *n.* 結論 conclusion.

kettei, *n.* 決定 decision; conclusion.

kettei suru, *vb.* 決定する decide; conclude.

ketten, *n.* 欠点 fault; blemish; shortcoming.

kewashii, *adj.* 険しい 1. steep. 2. stern.

kezuru, *vb.* 削る 1. shave. 2. sharpen. 3. cut down.

ki, *n.* 木 tree.

ki, *n.* 気 1. spirit; soul. 2. feeling. 3. intention; will.

kiatsu, *n.* 気圧 atmospheric pressure.

kiba, *n.* 牙 fang; tusk.

kiban, *n.* 基盤 foundation.

kibarashi, *n.* 気晴らし diversion; pastime.

kibi-kibi shita, *adj.* きびきび した energetic; witty.

kibin (na), *adj.* 機敏 (な) nimble; quick.

kibishii, *adj.* 厳しい stern; rigid.

kibo, *n.* 規模 scale.

kibō, *n.* 希望 hope; wish.

kibō suru, *vb.* 希望する hope; wish.

kibun, *n.* 気分 feeling; mood.

kichi, *n.* 基地 base; **gunji kichi** military base.

kichi, *n.* 吉 good fortune.

kichigai, *n., adj.* 気違い lunatic; insane.

kichin to, *adv.* きちんと properly; tidily.

kichō (na), *adj.* 貴重 (な) precious.

kidate, *n.* 気立て disposition; personality.

kidoru, *vb.* 気取る put on airs.

kieru, *vb.* 消える disappear; extinguish.

kifu, *n.* 寄付 contribution; donation.

ki ga au, *vb.* 気が合う feel comfortable or compatible with.

ki ga chiisai, *adj.* 気が小さ い timid.

ki ga chiru, *vb.* 気が散る be distracted.

kigaeru, *vb.* 着替える change clothes.

ki ga ii, *adj.* 気が良い good-natured.

kigakari, *n.* 気掛かり apprehension; concern.

ki ga kawaru, *vb.* 気が変わ る change one's mind.

ki ga ki de nai, *adj.* 気が気 でない anxious; uneasy.

ki ga kiku, *vb.* 気が利く be

sensitive; be considerate.

ki ga kuru'u, *vb.* 気が狂う go mad.

ki ga mijikai, *adj.* 気が短い short-tempered.

ki ga muku, *vb.* 気が向く feel like doing something.

ki ga omoi, *adj.* 気が重い depressed; discouraged.

ki ga suru, *vb.* 気がする imagine; feel; sense.

ki ga susumanai, *vb.* 気が すまない be reluctant.

ki ga tsuku, *vb.* 気が付く 1. become aware of; notice. 2. come to; regain consciousness.

ki ga tsuyoi, *adj.* 気が強い strong-willed.

ki ga yowai, *adj.* 気が弱い cowardly; timid.

kigen, *n.* 期限 deadline; term.

kigen, *n.* 起源 origin.

kigen, *n.* 機嫌 mood; feeling; humor; **ii kigen** cheerfulness; good-humor.

kigen, *n.* 紀元 era; **seireki kigen 1948** 1948 A.D.

kigenzen, *n.* 紀元前 (year) B.C.

kigō, *n.* 記号 sign; symbol.

kigyō, *n.* 企業 enterprise; company.

kihon, *n.* 基本 basics.

kihon-teki (na), *adj.* 基本的 (な) basic.

kiiroi, *adj.* 黄色い yellow.

kiji, *n.* 生地 fabric; textile; cloth.

kiji, *n.* 記事 newspaper article.

kijun, *n.* 基準 criterion; standard.

kikai, *n.* 機会 opportunity.

kikai, *n.* 機械 machine.

kikaku, *n.* 企画 project; plan.

kikaku, *n.* 規格 standard.

kikan, *n.* 器官 organ (body).

kikan, *n.* 機関 1. engine. 2. system. 3. agency.

kikan, *n.* 期間 duration; period.

kikazaru, *vb.* 着飾る dress up.

kiken na, *adj.* 危険な dangerous; risky.

kiki, *n.* 危機 crisis.

kikin, *n.* 飢饉 famine.

kikitori, *n.* 聞き取り dictation; listening.

kikitoru, *vb.* 聞き取る hear; understand.

kikō, *n.* 気候 weather; climate.

kikoeru, *vb.* 聞こえる 1. be audible. 2. sound; **hontō ni kikoeru** sound true.

kikoku suru, *vb.* 帰国する return to one's own country.

kiku, *n.* 菊 chrysanthemum.

kiku, *vb.* 聞く 1. hear; listen. 2. inquire; ask.

kiku, *vb.* 効く be effective.

kikubari, *n.* 気配り consideration.

kikyō, *n.* 帰郷 homecoming.

kimae, *n.* 気前 generosity; **kimae ga ii** generous.

kimagure (na), *adj.* 気紛れ (な) whimsical; capricious.

kimama (na), *adj.* 気まま (な) carefree.

kimari, *n.* 決まり rule.

kimaru, *vb.* 決まる be decided.

kimatsushiken, *n.* 期末試験 final examination.

kimeru, *vb.* 決める decide.

kimi, *pron.* 君 you (informal).

kimi no, *adj.* 君の your (informal).

kimochi, *n.* 気持ち feeling.

kimochi ga ii, 気持ち良い pleasant; comfortable.

kimono, *n.* 着物 kimono.

kimyō (na), *adj.* 奇妙 (な) strange.

kin, *n.* 金 gold.

kin, *n.* 菌 germ; fungus.

kinaga ni, *adv.* 気長に patiently.

kinchō, *n.* 緊張 nervousness; tension.

kindai, *n.* 近代 modern era.

kindai-teki (na), *adj.* 近代的 (な) modern.

kinen, *n.* 記念 memento; memorial; commemoration.

kin'en 禁煙 No Smoking.

kingaku, *n.* 金額 sum of money.

kingan, *n.* 近眼 nearsightedness.

kingyo, *n.* 金魚 goldfish.

ki ni iranai/kuwanai, 気に入らない／〜食わない dislike.

ki ni iru, *vb.* 気に入る like; favor.

ki ni naru/suru, *vb.* 気になる／〜する worry about; be concerned about.

kinjiru, *vb.* 禁じる prohibit.

kinjo, *n.* 近所 neighborhood.

kinko, *n.* 金庫 safe.

kinkyū, *n.* 緊急 emergency.

kin'niku, *n.* 筋肉 muscle.

kinō, *n.* 機能 function.

kinō, *n., adv.* 昨日 yesterday.

ki no doku (na), *adj.* 気の毒 (な) pitiful.

ki no hayai, *adj.* 気の早い imprudent; hasty.

kinoko, *n.* きのこ mushroom.

ki no nagai, *adj.* 気の長い patient.

kinpatsu, *n.* 金髪 blond hair.

kinsei, *n.* 金星 Venus (planet).

kinshi, *n.* 禁止 ban; prohibition.

kinshi, *n.* 近視 shortsightedness; nearsightedness.

kinu, *n.* 絹 silk.

kin'yōbi, *n.* 金曜日 Friday.

kinyū suru, *vb.* 記入する write in; enter.

kinzoku, *n.* 金属 metal.

kioku, *n.* 記憶 memory.

ki o kubaru, *vb.* 気を配る pay attention.

kioku suru, *vb.* 記憶する remember.

kion, *n.* 気温 (air) temperature.

ki o tsukeru, *vb.* 気をつける be careful.

ki o tsukete, *interj.* 気をつけて Take care! Watch out!

ki o ushinau, *vb.* 気を失う faint; lose consciousness.

kippari (to), *adv.* きっぱり (と) 1. once and for all. 2. point-blank.

kippu, *n.* 切符 ticket.

kirai (na) 嫌い (な) 1. *adj.* distasteful. 2. *vb.* dislike.

kira-kira suru, *vb.* きらきらする glitter; twinkle.

kiraku (na), *adj.* 気楽 (な) easygoing; carefree.

kirasu, *vb.* 切らす run out of; exhaust (supply).

kirau, *vb.* 嫌う dislike.

kirei (na), *adj.* きれい (な) 1. beautiful; pretty. 2. clean. 3. fair.

kireru, *vb.* 切れる 1. cut (well). 2. be disconnected. 3. run out of. 4. expire.

kiri, *n.* 霧 fog; mist.

kirikaeru, *vb.* 切り替える change; switch.

kirin, *n.* きりん giraffe.

kirisuto, *n.* キリスト (Pg. *Cristo*) Jesus Christ.

kirisutokyō, *n.* キリスト教 Christianity.

kiritaosu, *vb.* 切り倒す cut down (a tree).

kiritoru, *vb.* 切り取る cut off or out.

kiritsu suru, *vb.* 起立する stand up.

kiro, *n.* キロ (F. *kilo*) kilogram.

kiroku, *n.* 記録 document; record.

kiru, *vb.* 切る 1. cut. 2. turn off; hang up; stop.

kiru, *vb.* 着る put on; wear (clothes).

kiryoku, *n.* 気力 willpower; mental energy.

kisei, *n.* 規制 regulation; restriction.

kiseki, *n.* 奇蹟 miracle.

kiseru, *vb.* 着せる help someone dress.

kisetsu, *n.* 季節 season.

kisha, *n.* 記者 reporter.

kisha, *n.* 汽車 train with a steam locomotive.

kisha de, *adv.* 汽車で by train.

kisha kaiken, *n.* 記者会見 press conference.

kishi, *n.* 岸 shore.

kishō, *n.* 気象 weather.

kiso, *n.* 基礎 foundation; base; basics.

kisoku, *n.* 規則 rule; regulation.

kissaten, *n.* 喫茶店 coffee shop.

kisū, *n.* 奇数 odd number.

kita, *n.* 北 north.

kitachōsen, *n.* 北朝鮮 North Korea.

kitaeru, *vb.* 鍛える train; strengthen (oneself).

kitai suru, *vb.* 期待する expect.

kitanai, *adj.* 汚い 1. dirty. 2. unjust; mean.

kitchiri (to), *adv.* きっちり (と) 1. exactly. 2. on time. 3. tightly.

kitoku, *n.* 危篤 critical condition (health).

kitsuenseki, *n.* 喫煙席 smoking seat.

kitsui, *adj.* きつい 1. laborious; difficult. 2. tight-fitting. 3. stern; harsh.

kitsune, *n.* 狐 fox.

kitte, *n.* 切手 postage stamp.

kitto, *adv.* きっと for sure; without fail.

kiwamete, *adv.* 極めて extremely; very.

kiyō (na), *adj.* 器用 (な) dexterous; clever.

kiyoi, *adj.* 清い clear; pure.

kizamu, *vb.* 刻む cut; carve; mince; dice.

kizetsu suru, *vb.* 気絶する faint.

kizoku, *n.* 貴族 aristocracy; nobility.

kizu, *n.* 傷 1. scar; wound; injury. 2. defect.

kizuguchi, *n.* 傷口 wound.

kizukau, *vb.* 気遣う care for; worry; pay attention.

kizuku, *vb.* 気付く 1. find out; become aware of. 2. regain consciousness.

kizuku, *vb.* 築く establish; build.

kizuna, *n.* 絆 bond; tie.

kizutsukeru, *vb.* 傷つける hurt; injure; damage.

kizutsuku, *vb.* 傷つく be hurt; be injured; be damaged.

-kkai see **-kai.**

ko, *n.* 子 baby (human, animal); child.

-ko 個 (counter) **tamago goko** five eggs.

-ko 子 (suffix for woman's given name) **Michiko** Michiko.

kō, *adv.* こう this way; like this; so much like this.

-kō 港 port; **yokohamakō** Port of Yokohama.

kōban, *n.* 交番 police box.

kobosu, *vb.* こぼす spill; drop.

kobu, *n.* こぶ bump; hump; lump.

kobushi, *n.* 拳 fist.

kōbutsu, *n.* 好物 favorite food.

kōcha, *n.* 紅茶 black tea; **kōcha o ireru** prepare black tea.

kochira, *pron.* こちら this person; this place; this way.

kōchō, *n.* 校長 school principal.

kōchō (na, no), *adj.* 好調 (な、の) in good condition or form.

kōdai (na), *adj.* 広大 (な) vast.

kodai no, *adj.* 古代の ancient.

kodawaru, *vb.* 拘わる be fixated on something; be particular about.

kōdo, *n.* 高度 altitude.

kōdo (na, no), *adj.* 高度 (な、の) high-level; advanced.

kōdō, *n.* 行動 behavior; action.

kodoku, *n.* 孤独 solitude; isolation.

kōdoku suru, *vb.* 購読する subscribe.

kodomo, *n.* 子供 child(ren).

kodomorashii, *adj.* 子供らしい childlike.

koe, *n.* 声 1. voice; **ōkii (chiisai) koe** loud (soft) voice. 2. sound of (animal); **semi no koe** chirping of cicada. 3. opinion.

kōen, *n.* 公園 park.

kōen, *n.* 公演 performance.

kōen, *n.* 講演 speech; lecture.

kōenkai, *n.* 講演会 lecture.

koeru, vb. 越える 1. exceed; surpass. 2. step over; pass; cross.

koeru, vb. 肥える put on weight.

koeta, adj. 肥えた 1. overweight. 2. fertile.

kofū (na), adj. 古風 (な) antiquated; old-fashioned.

kōfuku (na, no), adj. 幸福 (な、の) happy.

kōfun suru, vb. 興奮する get excited.

kōgai, n. 郊外 suburb.

kōgai, n. 公害 environmental pollution.

kōgan, n. 睾丸 testicles.

kogara (na), adj. 小柄 (な) short and slim (person).

kogasu, vb. 焦がす scorch; burn.

kogata (no), adj. 小型 (の) small.

kōgeki suru, vb. 攻撃する attack; criticize.

kogeru, vb. 焦げる be scorched; be burned.

kōgi, n. 講義 lecture.

kōgi suru, vb. 抗議する protest.

kogitte, n. 小切手 check (bank).

kōgo, n. 口語 colloquial speech; spoken language.

kōgō, n. 皇后 Empress.

kogoeru, vb. 凍える be numb from the cold.

kōgo ni, adv. 交互に alternately; in turn.

kogoto, n. 小言 complaint; scolding.

kogu, vb. 漕ぐ row (boat).

kōgu, n. 工具 tool.

kōgyō, n. 工業 industry.

kōhai, n. 後輩 junior (in age, rank, or position).

kōhan, n. 後半 latter half.

kōhei (na), adj. 公平 (な) impartial; fair; unbiased.

kōhyō, n. 好評 favorable review; good reception.

koi, n. 恋 love; **koi o shiteiru** be in love.

koi, n. 鯉 carp.

koi, adj. 濃い 1. thick. 2. strong; **koi kōhī** strong coffee. 3. dark; deep.

kōi, n. 行為 deed; action.

kōi, n. 好意 goodwill; kindness.

koibito, n. 恋人 lover; boyfriend/girlfriend.

koi ni, adv. 故意に intentionally.

koinu, n. 小犬 puppy.

koishii, adj. 恋しい beloved; cherished.

kōishō, n. 後遺症 lingering effects (illness).

koji, n. 孤児 orphan.

koji, n. 小路 alley.

kōji, n. 工事 construction.

kōjichū 工事中 under construction; men at work.

kojiki, n. 乞食 beggar.

kojin, n. 個人 individual.

kojinmari shita, adj. 小じんまりした small and neat.

kojireru, vb. こじれる become complicated; worsen.

kōjitsu, n. 口実 pretext; excuse.

kojitsukeru, vb. こじつける distort.

kōjō, n. 向上 improvement.

kōjō, n. 工場 factory; plant.

kōjō suru, vb. 向上する improve.

kōka, n. 効果 effect; **kōka ga aru (nai)** effective (ineffective).

kōka (na), adj. 高価 (な) expensive.

kōkai suru, vb. 後悔する regret.

kōkan, n. 好感 good impression; **kōkan o idaku**

feel favorably disposed toward someone.

kōkan, n. 交換 exchange.

kōkan-ryūgakusei, n. 交換留学生 exchange student.

kōkanshu, n. 交換手 telephone operator.

kōkan suru, vb. 交換する exchange.

kōka-teki (na), adj. 効果的 (な) effective.

koke, n. 苔 moss.

kokei (no), adj. 固形 (の) solid.

kōken suru, vb. 貢献する contribute.

kōketsuatsu, n. 高血圧 high blood pressure.

kōkishin, n. 好奇心 curiosity.

kokka, n. 国歌 national anthem.

kokkai, n. 国会 Diet (legislative assembly).

kokkaigijidō, n. 国会議事堂 Diet Building.

kokki, n. 国旗 national flag.

kokkyō, n. 国境 border (between nations).

koko, n. ここ this place; here.

kōkō, n. 高校 senior high school.

kōkō, n. 孝行 filial piety.

kōkoku, n. 広告 advertisement.

kokonotsu, n. 九つ nine; nine years old.

kokoro, n. 心 spirit; heart; mind.

kokoroatari, n. 心当たり some information;

kokoroatari ga aru have something in mind; have some information.

kokorobosoi, adj. 心細い downhearted; forlorn.

kokorogurushii, adj. 心苦しい emotionally painful.

kokoromiru, vb. 試みる experiment; try.

kokoroyoku, adv. 快く gladly.

kokorozashi, n. 志 ambition; wish; goal.

kokorozukai, n. 心遣い thoughtfulness.

kokuban, n. 黒板 blackboard.

kokubetsushiki, n. 告別式 wake.

kōkūbin, n. 航空便 airmail; **kōkūbin de** via airmail.

kokudō, n. 国道 national highway.

kokugai de/ni, adv. 国外で／〜に abroad.

kōkūgaisha, n. 航空会社 airline.

kokugo, n. 国語 Japanese language; national language.

kokugojiten, n. 国語辞典 Japanese dictionary.

kokuhaku suru, vb. 告白する confess.

kokujin, n. 黒人 black person.

kokumin, n. 国民 people of a nation; citizen.

kokumin-kenkōhoken, n. 国民健康保険 national health insurance.

kokumin-sōseisan, n. 国民総生産 gross national product.

kokumotsu, n. 穀物 grain; cereal.

kokunai (no), adj. 国内 (の) domestic.

kokuren, n. 国連 United Nations.

kokurengun, n. 国連軍 United Nations forces.

kokuritsu (no), adj. 国立 (の) national.

kokusai, n. 国債 government bond.

kokusai-teki (na), *adj.* 国際的 (な) international.

kokusan (no), *adj.* 国産 (の) domestic; made in Japan.

kokusanhin, *n.* 国産品 domestic product.

kokuseki, *n.* 国籍 nationality.

kokuso suru, *vb.* 告訴する sue; accuse.

kokyō, *n.* 故郷 hometown.

kōkyo, *n.* 皇居 Imperial Palace.

kōkyōgakudan, *n.* 交響楽団 symphony orchestra.

kokyū, *n.* 呼吸 breathing; respiration; **jinkōkokyū** artificial respiration.

kōkyū (na), *adj.* 高級 (な) high-quality; high-class.

kokyū suru, *vb.* 呼吸する breathe; respire.

koma, *n.* こま top (toy).

komakai, *adj.* 細かい 1. small; minute. 2. meticulous; detailed.

komakaku, *adv.* 細かく minutely; in detail.

kōman (na), *adj.* 高慢 (な) arrogant; haughty.

komaru, *vb.* 困る 1. be in trouble; be annoyed; be at a loss. 2. be short of money.

kome, *n.* 米 uncooked white rice.

komekami, *n.* こめかみ temple (forehead).

komichi, *n.* 小道 alley; lane.

komoji, *n.* 小文字 small letter; lowercase letter.

kōmon, *n.* 肛門 anus.

komori, *n.* 子守 baby-sitter; baby-sitting.

komu, *vb.* 込む 1. be crowded. 2. be intricate.

komugi, *n.* 小麦 wheat.

komugiko, *n.* 小麦粉 wheat flour.

kōmuin, *n.* 公務員 civil servant.

kona, *n.* 粉 1. powder. 2. flour.

kōnai, *n.* 構内 grounds; premises.

kona-miruku, *n.* 粉ミルク powdered milk.

konasekken, *n.* 粉せっけん soap powder.

konban, *n.* 今晩 this evening; tonight.

konban wa, *interj.* 今晩は Good evening!

konbu, *n.* 昆布 kelp.

konchū, *n.* 昆虫 insect.

kondate, *n.* 献立 menu.

kondo, *n., adv.* 今度 1. this time. 2. next time.

kondo wa, *adv.* 今度は 1. this time. 2. next time.

kone, *n.* コネ (E.) connection.

koneko, *n.* 子猫 kitten.

kōnetsu, *n.* 高熱 high fever.

kōnetsuhi, *n.* 光熱費 utility charges.

kongaragaru, *vb.* こんがらがる become complicated; become entangled.

kongetsu, *n.* 今月 this month.

kongo, *adv.* 今後 hereafter.

kongō, *n.* 混合 mixture.

kōnin(sha), *n.* 後任(者) successor; replacement.

kōnin suru, *vb.* 公認する (publicly) authorize; approve.

kon(iro), *n.* 紺(色) navy blue.

konjō, *n.* 根性 1. will power. 2. character.

konkai, *n.* 今回 this time.

konki, *n.* 根気 patience; perseverance.

konkizuyoi, *adj.* 根気強い patient; tenacious.

konkyo, *n.* 根拠 source or basis (of a rumor, debate,

reasoning, etc.).

kon'na, *adj.* こんな such; this kind of.

kon'nan (na), *n.* 困難 (な) difficult.

kon'nichi, *n.* 今日 today.

kon'nichi no, *adj.* 今日の today's.

kon'nichi wa, *interj.* 今日は Good afternoon! Good morning!

kono, *adj.* この this.

kono aida, konaida, *adv.* この間, こないだ the other day; recently.

kono goro, *adv.* この頃 these days; currently.

kono-gurai/-kurai no, *adj.* この位の about this much.

kono hen ni, *adv.* この辺に in this neighborhood.

kono mae, *n.* この前 the last time; the other day.

kono mama ni suru, *vb.* このままにする leave (something) as it is.

konomashii, *adj.* 好ましい pleasant; desirable.

konomi, *n.* 木の実 nut; fruit.

konomi, *n.* 好み taste; preference.

konomu, *vb.* 好む like; favor.

kono tsugi (no) この次 (の) 1. *adj.* next. 2. *adv.* next time.

kono yō ni, *adv.* このように in this way; like this.

konpon, *n.* 根本 base; foundation.

konran, *n.* 混乱 confusion; chaos.

konsento, *n.* コンセント electrical outlet.

konshū, *n.* 今週 this week.

konwaku, *n.* 困惑 embarrassment; perplexity.

kon'ya, *n.* 今夜 this evening;

tonight.

kon'yaku, *n.* 婚約 engagement.

kon'yaku suru, *vb.* 婚約する become engaged; betrothed.

kōnyū, *n.* 購入 purchase.

kōon, *n.* 高温 high temperature.

koraeru, *vb.* 堪える endure.

korashimeru, *vb.* こらしめる punish.

kore, *pron.* これ this (object).

kore kara, *adv.* これから from now on.

kore made, *adv.* これまで until now.

korera, *pron.* これら these (objects).

kōri, *n.* 氷 ice.

koriru, *vb.* こりる learn a lesson; get sick of.

koritsu, *n.* 孤立 isolation.

kōritsu, *n.* 効率 efficiency.

koritsu suru, *vb.* 孤立する be isolated.

-koro 頃 1. (time) when; **chiisai-koro** when I was small. 2. variant of **-goro**; about (time).

korobu, *vb.* 転ぶ stumble; fall down.

korogaru, *vb.* 転がる roll over; lie around.

korogasu, *vb.* 転がす roll; knock down.

kōrogi, *n.* こうろぎ cricket (insect).

korokke, *n.* コロッケ (F.) potato croquette.

koromo, *n.* 衣 1. coating; breading (food). 2. clothes.

korosu, *vb.* 殺す murder; kill.

koru, *vb.* 凝る 1. be obsessed with; be absorbed in. 2. become stiff (neck).

kōru, *vb.* 凍る freeze.

kōryo, n. 考慮 consideration.

kōryo suru, vb. 考慮する think about; consider.

kōryoku, n. 効力 effect.

kōsai suru, vb. 交際する 1. associate with. 2. be friendly with; date.

kosame, n. 小雨 light rain.

kōsan suru, vb. 降参する surrender; give up.

kōsa suru, vb. 交差する intersect; cross.

kōsaten, n. 交差点 intersection; crossing.

kōsatsu suru, vb. 考察する consider; examine; ponder.

kosei, n. 個性 individuality; personality.

kōseibusshitsu, n. 抗生物質 antibiotic.

kosei-teki (na), adj. 個性的 (な) unique; individualistic.

koseki, n. 戸籍 family register.

koshi, n. 腰 waist; back; hip.

kōshi, n. 講師 lecturer; instructor.

koshikake, n. 腰掛け chair; seat; stool.

kōshiki ni, adv. 公式に officially.

kōshin, n. 行進 march.

kōshin suru, vb. 更新する renew.

koshi o kakeru, vb. 腰を掛ける sit down; take a seat.

koshitsu, n. 個室 private room (hospital); single room (hotel).

kōshitsu, n. 皇室 imperial family.

koshō, n. 胡椒 pepper (condiment).

koshō, n. 故障 breakdown (mechanical); malfunction.

kōshō, n. 交渉 1. negotiation; bargaining. 2. contact.

kōshoku (na), adj. 好色 (な) amorous; erotic; lecherous.

koshō suru, vb. 故障する break down (mechanical).

kōshū, n. 公衆 general public; the masses.

kōshūbenjo, n. 公衆便所 public toilet.

kosodate, n. 子育て child raising.

kōsō-kenchiku/-biru, n. 高層建築／〜ビル skyscraper.

koso-koso suru, vb. こそこそする behave sneakily.

kōsoku, n. 校則 school regulations.

kōsoku, n. 高速 high speed.

kōsokudōro, n. 高速道路 highway; freeway.

kossetsu suru, vb. 骨折する break a bone.

kossori (to), adv. こっそり (と) secretly; sneakily.

kosu, vb. 越す 1. exceed. 2. pass; cross. 3. move (residence).

kosu, vb. 漉す strain; filter.

kōsui, n. 香水 perfume.

kosuru, vb. 擦る rub; scrub.

kotae, n. 答え answer; solution.

kotaeru, vb. 答える answer; solution.

kotaeru, vb. 応える 1. respond. 2. affect.

kōtai, n. 交代 shift; alternation.

kōtai de, adv. 交代で in shifts; in turn.

kōtaigō, n. 皇太后 Empress Dowager.

kōtaishi, n. 皇太子 Crown Prince.

kōtai suru, vb. 交代する take one's shift or turn.

kotatsu, n. こたつ Japanese room heater covered with a quilt.

kōtei, n. 行程 process.

kōtei, n. 校庭 schoolyard.

kotei suru, vb. 固定する rivet; fix; stabilize.

koten, n. 個展 individual exhibition.

kōten suru, vb. 好転する improve.

kōtetsu, n. 鋼鉄 steel.

koto, n. 事 1. thing. 2. matter; affair. 3. event; occurrence.

koto, n. 古都 former capital (esp. Kyoto).

koto, n. 琴 Japanese thirteen-stringed musical instrument.

kotoba, n. 言葉 language; word.

-koto ga aru ことがある have done; **yonda-koto ga aru** have read.

kōtōgakkō, n. 高等学校 senior high school.

kotogotoku, adv. ことごとく without exception; entirely.

kotonaru, vb.異なる differ.

kotori, n. 小鳥 small bird.

kotoshi, n. 今年 this year.

kotowaru, vb. 断る decline; refuse.

kotowaza, n. ことわざ proverb.

kotsu, n. こつ knack; **kotsu o oboeru** get a feel for.

kōtsū, n. 交通 traffic; transportation.

kōtsūjiko, n. 交通事故 traffic accident.

kottō(hin), n. 骨董(品) antique; curio.

kou, vb. 乞う beg; ask.

kouma, n. 小馬 pony; colt.

kōun, n. 幸運 good luck.

kouri, n. 小売り retail.

koushi, n. 子牛 calf; **koushi no niku** veal.

kowagaru, vb. 怖がる feel scared (afraid, nervous).

kowai, adj. 怖い scared;

afraid; **hito ga kowai** afraid of people.

kowasu, vb. 壊す break; damage; destroy.

koya, n. 小屋 cabin; hut; shed.

koyomi, n. 暦 calendar.

koyubi, n. 小指 little finger; little toe.

koyūmeishi, n. 固有名詞 proper noun (grammar).

koyū no, adj. 固有の unique; distinctive.

kōza, n. 講座 academic course; lecture.

kōza, n. 口座 bank account; **kōza o hiraku** open a bank account.

kozara, n. 小皿 saucer; small plate.

kōzen to, adv. 公然と openly; publicly.

kozō, n. 小僧 1. boy. 2. novice priest.

kōzō, n. 構造 structure.

kōzui, n. 洪水 inundation; flood.

kozukai, n. 小遣 pocket money; allowance.

kozutsumi, n. 小包 parcel (sent by mail).

ku, n. 九 nine.

-ku 区 ward; **shinjukuku** Shinjuku Ward.

kubaru, vb. 配る 1. distribute; hand out. 2. deliver.

kubetsu, n. 区別 distinction; differentiation.

kubetsu suru, vb. 区別する distinguish; differentiate.

kubi, n. 首 neck; head.

kubikazari, n. 首飾り necklace.

kubi o kiru, vb. 首を切る 1. dismiss from a job. 2. behead; decapitate.

kubomi, n. 凹み hollow; crevice; depression.

kubomu, vb. 凹む sink.

kubun, n. 区分 classification; division.

kuchi, n. 口 1. mouth. 2. taste (sense of). 3. position (employment).

kuchibashi, n. くちばし beak; bill.

kuchibeni, n. 口紅 lipstick.

kuchibiru, n. 唇 lip(s).

kuchibue, n. 口笛 whistling.

kuchidome o suru, vb. 口止めをする bind someone to secrecy.

kuchigenka, n. 口喧嘩 argument.

kuchihige, n. 口髭 mustache.

kuchikomi de, adv. 口コミで by word of mouth.

kuchinashi, n. くちなし gardenia.

kuchi o dasu, vb. 口を出す interrupt; mind someone else's business.

kuchi o kiku, vb. 口をきく speak; talk.

kuchiru, vb. 朽ちる rot; decay.

kuchisaki dake, n. 口先だけ mere words; lip service.

kuchizuke, n. 口づけ kiss.

kūchū ni, adv. 空中に in midair.

kuda, n. 管 tube; pipe.

kudaku, vb. 砕く break; smash.

kudamono, n. 果物 fruit.

kudaranai, adj. 下らない 1. ridiculous; stupid. 2. worthless; petty.

kudari, n. 下り 1. descent; going down. 2. train from Tokyo.

kudarizaka, n. 下り坂 downward slope.

kudaru, vb. 下る 1. descend; go down.

kudasai, adv. 下さい please;

Michi o oshiete kudasai. Please show me the way.

Ocha kudasai. Tea, please.

Sushi kudasai. Sushi, please.

kudoi, adj. くどい repetitious; tedious; persistent.

kufū, n. 工夫 ingenuity.

kugatsu, n. 九月 September.

kugi, n. 釘 nail; peg.

kuginuki, n. 釘抜き nail puller.

kugiri, n. 区切り ending; stop; pause; **kugiri o tsukeru** leave off (work).

kugiru, vb. 区切る divide; mark off.

kuguru, vb. 潜る pass under or through.

kūhaku, n. 空白 blank.

kui, n. 悔い regret; **kui ga nokoru** have regrets.

kuichigai, n. 食い違い disparity; conflict (of opinion).

kuichigau, vb. 食い違う clash.

kuimono, n. 食い物 eats; grub.

kuiru, vb. 悔いる regret; repent.

kuisugi, n. 食い過ぎ overeating.

kuitomeru, vb. 食い止める hold back; stop.

kujaku, n. 孔雀 peacock; peahen.

kuji, n. くじ lottery; raffle.

kujiku, vb. 挫く 1. sprain (ankle, etc.). 2. discourage.

kujira, n. 鯨 whale.

kujō o iu, vb. 苦情を言う complain.

kūkan, n. 空間 space.

kuki, n. 茎 stem; stalk.

kūki, n. 空気 air; atmosphere.

kukkiri (to), adv. くっきり

(と) clearly.

kūkō, n. 空港 airport.

kuku, n. 九九 multiplication table.

kukuru, vb. 括る bind; bundle.

kuma, n. 熊 bear.

kumi, n. 組 1. group; team. 2. class (school).

kumiai, n. 組合 union; association.

kumiawaseru, vb. 組み合わせる combine; pair.

kumitateru, vb. 組み立てる build; assemble.

kumo, n. 蜘蛛 spider.

kumo, n. 雲 cloud.

kumo no su, n. 蜘蛛の巣 cobweb.

kumori, n. 曇り cloudy weather.

kumoru, vb. 曇る 1. become cloudy. 2. be in a gloomy mood.

kumu, vb. 汲む 1. get water (by scooping, pumping, etc.). 2. comprehend; discern.

kumu, vb. 組む 1. assemble. 2. unite; pair. 3. fold (arms); cross (legs). 4. make (a plan).

-kun 君 Mr.; Ms. (used in addressing younger people or colleagues in place of -**san** or -**sama**).

kuneru, vb. くねる twist; wind around.

kuni, n. 国 1. nation; country. 2. hometown.

kunren suru, vb. 訓練する train; drill.

kunshō, n. 勲章 medal; decoration.

kun(yomi), n. 訓(読み) Japanese reading of a Chinese character.

kura, n. 蔵, 倉 storehouse.

kuraberu, vb. 比べる compare.

kurage, n. くらげ jellyfish.

-kurai, -gurai くらい, ぐらい 1. about; approximately; almost. 2. something like. 3. as ... as.

kura-kura suru, vb. くらくらする feel giddy or dizzy.

kurasu, vb. 暮らす live; make a living.

kurayami, n. 暗闇 darkness.

kure, n. 暮れ 1. year-end. 2. nightfall.

kuregure mo, adj. くれぐれも sincere; **Kuregure mo minasama ni yoroshiku.** Be sure to give (my) sincere regards to everyone.

kureru, vb. 暮れる get dark; end; be absorbed in.

kuri, n. 栗 chestnut.

kurikaesu, vb. 繰り返す repeat.

kurīningu, n. クリーニング (E.) dry cleaning; **kurīningu ni dasu** send (clothes) to the dry cleaner.

kurinuku, vb. くり抜く hollow.

kuro, n. 黒 black.

kurō, n. 苦労 hardship; suffering; trouble.

kuroi, adj. 黒い black.

kurō suru, vb. 苦労する suffer hardship.

kuru, vb. 来る 1. come; arrive. 2. derive (from).

kuru-kuru, adv. くるくる round and round.

kuruma, n. 車 1. automobile; car; taxi. 2. wheel.

kuruma isu, n. 車椅子 wheelchair.

kurumi, n. 胡桃 walnut.

kurumu, vb. くるむ wrap.

kurushii, adj. 苦しい 1.

painful. 2. difficult; laborious.

kurushimeru, *vb.* 苦しめる harass; torture.

kurushimu, *vb.* 苦しむ feel pain; suffer; struggle.

kuru'u, *vb.* 狂う 1. go mad. 2. be obsessed with. 3. go wrong.

kusa, *n.* 草 grass.

kusai, *adj.* 臭い 1. smelly; stinking. 2. suspicious.

kusamura, *n.* 草むら grassy area.

kusari, *n.* 鎖 chain.

kusaru, *vb.* 腐る rot; spoil; be corrupted.

kuse, *n.* 癖 1. habit; **kuse ga tsuku** acquire a habit. 2. idiosyncratic behavior.

kūseki, *n.* 空席 1. vacant seat. 2. vacant position.

kusha-kusha (na, no), *adj.* くしゃくしゃ（な、の） wrinkled; crumpled.

kushami, *n.* くしゃみ sneeze.

kushami o suru, *vb.* くしゃみをする sneeze.

kushi, *n.* 櫛 comb.

kushi, *n.* 串 skewer.

kushiyaki, *n.* 串焼き skewered and grilled food.

kuso くそ 1. *n.* feces. 2. *interj.* Damn it! Shit!

kūsō, *n.* 空想 fantasy; imagination.

kūsō suru, *vb.* 空想する fantasize; imagine.

kusuguru, *vb.* くすぐる tickle.

kusu-kusu warau, *vb.* くすくす笑う giggle.

kusuri, *n.* 薬 1. medicine; pill; drug. 2. ointment. 3. good lesson; **Kusuri ni natta.** (I) learned a good lesson.

kusuri yubi, *n.* 薬指 third

finger; ring finger.

kutabaru, *vb.* くたばる die (pejorative usage).

kutabireru, *vb.* くたびれる 1. be fatigued. 2. become worn.

kutsu, *n.* 靴 shoe(s); **kutsu o haku** wear shoes; **kutsu o nugu** remove one's shoes.

kutsugaesu, *vb.* 覆す overturn; overthrow.

kutsu himo, *n.* 靴紐 shoelace.

kutsurogu, *vb.* 寛ぐ relax; make oneself at home.

kutsushita, *n.* 靴下 sock(s); **kutsushita nisoku** two pairs of socks.

kuttsuku, *vb.* くっ付く adhere to.

ku'u, *vb.* 食う 1. eat; bite; consume (vulgar). 2. support oneself; live. 3. cheat.

kuwaeru, *vb.* 加える add; include; **X o Y ni kuwaeru** add X to Y.

kuwaete, *adv.* 加えて on top of; in addition to.

kuwashii, *adj.* 詳しい 1. detailed; fully explained. 2. versed; knowledgeable; **kabuki ni kuwashii** versed in Kabuki.

(o)kuyami, *n.* （お）悔やみ condolence(s).

kuyashii, *adj.* 悔やしい mortifying.

kuyo-kuyo suru, *vb.* くよくよする brood.

kuzukago, *n.* 屑籠 wastebasket.

kuzusu, *vb.* 崩す 1. dismantle; pull down; destroy. 3. make change (money).

kyabetsu, *n.* キャベツ cabbage.

kyaku, *n.* 客 1. customer;

client; guest; visitor. 2. passenger.

kyakuhon, *n.* 脚本 screenplay; script.

kyakuma, *n.* 客間 parlor; drawing room.

kyakuseki, *n.* 客席 seat in the audience; passenger seat.

kyō, *n.* 今日 today.

kyōben, *n.* 教鞭 teaching; **kyōben o toru** to teach.

kyōbō (na), *adj.* 凶暴 (な) savage; ferocious.

kyōchō suru, *vb.* 強調する emphasize.

kyodai (na), *adj.* 巨大 (な) huge; colossal; enormous.

kyōdai, *n.* 兄弟 brother(s); sister(s).

kyōdo, *n.* 郷土 hometown; homeland.

kyōdō suru, *vb.* 協同する cooperate; work together.

kyōfu, *n.* 恐怖 fear; horror.

kyōgi, *n.* 競技 athletic competition.

kyōgijō, *n.* 競技場 athletic field; sports arena.

kyōgi suru, *vb.* 協議する discuss.

kyōhaku suru, *vb.* 脅迫する threaten; blackmail.

kyōhansha, *n.* 共犯者 accomplice.

kyohi suru, *vb.* 拒否する reject; refuse.

kyōiku, *n.* 教育 education.

kyōiku suru, *vb.* 教育する educate; teach.

kyōin, *n.* 教員 teacher.

kyojin, *n.* 巨人 giant.

kyōju, *n.* 教授 1. professor. 2. teaching.

kyoka, *n.* 許可 permission; approval; **kyoka o ataeru** give permission or approval.

kyōka, *n.* 教科 subject; course of study.

kyōkai, *n.* 教会 church.

kyōkai, *n.* 協会 association; organization.

kyōkai, *n.* 境界 boundary; border.

kyokashō, *n.* 許可証 license; permit.

kyōkasho, *n.* 教科書 textbook.

kyoka suru, *vb.* 許可する permit; approve; allow.

kyōkoku, *n.* 峡谷 canyon; ravine.

kyoku, *n.* 曲 musical composition; song.

kyoku, *n.* 局 office; **denwa kyoku** telephone exchange; **yūbin kyoku** post office.

kyokugen, *n.* 極限 limit.

kyokuryoku, *adv.* 極力 as much as possible; to the best of one's ability; **kyokuryoku sakeru** avoid as much as possible.

kyokusen, *n.* 曲線 curved line.

kyokutan (na), *adj.* 極端 (な) extreme.

kyokutan ni, *adv.* 極端に extremely.

kyokutō, *n.* 極東 Far East.

kyōkyū, *n.* 供給 supply.

kyōkyū suru, *vb.* 供給する supply; provide.

kyōmi, *n.* 興味 interest (in).

kyonen, *n.* 去年 last year.

kyōretsu (na), *adj.* 強烈 (な) intense; stunning; powerful.

kyori, *n.* 距離 distance.

kyoro-kyoro suru, *vb.* きょろきょろする look around anxiously.

kyōryoku suru, *vb.* 協力する cooperate; collaborate.

kyōryū, *n.* 恐竜 dinosaur.

kyōsanshugi, *n.* 共産主義 communism.

kyōsei suru, *vb.* 強制する compel; force.

kyōsei-teki (na), *adj.* 強制的 (な) compulsory.

kyōshi, *n.* 教師 teacher.

kyōshitsu, *n.* 教室 classroom.

kyōshuku suru, *vb.* 恐縮する 1. feel grateful. 2. feel embarrassed.

kyōsō, *n.* 競走 footrace.

kyōsō suru, *vb.* 競争する compete against; contest.

kyōtsū (no), *adj.* 共通 (の) common; mutual.

kyōwakoku, *n.* 共和国 republic.

kyōyō ga aru, *adj.* 教養がある cultured; learned.

kyōyū (no), *adj.* 共有 (の) jointly owned.

kyōzai, *n.* 教材 teaching materials.

kyū, *n.* 級 class; level; grade.

kyū (na), *adj.* 急 (な) 1. urgent. 2. sudden; unexpected. 3. steep; **kyū na sakamichi** steep slope. 4. rapid.

kyūgeki (na), *adj.* 急激 (な) 1. abrupt. 2. rapid.

kyūgyō suru, *vb.* 休業する close temporarily (business).

kyūjinkōkoku, *n.* 求人広告 help-wanted advertisement.

kyūjitsu, *n.* 休日 holiday.

kyūjo, *n.* 救助 rescue; relief.

kyūjū, *n.* 九十 ninety.

kyūka, *n.* 休暇 vacation

day(s); **kyūka o toru** take vacation or take day(s) off.

kyūkei suru, *vb.* 休憩する take a rest; take a break.

kyūkō, *n.* 急行 express train.

kyūkon, *n.* 球根 bulb (plant).

kyūkon suru, *vb.* 求婚する propose marriage.

kyūkutsu (na), *adj.* 窮屈 (な) 1. cramped; narrow; tight. 2. ill at ease.

kyūkyūbako, *n.* 救急箱 first-aid kit.

kyūkyūsha, *n.* 救急車 ambulance.

kyūri, *n.* きゅうり cucumber.

kyūryō, *n.* 給料 salary; pay; wages.

kyūsei, *n.* 旧姓 former name; maiden name.

kyūshiki (na, no), *adj.* 旧式 (な、の) old-fashioned; outdated.

kyūsho, *n.* 急所 1. key point; weak point; **kyūsho o tsuku** attack someone's weak point. 2. groin.

kyūshū suru, *vb.* 吸収する absorb; digest.

kyūyakuseisho, *n.* 旧約聖書 Old Testament.

kyūyō, *n.* 急用 urgent business.

kyūyō suru, *vb.* 休養する rest; recuperate.

kyūyu, *n.* 給油 refueling.

M

ma, *n.* 間 1. interval; pause; time. 2. space. 3. room.

mā, *interj.* まあ 1. Oh! Wow! 2. Well!

mabara (na), *adj.* 疎ら (な) sparse.

mabataki, *n.* まばたき blink.

maboroshi, *n.* 幻 illusion; chimera.

mabushii, *adj.* 眩しい dazzling; blinding.

mabuta, *n.* まぶた eyelid.

machi, *n.* 町 town.

machiaishitsu, *n.* 待合室 waiting room.

machiawaseru, *vb.* 待ち合わせる rendezvous.

machidōshii, *vb.* 待ち遠しい long for; be impatient for; look forward to; **ryokō ga machidōshii** look forward to a trip.

machigai, *n.* 間違い mistake.

machigau, *vb.* 間違う make a mistake.

machikaneru, *vb.* 待ち兼ねる wait eagerly for; look forward to.

mada, *adv.* 未だ 1. as yet; still. 2. not yet (with negative).

made, *art.* 迄 1. till; until; **ashita made** until tomorrow. 2. as far as; up to.

made ni, *art.* 迄に by (time); **ashita made ni** by tomorrow.

mado, *n.* 窓 window.

madoguchi, *n.* 窓口 ticket window.

mae 前 1. *n.* front; **ie no mae ni** in front of the house. 2. *prep., conj.* before; **goji mae ni** before five o'clock; **kare ga iku mae ni** before he leaves. 3. *adj.* ago; **mikka mae** three days ago.

mae (no), *adj.* 前 (の) 1. former; preceding. 2. facing.

-mae 前 order of (food); **sushi ichinin-mae** one order of sushi.

maebure, *n.* 前触れ advance notice; sign; harbinger.

maemotte, *adv.* 前以つて beforehand; in advance.

mae ni, *adv.* 前に formerly; before.

mafuyu, *n.* 真冬 midwinter.

magarikado, *n.* 曲がり角 street corner.

magaru, *vb.* 曲がる 1. turn; **kado o magaru** turn at the corner. 2. bend; warp.

mageru, *vb.* 曲げる 1. twist. 2. falsify.

magirawashii, *adj.* 紛らわしい confusing; misleading.

magireru, *vb.* 紛れる 1. be diverted. 2. be confused.

magiwa ni 間際に 1. *adv.* at the last moment. 2. *prep.* just before.

mago, *n.* 孫 grandchild.

magokoro, *n.* 真心 sincerity; heart and soul.

mago-mago suru, *vb.* まごまごする be bewildered; embarrassed.

magure(atari), *n.* まぐれ(当たり) good luck; fluke.

maguro, *n.* 鮪 tuna.

mahiru, *n.* 真昼 broad daylight; midday.

mahi suru, *vb.* 麻痺する be numbed; be paralyzed.

mahō, *n.* 魔法 magic; witchcraft.

mahōbin, *n.* 魔法びん thermos.

mahōtsukai, *n.* 魔法使い magician; wizard; **ozu no mahōtsukai** The Wizard of Oz.

mai, *n.* 舞 dance.

mai- 毎 each; every; **maiasa** every morning; **maiban** every evening (night).

-mai 枚 number suffix indicating counter for flat and thin items; **kami nimai** two pieces of paper.

maido 毎度 1. *n.* each time; every time. 2. *adv.* always.

maigo, *n.* 迷子 lost person.

maikai, *n.* 毎回 each time; every time.

mainen, *n., adv.* 毎年 every year.

mainichi, *n., adv.* 毎日 every day.

mairu, *vb.* 詣る make a pilgrimage; visit a sacred place.

mairu, *vb.* 参る 1. be defeated; surrender. 2. be fed up with.

maishū, *n., adv.* 毎週 every week.

maitoshi, *n., adv.* 毎年 every year.

maitsuki, *n., adv.* 毎月 every month.

majime (na), *adj.* 真面目 (な) 1. sincere; honest. 2. industrious. 3. serious.

majinai, *n.* 呪い incantation.

majiwari, *n.* 交わり friendship; association.

majiwaru, *vb.* 交わる 1. keep company with; mix with. 2. intersect.

majo, *n.* 魔女 witch.

makaseru, *vb.* 任せる entrust.

makasu, *vb.* 負かす defeat; beat.

makeru, *vb.* 負ける 1. be defeated; lose. 2. give a discount. 3. succumb to.

maki, *n.* 薪 firewood.

makiba, *n.* 牧場 meadow; pasture.

makikomu, *vb.* 巻き込む involve in; entangle in.

makimono, *n.* 巻き物 scroll painting.

makka (na), *adj.* 真赤 (な) 1. crimson. 2. downright.

makkura (na), *adj.* 真暗 (な) pitch dark.

makkuro (na), *adj.* 真黒 (な) jet-black.

makoto, *n.* 真 1. truth. 2. sincerity.

makoto ni, *adv.* 真に truly; really; very.

maku, *n.* 幕 1. theater

curtain. 2. act of a play.

maku, *vb.* 撒く sprinkle; scatter.

maku, *vb.* 巻く roll; wind.

maku, *vb.* 蒔く sow.

makura, *n.* 枕 pillow.

makuru, *vb.* まくる roll up.

mama, *adv.* まま as is; **sono mama ni suru** leave as is.

mā-mā (no), *adj.* まあまあ (の) so-so; passable.

mame, *n.* 豆 bean; pea.

mame, *n.* まめ blister.

mamonaku, *adv.* 間もなく before long; soon.

mamoru, *vb.* 守る 1. protect. 2. observe (rules); keep (promises).

man, *n.* 万 ten thousand; **niman** twenty thousand.

manabu, *vb.* 学ぶ learn; study.

manaita, *n.* まないた cutting board.

manbiki, *n.* 万引き shoplifting; shoplifter.

mane, *n.* 真似 imitation; mimicry.

maneku, *vb.* 招く invite.

maneru, *vb.* 真似る imitate; mimic.

manga, *n.* 漫画 cartoon; comic strip.

mangetsu, *n.* 満月 full moon.

ma ni au, *vb.* 間に合う 1. be in time for. 2. suffice.

man'ichi, *adv.* 万一 unlikely event.

man'in (no), *adj.* 満員 (の) filled to capacity.

man'naka, *n.* 真中 center; middle.

man'nenhitsu, *n.* 万年筆 fountain pen.

manshon, *n.* マンション (E. *mansion*) condominium; apartment; apartment building.

manten, n. 満点 perfect score.

manugareru, vb. 免れる be exempted from; avoid.

manuke, n. 間抜け fool.

manzoku suru, vb. 満足する be satisfied.

mare (na), adj. 稀 (な) unusual; rare.

mari, n. まり ball.

maru, n. 丸 circle.

maru de まるで 1. adv. absolutely. 2. conj. just like.

marui, adj. 丸い circular; globular; round.

maryoku, n. 魔力 magical power.

masaka, interj. まさか Impossible! That can't be!

masa ni 正に 1. adv. exactly; really. 2. prep. on the point of (doing).

masaru, vb. 勝る outclass; outdo.

masashiku, adv. 正しく undoubtedly.

masatsu, n. 摩擦 friction; rubbing.

mashi (na), adj. まし (な) better; preferable.

mashita ni, adv. 真下に directly underneath.

mashite, adv. まして let alone; not to mention.

masshiro (na), adj. 真白 (な) pure white.

massugu (na), adj. 真っ直ぐ (な) 1. straight. 2. honest.

masu, n. ます trout.

masu, vb. 増す increase.

masui, n. 麻酔 anesthesia.

masu-komi, n. マスコミ (E.) mass media.

masu-masu, adv. ますます increasingly.

mata, n. 股 thigh; groin.

mata また 1. adv. again; also. 2. conj. and; as well as.

matagaru, vb. またがる sit astride; extend (over).

matagu, vb. またぐ straddle.

mataseru, vb. 待たせる keep someone waiting.

matataku, vb. 瞬く blink; twinkle.

matataku ma ni, adv. 瞬く間に in an instant.

mata wa, conj. または or; either ... or.

matcha, n. 抹茶 powdered green tea.

mato, n. 的 1. target. 2. center (of attention).

matomeru, vb. まとめる 1. bundle together; compile. 2. finish; settle. 3. summarize.

matomete, adv. まとめて all together.

matomo (na), adj. まとも (な) 1. honest. 2. decent.

matsu, n. 松 pine tree.

matsu, vb. 待つ wait for; expect.

matsuge, n. まつげ eyelashes.

matsuri, n. 祭 festival.

matsuru, vb. 祭る deify; worship.

mattaku, adv. 全く indeed; really; utterly.

mau, vb. 舞う dance.

maue ni, adv., prep. 真上に directly above.

maushiro ni, adv., prep. 真後ろに directly behind.

mawari, n. 周り、回り circumference.

mawarimichi, n. 回り道 detour; roundabout way.

mawari ni, prep. まわりに around.

mawaru, vb. 回る 1. turn; reel; spin. 2. circulate.

mayaku, n. 麻薬 narcotic.

mayonaka, n. 真夜中 midnight.

mayou, vb. 迷う 1. lose

(direction); **michi ni mayou** lose one's way. 2. vacillate. 3. be captivated.

mayu, n. まゆ cocoon.

mayu(ge), n. 眉(毛) eyebrow.

mazeru, vb. 混ぜる mix.

mazo, n. マゾ (E.) masochism; masochist.

mazu, adv. 先ず 1. first of all. 2. possibly.

mazui, adj. まずい 1. bad tasting. 2. inadvisable.

mazushii, adj. 貧しい destitute; poor.

me, n. 芽 sprout.

me, n. 目 eye; discernment.

meate, n. 目当て prospect; aim.

mebae, n. 芽生え budding; awakening.

meboshi o tsukeru, vb. 目星をつける aim at.

mechakucha (na), adj. めちゃくちゃ (な) 1. chaotic. 2. irrational; nonsensical.

medama, n. 目玉 eyeball.

medatsu, vb. 目立つ stand out.

medetai, adj. めでたい 1. auspicious. 2. stupid.

megami, n. 女神 goddess.

megane, n. 眼鏡 eyeglasses.

me ga sameru, vb. 目が覚める wake up.

megumi, n. 恵み blessing; bounty.

megumu, vb. 恵む 1. give alms. 2. show mercy to.

meguriau, vb. 巡り会う encounter.

megusuri, n. 目薬 eye drops.

mei, n. 姪 niece.

meian, n. 名案 good idea; **meian ga aru** have a good idea.

meibo, n. 名簿 directory; list of names.

meibutsu, n. 名物 attraction.

meiga, n. 名画 masterpiece (painting, drawing, film).

meijin, n. 名人 expert; master.

meikaku (na), adj. 明確 (な) clear-cut; precise.

meimon (no), adj. 名門の renowned; prestigious.

meirei suru, vb. 命令する command; order.

meiru, vb. 滅入る feel depressed.

meisaku, n. 名作 masterpiece.

meisei, n. 名声 renown.

meishi, n. 名刺 calling card; business card.

meishi, n. 名詞 noun.

meishin, n. 迷信 superstition.

meisho, n. 名所 historic site; place of interest.

meishō, n. 名称 name; title.

meiwaku, n. 迷惑 annoyance; nuisance; trouble; **meiwaku o kakeru** inconvenience.

meiwaku (na), adj. 迷惑 (な) annoying; troublesome.

meiyo, n. 名誉 honor; glory.

mejirushi, n. 目印 landmark; sign.

mekakushi, n. 目隠し blindfold.

mekki, n. めっき gilding; plating.

mekkiri, adv. めっきり considerably.

mekura, n. 盲 1. blindness; blind person (not in polite use). 2. ignorance.

mekuru, vb. めくる turn over; turn (page).

memai, n. めまい dizziness; giddiness.

men, n. 面 1. mask; face; **men to mukatte** face to

face. 2. surface. 3. aspect. 4. page (newspaper).

men, *n.* 綿 cotton.

men, *n.* めん noodles.

mendō, *n.* 面倒 1. annoyance; difficulty. 2. care; **mendō o miru** take care of (someone).

mendōkusai, *adj.* 面倒臭い annoying; tiresome.

mendori, *n.* 雌鳥 hen.

menkai, *n.* 面会 interview; meeting.

menkyo, *n.* 免許 license.

me no mae de/ni, *adv.* 目の前で、〜に before one's very eyes.

menseki, *n.* 面積 area.

mentsu, *n.* メンツ face; honor; **mentsu o ushinau** lose face.

menzeihin, *n.* 免税品 duty-free item.

me o miharu, *vb.* 目を見張る stare.

me o tōsu, *vb.* 目を通す look over.

me o tsukeru, *vb.* 目を付ける notice; keep an eye on.

merikenko, *n.* メリケン粉 flour.

meshi, *n.* 飯 rice; food; meal (used by males).

meshiagaru, *vb.* 召し上がる eat; drink (polite).

mesu, *n.* 雌 female (animal).

metoru, *vb.* めとる marry (a woman).

metta ni, *adv.* 滅多に rarely; seldom.

meyasu, *n.* 目安 gauge; standard.

mezamashi(-dokei), *n.* 目覚まし(時計) alarm clock.

mezameru, *vb.* 目覚める wake up.

mezasu, *vb.* 目指す aim at.

mezurashii, *adj.* 珍しい rare; unusual.

mezurashiku, *adv.* 珍しく unusually; unexpectedly.

mezurashisō ni, *adv.* 珍しそうに curiously.

mi, *n.* 身 1. body. 2. person; **hitori mi** single person. 3. flesh; meat.

mi, *n.* 実 fruit; nut; **mi ga naru** bear fruit.

miageru, *vb.* 見上げる look upward.

miai, *n.* 見合い arranged marriage meeting.

miakiru, *vb.* 見飽きる tire of seeing.

mibōjin, *n.* 未亡人 widow.

mibunshōmeisho, *n.* 身分証明書 identification card.

miburi, *n.* 身振り gesture.

michi, *n.* 道 1. road; way. 2. means. 3. doctrine. 4. career.

michibiku, *vb.* 導く direct; guide; lead.

michiru, *vb.* 満ちる become full.

midara (na), *adj.* 淫ら (な) indecent.

midareru, *vb.* 乱れる 1. become chaotic; become disrupted. 2. be windblown (hair).

midasu, *vb.* 乱す disrupt; disturb.

midori, *n.* 緑 green.

mie o haru, *vb.* 見栄を張る be vain; pretend to be important.

mieru, *vb.* 見える 1. be able to see. 2. appear.

migaku, *vb.* 磨く 1. brush; shine; polish; **ha o migaku** brush one's teeth. 2. improve (a skill).

migaru (na), *adj.* 身軽 (な) 1. light; agile. 2. unburdened; without obligation.

migawari, *n.* 身代わり

substitute (person).

migi, n. 右 right-hand side or direction; **migi ni** on the right.

migigawa, n. 右側 right side.

migikiki (no), adj. 右利き (の) right-handed.

migomoru, vb. 身ごもる get pregnant.

migoto (na), adj. 見事 (な) wonderful; marvelous.

mihanasu, vb. 見放す forsake.

miharashi, vb. 見晴らし view; **miharashi ga ii** have a good view.

miharu, vb. 見張る stand guard; watch.

mihon, n. 見本 sample; example.

mijika (na, no), adj. 身近 (な、の) close at hand; closely related.

mijikai, adj. 短い short.

mijime (na), adj. 惨め (な) miserable.

mijuku (na), adj. 未熟 (な) immature; inexperienced.

mikake, n. 見掛け appearance; facade.

mikakeru, vb. 見掛ける catch sight of.

mikan, n. みかん mandarin orange.

mikata, n. 味方 supporter; ally; **mikata o suru** take someone's side.

mikata, n. 見方 viewpoint; **mikata o kaeru** change one's viewpoint.

mikazuki, n. 三日月 crescent moon.

miki, n. 幹 tree trunk.

mikka, n. 三日 the third day of the month; three days.

mikomi, n. 見込み prospect.

mikon (no), adj. 未婚 (の) unmarried.

mikudasu, vb. 見下す scorn.

mimai, n. 見舞い visit (to a sick or injured person).

mimamoru, vb. 見守る 1. watch over; protect; support. 2. follow (event).

-miman 未満 under; less than.

mimi, n. 耳 ear.

mimikazari, n. 耳飾り earring.

mimitabu, n. 耳たぶ earlobe.

mimoto, n. 身元 identity; lineage.

mina, pron. 皆 all; everyone; everything.

minami, n. 南 south.

minamoto, n. 源 origin; source.

minaosu, vb. 見直す reexamine; reconsider.

minarai, n. 見習い apprentice; apprenticeship.

minari, n. 身なり 1. clothes. 2. appearance.

minasu, vb. 見なす regard as; presume.

minato, n. 港 harbor; port.

mine, n. 峰 mountain peak.

minikui, adj. 醜い ugly.

minikui, adj. 見にくい hard to see; obscure.

mi ni tsukeru, vb. 身につける learn.

min'na de, adv. 皆で 1. all told; in sum. 2. all together.

minogasu, vb. 見逃す 1. overlook. 2. turn a blind eye to.

minoru, vb. 実る bear fruit; ripen.

minshuku, n. 民宿 private home providing food and lodging for travelers.

minshushugi, n. 民主主義 democracy.

minuku, vb. 見抜く see

through (someone).

minwa, n. 民話 folklore.

minyō, n. 民謡 folk song.

minzoku, n. 民族 ethnic group; race.

mioboe ga aru, vb. 見覚えがある recognize; remember.

miokuru, vb. 見送る see a person off.

miorosu, vb. 見下ろす overlook (scenery).

miotosu, vb. 見落とす overlook.

mirai, n. 未来 future.

miru, vb. 見る 1. look; see; watch. 2. take care of.

-miru みる try; **tabetemiru** try food.

miryoku-teki (na), adj. 魅力的 (な) fascinating; charming.

misaki, n. 岬 cape; promontory.

mise, n. 店 shop; store.

misebirakasu, vb. 見せびらかす show off; flaunt.

misemono, n. 見世物 attraction; show.

miseru, vb. 見せる show.

mishin, n. ミシン (E.) sewing machine.

mishiranu, adj. 見知らぬ unfamiliar.

miso, n. みそ fermented bean paste.

misoshiru, n. みそ汁 miso soup.

misuborashii, adj. みすぼらしい shabby; tattered.

misuteru, vb. 見捨てる abandon; forsake.

-mitai みたい resembling; seeming; **bakamitai** seeming silly.

mitasu, vb. 満たす fill (up); fulfill.

mitei (no), adj. 未定 (の) undecided.

mitomeru vb. 認める recognize; admit.

mitōshi, n. 見通し perspective; outlook.

mitsubachi, n. 蜜蜂 honeybee.

mitsukaru, vb. 見つかる be found; be caught.

mitsukeru, vb. 見つける find out; locate.

mitsumoru, vb. 見積もる estimate.

mittomonai, adj. みっともない disgraceful; shameful.

mittsu, n. 三つ three; three years old.

miuchi, n. 身内 relative.

miushinau, vb. 見失う lose sight of.

miwake, n. 見分け differentiation; distinction; **miwake ga tsukanai** unable to differentiate.

miwakeru, vb. 見分ける distinguish.

miwatasu, vb. 見渡す look out (over, across).

miyage, n. みやげ souvenir; present.

miyako, n. 都 capital.

mizo, n. 溝 ditch; groove; gap.

mizu, n. 水 water.

mizugi, n. 水着 bathing suit.

mizuiro, n. 水色 light blue.

mizumushi, n. 水虫 athlete's foot.

mizuumi, n. 湖 lake.

mo, parti. も 1. also; and. 2. even.

mō もう 1. adv. already; before long. 2. adj. another; more; **mō sannin** three more people.

mochi, n. もち Japanese rice cake.

mochiageru, vb. 持ち上げる lift up.

mochikomu, vb. 持ち込む bring in.

mochimono, n. 持ち物 belongings.

mochinushi, n. 持ち主 owner.

mochiron, adv. もちろん needless to say; of course.

mōchōen, n. 盲腸炎 appendicitis.

modoru, vb. 戻る return; revert.

modosu, vb. 戻す return; put back.

moeru, vb. 燃える burn.

mōfu, n. 毛布 blanket.

moguru, vb. 潜る dive; hide.

mohan-teki (na), adj. 模範的 (な) model.

mohaya, n. 最早 1. by now. 2. no longer (with negative).

moji, n. 文字 character; letter.

moji-moji suru, vb. もじもじする fidget.

mōjin, n. 盲人 blind person.

mōkaru, vb. 儲かる make a profit; be profitable.

mokei, n. 模型 model (train, etc.).

mōkeru, vb. 儲ける profit (from).

mokugeki suru, vb. 目撃する witness.

mokuhyō, n. 目標 goal; aim.

mokuji, n. 目次 table of contents.

mokuren, n. 木蓮 magnolia.

mokusei, n. 木星 Jupiter (planet).

mokusei (no), adj. 木製 (の) wooden.

mokuteki, n. 目的 purpose.

mokutekigo, n. 目的語 object (grammar).

mokuyōbi, n. 木曜日 Thursday.

mokuzai, n. 木材 lumber.

mokuzō (no), adj. 木造 (の) wooden.

momen, n. 木綿 cotton.

momiji, n. 紅葉 maple.

momo, n. 桃 peach.

momo, n. 腿 thigh.

momoiro, n. 桃色 pink.

momu, vb. 揉む rub; massage.

mon, n. 門 gate.

mondai, n. 問題 question; problem.

mongen, n. 門限 curfew.

monku, n. 文句 1. phrase; words. 2. complaint.

mono, n. 者 person.

mono, n. 物 thing; object.

monogatari, n. 物語 story; tale.

monomane, n. 物真似 mimicry; takeoff.

monosashi, n. 物差し gauge; scale.

monotarinai, adj. 物足りない unsatisfying.

monozuki (na), adj. 物好き (な) curious; peculiar.

morau, vb. 貰う 1. receive. 2. (as auxiliary verb) have something done for you.

moreru, vb. 漏れる leak.

mori, n. 森 woods; grove.

moriagaru, vb. 盛り上がる swell; rise.

moro ni, adv. もろに altogether.

moru, vb. 盛る fill; pile up.

moru, vb. 漏る leak.

mosha, n. 模写 copy (reproduction).

moshi, 1. adv. もし providing. 2. conj. if; in case.

mōshiageru, vb. 申し上げる say; speak; tell (humble).

mōshideru, vb. 申し出る offer, volunteer.

mōshikomi, n. 申し込み application.

mōshikomu, vb. 申し込む apply for.

moshiku wa, *conj.* もしくは or.

moshi-moshi, *interj.* もしもし 1. Hello. (telephone). 2. Excuse me. (to get someone's attention).

mōshiwake arimasen, *adj.* 申し訳ありません (I'm) sorry.

mōsō, *n.* 妄想 fantasy; delusion.

mōsu, *vb.* 申す say; speak; tell (humble).

motarasu, *vb.* もたらす bring about; yield.

motenashi, *n.* もてなし hospitality; entertainment.

motenasu, *vb.* もてなす entertain.

moteru, *vb.* もてる be popular.

moto, *n.* 元、本 1. base; origin; source. 2. principal (money).

moto, *adv.* 元 formerly.

motomeru, *vb.* 求める 1. ask; request. 2. buy.

moto-moto, *adv.* 元々 originally; from the outset.

moto wa, *adv.* 元は formerly; before.

motozuku, *vb.* 基づく be based on; derive from.

motsu, *vb.* 持つ 1. have; hold; own. 2. last.

motsureru, *vb.* もつれる tangle; become complicated.

mottainai, *adj.* 勿体ない 1. wasteful. 2. too good for.

-motte もって with; by way of; owing to.

motteiku, *vb.* 持って行く take along; take away.

motto, *adv.* もっと more.

mottomo, *adv.* 最も most; **mottomo kirei** most beautiful; **mottomo ōkii** biggest.

mottomo (na) もっとも (な) 1. *adj.* logical; rational; true. 2. *conj.* however; of course.

moya, *n.* もや haze; mist.

moyashi, *n.* もやし bean sprout.

moyasu, *vb.* 燃やす burn.

moyō, *n.* 模様 design; pattern.

mucha (na), *adj.* 無茶 (な) reckless; absurd; immoderate.

muchi, *n.* 鞭 whip.

muchi (na), *adj.* 無知 (な) ignorant.

muchū de, *adv.* 夢中で 1. madly; intently. 2. desperately.

muda (na), *adj.* 無駄 (な) useless; wasteful.

mudan de, *adv.* 無断で without permission.

mugai (na), *adj.* 無害 (な) harmless.

mugen (no), *adj.* 無限 (の) eternal; endless; infinite.

mugoi, *adj.* 酷い cruel; brutal.

mugon (no), *adj.* 無言 (の) speechless; silent.

muhyōjō (na, no), *adj.* 無表情 (な、の) expressionless; poker-faced.

muichimon (no), *adj.* 無一文 (の) penniless.

muimi (na), *adj.* 無意味 (な) meaningless; purposeless.

muishiki ni, *adv.* 無意識に unconsciously.

mujitsu, *n.* 無実 innocence (crime).

mujō (na), *adj.* 無情 (な) heartless; unfeeling.

mujōken de/ni, *adv.* 無条件 で、～に unconditionally.

mujun suru, *vb.* 矛盾する be inconsistent.

mukae ni iku, *vb.* 迎えに行く go to meet an arriving

passenger.

mukaeru, *vb.* 迎える meet; welcome.

mukai (no), *prep.* 向かい (の) across the street.

mukai no mise store across the street.

muka-muka suru, *vb.* むかむかする 1. feel nauseated. 2. feel disgusted.

mukashi (no), *adj.* 昔 (の) old; ancient; former.

mukashibanashi, *n.* 昔話 1. legend. 2. reminiscences.

mukau, *vb.* 向かう 1. head for. 2. face.

mukeiken (na, no), *adj.* 無経験 (な、の) inexperienced.

mukeru, *vb.* 向ける direct; project; turn.

muko, *n.* 婿 bridegroom; son-in-law.

mukō, *n.* 無効 invalidity.

mukō, *n.* 向こう 1. opposite side. 2. foreign country. 3. the other or opposite party.

mukō ni, *adv.* 向こうに over there.

muku, *vb.* 向く 1. look; turn to. 2. be suitable.

muku, *vb.* 剝く peel.

munashii, *adj.* 空しい empty; fruitless.

mune, *n.* 胸 chest; breast.

mura, *n.* 村 village.

muragaru, *vb.* 群がる flock; throng.

murasaki, *n.* 紫 purple.

mure, *n.* 群れ crowd; group; hoard.

muri, *n.* 無理 1. impossibility. 2. unreasonableness.

muri (na), *adj.* 無理 (な) 1. impossible. 2. unreasonable.

muryō (no), *adj.* 無料 (の) free of charge.

muryoku, *n.* 無力 powerlessness.

musaboru, *vb.* むさぼる devour.

musekinin (na), *adj.* 無責任 (な) irresponsible.

musen, *n.* 無線 wireless (electronics).

mushi, *n.* 虫 1. insect. 2. worm.

mushiatsui, *adj.* 蒸し暑い hot and humid.

mushiba, *n.* 虫歯 decayed tooth.

mushimegane, *n.* 虫眼鏡 magnifying glass.

mushin, *n.* 無心 1. innocence; honesty. 2. request for money.

mushinkei (na, no), *adj.* 無神経 (な、の) insensitive; indifferent.

mushiro, *adv.* むしろ rather.

mushiru, *vb.* むしる tear; pull out.

mushi suru, *vb.* 無視する ignore; disregard.

mushiyaki, *n.* 蒸し焼き baking in a covered pot.

mushoku (no), *adj.* 無色 (の) colorless.

mushoku (no), *adj.* 無職 (の) unemployed.

musu, *vb.* 蒸す 1. steam. 2. be hot and humid.

musū (no), *adj.* 無数 (の) countless; innumerable.

musubu, *vb.* 結ぶ 1. bind; connect; tie. 2. conclude. 3. form; organize.

musuko, *n.* 息子 son.

musume, *n.* 娘 daughter; girl.

mutto suru, *vb.* むっとする 1. take offense. 2. be muggy.

muttsu, *n.* 六つ 1. six (counter). 2. six years old.

muttsuri shita, *adj.* むっつりした sullen.

muyami ni, *adv.* 無暗に indiscriminately; recklessly.

muzai, *n.* 無罪 innocence (crime).

muzan (na) *adj.* 無残 (な) 1. heartless. 2. tragic.

muzukashii, *adj.* 難しい difficult.

muzu-muzu suru, *vb.* むずむずする feel itchy.

myaku, *n.* 脈 pulse; vein.

myō (na) *adj.* 妙 (な) 1. odd; strange. 2. unique.

myōji, *n.* 名字 family name.

N

na, *n.* 名 1. name. 2. fame.

-na な don't (do); **Miruna.** Don't look.

nabe, *n.* 鍋 pan; pot.

nabiku, *vb.* なびく 1. wave (in the wind). 2. be seduced; succumb.

nadameru, *vb.* なだめる calm down; soothe.

nadare, *n.* 雪崩 avalanche.

naderu, *vb.* 撫でる rub; stroke.

nado, *parti.* など 1. et cetera. 2. for instance. 3. such as.

nae, *n.* 苗 seedling.

nafuda, *n.* 名札 name tag.

nagagutsu, *n.* 長靴 knee-high boots (rubber or leather).

nagai, *adj.* 長い long.

naga'iki, *n.* 長生き longevity.

nagaku, *adv.* 長く long; for a long time.

nagame, *n.* 眺め view.

nagameru, *vb.* 眺める gaze; look at.

-nagara ながら 1. while; at the same time. 2. although; nevertheless.

nagare, *n.* 流れ flow; stream.

nagareboshi, *n.* 流れ星 meteor.

nagareru, *vb.* 流れる 1. flow; be washed away. 2. pass (time). 3. be called off.

nagasa, *n.* 長さ length.

nagashi, *n.* 流し kitchen

sink.

nagasode, *n.* 長袖 long-sleeved garment.

nagasu, *vb.* 流す 1. drain; pour; flush. 2. shed (tears). 3. wash away.

nageku, *vb.* 嘆く lament; grieve.

nageru, *vb.* 投げる 1. throw. 2. give up.

nagori, *n.* 名残 traces; remnants.

nagoyaka (na), *adj.* 和やか (な) gentle; peaceful.

naguru, *vb.* 殴る beat up; punch; slap.

nagusameru, *vb.* 慰める console; divert.

nai, *adv.* ない no; not.

naibu, *n.* 内部 inside; insider.

naika, *n.* 内科 internal medicine.

naikaku, *n.* 内閣 Cabinet.

naikaku-sōridaijin, *n.* 内閣総理大臣 (Japanese) prime minister.

naikō-teki (na), *adj.* 内向的 (な) introverted.

naisen, *n.* 内線 extension (telephone).

naisho, *n.* 内緒 secret.

naisō, *n.* 内装 interior decoration.

naiyō, *n.* 内容 1. content. 2. substance.

naizō, *n.* 内臓 internal organs.

najimi (no), adj. 馴染み (の) familiar; regular (customer).

najimu, vb. 馴染む 1. adapt. 2. become accustomed to.

naka, n. 中 1. inside. 2. middle.

naka, n. 仲 relationship; **naka ga ii** be on good terms.

naka de, prep. 中で among; in.

nakama, n. 仲間 colleague; friend; partner.

nakami, n. 中身 content; substance.

naka-naka, adv. なかなか 1. (with negative) not easily; not in the way one wishes. 2. quite.

nakanaori, n. 仲直り reconciliation.

-nakattara なかったら if not; if it had not been for.

nakayoshi, n. 仲良し close friend.

nakayubi, n. 中指 middle finger.

-nakereba-naranai なければならない see **-nakutewa-naranai.**

nakidasu, vb. 泣き出す start crying.

nakigoe, n. 泣き声 (human) weeping; sobbing; crying.

nakigoe, n. 鳴き声 (animal) howling; crying; chirping.

nakimushi, n. 泣き虫 crybaby.

nakōdo, n. 仲人 go-between; matchmaker.

naku, vb. 泣く (human) cry; weep.

naku, vb. 鳴く (animal) bark; chirp; cry.

nakunaru, vb. 亡くなる die.

nakunaru, vb. 無くなる run out; disappear.

nakusu, vb. 無くす lose.

-nakutewa-naranai なくて はならない 1. must; should; **Ika-nakutewa-naranai.** (I) must leave. 2. indispensable.

namae, n. 名前 name.

namahōsō, n. 生放送 live broadcast.

namaiki (na), adj. 生意気 (な) conceited.

namakemono, n. 怠け者 lazy person.

namakeru, vb. 怠ける be lazy.

nama no, adj. 生の 1. raw; uncooked. 2. live (performance).

namari, n. 鉛 lead (mineral).

namari, n. 訛 accent (pronunciation).

namazu, n. なまず catfish.

nameraka (na), adj. 滑らか (な) smooth; mellow.

nameru, vb. なめる 1. lick. 2. underestimate; insult.

nami, n. 波 wave.

namida, n. 涙 tears.

namiki, n. 並木 trees lining a street.

nami no, adj. 並の ordinary; usual.

nan 何 1. adj. what. 2. pron. what.

naname (no), adj. 斜め (の) diagonal; oblique.

nanatsu, n. 七つ 1. seven. 2. seven years old.

nanban, n. 何番 1. What number? 2. What ranking?

nanboku, n. 南北 north and south.

nan da, interj. 何だ 1. Is this all? 2. It's nothing!

nan da ka, adv. 何だか somehow.

nandemo 何でも pron. anything.

nan demo nai, interj. 何でもない It's nothing!

nando, n. 何度 how many

times.

nandomo, adv. 何度も many times.

nani, pron. 何 what.

nanika, pron. 何か 1. something. 2. anything.

nanimo, pron. 何も (with negative) nothing.

nanimokamo, pron. 何もかも everything.

nani shiro, adv. 何しろ anyway.

nani yori (mo), adv. 何より (も) more than anything.

nanji n. 何時 what time.

nankai n. 何回 how many times.

nankai mo adv. 何回も many times.

nankyoku, n. 南極 South Pole.

nannen n. 何年 what year; how many years; what grade (in school).

nannichi n. 何日 what day.

nannin, n. 何人 how many people.

-nanode なので because.

nanoka, n. 七日 seventh day of the month.

nansai, adv. 何歳 how old.

nanto, adv. 何と what; how.

nantoka, adv. 何とか somehow; some way or other.

nanto shitemo, adv. 何としても at any cost.

nao, adv. 尚 1. further; in addition. 2. still.

naosu, vb. 治す cure; heal.

naosu, vb. 直す correct; repair; alter.

-naosu なおす redo; do again.

-nara(ba) ならば if; in that case.

naraberu, vb. 並べる align; place side by side.

narabu, vb. 並ぶ form a line.

narau, vb. 習う learn; study.

narawashi, n. 習わし custom; tradition.

nareru, vb. 慣れる become accustomed to.

-nari ni なりに in one's own way.

naritatsu, vb. 成り立つ 1. consist of. 2. materialize.

nariyuki, n. 成り行き course of events.

naru, vb. なる 1. become; **sensei ni naru** become a teacher. 2. turn out; result in.

naru, vb. 生る bear fruit.

naru, vb. 鳴る chime; ring; sound.

narubeku, adv. なるべく as ... as possible; **narubeku hayaku** as soon as possible.

naruhodo, adv. なるほど indeed.

nasakebukai, adj. 情深い compassionate; kind.

nasakenai, adj. 情無い 1. disappointing; regrettable. 2. shameful.

nashi, n. 梨 pear.

-nashi de 無しで without.

nasu(bi), n. なす(び) eggplant.

natsu, n. 夏 summer.

natsukashii, adj. 懐かしい nostalgic; evocative of times past.

natsuyasumi, n. 夏休み summer vacation.

nattō, n. 納豆 fermented soybeans.

nattoku suru, vb. 納得する acquiesce; agree.

nawa, n. 縄 rope.

nawabari, n. 縄張り territory; turf.

nayamasu, vb. 悩ます annoy; worry.

nayami, n. 悩み distress; worry.

nayamu, vb. 悩む be troubled; be worried.

naze, adv. なぜ why.

nazeka, adv. なぜか somehow.

naze nara(ba), conj. なぜなら(ば) because.

nazo, n. 謎 enigma; riddle; **nazo o kakeru** pose a riddle.

nazo no, adj. 謎の enigmatic; mysterious.

nazukeru, vb. 名付ける name.

ne, n. 根 root.

ne, n. 値 price.

neagari, n. 値上がり price increase.

nebaru, vb. 粘る 1. persist. 2. be sticky.

nebusoku, n. 寝不足 lack of sleep.

nedan, n. 値段 price.

negau, vb. 願う ask; hope; pray; request.

negi, n. ねぎ green onion.

neji, n. ねじ screw.

nejiru, vb. ねじる twist.

nekki, n. 熱気 hot air; intensity; zeal.

nekkyō, n. 熱狂 enthusiasm; excitement.

neko, n. 猫 cat.

nemaki, n. 寝巻き pajamas; nightclothes.

nemui, adj. 眠い sleepy.

nemuru, vb. 眠る sleep.

-nen 年 1. year. 2. grade (in school).

nendai, n. 年代 1. age; generation. 2. date; period.

nendo, n. 粘土 clay.

nengajō, n. 年賀状 New Year's card.

nen'iri (na), adj. 念入り(な) elaborate; minute; meticulous.

nenjū 年中 1. n. the whole year. 2. adv. throughout the year; always.

nenkan 年間 1. n. era; period. 2. n. the whole year. 3. adj. annual.

nenkin, n. 年金 annuity; pension.

nenmatsu, n. 年末 year end.

nenrei, n. 年齢 age.

nenryō, n. 燃料 fuel.

nenshi, n. 年始 1. New Year's Day.

nenza, n. 捻挫 sprain.

nerau, vb. 狙う aim at; target.

neru, vb. 寝る sleep; go to bed.

neru, vb. 練る 1. knead. 2. plan carefully.

nesagari, n. 値下がり price decrease.

nēsan, n. 姉さん elder sister; Miss (familiar form of address).

nesshin (na), adj. 熱心 (な) ardent; enthusiastic.

nessuru, vb. 熱する heat.

nesugosu, vb. 寝過ごす oversleep.

netamu, vb. 妬む be jealous; envy.

netchū suru, vb. 熱中する be absorbed in; be enthusiastic about.

netsu, n. 熱 1. heat. 2. fever; 3. obsession; zeal.

nettai, n. 熱帯 tropics.

neuchi no aru, adj. 値打ちのある worthy; valuable.

nezumi, n. ねずみ mouse; rat.

nezumi'iro, n. ねずみ色 gray color.

ni, n. 二 two (number).

ni, parti. に 1. at; by; for; from; in; on; to. 2. per.

niau, vb. 似合う become; suit.

nibai, adv. 二倍 twice; twofold.

niban, n. 二番 second place.

nibui, adj. 鈍い dull; dim-witted.

nibun no ichi, n. 二分の一 half.

-nichi 日 day; date.

nichi-yōbi, n. 日曜日 Sunday.

nido, adv. 二度 twice; a second time.

nieru, vb. 煮える boil.

nigai, adj. 苦い bitter.

nigasu, vb. 逃がす let loose; lose.

nigate, n. 苦手 weak point; tough customer.

nigatsu, n. 二月 February.

nigeru, vb. 逃げる escape; run away.

nigiru, vb. 握る grasp; hold tight.

nigiyaka (na), adj. 賑やか(な) lively; crowded.

nigoru, vb. 濁る be unclear; be muddy.

nihon, n. 日本 Japan.

niisan, n. 兄さん elder brother.

niji, n. 虹 rainbow.

nijimu, vb. にじむ blur; run.

nijū, n. 二十 twenty.

nijū no, adj. 二重の double.

nikai, n. 二階 second floor.

nikibi, n. にきび acne; pimple.

nikki, n. 日記 diary; **nikki o tsukeru** keep a diary.

niko-niko suru, vb. にこにこする smile.

nikoyaka (na), adj. にこやか(な) sunny; beaming.

niku, n. 肉 1. meat. 2. flesh.

nikui, adj. 憎い hateful.

-nikui にくい difficult (to do); **kikinikui** difficult to hear.

nikumu, vb. 憎む hate; loathe.

nimaime, n. 二枚目 good-looking man.

nimono, n. 煮物 boiled food.

nimotsu, n. 荷物 baggage; cargo; load.

-nin 人 person; people; **sannin** three people.

ninau, vb. 担う carry; bear.

ninensei, n. 二年生 sophomore; second-grader.

ningen, n. 人間 human being.

ningyō, n. 人形 doll.

ninja, n. 忍者 spy; secret agent.

ninjin, n. にんじん carrot.

ninjō, n. 人情 sympathy; human feelings.

ninki, n. 人気 popularity.

nin'niku, n. にんにく garlic.

ninshinchūzetsu, n. 妊娠中絶 abortion.

ninshin suru, vb. 妊娠する become pregnant.

ninsō, n. 人相 looks; (facial) features.

nintai, n. 忍耐 patience.

ninzū, n. 人数 number of people.

niou, vb. 臭う、匂う smell of.

nippon, n. 日本 Japan.

niramu, vb. にらむ glare at.

niru, vb. 似る resemble; look like.

niru, vb. 煮る boil; cook.

nisan (no), adj. 二、三 (の) two or three.

nisei, n. 二世 1. Junior. 2. the Second (in royal line).

nisemono, n. 偽物 counterfeit; fake.

nisesatsu, n. 偽札 counterfeit banknote.

nishi, n. 西 west.

nittei, n. 日程 daily schedule.

niwa, n. 庭 garden; yard.

niwatori, n. 鶏 chicken.

nizukuri, n. 荷作り packing;

crating.

no, n. 野 field.

no, parti. の at; for; in; of; on; from.

nō, n. 脳 brain.

nō, n. 能 old-style Japanese theater (Noh).

nobasu, vb. 延ばす 1. extend. 2. postpone.

nobasu, vb. 伸ばす 1. enlarge; lengthen; stretch. 2. develop; cultivate. 3. straighten up.

noberu, vb. 述べる tell; state.

nobiru, vb. 伸びる 1. develop; grow. 2. be postponed. 3. be exhausted; collapse.

noboru, vb. 登る climb.

nochi (no), adj. 後 (の) later; future.

-node ので because.

nodo, n. 喉 throat.

nodoka (na), adj. のどか (な) peaceful.

nogasu, vb. 逃す let go; let escape.

nōgyō, n. 農業 agriculture.

nohara, n. 野原 field.

nokeru, vb. 退ける remove.

noko(giri), n. 鋸 hand or electric saw.

nokorazu, adv. 残らず entirely.

nokoru, vb. 残る stay behind; remain.

nokosu, vb. 残す leave; leave behind.

noku, vb. 退く step aside.

nomi, n. のみ chisel.

nomi, n. 蚤 flea.

-nomi のみ only.

nomikomu, vb. 飲み込む 1. swallow. 2. understand.

nomimono, n. 飲み物 beverage.

-nominarazu のみならず not only ... but also.

nomisugi, n. 飲み過ぎ excessive drinking.

nomiya, n. 飲み屋 bar.

nomu, vb. 飲む 1. drink; swallow; take (pills). 2. smoke.

nonbiri suru, vb. のんびり する be relaxed; be unhurried.

-noni のに 1. although; on the other hand. 2. if only; **Motto yasui to ii-noni.** If only it were cheaper.

noren, n. のれん shop curtain.

nori, n. 糊 starch.

nori, n. 海苔 dried seaweed sold in sheets.

noriba, n. 乗り場 taxi stand; train platform; bus stop.

norikaeru, vb. 乗り換える transfer.

norimono, n. 乗り物 vehicle.

nōritsu-teki (na), adj. 能率 的 (な) efficient.

noroi, n. 呪い curse; **noroi o kakeru** put a curse on (someone).

noroi, adj. のろい 1. slow (movement). 2. slow-witted.

noroma, n. のろま slow-witted person.

noru, vb. 乗る get on; ride; take (a train, taxi, etc.).

noru, vb. 載る 1. be printed. 2. be placed on.

nōryoku, n. 能力 ability; competence; skill.

noseru, vb. 乗せる 1. carry. 2. load. 3. transport.

noseru, vb. 載せる 1. put on top of. 2. publish (in a newspaper or journal).

nō sotchū, n. 脳卒中 stroke; apoplexy.

nōto, n. ノート (E.) notebook.

nozoite, *prep.* 除いて except.

nozoku, *vb.* 除く eliminate; remove.

nozoku, *n.* 覗く snoop.

nozomi, *n.* 望み hope; dream; wish; **nozomi ga kanau** dream comes true.

nozomu, *vb.* 望む hope; dream; wish.

nugu, *vb.* 脱ぐ remove (clothing).

nukasu, *vb.* 抜かす omit; overlook; skip.

nukemichi, *n.* 抜け道 1. byway. 2. loophole.

nukeru, *vb.* 抜ける 1. come off; fall out. 2. escape. 3. go through. 4. lack.

nuku, *vb.* 抜く 1. pull out. 2. outrun; surpass. 3. skip; eliminate. 4. open (a bottle).

nukumeru, *vb.* ぬくめる warm.

numa, *n.* 沼 swamp.

nuno, *n.* 布 cloth.

nurasu, *vb.* 濡らす wet.

nureru, *vb.* 濡れる get wet.

nuru, *vb.* 塗る paint; spread (butter).

nurui, *adj.* ぬるい lukewarm; tepid.

nusumareru, *vb.* 盗まれる be stolen.

nusumu, *vb.* 盗む steal.

nu'u, *vb.* 縫う sew.

nyō, *n.* 尿 urine.

nyōbō, *n.* 女房 one's wife.

nyūeki, *n.* 乳液 lotion.

nyūgaku, *n.* 入学 enrollment (school); matriculation.

nyū(gaku)shi(ken), *n.* 入(学)試(験) entrance examination.

nyūgan, *n.* 乳癌 breast cancer.

nyūin, *n.* 入院 hospitalization.

nyūin suru, *vb.* 入院する be hospitalized.

nyūjō, *n.* 入場 admission (to theater, arena, auditorium, etc.).

nyūkoku, *n.* 入国 immigration; entrance into a country.

nyūmon suru, *vb.* 入門する become a disciple or student.

nyūryoku suru, *vb.* 入力する input; enter (computer data).

nyūsha, *n.* 入社 joining a company.

nyūyoku suru, *vb.* 入浴する take a bath.

O

o, *n.* 尾 tail; **o o furu** wag a tail.

o-, *pref.* attached to nouns: (1) indicates that the object in question belongs to someone other than the speaker; (2) shows politeness; or (3) has become inseparable from certain nouns, such as **ocha** (tea).

ō, *n.* 王 king.

ōame, *n.* 大雨 heavy rain.

ōatari, *n.* 大当たり great success.

oba(san), *n.* 伯母(さん) aunt; middle-aged woman.

ōbā, *n.* オーバー (E.) overcoat.

obake, *n.* お化け ghost; monster.

obāsan, *n.* お婆さん grandmother; elderly woman.

obi, n. 帯 kimono sash.

obieru, vb. 怯える be frightened.

obitadashii, adj. おびただしい immense; abundant.

obiyakasu, vb. 脅かす menace; threaten.

ōbo, n. 応募 application; subscription.

oboeru, vb. 覚える 1. memorize; remember. 2. learn. 3. feel.

oboreru, vb. 溺れる drown.

ōbo suru, vb. 応募する apply for.

ocha, n. お茶 tea.

ōchaku (na), adj. 横着 (な) 1. impudent. 2. lazy.

ochiba, n. 落ち葉 fallen leaves.

ochikomu, vb. 落ち込む feel depressed.

ochiru, vb. 落ちる 1. come off; fall. 2. fail. 3. go downhill.

ochitsuki, n. 落ち着き 1. composure. 2. calmness; serenity.

ochitsuki no aru, adj. 落ち着きのある 1. self-possessed. 2. calm; serene.

ochitsuku, vb. 落ち着く 1. become calm; relax. 2. be settled.

odaiji ni, interj. Take care!

ōdanhodō, n. 横断歩道 pedestrian crossing; crosswalk.

odayaka (na), adj. 穏やか (な) calm; peaceful.

odeki, n. おでき swelling; eruption (skin).

odokasu, vb. 脅かす 1. frighten. 2. threaten.

odo-odo suru, vb. おどおどする be fearful; be nervous.

odori, n. 踊り dance.

ōdōri, n. 大通り main street.

odorokasu, vb. 驚かす surprise.

odoroku, vb. 驚ろく be surprised.

odoru, vb. 踊る dance.

odosu, vb. 脅す menace; threaten.

ōen suru, vb. 応援する support.

ōeru, n. オーエル (E. office lady) female office worker.

ōfuku, n. 往復 round trip.

ofukuro(san), n. お袋(さん) mother.

ogamu, vb. 拝む 1. pray. 2. worship; revere.

ōgata, n. 大型 large size.

ogawa, n. 小川 brook.

ōgesa (na), adj. 大げさ (な) exaggerated.

ōgi, n. 扇 folding fan.

oginau, vb. 補う supplement; compensate for.

ōgoe, n. 大声 loud voice.

ōgoe de in a loud voice.

ōgon, n. 黄金 gold.

ogori, n. 奢り treat; **Watashi no ōgori desu.** It's my treat.

ohayō (gozaimasu), interj. おはよう (ございます) Good morning!

ōhei (na), adj. 横柄 (な) arrogant; patronizing.

ōhi, n. 王妃 queen.

oi, n. 甥 nephew.

oi, interj. おい Hey!

ōi, adj. 多い 1. many; much. 2. frequent.

oidasu, vb. 追い出す expel; evict.

oikakeru, vb. 追いかける pursue; chase after.

oikomu, vb. 追い込む drive (into).

oikosu, vb. 追い越す 1. overtake. 2. surpass.

oimotomeru, vb. 追い求める pursue; seek after; long

for.

oinuku, vb. 追い抜く surpass; pass.

oishii, adj. おいしい delicious; tasty.

oishisō (na), adj. おいしそう (な) mouth-watering; appetizing.

ō'isogi de, adv. 大急ぎで in a great hurry.

oitsuku, vb. 追い付く catch up with; overtake.

oji(san), n. 伯父(さん) uncle.

ōji(sama), n. 王子(様) prince.

ojigi, n. お辞儀 bow (polite gesture).

ōjiru, vb. 応じる respond; comply with.

ojiisan, n. お爺さん grandfather; old man.

ōjo(sama), n. 王女(様) princess.

ojōsan, n. お嬢さん 1. young girl. 2. (someone else's) daughter.

oka, n. 丘、岡 hill.

okage(sama) de おかげ(さま)で 1. adv. thanks to; owing to. 2. conj. because.

okāsan, n. お母さん mother.

okashi, n. お菓子 confection; cake.

okashii, adj. おかしい 1. funny. 2. wrong; suspicious. 3. unusual; odd.

okasu, vb. 犯す 1. infringe. 2. violate; commit a crime; rape.

ōkata, adv. 大方 1. almost. 2. probably.

okawari, n. お代わり second helping.

okazu, n. おかず side dishes (served with rice).

okeru, prep. おける at; in; on.

oki'agaru, vb. 起き上がる

get up; stand up.

okiba, n. 置き場 storage space.

ōkii, adj. 大きい 1. big; large. 2. loud (voice).

okikaeru, vb. 置き換える replace; substitute.

-oki ni おきに every other; **ichi-nichi-oki ni** every other day.

okini'iri, n. お気に入り favorite thing or person.

okiru, vb. 起きる 1. get up; wake up. 2. happen.

ōkisa, n. 大きさ size.

okonai, n. 行い act; behavior.

okonau, vb. 行う perform; conduct.

okoraseru, vb. 怒らせる offend; anger.

okorippoi, adj. 怒りっぽい short-tempered.

okoru, vb. 起こる 1. originate; start. 2. happen; break out.

okoru, vb. 怒る get upset; get angry.

okosu, vb. 起こす 1. wake someone up. 2. start. 3. generate; cause; make (a fire).

oku, n. 奥 back; depths.

oku, n. 億 a hundred million.

oku, vb. 置く 1. put; place. 2. leave (as it is).

ōku, 多く 1. n. most. 2. adv. mainly.

okubyō (na), adj. 臆病 (な) timid.

okujō, n. 屋上 rooftop.

ōkurashō, n. 大蔵省 Finance Ministry.

okureru, vb. 遅れる 1. be behind schedule; be late for. 2. lag behind others. 3. (watch) lose time.

okuridasu, vb. 送り出す

send out; see (someone) out.

okurikaesu, *vb.* 送り返す send back.

okurimono, *n.* 贈り物 present; gift.

okuru, *vb.* 送る 1. send. 2. see off. 3. lead (a life); spend (time).

okusama, *n.* 奥様 1. (someone else's) wife. 2. married woman.

ōkute (mo), *adv.* 多くて (も) at most.

ōkyū-shochi/-teate, *n.* 応急処置、～手当 emergency measures; first- aid treatment.

omae, *pron.* お前 you (informal).

omamori, *n.* お守り amulet; talisman.

omatsuri, *n.* お祭り festival.

omawari(san), *n.* おまわり(さん) policeman.

omedeta, *n.* めでた happy event; marriage; pregnancy.

omedetō (gozaimasu), *interj.* おめでとう(ございます) Congratulations! Happy ...!; **Kekkon omedetō.** Congratulations on your marriage! **Tanjōbi omedetō.** Happy Birthday!

ōmisoka, *n.* 大晦日 New Year's Eve.

o-miyage, *n.* お土産 souvenir; present.

omocha, *n.* おもちゃ toy.

omoi, *n.* 思い 1. idea; thought; sentiment. 2. love.

omoi, *adj.* 重い 1. heavy. 2. serious; weighty.

omoidasu, *vb.* 思い出す recall; remember.

omoide, *n.* 思い出 recollection; memory.

omoidōri ni, *adv.* 思い通り に to one's satisfaction.

omoigakenaku, *adv.* 思いが けなく 1. unexpectedly. 2. without notice; suddenly.

omoikiri 思い切り 1. *n.* decision. 2. *adv.* to the utmost; to one's heart's content.

omoitsuku, *vb.* 思い付く hit upon an idea.

omoiyaru, *vb.* 思い遣る empathize; identify with; care about.

ōmoji, *n.* 大文字 capital letter.

omomi, *n.* 重み weight.

omo na, *adj.* 主な main; chief.

omoni, *n.* 重荷 burden.

omo ni, *adv.* 主に mainly; chiefly.

ōmono, *n.* 大物 1. trophy. 2. magnate; important figure.

omo-omoshii, *adj.* 重々しい grave; solemn.

omosa, *n.* 重さ weight.

omoshirogaru, *vb.* 面白がる enjoy; be amused by.

omoshirohanbun ni, *adv.* 面白 半分に for the fun of; for sport.

omoshiroi, *adj.* 面白い interesting; enjoyable; funny.

omote, *n.* 表 1. surface. 2. front. 3. outdoors.

omotedōri, *n.* 表通り main street.

omou, *vb.* 思う think; feel; intend.

omou zonbun, *adv.* 思う存分 to one's heart's content.

omowareru, *vb.* 思われる 1. seem. 2. be considered. 3. be loved.

omowazu, *adv.* 思わず unintentionally.

ōmu, *n.* おうむ parrot.

ōmukashi, *n.* 大昔 ages ago.

omutsu, *n.* おむつ diaper.

on, *n.* 恩 indebtedness; obligation; gratitude; **on ni kiru** feel indebted/grateful; **on ni kiseru** make someone feel indebted.

onaji, *adj.* 同じ same; equivalent to.

onajiku, *adv.* 同じく similarly.

onaka, *n.* お腹 belly; stomach; **onaka ga ōkii** be pregnant; be full.

onboro (no), *adj.* おんぼろ (の) worn-out; tattered.

onbu, *n.* おんぶ piggyback ride.

ondo, *n.* 温度 temperature.

ondokei, *n.* 温度計 thermometer.

onēsan, *n.* お姉さん elder sister.

ongaeshi, *n.* 恩返し returning a favor.

ongaku, *n.* 音楽 music.

oni, *n.* 鬼 1. devil. 2. cruel person.

oniisan, *n.* お兄さん elder brother.

onkyō, *n.* 音響 sound.

on'na, *n.* 女 woman.

on'nagata, *n.* 女方 female impersonator (kabuki).

on'na no ko, *n.* 女の子 girl.

ono, *n.* 斧 ax.

onsen, *n.* 温泉 hot spring.

onsetsu, *n.* 音節 syllable.

onshirazu (no), *adj.* 恩知らず (の) ungrateful.

onshitsu, *n.* 温室 greenhouse.

ō'otoko, *n.* 大男 giant; very tall man.

oppai, *n.* おっぱい 1. breast. 2. breast milk.

ōppira ni, *adv.* 大っぴらに openly.

ōraka (na), *adj.* おおらか (な) easygoing; bighearted.

oranda, *n.* オランダ Holland.

ore, *n.* 俺 I (male, informal).

orei, *n.* お礼 gratitude; thanks.

oreru, *vb.* 折れる 1. be broken. 2. give in.

ori, *n.* 檻 cage; cell.

origami, *n.* 折り紙 Japanese paper folding.

orikaesu, *vb.* 折り返す 1. turn back. 2. go back; return.

orimageru, *vb.* 折り曲げる bend; fold down.

oriru, *vb.* 降りる get off; descend; go or come down.

oritatami-shiki (no), *adj.* 折り畳み式 (の) collapsible; folding.

oroshi(uri), *n.* 卸し(売り) wholesale.

orosu, *vb.* 下ろす 1. bring down. 2. draw out (money).

oru, *vb.* 折る break.

oru, *vb.* 織る weave.

osaeru, *vb.* 押える 1. press down. 2. apprehend. 3. comprehend; master.

osaeru, *vb.* 抑える suppress; control.

Osaki ni dōzo. お先にどうぞ After you.

Osaki ni (shitsurei shimasu). お先に (失礼します) Please forgive my going first.

osamaru, *vb.* 収まる、納まる 1. be settled; be solved; **maruku osamaru** be settled satisfactorily. 2. be satisfied. 3. calm down.

osameru, *vb.* 収める、納める 1. put away (in a closet, chest, etc.). 2. conclude. 3. pay a bill or pay for merchandise.

osameru, *vb.* 治める reign;

administer.

osan, *n.* 大産 childbirth.

osanai, *adj.* 幼い 1. very young. 2. childish.

osarai o suru, *vb.* おさらいをする review.

ōsawagi, *n.* 大騒ぎ fuss; uproar.

oseibo, *n.* お歳暮 year-end gift.

oseji, *n.* お世辞 flattery.

osen, *n.* 汚染 pollution.

ōsetsu-ma/-shitsu, *n.* 応接間／〜室 drawing room.

oshaberi, *n.* おしゃべり 1. chatting. 2. talkative person; rumormonger.

oshare (na), *adj.* おしゃれ（な）fashion-conscious.

oshi, *n.* おし mute (person).

oshidasu, *vb.* 押し出す push out.

oshie, *n.* 教え teaching; dogma; doctrine.

oshieru, *vb.* 教える 1. teach. 2. show; tell.

oshii, *adj.* 惜しい unfortunate; regrettable.

oshi'ire, *n.* 押し入れ closet.

oshimai, *n.* お仕舞い ending; conclusion.

oshimu, *vb.* 惜しむ 1. regret. 2. begrudge.

oshinagasu, *vb.* 押し流す wash away.

oshinokeru, *vb.* 押し退ける jostle; elbow.

oshiroi, *n.* おしろい face powder.

oshitaosu, *vb.* 押し倒す knock down; push down.

oshitsubusu, *vb.* 押し潰す crush; squash.

oshitsukeru, *vb.* 押しつける coerce; push.

oshoku, *n.* 汚職 corruption (by officials).

ōshū, *n.* 欧州 Europe.

osoi, *adj.* 遅い 1. late. 2. slow.

osomatsu (na), *adj.* お粗末（な）crude; clumsy.

osoraku, *adv.* 恐らく perhaps; probably.

osore, *n.* 恐れ fear.

Osore'irimasu. 恐れ入ります I appreciate it. I am sorry.

osoreru, *vb.* 恐れる fear; be apprehensive.

osoroi de, *adv.* お揃いで all together.

osoroshii, *adj.* 恐ろしい frightening; terrible.

osoru, *vb.* 襲う attack.

ossharu, *vb.* おっしゃる say; tell (polite).

osu, *n.* 雄 male animal.

osu, *n.* 押す 1. press; push. 2. force.

ōsuji, *n.* 大筋 outline.

otafukukaze, *n.* お多福風邪 mumps.

otagai, *pron.* お互い each other; one another.

ōtai suru, *vb.* 応待する receive or wait on people.

otaku, *n.* お宅 1. *pron.* you (polite). 2. *n.* your house; your home.

otamajakushi, *n.* おたまじゃくし tadpole.

oteage, *n.* お手上げ helplessness; hopeless situation.

otearai, *n.* お手洗い bathroom; restroom.

otenba, *n.* お転婆 tomboy.

ōte no, *adj.* 大手の major (company).

oto, *n.* 音 sound.

ōtō, *n.* 応答 response; reply.

ōtobai, *n.* オートバイ motorcycle.

otogibanashi, *n.* お伽話 fairy tale.

otoko, *n.* 男 male; man.

otoko no ko, *n.* 男の子 boy.

otome, *n.* 乙女 maiden.

otomo suru, *vb.* お供する accompany.

otona, *n.* 大人 adult; grown-up.

otonashii, *adj.* おとなしい 1. quiet. 2. submissive.

otoroeru, *vb.* 衰える become infirm; decline.

otōsan, *n.* お父さん father.

otoshidama, *n.* お年玉 New Year's present.

otosu, *vb.* 落とす 1. drop. 2. lose. 3. decrease.

otōto, *n.* 弟 younger brother.

ototoi, *n.* おととい day before yesterday.

ototoshi, *n.* おととし year before last.

otozure, *n.* 訪れ visit; arrival.

otozureru, *vb.* 訪れる visit; arrive.

otsukai, *n.* お使い errand.

otto, *n.* 夫 husband.

ou, *vb.* 追う chase after; follow; pursue.

ou, *vb.* 負う 1. carry on one's back. 2. bear (responsibility); be indebted to. 3. sustain (injury).

ōu, *vb.* 覆う cover.

ō'uridashi, *n.* 大売り出し (bargain) sale.

oushi, *n.* 雄牛 bull.

owaru, *vb.* 終る end; finish; be over.

oya, *n.* 親 parent.

ōya, *n.* 大家 landlord.

oyabun, *n.* 親分 boss.

ōyake (no), *adj.* 公 (の) public; open.

oyako, *n.* 親子 parent and child.

oyasumi(nasai), *interj.* お休み(なさい) Good night!

oyayubi, *n.* 親指 thumb.

ōyō, *n.* 応用 application.

oyobi, *conj.* 及び and.

oyobosu, *vb.* 及ぼす affect; influence.

oyobu, *vb.* 及ぶ reach; extend to.

oyogi, *n.* 泳ぎ swimming.

oyogu, *vb.* 泳ぐ swim.

oyoso 凡そ 1. *n.* estimate; outline. 2. *adv.* approximately.

ōyō suru, *vb.* 応用する apply; put into practice.

ōyuki, *n.* 大雪 heavy snow.

ōzei, *n.* 大勢 crowd (of people).

ōzora, *n.* 大空 sky.

P

pachinko, *n.* パチンコ Japanese pinball game.

pāma, *n.* パーマ permanent wave; **pāma o kakeru** get a permanent.

pan, *n.* パン (Pg. pāo) bread.

pan-ko/-kuzu, *n.* パン粉、〜屑 breadcrumbs.

panku, *n.* パンク (E.) puncture; flat tire.

panku suru, *vb.* パンクする get a flat tire.

pansuto, *n.* パンスト (E.)

pantyhose.

pan'ya, *n.* パン屋 bakery; baker.

para-para furu, *vb.* ばらば ら降る rain lightly.

pari-pari suru, *vb.* ぱりぱり する crunch (cracker, etc.).

pasokon, *n.* パソコン (E.) personal computer.

pata-pata suru, *vb.* ばたば たする flap; flutter.

pāto, *n.* パート (E.) part-timer; part-time job.

patokā, n. パトカー (E.) patrol car.

patto, adv. ぱっと instantly; suddenly; in a flash.

patto shinai, vb. ぱっとしない be mediocre; be unspectacular.

peko-peko suru, vb. ぺこぺこする 1. flatter; fawn. 2. cringe.

penchi, n. ペンチ pliers.

penki, n. ペンキ (D. pek) paint.

penshon, n. ペンション (F. pension) small hotel.

pēpā-tesuto, n. ペーパーテスト written exam.

pera-pera shaberu, vb. ぺらぺらしゃべる chatter.

petenshi, n. ぺてん師 impostor; swindler.

pika-pika suru, vb. ぴかぴかする glisten; sparkle.

pīman, n. ピーマン (F. piment) green pepper.

pin-boke, n. ピンぼけ out-of-focus photograph.

pin-pin shite iru, adj. ぴんぴんしている healthy.

pinto, n. ピント (D. brandpunt) focus (camera).

piri-piri suru, vb. ぴりぴりする smart; sting.

pittari, adv. ぴったり 1. tightly. 2. exactly.

pittari suru, vb. ぴったりする fit perfectly.

piza(pai), n. ピザ(パイ) (It. pizza) pizza.

poro-shatsu, n. ポロシャツ (E.) polo shirt.

posuto, n. ポスト (E. post) mailbox.

potto naru, vb. ぽっとなる blush.

-ppai see **-hai.**

-ppiki see **-hiki.**

-ppon see **-hon.**

pun-pun suru, vb. ぷんぷんする 1. be indignant. 2. reek.

purin, n. プリン (E. pudding) caramel custard; flan.

puro, n. プロ (E.) professional.

pusshu-hon, n. プッシュホン (E.) touch-tone phone.

pyon-pyon haneru, vb. ぴょんぴょんはねる hop; skip.

R

-ra 等 plural indicator; and so on; **karera** they.

raigetsu, n. 来月 next month.

rainichi suru, vb. 来日する visit Japan.

raishū, n. 来週 next week.

rakkan-teki (na), adj. 楽観的 (な) optimistic.

raku, n. 楽 comfort; pleasure; relief.

rakuchaku, n. 落着 solution; settlement.

rakuda, n. ラクダ camel.

rakugaki, n. 落書き graffiti.

raku (na), adj. 楽 (な) comfortable; easy.

raku ni naru, vb. 楽になる 1. feel at ease. 2. be relieved (from pain).

raku-raku (to), adv. 楽々 (と) easily.

rāmen, n. ラーメン Chinese style noodles in broth.

ran, n. 蘭 orchid.

ran, n. 欄 column (newspaper).

ranbō (na), adj. 乱暴 (な) violent; disorderly.

-rashii らしい 1. seem;

appear; sound. 2. I hear (that). 3. befitting; **otokorashii** befitting a man.

rei, *n.* 霊 1. soul. 2. ghost.

rei, *n.* 零 zero.

rei, *n.* 礼 1. bow; salute. 2. gratitude; thanks.

rei, *n.* 例 example; **rei o ageru** give an example.

reibō, *n.* 冷房 air conditioning.

reigai, *n.* 例外 exception.

reigi, *n.* 礼儀 civility; etiquette.

reigi tadashii, *adj.* 礼儀正しい polite; well-mannered.

reihai, *n.* 礼拝 worship.

reikyaku suru, *vb.* 冷却する cool.

reinendōri, *adv.* 例年通り as usual; as in years past.

rei no, *adj.* 例の usual.

rei o suru, *vb.* 礼をする 1. bow; salute. 2. thank; express gratitude.

reisei (na), *adj.* 冷静 (な) calm; composed; level-headed.

reitōshokuhin, *n.* 冷凍食品 frozen food.

reitō suru, *vb.* 冷凍する freeze.

reizōko, *n.* 冷蔵庫 refrigerator.

reji, *n.* レジ (E.) register; cashier.

rekishi, *n.* 歴史 history.

rekishi-teki (na), *adj.* 歴史的 (な) historic; epoch-making.

ren'ai, *n.* 恋愛 romantic love.

renchū, *n.* 連中 group of people; crowd (social).

renga, *n.* 煉瓦 brick.

renketsu suru, *vb.* 連結する connect.

renkon, *n.* 蓮根 lotus root.

renkyū, *n.* 連休 consecutive days off (esp. three-day weekend).

renraku suru, *vb.* 連絡する contact; inform.

renshū suru, *vb.* 練習する practice; exercise; drill.

rensō suru, *vb.* 連想する associate; be reminded of.

rentogen, *n.* レントゲン (G. *Röntgen*) x-ray.

renzoku-teki (na), *adj.* 連続的 (な) continuous; consecutive.

ressha, *n.* 列車 train.

retsu, *n.* 列 row; line.

rettō, *n.* 列島 archipelago.

rettōkan, *n.* 劣等感 inferiority complex.

rieki, *n.* 利益 profit.

rien, *n.* 離縁 divorce.

rihatsuten, *n.* 理髪店 barber shop.

riji, *n.* 理事 director; member of the board.

rika, *n.* 理科 science (course).

rikai, *n.* 理解 understanding.

rikkōho suru, *vb.* 立候補する run for; be a candidate for.

rikō (na), *adj.* 利口 (な) clever; smart.

rikon suru, *vb.* 離婚する obtain a divorce.

riku, *n.* 陸 land.

rikugun, *n.* 陸軍 army.

rikutsu, *n.* 理屈 1. argument. 2. theory. 3. pretext.

rikutsu o iu, *vb.* 理屈を言う 1. argue. 2. theorize.

ringo, *n.* りんご apple.

rinji (no), *adj.* 臨時 (の) 1. temporary. 2. extraordinary. 3. emergency.

rinkaku, *n.* 輪郭 outline.

rinri, *n.* 倫理 ethics.

rippa ni, adv. 立派に admirably; wonderfully.

rippuku suru, vb. 立腹する become angry.

rirekisho, n. 履歴書 resume; curriculum vitae.

ririku suru, vb. 離陸する take off (flight).

riron-teki (na), adj. 理論的 (な) theoretical.

risei-teki (na), adj. 理性的 (な) rational.

rishi, n. 利子 interest (money).

risō-teki (na), adj. 理想的 (な) ideal.

risshō suru, vb. 立証する prove.

risu, n. りす squirrel.

ritsu, n. 率 percentage; proportion; rate.

rittai-teki (na), adj. 立体的 (な) three-dimensional.

riyō suru, vb. 利用する use; utilize.

riyū, n. 理由 reason; excuse.

rō, n. ろう wax.

roba, n. ろば donkey.

rōdō, n. 労働 manual labor.

rōdoku, n. 朗読 recitation; reading aloud.

rōgan, n. 老眼 farsightedness due to aging.

rōgankyō, n. 老眼鏡 reading glasses.

rōgo, n. 老後 old age.

roji, n. 路地 alley.

rōjin, n. 老人 elderly person.

rōjin-hōmu, n. 老人ホーム nursing home for the aged.

rōka, n. 廊下 corridor; hallway.

roka suru, vb. 濾過する filter.

rokkotsu, n. 肋骨 rib.

roku, n. 六 six.

rokuga suru, vb. 録画する videotape.

rokugatsu, n. 六月 June.

rokujū, n. 六十 sixty.

rokuon, n. 録音 sound recording.

rōmaji, n. ローマ字 Roman letter.

ron, n. 論 1. theory. 2. opinion; argument.

ronbun, n. 論文 essay; research paper; thesis; dissertation.

rōnin, n. 浪人 1. masterless samurai. 2. unemployed person. 3. high school graduate who has not yet passed a college entrance examination.

ronjiru, vb. 論じる argue; discuss.

ronri-teki (na), adj. 論理的 (な) logical.

ronsō, n. 論争 controversy; argument.

rōryoku, n. 労力 labor force.

rosen, n. 路線 route (transportation).

roshia, n. ロシア Russia.

roshutsu suru, vb. 露出する expose.

rōsoku, n. ろうそく candle.

rōsoku o tsukeru light a candle.

rōsu, n. ロース (E.) roast (meat).

roten, n. 露店 street vendor's stall.

rotenburo, n. 露店風呂 open-air bath.

rōya, n. 牢屋 prison; jail.

rui, n. 類 category; class; type.

ruigo, n. 類語 synonym.

ruijihin, n. 類似品 imitation.

rusu, n. 留守 absence (from home).

rusuban, n. 留守番 caretaker (during one's absence).

rusubandenwa, n. 留守番電話 answering machine.

ryaku, n. 略 abbreviation.

abridgement; omission.

ryaku suru, vb. 略する abbreviate; abridge; omit.

ryō, n. 猟 hunting.

ryō, n. 漁 fishing.

ryō, n. 寮 dormitory.

ryō, n. 量 quantity.

ryōdo, n. 領土 territory.

ryōgae, n. 両替 1. making change (money). 2. foreign currency exchange.

ryōga suru, vb. 凌駕する surpass.

ryōgawa, n. 両側 both sides.

ryohi, n. 旅費 travel expenses.

ryōhō 両方 1. pron. both. 2. n. both sides; both parties.

ryōjikan, n. 領事館 consulate; **amerika-ryōjikan** American consulate.

ryōkai suru, vb. 了解する agree; consent; understand.

ryokaku, n. 旅客 passenger; traveler.

ryokakuki, n. 旅客機 passenger airplane.

ryokan, n. 旅館 Japanese-style inn.

ryoken, n. 旅券 passport.

ryōkin, n. 料金 fare; fee; price.

ryokō suru, vb. 旅行する travel; take a trip; tour.

ryokucha, n. 緑茶 green tea.

ryōri suru, vb. 料理する cook; prepare a meal.

ryōsei, n. 両性 both sexes.

ryōshi, n. 漁師 fisherman.

ryōshin, n. 良心 conscience.

ryōshin, n. 両親 parents.

ryōshitsu, n. 良質 good quality.

ryōshūsho, n. 領収書 receipt.

ryōte, n. 両手 both hands.

ryōyō suru, vb. 療養する receive medical treatment; recuperate.

ryū, n. 竜 dragon.

ryūgaku, n. 留学 study abroad.

ryūgaku-sei, n. 留学生 foreign student.

ryūkō'okure (no), adj. 流行遅れ outdated.

ryūkō suru, vb. 流行する 1. be in vogue; be popular. 2. be prevalent; be rampant.

ryūkyūshotō, n. 琉球諸島 Ryukyu Islands; Okinawa.

ryūtsū, n. 流通 distribution.

ryūzan, n. 流産 1. miscarriage. 2. failure.

S

sa, n. 差 difference; gap; **nichibei no sa** difference between Japan and the U.S.

saba, n. 鯖 mackerel.

sabaku, n. 砂漠 desert.

sabaku, vb. さばく settle; pass judgment on.

sabetsu suru, vb. 差別する discriminate.

sabi, n. 錆 rust.

sabishii, adj. 寂しい 1. lonely. 2. desolate.

saboru, vb. さぼる 1. neglect

(one's job or duty). 2. cut class.

saboten, n. サボテン cactus.

sadameru, vb. 定める decide; prescribe.

sadō, n. 茶道 tea ceremony.

-sae さえ 1. even; **kodomo-sae** even a child. 2. if only; **Okane-sae areba.** If only I had money.

saezuru, vb. さえずる chirp; warble (birds).

sagaru, vb. 下がる 1. hang

(from). 2. go down; step backward. 3. drop.

sagasu, *vb.* 捜す look for.

sagi, *n.* さぎ heron.

sagi, *n.* 詐欺 fraud; hoax.

saguru, *vb.* 探る grope; look for; probe.

sagyō, *n.* 作業 work; operation.

sahō, *n.* 作法 etiquette; manners.

sahodo, *adv.* さほど (with negative) not very; not so much.

sai, *n.* 才 ability; talent.

sai- 再 re-; **saikon** remarriage.

-sai 歳, 才 age; years old; **rokusai** six years old.

sai'ai (no), *adj.* 最愛 (の) most cherished.

sai'aku (no), *adj.* 最悪 (の) worst; **sai'aku no bāi ni wa** in the worst case.

saibai, *n.* 栽培 cultivation (plants).

saiban, *n.* 裁判 trial; judgment.

saibō, *n.* 細胞 cell (biology).

saichū *prep.* 最中 in the midst of; during.

saidai (no), *adj.* 最大 (の) 1. biggest; largest; maximum. 2. best.

saifu, *n.* 財布 wallet; purse.

saigai, *n.* 災害 disaster.

saigo (no), *adj.* 最後 (の) last; final.

saihakkō, *n.* 再発行 reissue.

saihō, *n.* 裁縫 sewing.

saihōsō, *n.* 再放送 rerun (broadcasting).

saijitsu, *n.* 祭日 holiday.

saikai suru, *vb.* 再開する reopen; resume.

saikai suru, *vb.* 再会する meet again.

saiken, *n.* 債券 bond (finance).

saiken suru, *vb.* 再建する rebuild; revive; re-establish.

saikin, *n.* 細菌 bacterium; germ.

saikin, *adv.* 最近 recently; these days.

saikō (no), *adj.* 最高 (の) best; highest; supreme.

saikon, *n.* 再婚 remarriage.

saikon suru, *vb.* 再婚する remarry.

saikoro, *n.* さいころ die; dice.

saiku suru, *vb.* 細工する 1. devise. 2. manipulate.

saimu, *n.* 債務 debt.

sainan, *n.* 災難 misfortune; disaster.

sainō ga aru, *adj.* 才能がある able; gifted; talented.

sairyō no, *adj.* 最良の best.

saisan, *n.* 採算 profit; surplus; **saisan ga au** profitable.

saiseishi, *n.* 再生紙 recycled paper.

saisei suru, *vb.* 再生する 1. recycle. 2. be reborn; revive.

saishi, *n.* 妻子 family; wife and children.

saishin (no), *adj.* 最新 (の) latest; newest.

saisho, *n.* 最初 beginning.

saisho (no), *adj.* 最初 (の) first; earliest; original.

saishō (no), *adj.* 最少 (の) fewest; minimum.

saisho ni, *adv.* 最初に 1. first; at the outset. 2. first of all.

saishū (no), *adj.* 最終 (の) last; **saishūdensha** last train of the day.

saishū suru, *vb.* 採集する collect.

saisoku suru, *vb.* 催促する demand; urge.

saitei (no), *adj.* 最低 (の) 1.

lowest; minimum. 2. worst.

saiteki (na), adj. 最適 (な) most suitable; optimum.

saiten suru, vb. 採点する grade; mark.

saiwai, n. 幸い happiness; good luck.

saiyō suru, vb. 採用する 1. adopt; accept. 2. employ.

saizen (no), adj. 最善 (の) best.

saji, n. さじ spoon.

saji o nageru, vb. さじを投げる give up.

saka, n. 坂 slope; hill.

sakaba, n. 酒場 bar; pub.

sakaeru, vb. 栄える prosper; thrive.

sakai, n. 境 1. border; frontier. 2. boundary.

sakan (na), adj. 盛ん (な) 1. active; enthusiastic; energetic. 2. popular; thriving.

sakana, n. 肴 appetizer.

sakana, n. 魚 fish.

sakan ni, adv. 盛んに 1. actively; enthusiastically; energetically. 2. often. 3. lavishly.

sakanoboru, vb. 遡る 1. date back. 2. go upstream.

sakarau, vb. 逆らう oppose; disobey.

sakari, n. 盛り prime; height.

sakasama (no), adj. 逆さま (の) reverse; upside-down; topsy-turvy.

sakaya, n. 酒屋 1. liquor store. 2. sake maker.

sakazuki, n. 杯 sake cup.

sake, n. 酒 1. Japanese rice wine. 2. alcoholic drink.

sake, n. 鮭 salmon.

sakebu, vb. 叫ぶ scream; shout.

sakeru, vb. 避ける avoid.

sakeru, vb. 裂ける split; tear.

saki, n. 先 1. tip; point. 2. first. 3. future.

saki (no), adj. 先 (の) 1. former (position). 2. future.

sakihodo, adv. 先程 a short time ago.

saki ni, 先に 1. adv. ahead; formerly; **saki ni iku** precede. 2. prep. before; beyond.

sakiyuki, n. 先行き future; outlook.

sakka, n. 作家 writer.

sakkaku, n. 錯覚 illusion; misunderstanding.

sakki, adv. さっき a short time ago.

sakkyoku suru, vb. 作曲する compose (music).

saku, n. 策 1. plan; scheme. 2. device.

saku, n. 柵 fence.

saku, vb. 裂く split; tear.

saku, vb. 咲く blossom; flower.

sakuban, n., adv. 昨晩 last night.

sakubun, n. 作文 composition (writing).

sakuhin, n. 作品 creation; opus.

sakuin, n. 索引 index.

sakujitsu, n. 昨日 yesterday.

sakujo suru, vb. 削除する delete; eliminate.

sakumotsu, n. 作物 crops.

sakunen, n., adv. 昨年 last year.

sakura, n. 桜 cherry tree; cherry blossom.

sakuranbo, n. 桜ん坊 cherry.

sakusei suru, vb. 作製する draw up; prepare.

sakusen, n. 作戦 1. plan; strategy; **sakusen o tateru** devise a plan or strategy. 2. military operation.

sakuya, n., adv. 昨夜 last

night; yesterday evening.

-sama 様 Mr.; Mrs.; Ms.(formal).

samasu, vb. 冷ます cool.

samasu, vb. 覚ます awake.

samatageru, vb. 妨げる hinder; obstruct.

samazama (na, no), adj. 様々 (な、の) various.

same, n. 鮫 shark.

sameru, vb. 覚める 1. wake up. 2. become sober.

sameru, vb. 冷める cool off; become cold.

samonai to, adv. さもないと otherwise; if not.

samui, adj. 寒い chilly; cold.

samurai, n. 侍 Japanese warrior.

san, n. 三 three.

-san 様 Mr.; Mrs.; Ms.

sanbi suru, vb. 賛美する laud; praise.

sanbutsu, n. 産物 product.

sanfujinka, n. 産婦人科 obstetrics and gynecology.

sangatsu, n. 三月 March.

sangoshō, n. さんご礁 coral reef.

sangyō, n. 産業 industry.

sanjū, n. 三十 thirty.

sanka, n. 参加 participation.

sankaku, n. 三角 triangle.

sanka suru, vb. 参加する participate.

sankō ni suru, vb. 参考にする refer to.

sankōsho, n. 参考書 reference book.

sanmyaku, n. 山脈 mountain range; **arupusu-sanmyaku** the Alps.

sanpatsu, n. 散髪 haircut.

sanpo suru, vb. 散歩する go for a walk.

sanretsu suru, vb. 参列する attend; participate.

sansei suru, vb. 賛成する agree.

sanshō suru, vb. 参照する refer to; consult (dictionary).

sanso, n. 酸素 oxygen.

sansū, n. 算数 arithmetic.

sanzan (na) 散々 (な) 1. adj. devastating; terrible. 2. adv. devastatingly; severely.

sao, n. 竿 pole; rod.

sappari, adv. さっぱり not at all; **sappari wakaranai.** (I) don't understand it at all.

sappari shita, adj. さっぱり した 1. neat. 2. plain. 3. frank.

sappari suru, vb. さっぱり する feel refreshed.

sappūkei (na), adj. 殺風景 (な) bleak; insipid.

sara, n. 皿 dish; plate; saucer.

sara'araiki, n. 皿洗い機 automatic dishwasher.

saraigetsu, n. 再来月 the month after next.

sarainen, n. 再来年 the year after next.

saraishū, n. 再来週 the week after next.

sara ni, adv. 更に 1. again. 2. further; in addition.

sararīman, n. サラリーマン (E.) male salaried worker.

sarau, vb. さらう 1. kidnap. 2. dredge. 3. review.

saru, n. 猿 monkey.

saru, vb. 去る depart; leave.

sasa, n. 笹 bamboo grass.

sasaeru, vb. 支える 1. support; bolster. 2. maintain.

sasageru, vb. 捧げる dedicate; devote; offer; **inochi o sasageru** offer one's life; devote oneself.

sasayaka (na), adj. ささやか (な) modest; small.

sasayaki, n. ささやき whisper.

sasayaku, *vb.* ささやく whisper.

-saseru let one do; make one do; have one do; **hanasaseru** let someone speak.

sashi'ageru, *vb.* 差し上げる give; offer (polite).

sashidasu, *vb.* 差し出す 1. offer; present. 2. send.

sashikomu, *vb.* 差し込む 1. insert; plug in. 2. come in (sunlight).

sashimi, *n.* 刺し身 sliced raw fish or seafood.

sashizu, *n.* 指図 1. direction; instruction. 2. command; order.

sasou, *vb.* 誘う 1. invite. 2. entice. 3. incite.

sassa to, *adv.* さっさと quickly; swiftly.

sassoku, *adv.* 早速 immediately; at once.

sassuru, *vb.* 察する guess; imagine; sympathize.

sasu, *vb.* 指す point at; point to; indicate.

sasu, *vb.* 刺す stab; sting; bite (insect).

sasuga (ni), *adv.* さすが (に) indeed; as expected.

sasuru, *vb.* さする rub; stroke.

sate, *interj.* さて Well! Now!

sato, *n.* 里 1. hometown; village.

satō, *n.* 砂糖 sugar.

satogaeri, *n.* 里帰り married woman's visit to her family.

satori, *n.* 悟り enlightenment.

satoru, *vb.* 悟る realize; fathom; be enlightened.

satsu, *n.* 札 paper currency.

-satsu 冊 (counter for books) **ni-satsu** two books.

satsuei, *n.* 撮影 filming; photographing.

satsugai suru, *vb.* 殺害する kill; murder.

satsujin, *n.* 殺人 murderer.

satsumaimo, *n.* さつま芋 sweet potato.

sawagi, *n.* 騒ぎ 1. noise. 2. chaos; trouble; tumult.

sawagu, *vb.* 騒ぐ 1. make noise; be clamorous; be riotous. 2. make a fuss.

sawaru, *vb.* 触る touch; feel.

sawayaka (na), *adj.* さわやか (な) refreshing; pleasant.

sayō, *n.* 作用 1. action. 2. effect; **fukusayō** side effect.

sayōnara, *interj.* さようなら Goodbye.

sayō suru, *vb.* 作用する act on; work on.

sayū, *n.* 左右 right and left sides.

sayū suru, *vb.* 左右する influence.

sazukaru, *vb.* 授かる be endowed with; be blessed with.

sazukeru, *vb.* 授ける give; grant.

se, *n.* 背 1. back (body). 2. height (person); **Se ga takai.** (He) is tall.

sebiro, *n.* 背広 man's suit.

sebone, *n.* 背骨 backbone; spine.

sedai, *n.* 世代 generation; **sedai no sa** generation gap.

sei, *n.* 姓 family name; surname.

sei, *n.* 精 1. spirit; sprite. 2. vigor; energy; **sei o dasu** apply oneself.

sei, *n.* 背 height.

sei, *n.* 聖 1. holiness; sacredness. 2. Saint.

sei, *n.* せい fault; responsibility.

-sei 生 suffix indicating student level; **sannensei** third grader; junior;

daigaku-ichinensei
university freshman.

-sei 製 made in; made of;
nihon-sei made in Japan.

seibetsu, n. 性別 gender.

seibi, n. 整備 adjustment;
maintenance; repair.

seibo, n. 歳暮 year-end gift.

seibugeki, n. 西部劇
western (movie).

seibun, n. 成分 ingredient;
component.

seibutsu, n. 生物 living
creature.

seibutsugaku, n. 生物学
biology.

seichō suru, n. 成長する
grow; become mature.

seidai (na), adj. 盛大 (な) 1.
grandiose; pompous. 2.
thriving; successful; **seidai
na pāti** successful party.

sei de, prep. せいで because
of; owing to; **taifū no sei
de** because of the typhoon.

seido, n. 制度 system;
regime.

sei'eki, n. 精液 sperm.

sei'en, n. 声援 cheering;
encouragement; support;
seien o okuru cheer on.

seifu, n. 政府 government.

seifuku, n. 制服 uniform.

seigen, n. 制限 limit;
restriction; **seigensokudo**
speed limit.

seigen suru, vb. 制限する
limit; restrict.

seigi, n. 正義 justice.

seihantai (no), adj. 正反対
(の) diametrically opposite.

seihin, n. 製品 product.

seihōkei, n. 正方形 square
(geometry).

seihoku, n. 西北 northwest.

sei'i, n. 誠意 sincerity.

sei'ippai, adv. 精一杯 with
all one's might.

seiji, n. 政治 1. politics. 2.

administration;
government.

seijika, n. 政治家 politician;
statesman.

seijin, n. 成人 adult;
grownup.

seijitsu (na), adj. 誠実 (な)
sincere; faithful.

seijō (na), adj. 正常 (な)
normal.

seijuku shita, adj. 成熟した
mature; ripe.

seika, n. 成果 product; result
(of one's efforts).

seikai, n. 正解 correct
answer.

seikaku, n. 性格 personality;
disposition.

seikaku (na), adj. 正確 (な)
accurate; exact.

seikatsu, n. 生活 life;
livelihood.

seikatsuhi, n. 生活費 cost of
living.

seikatsu-suijun, n. 生活水
準 living standard.

seikei, n. 生計 livelihood;
living.

seikei(-shujutsu), n. 整形
(手術) plastic surgery;
orthopedic surgery.

seiketsu (na), adj. 清潔 (な)
clean.

seiki, n. 世紀 century;
jūnana-seiki seventeenth
century.

seiki, n. 性器 sex organ.

seikō, n. 成功 success.

seikō, n. 性交 sexual
intercourse.

seikō suru, vb. 成功する
succeed.

seiku, n. 成句 idiomatic
expression.

seikyōiku, n. 性教育 sex
education.

seikyū, n. 請求 claim;
demand; request.

seikyūsho, n. 請求書 bill;

invoice; written application.

seimei, n. 姓名 full name.

seimei, n. 生命 life.

seimeihoken, n. 生命保険 life insurance;

seimeihoken o kakeru insure someone's life.

seimitsu (na), adj. 精密 (な) 1. detailed; precise. 2. thorough.

seinan, n. 西南 southwest.

seinaru, adj. 聖なる holy; sacred.

seinen, n. 成年 adulthood;

seinen ni tassuru come of age.

seinen, n. 青年 young adult.

seinengappi, n. 生年月日 date of birth.

seinō, n. 性能 performance; efficiency.

seireki, n. 西暦 Anno Domini; A.D. (Christian calendar).

seiretsu suru, vb. 正列する form a line.

seiri, n. 生理 1. physiology. 2. menstruation.

seiri suru, vb. 整理する 1. arrange; consolidate; put in order. 2. retrench.

seiritsu suru, vb. 成立する be formed; be created; be established.

seiryō-inryōsui, n. 清涼飲料水 soft drink.

seiryoku, n. 勢力 power; influence.

seiryoku, n. 精力 energy; vigor; vitality.

seiryoku-teki (na), adj. 精力的 (な) energetic; vigorous.

seisabetsu, n. 性差別 sexual discrimination.

seisaku suru, vb. 制作する manufacture; make; produce.

seisan, n. 生産 production.

seisan suru, vb. 清算する settle (an account); clear a debt.

seisei dōdō to, adv. 正々堂々と aboveboard; openly; fairly and squarely.

seiseki, n. 成績 1. achievement; result; showing. 2. school grades.

seishiki (na, no), adj. 正式 (な、の) 1. formal. 2. official.

seishin, n. 精神 mind; soul; spirit.

seishinbyō, n. 精神病 mental illness.

seishinka, n. 精神科 psychiatry.

seishin-teki (na), adj. 精神的 (な) spiritual; mental.

seishitsu, n. 性質 nature; character.

seisho, n. 聖書 Bible.

seishokusha, n. 聖職者 priest; clergyman.

seishōnen, n. 青少年 juveniles; young people.

seishun, n. 青春 adolescence; youth.

seitai, n. 声帯 vocal cords.

seitaigaku, n. 生態学 ecology.

sei-teki (na), adj. 性的 (な) sexual; **sei-teki na iyagarase** sexual harassment.

seiten, n. 晴天 fair weather.

seito, n. 生徒 pupil; student.

seitō (na, no), adj. 正当 (な、の) 1. orthodox; legitimate. 2. just.

seiton suru, vb. 整頓する organize; tidy up.

seiyaku, n. 制約 restriction.

seiyō, n. 西洋 the West.

seiyō suru, vb. 静養する rest; recuperate.

seiza, n. 星座 constellation.

seiza, n. 正座 traditional

Japanese way of sitting on tatami (e.g., for tea ceremony).

seizei, adv. せいぜい at best; at most.

seizō, n. 製造 manufacture; production.

seizon, n. 生存 1. existence. 2. survival.

seizō suru, vb. 製造する manufacture; produce.

sekai, n. 世界 world; society.

seken, n. 世間 1. society. 2. other people. 3. way of the world.

sekenbanashi, n. 世間話 gossip; small talk.

seki, n. 籍 1. family register. 2. membership.

seki, n. 席 1. seat; **seki ni tsuku** take a seat. 2. occasion.

seki, n. 咳 cough.

sekidō, n. 赤道 equator.

sekidome, n. 咳止め cough medicine.

sekijūji, n. 赤十字 Red Cross.

sekinin, n. 責任 responsibility; **sekinin o toru** take responsibility.

sekininsha, n. 責任者 person in charge.

sekitan, n. 石炭 coal.

sekiyu, n. 石油 petroleum; oil; kerosene.

sekiyu-sutōbu, n. 石油ストーブ kerosene heater.

sekkachi (na), adj. せっかち (な) headlong; impatient; impetuous.

sekkaku, adv. せっかく 1. at great pains. 2. kindly.

sekkei, n. 設計 design; plan.

sekken, n. せっけん soap.

sekki, n. 石器 1. stoneware. 2. stone tool.

sekkin suru, vb. 接近する approach.

sekkō, n. 石膏 plaster.

sekkyō, n. 説教 admonishment; preaching; sermon.

sekkyoku-teki (na), adj. 積極的 (な) 1. aggressive. 2. positive.

sekkyō suru, vb. 説教する admonish; preach.

semai, adj. 狭い narrow; small.

semaru, vb. 迫る 1. draw near; come close. 2. urge.

semeru, vb. 責める 1. accuse; reproach. 2. torment.

semete, adv. せめて at least.

semi, n. 蟬 cicada.

sen, n. 線 1. line; **sen o hiku** draw a line. 2. tranportation line or track.

sen, n. 栓 bottle cap; cork; stopper.

sen, n. 千 thousand.

senaka, n. 背中 back (body).

senbei, n. せんべい rice cracker.

senbetsu, n. せんべつ farewell present.

senchaku jun ni, adv. 先着順に on a first-come, first-served basis.

senchō, n. 船長 captain (ship).

senden, n. 宣伝 advertisement; propaganda; publicity.

sendo, n. 鮮度 freshness.

sengen, n. 宣言 proclamation; declaration.

sengetsu, n., adv. 先月 last month.

sengo, n. 戦後 postwar period.

sen'i, n. 繊維 fiber.

sen'in, n. 船員 sailor; seaman; crew.

senjitsu, n., adv. 先日 yesterday; the other day.

senkō, n. 線香 incense.

senkoku, n. 宣告 sentence; judgment.

senkō suru, vb. 専攻する major; specialize; **bijinesu o senkō suru** major in business.

senkyo, n. 選挙 election.

senkyō, n. 宣教 missionary work.

senmei (na), n. 鮮明 (な) bright; clear; vivid.

senmenjo, n. 洗面所 restroom; bathroom.

senmon, n. 専門 specialty.

sen'nen suru, vb. 専念する concentrate; devote oneself to; focus on.

sen'nin (no), adj. 専任 (の) full-time.

sen'nō suru, vb. 洗脳する brainwash.

sen'nuki, n. 栓抜き corkscrew; bottle opener.

sen'nyūkan, n. 先入感 1. prejudice; preconception. 2. bias.

senobi suru, vb. 背伸びする stretch; stand on tiptoe.

senpai, n. 先輩 senior; elder; predecessor.

senpaku, n. 船舶 ship.

senpō, n. 先方 other person or party.

senpūki, n. 扇風機 electric fan.

senro, n. 線路 track; rail (train).

senryaku, n. 戦略 strategy; tactics.

sensai (na), adj. 繊細 (な) delicate; fragile; sensitive.

sensei, n. 先生 1. teacher; master. 2. doctor (M.D.). 3. title used when speaking of or to members of certain professions (lawyers, politicians).

sensha, n. 戦車 tank

(military vehicle).

senshi, n. 戦死 death in action.

senshinkoku, n. 先進国 advanced nation.

senshitsu, n. 船室 cabin; stateroom.

senshoku, n. 染色 dyeing.

senshu, n. 選手 athlete; athletic team member.

senshū, n., adv. 先週 last week.

senshuken, n. 選手権 championship.

senshutsu suru, vb. 選出する elect.

sensō, n. 戦争 battle; war.

sensu, n. 扇子 folding fan.

sensuikan, n. 潜水艦 submarine.

sentakuki, n. 洗濯機 washing machine.

sentaku suru, vb. 選択する choose; select.

sentan, n. 先端 1. tip; end. 2. vanguard.

sentan o iku, vb. 先端を行く be a front runner.

senten-teki (na), adj. 先天的 (な) congenital; inherent.

sentō, n. 先頭 lead; first place; **sentō ni tatsu** be in the lead.

sen'yō (no), adj. 専用 (の) exclusive; private.

senzai, n. 洗剤 detergent.

senzen, n. 戦前 prewar period.

senzo, n. 先祖 ancestor.

senzoku, n. 専属 exclusive contract.

seou, vb. 背負う 1. carry on one's back. 2. shoulder (burden).

seppuku, n. 切腹 Japanese ritual suicide; harakiri.

serifu, n. 台詞 lines (stage play).

sessei, n. 節制 temperance;

self-control.

sesse to, *adv.* せっせと diligently; industriously.

sesshi, *n.* 摂氏 Celsius; **sesshi sanjūnido** thirty-two degrees Celsius.

sesshoku suru, *vb.* 接触する 1. touch. 2. contact.

sessuru, *vb.* 接する 1. border on; adjoin. 2. encounter.

setake, *n.* 背丈 height.

setchakuzai, *n.* 接着剤 glue.

setchi suru, *vb.* 設置する install; set up.

setogiwa, *n.* 瀬戸際 1. last moment; **setogiwa de** at the last moment. 2. brink; **setogiwa ni tatsu** be on the brink of.

setomono, *n.* 瀬戸物 china; pottery.

setsu, *n.* 説 theory; opinion.

setsubi, *n.* 設備 equipment; facility.

setsudan suru, *vb.* 切断する cut; sever.

setsujitsu (na), *adj.* 切実 (な) keen; acute; sincere.

setsumei suru, *vb.* 説明する explain; illustrate.

setsuritsu suru, *vb.* 設立する establish; found.

setsuyaku suru, *vb.* 節約する economize; save.

setsuzoku, *n.* 接続 connection.

setsuzokushi, *n.* 接続詞 conjunction (grammar).

setsuzoku suru, *vb.* 接続する join; connect.

settei suru, *vb.* 設定する set up.

settōgo, *n.* 接頭語 prefix (grammar).

settoku, *n.* 説得 persuasion.

sewa, *n.* 世話 1. care; **sewa o suru** take care of (person). 2. inconvenience; trouble; **sewa o kakeru**

cause inconvenience or trouble.

shaberu, *vb.* しゃべる talk; chat; chatter.

shaburu, *vb.* しゃぶる suck.

shachō, *n.* 社長 company president.

shagamu, *vb.* しゃがむ squat.

shagaregoe, *n.* しゃがれ声 husky or hoarse voice.

sha'in, *n.* 社員 employee.

shaka, *n.* 釈迦 Buddha.

shakai, *n.* 社会 society.

shakaigaku, *n.* 社会学 sociology.

shakkin, *n.* 借金 debt; **shakkin o suru** incur a debt.

shakkuri, *n.* しゃっくり hiccup.

shako, *n.* 車庫 garage.

shaku (na, no), *adj.* 癪 (な、の) annoying; offensive.

shakuya, *n.* 借家 rented house.

shamen, *n.* 斜面 slope.

shamisen, *n.* 三味線 Japanese string instrument.

shamoji, *n.* しゃもじ rice ladle.

share, *n.* しゃれ joke.

sharin, *n.* 車輪 wheel.

sharyō, *n.* 車輌 vehicle.

shasen, *n.* 斜線 oblique line.

shashin, *n.* 写真 photograph; **shashin o toru** take a photograph.

shashō, *n.* 車掌 bus or train conductor.

shatai, *n.* 車体 body (car).

shatsu, *n.* シャツ (E.) shirt.

shi, *n.* 四 four.

shi, *n.* 死 death.

shi, *n.* 詩 poem.

shi, *n.* 市 city.

-shi 氏 Mr.; Mrs.; Ms.

shiageru, *vb.* 仕上げる complete; finish.

shiai, *n.* 試合 competition; game; match.

shiatsu, *n.* 指圧 Japanese massage using finger pressure.

shiawase (na), *adj.* 幸せ (な) happy.

shibafu, *n.* 芝生 lawn; turf.

shibai, *n.* 芝居 drama; play.

shibaraku, *adv.* 暫く 1. for a while. 2. for a long time.

shibaru, *vb.* 縛る tie; bind.

shiba-shiba, *adv.* しばしば frequently.

shibireru, *vb.* 痺れる become paralyzed; be numbed.

shibō, *n.* 死亡 death.

shibō, *n.* 脂肪 fat.

shibomu, *vb.* しぼむ wither away; fade.

shiboru, *vb.* 絞る 1. wring. 2. narrow down.

shibui, *adj.* 渋い 1. astringent. 2. chic. 3. sullen.

shibutoi, *adj.* しぶとい persistent; stubborn.

shichi, *n.* 七 seven.

shichigatsu, *n.* 七月 July.

shichijū, *n.* 七十 seventy.

shichimenchō, *n.* 七面鳥 turkey.

shichō, *n.* 市長 mayor.

shichō, *n.* 市庁 city office.

shidai ni, *adv.* 次第に gradually; by and by.

shidō, *n.* 指導 guidance; direction; advice.

shien, *n.* 支援 support.

shigaidenwa, *n.* 市外電話 long-distance call.

shigaisen, *n.* 紫外線 ultraviolet ray.

shigamitsuku, *vb.* しがみ付く cling to.

shigatsu, *n.* 四月 April.

shigeki, *n.* 刺激 stimulation.

shigemi, *n.* 繁み bush.

shigen, *n.* 資源 resources.

shigeru, *vb.* 繁る grow luxuriant.

shigoto, *n.* 仕事 job; work.

shigoto o suru, *vb.* 仕事をする work.

shigusa, *n.* しぐさ gesture; mannerism.

shigyōshiki, *n.* 始業式 opening ceremony.

shihai suru, *vb.* 支配する control; rule.

shihatsu, *n.* 始発 first train or bus.

shihei, *n.* 紙幣 paper money; bank note.

shihō, *n.* 四方 all directions.

shihonkin, *n.* 資本金 capital.

shi'in (shion), *n.* 子音 consonant.

shi'ireru, *vb.* 仕入れる purchase; stock.

shi'itake, *n.* しいたけ Japanese mushroom.

shijin, *n.* 詩人 poet.

shiji suru, *vb.* 支持する support.

shiji suru, *vb.* 指示する direct; indicate.

shijō, *n.* 市場 market.

shijū, *adv.* 始終 always; constantly.

shijūsō, *n.* 四重奏 quartet.

shika, *n.* 歯科 dentistry; dental clinic.

shika, *n.* 鹿 deer.

-shika しか only; **mizu-shika nomanai** drink only water.

shikai, *n.* 歯科医 dentist.

shikai(sha), *n.* 司会(者) 1. chairperson. 2. master of ceremonies.

shikaku, *n.* 資格 credentials; qualifications.

shikaku, *n.* 四角 square; rectangle.

shikameru, *vb.* しかめる

(kao o) shikameru frown.

shikamo adv. しかも on top of that; in addition; besides.

shikarareru, vb. 叱られる get scolded.

shikaru, vb. 叱る scold.

shikashi, conj. しかし however; but.

shikata, n. 仕方 way; method; **unten no shikata** the way to drive.

shikata ga nai, vb. 仕方がない 1. cannot be helped. 2. cannot help (doing).

shikei, n. 死刑 death penalty.

shiken, n. 試験 examination; test.

shiki, n. 式 1. ceremony; rite.

shiki, n. 四季 the four seasons.

shiki, n. 指揮 conducting; direction; command.

shikichi, n. 敷地 location; site.

shikijō, n. 式場 hall where ceremonies are held.

shikiri ni, adv. しきりに 1. often; frequently. 2. eagerly.

shikiru, vb. 仕切る divide; partition.

shikitari, n. しきたり convention; tradition; custom.

shikiten, n. 式典 ceremony.

shikkaku, n. 失格 elimination; disqualification.

shikkari, adv. しっかり firmly; tightly; strongly.

shikkari shita, adj. しっかりした 1. firm; stable. 2. reliable.

shikkari suru, vb. しっかりする 1. become strong. 2. get a hold on oneself.

shikke, n. 湿気 dampness; humidity.

shikomu, vb. 仕込む 1. train. 2. stock (merchandise).

shikō suru, vb. 思考する think; ponder.

shikō suru, vb. 施行する enact; enforce; carry out.

shiku, n. 詩句 verse.

shiku, vb. 敷く 1. lay out; spread. 2. enact.

shikujiri, n. しくじり blunder; mistake.

shikumi, n. 仕組み mechanism; device.

shikyū, n. 子宮 uterus; womb.

shikyū suru, vb. 支給する supply; provide.

shima, n. 島 island.

shima, n. 縞 stripe.

shimai, n. 姉妹 sisters.

shimaru, vb. 閉まる close; shut.

shimatsu suru, vb. 始末する 1. settle; dispose of. 2. clear.

shimatta, interj. しまった Damn!

shimau, vb. 仕舞う 1. put away. 2. close.

-shimau, vb. しまう finish (doing something); **tabeteshimau** finish eating (something).

shimei, n. 氏名 full name.

shimei suru, vb. 指名する appoint; nominate.

shimekiribi, n. 締め切り日 closing date; deadline.

shimeppoi, adj. 湿っぽい 1. damp; humid. 2. depressing.

shimeru, vb. 閉める close; shut.

shimeru, vb. 締める fasten (seat belt); tie (necktie); strangle; tighten.

shimesu, vb. 示す show; point out.

shimi, n. 染み stain.

shimo, n. 霜 frost.

shimon, n. 指紋 fingerprint.

shin, n. 芯 core; heart; center.

shin (no), adj. 真 (の) true; genuine; real.

shin- 新 new; **shinsekai** New World.

shina, n. 品 1. goods. 2. quality.

shinamono, n. 品物 1. merchandise. 2. article.

shinaosu, vb. しなおす do over again; try again.

shinayaka (na), adj. しなやか (な) pliant; supple.

shinbō, n. 辛抱 endurance; patience.

shinbōzuyoi, adj. 辛抱強い patient.

shinbun, n. 新聞 newspaper.

shinchō, n. 身長 a person's height.

shinchū, n. 心中 innermost thoughts.

shindai, n. 寝台 bed.

shindan, n. 診断 diagnosis.

shindo, n. 深度 depth (water).

shingaku, n. 神学 theology.

shingaku, n. 進学 entrance into a school of a higher level (e.g., university from high school).

shingō, n. 信号 traffic light; signal.

shingu, n. 寝具 futon; bedding.

shinin, n. 死人 dead person.

shinja, n. 信者 religious believer; member of a religious sect.

shinjin, n. 新人 newcomer.

shinjinbukai, adj. 信心深い devout.

shinjirarenai, adj. 信じられない unbelievable.

shinjitsu, n. 真実 fact; truth.

shinju, n. 真珠 pearl.

shinka, n. 進化 progress.

shinkansen, n. 新幹線 bullet train.

shinkaron, n. 進化論 theory of evolution.

shinkei, n. 神経 nerve (anatomy).

shinkeishitsu (na), adj. 神経質 (な) nervous; high-strung.

shinken (na), adj. 真剣 (な) earnest; sincere.

shinkiroku, n. 新記録 new record (in competition).

shinkō, n. 信仰 belief; religion.

shinkoku (na), adj. 深刻 (な) serious; grave.

shinkokyū, n. 深呼吸 deep breathing.

shinkon, n. 新婚 newlywed.

shinkonryokō, n. 新婚旅行 honeymoon.

shinkū, n. 真空 vacuum.

shinkyō, n. 心境 mind; feeling.

shinmitsu (na), adj. 親密 (な) intimate; close.

shin'nen, n. 新年 new year; **Shin'nen akemashite omedetō gozaimasu.** Happy New Year!

shin'nyū, n. 侵入 invasion.

shin'nyū-sei, n. 新入生 new student; freshman.

shinobu, vb. 忍ぶ endure.

shinpai suru, vb. 心配する be anxious; worry.

shinpan, n. 審判 refereeing; judgment.

shinpo, n. 進歩 progress.

shinpu, n. 神父 Christian priest.

shinrai suru, vb. 信頼する trust; rely on.

shinri, n. 真理 truth.

shinri, n. 心理 state of mind.

shinrigaku, n. 心理学 psychology.

shinrin, *n.* 森林 forest; woods.

shinro, *n.* 進路 course; route.

shinrui, *n.* 親類 relative.

shinryō, *n.* 診療 medical treatment.

shinsa, *n.* 審査 screening; examination.

shinsatsu, *n.* 診察 medical examination.

shinseki, *n.* 親戚 relative.

shinsen (na), *adj.* 新鮮 (な) fresh.

shinsetsu (na), *adj.* 親切 (な) kind.

shinshi, *n.* 紳士 gentleman.

shinshiki, *n.* 新式 new model; new style; new technique.

shinshitsu, *n.* 寝室 bedroom.

shinshutsu suru, *vb.* 進出する enter; branch out into; progress.

shintakuginkō, *n.* 信託銀行 trust bank.

shinto, *n.* 信徒 member of a religious organization.

shintō, *n.* 神道 Japanese religion based on animism and ancestor worship.

shinu, *vb.* 死ぬ die.

shinwa, *n.* 神話 mythology.

shin'yakuseisho, *n.* 新約聖書 New Testament.

shin'yō, *n.* 信用 trust; faith.

shin'yū, *n.* 親友 close friend.

shinzō, *n.* 心臓 heart.

shinzōhossa, *n.* 心臓発作 heart attack.

shio, *n.* 塩 salt.

shio, *n.* 潮 1. tide. 2. sea water.

shioreru, *vb.* しおれる 1. wilt; wither; droop. 2. feel depressed.

shiori, *n.* しおり 1. bookmark. 2. guidebook.

shippai suru, *vb.* 失敗する make a mistake; fail.

shippo, *n.* しっぽ tail.

shippu, *n.* 湿布 compress.

shiraberu, *vb.* 調べる 1. investigate; check. 2. consult; look up.

shiraga, *n.* 白髪 gray hair; white hair.

shirase, *n.* 知らせ notification; news.

shiraseru, *vb.* 知らせる notify; inform.

shiren, *n.* 試練 trial; ordeal.

shiri, *n.* 尻 1. buttocks. 2. bottom.

shiriau, *vb.* 知り合う meet; get acquainted.

shirigomi suru, *vb.* 尻込みする hesitate; shy away from.

shiritsu (no), *adj.* 市立 (の) municipal.

shiritsu (no), *adj.* 私立 (の) private.

shirizokeru, *vb.* 退ける 1. chase away; repel. 2. reject.

shirizoku, *vb.* 退く retreat.

shiro, *n.* 城 castle.

shiroi, *adj.* 白い white.

shiromi, *n.* 白身 white meat or fish.

shirōto, *n.* 素人 amateur.

shiru, *n.* 汁 1. soup. 2. juice.

shiru, *vb.* 知る know.

shirushi, *n.* 印 sign; symbol; indication.

shiryō, *n.* 資料 data; material.

shiryoku, *n.* 視力 eyesight.

shisan, *n.* 資産 assets.

shisei, *n.* 姿勢 posture; stance.

shiseikatsu, *n.* 私生活 private life.

shisen, *n.* 視線 gaze.

shisetsu, *n.* 施設 1. equipment. 2. facility; institution.

shisha, *n.* 死者 deceased.

shishō, *n.* 支障 hindrance;
  shishō o kitasu hinder.

shishobako, *n.* 私書箱 post
  office box.

shishū, *n.* 刺しゅう
  embroidery.

shishunki, *n.* 思春期
  adolescence; puberty.

shisō, *n.* 思想 thought; idea.

shisokonau, *vb.* しそこなう
  fail; make a mistake.

shison, *n.* 子孫 descendant.

shisshin suru, *vb.* 失神する
  faint.

shisso (na), *adj.* 質素 (な) 1.
  plain; simple. 2. frugal.

shisū, *n.* 指数 index;
  keizaishisū economic
  index.

shita, *n.* 舌 tongue.

shita, *n.* 下 bottom.

shitagatte, *adv.* 従って
  therefore.

shitagau, *vb.* 従う obey;
  follow.

shitagi, *n.* 下着 underwear.

shitai, *n.* 死体 dead body.

shitaku, *n.* 支度
  preparation.

shitamachi, *n.* 下町
  downtown.

shitamawaru, *vb.* 下回る be
  less than.

shita ni, *adv.* 下に below;
  beneath; under.

shitashii, *adj.* 親しい
  intimate; friendly.

shitashimu, *vb.* 親しむ
  become intimate with; make
  friends with.

shitau, *vb.* 慕う 1. adore. 2.
  yearn for.

shitei suru, *vb.* 指定する
  appoint; designate.

shiteki suru, *vb.* 指摘する
  point out.

shiten, *n.* 支店 branch
  (office, store).

shiten, *n.* 視点 viewpoint.

shitogeru, *vb.* し遂げる
  accomplish; complete.

shitsu, *n.* 質 quality.

-shitsu 室 room;
  kaigishitsu conference
  room.

shitsubō suru, *vb.* 失望する
  be disappointed.

shitsudo, *n.* 湿度 humidity.

shitsugai, *n.* 室外 outdoors.

shitsugyō, *n.* 失業
  unemployment.

shitsukeru, *vb.* 躾ける 1.
  train. 2. teach manners.

shitsu(k)koi, *adj.* しつ(つ)
  こい persistent; obstinate.

shitsumon, *n.* 質問
  question.

shitsunai, *n.* 室内 indoors.

shitsurei (na), *adj.* 失礼 (な)
  rude; discourteous.

shitsurei (shimasu), *vb.* 失
  礼 (します) 1. Excuse me.
  2. I must be going.

shitsurei suru, *vb.* 失礼する
  excuse oneself.

shitto, *n.* 嫉妬 jealousy.

shiwa, *n.* しわ wrinkle.

shiyakusho, *n.* 市役所 city
  office; city hall.

shiyō, *n.* 使用 use;
  employment.

shiyō suru, *vb.* 使用する
  use.

shizen, *n.* 自然 nature.

shizen (na, no), *adj.* 自然
  (な、の) natural;
  spontaneous; **shizen-
  shokuhin** natural foods.

shizuka (na), *adj.* 静か (な)
  1. quiet; silent. 2. calm.

shizumaru, *vb.* 静まる
  become calm; become quiet.

shizumu, *vb.* 沈む 1. set
  (sun, moon). 2. sink. 3.
  feel depressed.

shōbai, *n.* 商売 business;
  commerce.

shō, *n.* 章 chapter.

shōben, *n.* 小便 urine.

shōbō, *n.* 消防 firefighting.

shōbōshi, *n.* 消防士 firefighter.

shōbōsho, *n.* 消防署 firehouse.

shōbu, *n.* 勝負 game; fight; match.

shobun suru, *vb.* 処分する 1. get rid of; clear away. 2. expel; punish.

shochi suru, *vb.* 処置する deal with; treat.

shōchi suru, *vb.* 承知する 1. accept; consent. 2. understand.

shochō, *n.* 所長 director.

shodō, *n.* 書道 calligraphy (using a brush).

shōdoku, *n.* 消毒 sterilization.

shō-ene, *n.* 省エネ energy conservation.

shōga, *n.* 生姜 ginger.

shōgai, *n.* 障害 obstacle.

shōgai, *n.* 生涯 life; career.

shōgakkō, *n.* 小学校 elementary school.

shōgakukin, *n.* 奨学金 fellowship; scholarship; stipend.

shōgatsu, *n.* 正月 New Year; New Year's Day.

shōgeki, *n.* 衝撃 impact; shock.

shōgen suru, *vb.* 証言する testify; give evidence.

shogeru, *vb.* しょげる be dejected; be depressed.

shōgi, *n.* 将棋 Japanese chess.

shōgo, *n.* 正午 noon.

shōgun, *n.* 将軍 general; head of samurai government.

shōgyō, *n.* 商業 business; commerce.

shōhisha, *n.* 消費者 consumer.

shōhizei, *n.* 消費税 sales tax.

shōhin, *n.* 商品 goods; merchandise.

shōhyō, *n.* 商標 trademark.

shōji, *n.* 障子 Japanese paper and wood door or screen.

shōjiki (na), *adj.* 正直 (な) honest.

shōjiru, *vb.* 生じる 1. arise; occur. 2. bring about.

shojo, *n.* 処女 virgin.

shōjo, *n.* 少女 girl.

shōjō, *n.* 症状 1. condition of a patient. 2. symptom.

shojun, *n.* 初旬 first ten days of a month.

shoka, *n.* 初夏 early summer.

shōka, *n.* 消火 the extinguishing of a fire.

shōka, *n.* 消化 digestion (food and information).

shōkaki, *n.* 消火器 fire extinguisher.

shōkai suru, *vb.* 紹介する introduce.

shōka suru, *vb.* 消化する digest (food and information).

shōken, *n.* 証券 stocks; securities.

shoki, *n.* 書記 secretary; clerk.

shoki, *n.* 初期 beginning; initial stage.

shōki, *n.* 正気 sanity.

shōkin, *n.* 賞金 cash prize.

shokki, *n.* 食器 tableware (dishes; cups; flatware; chopsticks).

shokkidana, *n.* 食器棚 cupboard.

shōko, *n.* 証拠 evidence; proof; testimony.

shokuba, *n.* 職場 workplace.

shokubutsu, *n.* 植物 plant; vegetation.

shokudō, *n.* 食堂 dining

room; restaurant.

shokugyō, n. 職業 occupation; profession.

shokuji, n. 食事 meal.

shokuji o suru, vb. 食事をする dine.

shokunin, n. 職人 craftsperson; artisan.

shokupan, n. 食パン bread.

shokuryō(hin), n. 食料(品) food.

shokutaku, n. 食卓 dining table.

shokuyō (no), adj. 食用 (の) edible.

shokuyoku, n. 食欲 appetite; **shokuyoku ga aru** have an appetite.

shōkyoku-teki (na), adj. 消極的 (な) 1. passive. 2. negative.

shokyū, n. 初級 beginners' level.

shomei, n. 署名 signature.

shōmei, n. 照明 lighting.

shōmei, n. 証明 proof; identification.

shōmen, n. 正面 front.

shōmō suru, vb. 消耗する 1. consume. 2. use up; deplete.

shomotsu, n. 書物 book.

shonbori suru, vb. しょんぼりする be disheartened; be dejected.

shōnen, n. 少年 boy.

~~shonichi,~~ n. 初日 opening day; first day.

shōnika, n. 小児科 pediatrics.

shōnimahi, n. 小児麻痺 polio.

shōnin, n. 承認 approval; recognition; sanction.

shōnin, n. 証人 witness.

shōnin suru, vb. 承認する approve; recognize; sanction.

shōrai, n. 将来 future;

shōrai ga aru have a (bright) future.

shōri, n. 勝利 victory.

shori suru, vb. 処理する 1. handle; treat. 2. get rid of; dispose of.

shorui, n. 書類 document.

shōryaku suru, vb. 省略する abbreviate; omit.

shōryō (no), adj. 少量 (の) a bit of; a little.

shosai, n. 書斎 1. library (home). 2. study.

shoseki, n. 書籍 book.

shōsetsu, n. 小説 novel.

shoshiki, n. 書式 form; format (written).

shoshin, n. 初診 first visit to a doctor.

shōshin, n. 昇進 promotion.

shoshinsha, n. 初心者 beginner; novice.

shōsho, n. 証書 1. written instrument. 2. certificate.

shōshō 少々 1. adv. a bit; a little; **shōshō takai** a bit expensive. 2. a moment; **Shōshō omachi kudasai.** Please wait a moment.

shōsū, n. 少数 1. small number; minority. 2. decimal.

shōtai, n. 正体 1. true nature or self; **shōtai o arawasu** reveal one's true nature. 2. consciousness.

~~shōtai,~~ n. 招待 invitation.

shōtaijō, n. 招待状 invitation (letter, card); **shōtaijō o dasu** send invitations.

shotaimen, n. 初対面 first meeting.

shōtchū, adv. しょっちゅう always; constantly.

shoten, n. 書店 1. bookstore. 2. publishing company.

shōten, n. 焦点 focus; central issue; **(ni) shōten o**

awaseru focus (on).

shotō, *n.* 諸島 archipelago; islands.

shotoku, *n.* 所得 income.

shōtotsu suru, *vb.* 衝突する 1. crash; collide. 2. conflict.

shōyu, *n.* しょう油 soy sauce.

shoyū suru, *vb.* 所有する possess.

shozai, *n.* 所在 location; whereabouts.

shōzōga, *n.* 肖像画 portrait.

shozoku suru, *vb.* 所属する belong to.

shu, *n.* 主 1. the Lord (God). 2. master; lord.

shu, *n.* 種 species.

shū, *n.* 週 week; **konshū** this week.

shū, *n.* 州 province; state; **Yuta-shū** state of Utah.

shūchakueki, *n.* 終着駅 terminal (railroad).

shūchi (no), *adj.* 周知 (の) well-known.

shuchō suru, *vb.* 主張する assert; claim.

shūchū suru, *vb.* 集中する concentrate.

shudai, *n.* 主題 theme; topic.

shudan, *n.* 手段 means; way.

shūdan, *n.* 集団 group.

shūeki, *n.* 収益 revenue; profit.

shuen suru, *vb.* 主演する play a title role.

shufu, *n.* 主婦 housewife.

shūgakuryokō, *n.* 修学旅行 school trip.

shugei, *n.* 手芸 handicraft.

shugi, *n.* 主義 belief; ism; principle.

shugo, *n.* 主語 subject (grammar).

shūgō suru, *vb.* 集合する gather; congregate.

shugyō, *n.* 修業 1. training.

2. apprenticeship.

shūgyō, *n.* 終業 closing.

shūha, *n.* 宗派 religious sect.

shūhasū, *n.* 周波数 frequency.

shūhen, *n.* 周辺 1. neighborhood; vicinity. 2. circumference.

shūji, *n.* 習字 calligraphy.

shuji'i, *n.* 主治医 attending physician.

shujin, *n.* 主人 1. husband. 2. owner. 3. master; mistress.

shujinkō, *n.* 主人公 protagonist; hero; heroine.

shūjitsu, *n.* 週日 weekday.

shujutsu suru, *vb.* 手術する perform surgery.

shūkai, *n.* 集会 meeting.

shūkaku, *n.* 収穫 harvest; crop.

shūkan, *n.* 習慣 custom; habit.

-shūkan 週間 week(s); **nishūkan** two weeks.

shūkanshi, *n.* 週刊紙 weekly magazine.

shūketsu suru, *vb.* 終結する end.

shūki, *n.* 臭気 odor.

shūkin, *n.* 集金 bill collection.

shūki-teki (na), *adj.* 周期的 (な) cyclical; periodic.

shukka suru, *vb.* 出荷する ship; send.

shukketsu, *n.* 出血 bleeding.

shukkin suru, *vb.* 出勤する go to work.

shukkoku, *n.* 出国 departure from a country.

shukudai, *n.* 宿題 homework; assignment.

shukuhai, *n.* 祝杯 toast; celebration; **shukuhai o ageru** drink a toast.

shukuhaku suru, *vb.* 宿泊

する stay (hotel).

shukujitsu, n. 祝日 holiday.

shukusha, n. 宿舎 lodging.

shukushō, n. 縮小 reduction; cutback.

shūkyō, n. 宗教 religion.

shūkyū, n. 週休 regular days off.

shūmai, n. シューマイ steamed Chinese dumpling.

shūmatsu, n. 週末 weekend.

shumi, n. 趣味 1. hobby; diversion. 2. taste.

shūnen, n. 周年 anniversary.

shuniku, n. 朱肉 red ink used for seals.

shunin, n. 主任 director; head.

shūnin suru, vb. 就任する be appointed; be inaugurated.

shunkan-teki ni, adv. 瞬間的に momentarily.

shunō, n. 首脳 leader; top executive.

shūnyū, n. 収入 income.

shuppan, n. 出版 publication.

shuppan suru, vb. 出版する publish.

shuppatsu suru, vb. 出発する depart; start out.

shūri suru, vb. 修理する repair.

shurui, n. 種類 type; kind.

shūryō, n. 終了 ending; termination.

shusai suru, vb. 主催する sponsor.

shūsei suru, vb. 修正する correct; revise.

shūsekikairo, n. 集積回路 integrated circuit.

shūsen, n. 終戦 termination of a war.

shūshi始, n. 終始 1. n. beginning and ending. 2. adv. from

beginning to end; all the while.

shushō, n. 首相 prime minister.

shushoku, n. 主食 staple food.

shūshū suru, vb. 収集する collect; gather.

shussan suru, vb. 出産する give birth.

shusse, n. 出世 success; promotion; **shusse suru** succeed.

shusseki, n. 出席 attendance; **shusseki o toru** take attendance.

shusseki suru, vb. 出席する attend; be present.

shussha suru, vb. 出社する go to one's office.

shusshi, n. 出資 investment.

shusshin, n. 出身 1. birthplace; hometown. 2. former affiliation; alma mater.

shutchō, n. 出張 business trip.

shūten, n. 終点 last stop.

shuto, n. 首都 capital city.

shūto, n. しゅうと father-in-law.

shutoku suru, vb. 取得する acquire; obtain.

shūtome, n. 姑 mother-in-law.

shutsuen suru, vb. 出演する act (in a film or play).

shutsugen suru, vb. 出現する appear.

shutsujō suru, vb. 出場する participate; enter (a competition).

shutsuryoku, n. 出力 output.

shuwa, n. 手話 sign language.

shuyaku, n. 主役 leading

role.

shuyō (na), adj. 主要 (な) chief; major.

shūyō suru, vb. 収容する accommodate; take in.

shuzai suru, vb. 取材する collect information; do research.

shuzoku, n. 種族 race; tribe.

shūzoku, n. 習俗 custom.

sō, n. 層 1. layer. 2. class.

sō そう 1. adj. so. 2. adv. yes; so; in that way.

-sō そう seem; I hear (that); **yasashisō** seems easy.

soba, n. そば buckwheat; buckwheat noodles.

soba, n. 側 neighborhood; vicinity.

sōba, n. 相場 market; market price.

sobakasu, n. そばかす freckles.

soba ni 側に 1. prep. beside. 2. adv. close to; in the neighborhood of.

sōbetsukai, n. 送別会 farewell party.

sōbi, n. 装備 equipment.

sobieto, n. ソビエト Soviet Union; USSR.

sobo, n. 祖母 grandmother.

soboku (na), adj. 素朴 (な) simple; naive; unpretentious.

sōchi, n. 装置 equipment; device.

sochira そちら 1. pron. you. 2. n. over there.

-sō da そうだ I hear (that); **Ame ga furusō da.** I hear that it's going to rain.

sodachi, n. 育ち upbringing.

sōdan, n. 相談 advice; consultation.

sodateru, vb. 育てる raise; rear (child, plant, etc.).

sodatsu, vb. 育つ grow up; be brought up.

sode, n. 袖 sleeve.

soeru, vb. 添える attach to.

sofu, n. 祖父 grandfather.

sōgankyō, n. 双眼鏡 binoculars.

sōgen, n. 草原 prairie.

sōgi, n. 葬儀 funeral.

sōgo 相互 1. pron. each other; one another. 2. n. mutuality.

sōgō, n. 総合 total; whole.

sōgo no, adj. 相互の mutual; reciprocal.

sōgō suru, vb. 総合する synthesize; integrate.

sogu, vb. 削ぐ 1. shave off; slice. 2. diminish. 3. spoil.

sōgyō suru, vb. 操業する operate; run.

sōhō, n. 相方 both sides.

sōi, n. 相違 difference.

sōji, n. 掃除 cleaning; dusting; sweeping.

sōjiki, n. 掃除機 vacuum cleaner.

sōjū, n. 操縦 management; handling; operation.

sōjū suru, vb. 操縦する handle; operate.

sōki, n. 早期 early stage.

sōkin, n. 送金 remittance.

sokkenai, adj. そっけない 1. blunt. 2. unfriendly.

sokki, n. 速記 shorthand; stenography.

sokkuri そっくり 1. n. all. 2. adj. identical. 3. adv. altogether.

soko, n. 底 1. bottom; **kokoro no soko kara** from the bottom of one's heart. 2. shoe sole.

soko, n. そこ there; that place.

sōko, n. 倉庫 warehouse.

soko de そこで 1. conj. then. 2. adv. therefore; thereupon.

sokoku, n. 祖国 native country.

-sokonau 損なう fail to do something; **yomisokonau** fail to read.

sokora そこら 1. *adv.* thereabouts; around there. 2. *prep.* about.

soko-soko, *adv.* そこそこ barely; at most.

-soku 足 suffix indicating a pair (footwear); **kutsushita sansoku** three pairs of socks.

sokudo, *n.* 速度 speed.

sokuji (ni), *adv.* 即時 (に) without delay; instantly.

sokumen, *n.* 側面 side; aspect.

sokuryō, *n.* 測量 measurement; survey.

sokuseki (no), *adj.* 即席 (の) 1. instant. 2. improvised.

sokushi, *n.* 即死 instantaneous death.

sokutatsu, *n.* 速達 special delivery.

sokutei suru, *vb.* 測定する measure.

sokuza ni, *adv.* 即座に immediately.

sōkyū ni, *adv.* 早急に immediately; as soon as possible.

somaru, *vb.* 染まる 1. be dyed or stained. 2. be influenced.

sōmen, *n.* そうめん fine noodles.

someru, *vb.* 染める dye; tint.

somo-somo, *adv.* そもそも to begin with.

somuku, *vb.* 背く 1. rebel against; disobey. 2. violate.

son, *n.* 損 disadvantage; damage; loss.

sonaeru, *vb.* 供える offer (at an altar).

sonaeru, *vb.* 備える 1. prepare. 2. have; be

equipped with.

sōnan, *n.* 遭難 accident; disaster.

sonchō suru, *vb.* 尊重する respect; value.

songai, *n.* 損害 damage; loss.

sonkei suru, *vb.* 尊敬する respect.

son'na, *adj.* そんな that; that kind of; such.

sono, *adj.* その that; those.

sonoba de, *adv.* その場で on the spot.

sonogo, *adv.* その後 after that; afterward.

sono hen ni, *adv.* その辺に in the vicinity of.

sono hoka, *n.* その他 the rest; others.

sono kawari ni, *adv.* その代わりに instead.

sono kuse ni, *adv.* そのくせに nevertheless; yet.

sono mama, *adv.* そのまま as is.

sono uchi ni, *adv.* その内に 1. soon. 2. in the meantime.

sono ue (ni) その上 (に) 1. *prep.* besides. 2. *adv.* in addition; on top of that.

son suru, *vb.* 損する lose (money).

sōnyū suru, *vb.* 挿入する insert.

sonzai suru, *vb.* 存在する exist.

sō'on, *n.* 騒音 noise.

sora, *n.* 空 1. sky. 2. weather.

sora, *interj.* そら Hey!; Look!

sorasu, *vb.* 外らす 1. dodge. 2. turn away.

sore, *pron.* それ that.

sore de, *adv.* それで and then.

sore hodo, *adv.* それほど so much; **sore hodo takakunai** not so expensive.

sore kara それから 1. *conj.* and. 2. *adv.* afterward; since then.

sore made, *adv.* それまで till then.

soren, ソ連 Soviet Union.

sore ni それに 1. *prep.* besides. 2. *adv.* in addition; moreover.

sore to mo, *conj.* それとも or.

sore to naku, *adv.* それとな く indirectly; casually.

sorezore, *adv.* それぞれ individually; respectively.

sori, *n.* そり sleigh.

sōridaijin, *n.* 総理大臣 prime minister.

sorikaeru, *vb.* 反り返る bend back; warp.

sōritsu suru, *vb.* 創立する establish.

soroban, *n.* 算盤 abacus.

soroeru, *vb.* 揃える 1. arrange; prepare. 2. put in order; make complete. 3. make uniform.

soro-soro, *adv.* そろそろ 1. soon; now; **Soro-soro shitsurei shimasu.** I must be going. 2. slowly; **soro-soro aruku** walk slowly.

sorou, *vb.* 揃う 1. be complete. 2. be equal; be the same. 3. assemble.

soru, *vb.* 剃る shave.

sōryō, *n.* 送料 shipping charge; postage.

sōsaku suru, *n.* 捜索する investigate; search.

sōsaku suru, *n.* 創作する create; write.

sōsa suru, *vb.* 操作する operate a machine.

sōseiki, *n.* 創生記 Genesis (Bible).

sōseji, *n.* ソーセージ (E.) sausage.

sosen, *n.* 祖先 ancestor.

sōsetsu suru, *vb.* 創設する found; establish.

soshiki, *n.* 組織 organization; system.

sōshiki, *n.* 葬式 funeral.

sōshin, *n.* 送信 transmission.

soshite そして 1. *conj.* and. 2. *adv.* consequently.

soshitsu, *n.* 素質 potential; talent.

sōshoku, *n.* 装飾 decoration.

sōsō (ni), *adv.* 早々 (に) 1. immediately. 2. early.

sosogu, *vb.* 注ぐ 1. pour. 2. devote.

sosokkashii, *adj.* そそっか しい hasty; rash.

sosonokasu, *vb.* そそのかす instigate; agitate.

sōsū, *n.* 総数 total number.

sōtai-teki ni, *adv.* 総体的に relatively.

sotchi そっち 1. *pron.* you (informal). 2. *n.* over there.

sotchinoke ni suru, *vb.* そ っちのけにする neglect one's duties.

sotchoku (na), *adj.* 率直 (な) candid; frank; straightforward.

sotchū, *n.* 卒中 stroke (seizure).

sōtei suru, *vb.* 想定する assume; suppose.

soto, *n.* 外 exterior; outside; outdoors.

sotogawa, *n.* 外側 exterior; outside.

sotsugyō suru, *vb.* 卒業する graduate.

sotte 沿って 1. *prep.* along. 2. *adv.* in line with.

sotto, *adv.* そっと 1. softly; quietly. 2. secretly.

sotto shite oku, *vb.* そっと しておく leave alone; leave as is.

sou, *vb.* 添う 1. accompany.

2. marry. 3. satisfy; **kitai ni sou** satisfy one's expectations.

sou, vb. 沿う follow.

sowa-sowa to, adv. そわそわと restlessly; uneasily.

soyo kaze, n. そよ風 breeze.

sozai, n. 素材 ingredient; material.

sōzen, n. 騒然 commotion; turmoil.

sōzōryoku, n. 想像力 imagination.

sōzōryoku, n. 創造力 creativity.

sōzōshii, adj. 騒々しい noisy.

su, n. 酢 vinegar.

su, n. 巣 animal habitat: nest, cobweb, den, honeycomb.

sū, n. 数 number.

subarashii, adj. 素晴らしい wonderful; superb.

subayai, adj. 素早い nimble; speedy.

suberidai, n. 滑り台 sliding board.

suberu, vb. 滑る 1. slip; slide. 2. fail (an examination).

subete, n. 全て all; everything.

subete (no), adj. 全て (の) all.

sude ni, adv. 既に already.

suekko, n. 末っ子 youngest child.

suetsukeru, vb. 据え付ける install; set up.

sūgaku, n. 数学 mathematics.

sugaru, vb. すがる cling to; depend on.

suga-sugashii, adj. すがすがしい refreshing.

sugata, n. 姿 1. appearance; figure; features. 2. condition.

sugi, n. 杉 cedar.

-sugi 過ぎ past; over; **gojisugi** past five o'clock; **hachisugi** over twenty years old.

sugiru, vb. 過ぎる 1. pass by. 2. exceed. 3. expire.

-sugiru 過ぎる to excess; **nomi-sugiru** drink to excess.

sugoi, adj. すごい 1. amazing; wonderful. 2. awful; terrifying.

sugoku, adv. すごく very; awfully.

sugosu, vb. 過ごす (time) spend; pass.

sugu (ni), adv. すぐ (に) 1. immediately. 2. easily. 3. very; **sugu chikaku ni** very near to.

sugureta, adj. 優れた excellent.

suhada, n. 素肌 bare skin.

suiageru, vb. 吸い上げる pump up; suck up.

suibaku, n. 水爆 hydrogen bomb.

suibun, n. 水分 moisture; water.

suichoku (na), adj. 垂直 (な) perpendicular; vertical.

suichū de/ni, adv. 水中で、～に under water.

suiden, n. 水田 rice paddy.

suidō, n. 水道 water supply.

suidōsui, n. 水道水 tap water.

suiei, n. 水泳 swimming.

suigara, n. 吸い殻 cigarette butt.

suigin, n. 水銀 mercury.

suihanki, n. 炊飯器 rice cooker.

suihei (na, no), adj. 水平 (な、の) horizontal.

suiheisen, n. 水平線

horizon.

suijun, *n.* 水準 standard; level.

suika, *n.* 西瓜 watermelon.

suikomu, *vb.* 吸い込む inhale; absorb.

suimen, *n.* 水面 surface of water.

suimin, *n.* 睡眠 sleep.

suiminbusoku, *n.* 睡眠不足 lack of sleep.

suimin'yaku, *n.* 睡眠薬 sleeping pill.

suimono, *n.* 吸い物 Japanese-style soup.

suion, *n.* 水温 water temperature.

suiren, *n.* 水蓮 water lily.

suiri suru, *vb.* 推理する speculate; infer.

suiryokudenki, *n.* 水力電気 hydroelectricity.

suiryoku-hatsuden, *n.* 水力発電 hydroelectric power.

suisaiga, *n.* 水彩画 watercolor painting.

suisei, *n.* 水星 Mercury (planet).

suisen, *n.* 水仙 daffodil; narcissus.

suisenbenjo, *n.* 水洗便所 flush toilet.

suisen suru, *vb.* 推薦する recommend.

suisha, *n.* 水車 waterwheel.

suishin suru, *vb.* 推進する promote.

suishō, *n.* 水晶 crystal.

suiso, *n.* 水素 hydrogen.

suisō, *n.* 水槽 water tank.

suisoku suru, *vb.* 推測する assume; guess.

suisu, *n.* スイス Switzerland.

suitei suru, *vb.* 推定する assume; estimate.

suitō, *n.* 水筒 water bottle.

suitoru, *vb.* 吸い取る absorb; soak up.

suiyōbi, *n.* 水曜日 Wednesday.

suizokukan, *n.* 水族館 aquarium.

suji, *n.* 筋 1. streak (line). 2. fiber; muscle; tendon. 3. story line; logic. 4. lineage.

sūji, *n.* 数字 number; figure.

sujimichi, *n.* 筋道 rationality; reason; logic.

sukasazu, *adv.* すかさず immediately.

sukebe(i), *n.* 助平 lecher.

suki, *n.* 隙 1. gap; opening. 2. carelessness; inattentiveness.

suki 好き 1. *n.* fondness; love. 2. *adj.* favorite; fond. 3. *vb.* like; love.

sukima, *n.* 隙間 gap; hole.

sukitōtta, *adj.* 透き通った transparent; clear.

sukiyaki, *n.* すき焼き Japanese meat dish.

sukkari, *adv.* すっかり completely; thoroughly.

sukkiri suru, *vb.* すっきりする be satisfied; feel refreshed.

sukoshi 少し 1. *n.* a small amount. 2. *adv.* a little bit; slightly; for a short time.

sukoshi mo, *adv.* 少しも not at all (with negative).

sukoshi zutsu, *adv.* 少しずつ little by little.

suku, *vb.* 空く become empty.

sukui, *n.* 救い help; hope.

sukunai, *adj.* 少ない few.

sukunaku tomo, *adv.* 少なくとも at least.

suku'u, *vb.* 救う rescue.

suku'u, *vb.* 掬う scoop up.

sumanai, *adj.* 済まない inexcusable.

sumasu, *vb.* 済ます finish.

sumāto (na), *adj.* スマート(な) (E. *smart*) 1. stylish. 2. well-proportioned; slim.

sumi, n. 墨 Chinese ink.

sumi, n. 炭 charcoal.

sumi, n. 隅 corner; nook.

sumimasen, interj. すみません 1. I am sorry! Excuse me! 2. Thank you!

sumire, n. 菫 violet (plant).

sumiyaka (na), adj. 速やか (な) swift.

sumō, n. 相撲 Japanese wrestling.

sumomo, n. 李 Japanese plum.

sumu, vb. 住む reside.

sumu, vb. 済む 1. end. 2. manage; do without.

suna, n. 砂 sand.

sunahama, n. 砂浜 sandy beach.

sunao (na), adj. 素直 (な) 1. docile. 2. honest.

sunawachi 即ち 1. conj. or; that is. 2. adv. namely; in other words.

sune, n. すね shin.

suneru, vb. すねる sulk.

sunpō, n. 寸法 measurement.

sunzen de/ni, prep. 寸前で、〜に just before (time or place).

sūpā(māketto), n. スーパー(マーケット) (E.) supermarket.

supein, n. スペイン (E.) Spain.

supīdo-ihan, n. スピード違反 speeding violation.

suppai, adj. 酸っぱい sour.

sura, parti. すら even; **Hiragana sura yomenai.** (He) cannot even read hiragana.

sura-sura (to), adv. すらすら (と) fluently; easily; **nihongo o sura-sura hanasu** speak Japanese fluently.

sureru, vb. 擦れる 1. rub (against). 2. wear down. 3.

become jaded.

sure-sure, adj. すれすれ extremely close (location).

suri, n. すり pickpocket.

suriheru, vb. 磨り減る be worn down; be exhausted.

surikireru, vb. 擦り切れる wear out.

surimuku, vb. 擦りむく abrade; scrape.

surinukeru, vb. 擦り抜ける squeeze through.

suritsubusu, vb. 磨りつぶす grind down; mash.

suru, vb. する 1. do; play (games, sports, etc.). 2. make (into); **Kimi o shiawase ni suru.** (I'll) make you happy. 3. choose; decide on; **kore ni suru** choose or decide on this. 4. cost; **hyaku en suru** cost 100 yen. 5. have; get.

suru, vb. 刷る print.

surudoi, adj. 鋭い 1. acute; sharp. 2. insightful; keen.

suru-suru to, adv. するすると smoothly.

suru to, conj. すると and then.

susamajii, adj. すさまじい amazing; horrible.

sushi, n. 寿司 raw fish slices on rice.

suso, n. 裾 1. hem. 2. foot (of a mountain).

susugu, vb. すすぐ rinse.

susumeru, vb. 進める advance; promote.

susumeru, vb. 勧める advise; recommend.

susurinaku, vb. すすり泣く sob.

suteki (na), adj. 素敵 (な) great; wonderful.

suteru, vb. 捨てる throw away; abandon.

suto(raiki), n. スト(ライキ) (E.) (labor) strike.

su'u, *vb.* 吸う 1. breathe in; inhale; smoke. 2. absorb; suck up.

suwaru, *vb.* 座る sit down; take a seat.

suzu, *n.* 鈴 small bell.

suzume, *n.* 雀 sparrow.

suzuran, *n.* 鈴蘭 lily of the valley.

suzuri, *n.* 硯 inkstone for calligraphy.

suzushii, *adj.* 涼しい cool.

T

ta, *n.* 田 rice field.

ta (no), *adj.* 他 (の) other; another.

taba, *n.* 束 bunch; bundle.

tabemono, *n.* 食べ物 food.

tabenokoshi, *n.* 食べ残し leftover food.

taberu, *vb.* 食べる eat.

tabesugi, *n.* 食べ過ぎ overeating.

tabi, *n.* 足袋 Japanese-style socks.

tabi, *n.* 旅 traveling; trip;
   tabi o suru take a trip; travel.

-tabi ni 度に each time;
   kare ni au-tabi ni each time I see him.

tabi-tabi, *adv.* 度々 repeatedly; frequently.

tabun, *adv.* 多分 perhaps; probably.

tachi, *n.* 質 personality; nature; **tachi no warui** bad natured.

-tachi 達 (plural indicator)
   kodomotachi children.

tachiagaru, *vb.* 立ち上がる stand up.

tachiau, *vb.* 立ち合う witness; attend.

tachiba, *n.* 立場 position; situation.

tachigiki, *n.* 立ち聞き eavesdropping.

tachimachi, *adv.* たちまち instantly; on the spot.

tachiōjō suru, *vb.* 立ち往生 する be stuck; come to a standstill.

tachisaru, *vb.* 立ち去る leave.

tachiyoru, *vb.* 立ち寄る drop in: stop by; **bā ni tachiyoru** drop in at a bar.

tada, ただ 1. *adv.* only. 2. *conj.* but; however.

tada (no), *adj.* 只 (の) 1. free of charge. 2. ordinary.

tada de, *adv.* 只で free of charge.

tadaima, *adv.* 只今 1. at present. 2. soon.

tadaima, *interj.* ただいま I'm home!

tadashi, *conj.* ただし but, however.

tadashii, *adj.* 正しい correct; right.

tadayou, *vb.* 漂う drift.

tadoru, *vb.* 迪る follow; trace.

tadōshi, *n.* 他動詞 transitive verb.

taemanaku, *adv.* 絶え間な く constantly; incessantly.

taeru, *vb.* 耐える endure.

tagai 互い *pron.* each other; one another.

tagayasu, *vb.* 耕す till; cultivate (land).

tagiru, *vb.* たぎる boil.

tahatsu suru, *vb.* 多発する occur frequently.

tahō 他方 1. *n.* the other side. 2. *adv.* on the other hand.

tahōmen, *n.* 多方面

multifariousness.

tai, n. 鯛 sea bream.

tai, n. 隊 group; party.

tai, n. タイ Thailand.

-tai たい want to (do);
nihon ni ikitai want to go
to Japan.

taiatari suru, vb. 体当たり
する 1. throw oneself at. 2.
throw oneself into.

taibō (no), adj. 待望の
wished-for; eagerly awaited.

taido, n. 態度 attitude.

taifū, n. 台風 typhoon.

taigai, adv. 大概 mostly.

taihan, n. 大半 majority.

taiheiyō, n. 太平洋 Pacific
Ocean.

taihen 大変 1. adj. difficult.
2. adv. very; extremely.

taiho suru, vb. 逮捕する
arrest.

tai'iku, n. 体育 physical
training.

tai'ikukan, n. 体育館
gymnasium.

tai'in suru, vb. 退院する be
discharged from a hospital.

taiji, n. 胎児 fetus.

taiji suru, vb. 退治する
conquer; eliminate.

taijū, n. 体重 weight (of a
person).

taikai, n. 大会 convention.

taikaku, n. 体格 physical
build.

taiken suru, vb. 体験する
experience.

taiketsu suru, vb. 対決する
confront.

taiki, n. 大気 air;
atmosphere.

taiki suru, vb. 待機する
stand by.

taiko, n. 太鼓 drum.

taikō suru, vb. 対抗する
oppose; fight.

taikutsu (na), adj. 退屈 (な)
boring.

taikyū-ryoku/-sei, n. 耐久
力/～性 durability.

taimen, n. 対面 meeting.

taiō, n. 対応 handling;
treatment.

taionkei, n. 体温計
thermometer (clinical).

taiō suru, vb. 対応する deal
with.

taira (na), adj. 平ら (な) flat;
level.

tairiku, n. 大陸 continent.

tairitsu suru, vb. 対立する
confront.

tairyō, n. 大量 large
amount.

tairyoku, n. 体力 stamina.

taisaku, n. 対策 1. measures
(actions). 2. strategy;
taisaku o tateru plan a
strategy.

taisei, n. 体制 1. power;
government. 2. social or
economic structure.

taiseiyō, n. 大西洋 Atlantic
Ocean.

taisetsu (na), adj. 大切 (な)
1. important. 2. beloved.

taishikan, n. 大使館
embassy.

taishita, adj. 大した 1. great.
2. not very significant (with
negative).

taishite, adv. 大して not
very (with negative).

taishite, prep. 対して 1.
against. 2. in contrast to; as
opposed to. 3. toward.

taishitsu, n. 体質
disposition; nature.

taishō, n. 対象 object.

taishoku suru, vb. 退職する
resign, retire (from one's
job).

taisho suru, vb. 対処する
deal with.

taishō-teki (na), adj. 対照的
(な) diametrically opposite.

taisō, n. 体操 gymnastics;

exercise.

taisō, *adv.* 大層 very.

taisui, *adj.* 耐水 waterproof.

taitō (na, no), *adj.* 対等 (な、の) equal; fair.

taitoku suru, *vb.* 体得する master.

taiwa, *n.* 対話 conversation; dialogue.

taiwan, *n.* 台湾 Taiwan; Republic of China.

taiyō, *n.* 太陽 sun.

taizai suru, *vb.* 滞在する stay.

tajirogu, *vb.* たじろぐ flinch; recoil.

taka, *n.* 鷹 hawk.

takai, *adj.* 高い 1. high. 2. expensive. 2. loud (sound).

takamaru, *vb.* 高まる increase; rise.

takameru, *vb.* 高める raise.

takara, *n.* 宝 treasure.

takarakuji, *n.* 宝くじ lottery.

takasa, *n.* 高さ height.

take, *n.* 竹 bamboo.

takenoko, *n.* 竹の子 bamboo shoot.

taki, *n.* 滝 waterfall; cascade.

takkyū, *n.* 卓球 table tennis.

tako, *n.* たこ callus.

tako, *n.* 凧 kite; **tako o ageru** fly a kite.

tako, *n.* 蛸 octopus.

taku, *vb.* 炊く boil; cook.

taku, *vb.* 焚く burn (wood).

takuan, *n.* たくあん pickled Japanese radish.

takumashii, *adj.* たくましい 1. strong. 2. dependable.

takumi (na), *adj.* 巧みな skillful.

takuramu, *vb.* 企む plot; scheme.

takusan, *n.* 沢山 1. many; much. 2. more than enough.

takuwaeru, *vb.* 蓄える store; save.

tama, *n.* 玉 1. ball; bead. 2. bullet.

tamago, *n.* 卵 1. egg. 2. fish roe.

tamamono, *n.* 賜物 1. gift. 2. outcome; fruit.

tamanegi, *n.* 玉ねぎ onion.

tama ni, *adv.* たまに occasionally.

tamaranai, *adj.* たまらない 1. intolerable. 2. exciting.

tamaru, *vb.* 溜まる 1. accumulate; heap up. 2. be overdue.

tamashii, *n.* 魂 soul.

tama-tama, *adv.* たまたま by chance.

tame (ni), *conj.* 為 (に) 1. in order to; **eizu-bōshi no tame ni** in order to prevent AIDS; **kazoku o yashinau tame ni** in order to support one's family. 2. because of; owing to.

tame ni naru, *vb.* 為になる be beneficial; be useful.

tamerau, *vb.* ためらう hesitate.

tameru, *vb.* 貯める save; store.

tamesu, *vb.* 試す test; attempt.

tamotsu, *vb.* 保つ keep; maintain.

tan, *n.* たん phlegm.

tana, *n.* 棚 shelf.

tanabata, *n.* 七夕 Japanese festival (July 7).

tanbo, *n.* 田んぼ rice field.

tandoku de, *adv.* 単独で alone; independently.

tane, *n.* 種 1. seed. 2. source; cause.

tango, *n.* 単語 word.

tani, *n.* 谷 valley; ravine.

tan'i, *n.* 単位 1. (school course) credit; **tan'i o toru** earn credits. 2. unit.

tanin, *n.* 他人 1. stranger. 2. other people.

tanjō, *n.* 誕生 birth.

tanjōbi, *n.* 誕生日 birthday.

tanjunka suru, *vb.* 単純化する simplify.

tanka, *n.* 担架 stretcher.

tanken, *n.* 探険 exploration; expedition.

tanki, *n.* 短期 short term.

tanki (na), *adj.* 短気 (な) short-tempered.

tankidaigaku, *n.* 短期大学 junior college.

tankōbon, *n.* 単行本 book.

tankyū, *n.* 探究 pursuit; quest; research.

tan naru, *adj.* 単なる mere.

tan ni, *adv.* 単に merely; only.

tanō (na), *adj.* 多能 (な) versatile.

tanomi, *n.* 頼み 1. request. 2. reliance.

tanomu, *vb.* 頼む ask; request.

tanoshii, *adj.* 楽しい enjoyable; pleasant.

tanoshimaseru, *vb.* 楽しませる amuse; entertain.

tanoshimi ni suru, *vb.* 楽しみにする look forward to; anticipate.

tanpa, *n.* 短波 shortwave.

tanpaku (na), *adj.* 淡泊 (な) 1. simple (tastes). 2. nonchalant.

tanpaku(shitsu), *n.* 蛋白 (質) protein.

tanpopo, *n.* たんぽぽ dandelion.

tanri, *n.* 単利 simple interest.

tanseki, *n.* 胆石 gallstone.

tanshin, *n.* 単身 being alone; being separated (from one's family).

tanshuku suru, *vb.* 短縮する curtail; shorten.

tansu, *n.* たんす Japanese chest of drawers.

tansū, *n.* 単数 singular (grammar).

tansuikabutsu, *n.* 炭水化物 carbohydrate.

tantei, *n.* 探偵 detective work.

tantō, *n.* 担当 charge (duty).

tanuki, *n.* 狸 raccoon-like animal indigenous to Japan.

taoreru, *vb.* 倒れる 1. fall; faint. 2. become bankrupt.

tappitsu, *n.* 達筆 good penmanship.

tappuri, *adv.* たっぷり 1. abundantly. 2. as much as one likes.

tara, *n.* たら codfish.

tarai, *n.* たらい washbasin.

tarako, *n.* たら子 codfish roe.

tarappu, *n.* タラップ (D. *trap*) movable stairs.

tareru, *vb.* 垂れる hang down; sag.

tariru, *vb.* 足りる be sufficient.

taru, *n.* 樽 barrel; cask.

tarumu, *vb.* 弛む become loose; sag.

taryō, *n.* 多量 large quantity.

tashi, *n.* 足し supplement.

tashika (na), *adj.* 確か (な) 1. sure; secure. 2. reliable.

tashikameru, *vb.* 確かめる make sure; confirm.

tashō (no), *adj.* 多少 (の) a little.

tasogare, *n.* たそがれ twilight.

tassei suru, *vb.* 達成する achieve.

tassha (na), *adj.* 達者 (な) 1. skillful. 2. healthy.

tassuru, *vb.* 達する reach; become; **seinen ni tassuru** become an adult.

tasu, *vb.* 足す add.

tasū, *n.* 多数 majority; large number.

tasukeru, *vb.* 助ける help; support.

tataeru, *vb.* 賛える praise.

tatakau, *vb.* 戦う battle; fight.

tataku, *vb.* 叩く beat; strike.

tatami, *n.* 畳 Japanese straw floor mat.

tatamu, *vb.* 畳む fold.

tatari, *n.* たたり curse.

tate, *n.* 縦 length; height;
tate no sen 縦の線 vertical line.

tategaki, *n.* 縦書き vertical writing.

tategami, *n.* たてがみ mane.

tatekaeru, *vb.* 建て替える remodel (a building); rebuild.

tatekaeru, *vb.* 立て替える make a payment (for someone).

tatemono, *n.* 建物 building.

tateru, *vb.* 建てる 1. build. 2. put upright.

tatoeba, *adv.* 例えば for example.

tatsu, *vb.* 立つ 1. stand. 2. be built.

tatsumaki, *n.* 竜巻 tornado.

tatta (no), *adv.* たった (の) only.

taue, *n.* 田植え rice-planting.

tayori, *n.* 便り news; letter.

tayori, *n.* 頼り reliance.

tayori ni suru, *vb.* 頼りにする rely on.

tayoru, *vb.* 頼る rely on.

tazuneru, *vb.* 尋ねる 1. ask; inquire. 2. search for.

te, *n.* 手 1. hand. 2. means; way. 3. kind; type.

tearai, *n.* 手洗い restroom.

teara (na), *adj.* 手荒 (な) rough; harsh.

teashi, *n.* 手足 hands and feet; limbs.

teate, *n.* 手当て 1. allowance. 2. medical treatment.

teatsui, *adj.* 手厚い attentive.

tebanasu, *vb.* 手離す part with.

tebayaku, *adv.* 手早く quickly.

tebiki, *n.* 手引き instruction; manual.

tebukuro, *n.* 手袋 gloves.

techō, *n.* 手帳 pocket notebook.

tedashi (o) suru, *vb.* 手出し (を)する 1. meddle. 2. make advances to.

tedori, *n.* 手取り income after taxes.

tegaki, *n.* 手書き handwriting.

tegami, *n.* 手紙 letter;
tegami o dasu mail a letter.

tegaru (na), *adj.* 手軽 (な) easy; quick.

tegata, *n.* 手形 bill; check.

tegatai, *adj.* 手固い solid and steady; reliable.

tegoro (na), *adj.* 手頃 (な) 1. handy. 2. affordable.

tegotae, *n.* 手応え response;
ii tegotae ga aru get a good response.

tegowai, *adj.* 手ごわい difficult to deal with or overcome.

teguchi, *n.* 手口 method; trick.

tehai suru, *vb.* 手配する 1. arrange; prepare. 2. institute a search.

tehajime ni, *adv.* 手始めに to begin with; in the first place.

tehon, *n.* 手本 example; model.

tei'an, *n.* 提案 proposal.

teiden, *n.* 停電 power

failure.

teido, *n.* 程度 1. criterion; standard; **teido ga takai** high standard. 2. extent; **sono teido made** to that extent.

tei'in, *n.* 定員 capacity (people).

teiji, *n.* 定時 regular time.

teikanshi, *n.* 定冠詞 definite article.

teika suru, *vb.* 低下する drop; decrease.

teikei suru, *vb.* 提携する cooperate; form a partnership.

teiketsuatsu, *n.* 低血圧 low blood pressure.

teiki, *n.* 定期 routine; regularity.

teikibin, *n.* 定期便 scheduled flight.

teikiken, *n.* 定期券 commutation ticket.

teikinri, *n.* 低金利 low interest.

teikō, *n.* 抵抗 resistance; defiance.

teikoku, *n.* 帝国 empire.

teikō suru, *vb.* 抵抗する resist; rebel.

teikyō suru, *vb.* 提供する offer; provide; sponsor.

teikyūbi, *n.* 定休日 regular day off.

teinei (na), *adj.* 丁寧 (な) 1. polite; courteous. 2. careful.

teinei ni, *adv.* 丁寧に 1. politely; courteously. 2. carefully.

teinen, *n.* 停年 retirement age.

teion, *n.* 低温 low temperature.

te'ire, *n.* 手入れ 1. care. 2. police raid.

te'ire suru, *vb.* 手入れする take care of.

teisai, *n.* 体裁 appearance; looks.

teisei, *n.* 訂正 correction.

teisen, *n.* 停戦 cease-fire.

teisetsu, *n.* 定説 established theory.

teisha, *n.* 停車 stopping (vehicle).

teishoku, *n.* 定食 set meal; table d'hôte.

teishu, *n.* 亭主 husband.

teishutsu suru, *vb.* 提出する hand in; submit.

tejika (na, no), *adj.* 手近 (な、の) 1. nearby. 2. familiar.

tejina, *n.* 手品 magic trick.

tejō, *n.* 手錠 handcuffs.

tejun, *n.* 手順 process; arrangement.

teki, *n.* 敵 enemy; opponent.

-teki (na) 的 (な) (adjectival suffix) -ic; -ing; -ish; -like, etc.; **shinbi-teki na** aesthetic.

tekihatsu suru, *vb.* 摘発する expose; disclose.

teki'i, *n.* 敵意 hostility.

tekiō suru, *vb.* 適応する adapt oneself to.

tekipaki (to), *adv.* てきぱき (と) 1. efficiently. 2. quickly.

teki suru, *vb.* 適する fit; be suitable.

tekisuto, *n.* テキスト (E.) textbook.

tekitai suru, *vb.* 敵対する oppose; fight.

tekitō (na), *adj.* 適当 (な) 1. appropriate; suitable. 2. reasonable.

tekkin-konkurīto, *n.* 鉄筋コンクリート reinforced concrete.

tekkyō, *n.* 鉄橋 iron bridge.

teko, *n.* てこ lever.

tekozuru, *vb.* てこずる have difficulty dealing with.

tekubi, *n.* 手首 wrist.

tema, *n.* 手間 (a lot of) time; trouble; **tema ga kakaru** require a lot of time and trouble.

tēma, *n.* テーマ (E.) theme; topic.

temae, *n.* 手前 1. front. 2. this side. 3. social propriety.

temane, *n.* 手真似 gesture.

temari, *n.* 手まり Japanese handball.

temawarihin, *n.* 手回り品 personal belongings.

temawashi, *n.* 手回し preparations; arrangements.

temijika ni, *adv.* 手短かに briefly.

-temo ても even if; **okane ga nakutemo** even if (I) don't have any money.

temoto ni, *adv.* 手元に at hand.

ten, *n.* 天 sky; heaven.

ten, *n.* 点 1. dot; period; point. 2. grade; mark; score. 3. item.

tenaoshi, *n.* 手直し correction; touching up.

tenareta, *adj.* 手馴れた skillful; experienced.

tenbō, *n.* 展望 1. prospect. 2. vista.

tendon, *n.* 天丼 tempura on rice.

tengoku, *n.* 天国 paradise; heaven.

tengyō, *n.* 転業 career change.

te ni amaru, *vb.* 手に余る be unmanageable.

te ni ireru, *vb.* 手に入れる obtain.

tenjō, *n.* 天井 ceiling.

tenka, *n.* 点火 ignition; lighting.

tenkai, *n.* 展開 development.

tenkan suru, *vb.* 転換する change; convert.

tenka suru, *vb.* 点火する ignite; light; fire up.

tenkei-teki (na), *adj.* 典型 的 (な) typical.

tenken suru, *vb.* 点検する inspect.

tenki, *n.* 天気 weather; good weather.

tenkin, *n.* 転勤 job transfer.

tenkiyohō, *n.* 天気予報 weather forecast.

tenkō, *n.* 天候 weather.

tenmetsu suru, *vb.* 点滅す る go on and off; blink.

tenmongaku, *n.* 天文学 astronomy.

ten'nen (no), *adj.* 天然 (の) natural; **ten'nenshigen** natural resources.

ten'nō, *n.* 天皇 emperor of Japan.

tenpuku suru, *vb.* 転覆する capsize; overturn.

tenpura, *n.* 天ぷら tempura (Japanese deep-fried dish).

tensai, *n.* 天才 genius.

tensen, *n.* 点線 dotted line.

tenshi, *n.* 天使 angel.

tenshoku, *n.* 転職 job or career change.

tenshu, *n.* 店主 shop owner.

tensū, *n.* 点数 points; score.

tenteki, *n.* 点滴 intravenous drip.

tentōmushi, *n.* てんとう虫 ladybug.

tenugui, *n.* 手拭い Japanese-style towel.

te o dasu, *vb.* 手を出す 1. get involved in. 2. meddle.

teokure, *n.* 手遅れ occurring too late.

teppen, *n.* てっぺん top; summit.

teppō, *n.* 鉄砲 gun.

tera, *n.* 寺 temple.

terasu, vb. 照らす illuminate; light.

terebi, n. テレビ (E.) television set.

terebi-bangumi, n. テレビ 番組 television program.

teru, vb. 照る shine.

tesage, n. 手提げ 1. shopping bag. 2. briefcase.

tesō(mi), n. 手相(見) palm reading.

tesū, n. 手数 pains; trouble.

tesuri, n. 手すり handrail.

tesūryō, n. 手数料 handling fee; commission.

tetsu, n. 鉄 iron.

tetsubō, n. 鉄棒 iron bar.

tetsudai, n. 手伝い 1. helper. 2. help.

tetsudau, vb. 手伝う help.

tetsudō, n. 鉄道 railroad.

tetsugaku, n. 哲学 philosophy.

tetsuke(kin), n. 手付け(金) deposit (money).

tetsuzuki, n. 手続き procedure.

tettai suru, vb. 撤退する withdraw.

tewatasu, vb. 手渡す hand to; submit.

tezukuri (no), adj. 手作り (の) handmade; homemade.

to, n. 戸 door.

to, parti. と 1. conj. and; **anata to watashi** you and me. 2. prep. with; **haha to** with my mother. 3. conj. when; **uchi ni kaeru to** when I came back home. 4. conj. if; **ame ga furu to** if it rains.

tō, n. 十 ten; ten years old.

tō, n. 塔 pagoda; tower.

tō, n. 党 group; political party.

-tō 等 1. etc.; **sushi, sashimitō** sushi, sashimi, etc. 2. place (competition);

nitō second place.

tōan, n. 答案 answer sheet (used during examination).

tobasu, vb. 飛ばす 1. fly; speed. 2. skip over.

tobikiri (no), adj. とびきり (の) exceptional; outstanding.

tobikomu, vb. 飛び込む dive into; jump into.

tobimawaru, vb. 飛び回る jump around; fly around.

tobira, n. 扉 1. door. 2. title page.

tōbō, n. 逃亡 escape; flight.

tobokeru, vb. とぼける feign innocence or ignorance.

toboshii, adj. 乏しい scarce.

tobu, vb. 飛ぶ 1. fly. 2. skip (number, page).

tobu, vb. 跳ぶ jump; leap.

tōbu, n. 頭部 head.

tōbu, n. 東部 eastern region.

tōbun, n. 糖分 sugar.

tōbun suru, vb. 等分する divide equally.

tōchaku suru, vb. 到着する arrive.

tochi, n. 土地 1. land; soil. 2. locality.

tochū de, adv. 途中で 1. en route. 2. in the middle.

todaeru, vb. 途絶える cease; end.

tōdai, n. 灯台 lighthouse.

todana, n. 戸棚 cupboard.

todoku, vb. 届く reach; be received.

todomaru, vb. 留まる stay.

todomeru, vb. 止める 1. put an end to. 2. detain.

todoroku, vb. とどろく 1. roar; thunder. 2. resound; spread (fame). 3. throb.

tōei suru, vb. 投影する project.

tōfu, n. 豆腐 tofu; bean curd.

togameru, vb. 咎める

blame.

tōgarashi, *n.* 唐辛子 hot pepper.

togatta, *adj.* 尖った pointed.

toge, *n.* とげ thorn.

tōge, *n.* 峠 1. mountain pass or peak. 2. crucial point.

togeru, *vb.* 遂げる accomplish.

togireru, *vb.* 途切れる discontinue; halt.

tōgō suru, *vb.* 統合する combine; unite.

togu, *vb.* 研ぐ 1. sharpen. 2. wash (rice).

toguchi, *n.* 戸口 doorway.

tōhō, *pron.* 当方 I; we.

toho de, *adv.* 徒歩で on foot.

tōhoku, *n.* 東北 northeast.

tohō ni kureru, *vb.* 途方に暮れる be at a loss.

tōhyō, *n.* 投票 vote; voting.

toi, *n.* 問い question.

tōi, *adj.* 遠い distant; far.

toi'awaseru, *n.* 問い合わせ inquire; refer to.

toiki, *n.* 吐息 sigh.

tōitsu, *n.* 統一 1. standardization. 2. unification.

-to iu という named; called; **Keiji-to iu hito** a person called Keiji.

-to iu noni というのに although; **ikuna-to iu noni** although I say "don't go."

tōji, *n.* 当時 old days; those days; **tōji wa** in those days.

tojikomeru, *vb.* 閉じ込める confine; shut up.

tojikomoru, *vb.* 閉じこもる shut oneself up.

tojimari suru, *vb.* 戸締りする lock the door(s) and window(s).

tojiru, *vb.* 閉じる 1. close; shut. 2. end.

tōjitsu, *n.* 当日 that day;

designated day;

tōjitsukagiri valid only for that day; **tōjitsuken** ticket sold on the day of the performance.

tōjōjinbutsu, *n.* 登場人物 cast; characters (play, story).

tōka, *n.* 十日 tenth day of the month.

tokai, *n.* 都会 city.

tokasu, *vb.* 溶かす melt; dissolve; liquefy.

tōka suru, *vb.* 投下する 1. drop; discharge. 2. invest.

tokei, *n.* 時計 clock; watch.

tokekomu, *vb.* 溶け込む adjust; blend in with.

tokeru, *vb.* 溶ける melt; dissolve.

tokeru, *vb.* 解ける 1. untie; undo. 2. solve.

tōketsu, *n.* 凍結 freezing.

toki, *n.* 時 1. time. 2. opportunity; timing.

-toki とき when; **kare ga nihon ni itta-toki** when he visited Japan.

tōki, *n.* 冬期 winter; **tōki-orinpikku** Winter Olympic Games.

tōkibi, *n.* とうきび corn (food).

tokidoki, *adv.* 時々 sometimes; now and then.

tokifuseru, *vb.* 説き伏せる persuade; convince.

tokimeku, *vb.* ときめく throb.

toki ni wa, *adv.* 時には sometimes.

tokkun, *n.* 特訓 crash course.

tokku ni, *adv.* とっくに a long time ago; already.

tokkyo, *n.* 特許 patent.

tokkyū, *n.* 特急 express train.

toko, *n.* 床 1. floor. 2. bed.

tōkō, *n.* 登校 attendance at

school.

tokonoma, n. 床の間 alcove (for hanging scrolls or for ikebana).

tokoro, n. 所 1. place. 2. part. 3. address; house.

-tokoro ところ 1. on the point of; almost; **shinu-tokoro** on the point of death. 2. just when; **tabeteiru-tokoro** just when (I) was eating.

tokoro de, adv. ところで by the way.

tokoro ga, conj. ところが but.

tokoya, n. 床屋 barbershop.

toku, n. 得 benefit; profit.

toku, vb. 解く 1. solve. 2. undo. 3. dismiss. 4. absolve.

tokubetsu (na, no), adj. 特別 (な、の) special; exceptional.

tokuchō, n. 特徴 characteristic; special feature.

tokudai, n. 特大 extra-large size.

tokugi, n. 特技 one's special talent.

tokui (na), adj. 得意 (な) 1. skillful. 2. elated.

tokui(saki), n. 得意(先) good customer.

tokumei (no), adj. 匿名 (の) anonymous.

toku ni, adv. 特に especially; particularly.

tokushitsu, n. 特質 peculiarity; characteristic.

tokushoku, n. 特色 distinguishing characteristic.

tokushu (na), adj. 特殊 (な) unique; peculiar; special.

toku suru, vb. 得する benefit; profit.

tokutei (no), adj. 特定 (の) particular; specific.

tokuten, n. 得点 marks; score.

tokuyū (na, no), adj. 特有 (な、の) unique; peculiar.

Tōkyō, n. 東京 Tokyo.

tomadou, vb. とまどう be disoriented; be bewildered.

tomarikyaku, n. 泊まり客 overnight guest.

tomaru, vb. 止まる stop.

tomaru, vb. 泊まる stay overnight (house, hotel).

tomato, n. トマト (E.) tomato.

tōmawari suru, vb. 遠回りする make a detour; go a roundabout way.

tōmei (na), adj. 透明 (な) transparent; **tōmeiningen** invisible man.

tomeru, vb. 止める stop; discontinue; turn off.

tomeru, vb. 留める fasten; button; attach.

tomeru, vb. 泊める lodge someone overnight.

tomi, n. 富 wealth.

tōmin, n. 冬眠 hibernation.

tomo, n. 友 friend.

-tomo 共 both; **futari-tomo** both (of us).

-tomo とも even though; whatever (whoever, whichever, etc.) may ...; **nani ga okorō-tomo** whatever may happen.

tomodachi, n. 友達 friend.

tomokaku, adv. ともかく 1. anyway; in any case. 2. aside from.

tomo ni 共に 1. adj. both. 2. adv. together.

tōmorokoshi, n. とうもろこし corn (food).

tomu, vb. 富む be rich; be wealthy; prosper.

tōnan, n. 盗難 burglary; robbery.

tōnan, n. 東南 southeast.

tōnan-ajia, n. 東南アジア Southeast Asia.

tonari (no), adj. 隣 (の) next-door; next.

tonbo, n. とんぼ dragonfly.

tondemonai とんでもない 1. adj. horrible; surprising. 2. adj. unreasonable. 3. interj. My pleasure! 4. interj. Not a chance!

tō ni, adv. とうに already; a long time ago.

tonikaku, adv. とにかく 1. anyway. 2. really; indeed.

tonkatsu, n. 豚カツ pork cutlet.

tōnyōbyō, n. 糖尿病 diabetes.

toppa suru, vb. 突破する break through.

toppatsu-teki (na), adj. 突発的 (な) unpredictable; unexpected.

tora, n. 虎 tiger.

toraeru, vb. 捕える、捉える 1. arrest; capture. 2. understand.

toranpu, n. トランプ playing cards; card game.

toreru, vb. とれる 1. be caught (fish, etc.); be harvested. 2. come off. 3. go away; vanish.

tori, n. 鳥 1. bird. 2. poultry.

tōri, n. 通り 1. street; avenue. 2. understanding.

-tōri (ni) とおりに as; Watashi no iu-tōri ni shiro. Do as I say! sensei no ossharu-tōri ni as the teacher says.

toriatsukau, vb. 取り扱う handle; treat.

toriawase, n. 取り合わせ assortment; combination.

torichigaeru, vb. 取り違える misunderstand.

toridasu, vb. 取り出す take out; extract.

torihada, n. 鳥肌 goose pimples; **torihada ga tatsu** get goose pimples.

torihazusu, vb. 取り外す take off; remove.

tori'ireru, vb. 取り入れる 1. take in; take up; use. 2. harvest.

torikaesu, vb. 取り返す recover; take back.

torikesu, vb. 取り消す cancel; repeal.

tōrikosu, vb. 通り超す go beyond.

torikumu, vb. 取り組む 1. wrestle with. 2. deal with.

torimaku, vb. 取り巻く surround.

torimidasu, vb. 取り乱す lose control; be confused.

torimodosu, vb. 取り戻す get back.

torinasu, vb. 取りなす mediate.

tōrinukeru, vb. 通り抜ける pass through.

torisageru, vb. 取り下げる withdraw.

torishimaru, vb. 取り締まる control; oversee.

tōrisugiru, vb. 通り過ぎる pass by; pass over.

toritome ga nai, adj. とりとめがない meandering; incoherent.

toritsugu, vb. 取り次ぐ convey; transmit.

toritsukeru, vb. 取り付ける install; equip.

toriwake, adv. とりわけ above all; especially.

toriwakeru, vb. 取り分ける divide; distribute.

toriyameru, vb. 取り止める cancel.

toro, n. tuna meat prized for its oil content (sushi).

tōroku suru, vb. 登録する register; enroll.

tōron suru, *vb.* 討論する debate; discuss.

toru, *vb.* 取る 1. get; take; pick up. 2. eat; take (food, medicine, etc.). 3. take (course). 4. steal; rob. 5. subscribe.

toru, *vb.* 撮る take (a photograph).

tōru, *vb.* 通る 1. pass through or by. 2. pass (examination).

toruko, *n.* トルコ Turkey.

tōsan, *n.* 父さん one's father (daddy).

toshi, *n.* 年 age; year.

toshi, *n.* 都市 city.

tōshi, *n.* 投資 investment.

tōshibangō, *n.* 通し番号 serial number.

toshigoro, *n.* 年頃 1. marriageable age. 2. puberty.

toshin, *n.* 都心 city center.

toshishita (no), *adj.* 年下 (の) younger.

toshitsuki, *n.* 年月 time; years.

toshiue (no), *adj.* 年上 (の) senior; older.

toshiyori (no), *adj.* 年寄り (の) elderly.

toshokan, *n.* 図書館 library.

tōshu, *n.* 投手 pitcher (baseball).

tosō, *n.* 塗装 coat of paint.

tōsō, *n.* 闘争 1. fight. 2. labor strike.

tossa ni, *adv.* とっさ (に) on the spot; impromptu.

tōsu, *vb.* 通す 1. let someone pass; pass (an object) through. 2. admit; show in. 3. penetrate.

totan ni, *adv.* 途端に at the very moment.

tōtei, *adv.* 到底 (with negative) not by any means; not at all.

totemo, *adv.* とても very.

tōtō, *adv.* とうとう at last; after all.

tōtoi, *adj.* 尊い 1. sacred. 2. important; valuable.

totonou, *vb.* 整う, 調う 1. be in order. 2. be ready.

totsugeki, *n.* 突撃 charge; assault.

totsugu, *vb.* 嫁ぐ get married (bride).

totsunyū suru, *vb.* 突入する enter; rush into.

totsuzen (no), *adj.* 突然 (の) abrupt; sudden.

totte, *n.* 取っ手 doorknob; handle.

-totte とって for; to;

watashi ni-totte to me.

totteoku, *vb.* 取って置く set aside.

tou, *vb.* 問う ask; inquire.

tōyō, *n.* 東洋 East; Orient.

tōyōjin, *n.* 東洋人 Oriental (person).

tōyu, *n.* 灯油 kerosene.

tōzai, *n.* 東西 east and west; East and West.

tōzainanboku, *n.* 東西南北 four directions; north, south, east, and west.

tozan, *n.* 登山 mountain climbing.

tōzen, *adv.* 当然 naturally.

tsuba(ki), *n.* 唾 saliva.

tsubaki, *n.* 椿 camellia.

tsubame, *n.* つばめ swallow (bird).

tsubasa, *n.* 翼 wing.

tsubo, *n.* 壺 jar; pot; urn.

tsubomi, *n.* つぼみ bud.

tsubu, *n.* 粒 grain.

tsubureru, *vb.* つぶれる 1. be crushed. 2. go bankrupt.

tsuburu, *vb.* つぶる close (eyes).

tsubusu, *vb.* つぶす 1. crush; mash. 2. kill (time). 3. wreck.

tsubuyaku, vb. 呟く mumble; mutter.

tsuchi, n. 土 soil; earth.

tsūchi suru, vb. 通知する notify.

-tsudo つど every time; **unten suru sono-tsudo** every time (I) drive.

tsudou, vb. 集う gather; meet.

tsue, n. 杖 walking stick; cane.

tsūgaku suru, vb. 通学する attend school.

tsugeru, vb. 告げる tell; inform.

tsugi, n. 次 next.

tsugi-tsugi to/ni, adv. 次々 と、〜に one after another.

tsugō ga warui, adj. 都合が 悪い inconvenient.

tsugō ga yoi/ii, adj. 都合が 良い、〜いい convenient.

tsugu, vb. 注ぐ pour (tea, coffee, etc.).

tsugumu, vb. つぐむ shut (mouth).

tsugunau, vb. 償う compensate.

tsui, adv. つい 1. accidentally; in spite of oneself. 2. just; only.

-tsuide 次いで second to; **nihon ni-tsuide** second to Japan.

tsuide ni, adv. ついでに 1. incidentally. 2. in passing; while (I'm) on the subject.

tsuika suru, vb. 追加する add.

tsuikyū suru, vb. 追求する pursue; chase.

tsui ni, adv. 遂に finally; in the end; after all.

tsuiraku, n. 墜落 1. plane crash. 2. fall.

tsuiseki suru, vb. 追跡する chase.

tsuishin, n. 追伸 postscript.

tsuitachi, n. 一日 first day of the month.

-tsuite ついて about; on; **kabuki ni-tsuite hanasu** talk about kabuki.

tsuite'iku, vb. ついて行く 1. follow. 2. keep up with. 3. accompany.

tsuitekuru, vb. ついて来る 1. come along with. 2. follow.

tsuitotsu suru, vb. 追突する collide.

tsūjiru, vb. 通じる 1. lead to. 2. reach by telephone. 3. communicate; make oneself understood. 4. be knowledgeable.

tsūjite, prep. 通じて 1. by way of. 2. through; throughout.

tsūjō, adv. 通常 usually.

tsūka, n. 通過 transit; passage.

tsukaeru, vb. 仕える serve.

tsukaeru, vb. 使える be usable.

tsukai, n. 使い 1. errand; **tsukai ni iku** go on an errand. 2. messenger.

tsukaihatasu, vb. 使い果た す use up.

tsukaikata, n. 使い方 the way to use.

tsukaikonasu, vb. 使いこな す master; use skillfully.

tsukaisute (no), adj. 使い捨 て (の) disposable; **tsukaisute kamera** disposable camera.

tsukamaeru, vb. 捕まえる capture; catch.

tsukamu, vb. つかむ grasp; grip.

tsuka no ma (no), adj. 束の 間 (の) momentary; brief; ephemeral.

tsūkan suru, vb. 痛感する feel keenly.

tsukareru, vb. 疲れる get tired; become fatigued.

tsukaru, vb. 浸かる be soaked in.

tsūka suru, vb. 通過する pass; go through.

tsukau, vb. 使う 1. use. 2. employ (person). 3. spend; **hyakuen tsukau** spend one hundred yen.

tsukemono, n. 漬物 pickled vegetables.

tsukeru, vb. 付ける 1. attach. 2. install. 3. follow; pursue. make an entry.

tsukeru, vb. 点ける light; turn on.

tsukeru, vb. 漬ける 1. soak. 2. marinate.

tsuketasu, vb. 付け足す add.

tsuki, n. 月 1. moon. 2. month.

tsukiau, vb. 付き合う associate with.

tsukidasu, vb. 突き出す push out; thrust out.

tsukideru, vb. 突き出る stick out; protrude.

tsukihanasu, vb. 突き放す 1. abandon. 2. push off.

tsukihi, n. 月日 time; years.

tsukikaesu, vb. 突き返す 1. push back. 2. send back; turn down.

tsukimatou, vb. 付きまとう 1. follow; shadow. 2. haunt.

tsukimi, n. 月見 moon-viewing party.

tsūkin, n. 通勤 commuting.

tsūkindensha, n. 通勤電車 commuter train.

tsukiotosu, vb. 突き落とす push over.

tsukiru, vb. 尽きる be used up.

tsukisasu, vb. 突き刺す stab; pierce; skewer.

tsukisoi, n. 付き添い attendant; nurse.

tsukisou, vb. 付き添う 1. accompany. 2. take care of.

tsukitaosu, vb. 突き倒す push down.

tsukitobasu, vb. 突き飛ばす push away; send flying.

tsukitomeru, vb. 突き止める find out; locate; ascertain.

tsukiyo, n. 月夜 moonlit night.

tsukizuki (no), adj. 月々(の) monthly.

tsukkomu, vb. 突っ込む 1. thrust into. 2. jump into.

tsūkō, n. 通行 traffic.

tsūkōdome, n. 通行止め road closed (sign).

tsuku, vb. 着く 1. arrive. 2. come in contact with.

tsuku, vb. 点く 1. be lit; be ignited. 2. be turned on (television, lights).

tsuku, vb. 付く 1. adhere; stick. 2. be added; come along with.

tsuku, vb. 突く 1. poke; push; thrust. 2. use (for support).

tsukue, n. 机 desk.

tsukuri, n. 造り、作り structure.

tsukuribanashi, n. 作り話 fiction; lie.

tsukurikaeru, vb. 作り替える remodel; remake.

tsukurikata, n. 作り方 recipe.

tsukurinaosu, vb. 作り直す remodel; remake.

tsukuru, vb. 作る 1. make; produce. 2. prepare (food). 3. build. 4. grow (plants).

tsukusu, vb. 尽くす 1. use up. 2. exert oneself.

tsuma, n. 妻 one's own wife.

tsumami, n. つまみ 1. knob. 2. pinch; **shio hito**

tsumami a pinch of salt. 3. appetizer.

tsumaranai, adj. つまらない 1. dull; uninspiring. 2. petty; unimportant.

tsumari, adv. つまり namely; in short.

tsumaru, vb. 詰まる 1. be full; be congested. 2. be at a standstill.

tsumasaki de, adv. 爪先で on tiptoe.

tsumayōji, n. 爪揚子 toothpick.

tsumazuku, vb. つまずく 1. stumble; trip. 2. blunder.

tsume, n. 爪 nail; claw.

tsumeru, vb. 詰める fill; stuff; pack into.

tsumetai, adj. 冷たい 1. chilly; cold. 2. cold-hearted.

tsumi, n. 罪 sin; crime.

tsumiageru, vb. 積み上げる pile up; accumulate.

tsumikasaneru, vb. 積み重ねる stack; amass.

tsumori, n. つもり intention; expectation.

tsumu, vb. 積む 1. heap up; accumulate. 2. load.

tsumu, vb. 摘む pick (tea, cotton, etc.).

tsuna, n. 綱 rope.

tsunagu, vb. つなぐ 1. connect; link. 2. fasten; tie.

tsunami, n. 津波 tsunami.

tsune ni, adv. 常に always; continually.

tsuneru, vb. つねる pinch.

tsuno, n. 角 1. horn; antler. 2. feeler.

tsura, vb. 面 face (slang).

tsurai, adj. 辛い tormenting; painful.

tsurara, n. 氷柱 icicle.

-tsurete つれて as; **nihon ga tomu ni-tsurete** as Japan becomes more prosperous.

tsureteiku, vb. 連れて行く usher; take (a person) with one.

tsuri, n. 釣り fishing.

tsuriau, vb. 釣り合う balance; be well matched.

tsuri(sen), n. 釣り(銭) change (money).

tsūro, n. 通路 passageway.

tsuru, n. 鶴 crane (bird).

tsuru, vb. 吊る suspend; hang up.

tsuru, vb. 釣る fish.

tsurusu, vb. 吊るす suspend; hang up.

tsūsanshō, n. 通産省 MITI (Ministry of International Trade and Industry).

tsūsetsu ni, adv. 痛切に acutely.

tsūshin, n. 通信 correspondence; communication.

tsutaeru, vb. 伝える 1. tell; inform; convey. 2. hand down. 3. transmit.

tsutomeru, vb. 勤める work for a company.

tsutomeru, vb. 務める discharge one's duty.

tsutomeru, vb. 努める make an effort.

tsutsu, n. 筒 cylinder.

tsutsuji, n. つつじ azalea.

tsutsuku, vb. つつく peck; poke.

tsutsumigami, n. 包み紙 wrapping paper.

tsutsumu, vb. 包む wrap.

tsutsushimu, vb. 慎む 1. be discreet. 2. refrain from.

tsūwa, n. 通話 telephone call.

tsūya, n. 通夜 wake (for the deceased).

tsuya, n. 艶 luster.

tsūyaku, n. 通訳 interpreter; interpretation.

tsuyoi, adj. 強い strong.
tsuyomeru, vb. 強める 1. strengthen. 2. emphasize.
tsuyosa, n. 強さ strength; power.
tsūyō suru, vb. 通用する be valid; be useful; be acceptable; be used.
tsuyu, n. 梅雨 rainy season.

tsuyu, n. 汁 Japanese-style soup or sauce.
tsuyu, n. 露 dew.
tsuzukeru, vb. 続ける continue.
tsuzuku, vb. 続く 1. be continued. 2. adjoin.
tsuzuru, vb. 綴る spell; write.

U

u, n. 鵜 cormorant.
ubaguruma, n. 乳母車 baby carriage; stroller.
ubai'au, vb. 奪い合う fight over.
ubau, vb. 奪う 1. rob. 2. fascinate.
uchi, n. 内 1. inside; insider. 2. one's family; one's organization.
uchi うち 1. prep. in; among; within; **kazoku no uchi de** within one's family. 2. conj. while; **atsui uchi ni** while it is hot.
uchiageru, vb. 打ち上げる 1. wash ashore. 2. launch; shoot off. 3. finish; close (a performance).
uchiakeru, vb. 打ち明ける confide in.
uchiawaseru, vb. 打ち合わせる make preliminary arrangements.
uchigawa, n. 内側 inside.
uchikaesu, vb. 打ち返す strike back.
uchiki (na), adj. 内気 (な) shy.
uchikiru, vb. 打ち切る discontinue; break off.
uchitaosu, vb. 打ち倒す strike down.
uchitokeru, vb. 打ち解ける cast off one's reserve.
uchitsukeru, vb. 打ち付ける

hammer.
uchiwa, n. うちわ nonfolding fan.
uchiyaburu, vb. 打ち破る 1. break. 2. conquer.
uchū, n. 宇宙 universe; outer space.
uchūhikōshi, n. 宇宙飛行士 astronaut.
ude, n. 腕 1. arm. 2. skill.
udedokei, n. 腕時計 wristwatch.
udezuku de, adv. 腕ずくで by force.
udon, n. うどん Japanese noodles.
ue 上 1. n. top; surface; **tsukue no ue ni** on (top of) the desk. 2. n. upper part; person ranking above others. 3. prep. above; on; over. 4. adv. up.
uekibachi, n. 植木鉢 flowerpot.
ueru, vb. 飢える starve.
ugai, n. うがい gargling.
ugoku, vb. 動く 1. move; stir. 2. change; vary. 3. operate.
uguisu, n. うぐいす Japanese bush warbler.
ukaberu, vb. 浮かべる set afloat.
ukabu, vb. 浮かぶ 1. float. 2. surface.
ukagau, vb. 伺う 1. visit. 2.

ask.

ukaru, vb. 受かる pass (exam).

ukeireru, vb. 受け入れる accept.

ukemi, n. 受身 1. passivity. 2. passive voice.

ukeru, vb. 受ける 1. catch; get; receive. 2. take (exam, class, etc.). 3. be affected; suffer from.

uketamawaru, vb. 承る 1. hear. 2. be told.

uketoru, vb. 受け取る 1. receive. 2. interpret.

uketsugu, vb. 受け継ぐ inherit; succeed to.

uketsuke, n. 受け付け 1. acceptance. 2. receptionist; reception desk.

ukibori, n. 浮き彫り relief (carving).

uki-uki suru, vb. うきうきする be excited.

ukiyoe, n. 浮世絵 premodern Japanese woodblock print.

ukkari, adv. うっかり carelessly.

uku, vb. 浮く float.

uma, n. 馬 horse.

umai, adj. うまい 1. delicious. 2. skillful. 3. promising; successful.

umareru, vb. 生まれる be born.

umaretsuki, adv. 生まれつき by birth; by nature.

umaru, vb. 埋る be buried in; be filled with; **hana de umaru** be filled with flowers.

ume, n. 梅 plum.

umeboshi, n. 梅干し pickled Japanese plum.

umeru, vb. 埋める bury.

umi, n. 海 sea; ocean.

umibe, n. 海辺 beach; seashore.

umoreru, vb. 埋もれる be buried in.

umu, vb. 産む、生む give birth; produce; lay (egg).

un, n. 運 luck; fortune; **un ga ii** lucky; **un ga warui** unlucky.

un, interj. うん Yes! That's right!

unagasu, vb. 促す urge.

unagi, n. うなぎ eel.

una(gi)don(buri), n. うな(ぎ)丼 grilled eel served over rice.

unajū, n. うな重 grilled eel served over rice in a lacquer box.

unazuku, vb. 頷く 1. nod. 2. agree.

unchin, n. 運賃 fare (transportation).

undō, n. 運動 1. exercise; sport. 2. action; movement. 3. campaign.

undōgutsu, n. 運動靴 athletic shoes; sneakers.

un'ei suru, vb. 運営する manage; operate.

uni, n. うに sea urchin (sushi).

unmei, n. 運命 destiny.

unsō, n. 運送 shipment; transportation.

unten suru, vb. 運転する drive a car; operate a machine.

unuboreru, vb. うぬぼれる be conceited.

unzari suru, vb. うんざりする get disgusted with; become fed up with.

uo, n. 魚 fish.

uoichiba, n. 魚市場 fish market.

uppun, n. うっぷん anger; frustration; **uppun o harasu** vent one's anger.

ura, n. 裏 1. back; rear. 2. reverse. 3. hidden aspect.

uragaesu, *vb.* 裏返す turn over; turn inside out.

uragawa, *n.* 裏側 reverse side.

uragiru, *vb.* 裏切る betray; deceive.

uramu, *vb.* 恨む bear a grudge.

uranai, *n.* 占い fortune-telling.

urayamashii, *adj.* 羨ましい envious.

urei, *n.* 憂い、愁い melancholy; sorrow.

ureru, *vb.* 売れる sell; be in demand.

ureshii, *adj.* 嬉しい happy.

uriba, *n.* 売り場 counter; box office; department; **bunbōgu uriba** stationery department.

urikireru, *vb.* 売り切れる be sold out.

uroko, *n.* うろこ scale (fish).

urotsuku, *vb.* うろつく loiter; hover.

uru, *vb.* 売る sell.

urumu, *vb.* 潤む moisten; be blurred.

uruou, *vb.* 潤う 1. profit. 2. become moist.

urusai, *adj.* うるさい 1. annoying. 2. noisy. 3. fussy; meticulous. 4. inquisitive.

urushi, *n.* 漆 lacquer; lacquerware.

usabarashi, *n.* 憂さ晴らし diversion; distraction.

usagi, *n.* 兎 rabbit.

ushi, *n.* 牛 cow; bull.

ushinau, *vb.* 失う lose.

ushiro, *n.* 後ろ back; rear.

ushiro ni/de 後ろに、〜で 1. *prep.* behind. 2. *adv.* at the back.

uso, *n.* 嘘 lie.

uso (o) tsuku, *vb.* 嘘 (を) 吐く tell a lie.

usotsuki, *n.* 嘘吐き liar.

usu- 薄 1. thin; light; **usuaoi** light blue. 2. somewhat.

usugurai, *adj.* 薄暗い dim.

usui, *adj.* 薄い thin; light; weak.

uta, *n.* 歌 song.

utagau, *vb.* 疑う doubt; suspect.

utau, *vb.* 歌う sing.

uten, *n.* 雨天 rainy weather.

uto-uto suru, *vb.* うとうとする doze.

utsu, *vb.* 打つ 1. beat; hit; strike. 2. impress; touch (the heart).

utsu, *vb.* 撃つ fire (gun).

utsubuse, *n.* うつぶせ lying on one's stomach.

utsukushii, *adj.* 美しい beautiful.

utsumuku, *vb.* うつむく look down; hang one's head.

utsuri, *n.* 映り、写り reflection; image (on screen).

utsurikawaru, *vb.* 移り変わる change.

utsuru, *vb.* 移る 1. change; move. 2. be infected with.

utsuru, *vb.* 映る、写る be shown (on screen); be reflected.

utsushi, *n.* 写し copy.

utsusu, *vb.* 写す take (photograph); copy.

utsuwa, *n.* 器 1. container (bowl, plate, etc.); receptacle. 2. ability.

uttaeru, *vb.* 訴える 1. sue; appeal. 2. complain of.

uttori suru, *vb.* うっとりする be spellbound.

uttōshii, *adj.* うっとうしい gloomy; depressing.

uwagi, *n.* 上着 jacket.

uwaki, *n.* 浮気 extramarital affair; infidelity.

uwamawaru, vb. 上回る surpass; exceed.

uwa no sora de, adv. 上の空で absent-mindedly.

uwasa (o) suru, vb. 噂(を)する spread a rumor; gossip.

uyamau, vb. 敬う respect; venerate.

uya-uyashii, adj. 恭々しい deferential.

uzukumaru, vb. うずくまる crouch.

uzumaki, n. 渦巻き whirlpool.

uzumakijō (no), adj. 渦巻き状 (の) spiral.

uzumeru, vb. 埋める fill up; bury (face).

W

wa, n. 輪 round shape (ring, circle, wheel, etc.).

wabiru, vb. 詫びる apologize.

wabishii, adj. わびしい dreary; lonely.

wadai, n. 話題 topic.

waeijiten, n. 和英辞典 Japanese-English dictionary.

wafū, n. 和風 Japanese style.

wafuku, n. 和服 Japanese clothing; kimono.

waga- 我が one's (my, our, etc.); **wagasha** our company; **wagaya** my house.

wagamama (na), adj. 我がまま (な) selfish; spoiled.

wa-gomu, n. 輪ゴム rubber band.

wairo, n. 賄賂 bribe.

waisetsu (na), adj. わいせつ (な) obscene.

wai-shatsu, n. ワイシャツ (E.) dress shirt.

wakaba, n. 若葉 young leaf.

wakagaeru, vb. 若返る be rejuvenated.

wakai, adj. 若い young; immature.

wakai suru, vb. 和解する come to terms with.

wakamono, n. 若者 young person.

wakaranai, vb. 分からない not understand.

wakarazuya, n. 分からず屋 obdurate or obstinate person.

wakareru, vb. 別れる separate from; divorce; leave.

wakari, n. 分かり understanding.

wakarikitta, adj. 分かりきった obvious.

wakarinikui, adj. 分かりにくい puzzling; incomprehensible.

wakariyasui, adj. 分かりやすい easy to understand.

wakaru, vb. 分かる understand; know; recognize.

wakasa, n. 若さ youth; youthfulness.

wakasu, vb. 沸かす 1. boil; simmer. 2. excite.

waka-wakashii, adj. 若々しい youthful.

wake, n. 訳 1. reason. 2. meaning.

wakemae, n. 分け前 share.

wakenai, adj. 訳ない easy.

wakeru, vb. 分ける 1. divide. 2. share. 3. categorize.

waki, n. 脇 side.

wakiagaru, vb. 沸き上がる come or go up; rise.

wakimaeru, vb. 弁える discern; understand.

waki ni 脇に 1. *prep.* at the side of; beside. 2. *adv.* alongside.

waku, *n.* 枠 1. frame; framework. 2. limit.

waku, *vb.* 沸く 1. boil. 2. be enthusiastic.

wakuchin, *n.* ワクチン (G. *Vakzin*) vaccine.

wakusei, *n.* 惑星 planet.

waku-waku suru, *vb.* わくわくする be excited.

wameku, *vb.* 喚く yell; shriek.

wan, *n.* 湾 gulf; bay.

wana, *n.* 罠 snare; trap.

wana ni kakaru, *vb.* 罠にかかる be caught in a trap.

wani, *n.* わに crocodile; alligator.

wanpaku (na), *adj.* 腕白 (な) naughty.

wāpuro, *n.* ワープロ (E.) word processor.

wara, *n.* わら straw.

waraimono, *n.* 笑い者 laughingstock.

warau, *vb.* 笑う laugh; smile.

waremono, *n.* 割れ物 fragile article.

warera, *pron.* 我ら we.

wareru, *vb.* 割れる break; crack; split.

ware-ware, *pron.* 我々 we.

wari, *n.* 割 rate; percent; ten percent; **gowari** fifty percent.

wariai, *n.* 割合 ratio; percentage; proportion.

wariate, *n.* 割り当て allotment; allocation.

waribashi, *n.* 割りばし disposable wooden chopsticks.

waribiki, *n.* 割り引き discount.

warikan, *n.* 割り勘 Dutch treat.

warikirenai 割りきれない 1. indivisible. 2. unconvincing; unsatisfactory.

warikiru, *vb.* 割りきる give a logical explanation.

warikomu, *vb.* 割り込む break into; cut in.

wari ni 割に 1. *adv.* comparatively; proportionately. 2. *prep.* considering; **toshi no wari ni** considering (his) age.

waru, *n.* 悪 scoundrel.

waru, *vb.* 割る 1. break; split. 2. divide. 3. go below (score, value).

warui, *adj.* 悪い bad; wrong.

warukuchi, *n.* 悪口 slander; abuse.

warumono, *n.* 悪者 scoundrel.

wasabi, *n.* わさび Japanese horseradish.

washi, *n.* わし eagle.

washi, *n.* 和紙 Japanese paper.

washitsu, *n.* 和室 Japanese-style room.

washoku, *n.* 和食 Japanese meal.

wasuremono, *n.* 忘れ物 lost item; item left behind.

wasureppoi, *adj.* 忘れっぽい forgetful.

wasure-rarenai, *adj.* 忘れられない unforgettable.

wasureru, *vb.* 忘れる 1. forget. 2. leave behind.

wata, *n.* 綿 cotton.

watagashi, *n.* 綿菓子 cotton candy.

watakushi, *pron.* 私 I.

wataridori, *n.* 渡り鳥 migratory bird.

wataru, *vb.* 渡る 1. cross; pass. 2. be given; be obtained.

watashi, *pron.* 私 I.

watashi (no), *adj.* 私 (の) my.

watashitachi, *pron.* 私達 we.

watashitachi (no), *adj.* 私達 (の) our.

watasu, *vb.* 渡す 1. pass; hand over. 2. carry across.

waza, *n.* 技 skill; technique.

waza to, *adv.* わざと intentionally.

waza-waza, *adv.* わざわざ purposely.

wazuka (ni), *adv.* わずか (に) 1. barely; slightly. 2. only.

wazurau, *vb.* 患う suffer (from illness).

wazurau, *vb.* 煩らう worry about.

Y

ya, *n.* 矢 arrow.

ya や and; **hanaya tori** flowers and birds.

-ya 屋 shop; **hanaya** florist.

yā, *interj.* やあ Hi!

yaban (na), *adj.* 野蛮 (な) barbarous; uncivilized.

yabu, *n.* やぶ bush; thicket.

yabureru, *vb.* 敗れる be defeated; lose.

yaburu, *vb.* 破る 1. tear; break. 2. violate.

yachin, *n.* 家賃 house rent; room rent.

yado, *n.* 宿 lodging; hotel; inn.

yagai, *n* 野外 outdoors; **yagai-konsāto** outdoor concert.

yagate, *adv.* やがて before long; soon.

yagi, *n.* 山羊 goat.

yahari, *adv.* やはり 1. after all. 2. again.

yajirushi, *n.* 矢印 arrow (on map or sign).

yakamashii, *adj.* やかましい 1. noisy. 2. controversial; **yakamashī jiken** controversial case. 3. particular.

yakan, *n.* やかん kettle.

yakan, *n.* 夜間 nighttime.

yake, *n.* やけ desperation; **yake o okosu** surrender to desperation.

yakedo, *n.* 火傷 burn (injury).

yakei, *n.* 夜景 night view.

yake ni, *adv.* やけに 1. awfully. 2. desperately.

yakimeshi, *n.* 焼き飯 fried rice.

yakimochi, *n.* 焼きもち jealousy.

yakimono, *n.* 焼き物 chinaware; earthenware; pottery.

yakiniku, *n.* 焼き肉 broiled (grilled, roasted) meat.

yakisoba, *n.* 焼きそば fried noodles.

yakitori, *n.* 焼き鳥 grilled skewered chicken and vegetables.

yakkai (na), *adj.* 厄介 (な) troublesome; awkward.

yakkyoku, *n.* 薬局 drugstore; pharmacy.

yaku, *vb.* 焼く 1. burn or char (broil, grill, toast, etc.). 2. get a suntan. 3. print (photograph). 4. bake (pottery).

yaku, *adv.* 約 about; approximately.

yakudatsu, *vb.* 役立つ be useful; be helpful.

yakume, *n.* 役目 responsibility; function;

role.

yakumi, *n.* 薬味 spice.

yaku ni tatsu, *vb.* 役に立つ be useful; be helpful.

yakusō, *n.* 薬草 medicinal herb.

yakusoku, *n.* 約束 1. promise; **yakusoku o mamoru** keep one's promise. 2. appointment; **hoka no yakusoku ga aru** have another appointment.

yakusu, *vb.* 訳す translate; **nihongo ni yakusu** translate into Japanese.

yakuwari, *n.* 役割り role.

yakuza, *n.* やくざ hoodlum; gangster.

yakuzaishi, *n.* 薬剤師 pharmacist.

yakyū, *n.* 野球 baseball.

yama, *n.* 山 1. mountain; hill; pile. 2. speculation. 3. crisis; climax.

yamai, *n.* 病 disease; sickness.

yamamori (no), *adj.* 山盛り (の) abundant; heaping.

yamanobori, *n.* 山登り mountain climbing.

yameru, *vb.* 止める stop; give up.

yameru, *vb.* 辞める resign; quit.

yami, *n.* 闇 darkness.

yamome, *n.* やもめ widow.

yamu, *vb.* 止む stop; cease.

yamu o enai, *adj.* やむを得ない inevitable; unavoidable.

yanagi, *n.* 柳 willow.

yancha (na), *adj.* やんちゃ (な) mischievous.

yane, *n.* 屋根 roof.

yanushi, *n.* 家主 landlady; landlord.

yaoya, *n.* 八百屋 store selling vegetables and fruit; produce stand.

yappari, *adv.* やっぱり 1. after all. 2. again.

yare-yare, *interj.* やれやれ 1. Thank goodness that's over! 2. Good grief!

yari, *n.* 槍 spear.

yarikake (no), *adj.* やりかけ (の) unfinished.

yarikata, *n.* やり方 way of doing something; procedure.

yarinaosu, *vb.* やり残す redo.

yarisokonau, *vb.* やり損なう fail.

yaritogeru, *vb.* やり遂げる accomplish.

yarō, *n.* 野郎 1. man; guy (slang). 2. rascal.

yaru, *vb.* やる 1. give (informal). 2. do. 3. get along.

yaruki, *n.* やる気 determination.

yasai, *n.* 野菜 vegetable.

yasashii, *adj.* 易しい easy.

yasashii, *adj.* 優しい 1. kind; gentle. 2. graceful.

yasei (no), *adj.* 野性 (の) wild (animal, plant).

yaseru, *vb.* やせる 1. lose weight; become thin. 2. become barren.

yaseta, *adj.* やせた 1. slender; thin. 2. barren.

yashinau, *vb.* 養う feed; nourish; support; cultivate.

yasui, *adj.* 安い cheap; inexpensive.

-yasui 易い 1. easy (to do); **tsukai-yasui** easy to use. 2. easily; **okoriyasui** easily angered.

yasumono, *n.* 安物 cheap item.

yasumu, *vb.* 休む 1. take a break or rest; relax. 2. be absent from. 3. sleep.

yasuragu, *vb.* 安らぐ feel at

peace.

yasuraka ni, *adv.* 安らかに peacefully.

yasuri, *n.* やすり file (tool).

yasu-yasu to, *adv.* やすやすと easily.

yatai, *n.* 屋台 street food vendor.

yatara (ni, to), *adv.* やたら (に、と) 1. at random. 2. excessively.

yatou, *vb.* 雇う employ; hire.

yatsu 奴 (slang) 1. *pron.* he; she. 2. *n.* that person. 3. *n.* fellow.

yatsuatari suru, *vb.* 八つ当りする vent one's anger at random.

yatsura, *pron.* 奴ら they (slang).

yattekuru, *vb.* やって来る 1. arrive. 2. turn up.

yattemiru, *vb.* やってみる try; make an attempt.

yatto, *adv.* やっと 1. barely; somehow. 2. finally.

yattsu, *n.* 八つ eight; eight years old.

yawaragu, *vb.* 和らぐ soften; become less severe.

yawarakai, *adj.* 柔らかい soft; tender.

yaya, *adv.* やや somewhat; a little bit.

yayakoshii, *adj.* ややこしい complicated; difficult.

yo, *n.* 夜 night.

yo, *n.* 世 1. world; society. 2. life. 3. epoch; reign.

yō, *n.* 用 1. business; job. 2. errand.

yō 様 look like; sound like; **Hontō no yō desu.** (It) sounds true.

-yō 用 for the use of; **kodomoyō** for the use of children.

yoake, *n.* 夜明け daybreak.

-yōbi 曜日 day of the week;

sui-yōbi Wednesday.

yobidasu, *vb.* 呼び出す call; summon.

yobikakeru, *vb.* 呼び掛ける call to yo; appeal.

yobimono, *n.* 呼び物 attraction; main event.

yobina, *n.* 呼び名 name; alias.

yobō, *n.* 予防 prevention.

yōbō, *n.* 要望 demand; request.

yobōchūsha, *n.* 予防注射 vaccination.

yobō suru, *vb.* 予防する prevent.

yobu, *vb.* 呼ぶ 1. call. 2. send for. 3. invite.

yobun (no), *adj.* 余分 (の) extra; spare.

yōbun, *n.* 養分 nutriment.

yobun ni, *adv.* 余分に extra; too much.

yochi, *n.* 余地 room; space.

yōchi (na), *adj.* 幼稚 (な) childish; puerile.

yōchien, *n.* 幼稚園 kindergarten.

yochi suru, *vb.* 予知する predict; foresee.

yodare, *n.* 涎 saliva; drool.

yodōshi de, *adv.* 夜通しで all night.

yōfū (no), *adj.* 洋風 (の) Western-style.

yofuke, *n.* 夜更け late night; after midnight.

yōfuku, *n.* 洋服 Western-style clothes.

yoga, *n.* ヨガ (Hindi) yoga.

yōgo, *n.* 用語 (technical) terminology; jargon.

yogosu, *vb.* 汚す soil; stain.

yōguruto, *n.* ヨーグルト (E.) yogurt.

yōhin, *n.* 用品 1. supplies. 2. utensils.

yohō, *n.* 予報 forecast.

yohodo, *adv.* 余程

considerably.

yoi, *n.* 酔い drunkenness; intoxication.

yoi, *adj.* 良い good.

yōi, *n.* 用意 preparation.

yōiku suru, *vb.* 養育する raise; bring up.

yōin, *n.* 要因 factor.

yōi suru, *vb.* 用意する prepare.

yōji, *n.* 用事 business; errand.

yōji, *n.* 幼児 young child.

yojinoboru, *vb.* よじ登る climb; scale.

yōjin suru, *vb.* 用心する be careful; be cautious.

yojireru, *vb.* よじれる become twisted.

yōka, *n.* 八日 eighth day of the month; eight days.

yokan, *n.* 予感 premonition; presentiment.

yokei (na), *adj.* 余計 (な) excessive; unnecessary.

yokeru, *vb.* 避ける avoid.

yoki, *n.* 予期 expectation; prediction.

yōki, *n.* 容器 receptacle; container.

yōki (na), *adj.* 陽気 (な) merry; happy-go-lucky.

yokin, *n.* 預金 bank deposit.

yokka, *n.* 四日 fourth day of the month; four days.

yoko, *n.* 横 side; width.

yokodori suru, *vb.* 横取りする steal; snatch away.

yokogao, *n.* 横顔 profile.

yokogiru, *vb.* 横切る cross; cut across.

yokoku, *n.* 予告 advance notice.

yokoku suru, *vb.* 予告する give advance notice.

yokomichi, *n.* 横道 side road.

yōkoso, *interj.* ようこそ Welcome!

yokosu, *vb.* よこす give; send.

yokotaeru, *vb.* 横たえる lay down.

yokozuna, *n.* 横綱 grand champion (sumo).

yoku, *adv.* よく 1. well. 2. often. 3. thoroughly.

yoku- 翌 the next; the following; **yokushū** the following week.

yokubari (na), *adj.* 欲張り (な) greedy.

yokubaru, *vb.* 欲張る be greedy.

yokubō, *n.* 欲望 ambition; desire.

yokujitsu, *n.* 翌日 the next day.

yokushitsu, *n.* 浴室 bathroom.

yōkyū suru, *vb.* 要求する request; demand.

yōma, *n.* 洋間 Western-style room.

yome, *n.* 嫁 bride; daughter-in-law (used by husband's parents).

yomigaeru, *vb.* 蘇る revive; rise from the dead.

yomikaki, *n.* 読み書き reading and writing.

yomite, *n.* 読み手 reader.

yōmō, *n.* 羊毛 wool.

yomu, *vb.* 読む read.

yō (na, ni) 様 (な・に) as; like; sounding like; resembling; **yume no yō na hanashi** story resembling a dream (unlikely story); **anata no iu yō ni** as you say.

yon, *n.* 四 four.

yonaka, *n.* 夜中 middle of the night.

yonensei, *n.* 四年生 fourth grader; college senior.

yō ni ように in order to; **seikō suru yō ni** in order

yonjū, *n.* 四十 forty.

yo no naka, *n.* 世の中 life; society; world.

yopparau, *vb.* 酔っ払う get drunk.

yoppodo, *adv.* よっぽど considerably.

yōrei, *n.* 用例 example; illustration.

yore-yore (no), *adj.* よれよれ (の) ragged; tattered.

yori より 1. *conj.* than; **are yori ii** better than that. 2. *prep.* from; since. 3. *adv.* more; **yori tanoshiku naru** become more enjoyable.

yorimichi, *n.* 寄り道 stopping off; breaking of a journey.

yorisou, *vb.* 寄り添う lean on someone; draw near to someone (physically).

yoritsuku, *vb.* 寄り付く approach; come or go closer.

yorokeru, *vb.* よろける stagger; reel.

yorokobu, *vb.* 喜ぶ be happy; be delighted.

yoromeku, *vb.* よろめく stagger; wobble.

yōroppa, *n.* ヨーロッパ (Pg. *Europa*) Europe.

yoroshii, *adj.* よろしい good.

yoroshiku よろしく 1. *adv.* well. 2. *interj.* Pleased to meet you.

yoru, *n.* 夜 night.

yoru, *vb.* 寄る 1. go closer. 2. drop in at. 3. gather.

yoru to よると according to; **nyūsu ni yoru to** according to the news.

yōryō, *n.* 容量 capacity.

yōryō ga ii, *adj.* 要領がいい clever; smart; dexterous.

yōryō ga warui, *adj.* 要領が

悪い clumsy.

yōsai, *n.* 洋裁 sewing (Western-style clothes).

yosan, *n.* 予算 budget.

yoseatsumeru, *vb.* 寄せ集める collect.

yōsei, *n.* 妖精 elf; fairy.

yōsei suru, *vb.* 要請する demand; request.

yoseru, *vb.* 寄せる 1. bring closer; gather. 2. send.

yōsha suru, *vb.* 容赦する forgive.

yoshi, *interj.* よし Good!

yōshi, *n.* 養子 adopted child.

yōshi, *n.* 用紙 blank printed form.

yōshiki, *n.* 洋式 Western style.

yōshoku, *n.* 洋食 Western-style meal.

yoso, *n.* よそ another place.

yosō, *n.* 予想 expectation; speculation; **yosō ni hanshite** contrary to one's expectation.

yosōgai ni, *adv.* 予想外に unexpectedly.

yusomono, *n.* よそ者 stranger.

yoso-yososhii, *adj.* よそよそしい distant; unfriendly.

yōsu, *n.* 様子 condition; state.

yōsuru ni, *adv.* 要するに in short.

yotei, *n.* 予定 schedule; plan; **yoteidōri** on schedule.

yōto, *n.* 用途 usage; application.

yotsukado, *n.* 四つ角 intersection (road).

yotte, *adv.* よって therefore.

yotto, *n.* ヨット (E.) yacht.

yottsu, *n.* 四つ four; four years old.

you, *vb.* 酔う 1. get drunk; get intoxicated. 2. suffer

from motion sickness.

yowai, *adj.* 弱い weak.

yowami, *n.* 弱み weak point.

yowamushi, *n.* 弱虫 coward.

yowane, *n.* 弱音 complaining.

yoyaku, *n.* 予約 appointment; reservation; **yoyaku o toru/suru** make an appointment; make a reservation.

yōyaku, *adv.* 漸く 1. finally. 2. barely; somehow.

yoyū, *n.* 余裕 1. room; space. 2. compcsure.

yu, *n.* 湯 hot water.

yūbe, *n.* 夕べ 1. evening. 2. yesterday evening.

yubi, *n.* 指 finger; toe.

yūbin, *n.* 郵便 mail.

yūbinbangō, *n.* 郵便番号 zip code.

yūbinkyoku, *n.* 郵便局 post office.

yubisaki, *n.* 指先 fingertip.

yubisasu, *vb.* 指差す point to (with a finger).

yubiwa, *n.* 指輪 ring (jewelry); **kekkonyubiwa** wedding ring.

yūdachi, *n.* 夕立 shower (rain).

yūdai (na), *adj.* 雄大 (な) grand; grandiose.

yudaneru, *vb.* 委ねる entrust.

yudan suru, *vb.* 油断する be inattentive; be off guard.

yudayajin, *n.* ユダヤ人 Jew.

yudayakyō, *n.* ユダヤ教 Judaism.

yuderu, *vb.* ゆでる boil.

yudetamago, *n.* ゆで玉子 boiled egg.

yūeki (na), *adj.* 有益 (な) beneficial; useful.

yūenchi, *n.* 遊園地 amusement park.

yūfuku (na), *adj.* 裕福 (な) wealthy.

yūga (na), *adj.* 優雅 (な) elegant.

yūgai (na), *adj.* 有害 (な) harmful.

yugamu, *vb.* 歪む be bent; be distorted.

yūgata, *n.* 夕方 evening.

yūgure, *n.* 夕暮れ early evening; twilight.

yūhi, *n.* 夕日 setting sun.

yuigon, *n.* 遺言 will; deathbed instructions.

yui-itsu (no), *adj.* 唯一 (の) only; exclusive.

yūjin, *n.* 友人 friend.

yūjō, *n.* 友情 friendship.

yuka, *n.* 床 floor.

yukai (na), *adj.* 愉快 (な) pleasant; cheerful.

yūkai suru, *vb.* 誘拐する abduct.

yūkan, *n.* 夕刊 evening paper.

yūkan (na), *adj.* 勇敢 (な) brave.

yukata, *n.* 浴衣 informal summer kimono.

yuki, *n.* 雪 snow.

-yuki (no) 行き bound for (transportation); **Narayuki no densha** train bound for Nara.

yūki, *n.* 勇気 courage; **yūki o dasu** get up one's courage.

yukidaruma, *n.* 雪だるま snowman.

yukidomari, *n.* 行き止まり dead end.

yukiguni, *n.* 雪国 snow country.

yukizumari, *n.* 行き詰まり impasse; deadlock.

yukkuri, *adv.* ゆっくり 1. slowly. 2. leisurely.

yukkuri suru, *vb.* ゆっくりする 1. relax; rest. 2. take

one's time.

yūkō, n. 友好 friendship.

yūkō (na), adj. 有効 (な) valid; effective.

yuku, vb. 行く go.

yukuefumei, adj. 行方不明 missing (person).

yume, n. 夢 dream; **yume ga aru** have a dream.

yūmei (na), adj. 有名 (な) famous.

yumi, n. 弓 bow (archery).

yūnō (na), adj. 有能 (な) able; competent.

yunyū, n. 輸入 import.

yunyūhin, n. 輸入品 imported goods.

yurai, n. 由来 origin.

yūrei, n. 幽霊 ghost.

yureru, vb. 揺れる sway; shake.

yuri, n. 百合 lily.

yūri (na), adj. 有利 (な) advantageous; favorable.

yurikago, n. 揺りかご cradle; bassinet.

yurui, adj 緩い 1. lax; loose. 2. slow.

yurumu, vb. 緩む abate; become loose.

yurusu, vb 許す 1. forgive. 2. accept; permit.

yuruyaka (na), adj. 緩やか (な) 1. loose. 2. lenient. 3. slow.

yūryō (na), adj. 優良 (な) excellent.

yūryō (no), adj. 有料 (の)

pay (TV, phone, toilet, etc.); toll (road).

yūryoku (na), adj. 有力 (な) influential; powerful.

yūsen suru, vb. 優先する give priority to.

yūsen-terebi, n. 有線テレビ cable TV.

yūshoku, n. 夕食 evening meal.

yūshō suru, vb. 優勝する win (first place).

yūshū (na), adj. 優秀 (な) outstanding; prominent.

yushutsu, n. 輸出 export.

yusō, n. 輸送 shipment; transportation.

yūsō, n. 郵送 mailing.

yusugu, n. ゆすぐ rinse.

yusuru, n. 強請る blackmail.

yusuru, vb. 揺する shake.

yutaka (na), adj. 豊か (な) rich.

yutori, n. ゆとり 1. space; room. 2. ease.

yū'utsu, n. 憂うつ depression; melancholy.

yuwakashi, n. 湯沸かし teakettle.

yūwaku suru, vb. 誘惑する seduce; tempt.

yūyake, n. 夕焼け sunset.

yūzai (no), adj. 有罪 (の) guilty (criminal).

yuzuru, vb. 譲る 1. give way. 2. hand over. 3. sell. 4. bequeath.

Z

za, n. 座 1. seat; **za ni tsuku** take a seat. 2. post; position; **sōri no za ni tsuku** assume the position of prime minister.

zabuton, n. 座布団 floor cushion.

zai, n. 財 wealth; **zai o nasu** make a fortune.

zaigaku, n. 在学 school enrollment.

zaiko, n. 在庫 stock; inventory.

zaimoku, n. 材木 lumber;

timber.

zainin, n. 罪人 criminal; sinner.

zairyō, n. 材料 material; ingredient.

zaisan, n. 財産 assets; fortune; property.

zakkaten, n. 雑貨店 variety store.

zakkubaran (na, no), adj. ざっくばらん (な、の) frank; straightforward.

zakuro, n. ざくろ pomegranate.

zandaka, n. 残高 outstanding balance.

zangyaku (na), adj. 残虐 (な) cruel; inhuman.

zangyō, n. 残業 overtime work.

zankoku (na), adj. 残酷 (な) brutal; atrocious.

zan'nen (na), adj. 残念 (な) disappointing; regrettable.

zantei-teki ni, adv. 暫定的 に for the moment; tentatively.

zara-zara suru, vb. ざらざら する 1. feel rough. 2. be sandy.

zarigani, n. ざりがに crayfish.

zaru, n. ざる bamboo colander.

zaseki, n. 座席 seat (transportation, theater).

zasetsu suru, vb. 挫折する be frustrated; collapse; fail.

zashiki, n. 座敷 Japanese-style room with tatami flooring.

zasshi, n. 雑誌 magazine; periodical.

zassō, n. 雑草 weeds.

zatsu (na), adj. 雑 (な) crude; sloppy.

zatsuon, n. 雑音 noise; static.

zatto, adv. ざっと 1. roughly; approximately. 2. briefly.

zawameku, vb. ざわめく rustle; be noisy.

zehi, adv. 是非 by all means; definitely; really.

zei, n. 税 tax; duty.

zeikan, n. 税関 customs office.

zeikin, n. 税金 tax; duty.

zeiniku, n. 贅肉 body fat.

zeitaku (na), adj. 贅沢 (な) extravagant; luxurious.

zekkō (no), adj. 絶好 (の) propitious; ideal; wished-for.

zemi(nā), n. ゼミ(ナー) (G. Zeminar) seminar.

zen, n. 禅 Zen Buddhism.

zen, n. 善 good; right; virtue.

zen 前 1. adj. ex-; former; **zendaigishi** former Diet member. 2. prep. before; in front of; **ganzen de** before my eyes.

zen- 全 all; whole; **zensekai** the whole world.

zenbu 全部 1. pron. all; everything. 2. adj. all.

zenbu de, adv. 全部で in all; everything included.

zenchishi, n. 前置詞 preposition.

zendo, n. 全土 whole country; whole area.

zengaku, n. 全額 entire amount (money).

zengo (ni), adv. 前後 (に) 1. in front and behind; back and forth. 2. about; **hyaku-doru zengo** about one hundred dollars.

zenhan, n. 前半 first half.

zen'in, n. 全員 all members; everyone.

zenjitsu, n. 前日 previous day.

zenkai, n. 前回 last time.

zenkei, n. 前景 foreground.

zenki, *n.* 前期 first term.

zenki (no), *adj.* 前記 (の) above-mentioned.

zenkoku, *n.* 全国 entire nation.

zen'nen, *n.* 前年 previous year.

zen'nin, *n.* 善人 good person.

zenpan ni, *adv.* 全般に as a whole; in general.

zenpō ni, *n.* 前方に in front; ahead; forward.

zenryaku, *n.* 前略 salutation in a letter indicating that the writer is dispensing with formalities.

zenryoku o tsukusu, *vb.* 全力を尽くす do one's utmost.

zensai, *n.* 前菜 appetizer; hors d'oeuvre.

zensekai, *n.* 全世界 the whole world.

zensen, *n.* 前線 front line.

zenshin, *n.* 全身 the entire body (human).

zenshin suru, *vb.* 前進する 1. move forward. 2. make progress.

zenshū, *n.* 全集 complete literary works.

zensoku, *n.* ぜん息 asthma.

zentai, *n.* 全体 whole.

zentai de, *adv.* 全体で in all; all told.

zen'ya, *n.* 前夜 previous evening or night; eve.

zen-zen, *adv.* ぜんぜん 1. entirely. 2. (with negative) never; not at all; **Sake o zen-zen nomanai.** (I) never drink sake.

zettai (ni), *adv.* 絶対 (に) 1. absolutely; definitely. 2. by any means.

zō, *n.* 象 elephant.

zō, *n.* 像 image; portrait; statue.

zōge, *n.* 象牙 ivory.

-zoi ni 沿いに along;

kawazoi ni along the river.

zōka, *n.* 造花 artificial flowers.

zōka suru, *vb.* 増加する increase.

zōkin, *n.* 雑巾 dustcloth; cleaning cloth.

zokkō suru, *vb.* 続行する continue.

-zoku 族 1. family; class; race; tribe; **kizoku** noble family or class.

zoku ni, *adv.* 俗に generally; commonly.

zoku suru, *vb.* 属する belong; **kyōsan tō ni zoku suru** belong to the Communist Party.

zoku-zoku (to), *adv.* 続々 (と) one after another.

zoku-zoku suru, *vb.* ぞくぞくする 1. feel chilly. 2. be excited.

zonbun (ni), *adv.* 存分 (に) fully; to one's heart's content.

zonjiru, *vb.* 存じる know.

zōri, *n.* 草履 Japanese sandals.

zōsensho, *n.* 造船所 shipyard.

zotto suru, *vb.* ぞっとする shudder; be scared; be disgusted.

zu, *n.* 図 drawing; illustration; picture.

zubanukeru, *vb.* ずば抜ける excel; be outstanding.

zubon, *n.* ズボン (F. *Jupon*) pants; trousers.

zubon-tsuri, *n.* ズボン吊り suspenders.

zubunure (no), *adj.* ずぶ濡れ (の) soaking wet.

zubutoi, *adj.* 図太い audacious; brazen.

zuga, *n.* 図画 drawing; painting.

zugaikotsu, *n.* 頭蓋骨 skull.

zuibun, *adv.* 随分 very.

zujō ni, *adv.* 頭上に overhead.

zukai, *n.* 図解 illustration.

zukan, *n.* 図鑑 picture book.

zukei, *n.* 図形 drawing; figure.

zuki-zuki suru, *vb.* ずきずきする smart; throb.

-zukume ずくめ full of; **ii koto-zukume** full of good things.

zumen, *n.* 図面 blueprint; design.

zunguri shita, *adj.* ずんぐりした short and stocky.

zunō, *n.* 頭脳 brains; head.

zurari to, *adv.* ずらりと in a row.

zurasu, *vb.* ずらす move or shift (location, schedule).

zure, *n.* ずれ gap.

zureru, *vb.* ずれる shift out of place; deviate; stray.

zurui, *adj.* ずるい dishonest; sly.

zusan (na), *adj.* ずさん（な） sloppy; neglectful.

-zutsu, *parti.* ずつ 1. by (one by one, little by little, etc.); **hitori zutsu** one by one (people). 2. (for) each; **ringo futatsu zutsu** two apples (for) each (person).

zutsū, *n.* 頭痛 headache; **zutsū ga suru** have a headache.

zutto, *adv.* ずっと 1. always; all the while; all the way. 2. very much; far more; **zutto omoshiroi** far more interesting.

A

a, *art*. 1. hitotsu (no) 一つ (の) (one thing); hitori (no) 一人 (の) (one person). 2. aru 或る (a certain).

abalone, *n*. awabi あわび.

abandon, *vb*. 1. akirameru あきらめる; yameru 止める (give up). 2. misuteru 見捨る (forsake).

abate, *vb*. 1. osamaru 治まる (calm). 2. herasu 減らす; sageru 下げる (decrease).

abbreviate, *vb*. shōryaku suru 省略する.

abdomen, *n*. fukubu 腹部; onaka お腹.

abduct, *vb*. yūkai suru 誘拐する.

abhor, *vb*. nikumu 憎む.

abide, *vb*. 1. nokoru 残る; iru 居る (stay). 2. sumu 住む (reside).

ability, *n*. 1. nōryoku 能力 (competence). 2. sainō 才能 (talent).

ablaze, *adj*. 1. moeteiru 燃えている (on fire). 2. kōfun shiteiru 興奮している (excited).

able, *adj*. 1. yūnō (na) 有能 (な) (competent). 2. dekiru 出来る (able to do); **able to speak** hanasu koto ga dekiru.

abnormal, *adj*. ijō (na) 異常 (な).

aboard, *adv*. ... ni notte ... に乗って (bus, train, ship).

abolish, *vb*. haishi suru 廃止する.

abort, *vb*. 1. (ninshin)

chūzetsu suru (妊娠) 中絶する (end pregnancy). 2. ryūzan suru 流産する (miscarry). 3. shippai suru 失敗する (fail). 4. chūdan suru 中断する (discontinue).

about, 1. *adv*. daitai 大体; oyoso 凡そ; yaku 約; -gurai/-kurai -位 (approximately); **about five people** gonin-gurai 五人位. 2. *prep*. -goro -頃 (around); ... ni tsuite ... について (concerning); **about this book** kono hon ni tsuite この本について.

above, *adv., prep*. (...yori, no) ue ni (...より、の) 上に.

abrasion, *n*. 1. mametsu 磨滅 (wearing down). 2. surikizu 擦り傷 (injury, scratch).

abridge, *vb*. tanshuku suru 短縮する (shorten); herasu 減らす (decrease).

abroad, *adv*. gaikoku de/ni 外国で/に; kaigai de/ni 海外で/に.

abrupt, *adj*. kyū (na) 急 (な); totsuzen (no) 突然 (の).

absent, *adj*. inai いない (na); rusu (no) 留守 (の) (out for a while from office, home); **be absent** rusu ni suru 留守にする; yasumu 休む.

absent-minded, *adj*. bon'yari shita ぼんやりした.

absolute, *adj*. zettai-teki

(na) 絶対的 (な); zettai (no) 絶対 (の).

absorb, vb. kyūshū suru 吸収する; nomikomu 飲み込む; **be absorbed (in)** ...ni bottō suru ...に没頭する.

abstain, vb. hikaeru 控える; tsutsushimu 慎む.

absurd, adj. fugōri (na) 不合理 (な); bakageta 馬鹿げた.

abundant, adj. hōfu (na) 豊富 (な); takusan (no) 沢山 (の).

abuse, 1. n. gyakutai 虐待 (maltreatment); akuyō 悪用 (misuse). 2. vb. gyakutai suru 虐待する; akuyō suru 悪用する.

academic, adj. 1. gakumon (no) 学問 (の) (scholastic). 2. daigaku (no) 大学 (の) (of a university).

academy, n. gakuen 学園.

accelerate, vb. kasoku suru 加速する.

accelerator, n. akuseru アクセル.

accent, n. 1. kyōchō 強調 (emphasis). 2. namari 訛 (local speech).

accept, vb. ukeireru 受け入れる; shōdaku suru 承諾する (agree to); uketoru 受け取る (receive).

acceptable, adj. 1. ii いい; kekkō (na) 結構 (な) (agreeable). 2. mā-mā (no) まあまあ (の) (bearable).

access, n. sekkin 接近 (approach); chikazuku hōhō 近づく方法 (means of approach); **have access to** te ni hairu 手に入る.

accessory, n. sōshingu 装身具.

accident, n. jiko 事故; **by accident** gūzen ni 偶然に (coincidental); fui ni 不意に (unintentional).

acclimate, vb. nareru 慣れる; jun'nō suru 順応する.

accommodate, vb. 1. bengi o hakaru 便宜を図る (oblige). 2. tomeru 泊める (lodge). 3. tekiō saseru 適応させる (adapt).

accompany, vb. 1. otomo suru お供する; dōkō suru 同行する (go with). 2. tsuite kuru ついて来る (come with). 3. bansō suru 伴奏する (music).

accomplice, n. kyōhansha 共犯者.

accomplish, vb. nashitogeru 成し遂げる; kansei suru 完成する.

accord, 1. n. itchi 一致; chōwa 調和 (harmony); kyōtei 協定 (agreement); **of one's own accord** jihatsu-teki ni 自発的に. 2. vb. itchi suru 一致する; chōwa suru 調和する.

according to, prep. ...ni yoruto/yoreba ...によると／よれば (quotation). 2. ...ni shitagatte ...に従って (based on).

accordingly, adv. shitagatte 従って; sorede それで.

accost, vb. hanashikakeru 話しかける.

account, 1. n. riyū 理由 (reason); hanashi 話 (narration); hōkoku 報告 (report); yokinkōza 預金口座 (bank account); kanjō 勘定 (bill). 2. vb. kazoeru 数える (calculate); hanasu 話す (narrate); **account for** setsumei suru 説明する (explain).

accountable, adj. 1. sekinin ga aru 責任がある (responsible). 2. setsumei dekiru 説明出来る (explicable).

accountant, n. kaikei-shi/-gakari 会計士/〜係.

accurate, adj. seikaku (na) 正確 (な).

accuse, vb. semeru 責める.

accustom, vb. narasu 慣らす; **get accustomed to** ...ni nareru.

ache, 1. n. itami 痛み. 2. vb. itamu 痛む.

achieve, vb. tassei suru 達成する.

acid, 1. n. san 酸. 2. adj. sansei (no) 酸性 (の) (acidic); suppai 酸っぱい (sour).

acknowledge, vb. mitomeru 認める; shōnin suru 承認する.

acorn, n. donguri どんぐり.

acoustics, n. onkyō 音響.

acquaint, vb. shiraseru 知らせる; **be acquainted with** (...o) shitte-iru (...を) 知っている; **get acquainted with** (...to) shiriai ni naru (...と) 知り合いになる (person); ...ni nareru ...に慣れる (get accustomed to).

acquaintance, n. shiriai 知り合い; chijin 知人.

acquire, vb. 1. eru 得る (get). 2. shūtoku suru 習得する (learn).

acquit, vb. 1. menjiru 免じる (release). 2. furumau ふるまう (behave).

acrobat, n. kyokugei 曲芸.

across, adv., prep. 1. (...o) yokogitte (...を) 横切って; (...no) mukō ni (...の) 向こうに; **go across** yokogiru.

act, 1. n. okonai 行ない; kōdō 行動 (behavior); maku 幕 (theater). 2. vb. suru する (do); furumau ふるまう (behave); engi suru 演技する (theater).

acting, 1. n. engi 演技;

shibai 芝居. 2. adj. dairi (no) 代理 (の) (substitute).

active, adj. kappatsu (na) 活発 (な); katsudō-teki (na) 活動的 (な).

activity, n. katsudō 活動; undō 運動.

actor, n. haiyū 俳優 (male, female); danyū 男優 (male).

actress, n. joyū 女優.

actual, adj. 1. genjitsu (no) 現実 (の) (real). 2. ima (no) 今 (の) (present).

actually, adv. genjitsu ni 現実に; jitsu wa 実は.

acupuncture, n. hari (chiryō) 針(治療).

acute, adj. 1. surudoi 鋭い (sharp); hageshii 激しい (intense). 2. setsujitsu (na) 切実 (な) (critical). 3. kyūsei (no) 急性 (の) (disease).

adapt, vb. 1. tekiō saseru 適応させる (make fit). 2. kyakushoku suru 脚色する (rewrite).

add, vb. tasu 足す; kuwaeru 加える; **add up** gōkei suru 合計する.

addict, n. chūdoku(sha) 中毒(者); **drug addict** mayaku-chūdoku.

addition, n. tsuika 追加 (extra); tashizan 足し算 (mathematics); **in addition** sono ue ni その上に; **in addition to** ...ni kuwaete ...に加えて; mata また.

address, 1. n. jūsho 住所 (location); enzetsu 演説 (speech). 2. vb. jūsho o kaku 住所を書く (address a letter); hanashikakeru 話しかける (speak to); torikumu 取り組む (handle).

addressee, n. uketorinin 受け取り人.

adequate, adj. jūbun (na) 十

分 (な).

adhere, vb. 1. kuttsuku くっつく (glue). 2. yaritōsu やり通す; mamoritōsu 守り通す (be faithful).

adjective, n. keiyōshi 形容詞.

adjust, vb. 1. chōsetsu suru 調節する; awaseru 合わせる (tune, regulate). 2. totonoeru 整える (organize).

administration, n. 1. kanri 管理 (management); keiei 経営 (business); gyōsei 行政 (governing). 2. shikō 施行 (practice).

admirable, adj. subarashii 素晴らしい.

admire, vb. shōsan suru 賞賛する; tataeru 称える (praise); kanshin suru 感心する (be impressed); miageru 見上げる (look up to).

admission, n. 1. nyūjōkyoka 入場許可 (entrance admission); nyūgakukyoka 入学許可 (school admission). 2. nyūjōryō 入場料 (admission fee).

admit, vb. 1. ukeireru 受け入れる (allow). 2. mitomeru 認める (confess).

admonish, vb. chūi suru 注意する; isameru 諌める.

adolescent, n., adj. seinen (no) 青年 (の).

adopt, vb. 1. saiyō suru 採用する (use). 2. yōshi ni suru 養子にする (adopt a child).

adorable, adj. kawaii 可愛い.

adore, vb. 1. sūhai suru 崇拝する (honor). 2. netsuai suru 熱愛する (love).

adult, n., adj. otona (no) 大人 (の); seijin (no) 成人 (の).

adulterate, vb. shitsu o sageru 質を下げる.

adultery, n. kantsū 姦通; fugi 不義.

advance, 1. n. shinpo 進歩 (progress); zenshin 前進 (moving forward); shōshin 昇進 (promotion); maekin 前金 (money); **in advance** maemotte 前もって. 2. vb. shinpo suru 進歩する (progress); susumu 進む (move forward); shōshin suru 昇進する (promote).

advanced, adj. susunda 進んだ (progressed); jōkyū (no) 上級 (の) (at higher level).

advantage, n. yūri 有利; **take advantage of** (....o) riyō suru (...を) 利用する (utilize).

adventure, n. bōken 冒険.

adverb, n. fukushi 副詞.

adversary, n. teki 敵 (enemy); kyōsōaite 競争相手 (rival).

advertisement, n. 1. senden 宣伝; kōkoku 広告 (promotion). 2. tsūkoku 通告 (notice).

advisable, adj. nozomashii 望ましい (desirable); kenmei (na) 賢明 (な).

advise, vb. jogen suru 助言する.

adviser, advisor, n. kaunserā カウンセラー; jogensha 助言者; sōdansha 相談者.

aerial, 1. n. antena アンテナ. 2. adj. kūki (no) 空気 (の) (air); kōkūki (no) 航空機 (の) (airplane).

afar, adv. tōku ni 遠くに; **from afar** tōku kara 遠くから.

affair, n. 1. shigoto 仕事; yōji 用事 (business). 2. jiken 事件 (event). 3. love

affair ren'ai 恋愛.

affect, vb. 1. eikyō suru 影響する (influence). 2. kandō saseru 感動させる (move). 3. furi o suru 振りをする (pretend).

affected, adj. 1. eikyō sareta 影響された (influenced). 2. kidotta 気取った (pretentious). 3. misekake (no) 見せかけ (の) (feigned).

affection, n. aichaku 愛着.

affiliate, 1. n. kankeisha 関係者 (affiliated person); kankeidantai 関係団体 (affiliated organization). 2. vb. kankei saseru/suru 関係させる／する (associate); kanyū saseru 加入させる (join).

affirm, vb. kōtei suru 肯定する; dangen suru 断言する.

affirmative, 1. n. kōteibun 肯定文 (sentence). 2. adj. kōtei-teki (na) 肯定的 (な); dantei-teki (na) 断定的 (な).

affluence, n. 1. tomi 富 (wealth). 2. yutakasa 豊かさ (abundance).

afford, vb. 1. (okane, jikan ga) aru (お金、時間が) 有る (have money, time). 2. yoyū ga aru 余裕が有る (handle). 3. ataeru 与える (supply).

afraid, adj. 1. kowai 怖い; osoroshii 恐ろしい (frightened); **be afraid of** ...ga kowai/shinpai ...が怖い／心配. 2. shinpai (na) 心配 (な) (worried). 3. zan'nen (na) 残念 (な) (sorry).

after, 1. adv ato de/ni 後で／に (afterward, later); ushiro de/ni 後ろで／に (behind). 2. prep. (...no) ato de/ni (...の)後で／に (later

than); (...no) ushiro de/ni (...の)後ろで／に (behind); ...ni naratte に倣って (following). 3. conj. sorekara それから; (...shita) ato de (...した) 後で.

afterlife, n. 1. raise 来世 (next life). 2. ban'nen 晩年 (later years).

afternoon, n. gogo 午後; **good afternoon** kon'nichiwa 今日は.

afterward, adv. ato de/ni 後で／に.

again, adv. mata 又; futatabi 再び.

against, prep. 1. ...ni taishite ...に対して (in competition with). 2. ...ni sakaratte ...に逆らって (in opposition to). 3. mukatte 向かって (toward). 4. ...ni motarete ...にもたれて (lean upon).

agape, adv. akirete あきれて; azen to shite 唖然として.

age, 1. n. toshi 年; nenrei 年齢 (of a man or animal); nensū 年数 (of inanimate objects); jidai 時代 (era); **of age** seijin 成人; **old age** rōnen 老年. 2. vb. toshi o toru 年をとる (advance in years); fukeru 老ける (get old); jukusuru 熟する (mature).

agency, n. 1. dairiten 代理店 (agent company); **travel agency** ryokōdairiten 旅行代理店. 2. jimusho 事務所 (office). 3. hataraki 働き (function).

agent, n. 1. dairi(nin) 代理 (人) (acting person); dairiten 代理店 (firm). 2. daihyōsha 代表者 (representative). 3. yakunin 役人 (government agent). 4. dōin 導因 (cause).

aggravate, vb. 1. akka saseru 悪化させる

(exacerbate). 2. ira-ira saseru いらいらさせる (annoy).

aggression, n. shinryaku 侵略; kōgeki 攻撃.

agile, adj. kibin (na) 機敏 (な); keikai (na) 軽快 (な).

agitate, vb. 1. yuriugokasu 揺り動かす (move). 2. dōyō saseru 動揺させる (perturb). 3. uttaeru 訴える (argue). 4. sendō suru 扇動する (manipulate).

ago, adj., adv. mae ni 前に; **two days ago** futsuka mae ni.

agony, n. kurushimi 苦しみ; kutsū 苦痛.

agree, vb. 1. dōi suru 同意する; sansei suru 賛成する (consent). 2. itchi suru 一致する (concur).

agreeable, adj. kokochi yoi 心地良い; tanoshii 楽しい.

agricultural, adj. nōgyō (no) 農業 (の); nōkō (no) 農耕 (の).

agriculture, n. nōgyō 農業.

ahead, adv. mae ni 前に; saki ni 先に; **straight ahead** massugu saki ni まっすぐ先に; **Go ahead.** Osaki ni dōzo お先にどうぞ. (After you.)

aid, 1. n. enjo 援助. 2. vb. enjo suru 援助する.

AIDS, n. eizu エイズ.

ail, vb. 1. itamu 痛む (pain). 2. komaru 困る (trouble). 3. wazurau 患う (ill).

ailment, n. byōki 病気.

aim, 1. n. mokuteki 目的 (purpose); mato 的 (goal). 2. vb. nerau 狙う (point); mezasu 目指す (intend).

aimless, adj. mokuteki ga nai 目的がない.

air, 1. n. kūki 空気 (gas); yōsu 様子; fūsai 風采

(impression); sora 空 (sky); merodī メロディー (tune); **in the open air** soto de/ni 外で/に. 2. vb. kaze o tōsu 風を通す (dry).

air base, n. kūgunkichi 空軍基地.

air-conditioned, adj. reidanbō (tsuki) (no) 冷暖房 (付) (の).

air-conditioner, n. eakon エアコン; reidanbōki 冷暖房機.

airmail, n. kōkūbin 航空便.

airplane, n. hikōki 飛行機.

airport, n. kūkō 空港.

airsick, adj. hikōyoi 飛行機酔い.

aisle, n. tsūro 通路.

alarm, 1. n. keihō 警報 (signal); osore 恐れ (fear). 2. vb. keihō o dasu 警報を出す (signal); odorokaseru 驚ろかせる (scare).

alarm clock, n. mezamashi-dokei 目覚まし時計.

alas, interj. aa ああ.

album, n. arubamu アルバム; -chō -帳; **picture album** shashin-chō 写真帳.

alcohol, n. arukōru アルコール; sake 酒.

alcoholic, 1. adj. arukōru-chūdoku (no) アルコール中毒 (の) (addicted); sake (no) 酒 (の) (of alcohol). 2. n. aru(kōru) chū(doku) アル (コール)中(毒).

alert, 1. n. keihō 警報 (alarm); yōjin 用心 (vigilance). 2. adj. nukeme nai 抜け目ない (thoroughly attentive); yōjinbukai 用心深い (vigilant). 3. vb. yōjin saseru 用心させる; keikoku suru 警告する.

alias, n. betsumei 別名.

alien, 1. adj. gaikoku (no) 外国 (の) (of a foreign

country); awanai 合わない
(strange); hantai (no) 反対
(の) (adverse). 2. n.
gaikokujin 外国人
(foreigner); yosomono よそ
者 (outsider).

alienate, vb. sogai suru 疎外
する; tōzakeru 遠ざける.

align, vb. naraberu 並べる;
soroeru 揃える.

alike, adj. 1. nita 似た;
niteiru 似ている (similar).
2. onaji 同じ (same).

alive, adj. ikiteiru 生きてい
る (living); iki-iki shiteiru 生
き生きしている (lively).

all, 1. pron. subete 全て;
min'na 皆; zenbu 全部;
after all kekkyoku 結局;
Not at all. Dōitashimashite.
どういたしまして (Don't
mention it.). 2. adj. subete
(no) 全て (の); min'na (no)
皆 (の); zenbu (no) 全部
(の). 3. adv. sukkari すっか
り; mattaku 全く; **all of a
sudden** totsuzen 突然.

all-around, adj. 1. tasai (na)
多才 (な); ban'nō (na, no)
万能 (な、の) (extremely
capable). 2. kanzen (na) 完
全 (な) (complete).

allegiance, n. 1. chūsei 忠誠
(loyalty). 2. gimu 義務
(duty).

allergic, adj. arerugīsei (no)
アレルギー性 (の).

allergy, n. kyozetsuhan'nō
拒絶反応.

alley, n. yokochō 横町;
komichi 小道.

alliance, n. dōmei 同盟;
engumi 縁組.

alligator, n. wani わに.

allocate, vb. (wari)ateru 割)
当てる.

all-out, adj. tettei-teki (na)
徹底的 (な).

allow, vb. 1. yurusu 許す

(permit). 2. ataeru 与える
(give). 3. mitomeru 認める
(admit).

allowance, n. 1. kyoka 許可
(permission). 2. hiyō 費用;
teate 手当て (expense). 3.
wariate 割り当て
(allotment). 4. kozukai 小
遣い (spending money). 5.
make allowance for (...o)
kōryo suru (...を) 考慮する.

alloy, n. gōkin 合金.

all right, 1. adj. yoroshii よ
ろしい (good); daijōbu (na)
大丈夫 (な) (safe, OK). 2.
interj. ii いい; daijōbu 大丈
夫.

ally, 1. n. dōmeikoku 同盟国
(allied nation); kyōryokusha
協力者 (supporter). 2. vb.
dōmei suru 同盟する; en o
musubu 縁を結ぶ (establish
relations).

almond, n. āmondo アーモ
ンド.

almost, adv. hotondo ほとん
ど; daitai 大体.

alone, 1. adj. hitori (no) 一
人 (の) (person); ...nomi ...
のみ (only). 2. adv. hitori de
一人で; **leave alone** hitori
ni shiteoku (person); hotte
oku 放っておく.

along, 1. adv. issho ni 一緒に
(together); **all along** zutto
ずっと; **get along with**
(...to) umaku yatte iku (...
と) うまくやっていく. 2.
prep. ...ni sotte ...に沿って
(over the length of); ...ni
awasete ...に合わせて (in
accordance with).

alongside, adv., prep. (...o)
narande (...と) 並んで;
(...no) soba ni (...の) 側に.

aloud, adv. koe o dashite 声
を出して.

alphabetical, adj.
arufabetto(jun) (no) アルフ

アベット(順) (の).

already, *adv.* mō もう; sude ni 既に.

also, *adv.* mo も; mata 又.

alter, *vb.* 1. kaeru 変える (change). 2. naosu 直す (alter size).

alternate, 1. *adj.* kōgo (no) 交互 (の) (by turns); hitotsuoki (no) 一つおき (の) (every other). 2. *n.* kawari 代わり (substitute). 3. *vb.* kaeru 代える; kawaru 代わる (change); kōtai de suru 交代でする (do by turns).

alternative, 1. *adj.* kawari (no) 代わり (の). 2. *n.* kawari 代わり (substitute); sentaku 選択 (choice).

although, *conj.* ...desuga ...ですが; ...dakedo ...だけど.

altitude, *n.* kōdo 高度; takasa 高さ.

altogether, *adv.* 1. zenbu de 全部で (in all). 2. mattaku 全く (completely). 3. zentai ni 全体に (as a whole).

aluminum, *n.* arumi(niumu) アルミ(ニウム).

alumni, *n.* sotsugyōsei 卒業生.

always, *adv.* itsumo いつも.

a.m., gozen 午前; **nine a.m.** gozen kuji.

amateur, *n.* amachua アマチュア; shirōto 素人.

amaze, *vb.* odorokaseru 驚かせる; **be amazed at** ...ni odoroku ...に驚く.

ambassador, *n.* taishi 大使.

ambiguous, *adj.* aimai (na) 曖昧 (な); bon'yari shita ぼんやりした.

ambition, *n.* yashin 野心; iyoku 意欲.

ambulance, *n.* kyūkyūsha 救急車.

ambush, 1. *n.* machibuse 待ち伏せ; fui'uchi 不意打ち. 2. *vb.* machibuse suru 待ち伏せする.

amend, *vb.* kaisei suru 改正する; aratameru 改める.

America, *n.* amerika アメリカ (U.S.).

American, 1. *n.* amerikajin アメリカ人. 2. *adj.* amerika (no) アメリカ (の) (of the U.S.); amerikajin (no) アメリカ人 (の) (of an American).

amiable, *adj.* shinsetsu (na) 親切 (な) (kind); yūkō-teki (na) 友好的 (な) (friendly).

amiss, 1. *adj.* hazure (no) 外れ (の); machigai (no) 間違い (の). 2. *adv.* hazurete 外れて; machigatte 間違って; **take amiss** waruku toru 悪くとる; gokai suru 誤解する.

amnesia, *n.* kioku sōshitsu 記憶喪失; kenbōshō 健忘症.

amnesty, 1. *n.* onsha 恩赦. 2. *vb.* onsha o ataeru 恩赦を与える.

among, *prep.* (...no) aida de/ni (...の) 間で／に (between); (...no) naka de/ni (...の) 中で／に (in the midst of).

amorous, *adj.* 1. aijōbukai 愛情深い (affectionate). 2. ren'aichū (no) 恋愛中 (の) (in love). 3. kōshoku (na) 好色 (な) (lecherous).

amount, 1. *n.* gōkei 合計. 2. *vb.* **amount to** ...ni tassuru ...に達する; ...ni naru ...になる.

amplify, *vb.* kakudai suru 拡大する; hirogeru 拡げる.

amputate, *vb.* kiru 切る; setsudan suru 切断する.

amusement, *n.* tanoshimi 楽しみ; goraku 娯楽.

amusing, *adj.* tanoshii 楽しい; okashii おかしい.

an, *art.* see **a.**

analysis, *n.* bunseki 分析.

analyze, *vb.* bunseki suru 分析する.

anatomy, *n.* shikumi 仕組み (system); kaibō 解剖 (dissect); bunseki 分析 (analysis).

ancestor, *n.* sosen 祖先; senzo 先祖.

anchor, 1. *n.* ikari 錨. 2. *vb.* tomeru 留める (fasten); teihaku suru 停泊する (anchor boat); ikari o orosu 錨を下ろす (lower anchor).

ancient, 1. *n.* kodaijin 古代人. 2. *adj.* kodai (no) 古代 (の); ōmukashi (no) 大昔 (の) (of ancient times); rōjin (no) 老人 (の) (of an elderly person).

and, *conj.* soshite そして; ...to ...と.

anemia, *n.* hinketsu(shō) 貧血(症).

anesthetic, *n.* masui 麻酔.

angel, *n.* tenshi 天使.

anger, 1. *n.* ikari 怒り. 2. *vb.* okoraseru 怒らせる (provoke); okoru 怒る (get angry).

angle, *n.* kakudo 角度; **right angle** chokkaku 直角.

anguish, *n.* kurushimi 苦しみ; kunō 苦悩.

animal, *n.* dōbutsu 動物.

animation, *n.* 1. animēshon アニメーション; mangaeiga 漫画映画 (animated film). 2. kakki 活気 (liveliness).

ankle, *n.* kurubushi くるぶし; ashikubi 足首.

annihilate, *vb.* zenmetsu saseru 全滅させる.

anniversary, *n.* kinenbi 記念日.

announce, *vb.* kōhyō suru

公表する; shiraseru 知らせる.

annoying, *adj.* meiwaku (na) 迷惑 (な); yakkai (na) 厄介 (な).

annual, 1. *adj.* (ichi)nen (no) (一)年 (の) (yearly); maitoshi (no) 毎年 (の) (recurring yearly). 2. *n.* nenkan 年鑑 (publication).

anonymous, *adj.* mumei (no) 無名 (の); tokumei (no) 匿名 (の).

another, *adj., pron.* mō hitori (no) もう一人 (の) (person); mō hitotsu (no) もう一つ (の) (thing).

answer, 1. *n.* kotae 答え (reply to a question); henji 返事 (response). 2. *vb.* kotaeru 答える; henji suru 返事する.

ant, *n.* ari 蟻.

antagonize, *vb.* teki ni mawasu 敵に回す (make enemy); tairitsu suru 対立する (oppose).

Antarctica, *n.* nankyoku(tairiku) 南極(大陸).

anthem, *n.* 1. kokka 国歌 (national anthem). 2. seika 聖歌 (church music).

anthropology, *n.* jinruigaku 人類学.

anti-, han- 反-; **han-shakai-teki** antisocial.

antibiotic, *n.* kōseibusshitsu 抗生物質.

anticipate, *vb.* 1. kitai suru 期待する (expect). 2. yoki suru 予期する (foresee).

antics, *n.* hyōkin ひょうきん.

antique, *n.* kottō(hin) 骨董(品).

antler, *n.* tsuno 角.

anus, *n.* kōmon 肛門.

anxious, *adj.* 1. shinpai (na)

心配 (な) (worried). 2.
nesshin (na) 熱心 (な)
(eager).

any, 1. *adj., pron.*
(affirmative sentence)
nandemo 何でも (anything
at all); subete 全て
(everything); daredemo 誰
でも (anyone, everyone);
(negative sentence) nanimo
何も (not anything);
daremo 誰も (not anybody);
(interrogative, conditional
sentence) nanika 何か
(anything, something);
dareka 誰か (anyone,
someone). 2. *adv.* **any
longer/more** mohaya
...nai) 最早 (...ない); mō
(...nai) もう (...ない).

anybody, *pron.* 1.
(affirmative sentence)
daredemo 誰でも. 2.
(negative sentence) daremo
誰も. 3. (interrogative,
conditional sentence)
dareka 誰か.

anyhow, *adv.* 1. tonikaku と
にかく (in any case). 2.
zehi 是非 (under any
circumstances).

anyone, *pron.* see **anybody**.

anything, 1. *pron.*
(affirmative sentence)
nandemo 何でも; (negative
sentence) nanimo 何も;
(interrogative, conditional
sentence) nanika 何か. 2.
adv. (affirmative sentence)
sukoshiwa 少しは; (negative
sentence) sukoshimo 少し
も.

anyway, *pron.* see **anyhow**.

anywhere, *adv.* 1.
(affirmative sentence) doko
demo どこでも. 2.
(interrogative, conditional
sentence) doko ka どこか.
3. (negative sentence) doko

nimo (...nai) どこにも (...な
い).

apart, *adv.* 1. bara-bara ni ば
らばらに (into pieces); **take
apart** bara-bara ni suru ば
らばらにする; bunkai suru
分解する. 2. hanarete 離れ
て (away from). 3. kobetsu
ni 個別に (individually).

apartment, *n.* apāto アパー
ト.

apathy, *n.* 1. mukanjō 無感
情. 2. mukanshin 無関心.

ape, 1. *n.* saru 猿. 2. *vb.*
mane suru 真似する.

apiece, *adv.* 1. hitotsu (ni
tsuki) 一つ (に付き) (per
piece). 2. hitori (ni tsuki) 一
人 (に付き) (per person).

apologize, *vb.* 1. ayamaru 謝
る. 2. benmei suru 弁明す
る.

apology, *n.* 1. shazai 謝罪.
2. benmei 弁明.

apparatus, *n.* 1. kikai 器械;
sōchi 装置 (instrument). 2.
kikō 機構; kikan 機関
(system).

apparent, *adj.* akiraka (na)
明らか (な).

appeal, 1. *n.* uttae 訴え;
yōsei 要請 (entreaty);
miryoku 魅力 (attraction);
kōso 控訴 (court petition).
2. *vb.* uttaeru 訴える; yōsei
suru 要請する; hikitsukeru
引き付ける (attract); kōso
suru 控訴する.

appear, *vb.* 1. arawareru 現
れる; deru 出る (show up,
come into sight). 2. (...no
yō ni) mieru (...のように) 見
える (seem).

appearance, *n.* 1. tōjō 登場;
shutsugen 出現 (showing
up). 2. gaiken 外見; yōsu 様
子 (outward show).

append, *vb.* tsukeru 付ける;
tsuketasu 付け足す.

appendicitis, *n.* mōchōen 盲腸炎; chūsuien 虫垂炎.

appetite, *n.* shokuyoku 食欲.

appetizer, *n.* zensai 前菜.

appetizing, *adj.* oishisō (na) おいしそう (な).

applause, *n.* kassai 喝采; hakushu 拍手.

apple, *n.* ringo りんご.

appliance, *n.* kigu 器具; kikai 器械.

application, *n.* 1. mōshikomi 申し込み; ōbo 応募 (request). 2. shiyō 使用 (use). 3. ōyō 応用 (derived use). 4. mōshikomi yōshi 申し込み用紙; mōshikomisho 申し込み書 (form).

apply, *vb.* 1. tsukeru 付ける (put on). 2. tsukau 使う (use). 3. **apply to** ōyō suru 応用する. 4. **apply for** mōshikomu 申し込む; ōbo suru 応募する.

appointment, *n.* 1. ninmei 任命. 2. shitei 指定. 3. yakusoku 約束, yoyaku 予約 (meeting).

appraise, *vb.* hyōka suru 評価する; kantei suru 鑑定する.

appreciate, *vb.* 1. kansha suru 感謝する (thank). 2. (takaku) hyōka suru (高く) 評価する; kanshō suru 鑑賞する (value). 3. sassuru 察する (be aware). 4. kachi o ageru 価値を上げる (raise value).

appreciation, *n.* 1. kansha 感謝. 2. hyōka 評価; kanshō 鑑賞. 3. ninshiki 認識 (recognition). 4. kachi no zōka 価値の増加.

apprehend, *vb.* 1. sassuru 察する; kizuku 気づく (perceive). 2. shinpai suru

shinpai suru (worry). 3. taiho suru 逮捕する (arrest).

apprehension, *n.* 1. shinpai 心配; fuan 不安 (worry). 2. taiho 逮捕 (arrest).

apprentice, *n.* deshi 弟子; minarai 見習い.

approach, 1. *n.* sekkin 接近; chikazuki 近づき (coming near); hōhō 方法 (method); shudan 手段 (means). 2. *vb.* sekkin suru 接近する; chikazuku 近づく; kōshō suru 交渉する (discuss); torikakaru 取り掛かる (begin).

appropriate, 1. *adj.* fusawashii ふさわしい (suitable). 2. *vb.* ateru 当てる (set aside); nusumu 盗む (steal).

approve, *vb.* shōnin suru 承認する; sansei suru 賛成する.

approximate, *adj.* daitai (no) 大体 (の); chikai 近い.

apricot, *n.* anzu 杏.

April, *n.* shi-gatsu 四月.

apron, *n.* epuron エプロン; maekake 前掛け.

apt, *adj.* 1. -yasui 易い; (...no) keikō ga aru (...の) 傾向がある (inclined, tending); **apt to get upset** okori-yasui. 2. tekisetsu (na) 適切 (な) (fitting).

aquarium, *n.* 1. suisō 水槽 (fishbowl); suizokukan 水族館 (fish museum).

Arabia, *n.* arabia アラビア.

Arabic, *n.* arabiago アラビア語.

arbitrary, *adj.* 1. shukan-teki (na) 主観的 (な) (subjective). 2. katte (na) 勝手 (な) (unreasonable).

arbitration, *n.* chōtei 調停; chūsai 仲裁.

arbor, *n.* kokage 木陰.

arc, *n.* enko 円弧.

arcade, *n.* ākēdo アーケード; shōtengai 商店街.

arch, *n.* āchi アーチ; yumigata 弓形.

archaeology, *n.* kōkogaku 考古学.

archer, *n.* ite 射手.

archipelago, *n.* rettō 列島; guntō 群島.

architecture, *n.* 1. kenchikugaku 建築学 (profession, study). 2. kenchiku 建築 (building, construction). 3. kenchiku-yōshiki 建築様式 (style).

archives, *n.* 1. kiroku 記録. 2. kiroku(hozon)sho 記録 (保存)書.

arctic, 1. *n.* **Arctic** hokkyoku 北極. 2. *adj.* hokkyoku (no) 北極 (の).

area, *n.* 1. chiku 地区; chi'iki 地域 (region). 2. bun'ya 分野 (field). 3. tokoro 所 (section, space).

area code, *n.* shigaikyokubang 市外局番.

arena, *n.* kyōgijō 競技場.

argue, *vb.* 1. giron suru 議論する; noberu 述べる (debate, state). 2. iiarasou 言い争う (dispute). 3. shuchō suru 主張する (reason).

arise, *vb.* 1. okoru 起こる; shōjiru 生じる (occur). 2. tachiagaru 立ち上がる (get up).

aristocratic, *adj.* kizoku (no) 貴族 (の); kizoku-teki (na) 貴族的 (な).

arithmetic, *n.* 1. sansū 算数 (study). 2. keisan 計算 (figuring).

arm, *n.* 1. ude 腕 (limb); buki 武器 (weapon). 2. *vb.* busō suru 武装する.

armchair, *n.* hijikakeisu 肘

掛け椅子.

armful, *n.* ude ippai 腕一杯.

armor, *n.* yoroi 鎧.

armpit, *n.* waki no shita 脇の下.

army, *n.* rikugun 陸軍.

aroma, *n.* kaori 香り.

around, 1. *adv.* shūi ni 周囲に; gururi to ぐるりと (in a circle); shihō ni 四方に (on every side); fukin ni 付近に (nearby); daitai 大体; yaku 約 (approximately). 2. *prep.* ...no mawari ni ...のまわりに (surrounding); ...no fukin ni ...の付近に (near); -goro -頃 (time); **around noon** jūniji-goro.

arouse, *vb.* 1. shigeki suru 刺激する (stir). 2. okosu 起こす; mezamesaseru 目覚めさせる (awaken).

arrange, *vb.* 1. seiri suru 整理する (put in order). 2. yōi suru 用意する; junbi suru 準備する (prepare). 3. ikeru 生ける (flowers).

arrest, 1. *n.* taiho 逮捕 (seizure); soshi 阻止 (stoppage). 2. *vb.* taiho suru 逮捕する; soshi suru 阻止する.

arrive, *vb.* tsuku 着く; tōchaku suru 到着する.

arrogant, *adj.* gōman (na) 傲慢 (な).

arrow, *n.* 1. ya 矢. 2. yajirushi 矢印 (figure).

arson, *n.* hōka 放火.

art, *n.* 1. geijutsu 芸術; bijutsu 美術; **art gallery** garō 画廊. 2. gijutsu 技術 (skill).

artery, *n.* dōmyaku 動脈.

arthritis, *n.* kansetsuen 関節炎.

article, *n.* 1. kiji 記事 (writing). 2. mono 物 (thing). 3. kanshi 冠詞

(grammar).

artificial, adj. 1. jinkō (no) 人工 (の); jinkō-teki (na) 人工的 (な) (man-made). 2. nisemono (no) 偽物 (の) (fake).

artillery, n. taihō 大砲.

artist, n. geijutsuka 芸術家.

artless, adj. shizen (na) 自然 (な); soboku (na) 素朴 (な).

as, 1. adv. onaji kurai 同じくらい; **as much as** ...to onaji kurai ...と同じくらい; **as yet** ima made no tokoro 今までのところ; **as well** mata また. 2. prep. ...no yōni ...のように (like); ...toshite ...として (in the role of); **as for** ...ni tsuite wa ...については; **as of** ...kara ...から. 3. conj. yō ni ように (in the way that); toki とき (when); nanode なので (because); dakara だから (though); dakedo だけど (though); **as if** marude ...no yō ni まるで...のように; **as well as** ...to onajiku ...と同じく; **as long as** ...kagiri ...かぎり; **as soon as** ...to sugu ni ...とすぐに.

ascend, vb. noboru 上る; agaru 上がる.

ascent, n. 1. jōshō 上昇. 2. nobori kaidan 上り階段 (stair); nobori michi 上り道 (slope).

ash, n. hai 灰.

ashamed, adj. hazukashii 恥ずかしい; **be ashamed of** (o) hajiru (を)恥じる.

ashore, adv. kishi/riku de 岸／陸で (on shore); kishi/riku ni 岸／陸に (to shore); **go ashore** jōriku suru 上陸する.

ashtray, n. haizara 灰皿.

Asia, n. ajia アジア.

aside, 1. n. bōhaku 傍白 (in a play). 2. adv. waki ni 脇に

(to one side); hanashite 離して (separate); **aside from** (o/wa) nozoite (を／は)除いて (except for); sono ue ni その上に (besides).

ask, vb. 1. kiku 聞く; tazuneru 尋ねる; shitsumon suru 質問する (question, inquire). 2. tanomu 頼む; motomeru 求める (request). 3. maneku 招く (invite).

asleep, adj. nemutteiru 眠っている; **fall asleep** nemuru 眠る.

aspect, n. 1. mikake 見かけ; yōsu 様子 (appearance). 2. jōtai 状態 (condition). 3. kyokumen 局面 (phase). 4. mikata 見方 (view).

asphyxiate, vb. chissoku saseru 窒息させる.

aspire, vb. akogareru 憧れる; mezasu 目指す.

assassinate, vb. ansatsu suru 暗殺する.

assault, 1. n. kōgeki 攻撃 (attack); bōkō 暴行 (violence); gōkan 強姦 (rape). 2. vb. kōgeki suru 攻撃する; bōkō o kuwaeru 暴行を加える; gōkan suru 強姦する.

assemble, vb. atsumeru 集める (bring together); atsumaru 集まる (come together); kumitateru 組立てる (put together).

assembly line, n. nagaresagyō 流れ作業.

assent, 1. n. dōi 同意. 2. vb. dōi suru 同意する.

assert, vb. 1. dangen suru 断言する (declare). 2. shuchō suru 主張する (claim).

assess, vb. 1. kazeiひhyōka suru 課税評価する (for tax). 2. hyōka suru 評価する (evaluate).

asset, n. 1. riten 利点

(valuable quality). 2. zaisan 財産 (valuable item).

assets, *n.* zaisan 財産; shisan 資産.

assign, *vb.* 1. wariateru 割り当てる (allocate). 2. shitei suru 指定する (designate time, place, etc.). 3. ninmei suru 任命する (designate a person).

assignment, *n.* 1. ninmu 任務 (job). 2. ninmei 任命 (act of assigning). 3. shukudai 宿題 (homework).

assist, *vb.* tasukeru 助ける; enjo suru 援助する.

assistant, *vb.* joshu 助手.

associate, 1. *n.* nakama 仲間; kyōdōsha 共同者. 2. *vb.* rensō suru 連想する (relate). 2. te o musubu 手を結ぶ (unite). 3. tsukiau 付き合う (keep company).

association, *n.* 1. kai 会; dantai 団体 (organization). 2. kankei 関係 (relationship).

assorted, *adj.* iro-iro (na, no) いろいろ (な、の).

assume, *vb.* 1. katei suru 仮定する (suppose). 2. hikiukeru 引き受ける (undertake). 3. (...no) furi o suru (...の) 振りをする (pretend).

assumption, *n.* 1. katei 仮定; suitei 推定 (supposition). 2. hikiuke 引き受け (undertaking).

assure, *vb.* 1. dangen suru 断言する. 2. hoshō suru 保障する. 3. tashikameru 確かめる (make sure).

asthma, *n.* zensoku ぜん息.

astigmatism, *n.* ranshi 乱視.

astonish, *vb.* odorokaseru 驚ろかせる; **be astonished** odoroku 驚ろく.

astrology, *n.* hoshi uranai 星占い.

astronaut, *n.* uchūhikōshi 宇宙飛行士.

astronomy, *n.* tenmongaku 天文学.

at, *prep.* de で; ni に; e へ.

atheist, *n.* mushinronsha 無神論者.

athlete, *n.* undōsenshu 運動選手; kyōgisha 競技者.

athletics, *n.* undō 運動; kyōgi 競技.

Atlantic, 1. *adj.* taiseiyō (no) 大西洋 (の). 2. *n.* taiseiyō 大西洋.

atlas, *n.* chizuchō 地図帳.

atmosphere, *n.* 1. taiki 大気 (air). 2. fun'iki 雰囲気 (mood).

atom, *n.* genshi 原子.

atomic bomb, *n.* genshibakudan 原子爆弾; genbaku 原爆.

atone, *vb.* tsugunau 償う.

attach, *vb.* tsukeru 付ける (join); musubu 結ぶ (tie).

attached, *adj.* 1. suki (na) 好き (な); aichaku ga aru 愛着がある (feel affection for). 2. fuzoku (no) 付属 (の) (connected to)

attachment, *n.* 1. toritsuke 取り付け (fastening). 2. toritsukehin 取り付け品 (fastened item). 3. aijō 愛情; aichaku 愛着 (fondness).

attack, 1. *n.* kōgeki 攻撃 (assault); hossa 発作 (seizure); bōkō 暴行 (assault). 2. *vb.* kōgeki suru 攻撃する; torikakaru 取り掛かる (set about doing).

attempt, 1. *n.* kokoromi 試み. 2. *vb.* kokoromiru 試みる.

attend, *vb.* 1. shusseki suru 出席する (be present at); kayou 通う (frequent). 2. tomonau 伴う (go with). 3.

sewa o suru 世話をする (take care of). 4. ki o tsukeru 気を付ける (take heed).

attendant, 1. adj. fuzui (no) 付随 (の) (connected); (o)tomo (no) お供 (の) (accompanying); shusseki (no) 出席 (の) (present). 2. n. tsukisoinin 付き添い人 (attending person); otomo お供 (person accompanying); shussekisha 出席者 (person present); an'naigakari 案内係り (public helper).

attention, n. 1. chūmoku 注目 (directing mind); chūi 注意 (careful notice). 2. omoiyari 思い遣り; hairyo 配慮 (consideration, care).

attic, n. yaneurabeya 屋根裏部屋.

attitude, n. 1. taido 態度 (orientation, manner). 2. shisei 姿勢 (posture).

attorney, n. bengoshi 弁護士 (lawyer).

attraction, n. 1. miryoku 魅力 (attractive quality). 2. hikitsukeru chikara 引き付ける力 (attractive power). 3. inryoku 引力 (attracting force). 4. yobimono 呼び物 (spectacle).

attractive, adj. miryoku-teki (na) 魅力的 (な) (fascinating); kakkoii かっこいい (good-looking).

attribute, 1. n. zokusei 属性; tokushitsu 特質 (characteristic). 2. vb. ...ni yoru to kangaeru ...による と考える (assign to).

auction, n. kyōbai 競売.

audible, adj. kikoeru 聞こえる.

audience, n. chōshū 聴衆 (listener); kankyaku 観客

(theatergoer); kanshū 観衆 (viewer); dokusha 読者 (reader).

auditorium, n. kōdō 講堂; kaikan 会館.

August, n. hachigatsu 八月.

aunt, n. oba(san) 伯母(さん).

auspicious, adj. 1. saisaki ga ii 幸先がいい (fortunate). 2. yūbō (na) 有望 (な) (promising).

Australia, n. ōsutoraria オーストラリア.

authentic, adj. 1. tashika (na) 確か (な) (reliable). 2. honmono (no) 本物 (の) (genuine).

author, n. sakusha 作者; chosha 著者.

authority, n. ken'i 権威 (power to judge); ken'isha 権威者 (person with power); tōkyoku 当局 (legal power).

authorship, n. 1. chojutsugyō 著述業 (occupation). 2. sakusha 作者; dedokoro 出所 (personal origin).

autobiography, n. ji(jo)den 自(叙)伝.

automatic, adj. jidō (no) 自動 (の).

automation, n. jidōsōchi 自動装置.

automobile, n. jidōsha 自動車.

autumn, n. aki 秋.

auxiliary verb, n. jodōshi 助動詞.

available, adj. 1. te ni hairu 手に入る; aru 有る (obtainable, at hand). 2. au koto ga dekiru 会う事が出来る (ready to be seen); jikan ga aru 時間がある (not busy).

avalanche, n. nadare 雪崩.

avenge, vb. fukushū suru 復讐

讐する.

avenue, n. 1. ōdōri 大通り;
...gai ...街 (street); **Fifth
Avenue** gobangai. 2.
(sekkin)shudan (接近)手段
(approach).

average, 1. n. heikin 平均.
2. adj. heikin (no) 平均 (の)
(of an average); futsū (no)
普通 (の) (ordinary). 3. vb.
heikin ...ni naru 平均...にな
る.

aviation, n. hikōjutsu 飛行
術; kōkūjutsu 航空術.

avoid, vb. 1. nogareru 逃れ
る (escape). 2. sakeru 避け
る (keep away).

awake, 1. adj. okiteiru 起き
ている (not sleeping).
2. kizuiteiru 気づいている
(conscious). 3. vb. mezameru
目覚める (wake up).

award, 1. n. shō 賞 (prize);
baishōkin 賠償金 (by
judicial decree). 2. vb.
ataeru 与える.

aware, adj. kizuiteiru 気付い

ている.

away, 1. adv. yoso/hoka ni
余所／他に (from this or
that place, in another
direction, in another place);
hanarete 離れて (at a
distance, apart); kiete 消え
て (to nothing). 2. adj. rusu
(no) 留守 (の) (absent);
hanareteiru 離れている
(distant).

awful, adj. 1. kowai 怖い;
osoroshii 恐ろしい
(dreadful). 2. hidoi ひどい;
warui 悪い (bad).

awhile, adv. shibaraku 暫く.

awkward, adj. 1. gikochinai
ぎこちない; bukakkō (na)
無格好 (な) (clumsy). 2.
muzukashii 難しい
(difficult). 3. kimazui 気ま
ずい (embarrassing).

awning, n. hiyoke 日除け.

ax, axe, n. ono 斧.

axis, n. jiku 軸; chūshinsen
中心線.

azalea, n. tsutsuji つつじ.

B

babble, 1. n. oshaberi おしゃ
べり (excessive talk). 2. vb.
makushitateru まくしたて
る (speak fast); shaberu しゃ
べる (talk excessively).

baby, n. aka-chan 赤ちゃん;
nyūji 乳児.

babysitter, n. komori 子守
り.

bachelor, n. dokushindansei
独身男性.

back, 1. n. se(naka) 背(中)
(of person, animal, chair);
ura 裏 (reverse side); oku 奥
(farthest from front); **in
back of** (...no) ushiro ni/de
(...の) 後ろに／で. 2. vb.
shiji suru 支持する

(sponsor); atomodori/bakku
suru 後戻り／バックする
(move backward). 3. adj.
ushiro no 後ろの (in the
rear); mukashi/mae (no)
昔／前 (の) (of the past). 4.
adv. ushiro ni/de 後ろに／で
(at the rear); mukashi 昔 (in
the past).

backbone, n. 1. sebone 背
骨; sekitsui 脊椎 (spine). 2.
kikotsu 気骨 (strength of
character). 3.
daikokubashira 大黒柱
(main support).

background, n. 1. haikei 背
景 (backdrop, background
circumstance). 2. keireki 経

歴 (personal background);
umare 生まれ (person's
origin). 3. rekishi 歴史
(historical background).

backpack, n. ryukkusakku
リュックサック;
nappusakku ナップサック.

backward, 1. adj.
ushiromuki (no) 後ろ向き
(の) (toward the rear);
gyaku (no) 逆 (の)
(reversed); okureta 遅れた
(behind in time or
development). **2.** adv.
ushiro no hō ni 後ろの方に
(toward the rear); ushiro
kara 後ろから (from
behind); kako ni 過去に (in
the past); hantai ni 反対に
(reverse of).

backyard, n. uraniwa 裏庭.

bacon, n. bēkon ベーコン.

bad, adj. warui 悪い (not
good, wicked, harmful);
akushitsu (na, no) 悪質 (な、
の) (wicked nature);
machigai (no) 間違い (の)
(incorrect); kusatta 腐った
(spoiled).

badger, 1. n. anaguma 穴熊.
2. vb. shitsukoku iu しつこ
く言う.

bag, 1. n. fukuro 袋; tesage
手下げ; kaban 鞄. **2.** vb.
fukuro ni ireru 袋に入れる
(put in a bag).

baggage, n. tenimotsu 手荷
物.

baggy, adj. dabu-dabu shita
だぶだぶした.

bait, 1. n. esa 餌 (food); otori
おとり (allurement). **2.** vb.
esa o tsukeru 餌を付ける
(food); obikiyoseru 誘き寄
せる (entice).

bake, vb. yaku 焼く.

baker, n. panya パン屋.

bakery, n. panya パン屋.

baking powder, n.

fukurashiko ふくらし粉.

balance, 1. n. hakari 秤
(scale); baransu バランス;
tsuriai 釣合 (equilibrium);
sashihiki-zandaka 差引き残
高 (account balance). **2.** vb.
hakaru 計る (weigh, value);
tsuriawaseru 釣合わせる
(make equal); sōsai suru 相
殺する (offset); shūshi o
kessan suru 収支を決算する
(adjust account).

bald, adj. hageta 禿げた;
hage (no) 禿げ (の).

baldness, n. hage 禿.

ball, n. 1. kyū 球; tama 玉
(spherical object). 2.
butōkai 舞踏会 (dance).

ballad, n. barādo バラード;
min'yō 民謡.

balloon, n. fūsen 風船 (toy);
kikyū 気球 (hot air).

ballot, 1. n. tōhyōyōshi 投票
用紙 (form); sōtōhyō(sū) 総
投票(数) (total votes). **2.** vb.
tōhyō suru 投票する (vote).

ballpoint pen, n. hōru•pen
ボールペン.

bamboo, n. take 竹.

bamboo shoot, n. takenoko
竹の子.

ban, 1. n. kinshi 禁止. **2.** vb.
kinshi suru 禁止する.

band, 1. n. himo 紐
(material for binding); dan
団 (group); gakudan 楽団
(orchestra). **2.** vb. **band
together** danketsu suru 団
結する.

bandage, 1. n. hōtai 包帯.
2. vb. hōtai o suru 包帯をす
る.

bang, 1. n. batan/ban/
doshin/don ばたん／ばん／
どしん／どん (loud noise);
maegami 前髪 (hair bangs).
2. vb. oto o tateru 音をたて
る (make noise); (gatan to)
butsukeru (がたんと) ぶつ

けろ (hit against); tsuyoku utsu 強く打つ (strike).

banish, vb. 1. tsuihō suru 追放する (exile). 2. oidasu 追い出す (drive away).

bank, 1. n. ginkō 銀行 (financial institution); kishi 岸; tsutsumi 堤 (river bank); moritsuchi 盛り土 (heap or mass). 2. vb. yokin suru 預金する (deposit).

bankrupt, 1. n. hasansha 破産者 (person). 2. adj. hasan shita 破産した (insolvent); **go bankrupt** hasan suru 破産する.

banner, n. hata 旗.

banquet, n. utage 宴; enkai 宴会.

bar, 1. n. bō 棒 (long object); katamari 塊 (piece of solid material); shōgai 障害 (obstacle); kan'nuki 門 (bolt); sakaba 酒場 (barroom); cauntā カウンター (counter); suji 筋 (stripe). 2. vb. shimeru 締める (close); samatageru 妨げる (block); shimedasu 締め出す (exclude).

barbarian, n. yabanjin 野蛮人.

barber, n. tokoya 床屋.

barbershop, n. tokoya 床屋; rihatsuten 理髪店.

bare, 1. adj. hadaka (no) 裸(の) (uncovered); (...no) nai (...の)ない (empty); kōzen (no) 公然(の) (unconcealed); tatta (no) たった(の) (mere). 2. vb. sarasu 曝す; arawa ni suru あらわにする (lay bare).

barefoot, adj. hadashi (no) はだし(の).

barely, adv. karōjite 辛うじて; nantoka 何とか.

bargain, 1. n. baibai-keiyaku 売買契約 (commercial

agreement); kōshō 交渉 okaidoku(hin) お買い得(品) (advantageous purchase). 2. vb. torihiki/kōshō suru 取り引き/交渉する (negotiate).

bark, 1. n. juhi 樹皮 (tree); hoegoe 吠え声(dog). 2. vb. hoeru 吠える (dog).

barley, n. ōmugi 大麦.

barn, n. naya 納屋; kachikugoya 家畜小屋.

barracks, n. heisha 兵舎.

barrel, n. taru 樽.

barrier, n. 1. shōgai 障害 (obstacle); saku 柵 (fence).

bartender, n. bāten バーテン.

base, 1. n. moto 元, soko 底 (bottom); kiso 基礎 (foundation); fumoto 麓 (foot of mountain); konkyo 根拠 (basis); kichi 基地 (military). 2. adj. iyashii 卑しい (despicable); tsumaranai つまらない (worthless). 3. vb. motozuku 基づく; **be based on** ...ni motozuku.

baseball, n. yakyū 野球.

basement, n. chika(shitsu) 地下(室); chikai 地階.

bash, 1. n. ichigeki 一撃 (heavy blow); pātī パーティ (party). 2. vb. naguru 殴る.

bashful, adj. hazukashii 恥ずかしい; uchiki (na) 内気(な).

basic, adj. kihon-teki (na) 基本的(な).

basin, n. tarai たらい; hachi 鉢; sen'menki 洗面器.

basis, n. kihon 基本; kiso 基礎.

basket, n. kago 籠.

bat, n. kōmori こうもり

(animal).

bath, n. (o)furo (お)風呂; basu バス.

bathe, vb. 1. (o)furo ni hairu (お)風呂に入る (take a bath); abiru 浴びる; tsukaru 浸かる (immerse).

bathing suit, n. mizugi 水着.

bathroom, n. 1. furoba 風呂場 (for bathing). 2. otearai お手洗い (rest room).

batter, 1. n. koromo 衣 (food coating). 2. vb. tsuzukete utsu 続けて打つ (beat); tsubusu 潰す; uchikowasu 打ち壊す (damage).

battery, n. batterī バッテリー (for vehicles); denchi 電池 (for appliances).

battle, 1. n. sentō 戦闘; tatakai 戦い. 2. vb. tatakau 戦う.

bawl, vb. 1. wameku 喚く (cry out); donaru どなる (yell). 2. **bawl out** shikaru 叱る.

bay, n. wan 湾 (water).

bazaar, n. ichi 市.

be, vb. iru/imasu 居る／居ます; aru/arimasu 有る／有ります; dearu/desu である／です.

beach, n. hama 浜; kishibe 岸辺.

bead, n. bīzu ビーズ (decoration); tama 玉 (drop).

beak, n. kuchibashi くちばし.

beam, 1. n. hari 梁 (structure); kōsen 光線 (light). 2. vb. hikaru 光る (emit light); hohoemu 微笑む (smile).

bean, n. mame 豆.

bear, 1. n. kuma 熊. 2. vb. umu 産む (bear a child);

sasaeru 支える (support); hakobu 運ぶ (carry); taeru 耐える (endure); **bear down** osaetsukeru 押さえつける; **bear in mind** oboete oku 覚えておく; **bear out** jisshō suru 実証する; **bear up** ganbaru 頑張る.

beard, n. ago hige あご髭.

bearing, n. 1. monogoshi 物腰; taido 態度 (manner). 2. kankei 関係 (relation). 3. gaman 我慢 (patience).

beast, n. ke(da)mono 獣; dōbutsu 動物.

beat, 1. n. kodō 鼓動 (heartbeat); hyōshi 拍子 (rhythm); junkai 巡回 (patrol route). 2. vb. utsu 打つ (strike, dash against); butsu 打つ (hit a person); tataku 叩く (hit repeatedly); kakimazeru 掻き混ぜる (stir); hyōshi o toru 拍子を取る (rhythm); uchimakasu 打ち負かす (defeat).

beautiful, adj. utsukushii 美しい; kirei (na) きれい (な).

beauty, n. 1. bi 美. 2. bijin 美人 (woman). 3. **beauty parlor** biyōin 美容院.

because, conj. nazenara なぜなら...; node ので; (...da)kara (...だ) から; **because of** (...no) tame ni (...の) 為に.

beckon, vb. temaneki suru 手招きする.

become, vb. 1. ...ni naru ...になる (come to be). 2. (ni)au (に)合う (suit).

bed, n. shindai 寝台.

bedroom, n. shinshitsu 寝室.

bee, n. mitsubachi 密蜂 (honeybee); hachi 蜂 (bee).

beef, n. gyūniku 牛肉.

beefsteak, n. bifuteki ビフテキ

テキ.

beehive, *n.* hachi no su 蜂の巣.

before, 1. *adv.* mae ni 前に (in front, previously); izen 以前 (previously). 2. *prep.* (...no) mae ni/de (...の) 前に／で (in front of, in the presence of); (...yori) mae ni (...より) 前に (previous to). 3. *conj.* (...suru) mae ni (...する) 前に.

beforehand, *adv.* maemotte 前もって.

beg, *vb.* 1. kou 請う (ask for charity). 2. tanomu 頼む (ask).

beggar, *n.* kojiki 乞食.

begin, *vb.* hajimeru 始める (cause to start); hajimaru 始まる (start to move or act).

beginner, *n.* shoshinsha 初心者.

beginning, *n.* hajime 初め.

behalf, *n.* **in/on one's behalf** (...no) tame ni (...の)為に (for someone); **on behalf of** (...o) daihyō shite (...を) 代表して (as representative); ...ni kawatte ...に代わって (as proxy).

behave, *vb.* 1. furumau ふるまう (conduct oneself). 2. gyōgi yoku suru 行儀良くする (act properly).

behead, *vb.* kubi o kiru 首を切る.

behind, 1. *adv.* ushiro/ato ni 後ろ／後に (at the back); okurete 遅れて (slow); **be behind** okurete-iru. 2. *prep.* (...no) ushiro ni (...の) 後ろに (at the back of); (...no) ato de (...の) 後で (later than). 3. *n.* (o)shiri (お)尻 (buttocks).

behold, 1. *vb.* miru 見る. 2. *interj.* miyo 見よ.

belated, *adj.* okureta 遅れた.

belch, *n.* geppu げっぷ.

belief, *n.* 1. shin'nen 信念 (conviction). 2. shinrai 信頼 (trust). 3. shinjin 信心 (religious tenet).

believe, *vb.* shinjiru 信じる (accept as true, trust). 2. (...to) kangaeru (...と) 考える (suppose). 3. **make believe** (...no) furi o suru (...の) 振りをする.

bell, *n.* 1. kane 鐘. 2. doaberu ドアベル; chaimu チャイム (doorbell). 3. suzu 鈴 (small bell).

bellboy, *n.* bōi(san) ボーイ (さん).

bellow, 1. *n.* hoegoe 吠え声; todoroki とどろき. 2. *vb.* hoeru 吠える; todoroku とどろく.

belly, *n.* onaka お腹; hara 腹.

beloved, *adj.* aisuru 愛する; taisetsu (na) 大切 (な).

below, 1. *adv.* shita ni/de 下に／で. 2. *prep.* (...no/yori) shita ni/de (...の／より) 下に／で; (...yori) hikui (...より) 低い.

bench, *n.* nagaisu 長椅子.

bend, 1. *n.* magari 曲がり (curve). 2. *vb.* magaru 曲がる (become curved); mageru 曲げる (curve something); makasu 負かす (cause to submit).

beneath, *prep.* (...no) shita ni/de (...の) 下に／で; (...yori) hikui (...より) 低い (lower than, under, unworthy of).

benefit, 1. *n.* jizen 慈善 (kind act); rieki 利益 (advantage); teate 手当て (payment). 2. *vb.* tame ni naru 為になる (do good for); toku suru 得する (gain advantage).

bent, 1. *adj.* magatta 曲がった (not straight); hinekureta ひねくれた (crooked attitude); **bent on** kesshin shiteiru 決心している (resolved). 2. *n.* keikō 傾向 (inclination); sainō 才能 (talent).

berry, *n.* **mulberry** kuwa no mi 桑の実; **raspberry** ki'ichigo 木苺; **strawberry** ichigo 苺.

beside, *prep.* 1. (...no) soba ni/de (...の) 側に／で (at the side of). 2. (...to) kurabete (...と) 比べて (compared with).

besides, 1. *adv.* soreni それに (also); sono ue ni その上に (in addition). 2. *prep.* (...no) hoka ni (...の) 他に (other than). 3. (...ni) kuwaete (...に) 加えて (in addition to).

best, 1. *adj.*, *adv.* ichiban ii 一番良い; sairyō (no) 最良 (の); **at best** yokutemo 良くても. 2. *n.* saizen 最善; **do one's best** saizen o tsukusu 最善を尽くす.

bet, 1. *n.* kakekin 掛金 (money). 2. *vb.* kakeru 賭ける (risk money or thing); **I bet...** kitto ... dearu きっと...である.

betray, *vb.* 1. uragiru 裏切る (be unfaithful). 2. bakuro suru 暴露する (disclose).

betrothal, *n.* kon'yaku 婚約.

better, 1. *adj.* motto ii もっと良い (of superior quality); kibun ga ii 気分が良い (healthy). 2. *vb.* kairyō suru 改良する.

between, 1. *adv.* aida ni 間に. 2. *prep.* (...no) aida/naka de (ni, o) (...の) 間／中で (に、を).

beverage, *n.* nomimono 飲物.

beware, 1. *vb.* yōjin suru 用心する; ki o tsukeru 気を付ける. 2. *interj.* Ki o tsukete/tsukenasai 気を付けて／付けなさい.

beyond, 1. *n.* anoyo あの世; raise 来世 (afterlife). 2. *adv.* mukō ni 向こうに (farther away). 3. *prep.* (...no) mukō ni (...の) 向こうに (on the farther side of); (...o) sugite (...を) 過ぎて (past); (...o) koete (...を) 超えて (outside the limits of); te no todokanai 手の届かない (outside the reach of); (...no) ue ni (...の) 上に (surpassing).

bias, 1. *n.* henken 偏見 (prejudice); shasen 斜線 (slanted line); **on the bias** naname ni 斜めに. 2. *vb.* henken o motaseru 偏見をもたせる.

bib, *n.* yodarekake 涎掛け.

bicycle, *n.* jitensha 自転車.

bifocal, *adj.* enkinryōyō (no) 遠近両用 (の).

big, *adj.* 1. ōkii 大きい (large, loud). 2. jūyō (na) 重要 (な) (important). 3. hijō na 非常な (outstanding).

bigotry, *n.* henken 偏見; henkutsu 偏屈.

big shot, *n.* ōmono 大物.

big toe, *n.* (ashi no) oyayubi (足の) 親指.

bilateral, *adj.* ryōhō/sōhō (no) 両方／双方 (の).

bilingual, *adj.* nikakokugo (no) 二ヵ国語 (の).

bill, 1. *n.* seikyūsho 請求書; kanjō 勘定 (statement of money owed); satsu 札; shihei 紙幣 (money); hōan 法案 (proposed law); kōkoku 広告 (notice);

kuchibashi くちばし (beak). 2. vb. **seikyūsho o okuru** 請求書を送る.

billboard, n. **kōkokuban** 広告板.

billfold, n. **saifu** 財布; **satsuire** 札入れ.

billiards, n. **tamatsuki** 玉突き.

billion, n. 1. (U.S.) **jūoku** 十億 (a thousand million). 2. (Brit.) **chō** 兆 (a million million).

bin, n. **hako** 箱 (container); **chozōsho** 貯蔵所 (granary).

bind, vb. 1. **musubu** 結ぶ; **tsunagu** つなぐ; **shibaru** 縛る (unite, tie). 2. **maku** 巻く (encircle). 3. **seihon suru** 製本する (make book).

binoculars, n. **sōgankyō** 双眼鏡.

biography, n. **denki** 伝記.

biology, n. **seibutsugaku** 生物学.

bird, n. **tori** 鳥.

birth, n. 1. **tanjō** 誕生 (fact of being born); **shussan** 出産 (act of being born); **by birth umaretsuki** 生まれつき; **give birth to** (...o) **umu** (...を) 産む. 2. **umare** 生まれ (lineage).

birthday, n. **tanjōbi** 誕生日.

bit, n. 1. **shōryō** 少量; **a bit sukoshi** 少し; **chotto** ちょっと. 2. **kiri** 錐 (drill). 3. **bitto** ビット (computers).

bite, 1. n. **kamitsuki** 噛みつき (act of biting); **sashikizu** 刺し傷 (insect); **hitokuchi** 一口 (food). 2. vb. **kamu** 噛む (with teeth); **sasu** 刺す (insect).

bitter, adj. 1. **nigai** 苦い (of harsh taste). 2. **kurushii** 苦しい; **tsurai** 辛い (unbearable). 3. **kibishii** 厳しい (severe).

black, 1. adj. **kuroi** 黒い (color); **hada no kuroi** 肌の黒い (having dark skin); **kurai** 暗い (without light, gloomy). 2. n. **kuro(iro)** 黒(色) (color); **kokujin** 黒人 (black race or person).

blackberry, n. **ki'ichigo** 木苺.

blackboard, n. **kokuban** 黒板.

blackmail, 1. n. **yusuri** 強請. 2. vb. **yusuru** 強請る.

black market, n. **yami'ichi** 闇市.

blackout, n. 1. **teiden** 停電 (electricity). 2. **kioku-sōshitsu** 記憶喪失 (amnesia).

bladder, n. **bōkō** 膀胱.

blade, n. 1. **ha** 刃 (knife). 2. **ha** 葉 (leaf).

blame, 1. n. **hinan** 非難 (censure); **sekinin** 責任 (responsibility). 2. vb. **semeru** 責める; **togameru** 咎める (censure); **be to blame for** (...no) **sekinin ga aru.**

bland, adj. 1. **odayaka (na)** 穏やか(な) (agreeable). 2. **ajikenai** 味気ない (insipid).

blank, 1. n. **kūhaku** 空白 (space to be filled in); **hakushi** 白紙 (paper without writing). 2. adj. **kūhaku (no)** 空白 (の); **hakushi (no)** 白紙 (の); **muhyōjō (na)** 無表情 (な) (no facial expression); **garanto shita** がらんとした (emotionless, empty).

blanket, n. **mōfu** 毛布.

blare, 1. n. **yakamashii hibiki** 喧しい響き. 2. vb. **yakamashiku hibiku** 喧しく響く.

blast, 1. n. **toppū** 突風 (wind); **bakuhatsu** 爆発

(explosion); hibiki 響き (horn); **full blast** zen'ryoku de 全力で. 2. vb. uchikowasu 打ち壊す (destroy); bakuha suru 爆破する (blow up).

blaze, 1. n. hono'o 炎 (flame); kagayaki 輝き (glow). 2. vb. moeru 燃える (burn); kagayaku 輝く (shine).

bleach, 1. n. hyōhakuzai 漂白剤. 2. vb. hyōhaku suru 漂白する.

bleed, vb. shukketsu suru 出血する.

blend, 1. n. burendo ブレンド; kongō 混合. 2. vb. mazeru 混ぜる.

bless, vb. 1. (shukufuku o) inoru (祝福を) 祈る (request divine favor for). 2. (megumi o) sazukeru (恵みを) 授ける (endow). 3. tataeru 賛える (praise).

blind, 1. n. hiyoke 日除け (window shade). 2. adj. mō(moku) (no) 盲(目) (の) (unable to see). 3. vb. mienaku suru 見えなくする (cause to not see).

blindfold, 1. n. mekakushi 目隠し. 2. vb. mekakushi o suru 目隠しをする.

blink, 1. n. matataki 瞬き (blinking, glimmer). 2. vb. mabataki suru 瞬きする (wink).

blister, n. mizubukure 水ぶくれ.

blizzard, n. fubuki 吹雪.

block, 1. n. burokku ブロック; katamari 塊 (solid mass); shōgai 障害 (obstacle); -chōme -丁目 (city block); tsumiki 積み木 (toy). 2. vb. fusagu 塞ぐ; samatageru 妨げる (obstruct).

blockade, 1. n. fūsa 封鎖.

2. vb. fūsa suru 封鎖する.

blond, adj. kinpatsu (no) 金髪 (の).

blood, n. 1. chi 血; ketsueki 血液 (liquid). 2. ketsuen 血縁 (family relation); kettō 血統 (lineage).

blood pressure, n. ketsuatsu 血圧.

bloodshot, adj. jūketsu 充血.

blood type, n. ketsuekigata 血液型.

blood vessel, n. kekkan 血管.

bloom, 1. n. hana 花 (flower); kaika 開花 (blossoming). 2. vb. hana saku 花咲く; kaika suru 開花する.

blossom, 1. n. hana 花. 2. vb. hana saku 花咲く.

blow, 1. n. tsuyoi kaze 強い風 (blast of wind); dageki 打撃 (stroke, shock). 2. vb. fuku 吹く (wind); narasu 鳴らす (instrument); **blow one's nose** hana o kamu 鼻をかむ; **blow up** kanshaku o okosu 癇癪を起こす (lose temper); bakuha suru 爆破する (explode); hikinobasu 引き伸ばす (enlarge photograph).

blowfish, n. fugu ふぐ.

blowout, n. panku パンク (puncture).

blue, 1. adj. aoi 青い (color); yū'utsu (na) 憂うつ (な) (melancholy). 2. n. ao(iro) 青(色) (color).

blueprint, n. aojashin 青写真 (drawing); keikaku 計画 (plan).

blunder, 1. n. shikujiri しくじり; machigai 間違い. 2. vb. shikujiru しくじる.

blunt, 1. adj. nibui 鈍い (dull); sotchoku (na) 率直

(な) (frank). 2. *vb.* nibuku
suru 鈍くする.

blur, 1. *n.* fusenmei 不鮮明;
kasumi霞 (indistinctness).
2. *vb.* bokasu ぼかす
(obscure); kasumu 霞む
(become indistinct).

blush, 1. *n.* sekimen 赤面.
2. *vb.* akaku naru 赤くなる
(redden); haji'iru 恥じ入る
(feel shame).

board, 1. *n.* ita 板 (timber,
sheet of wood); i'inkai 委員
会 (managing group). 2. *vb.*
noru 乗る (go aboard);
geshuku saseru 下宿させる
(take in boarder).

boarding pass, *n.* tōjōken
搭乗券.

boast, 1. *n.* jiman 自慢. 2.
vb. jiman suru 自慢する.

boat, *n.* bōto ボート; kobune
小船.

bob, *vb.* 1. jōge ni ugoku 上
下に動く (move). 2.
mijikaku suru 短くする (cut
short).

bobby pin, *n.* hea-pin ヘア
ピン.

body, *n.* 1. karada 体
(physical structure); shitai
死体 (corpse). 2. hontai 本
体 (main mass). 3. dantai
団体 (group).

bodyguard, *n.* yōjinbō 用心
棒.

boil, 1. *n.* futtō 沸騰 (water);
dekimono 出来物 (sore). 2.
vb. futtō suru 沸騰する
(reach boiling point); niru
煮る (cause to boil); ikaru
怒る (be angry).

bold, *adj.* 1. daitan (na) 大胆
(な) (daring). 2.
atsukamashii 厚かましい
(immodest). 3. medatsu 目
立つ (conspicuous). 4.
futoji (no) 太字 (の)
(boldface type).

bolt, 1. *n.* kan'nuki 閂 (bar);
inazuma 稲妻
(thunderbolt); tōsō 逃走
(flight). 2. *vb.* shimeru 締め
る (fasten); nigeru 逃げる
(run away).

bomb, 1. *n.* bakudan 爆弾
(missile); shippai 失敗
(failure). 2. *vb.* bakugeki
suru 爆撃する (attack);
shippai suru 失敗する (fail).

bond, *n.* 1. kizuna 絆 (tie
between people). 2.
setchakuzai 接着剤 (glue).
3. saiken 債券 (financial).

bone, 1. *n.* hone 骨. 2. *vb.*
hone o toru 骨を取る.

bonfire, *n.* takibi 焚き火.

bonus, *n.* bōnasu ボーナス;
shōyokin 賞与金.

book, 1. *n.* hon 本 (bound);
kaikeibo 会計簿 (account
book). 2. *vb.* kinyū suru 記
入する (record); yoyaku
suru 予約する (reserve).

bookcase, *n.* honbako 本箱.

booklet, *n.* panfuretto パン
フレット.

bookseller, *n.* honya 本屋;
shoten 書店.

bookstore, *n.* honya 本屋;
shoten 書店.

boom, 1. *n.* gō'on 轟音
(sound). 2. kōkeiki 好景気
(growth).

boost, 1. *n.* oshiage 押し上げ
(upward push); ato'oshi 後
押し (aid); jōshō 上昇
(increase, rise). 2. *vb.*
mochiageru 持ち上げる
(lift); ato'oshi suru 後押しす
る (aid); neage suru 値上げ
する (raise price); ageru 上
げる (increase).

boot, *n.* nagagutsu 長靴.

booth, *n.* 1. koshitsu 小室
(compartment). 2. yatai 屋
台 (street vendor).

border, 1. *n.* kokkyō 国境

(national border); sakai (boundary). 2. fuchi 縁 (margin). 2. vb. fuchi o tsukeru 縁を付ける; **border on** sessuru 接する.

bore, 1. n. ana 穴 (hole); tsumaranai hito つまらない 人 (person). 2. vb. ana o akeru 穴を開ける (hole); taikutsu saseru 退屈させる (weary).

boring, adj. taikutsu (na) 退 屈 (な); tsumaranai つまら ない.

born, adj. umaretsuki (no) 生まれつき (の) (by nature); **be born** umareru 生まれる.

borrow, vb. kariru/karu 借 りる／借る.

bosom, n. 1. mune 胸 (breast). 2. kokoro 心 (center of feelings).

boss, 1. n. jōshi 上司 (superior). 2. bosu ボス; oyabun 親分 (group leader).

botany, n. shokubutsugaku 植物学.

both, 1. pron. dochira mo ど ちらも; ryōhō 両方 (two). 2. adj. ryōhō (no) 両方 (の).

bother, 1. n. yakkai 厄介 (trouble); meiwaku 迷惑 (annoyance). 2. vb. nayamaseru 悩ませる (trouble); meiwaku o kakeru 迷惑をかける (annoy).

bottle, 1. n. bin 瓶. 2. vb. bin ni tsumeru 瓶につめる.

bottom, n. 1. soko 底. 2. (o)shiri (お)尻 (buttocks).

bounce, 1. n. hanekaeri 跳 ね返り (spring). 2. vb. hanekaeru 跳ね返る (spring back), tobiagaru 飛び上がる (jump up).

bound, adj. shibararete-iru 縛られている (tied up);

gimu ga aru 義務がある (obligated); tojita 綴じた (fastened); **bound for** (...) iki (no) (...) 行き (の).

boundary, n. 1. sakai 境; kyōkai 境界 (border). 2. genkai 限界 (limit).

bouquet, n. hanataba 花束.

bout, n. 1. shōbu 勝負 (contest). 2. kikan 期間 (period).

bow, 1. n. ojigi お辞儀 (salutation); hesaki 舳先 (ship); yumi 弓 (archery, violin); chōmusubi 蝶結び (ribbon). 2. vb. atama o sageru 頭を下げる (bend down); ojigi o suru お辞儀 をする (salute); mageru 曲 げる (curve).

bowels, n. chō 腸 (intestine); **bowel movement** bentsū 便通.

bowl, 1. n. (o)wan (お)椀 (round dish); chawan 茶碗 (rice bowl); donburi 丼 (big round dish); bōru ボール (mixing bowl). 2. vb. bōringu o suru ボーリング をする (sport).

bow tie, n. chō-nekutai 蝶ネ クタイ.

box, 1. n. hako 箱 (container); sajikiseki 桟敷 席 (in theater). 2. vb. hako ni ireru 箱に入れる (put into a box); naguru 殴る (strike); bokushingu o suru ボクシングをする (sport).

box office, n. kippu'uriba 切 符売場.

boy, n. otoko no ko 男の子; shōnen 少年.

boyfriend, n. kare(shi) 彼 (氏); koibito 恋人.

brace, n. sasae 支え (support). 2. vb. hokyō suru 補強する (reinforce).

bracelet, n. udewa 腕輪.

brag, 1. *n.* jiman 自慢. 2. *vb.* jiman suru 自慢する.

braid, 1. *n.* kumihimo 組み紐 (rope); osagegami おさげ髪; mitsuami 三つ編み (hair). 2. *vb.* kumu 組む; amu 編む.

brain, *n.* 1. nō 能. 2. chisei 知性; zunō 頭脳 (intelligence).

brake, 1. *n.* burēki ブレーキ. 2. *vb.* burēki o kakeru ブレーキをかける.

branch, 1. *n.* koeda 小枝 (tree); bumon 部門 (division); shiryū 支流 (river); **branch office** shisha/shiten 支社／支店. 2. *vb.* wakareru 分かれる.

brand, *n.* shōhyō 商標 (trademark); yaki'in 焼き印 (burned mark). 2. *vb.* yakitsuku 焼き付く (impress indelibly); omei o kiseru 汚名を着せる (stigmatize).

brandish, *vb.* furimawasu 振り回す.

brand-new, *adj.* ma'atarashii 真新しい.

brash, *adj.* 1. mukōmizu (na, no) 向こう見ず (な、の) (hasty). 2. namaiki (na) 生意気 (な) (rude).

brass, *n.* shinchū 真ちゅう (metal).

brassiere, *n.* burajā ブラジャー.

brave, *adj.* yūkan (na) 勇敢 (な).

brawl, 1. *n.* kenka けんか. 2. *vb.* kenka suru けんかする.

Brazil, *n.* burajiru ブラジル.

bread, *n.* 1. pan パン (food). 2. seikei 生計 (livelihood).

breadth, *n.* haba 幅; hirosa 広さ.

break, 1. *n.* yabure 破れ (rupture); sakeme 裂け目

(gap); kyūkei 休憩 (rest). 2. *vb.* kowasu 壊す; kudaku 砕く (separate into parts); kowasu 壊す (make useless); yaburu 破る (violate, tear); oru 折る (fracture, break off); sakeru 裂ける; kudakeru 砕ける (become ruptured or separated); wareru 割れる (become cracked); kowareru 壊れる (become useless); yabureru 破れる (become torn); oreru 折れる (become fractured or broken off).

breakfast, 1. *n.* asagohan 朝御飯; chōshoku 朝食. 2. *vb.* asa gohan o taberu 朝御飯を食べる.

breakup, *n.* 1. wakare 別れ (end of relationship). 2. kaitai 解体 (disintegration).

breast, *n.* 1. mune 胸 (chest). 2. chichi 乳 (milk gland). 3. kyōchū 胸中 (feelings).

breath, *n.* iki 息; **catch one's breath** iki o nomu; **hold one's breath** iki o tomeru; **out of breath** iki ga kireru.

breathe, *vb.* iki o suru 息をする.

breed, 1. *n.* hinshu 品種; shuzoku 種族 (sort); kettō 血統 (lineage). 2. *vb.* umu 産む (produce); kau 飼う (raise); sodateru 育てる (raise).

breeze, *n.* soyokaze そよ風.

brew, 1. *n.* jōzō 醸造. 2. *vb.* jōzō suru 醸造する (beer); ireru 入れる (tea).

bribe, 1. *n.* wairo 賄賂. 2. *vb.* baishū suru 買収する.

brick, *n.* renga 煉瓦.

bride, *n.* shinpu 新婦; hanayome 花嫁.

bridegroom, *n.* shinrō 新郎; hanamuko 花婿.

bridge, n. hashi 橋.

bridle, vb. seigyo suru 制御する (control).

brief, 1. adj. mijikai 短い (short); kanketsu (na) 簡潔 (な) (concise). 2. n. yōshi/yōyaku 要旨／要約 (outline, concise statement). 3. vb. temijika ni iu 手短に言う (inform in advance).

briefcase, n. kaban 鞄.

bright, adj. 1. akarui 明るい (filled with light, happy); hikaru 光る; kagayaku 輝く (shining). 2. kagayakashii 輝かしい (glorious). 3. atama ga ii 頭が良い (clever, intelligent, wise). 4. azayaka (na) 鮮やか (な) (bright color).

brilliant, adj. 1. kagayaiteiru 輝いている (bright). 2. subarashii 素晴らしい (splendid).

brim, n. 1. fuchi 縁. 2. tsuba つば (hat).

bring, vb. 1. tsuretekuru 連れて来る (a person); mottekuru 持って来る (a thing). 2. michibiku 導く (lead). **bring about** motarasu もたらす; **bring up** sodateru 育てる.

brink, n. 1. fuchi 縁; hashi 端 (edge); setogiwa 瀬戸際 (verge).

brisk, adj. 1. kakki ga aru 活気がある (quick and active). 2. sawayaka (na) さわやか (な) (sharp and stimulating).

Britain, n. igirisu イギリス; eikoku 英国.

brittle, adj. wareyasui 割れ易い; moroi 脆い.

broad, adj. 1. (haba)hiroi (幅)広い (wide, vast). 2. ōmaka (na) 大まか (な) (general). 3. kandai (na) 寛大 (な) (tolerant).

broadcast, 1. n. hōsō 放送. 2. vb. hōsō suru 放送する (radio, TV); hiromeru 広める (make known).

brochure, n. panfuretto パンフレット.

broil, vb. aburu あぶる.

broken, adj. 1. kowareta 壊れた (out of order). 2. wareta 割れた (in fragments); oreta 折れた (fractured); yabureta 破れた (torn, disrupted).

broker, n. nakagainin 仲買人.

brokerage, n. shōkengaisha 証券会社.

bronchitis, n. kikanshien 気管支炎.

bronze, n. seidō 青銅.

brood, 1. n. hina ひな (chicks). 2. vb. kangaekomu 考え込む (ponder).

brook, n. ogawa 小川.

broom, n. hōki 箒.

broth, n. dashi だし; sūpu スープ.

brother, n. 1 kyōdai 兄弟. 2. ani 兄; oniisan お兄さん (older brother). 3. otōto 弟 (younger brother).

brother-in-law, n. giri no kyōdai 義理の兄弟.

brow, n. 1. hitai 額 (forehead). 2. mayu まゆ (eyebrow).

brown, 1. adj. chairoi 茶色い. 2. n. chairo 茶色.

browse, vb. 1. hiroiyomi suru 拾い読みする (read). 2. miaruku 見歩く (look at goods leisurely).

bruise, 1. n. uchikizu 打ち傷; aza 痣. 2. vb. utsu 打つ; aza ga dekiru 痣ができる.

brush, 1. n. fude 筆 (for painting). 2. vb. burashi o kakeru ブラシを掛ける (clean with brush);

kasumeru 掠める (touch
lightly); **brush up** benkyō
shinaosu 勉強し直す
(knowledge).
brutal, *adj.* 1.
zan'nin/zankoku (na) 残
忍／残酷 (na) (cruel). 2.
muchakucha (na) むちゃく
ちゃ (な) (unreasonable).
bubble, 1. *n.* awa 泡 (foam);
shabondama シャボン玉
(soap bubble). 2. *vb.*
awadatsu 泡立つ.
buckwheat, *n.* soba そば
(grain); sobako そば粉
(flour).
bud, 1. *n.* tsubomi つぼみ;
me 芽. 2. *vb.* tsubomi/me ga
deru つぼみ／芽が出る.
Buddhism, *n.* bukkyō 仏教.
buddy, *n.* nakama 仲間.
budget, 1. *n.* yosan 予算.
2. *vb.* yosan o kumu 予算を
組む.
bug, *n.* mushi 虫 (insect).
build, 1. *n.* tsukuri 造り
(structure). 2. *vb.* tateru 建
てる (construct); kizuku 築
く (base, develop).
building, *n.* tatemono 建物;
biru ビル.
built-in, *n.* tsukuritsuke
(no) 造り付け (の)
(furniture); naizō (no) 内蔵
(の) (mechanics).
bulb, *n.* 1. denkyū 電球
(light bulb). 2. kyūkon 球根
(root).
bulge, 1. *n.* fukurami 膨ら
み. 2. *vb.* fukureru 膨れる;
tsukideru 突き出る.
bull, *n.* oushi 牡牛.
bullet, *n.* dangan 弾丸;
teppō no tama 鉄砲の玉.
bulletin, *n.* hōkoku 報告;
tsūchi 通知.
bulletin board, *n.* keijiban
掲示板.
bull's-eye, *n.* mato 的.

bully, 1. *n.* ijimekko いじ
めっこ. 2. *vb.* ijimeru いじ
める (abuse); ibaru 威張る
(be arrogant).
bump, 1. *n.* shōtotsu 衝突
(blow); kobu 瘤 (swelling).
2. *vb.* butsukaru ぶつかる;
utsu 打つ (strike); **bump
into** ...ni dekuwasu ...に出
くわす (come across).
bun, *n.* 1. kashi-pan 菓子パ
ン (sweet bread); rōrupan
ロールパン (roll).
2. sokuhatsu 束髪 (hair).
bunch, *n.* 1. taba 束; fusa 房
(cluster). 2. mure 群れ
(group of people).
bundle, 1. *n.* taba 束;
tsutsumi 包み (package).
2. *vb.* tabaneru 束ねる
(bind); tsutsumu 包む
(wrap); **bundle up** kikomu
着込む (dress); matomeru
まとめる (gather).
bunk, *n.* shindai 寝台.
bunny, *n.* (ko)usagi (子)兎.
burden, 1. *n.* omoni 重荷
(spiritual or material
burden); yakkai 厄介
(trouble). 2. *vb.* omoni o
owaseru 重荷を負わせる
(load); wazurawasu 煩わす
(trouble).
burglar, *n.* gōtō 強盗.
burn, 1. *n.* yakedo 火傷
(injury). 2. *vb.* moeru 燃え
る (be on fire, be excited);
moyasu 燃やす (consume
with fire); yaku 焼く (broil,
grill); kogasu 焦がす
(scorch); yakedo suru 火傷
する (injure).
burp, 1. *n.* geppu げっぷ.
2. *vb.* geppu o suru げっぷを
する.
burst, 1. *n.* haretsu 破裂
(rupture); bakuhatsu 爆発
(explosion). 2. *vb.* haretsu
suru 破裂する (break

violently); **bakuhatsu suru** 爆発する (explode); **burst into** totsuzen/issei ni shidasu 突然／いっせいにしだす.

bury, vb. umeru 埋める (in the ground); hōmuru 葬る (in a grave).

bus, n. basu バス; **catch a bus** basu ni maniau.

bush, n. shigemi 茂み; yabu やぶ (shrub, thicket).

business, n. 1. bijinesu ビジネス; shōbai 商売; eigyō 営業 (commerce, trade); **business hours** eigyōjikan 営業時間. 2. shigoto 仕事 (profession, work). 3. yōken 用件 (personal concern).

bust, n. 1. mune 胸 (bosom). 2. kyōzo 胸像 (sculpture).

busy, 1. adj. isogashii 忙しい (actively employed); kōtsū ga ōi 交通が多い (street); hanashichū (no) 話し中 (の) (telephone). 2. vb. **busy oneself** isoshimu いそしむ.

but, 1. prep. (...o) nozoite (...を) 除いて (other than). 2. conj. dakedo だけど; shikashi しかし; ga が (however).

butcher shop, n. nikuya 肉屋.

butler, n. shitsuji 執事.

butt, n. 1. moto 元 (end); suigara 吸殻 (cigarette end). 2. (o)shiri (お)尻 (buttocks).

butterfly, n. chōcho 蝶々.

buttocks, n. (o)shiri (お)尻.

buttress, 1. n. sasae 支え (support). 2. vb. sasaeru 支える (support); hōkyō suru 補強する (strengthen).

buy, 1. vb. kau 買う. 2. n. kaimono 買物.

buzz, 1. n. bun-bun to iu oto ぶんぶんという音 (bee); zawameki ざわめき (voices). 2. vb. bun-bun suru ぶんぶんする; zawameku ざわめく; buzā o osu ブザーを押す (signal with buzzer).

by, 1. prep. ...ni yotte ...によって; de で (by means of); (...no) chikaku/soba ni (...の) 近く/側に (near to); made ni までに (not later than); ... o tōshite ...を通して (through); ...zutsu ...ずつ (after); **little by little** sukoshi zutsu すこしずつ; **by oneself** hitori de 一人で. 2. adv. soba ni 側に (near); sugite 過ぎて (past); **by and by** yagate やがて; **by and large** ippan ni 一般に.

bye-bye, interj. sayonara さよなら; bai-bai バイバイ.

C

cab, n. takushī タクシー (taxi).

cabin, n. koya 小屋 (small house).

cabinet, n. 1. todana 戸棚 (furniture). 2. naikaku 内閣 (government).

cable, n. futozuna 太綱 (hawser).

cable television, n. yūsen-terebi 有線テレビ.

cache, n. kakushibasho 隠し場所 (hiding place).

cactus, n. saboten サボテン.

café, n. 1. kissaten 喫茶店 (tea or coffee parlor). 2. keishokudō 軽食堂 (restaurant).

cage, n. torikago 鳥籠 (bird cage); ori 檻 (large cage).

calculate, vb. 1. keisan suru 計算する (compute). 2. **be calculated to ...** o neratte iru ...を狙っている.

calculator, n. dentaku 電卓 (pocket calculator).

calf, n. 1. fukurahagi ふくら脛 (part of leg). 2. koushi 子牛 (young cow or bull).

calisthenics, n. biyōtaisō 美容体操.

call, 1. n. denwa 電話 (phone call); hōmon 訪問 (visit); shōshū 召集 (summons); yobigoe 呼び声 (shout); nakigoe 鳴き声 (call of a bird). 2. vb. denwa suru 電話する (phone); hōmon suru 訪問する (visit); yobu 呼ぶ (summon); nazukeru 名付ける (name); **call back** ato de mata denwa suru 後でまた電話する (phone); **call on** ... o hōmon suru 訪問する (visit); **call off** kyanseru suru キャンセルする (cancel).

caller, n. hōmonsha 訪問者 (visitor).

calm, 1. adj. heisei (na) 平静 (な) (undisturbed); odayaka (na) 穏やか (な) (not windy, not rough). 2. vb. nadameru 宥める (make calm, as a baby, etc.); shizumeru 静める (make quiet or peaceful); **calm down** shizuka ni naru 静かになる (become quiet).

camel, n. rakuda ラクダ.

camellia, n. tsubaki 椿.

camp, 1. n. kyanpujō キャンプ場 (campground); kichi 基地 (military camp); habatsu 派閥 (faction). 2. vb. kyanpu o suru キャンプをする (go camping).

campaign, 1. n. undō 運動 (political action);

senkyoundō 選挙運動 (electioneering); gunji-kōdō 軍事行動 (military operation). 2. vb. undō suru 運動する.

campus, n. kyanpasu キャンパス.

can, vb. 1. dekiru 出来る (be able); **can do** suru koto ga dekiru することが出来る. 2. shitemo ii してもいい (be allowed to do).

can, 1. n. kan 缶; **canned food** kanzume 缶詰め; **can opener** kankiri 缶切り. 2. vb. kanzume ni suru 缶詰めにする.

Canada, n. kanada カナダ.

canal, n. unga 運河.

cancer, n. gan 癌.

candid, adj. sotchoku (na) 率直 (な).

candidate, n. kōhosha 候補者.

candle, n. rōsoku 臘燭.

candleholder, n. rōsokutate 臘燭立て.

cane, 1. n. kuki 茎 (stalk); satōkibi 砂糖きび (sugarcane); take 竹 (bamboo); tsue 杖 (for walking). 2. vb. muchiutsu 鞭打つ (beat).

canister, n. kan 缶 (food container).

canned goods, n. kanzume shokuhin 缶詰め食品.

cannon, n. taihō 大砲 (gun).

cannot, vb. dekinai 出来ない.

canopy, n. tengai 天蓋.

cantaloupe, n. meron メロン.

canyon, n. kyōkoku 峡谷.

cap, 1. n. bōshi 帽子 (head covering); futa 蓋 (lid). 2. vb. ōu 覆う (cover); shinogu 凌ぐ (surpass).

capable, adj. 1. yūnō (na) 有

能 (な) (competent). **2. be capable of** ... ga dekiru ...が出来る (can do); ... kanōsei ga aru ... 可能性がある (be disposed to).

capacity, n. 1. shūyōnōryoku 収容能力 (amount contained). 2. seisanryoku 生産力 (amount produced). 3. nōryoku 能力 (ability). 4. shikaku 資格 (position).

cape, n. misaki 岬 (geography).

caper, vb. tobimawaru 飛び回る.

capital, n. 1. shuto 首都 (capital city). 2. shihonkin 資本金 (money). 3. ōmoji 大文字 (capital letter).

capitalize, vb. ōmoji de kaku 大文字で書く (write in capitals); **capitalize on** ... o riyō suru ... を利用する (take advantage of).

capsize, vb. tenpuku suru 転覆する.

captivate, vb. miwaku suru 魅惑する.

capture, vb. toraeru 捕える (seize, record).

car, n. 1. kuruma 車 (automobile). 2. sharyō 車両 (train car).

carbohydrate, n. tansuikabutsu 炭水化物.

carbon, n. tanso 炭素; **carbon paper** kābonshi カーボン紙.

carbonated, adj. tansan iri (no) 炭酸入り (の); **carbonated water** tansansui 炭酸水.

carbon dioxide, n. nisankatanso 二酸化炭素.

card, n. 1. kādo カード (index). 2. meishi 名刺 (calling card). 3. toranpu トランプ (playing card); **play**

cards toranpu o suru トランプをする.

cardboard, n. bōru-gami ボール紙.

care, 1. n. shinpai 心配 (worry); chūi 注意 (caution); kantoku 監督 (supervision); hogo 保護 (protection); **Take care!** Ki o tsukete. 気をつけて。 2. vb. **care (about)** (... o) ki ni suru (... を) 気にする (mind); (... o) shinpai suru (... を) 心配する (worry); **care for** ... ga suki ... が好き (like); **take care of** ... no mendō o miru ... の面倒を見る (look after, be responsible for).

career, n. shokugyō 職業.

carefree, adj. shinpai ga nai 心配がない.

careful, adj. chūibukai 注意深い; **be careful** chūi suru 注意する.

careless, adj. 1. fuchūi (na) 不注意 (な) (inattentive). 2. iikagen (na) いい加減 (な) (sloppy).

caretaker, n. 1. hogosha 保護者 (guardian). 2. kanrinin 管理人 (of a building).

cargo, n. tsumini 積荷.

carnivorous, adj. nikushoku (no) 肉食 (の).

carousel, n. kaiten mokuba 回転木馬.

carpenter, n. daiku 大工.

carpet, n. jūtan 絨毯.

carriage, n. 1. basha 馬車 (horse drawn carriage). 2. mi no konashi 身のこなし (deportment).

carrot, n. ninjin 人参.

carry, vb. 1. hakobu 運ぶ (transport). 2. tazusaeru 携える (take with one). 3. tomonau 伴う (entail, involve). 4. **carry the weight of** ...sasaeru ...支える (support); **be carried away** ware o wasureru 我を忘れる (lose control); **carry on** tsuzukeru 続ける (continue); **carry out** jikkō suru 実行する (put into action).

cart, n. teoshiguruma 手押し車 (handcart).

cartilage, n. nankotsu 軟骨.

cartoon, n. manga 漫画 (drawing); anime アニメ (animated cartoon).

cartoonist, n. mangaka 漫画家.

carve, vb. 1. horu 彫る (wood). 2. kirikaeru 切り分ける (meat).

case, n. 1. kēsu ケース (container). 2. jitsurei 実例 (instance). 3. ba'ai 場合 (situation). 4. jiken 事件 (event). 5. kanja 患者 (medical patient). 6. soshō 訴訟 (lawsuit). 7. kaku 格 (grammar). 8. **in any case** tonikaku とにかく; **just in case** ... ni sonaete... に備えて; **in case of** ... no ba'ai niwa... の場合には.

cash, 1. n. genkin 現金; **in cash** genkin de; **cash register** reji レジ. 2. vb. genkinka suru 現金化する (convert into cash); **cash in on** ...riyō suru ...利用する (take advantage of).

cask, n. taru 樽.

casket, n. 1. hitsugi 棺 (coffin). 2. hōsekibako 宝石箱 (jewel box).

cast, 1. n. kyasuto キャスト (performers); igata 鋳型 (mold); gibusu ギブス (orthopedic). 2. vb. nageru 投げる (throw); yaku ni tsukeru 役につける (hire to

perform); igata ni ireru 鋳型に入れる (mold); tōhyō suru 投票する (cast a vote).

caste, n. kaikyū 階級.

castle, n. shiro 城.

casual, adj. 1. kajuaru (na) カジュアル (な) (informal). 2. kiraku (na) 気楽 (な) (not caring, not serious). 3. gūzen (no) 偶然 (の) (accidental).

casualty, n. 1. jiko 事故 (accident). 2. giseisha 犠牲者 (victim). 3. fushōsha 負傷者 (wounded person).

cat, n. neko 猫.

cataract, n. 1. bakufu 瀑布 (water). 2. hakunaishō 白内障 (eye).

catastrophe, n. hakyoku 破局; sainan 災難.

catch, vb. 1. toraeru 捕らえる (get hold of, capture). 2. toru 捕る (fish). 3. ... ni kakaru ...にかかる (contract, as an illness). 4. ... ni ma ni au ...に間に合う (get aboard on time). 5. hiku 引く (attract). 6. wakaru 分かる (grasp mentally). 7. kikoeru 聞こえる (hear correctly).

catch cold kaze o hiku 風邪を引く; **catch sight of** o mikakeru ...を見かける; **catch up with** ... ni oitsuku ...に追いつく.

cater, vb. 1. shidashi o suru 仕出しをする (food). 2. **cater to** ... ni awaseru ...に合わせる.

caterpillar, n. imomushi 芋虫 (not furry); kemushi 毛虫 (furry).

catfish, n. namazu なまず.

cattle, n. kachiku 家畜.

cause, 1. n. gen'in 原因 (basis); riyū 理由 (reason); shin'nen 信念 (strong belief). 2. vb. hikiokosu 引き起こす.

caustic, adj. 1. fushokusei (no) 腐食性 (の) (corrosive). 2. hiniku tappuri (no) 皮肉たっぷり (の) (sarcastic).

caution, 1. n. keikoku 警告 (warning); yōjin 用心 (carefulness). 2. vb. keikoku suru 警告する (warn).

cave, cavern, n. dōkutsu 洞窟.

cavity, n. 1. ana 穴 (hole). 2. mushiba (no ana) 虫歯 (の穴) (dental).

cease, vb. yameru やめる.

cedar, n. sugi 杉.

ceiling, n. tenjō 天井.

celebrate, vb. iwau 祝う.

celebrity, n. yūmeijin 有名人.

celestial, adj. 1. tentai (no) 天体 (の) (of the sky or space). 2. tengoku-teki (na) 天国的 (な) (of heaven).

cell, n. 1. rōya 牢屋 (prison). 2. saibō 細胞 (biology).

cellar, n. chika sōko 地下倉庫.

cemetery, n. bochi 墓地.

census, n. kokuseichōsa 国勢調査.

centennial, n. hyakushūnen 百周年.

center, 1. n. chūshin 中心 (middle point, chief person). 2. vb. chūshin ni sueru 中心にすえる (place in middle).

centigrade, n. sesshi 摂氏.

central, adj. 1. chūshin (no) 中心 (の) (of or at center). 2. saijūyō (na) 最重要 (な) (most important).

centralize, vb. shūchū suru 集中する.

century, n. seiki 世紀; **nineteenth century** jūkyū seiki.

ceramic, adj. tōsei (no) 陶製

(の).

ceramics, n. tōki 陶器.

ceremony, n. 1. shiki 式 (act); gishiki 儀式 (ritual).

certain, adj. 1. tashika (na) 確か (な) (sure); **make certain** tashikameru. 2. ikubun ka (no) 幾分か (の) (some).

certificate, n. shōmeisho 証明書.

chain, n. 1. kusari 鎖 (connected rings); renzoku 連続 (series). 2. vb. kusari de tsunagu 鎖でつなぐ (fasten).

chain reaction, n. rensahannō 連鎖反応.

chair, 1. n. isu 椅子 (furniture); gakubuchō 学部長 (university department head); i'inchō 委員長 (committee leader). 2. vb. i'inchō o tsutomeru 委員長を勤める (preside over committee).

chamber, n. 1. heya 部屋 (room). 2. kaigisho 会議所 (assembly room). 3. giin 議員 (legislative body).

champion, n. yūshōsha 優勝者.

chance, 1. n. kikai 機会 (opportunity); un 運; gūzen 偶然 (fate, luck); kanōsei 可能性 (possibility); kake 賭け (risk); **by chance** gūzen ni. 2. adj. gūzen (no) 偶然 (の) (accidental). 3. vb. kakeru 賭ける (risk).

change, 1. n. henka 変化 (in condition); henkō 変更 (alteration); kōkan 交換 (exchange); (o)tsuri (お) 釣り (from bill payment); kozeni 小銭 (small change); kigae 着替え (of clothes); **for a change** kibun tenkan ni 気分転換に (change of mood). 2. *vb.* kawaru/kaeru 変わる／変える (alter/cause to alter in condition); kōkan suru 交換する (exchange); ryōgae suru 両替する (currency); kigaeru 着替える (clothes).

channel, 1. *n.* kaikyō 海峡 (geography); suiro 水路 (for liquid); michi 道 (route). 2. *vb.* furimukeru ふり向ける (direct); tsukisusumu 突き進む (clear a way).

chapter, *n.* 1. shō 章 (book). 2. shibu 支部 (branch of a society).

character, *n.* 1. seikaku 性格 (personal nature). 2. tōjōjinbutsu 登場人物 (in play, novel, etc.). 3. hinsei 品性 (moral strength). 4. hito 人 (person). 5. moji 文字 (written or printed symbol).

characteristic, 1. *adj.* tokuchō-teki (na) 特徴的 (な). 2. *n.* tokuchō 特徴.

charcoal, *n.* sumi 炭.

charge, 1. *n.* ryōkin 料金 (price); sekinin 責任 (responsibility); hihan 批判 (accusation); kōgeki 攻撃 (attack); kokuso 告訴 (legal); **be in charge of** ... no sekinin ga aru. 2. *vb.* kōgeki suru 攻撃する (attack); kokuso suru 告訴する (legal); jūden suru 充電する (charge a battery).

charity, *n.* 1. jizen 慈善 (aid); kifu 寄付 (donation). 2. jihishin 慈悲心 (benevolence); yasashisa 優しさ (kindness). 3. jizendantai 慈善団体 (benevolent organization).

charm, 1. *n.* miryoku 魅力 (fascination); mayoke 魔よけ (amulet, talisman). 2.

jumon 呪文 (incantation). 2. *vb.* miwaku suru 魅惑する (fascinate).

charming, *adj.* miryoku-teki (na) 魅力的 (な) (fascinating).

chart, 1. *n.* zu 図; hyō 表 (diagram, map, table); gurafu グラフ (graph). 2. *vb.* zushi suru 図示する.

chase, 1. *n.* tsuiseki 追跡. 2. *vb.* tsuiseki suru 追跡する (go after); **chase away** oiharau 追い払う (drive away).

chatter, 1. *n.* oshaberi おしゃべり. 2. *vb.* shaberimakuru しゃべりまくる (talk); gaku-gaku naru がくがく鳴る (teeth).

chatterbox, *n.* oshaberiya おしゃべり屋.

chauvinism, *n.* chō-aikoku-shugi 超愛国主義 (extreme patriotism); **male chauvinism** danseiyūi-shugi 男性優位主義 (ideology of male supremacy); joseibesshi 女性蔑視 (woman-hating).

cheap, *adj.* 1. yasui 安い (inexpensive). 2. yasuppoi 安っぽい (of low quality).

cheat, *vb.* 1. damasu だます (deceive). 2. kan'ningu o suru カンニングをする (cheat on examination).

check, 1. *n.* tenken 点検 (test or inspection); yokusei 抑制 (control); kogitte 小切手 (bank); shōgō no shirushi 商号の印 (mark); kōshimoyō 格子模様 (pattern). 2. *vb.* shiraberu 調べる (control); yokusei suru 抑制する (control); shirushi o tsukeru 印をつける (mark).

cheek, *n.* hoho 頬.

cheer, 1. *n.* seien 声援

(shout of encouragement); yorokobi 喜び (gladness). 2. vb. kansei o okuru 歓声を送る (shout encouragement); yorokobaseru 喜ばせる (gladden).

cheerful, adj. tanoshii 楽しい.

Cheers! interj. Kanpai! 乾杯. (when drinking).

chemical, 1. n. kagakubusshitsu 化学物質. 2. adj. kagaku (no) 化学 (の) (of chemistry).

chemistry, n. kagaku 化学.

cherish, vb. daiji ni suru 大事にする.

cherry, n. 1. sakuranbo 桜ん坊 (fruit). 2. sakura 桜 (tree).

chest, n. 1. mune 胸 (body). 2. hako 箱 (box); **chest of drawers** tansu たんす.

chestnut, n. kurumi くるみ.

chew, vb. kamu 嚙む (food).

chicken, n 1. keiniku 鶏肉 (meat). 2. niwatori 鶏 (bird).

chief, 1. n. -chō 長 (head); shūchō 酋長 (head of tribe). 2. adj. shuyō (na) 主要 (な) (most important); daiichi (no) 第一 (の) (ranked highest).

chiefly, adv. omo ni 主に.

child, n. ko(domo) 子(供).

childbirth, n. shussan 出産.

childish, adj. yōchi (na) 幼稚 (な).

chili pepper, n. tōgarashi 唐辛子.

chilly, adj. 1. samui 寒い (cold). 2. hiyayaka (na) 冷ややか (な) (unfriendly).

chimney, n. entotsu 煙突.

chin, n. ago あご.

china, n. tōjiki 陶磁器 (ceramic ware).

China, n. chūgoku 中国.

chip, 1. n. kakera 欠けら (small piece); kakeato 欠け跡 (broken piece); chippu チップ (computer). 2. vb. kakeru 欠ける (dent, break off); kizutsukeru 傷つける (make dent, cause to break off).

chirp, 1. n. saezuri さえずり. 2. vb. saezuru さえずる.

chive, n. asatsuki あさつき.

chlorine, n. enso 塩素.

chock-full, adj. manpai (no) 満杯 (の).

choice, 1. n. sentaku 選択 (preference); eranda hito 選んだ人 (chosen person); eranda mono 選んだ物 (chosen thing); **make one's choice** erabu 選ぶ; **have no choice** shikata ga nai 仕方がない. 2. adj. yorinuki (no) 選り抜き (の) (picked).

choir, n. gasshōtai 合唱隊 (group).

choke, vb. 1. musebu 咽ぶ (struggle to breathe). 2. chissoku suru 窒息する (be unable to breathe). 3. iki o tomeru 息を止める (stop breathing); shimekorosu 絞め殺す (kill). 4. fusagu 塞ぐ (block).

choose, vb. 1. erabu 選ぶ (pick). 2. kimeru 決める (decide).

choppy, adj. shiketeiru しけている (sea).

chopsticks, n. hashi 箸.

chorale, n. gasshōkyoku 合唱曲.

chord, n. waon 和音.

chore, n. zatsuyō 雑用.

choreography, n. furitsuke 振り付け.

chorus, n. gasshō 合唱.

Christ, n. iesu(-kirisuto) イエス(-キリスト); kirisuto キリスト.

Christian, 1. *n.* kurisuchan クリスチャン. 2. *adj.* kirisuto-kyō (no) キリスト教 (の).

Christianity, *n.* kirisuto-kyō キリスト教.

chromosome, *n.* senshokutai 染色体.

chronic, *adj.* mansei-teki (na) 慢性的 (な) (illness, problem).

chronicle, *n.* nendaiki 年代記.

chubby, *adj.* kobutori (no) 小太り (の).

chuckle, 1. *n.* kusu-kusu warai くすくす笑い. 2. *vb.* kusu-kusu warau くすくす笑う.

chunk, *n.* 1. taihan 大半 (big portion). 2. ōkii katamari 大きい塊 (big lump).

church, *n.* kyōkai 教会.

churn, *vb.* kakitateru かき立てる; **churn out** tairyōseisan suru 大量生産する.

cicada, *n.* semi 蟬.

cider, *n.* ringoshu りんご酒.

cigarette, *n.* tabako 煙草; **cigarette case** tabakoire; **cigarette lighter** raitā ライター.

cinema, *n.* eiga 映画.

cipher, *n.* 1. zero ゼロ (number). 2. angō 暗号 (code).

circle, 1. *n.* wa 輪; en 円; maru 丸 (shape). 2. *vb.* wa de kakomu 輪で囲む (enclose); mawaru 回る (go around).

circuit, *n.* 1. kairo 回路 (electrical path). 2. isshū 一周 (journey around).

circulate, *vb.* 1. nagareru 流れる (flow). 2. ugokimawaru 動き回る (move around). 3.

hiromaru 広まる (spread).

circumference, *n.* 1. enshū 円周 (outer boundary of a circular area). 2. enshū no nagasa 円周の長さ (length of outer boundary).

circumstance, *n.* 1. jōkyō 状況 (condition). 2. koto 事 (fact). 3. **depend on the circumstances** jōkyō ni yoru; **under the circumstances** sonna jōkyō dewa; **under no circumstances** nani ga attemo 何があっても.

cistern, *n.* suisō 水槽.

cite, *vb.* in'yō suru 引用する (quote).

citizen, *n.* 1. shimin 市民 (of a city or nation); kokumin 国民 (a nation). 2. jūnin 住人 (inhabitant, resident).

city, *n.* 1. shi 市 (large town). 2. tokai 都会 (metropolis).

civilization, *n.* bunmei 文明.

claim, *n.* 1. yōkyū 要求 (demand); shuchō 主張 (assertion); shinkoku 申告 (insurance claim); kenri 権利 (right, title). 2. *vb.* yōkyū suru 要求する (demand); shuchō suru 主張する (assert); shinkoku suru 申告する (make insurance claim).

clam, *n.* kai 貝; hamaguri 蛤.

clamber, *vb.* yojinoboru よじ登る.

clamor, 1. *n.* kensō 喧騒 (loud noise); fuhei 不平 (complaint). 2. *vb.* sawagitateru 騒ぎ立てる (make noise).

clamp, 1. *n.* koteikigu 固定器具. 2. *vb.* kotei suru 固定する; **clamp down on** ... o torishimaru ... を取り締ま

る.

clan, *n.* ichizoku 一族.

clang, *vb.* naru 鳴る (make a sound); narasu 鳴らす (cause to sound).

clap, *vb.* hakushu suru 拍手する (applaud).

clarification, *n.* setsumei 説明.

clarity, *n.* 1. meiryōsa 明瞭さ (clearness). 2. tōmeisa 透明さ (transparency).

clash, 1. *n.* fuitchi 不一致 (disagreement); arasoi 争い (fight). 2. *vb.* awanai 合わない (disagree); arasou 争う (fight).

clasp, 1. *n.* tomegane 留め金 (fastener); hōyō 抱擁 (hug); nigiru koto 握ること (act of gripping). 2. *vb.* tomeru 留める (fasten); daku 抱く (hug); nigiru 握る (grip).

class, *n.* 1. kaikyū 階級 (rank, caste). 2. burui 部類 (group). 3. tō(kyū) 等(級) (level of quality).

classic, 1. *n.* koten 古典 (established classic); meisaku 名作 (masterpiece). 2. *adj.* ichiryū (no) 一流 (の) (superior); tenkei-teki (na) 典型的 (な) (model).

classical, *adj.* 1. koten (no) 古典 (の) (of an established classic); **classical music** kurasshikku ongaku クラシック音楽. 2. koten-teki (na) 古典的 (な) (classic in nature).

classify, *vb.* bunrui suru 分類する.

classmate, *n.* dōkyūsei 同級生.

classroom, *n.* kyōshitsu 教室.

clatter, *vb.* kata-kata naru カタカタ鳴る.

claw, *n.* tsume 爪.

clay, *n.* nendo 粘土.

clean, 1. *adj.* kirei (na) きれい (な) (free from dirt); seiketsu (na) 清潔 (な) (sanitary); kiyoraka (na) 清らか (な) (free from vice); meikaku (na) 明確 (な) (trim). 2. *vb.* kirei ni naru/suru きれいになる／する (become/make clean); sōji suru 掃除する (tidy up).

cleanse, *vb.* 1. kiyomeru 清める (make clean or pure). 2. shōdoku suru 消毒する (sterilize).

clear, 1. *adj.* sundeiru 澄んでいる (sky, water, eyes); hare (no) 晴れ (の) (weather); tōmei (na) 透明 (な) (transparent); meihaku (na) 明白 (な) (evident); meikai (na) 明快 (な) (easily perceived); hakkiri shiteiru はっきりしている (clear-cut). 2. *vb.* hareru 晴れる (weather); katazukeru 片付ける (clear away); kansai suru 完済する (pay in full); koeru 超える (pass beyond).

clearing, *n.* akichi 空き地 (land).

clergyman, *n.* bokushi 牧師.

clerk, *n.* 1. jimuin 事務員 (office employee). 2. ten'in 店員 (store employee).

clever, *adj.* rikō (na) 利口 (な).

click, *n.* kachiri to iu oto かちりという音.

client, *n.* 1. irainin 依頼人 (legal). 2. kyaku 客 (customer).

cliff, *n.* gake 崖.

climate, *n.* 1. kikō 気候 (weather). 2. jōkyō 状況 (condition).

climb, *vb.* noboru 登る; agaru 上がる.

clinch, *vb.* ... no ketchaku o

tsukeru ... の決着をつける (settle decisively).

cling, vb. shigamitsuku しがみつく (hold on firmly).

clinic, n. shinryōsho 診療所.

clip, 1. n. **paper clip** kamibasami 紙鋏. **2.** vb. kurippu de tomeru クリップで留める (fasten with a clip); kiru 切る (cut paper, cloth, etc.); karu 刈る (cut hair, wool, etc.).

cloak, 1. n. manto マント. **2.** vb. kakusu 隠す (conceal).

clock, n. tokei 時計; **alarm clock** mezamashi-dokei 目覚まし時計; **around the clock** nijūyojikan 二十四時間.

clockwise, adv. migimawari ni 右回りに; **counterclockwise** hidarimawari ni 左回りに.

clog, 1. n. kigutsu 木靴 (wooden shoe); geta 下駄 (Japanese wooden shoe). **2.** vb. tsumaru 詰まる (become blocked).

close, 1. n. owari 終わり (end). **2.** vb. shimeru 閉める (shut); shimaru 閉まる (be shut); oeru 終える (bring to an end); **close down** heisa suru 閉鎖する; **close in** torikakomu 取り囲む. **3.** adj. chikai 近い (near); shitashii 親しい (intimate); **be close to** ... ni chikai. **4.** adv. chikaku ni 近くに (near); **close to** hotondo ほとんど (almost).

closet, n. oshiire 押入れ (small room); tansu たんす (cabinet).

cloth, n. nuno 布.

clothe, vb. fuku o kiseru 服を着せる.

clothes, clothing, n. fuku 服.

cloud, n. kumo 雲.

cloudy, adj. **1.** kumori (no) 曇り (の) (full of clouds). **2.** nigotteiru 濁っている (not clear).

clown, n. dōkeshi 道化師.

clue, n. itoguchi 糸口.

clump, n. katamari 塊.

clumsy, adj. **1.** bukiyō (na) 不器用 (な) (unskillful). **2.** bukakkō (na) 不格好 (な) (ungraceful).

clutch, 1. n. kuratchi クラッチ (car); tsukamari つかまり (tight hold). **2.** vb. tsukamu つかむ (hold tight).

clutter, vb. chirakasu 散らかす.

coach, 1. n. basha 馬車 (horse-drawn carriage); basu バス (bus); ekonomī-kurasu エコノミークラス (economy class); kōchi コーチ (sports). **2.** vb. shidō suru 指導する (advise).

coal, n. sekitan 石炭.

coarse, adj. **1.** arai 粗い (rough). **2.** soya (na) 粗野 (な) (vulgar).

coast, n. kaigan 海岸.

coax, vb. settoku suru 説得する (persuade).

cobweb, n. kumo no su 蜘蛛の巣.

cock, n. ondori 雄鶏 (rooster).

cockpit, n. sōjūshitsu 操縦室 (of plane).

cockroach, n. gokiburi ごきぶり.

cocky, adj. unubore (no) うぬぼれ (の).

cocoon, n. mayu まゆ.

cod, n. tara たら.

coddle, vb. amayakasu 甘やかす.

code, n. **1.** angō 暗号 (secret words); fugō 符号 (signals). **2.** hōten 法典 (collection of laws).

coexist, *vb.* kyōzon suru 共存する.

coffin, *n.* hitsugi 棺.

coherent, *adj.* ikkansei ga aru 一貫性がある.

coil, 1. *n.* wa 輪 (ring); koiru コイル (electrical). 2. *vb.* maku 巻く.

coin, 1. *n.* kōka 硬貨 (money). 2. *vb.* chūzō suru 鋳造する (coin money); tsukuru 創る (invent).

coincidence, *n.* gūzen no itchi 偶然の一致.

coitus, *n.* seikō 性交.

colander, *n.* zaru ざる; mizukoshi 水こし.

cold, 1. *n.* samusa 寒さ (absence of heat); kaze 風邪 (illness); **catch cold** kaze o hiku 風邪を引く. 2. *adj.* samui 寒い (cold weather, low temperature); tsumetai 冷たい (cold to the touch, unfriendly).

coldblooded, *adj.* reikoku (na) 冷酷 (な) (callous).

collaborate, *vb.* kyōryoku suru 協力する (work together); gassaku suru 合作する (write or produce together).

collapse, *vb.* 1. kowareru 壊れる; hōkai suru 崩壊する (fall or cave in). 2. taoreru 倒れる (faint). 3. shippai suru 失敗する (fail). 4. oritatameru 折りたためる (fold together compactly).

collar, *n.* 1. eri 襟 (garment). 2. kubiwa 首輪 (dog).

collarbone, *n.* sakotsu 鎖骨.

colleague, *n.* dōryō 同僚.

collect, *vb.* 1. atsumeru 集める (accumulate); atsumaru 集まる (come together). 2. shūkin suru 集金する (receive or compel

payment). 3. shūhai suru 集配する (mail).

collected, *adj.* reisei (na) 冷静 (な) (calm).

collective, *adj.* 1. kyōdō (no) 共同 (の) (joint). 2. dantai (no) 団体 (の); shūdan (no) 集団 (の) (by a group); **collective bargaining** dantaikōshō 団体交渉.

college, *n.* daigaku 大学.

collide, *vb.* shōtotsu suru 衝突する.

colon, *n.* 1. daichō 大腸 (anatomy). 2. koron コロン (punctuation).

color, 1. *n.* iro 色 (hue); enogu 絵の具 (for painting); kaoiro 顔色 (complexion). 2. *vb.* iro o tsukeru 色をつける (give color to); irozuku 色づく (take on color); akaku naru 赤くなる (blush); yugameru 歪める (distort in telling).

colt, *n.* osu no kouma 雄の子馬.

column, *n.* 1. hashira 柱 (pillar). 2. ran 欄 (area of print).

comb, 1. *n.* kushi 櫛. 2. *vb.* kushi de toku 櫛でとく.

combination, *n.* 1. gōdō 合同 (alliance). 2. kumiawase 組み合わせ (matching, pairing). 3. kumiawase-bangō 組み合わせ番号 (number for a lock).

combine, *vb.* 1. musubi-tsuku/tsukeru 結びつく／～つける (become/make united). 2. mazeru 混ぜる (mix). 3. kumiawaseru 組み合わせる (match, pair).

come, *vb.* 1. kuru 来る (approach). 2. tsuku 着く (arrive). 3. naru なる (become). 4. **come about**

okoru 起こる (happen); **come across** dekuwasu 出くわす (meet, find); **come back** kaeru 帰る (return); fukki suru 復帰する (revert; return to a former position, prosperity, etc.); **come down** oriru 降りる (descend); **come from** ...kara kuru; **come in** ... ni hairu ... に入る (enter); **Come in!** Dōzo ohairi kudasai; **come out** deru 出る (appear, be published); **come to** ... ni tassuru ... に達する (total); **come up** wadai ni noboru 話題にのぼる (be referred to).

comeback, n. fukki 復帰.

comet, n. suisei 彗星.

comfort, 1. n. nagusami 慰み (consolation); kaiteki 快適; anraku 安楽 (ease). 2. vb. nagusameru 慰める (console, cheer).

comfortable, adj. 1. kaiteki (na) 快適 (な) (cozy, complacent). 2. raku (na) 楽 (な) (easy, untroubled). 3. jūbun (na) 十分 (な) (affluent).

comforter, n. uwabuton 上布団 (quilt).

comic, 1. n. manga 漫画 (book); kigekihaiyū 喜劇俳優 (comedian). 2. adj. kokkei (na) 滑稽 (な) (funny).

comic strip, n. sūkomamanga 数コマ漫画.

command, 1. n. meirei 命令 (order); tōsotsu 統率 (leadership, authority); nōryoku 能力 (facility, ability). 2. vb. meirei suru 命令する (order); ... o tōsotsu suru ... を統率する (have authority over).

commemorate, vb. kinen

suru 記念する.

commencement, n. 1. kaishi 開始 (beginning). 2. sotsugyōshiki 卒業式 (graduation ceremony).

commend, vb. homeru ほめる.

commerce, n. shōgyō 商業 (business); bōeki 貿易 (foreign trade).

commit, vb. 1. okasu 犯す (perform, do); **commit a crime** tsumi o okasu; **commit suicide** jisatsu suru 自殺する 2. yudaneru 委ねる (entrust). 3. **commit oneself (to do)** (... suru to) chikau (...すると) 誓う (pledge oneself); **commit oneself (to something)** ... ni uchikomu ... に打ち込む (devote oneself).

commitment, n. 1. sekinin 責任 (responsibility). 2. chikai 誓い (pledge). 3. kenshin 献身 (devotion).

committee, n. iinkai 委員会.

common, adj. 1. kyōtsū (no) 共通 (の) (shared by all). 2. arifurete-iru ありふれている (ordinary); futsū (no) 普通 (の) (usual). 3. kōkyō (no) 公共 (の) (public). 4. gehin (na) 下品 (な) (vulgar).

commonplace, adj. futsū (no) 普通 (の) (usual); arifureteiru ありふれている (ordinary).

common sense, n. jōshiki 常識.

commotion, n. 1. dōyō 動揺 (tumult). 2. sōdō 騒動 (upheaval).

communication, n. 1. dentatsu 伝達 (act of communicating); renraku 連

絡 (getting in touch). 2. ishisōtsū 意志疎通 (interchange of thoughts). 3. messēji メッセージ (message).

communism, *n.* kyōsanshugi 共産主義.

community, *n.* 1. kyōdōtai 共同体 (social group). 2. kinjo 近所 (neighborhood); chiiki 地域 (area). 3. shakai 社会 (the public).

commute, *vb.* 1. kayou 通う (travel). 2. genkei suru 減刑する (commute a penalty).

commuter, *n.* tsūkinsha 通勤者.

companion, *n.* 1. tomo 友 (comrade). 2. nakama 仲間 (associate). 3. tsure 連れ (traveling companion). 4. katahō 片方 (one of a pair).

company, *n.* 1. kaisha 会社 (corporation, enterprise). 2. nakamazukiai 仲間付き合い (camaraderie, companionship). 3. tsukiai aite 付き合い相手 (companions). 4. **keep/part company with** ... to tsukiau/wakareru ... と付き合う／別れる.

comparatively, *adv.* hikaku-teki ni 比較的に.

compare, *vb.* 1. hikaku suru 比較する (contrast). 2. tatoeru たとえる (liken).

compassion, *n.* dōjō 同情.

compensate, *vb.* 1. tsugunau 償う (make up for). 2. ... ni hoshō suru ... に補償する (make payment to); baishō suru 賠償する (make amends).

competence, *n.* nōryoku 能力.

competent, *adj.* yūnō (na) 有能 (な).

competition, *n.* 1. kyōsō 競争 (rivalry). 2. kyōgikai 競技会 (match, race, tournament); konkūru コンクール (music or art contest).

compile, *vb.* henshū suru 編集する; matomeru まとめる (put together in one book or work).

complacency, *n.* jikomanzoku 自己満足.

complain, *vb.* 1. fuhei o iu 不平を言う (express discontent); kujō o iu 苦情を言う (remonstrate). 2. uttaeru 訴える (accuse, report).

complement, 1. *n.* kakkō no toriawase 格好の取り合わせ (ideal counterpart); hojū 補充 (supplement); hogo 補語 (grammar). 2. *vb.* tsuriau 釣り合う (counterbalance); hojū suru 補充する (supplement).

complete, 1. *adj.* kanzen (na) 完全 (な) (perfect); mattaku (no) 全く (の) (entire). 2. *vb.* kanzen ni suru 完全にする (make perfect); kansei suru 完成する (achieve, finish); owaraseru 終わらせる (bring to an end).

completion, *n.* 1. kansei 完成 (achievement). 2. owari 終わり (end).

complexion, *n.* kaoiro 顔色.

complicated, *adj.* 1. fukuzatsu (na) 複雑 (な) (complex). 2. muzukashii 難しい (difficult).

compliment, 1. *n.* sanji 賛辞 (expression of praise); aisatsu 挨拶 (regards). 2. *vb.* homeru ほめる (express praise).

complimentary, *adj.* 1.

sanji (no) 賛辞 (の) (of praise). 2. muryō (no) 無料 (の) (given free).

comply, vb. **comply with** ... ni shitagau ... に従う (obey); ... o mamoru ... を守る (observe).

component, n. bubun 部分.

composer, n. sakkyokuka 作曲家 (music).

composition, n. 1. kumitate 組み立て (combination). 2. sakubun 作文 (short essay); sakkyoku 作曲 (act of writing music); kyoku 曲 (music).

compound, 1. n. fukugōbutsu 複合物 (combined parts). 2. adj. fukugō (no) 複合 (の) (made of parts). 3. vb. kumiawaseru 組み合わせる (combine); fuyasu 増やす (increase).

comprehend, vb. rikai suru 理解する.

comprehensive, adj. hōkatsu-teki (na) 包括的 (な) (inclusive).

compress, vb. 1. asshuku suru 圧縮する (press together). 2. chijimeru 縮める (abridge, reduce).

compromise, n. dakyō 妥協 (agreement by mutual concession). 2. vb. dakyō suru 妥協する (agree).

compulsory, adj. 1. kyōsei-teki (na) 強制的 (な). 2. hisshū (no) 必修 (の) (of a school subject).

computer science, n. konpyūtā-kagaku コンピューター科学.

comrade, n. 1. nakama 仲間 (close companion). 2. dōshi 同志 (fellow member).

conceal, vb. kakusu 隠す.

conceivable, adj.

kangaerareru 考えられる.

concentrate, vb. 1. ... ni shūchū suru ... に集中する (give full attention). 2. nōshuku suru 濃縮する (make denser).

concept, n. gainen 概念 (general idea).

concern, 1. n. kanshinji 関心事 (matter that concerns); shinpai 心配 (worry); jigyō 事業 (business). 2. vb. ... ni kansuru ... に関する (relate to); ... ni eikyō o ataeru ... に影響を与える (have an effect on); shinpai saseru 心配させる (worry); **concern oneself with** ... ni kankei suru ... に関係する.

concert, n. ensōkai 演奏会.

concerto, n. kyōsōkyoku 協奏曲.

concession, n. 1. jōho 譲歩 (act of yielding). 2. tokken 特権 (right yielded).

concise, adj. kanketsu (na) 簡潔 (な).

conclude, vb. 1. oeru 終える (end). 2. torikimeru 取り決める (settle). 3. ketsuron o kudasu 結論を下す (judge, infer). 4. kimeru 決める (decide, determine).

conclusion, n. 1. ketsuron 結論 (final decision). 2. owari 終わり (ending); **in conclusion** owari ni. 3. teiketsu 定結 (final agreement or settlement).

concord, n. 1. yūkō 友好 (friendship). 2. itchi 一致 (agreement). 3. heiwa 平和 (peace).

concurrent, adj. 1. dōji ni okoru 同時に起こる (simultaneous). 2. onaji (no) 同じ (の) (same, in agreement).

condemn, vb. 1. hinan suru

非難する (denounce). 2. yūzai o senkoku suru 有罪を宣告する (find guilty). 3. futekitō to handan suru 不適当と判断する (judge unfit).

condense, vb. 1. yōyaku suru 要約する (summarize). 2. ekika suru 液化する (change vapor to liquid). 3. koku suru 濃くする (concentrate).

condescend, vb.

condescend to do
...otakaku tomatte ... suru お高くとまって... する (do arrogantly);
onkisegamashiku ... suru 恩着せがましく... する (do patronizingly).

condiment, n. yakumi 薬味.

condition, n. 1. jōtai 状態 (state of being); kenkōjōtai 健康状態; chōshi 調子 (state of health); **out of condition** chōshi ga warui. 2. jōken 条件 (requirement); **on condition that** ... no jōken de.

condolence, n. (o)kuyami (お)悔やみ (on occasion of death).

condone, vb. 1. mokunin suru 黙認する (approve tacitly). 2. yurusu 許す (forgive). 3. minogasu 見のがす (overlook).

conduct, 1. n. furumai 振るまい (behavior); un'ei 運営 (management). —vb. un'ei suru 運営する (manage, run); michibiku 導く; hiki'iru 率いる (direct, lead); dendō suru 伝達する (transfer heat, electricity, etc.); shiki suru 指揮する (act as musical conductor); okonau 行う (carry on);

conduct oneself furumau.

cone, n. 1. ensuikei 円錐形 (form). 2. aisukurīmu-ire アイスクリーム入れ (ice cream cone). 3. matsukasa 松かさ (pine cone).

conference, n. kaigi 会議.

confess, vb. 1. kokuhaku suru 告白する (reveal one's secret). 2. jihaku suru 自白する (admit one's crime). 3. mitomeru 認める (admit).

confide, vb. 1. uchiakeru 打ち明ける (impart secrets or private matters). 2. shin'yō suru 信用する (place trust in)

confidence, n. 1. shin'yō 信用 (trust). 2. jishin 自信 (self-confidence). 3. himitsu 秘密 (secret); **in confidence** naisho de 内緒で.

confirm, vb. 1. kakunin suru 確認する (make certain). 2. tsuyomeru 強める (strengthen).

confiscate, vb. bosshū suru 没収する (seize by public authority).

conflict, 1. n. tatakai 戦い (battle); sensō 戦争 (war); kenka 喧嘩 (quarrel); tairitsu 対立 (antagonism, discord). 2. arasou 争う (fight); tairitsu suru 対立する (oppose); kuichigau 食い違う (differ, disagree).

conform, vb. 1. shitagau 従う (obey). 2. itchi suru 一致する; (be in agreement); itchi saseru 一致させる (bring into agreement). 3. au 合う (be in accord or harmony); awaseru 合わせる (bring into agreement or harmony).

confront, vb. 1. tachimukau 立ち向かう (face

courageously, make effort).
2. tairitsu suru 対立する
(face hostilely). 3.
chokumen suru 直面する
(encounter).

confuse, vb. 1. kondō suru
混同する (mix up). 2.
konran saseru 混乱させる
(throw into disorder). 3.
tomadowaseru 戸惑わせる
(bewilder).

confusion, n. 1. kondō 混同
(mix-up). 2. konran 混乱
(disorder). 3. tomadoi 戸惑
い (bewilderment).

congenial, adj. 1. kimochi
ga ii 気持ちが良い
(pleasant). 2. tekishite iru
適している (suitable).

congestion, n. 1. kōtsūjūtai
交通渋滞 (traffic). 2.
hanazumari 鼻づまり
(nasal).

congratulations, 1. n. iwai
no kotoba 祝いの言葉. 2.
interj. Omedetō おめでとう.

congregation, n. 1.
atsumari 集まり (assembly).
2. shūkai 集会 (meeting).

congress, n. 1. kaigi 会議
(meeting). 2. kokkai 国会
(national legislative body);
gikai 議会 (U.S. Congress).

conjunction, n. 1.
setsuzokushi 接続詞
(grammar). 2. renketsu 連
結 (act of conjoining); **in
conjunction with ...** to
tomo ni ... と共に (together
with).

con man, n. sagishi 詐欺師.

connect, vb. 1. tsunagu 繋ぐ
(link, establish telephone
communication). 2.
renraku suru 連絡する
(buses, trains, etc.). 3.
kanrenzukeru 関連づける
(associate).

conquer, vb. seifuku suru 征

服する.

conscience, n. ryōshin 良心.

conscious, adj. 1. ishiki ga
aru 意識がある (aware). 2.
ishiki-teki (na) 意識的 (な)
(intentional).

consecutive, adj. renzoku
(no) 連続 (の).

consent, 1. n. gōi 合意
(agreement); kyoka 許可
(permission). 2. vb. gōi suru
合意する (agree); kyoka
suru 許可する (permit).

consequence, n. 1. kekka 結
果 (result). 2. jūyōsei 重要
性 (importance); **of
consequence** jūyō (na); **of
little consequence** jūyō de
nai.

conservation, n. 1. hozon
保存 (preservation). 2.
setsuyaku 節約 (controlled
utilization).

conservative, 1. n. hoshuha
保守派. 2. adj. hoshu-teki
(na) 保守的 (な) (favoring
existing conditions);
shinchō (na) 慎重 (な)
(cautious); hikaeme (na) 控
え目 (な) (modest).

conserve, vb. 1. hozon suru
保存する (keep intact). 2.
setsuyaku suru 節約する
(save).

consider, vb. 1. jukkō suru
熟考する (think over);
kangaeru 考える (think
about). 2. kentō suru 見当
する (examine). 3. ... to
minasu ... と見なす; ... to
omou と思う (deem);
consider expensive takai
to omou 高いと思う.

considerate, adj. omoiyari
ga aru 思いやりがある.

consign, vb. 1. okuru 送る
(ship). 2. yudaneru 委ねる
(entrust). 3. hikiwatasu 引
き渡す (hand over).

consist, vb. **consist of ...** kara naru ... からなる.

consistency, n. 1. ikkansei 一貫性 (constancy). 2. katasa 固さ (degree of firmness); kosa 濃さ (degree of density).

console, vb. nagusameru 慰める.

consolidate, vb. 1. tsuyomeru 強める (make firm); tsuyomaru 強まる (become firm). 2. gappei suru 合併する (unite, as companies).

consonant, n. shi'in 子音.

conspicuous, adj. medatsu 目立つ.

conspire, vb. 1. kyōbō suru 共謀する (plot together). 2. kyōryoku suru 協力する (act together).

constant, adj. 1. ittei (no) 一定 (の) (fixed). 2. taemanai 絶え間ない (uninterrupted). 3. seijitsu (na) 誠実 (な) (faithful).

constellation, n. seiza 星座.

constipation, n. benpi 便秘.

constraint, n. 1. seigen 制限 (restriction). 2. yokusei 抑制 (repression of natural feelings). 3. kyūkutsusa 窮屈さ (unnatural restraint in manner).

construct, vb. 1. kensetsu suru 建設する (build). 2. kumitateru 組み立てる (form).

construction, n. 1. kensetsu 建設 (act of constructing); **under construction** kensetsuchū (no) 建設中 (の). 2. tatemono 建て物 (building). 3. kōzō 構造 (structure). 4. kensetsugyō 建設業 (industry).

constructive, adj. kensetsu-teki (na) 建設的 (な).

consulate, n. ryōjikan 領事館.

consult, vb. 1. ... ni sōdan suru ... に相談する (ask advice of). 2. (isha ni) mite morau (医者に) 見てもらう (be checked by, e.g., doctor). 3. shiraberu 調べる (refer to, e.g., dictionary).

consume, vb. 1. tsukaihatasu 使い果たす (use up). 2. taberu 食べる (eat); nomu 飲む (drink). 3. shōhi suru 消費する (buy goods, etc.). 4. rōhi suru 浪費する (waste).

contact, 1. n. sesshoku 接触 (touching); renraku 連絡 (communication); **make contact with ...** to renraku o toru ... と連絡をとる. 2. vb. ... to sesshoku suru ... と接触する (touch); ... to renraku o toru ... と連絡をとる (communicate with).

contagious, adj. 1. densensei (no) 伝染性 (の) (transmittable). 2. kansen shiyasui 感染し易い (infectious).

contain, vb. 1. ... ga haitteiru ... が入っている (have within). 2. fukumu 含む (include). 3. osaeru 抑える (hold back).

contaminate, vb. osen suru 汚染する.

contemplate, vb. 1. kangaeru 考える (think about). 2. yoku kangaeru よく考える (consider thoroughly). 3. yoku miru よく見る (look at with attention). 4. keikaku suru 計画する (intend).

contemporary, 1. n. dōjidaijin 同時代人. 2. adj. dōjidai (no) 同時代 (の) (of same period); gendai (no)

現代 (の) (modern).

contend, 1. *n.* kisou 競う (compete). 2. tatakau 戦う (fight). 3. giron suru 議論する (dispute). 4. shuchō suru 主張する (assert).

content, *n.* naiyō 内容 (subject); nakami 中身 (what is contained); **table of contents** mokuji 目次.

content, 1. *n.* **to one's heart's content** omouzonbun ni 思う存分に. 2. *adj.* **be content (with)** (... de) manzoku shiteiru (... で) 満足している. 3. *vb.* manzoku saseru 満足させる; **content oneself (with)** (... de) manzoku suru (... で) 満足する.

contest, 1. *n.* konkūru コンクール (competition for a prize); takakai 戦い (struggle); giron 議論 (dispute). 2. *vb.* kisou 競う (compete with); arasou 争う (fight for); ... ni igi o tonaeru ... に異議を唱える (argue about).

context, *n.* 1. bunmyaku 文脈 (surrounding words). 2. mawari no jōkyō 周りの状況 (surrounding circumstances).

continence, *n.* 1. jisei 自制 (self-restraint). 2. kin'yoku 禁欲 (abstinence).

continent, *n.* tairiku 大陸 (major land mass).

contingent, *adj.* **contingent on** ... shidai ... 次第 (dependent on).

continue, *vb.* tsuzuku 続く (go on); tsuzukeru 続ける (carry on, extend).

continuous, *adj.* togireru koto ga nai 途切れる事がない.

contour, *n.* rinkaku 輪郭.

contraceptive, *n.* hiningu 避妊具 (device); hinin'yaku 避妊薬 (pill).

contract, 1. *n.* keiyaku 契約 (agreement); keiyakusho 契約書 (written form). 2. *vb.* keiyaku suru 契約する (agree); chijimu 縮む (become smaller or shorter); chijimeru 縮める (cause to become smaller or shorter); ... ni kakaru ... にかかる (catch, as disease).

contradict, *vb.* 1. ... ni hantai suru ... に反対する (assert the opposite of). 2. hitei suru 否定する (deny). 3. ... to kuichigau ... と食い違う (be inconsistent).

contraption, *n.* shikake 仕掛け.

contrary, *n.* hantai 反対 (opposite); **on the contrary** hantai ni 反対に; kaette かえって; **to the contrary** chigau fū ni 違う風に (differently). 2. *adj.* hantai (no) 反対 (の); gyaku (no) 逆 (の) (opposite); hinekurete-iru ひねくれている (perverse); **contrary to** ... ni hanshite ... に反して.

contrast, 1. *n.* chigai 違い (difference). 2. *vb.* kuraberu 比べる (compare); chigau 違う (differ).

contribute, *vb.* 1. kifu suru 寄付する (donate). 2. kikō suru 寄稿する (write a work under contract). 3.

contribute to ... ni kōken suru ... に貢献する (to be an important factor in).

control, 1. *n.* shihai 支配 (domination); kanri 管理 (management); yokusei 抑制 (restraint); **get under control** seigyo suru 制御す

る. 2. *vb.* shihai suru 支配す
る (dominate); kanri suru 管
理する (manage); yokusei
suru 抑制する (restrain);
control oneself jibun o
osaeru 自分を抑える.

convalesce, *vb.* kaifuku suru
回復する.

convenient, *adj.* 1. benri
(na) 便利 (な) (handy). 2.
kōtsugō (na) 好都合 (な)
(favorable).

convention, *n.* 1. shūkan 習
慣 (accepted usage). 2.
taikai 大会 (meeting).

converge, *vb.* shūchū suru
集中する (concentrate);
shūsoku suru 収束する
(mathematics).

conversation, *n.* kaiwa 会
話.

convert, 1. *n.* kaishūsha 改
宗者 (religion). 2. *vb.*
kaishū suru 改宗する
(become a convert); kaishū
saseru 改宗させる (cause to
convert); kaeru 変える
(change); kaesaseru 変えさ
せる (cause to change).

convex, *adj.* totsumen (no)
凸面 (の).

convey, *vb.* 1. hakobu 運ぶ
(carry); 2. tsutaeru 伝える
(transmit).

conviction, *n.* 1. shin'nen
信念 (firm belief). 2. yūzai
no hanketsu 有罪の判決
(legal guilt).

convince, *vb.* 1. settoku
suru 説得する (persuade).
2. shinji saseru 信じさせる
(cause to believe).

convulsion, *n.* keiren けい
れん.

cook, *vb.* ryōri suru 料理す
る (prepare by heating);
cook up detchiageru でっ
ち上げる (fabricate).

cookbook, *n.* ryōri no hon

料理の本.

cooking, *n.* ryōri 料理.

cool, 1. *adj.* suzushii 涼しい
(temperature); tsumetai 冷
たい (unaffectionate or
unfriendly); reisei (na) 冷静
(な) (detached). 2. *vb.* hieru
冷える (become chilled);
hiyasu 冷やす (make
chilled); sameru 冷める
(become cooler); samasu 冷
ます (make cooler).

cooperate, *vb.* kyōryoku
suru 協力する.

cooperative, 1. *n.*
kyōdōkanri-bunjō-manshon
共同管理分譲マンション
(apartment); kyōdō-kumiai
協同組合 (business). 2. *adj.*
kyōdō (no) 協同 (の)
(working together);
kyōryoku-teki (na) 協力的
(な) (helpful).

coordinate, *vb.* awaseru 合
わせる.

cop, *n.* keikan 警官.

cope, *vb.* **cope with** ... o
umaku shori suru ... をうま
く処理する.

copper, *n.* dō 銅.

copy, 1. *n.* kopī コピー
(duplicate); -bu -部
(newspaper, magazine);
-satsu -冊 (book); **two
copies of a book** hon
nisatsu 本2冊. 2. *vb.* kopī o suru
コピーをする (make copy);
mohō suru 模倣する
(imitate); kakiutsusu 書き写
す (transcribe).

copyright, *n.* chosakuken 著
作権.

coquettish, *adj.* adappoi あ
だっぽい.

coral, *n.* sango 珊瑚.

cordial, 1. *n.* rikyūru リキュ
ール (liqueur). 2. *adj.*
atatakai 暖かい (friendly).

corduroy, *n.* kōruten コール

テン。

core, *n.* 1. shin 芯 (of fruit). 2. kakushin 核心 (essential part).

corkscrew, *n.* sen'nuki 栓抜き。

corn, *n.* 1. tōmorokoshi とうもろこし (food). 2. uonome 魚の目 (growth on foot).

corner, 1. *n.* kado 角 (intersection; angle); hashi 端 (margin); sumi 隅 (niche, nook); **cut corners** tettoribayaku sumaseru てっとり早く済ませる (do a quick job). 2. *vb.* oitsumeru 追い詰める (trap).

cornerstone, *n.* kiban 基盤.

corporal, *adj.* nikutai (no) 肉体 (の); **corporal punishment** taibatsu 体罰.

corporate, *adj.* 1. kigyō (no) 企業 (の) (of a corporation). 2. dantai (no) 団体 (の) (of a group).

corporation, *n.* kigyō 企業 (business organization).

corpse, *n.* shitai 死体.

corral, 1. *n.* kakoi 囲い. 2. *vb.* kakoi ni ireru 囲いに入れる (put in a corral); kakutoku suru 獲得する (seize).

correct, 1. *adj.* tadashii 正しい (right); seikaku (na) 正確 (な) (accurate). 2. *vb.* tadasu 正す (make right).

correspond, *vb.* 1. itchi suru 一致する (match). 2. sōtō suru 相当する (be analogous). 3. buntsū suru 文通する (communicate by letters).

corridor, *n.* rōka 廊下.

corrode, *vb.* fushoku suru/saseru 腐食する／させる.

corrupt, 1. *adj.* daraku shiteiru 堕落している (depraved); kusatte-iru 腐っている (decayed). 2. *vb.* daraku suru/saseru 堕落する／させる (become/make depraved); kusareru 腐れる (become decayed); kusaraseru 腐らせる (make decayed); baishū suru 買収する (bribe); kegareru 汚れる (become tainted).

cosmetic, 1. *n.* keshōhin 化粧品 (powder, lotion, etc.). 2. *adj.* hyōmen-teki (na) 表面的 (な) (superficial).

cosmic, *adj.* uchū (no) 宇宙 (の).

cosmopolitan, *adj.* sekai-teki (na) 世界的 (な) (global); kokusai-teki (na) 国際的 (な) (international).

cosmos, *n.* uchū 宇宙.

cost, 1. *n.* hiyō 費用 (expenditure); kakaku 価格 (price paid); **cost of living** seikatsuhi 生活費; **at all costs** dōshitemo どうしても; **at the cost of** ... o gisei ni shite ... を犠牲にして. 2. *vb.* ... ga kakaru ... がかかる (require payment of); yōsuru 要する (require effort, time).

costume, *n.* ishō 衣装.

cottage, *n.* koya 小屋.

cotton, *n.* 1. wata 綿 (plant, wadding). 2. momen 木綿 (cloth).

cough, 1. *n.* seki 咳. 2. *vb.* seki o suru 咳をする.

council, *n.* i'inkai 委員会 (committee); kaigi 会議 (assembly).

counsel, 1. *n.* bengoshi 弁護士 (lawyer); sōdan 相談 (advice); chūkoku 忠告 (caution). 2. *vb.* jogen o ataeru 助言を与える (give advice); sōdan suru 相談する (get advice); chūkoku suru 忠告する (caution).

count, 1. *n.* keisan 計算 (act of counting); sōsū 総数 (total number); hakushaku 伯爵 (title). 2. *vb.* kazoeru 数える (determine number); taisetsu de aru 大切である (be important); fukumu 含む (include); ... to minasu ... とみなす (consider); **count on** ... o ate ni suru ... を当てにする.

countdown, *n.* byō yomi 秒読み.

countenance, 1. *n.* kaotsuki 顔付き (facial expression); kaodachi 顔立ち (facial features). 2. *vb.* yurusu 許す (allow).

counteract, *vb.* chūwa suru 中和する.

counterattack, *vb.* hangeki suru 反撃する.

counterfeit, 1. *n.* nisemono 偽せ物 (a fake). 2. *vb.* gizō suru 偽造する (fake).

countess, *n.* hakushakufujin 伯爵夫人.

country, *n.* 1. kuni 国 (nation; homeland). 2. kokumin 国民 (people of a country). 3. inaka 田舎 (rural district).

countryside, *n.* inaka 田舎.

county, *n.* gun 郡.

couple, 1. *n.* fūfu 夫婦 (married couple); futari 二人 (two people); futatsu 二つ (two things). 2. *vb.* tsunagu つなぐ (connect, fasten); hitotsu ni naru/suru 一つになる／する (become/make united).

courage, *n.* yūki 勇気.

courier, *n.* kyūshi 急使.

course, 1. *n.* michi 道 (route); hōkō 方向 (direction); kōza 講座 (set of lectures); **in the course of**

... no aida ni ... の間に. 2. *adv.* **of course** mochiron もちろん (needless to say).

court, 1. *n.* nakaniwa 中庭 (patio); ōkyū 王宮 (palace); hōtei 法廷 (law court); **settle out of court** jidan ni suru 示談にする; **take into court** saibanzata ni suru 裁判沙汰にする. 2. *vb.* ... no kigen o toru ... の機嫌をとる (flatter); kyūai suru 求愛する (woo).

courteous, *adj.* 1. reigi tadashii 礼儀正しい (good-mannered). 2. teinei (na) 丁寧 (na) (polite).

courtesy, *n.* 1. reigi 礼儀 (good manners). 2. teineisa 丁寧さ (politeness).

courthouse, *n.* saibansho 裁判所.

cousin, *n.* itoko いとこ.

covenant, *n.* seiyaku 誓約.

cover, 1. *n.* kabā カバー (anything that covers); futa 蓋 (lid, top). 2. *vb.* ōu 覆う (place something on, spread over); ... ni futa o suru ... に蓋をする (put a lid on); kurumu くるむ (wrap); **cover up** kakusu 隠す (hide).

coverage, *n.* hōdō 報道 (journalism).

cover charge, *n.* 入場料 (for a show).

covering, *n.* ōi 覆い.

covet, *vb.* hoshigaru 欲しがる.

covetous, *adj.* don'yoku (na) 貪欲 (な).

cow, *n.* 1. mesu 雌 (female animal). 2. nyūgyū 乳牛 (female bovine animal).

coward, *n.* okubyōmono 臆病者.

cozy, *adj.* igokochi ga ii 居心地がいい.

crab, n. kani 蟹 (crustacean).

crabby, adj. kimuzukashii 気難しい (peevish).

crack, 1. n. hibi ひび (crevice); sakeme 裂け目 (opening); wareme 割れ目 (chink); wareru oto 割れる音 (noise). 2. vb. hibi ga hairu ひびが入る (fracture); waru 割る (break something); wareru 割れる (break open). **crack down** torishimaru 取り締まる.

crackle, n. pachi-pachi to iu oto パチパチという音 (sound).

cradle, n. yurikago ゆりかご.

craft, n. 1. gijutsu 技術 (skill). 2. kōgei 工芸 (industrial arts). 3. shokugyō 職業 (profession). 4. fune 船 (boat).

craftsman, n. shokunin 職人.

crafty, adj. zurugashikoi ずる賢い.

crag, n. kewashii iwa 険しい岩.

cram, vb. tsumekomu 詰め込む (stuff, prepare for examination).

cramp, n. keiren けいれん (spasm); ikeiren 胃けいれん (stomach spasm).

cranium, n. zugaikotsu 頭蓋骨.

crash, 1. n. tsuiraku 墜落 (fall); shōtotsu 衝突 (collision); tōsan 倒産 (bankruptcy); gachan to iu oto がちゃんという音 (sound of breaking). 2. vb. tsuiraku suru 墜落する (fall); shōtotsu suru 衝突する (collide); hasan suru 破産する (go bankrupt).

crave, vb. hoshigaru 欲しがる.

crawfish, n. zarigani ざりがに.

crawl, 1. n. noroi ugoki のろい動き (slow movement); kurōru クロール (swimming stroke). 2. vb. hau 這う (move slowly, creep).

crayfish, n. zarigani ざりがに.

craze, 1. n. dairyūkō 大流行 (fad). 2. vb. kuruwaseru 狂わせる (make insane); nekkyō saseru 熱狂させる (make excited).

crazy, adj. 1. nekkyō (no) 熱狂 (の) (insane). 2. baka (na) 馬鹿 (な) (silly). 3. **crazy about** ... ni muchū (no) ... に夢中 (の).

creak, 1. n. kishiru oto きしる音. 2. vb. kishiru きしる.

crease, 1. n. shiwa しわ (wrinkle); orime 折り目 (fold). 2. vb. shiwa ni suru しわにする (wrinkle); shiwa ni naru しわになる (become wrinkled); oru 折る (fold).

create, vb. 1. sōzō suru 創造する (cause to exist). 2. hikiokosu 引き起こす (cause to happen).

creature, n. 1. dōbutsu 動物 (animal). 2. hito 人 (person).

credence, n. shin'yō 信用; **give credence to** ... o shinjiru ... を信じる.

credibility, n. kakujitsusei 確実性.

credible, adj. 1. shinjirareru 信じられる (trustworthy). 2. kakujitsu (na) 確実 (な) (reliable).

credit, 1. n. tsuke 付け (for buying); tan'i 単位 (for a degree); shin'yō 信用 (belief); shōsan 賞賛 (commendation); hokori 誇り (honor); **on credit**

kurejitto de; tsuke de; **give credit to** ... o shinjiru ... を信じるの; **do credit to** ... no hokori to naru. 2. *vb.* shinjiru 信じる (believe); kurejitto ni suru クレジットにする (credit an account); **credit to** ... no yue de aru to suru ...の故であるとする (ascribe to); **credit (someone) with** ... o sonaeteiru ... を備えている.

creek, *n.* ogawa 小川.

creep, *vb.* 1. hau 這う (crawl). 2. shinobiyoru 忍び寄る (sneak).

cremate, *vb.* kasō ni suru 火葬にする.

crescent, *n.* mikazuki 三日月 (moon).

crest, *n.* 1. tosaka とさか (bird). 2. itadaki 頂 (top). 3. mon 紋 (heraldic device).

crew, *n.* 1. norikumiin 乗組員 (ship, airplane, etc.). 2. kurū-han クルー班 (group of workers).

crib, *n.* bebī-beddo ベビーベッド (bed).

cricket, *n.* kōrogi こおろぎ (insect).

crime, *n.* 1. hanzai 犯罪 (unlawful act); **commit a crime** hanzai o okasu. 2. tsumi 罪 (sin).

crimson, 1. *adj.* shinku (no) 真紅 (の). 2. *n.* shinku 真紅.

cripple, 1. *n.* shitai-fujiyūsha 肢体不自由者. 2. *vb.* fugu ni suru 不具にする (make lame); funō ni suru 不能にする (disable).

crisis, *n.* kiki 危機.

crisp, *adj.* 1. tekipaki to shiteiru てきぱきとしている (brisk, decided). 2. meikai (na) 明解 (な) (lively, pithy). 3. pari-pari shiteiru ぱりぱりしている (hard but

easily breakable). 4. shaki-shaki shite-iru しゃきしゃきしている (firm and fresh).

criterion, *n.* kijun 基準.

critic, *n.* 1. hihyōka 批評家 (reviewer). 2. hihansha 批判者 (antagonist).

criticize, *vb.* 1. hihyō suru 批評する (critique). 2. hihan suru 批判する (reproach).

croak, *vb.* 1. kā-kā naku かーかー鳴く (crow); kero-kero naku けろけろ鳴く (frog). 2. shagaregoe de iu しゃがれ声で言う (speak with a hoarse voice).

crochet, *n.* kagibariami かぎ針編み.

crocodile, *n.* wani わに.

crooked, *adj.* 1. fushōjiki (na) 不正直 (な) (dishonest). 2. magatteiru 曲がっている (curved).

crop, 1. *n.* sakumotsu 作物 (produce); shūkaku 収穫 (yield). 2. *vb.* karikomu 刈り込む (cut short); **crop up** shōjiru 生じる (appear).

cross, 1. *n.* jūji 十字 (cross symbol); jūjika 十字架 (the cross of Christianity). 2. *adj.* fukigen (na) 不機嫌 (な) (ill-humored). 3. *vb.* yokogiru 横切る (go or pass across); majiwaru 交わる (intersect); hantai suru 反対する (oppose); **cross out** sen o hiite kesu 線をひいて消す; **cross one's arms** ude o kumu 腕を組む; **cross oneself** jūji o kiru 十字をきる.

cross-eyed, *adj.* yorime (no) 寄り目 (の).

crossing, *n.* 1. kōsaten 交差点 (intersection). 2. ōdanhodō 横断歩道 (crosswalk).

crossroads, n. jūjiro 十字路.

cross section, n. danmen 断面.

crosswalk, n. ōdanhodō 横断歩道.

crotch, n. mata 股.

crouch, vb. mi o kagameru 身をかがめる.

crow, n. karasu 烏.

crowd, 1. n. gunshū 群衆 (large group of people). **2.** vb. muragaru 群がる (throng); oshikomu 押し込む (push forward); mitasu 満たす (fill).

crowded, adj. kondeiru 混んでいる.

crown, 1. n. ōkan 王冠 (coronet); ōken 王権 (sovereignty); chōten 頂点 (top); atama 頭 (head); shikan 歯冠 (of tooth). **2.** vb. sokui saseru 即位させる (invest with sovereignty); ōu 覆う (cover).

crucial, adj. **1.** jūdai (na) 重大 (な) (important). **2.** kettei-teki (na) 決定的 (な) (determining).

crucify, vb. haritsuke ni suru はりつけにする.

crude, adj. **1.** bukiyō (na) 不器用 (な) (clumsy). **2.** soya (na) 粗野 (な) (coarse). **3.** mikakō (no) 未加工 (の) (unprocessed).

cruel, adj. **1.** zankoku (na) 残酷 (な) (heartless). **2.** hidoi ひどい (causing pain).

cruelty, n. **1.** zankokusa 残酷さ (heartlessness). **2.** hidosa ひどさ (painfulness).

crumb, n. pankuzu パン屑 (bread crumb); kuzu 屑 (morsel).

crumble, vb. **1.** hōkai suru 崩壊する (collapse). **2.** konagona ni suru 粉々にする (break into pieces).

crunch, vb. kamikudaku 噛み砕く (chew noisily).

crusade, n. **1.** undō 運動 (political campaign). **2.** jūjigun 十字軍 (Christian military expedition).

crush, 1. n. hitogomi 人混み (crowd); **have a crush on** ... ni muchū ni naru ... に夢中になる. **2.** vb. oshitsubusu 押し潰す (break by pressing); tsumekakeru 詰め掛ける (crowd).

crust, n. kawa 皮 (bread, pie). **2.** chikaku 地殻 (surface of the earth).

crutch, n. matsubazue 松葉杖.

cry, 1. n. sakebi 叫び (scream); nakigoe 泣き声 (weeping); nakigoe 鳴き声 (animal cry). **2.** vb. sakebu 叫ぶ (scream); naku 泣く (weep); naku 鳴く (animal cry).

cryptic, adj. **1.** himitsu (no) 秘密 (の) (secret). **2.** nazo ni michite-iru 謎に満ちている (mysterious).

cub, n. **1.** ko 子 (young animal).

cube, n. **1.** sanjō 三乗 (mathematics). **2.** rippōtai 立方体 (solid bounded by six squares).

cubic, adj. rippō (no) 立方 (の).

cuckoo, n. kakkō かっこう (bird).

cucumber, n. kyūri きゅうり.

cue, n. aizu 合図 (signal).

cuff, n. sodeguchi 袖口 (sleeve); orikaeshi 折り返し (pants).

cuisine, n. ryōri 料理.

culinary, adj. ryōri (no) 料理 (の).

culminate, vb. **1.** chōten ni

tassuru 頂点に達する (reach the highest point). 2.

culminate in ... ni owaru ... に終わる (result in).

culprit, *n.* hanzainin 犯罪人.

cultivate, *vb.* 1. tagayasu 耕す (till, plow). 2. kaihatsu suru 開発する (develop).

culture, *n.* 1. kyōyō 教養 (cultivation of the mind). 2. bunmei 文明; bunka 文化 (civilization, arts, etc.).

cumbersome, *adj.* ōkisugiru 大き過ぎる (too big).

cumulative, *adj.* ruiseki (no) 累積 (の).

cunning, *adj.* 1. zurugashikoi ずる賢い (clever). 2. zurui ずるい (sly).

cupboard, *n.* shokkidana 食器棚.

cure, 1. *n.* chiryō 治療 (remedy); kaifuku 回復 (restoration to health). 2. *vb.* chiryō suru 治療する (treat a patient); naosu 治す (restore to health).

curfew, *n.* 1. mongen 門限 (home, dormitory). 2. yakangaishutsu-kinshirei 夜間外出禁止令 (governmental).

curiosity, *n.* kōkishin 好奇心.

currency, *n.* 1. tsūka 通貨 (money). 2. tsūyō 通用 (prevalence); **gain currency** tsūyō suru.

current, 1. *n.* nagare 流れ (stream); suiryū 水流 (water); denryū 電流 (electricity). 2. *adj.* genzai (no) 現在 (の) (of today); tsūyō shiteiru 通用している (prevailing); **current events** jiji hinde.

curse, 1. *n.* noroi 呪い (wish that evil befall someone);

nonoshiri ののしり (profane oath). 2. *vb.* norou 呪う (wish evil upon); nonoshiru ののしる (swear).

cursory, *adj.* iikagen (na) 好い加減 (な).

curt, *adj.* bukkirabō (na) ぶっきらぼう (な).

curtail, *vb.* kiritsumeru 切り詰める.

curve, *n.* kyokusen 曲線 (line). 2. *vb.* magaru/mageru 曲がる／曲げる (bend/cause to bend).

custard, *n.* purin プリン (caramel custard); kasutādo カスタード (custard in general).

custodian, *n.* 1. hogosha 保護者 (guardian). 2. kanrinin 管理人 (caretaker).

custom, *n.* shūkan 習慣.

customary, *adj.* 1. futsū 普通 (usual). 2. itsumo no いつもの (habitual).

customer, *n.* (o)kyaku (お)客.

customs, *n.* 1. zeikan 税関 (office). 2. kanzei 関税 (tax).

cut, 1. *n.* kirikizu 切り傷 (wound); sakugen 削減 (reduction). 2. *vb.* kiru 切る (wound, divide); kireru 切れる (be sharp); mijikaku suru 短くする (shorten); **cut across** yokogiru 横切る.

cute, *adj.* kawaii 可愛い.

cutlet, *n.* katsu(retsu) カツ(レツ).

cutting, *n.* 1. kiru koto 切ること (act of cutting). 2. kirinuki 切り抜き (clipping). 3. kirieda 切り枝 (cut stem).

cycle, *n.* 1. shūki 周期 (regular occurrence, recurring time). 2. jitensha 自転車 (bicycle).

cyclical, *adj.* shūki-teki (na)

周期的 (な) (occurring regularly).

cylinder, *n.* entō 円筒; enchūkei 円柱形 (round elongated solid).

cynical, *adj.* hinikuppoi 皮肉

つぽい (distrustful, skeptical).

cynicism, *n.* reishō-teki na taido 冷笑的な態度 (cynical disposition).

cypress, *n.* itosugi 糸杉.

D

dab, *vb.* karuku ateru 軽く当てる.

dad, *n.* otōsan お父さん; papa パパ.

dagger, *n.* tantō 短刀.

daily, 1. *n.* nikkanshi 日刊紙 (newspaper). 2. *adj.* mainichi (no) 毎日 (の). 3. *adv.* mainichi 毎日.

dainty, *adj.* kyasha (na) 華奢 (な).

dairy, *n.* 1. nyūseihinten 乳製品店 (store). 2. rakunōjō 酪農場 (farm).

daisy, *n.* hinagiku ひな菊.

dally, *vb.* 1. guzu-guzu suru ぐずぐずする (delay). 2. tawamureru 戯れる (flirt).

damage, 1. *n.* songai 損害. 2. *vb.* songai o ataeru 損害を与える.

dame, *n.* 1. on'na no hito 女の人 (woman). 2. kifujin 貴婦人 (woman of rank).

damn, 1. *vb.* jigoku ni otosu 地獄に落とす (condemn to hell); kokuhyō suru 酷評する (declare bad). 2. *interj.* Chikushō 畜生.

damned, 1. *adj.* mattaku (no) 全く (の) (utter); norowarete iru 呪われている (cursed); **damned fool** mattaku no baka. 2. *adv.* mattaku 全く (extremely).

damp, *adj.* shimeppoi 湿っぽい.

dampness, *n.* shikke 湿気.

dance, 1. *n.* odori 踊り

(dancing). 2. *vb.* odoru 踊る.

dancer, *n.* odorite 踊り手.

dandelion, *n.* tanpopo たんぽぽ.

dandruff, *n.* fuke ふけ.

danger, *n.* 1. kiken 危険 (exposure to harm); kiki 危機 (threat). **be in danger of** (... no) osore ga aru (... の) 恐れがある; **in danger** kitoku 危篤 (critically ill); **out of danger** kiki o dassuru 危機を脱する.

dangerous, *adj.* kiken (na) 危険 (な).

dangle, *vb.* 1. burasagaru/ burasageru ぶら下がる/ぶら下げる (hang/cause to hang). 2. bura-bura suru/saseru ぶらぶらする/させる (swing/cause to swing).

dare, *vb.* 1. idomu 挑む (face boldly); unagasu 促す (challenge a person). 2. (... suru) yūki ga aru (... する) 勇気がある (have courage).

daring, 1. *adj.* yūkan (na) 勇敢 (な) (brave); daitan (na) 大胆 (な) (bold). 2. *n.* yūki 勇気 (bravery).

dark, 1. *n.* kurayami 暗闇 (absence of light); yūgure 夕暮 (nightfall); **after dark** yūgure no ato; **in the dark** shiranai 知らない (ignorant). 2. *adj.* kurai 暗い (having no light);

kuroppoi 黒っぽい (blackish); iroguro (no) 色黒 (の) (swarthy); **Dark Ages** ankokujidai 暗黒時代.

darling, 1. *n.* anata あなた (wife addressing husband); itoshii hito 愛しい人 (loved one). 2. *adj.* itoshii 愛しい (beloved).

dart, 1. *n.* nageya 投げ矢 (arrow); tosshin 突進 (dash). 2. *vb.* tosshin suru 突進する (walk or run swiftly); satto ... suru さっと... する (act suddenly and quickly).

dash, 1. *n.* tosshin 突進 (run); **a dash of** shō-shō (no) 少々 (の). 2. *vb.* isogu 急ぐ (hurry); nagetsukeru 投げつける (throw violently against); kudaku 砕く (destroy).

dashboard, *n.* keibain 計器盤 (car).

date, 1. *n.* nengappi 年月日; hizuke 日付 (particular time); yakusoku 約束 (appointment); dēto デート (with member of opposite sex); **date of birth** seinengappi; **out of date** jidaiokure 時代おくれ (old-fashioned); kigengire 期限切れ (invalid); **to date** ima made no tokoro 今までのところ. 2. *vb.* hi o kimeru 日を決める (fix the date for); hizuke ga aru 日付がある (show the date of); hizuke o kaku 日付を書く (write the date on); furuku naru 古くなる (become out of date); dēto suru デートする (go on a date).

daughter, *n.* musume 娘.
daughter-in-law, *n.* yome 嫁.
dawdle, *vb.* 1. bura-bura

suru ぶらぶらする (waste time). 2. guzu-guzu suru 愚図愚図する (be slow).

dawn, 1. *n.* yoake 夜明け. 2. *vb.* yo ga akeru 夜が明ける (begin to grow light); kizuku 気付く (notice, realize); **It dawned on me that** ... ni kizuita.

day, *n.* 1. hi 日 (24 hours). 2. hiru(ma) 昼(間) (daytime). 3. **all day** ichinichijū 一日中; **day after day** mainichi 毎日; **day after tomorrow** asatte あさって; **day before yesterday** ototoi おととい; **every day** mainichi 毎日; **every other day** ichinichi oki ni 一日おきに; **the next day** yokujitsu 翌日; **one day** itsuka いつか (someday); ichinichi 一日 (single day); **the other day** senjitsu 先日; **these days** konogoro この頃.

day-care center, *n.* hoikusho 保育所.

daylight, *n.* hi no hikari 日の光; nikkō 日光.

daylight saving time, *n.* samā-taimu サマータイム.

daytime, *n.* hiru (ma) 昼(間).

dead, *adj.* 1. shindeiru 死んでいる (no longer alive or active). 2. sutareteiru すたれている (obsolete, in decline). 3. mukankaku (no) 無感覚 (の) (bereft of sensation). 4. kireteiru きれている (without power or charge); ugokanai 動かない (no longer functioning).

deaden, *vb.* osaeru 抑える; yowameru 弱める (lower intensity).

dead end, *n.* ikidomari 行き止まり.

deadline, *n.* shimekiri 締め切り; kigen 期限.

deadly, *adj.* 1. chimei-teki (na) 致命的 (な) (fatal); shi o motarasu 死をもたらす (lethal). 2. tsūretsu (na) 痛烈 (な) (unrelenting).

deaf, *adj.* 1. mimi ga kikoenai 耳が聞こえない. 2. **turn a deaf ear to** ... ni mimi o kasanai ... に耳を貸さない.

deaf-mute, *n.* rōasha 聾唖者.

deal, 1. *n.* torihiki 取り引き (commerce); **a good/great deal** ii kaimono 買い物 (a bargain). 2. *vb.* kubaru 配る (distribute); **deal with** ... ni taisho suru ... に対処する (handle, treat); ... to torihiki o suru ... と取り引きをする (commerce); **deal in** ... o atsukau ... を扱う (commerce).

dear, *adj.* 1. taisetsu (na) 大切 (な) (precious). 2. takai 高い (expensive). 3. haikei 拝啓 (salutation in letters).

death, *n.* 1. shi 死 (end of life); 2. owari 終わり (end).

debase, *vb.* hinshitsu o sageru 品質を下げる (reduce quality); kachi o sageru 価値を下げる (devalue).

debate, 1. *n.* tōron 討論. 2. *vb.* hanashiau 話し合う; tōron suru 討論する.

debilitate, *vb.* suijaku saseru 衰弱させる.

debit, *n.* kari'iregaku 借入額 (borrowed money).

debris, *n.* gareki がれき (rubble); zangai 残骸 (ruins).

debt, *n.* 1. shakkin 借金; fusai 負債 (money); **be in debt** shakkin ga aru. 2.

ongi 恩義 (obligation).

debtor, *n.* fusaisha 負債者.

decade, *n.* jūnenkan 十年間.

decapitate, *vb.* kubi o haneru 首をはねる.

decay, 1. *n.* otoroe 衰え (decline); mushiba 虫歯 (teeth); fuhai 腐敗 (rot). 2. *vb.* otoroeru 衰える (decline); mushiba ni naru 虫歯になる (teeth); areru 荒れる (crumble); fuhai suru 腐敗する (rot).

deceit, *n.* 1. itsuwari 偽り (deception). 2. sagi 詐欺 (fraud).

deceive, *vb.* damasu だます.

December, *n.* jūnigatsu 十二月.

decency, *n.* 1. reigi tadashisa 礼儀正しさ (courteousness). 2. jōhinsa 上品さ (propriety).

decent, *adj.* 1. reigi tadashii 礼儀正しい (respectable, courteous). 2. jōhin (na) 上品 (な) (not obscene). 3. ii いい (good). 4. shinsetsu (na) 親切 (な) (kind).

decentralize, *vb.* bunsan suru 分散する.

decide, *vb.* 1. kimeru 決める; kettei suru 決定する (conclude, settle, etc.); kesshin suru 決心する (make up one's mind). 2. hanketsu o kudasu 判決を下す (law). 3. kaiketsu suru 解決する (solve).

decimal, *adj.* 1. shōsū (no) 小数 (の) (of tenths). **decimal point** shōsūten. 2. jusshinhō (no) 十進法 (の) (of tens).

decision, *n.* 1. kettei 決定; ketsuron 結論 (conclusion, settlement); kesshin 決心 (making up one's mind); **reach a decision** ketsuron ni tassuru. 2. hanketsu 判決 (law).

decisive, *adj.* 1. kettei-teki (na) 決定的（な）(determining). 2. dankotaru 断固たる (resolute).

declare, *vb.* 1. sengen suru 宣言する (proclaim). 2. shinkoku suru 申告する (at Customs, etc.). 3. dangen suru 断言する (affirm).

decline, 1. *n.* genshō 減少 (decrease); botsuraku 没落 (downfall); suijaku 衰弱 (of health). 2. *vb.* jitai suru 辞退する (refuse); otoroeru 衰える (diminish, weaken); sagaru 下がる (drop).

decompose, *vb.* 1. kusaru 腐る (become rotten). 2. bunkai suru 分解する (separate into parts).

decorate, *vb.* 1. kazaru 飾る (adorn). 2. naisō o suru 内装をする (house). 3. kunshō o ataeru 勲章を与える (military).

decoy, *n.* otori おとり.

decrease, 1. *n.* genshō 減少 (decreasing). 2. *vb.* heru/herasu 減る／減らす (become/make less in quantity); sagaru/sageru 下がる／下げる (become/make less in quality or degree).

decree, 1. *n.* meirei 命令 (command). 2. *vb.* meijiru 命じる.

dedicate, *vb.* sasageru 捧げる (devote, give, inscribe in honor of someone);
dedicate oneself to ... ni mi o sasageru (devote oneself to); ... ni sen'nen suru ... に専念する (be absorbed in).

deduce, *vb.* suitei suru 推定する.

deduct, *vb.* sashihiku 差し引く.

deed, *n.* 1. okonai 行い (action). 2. shōsho 証書 (legal title).

deem, *vb.* ... to minasu/omou ... と見なす／思う (consider/think).

deep, *adj.* 1. fukai 深い (extending far down, profound); okuyuki ga aru 奥行きがある (extending far into the rear). 2. koi 濃い (dark). 3. **in deep** hamarikonde はまり込んで; **in deep water** hijō ni komatte 非常に困って.

deer, *vb.* shika 鹿.

default, 1. *n.* taiman 怠慢 (neglect); furikō 不履行 (failure to meet legal obligation); **win by default** fushenshō suru 不戦勝する. 2. *vb.* okotaru 怠る (fail to meet obligation).

defeat, 1. *n.* haiboku 敗北 (act of losing). 2. *vb.* makasu 負かす (overthrow).

defect, 1. *n.* kekkan 欠陥 (imperfection); ketten 欠点 (fault). 2. *vb.* bōmei suru 亡命する (forsake one's country).

defend, *vb.* 1. mamoru 守る (protect). 2. benmei suru 弁明する (justify). 3. bengo suru 弁護する (law).

defense, *n.* 1. bōei 防衛 (resistance to attack). 2. bengo 弁護 (defending argument).

defensive, *adj.* 1. bōeiyō (no) 防衛用（の）(used for defending). 2. benkaigamashii 弁解がましい (attitude). 2. **be on the defensive** mamori ni mawaru 守りに回る.

defiance, n. hankō 反抗 (bold resistance); **in defiance of** ... ni sakaratte ... に逆らって.

deficient (in), adj. 1. (... ga) tarinai (... が) 足りない (insufficient, lacking). 2. ... ni kakeru ... に欠ける (defective).

defile, vb. 1. kegasu 汚す (befoul). 2. bōtoku suru 冒瀆する (desecrate).

define, vb. 1. teigi suru 定義する (state meaning of). 2. meikaku ni suru 明確にする (clarify).

definite, adj. meikaku (na) 明確 (な) (clear).

definition, n. 1. teigi 定義 (statement that defines). 2. meikakusa 明確さ (clearness).

definitive, adj. saigo (no) 最後 (の) (final); kettei-teki (na) 決定的 (な) (conclusive).

deflect, vb. soreru/sorasu そ れる／そらす (turn/cause to turn from true course).

deformity, n. 1. fugu 不具 (physical impairment). 2. kikei 奇形 (abnormally formed part).

defray, vb. shiharau 支払う.

defrost, vb. 1. shimo o tokasu 霜を溶かす (de-ice). 2. kaitō suru 解凍する (unfreeze).

defy, vb. teikō suru 抵抗する (challenge).

degenerate, 1. adj. daraku shiteiru 堕落している (corrupt). 2. vb. daraku suru 堕落する (become corrupt); akka suru 悪化す る (deteriorate).

degrade, vb. 1. otoshimeru 貶める (humiliate). 2.

sageru 下げる (debase, lower).

degree, n. 1. do 度 (intensity, angle, temperature). 2. teido 程度 (extent); **to a certain degree** aru teido ある程度; **by degrees** jojo ni 徐々に. 3. gakui 学位 (academic achievement).

deify, vb. shinkakuka suru 神格化する.

deity, n. kami 神.

dejected, adj. rakutan shiteiru 落胆している.

delay, 1. n. okure 遅れ. 2. vb. enki suru 延期する (postpone); temadoraseru 手間取らせる (hinder).

delegate, 1. n. daihyō 代表 (representative); dairi 代理 (proxy). 2. vb. daihyō to shite okuru 代表として送る (send as a representative); inin suru 委任する (commit to another).

delete, vb. kesu 消す.

deliberate, 1. adj. koi (no) 故意 (の) (intentional); shinchō (na) 慎重 (な) (cautious); yūchō (na) 悠長 (な) (unhurried). 2. vb. shingi suru 審議する (discuss); jukkō suru 熟考す る (reflect).

delicacy, n. 1. sensaisa 繊細 さ (fineness). 2. chinmi 珍 味 (food).

delicate, adj. 1. sensai (na) 繊細 (な) (dainty and fragile). 2. bimyō (na) 微妙 (な) (requiring tact).

delicious, adj. oishii おいし い.

delight, 1. n. yorokobi 喜び. 2. vb. tanoshimaseru 楽しま せる; **delight in** ... o tanoshimu.

delightful, adj. tanoshii 楽

しい.

delinquency, n. hikō 非行 (wrongdoing by youth).

delirious, adj. seishinsakuran (no) 精神錯乱 (の) (deranged).

deliver, vb. 1. haitatsu suru 配達する (convey); tewatasu 手渡す (hand over). 2. kaihō suru 解放する (free). 3. enzetsu suru 演説する (speak in public). 4. motarasu もたらす (produce). 5. osan o tasukeru お産を助ける (deliver a baby).

delivery, n. haitatsu 配達 (act of conveying). 2. osan お産 (childbirth). 3. kaihō 解放 (liberation). 4. enzetsu no shikata 演説の仕方 (style of public speaking).

delude, vb. damasu だます.

deluge, n. 1. kōzui 洪水 (flood). 2. gōu 豪雨 (heavy rain).

delusion, n. sakkaku 錯覚 (misconception).

delve, vb. saguru 探る.

demand, 1. n. yōkyū 要求 (requirement); shuchō 主張 (claim); juyō 需要 (commerce); **be in great demand** juyō ga ōi. 2. vb. yōkyū suru 要求する; shuchō suru 主張する.

demeanor, n. furumai ふるまい.

democracy, n. 1. minshushugi 民主主義 (social equality). 2. minshushugi kokka 民主主義国家 (democratic country).

democratic, adj. minshuteki (na) 民主的 (な) (of democracy).

demolish, n. torikowasu 取り壊す (tear down); tsubusu

tsubusu (crush).

demon, n. akurei 悪霊.

demonstrate, vb. 1. shimesu 示す (show); arawasu 表わす (express). 2. shōmei suru 証明する (prove); setsumei suru 説明する (explain). 3. demo o suru デモをする (parade).

demonstration, n. 1. jitsuen 実演 (display, exhibition). 2. setsumei 説明 (explanation). 3. demo デモ (political).

demote, vb. chii o sageru 地位を下げる.

demure, adj. 1. hikaeme (na) 控え目 (な) (shy and modest). 2. torisumashite-iru とりすましている (coyly sedate).

den, n. 1. dōkutsu 洞窟 (home of wild animal or criminal). 2. gorakushitsu 娯楽室 (family room).

denial, n. 1. hitei 否定 (negation). 2. kyohi 拒否 (refusal).

denomination, n. 1. kaheikachi 貨幣価値 (value of monetary unit). 2. meishō 名称 (name). 3. shūha 宗派 (religion).

denote, vb. shimesu 示す (indicate); imi suru 意味する (mean).

denounce, vb. hinan suru 非難する.

dense, adj. 1. misshū shiteiru 密集している (crowded). 2. koi 濃い (thick). 3. nibui 鈍い (slow).

dent, 1, n. hekomi 凹み; kubomi 窪み (depression). 2. vb. hekomaseru 凹ませる.

dental, adj. ha (no) 歯 (の).

dentistry, n. shikaigaku 歯科医学.

denture, n. ireba 入れ歯.

denunciation, n. hinan 非難.

deny, vb. 1. kyozetsu suru 拒絶する (refuse to agree or give). 2. hitei suru 否定する (negate).

depart, vb. 1. saru 去る; iku 行く (go away); deru 出る (train, etc.). 2. shinu 死ぬ (die).

department, n. ka 課 (business, etc.); gakubu 学部 (university).

departure, n. shuppatsu 出発 (act of leaving).

depend, vb. **depend on** 1. ... ni tayoru ... に頼る (rely on); ... o ate ni suru ... を当てにする (count on). 2. shin'yō suru 信用する (trust). 3. ... shidai de aru ... 次第である (be contingent on).

dependent, 1. n. fuyōkazoku 扶養家族 (family). 2. adj. ... shidai (no) ... 次第 (の) (contingent); izon shiteiru 依存している (supported).

depict, vb. egaku 描く.

deplete, vb. herasu 減らす (lessen); kara ni suru 空にする (empty).

deplore, vb. kanashimu 悲しむ (lament).

deposit, 1. n. yokin 預金 (bank); tetsukekin 手付け金; hoshōkin 保証金 (for purchasing something); shikikin 敷金 (for renting an apartment). 2. vb. oku 置く (place); yokin suru 預金する.

depot, n. 1. eki 駅 (station). 2. sōko 倉庫 (storehouse).

deprecate, vb. 1. hantai suru 反対する (protest). 2. hinan suru 非難する

(express disapproval).

depress, vb. 1. ochikomaseru 落ち込ませる (make despondent). 2. yowameru 弱める (weaken). 3. osu 押す (press inward).

depressed, adj. 1. ochikondeiru 落ち込んでいる (despondent). 2. fukeiki (no) 不景気 (の) (economy).

depth, n. 1. fukasa 深さ (distance down); okuyuki 奥行き (distance to the back). 2. fukami 深み (profundity). 3. **in depth** tettei-teki ni 徹底的に (thoroughly).

deputy, n. dairi 代理 (proxy).

derail, vb. dassen suru/saseru 脱線する／させる (run/cause to run off rails).

derange, vb. ki o kuruwaseru 気を狂わせる (make insane); **be deranged** kurutteiru 狂っている.

derivative, n. 1. haseigo 派生語 (word). 2. haseibutsu 派生物 (something derived).

derive from, vb. 1. ... ni yurai suru ... に由来する (originate from). 2. ... kara kuru ... から来る (come or stem from). 3. ... kara eru ... から得る (obtain from).

descend, vb. 1. kudaru 下る; oriru 降りる (move down); shizumu 沈む (settle, sink). 2. **descend from** (... no) shison de aru (... の) 子孫である (be a descendant of).

descendant, n. shison 子孫.

descent, n. 1. kudarizaka 下り坂 (slope); kakei 家系 (lineage).

describe, vb. byōsha suru 描写する (depict); setsumei

desert, 1. *n.* sabaku 砂漠 (sand). 2. *vb.* misuteru 見捨てる (abandon); dassō suru 脱走する (military).

deserve, *vb.* ... ni atai suru ... に値する (be worthy of).

design, 1. *n.* sekkei 設計 (blueprint); keikaku 計画 (plan, project); ito 意図 (intention); keiryaku 計略 (plot). 2. *vb.* sekkei suru 設計する; keikaku suru 計画する; ito suru 意図する.

designate, *vb.* 1. shimesu 示す (indicate). 2. ninmei suru 任命する (appoint).

designer, *n.* dezainā デザイナー (of a dress, etc.); sekkeisha 設計者 (of a house, machine, etc.).

desirable, *adj.* nozomashii 望ましい.

desire, 1. *n.* netsubō 熱望 (strong wish); yokubō 欲望 (lust, greed). 2. *vb.* netsubō suru 熱望する (wish strongly); yokubō suru 欲望する (lust, be greedy).

desist, *vb.* yameru 止める (stop); **desist from doing** ... suru koto o yameru ... することを止める.

desk, *n.* tsukue 机 (furniture).

despair, 1. *n.* zetsubō 絶望. 2. *vb.* zetsubō suru 絶望する.

desperado, *n.* kyōakuhan 凶悪犯 (reckless criminal).

desperate, *adj.* 1. zetsubō-teki (na) 絶望的 (な) (hopeless). 2. hisshi (no) 必死 (の) (frantic); **be**

desperate for hisshi ni ... o motomeru 必死に... を求める.

despise, *vb.* keibetsu suru 軽蔑する.

despite, *prep.* ... nimo kakawarazu ... にもかかわらず.

despondent, *adj.* ochikondeiru 落ち込んでいる (dejected); hikan-teki (na) 悲観的 (な) (pessimistic).

destination, *n.* mokutekichi 目的地 (trip); atesaki 宛先 (mail).

destiny, *n.* unmei 運命.

destitute, *adj.* 1. gokuhin (no) 極貧 (の) (extreme poverty). 2. nai 無い (deprived).

destroy, *vb.* 1. hakai suru 破壊する (ruin, end). 2. korosu 殺す (kill).

detach, *vb.* hazusu 外す (separate).

detail, 1. *n.* shōsai 詳細; **in detail** kuwashiku 詳しく. 2. *vb.* kuwashiku hanasu 詳しく話す (relate in detail).

detain, *vb.* 1. horyū suru 保留する (keep from proceeding). 2. tojikomeru 閉じ込める (confine).

detective, *n.* tantei 探偵 (investigator); keibu 警部 (police); **detective novel** tanteishōsetsu.

deter, *vb.* samatageru 妨げる.

detergent, *n.* senzai 洗剤.

deteriorate, *vb.* akka suru 悪化する.

determination, *n.* 1. ketsui 決意 (fortitude). 2. kettei 決定 (conclusion).

detonate, *vb.* bakuhatsu suru/saseru 爆発する／させる (erupt/cause to erupt).

detour, n. ukairo 迂回路; mawarimichi 回り道.

detract, vb. sokonau 損う (spoil); **detract from** ... o sokonau.

devastating, adj. 1. kaimetsu-teki (na) 壊滅的 (な) (completely destructive). 2. shokku (na) ショック (な) (shocking).

develop, vb. 1. sodatsu/sodateru 育つ/育てる (grow/cause to grow); hatten suru/saseru 発展する／させる (evolve or advance/cause to evolve or advance). 2. genzō suru 現像する (photo).

device, n. 1. kufū 工夫 (contrivance). 2. keikaku 計画 (plan).

devil, n. akuma 悪魔.

devious, adj. 1. magarikunette-iru 曲がりくねっている (circuitous). 2. kōkatsu (na) 狡猾 (な) (underhanded).

devise, vb. kangaetsuku 考えつく (form a plan, contrive).

devote, vb. 1. sasageru 捧げる (consecrate, commit). 2. ateru 充てる (set aside). **devote oneself to** ... ni sen'nen suru ... に専念する (immerse oneself in); ... ni mi o sasageru ... に身を捧げる (commit oneself to).

devotion, n. 1. sasageru koto 捧げること; kenshin 献身 (consecration, act of consigning). 2. aichaku 愛着 (attachment). 3. shinjin 信心 (religious faith).

devout, adj. 1. nesshin (na) 熱心 (な) (ardent). 2. shinjinbukai 信心深い (pious).

dew, n. tsuyu 露.

diabetes, n. tōnyōbyō 糖尿病.

diagnosis, n. shindan 診断.

diagram, n. zuhyō 図表 (chart, plan).

dial, 1. n. mojiban 文字盤 (clock, watch); tsumami つまみ (knob); 2. vb. denwa suru 電話する (phone).

dialect, n. hōgen 方言.

dialogue, n. taiwa 対話.

diameter, n. chokkei 直径.

diaper, n. omutsu おむつ.

diaphragm, n. ōkakumaku 横隔膜 (muscle).

diarrhea, n. geri 下痢.

diary, n. nikki 日記; **keep a diary** nikki o tsukeru 日記をつける.

dice, n. saikoro さいころ.

dictate, vb. 1. kakitoraseru 書き取らせる (say something to be written down). 2. meirei suru 命令する (command).

diction, n. hanashikata 話し方 (style of speaking).

dictionary, n. jiten 辞典; jisho 辞書.

die, 1. n. saikoro さいころ (singular of dice); daisu ダイス (machining). 2. vb. shinu 死ぬ (person, animal); kareru 枯れる (plant); owaru 終わる (cease); **die away** jojo ni kieteiku 徐々に消えて行く; **be dying for/to** ... ga totemo hoshii/shitai ... がとても欲しい／したい; **die of** ... de shinu; **die down** yowamaru 弱まる; **die out** shinitaeru 死に絶える.

diet, n. 1. tabemono 食べ物 (food); daietto (shokuhin) ダイエット(食品) (food chosen for health, etc.); **go on a diet** daietto o suru. 2. **Diet** kokkai 国会 (Japanese legislative assembly).

differ, *vb.* 1. kotonaru 異なる (be unlike). 2. iken ga kotonaru 意見が異なる (disagree).

different, *adj.* 1. chigau 違う (unlike). 2. iro-iro (na) 色々 (な) (various).

difficult, *adj.* 1. muzukashii 難しい (hard to do). 2. kimuzukashii 気難しい (unfriendly).

diffuse, 1. *adj.* bunsan-teki (na) 分散的 (な) (spread out). 2. *vb.* bunsan suru/saseru 分散する/させる (spread out/cause to spread out).

dig, *vb.* 1. horu 掘る (shovel, excavate); **dig up** horiokosu 掘り起こす (excavate). 2. sagashidasu 捜し出す (find out).

digest, 1. *vb.* shōka suru 消化する (absorb, comprehend).

digestion, *n.* shōka 消化 (absorption, comprehension).

digit, *n.* 1. keta 桁 (number). 2. yubi 指 (finger, toe).

dignity, *n.* 1. igen 威厳 (stateliness); kihin 気品 (nobleness).

dike, *n.* 1. teibō 堤防 (bank, wall). 2. mizo 溝 (ditch).

dilapidated, *adj.* onboro (no) おんぼろ (の).

dilate, *vb.* hirogaru/hirogeru 広がる/広げる (expand/cause to expand).

diligent, *adj.* kinben (na) 勤勉 (な).

dilute, *vb.* 1. usumeru 薄める (thin). 2. yowameru 弱める (weaken).

dim, 1. *adj.* usugurai 薄暗い (not bright); fumeiryō (na)

不明瞭 (な) (indistinct). 2. *vb.* usuguraku naru/suru 薄暗くなる/する (become/make dim).

dimension, *n.* 1. sunpō 寸法 (measurement). 2. ōkisa 大きさ (magnitude, size).

diminish, *vb.* 1. heru/herasu 減る/減らす (decrease/cause to decrease). 2. yowamaru/yowameru 弱まる/弱める (wane/cause to wane).

dimple, *n.* ekubo えくぼ.

dine, *vb.* shokuji o suru 食事をする; **dine out** gaishoku suru 外食する.

diner, *n.* 1. kyaku 客 (customer). 2. keishokudō 軽食堂 (restaurant). 3. shokudōsha 食堂車 (dining car).

dinner, *n.* 1. shokuji 食事 (meal); chūshoku 昼食 (lunch); yūshoku 夕食 (evening meal). 2. seisan 正餐 (formal dinner).

dinosaur, *n.* kyōryū 恐竜.

dip, 1. *n.* kudarizaka 下り坂 (slope). 2. *vb.* ireru 入れる; tsukeru 浸ける (plunge); sukuiageru すくい上げる (scoop); sagaru 下がる (slope down).

diploma, *n.* sotsugyō shōsho 卒業証書.

direct, 1. *adj.* massugu (na, no) 真っ直ぐ (な、の) (straight); chokusetsu (no) 直接 (の) (immediate, nothing in between); chokkō (no) 直行 (の) (transportation); sotchoku (na) 率直 (な) (straightforward). 2. *vb.* hōkō o oshieru 方向を教える (guide, tell the way to); kantoku suru 監督する (control, manage); shiji suru

指示する (command); mukeru 向ける (turn).

direction, *n.* 1. hōkō 方向 (course). 2. shiji 指示 (instruction[s]); adobaisu アドバイス (advice). 3. kantoku 監督 (movies). 4. enshutsu 演出 (theater). 5. **in all directions** shihō ni 四方に; **under the direction of** (... no) shiji no moto ni.

director, *n.* 1. kantoku 監督 (movies). 2. jūyaku 重役 (business). 3. kanrisha 管理者 (one who directs).

directory, *n.* jūshoroku 住所録 (addresses); meibo 名簿 (names); denwachō 電話帳 (telephone numbers).

dirt, *n.* 1. yogore 汚れ (filth). 2. tsuchi 土 (earth).

dirty, *adj.* 1. kitanai 汚ない (unclean, ignoble); **dirty trick[s]** kitanai teguchi. 2. hiwai (na) 卑猥 (な) (indecent).

disabled, *n.* shintai shōgaisha 身体障害者 (people).

disagree, *vb.* 1. iken ga awanai 意見が合わない (disagree with). 2. itchi shinai 一致しない (differ).

disappear, *vb.* 1. kieru 消える (go out of sight). 2. nakunaru なくなる (become lost).

disappointed, *adj.* **be disappointed with** ... ni gakkari suru ... にがっかりする.

disapprove, *vb.* 1. hinin suru 否認する; ... ni hantai suru ... に反対する. 2. hihan suru 批判する.

disarray, *n.* midare 乱れ (clothing); ranzatsu 乱雑 (room, house, etc.); **in**

disarray midarete.

disaster, *n.* sainan 災難 (great misfortune); daisaigai 大災害 (catastrophe, natural disaster).

disband, *vb.* kaisan suru 解散する.

disbelief, *n.* utagai 疑い.

discard, *vb.* suteru 捨てる (thing); misuteru 見捨てる (person).

discern, *vb.* 1. mitomeru 認める (notice). 2. shikibetsu suru 識別する (distinguish).

disciple, *n.* deshi 弟子.

discipline, 1. *n.* tanren 鍛練 (training in rules); kiritsu 規律 (subjection to rules); chōbatsu 懲罰 (punishment); senmonbun'ya 専門分野 (specialty). 2. *vb.* kunren suru 訓練する (train); bassuru 罰する (punish).

disclose, *vb.* akiraka ni suru 明らかにする (reveal); bakuro suru 暴露する (expose); shiraseru 知らせる (make known).

discolor, *vb.* henshoku suru 変色する.

discomfort, *n.* fukaikan 不快感 (uncomfortable sensation); fukai 不快 (lack of comfort).

disconnect, *vb.* 1. kirihanasu 切り放す (separate). 2. kiru 切る (cut off telephone, etc.). 3. tatsu 絶つ (cut off).

discontent, *n.* fuman 不満.

discontinue, *vb.* yameru 止める.

discord, *n.* 1. fuitchi 不一致 (disagreement); fuwa 不和 (strife). 2. fukyō waon 不協和音 (music).

discount, 1. *n.* waribiki 割引. 2. *vb.* waribiki suru 割引

する.

discourage, vb. 1. kujikesaseru 挫けさせる (deprive of will); rakutan saseru 落胆させる (dishearten). 2. kinjiru 禁じる (prohibit). 3. omoi todomaraseru 思いとどまらせる (dissuade).

discourse, n. 1. kōen 講演 (lecture). 2. giron 議論 (discussion).

discover, vb. hakken suru 発見する.

discredit, vb. 1. shin'yō o nakusu 信用を無くす (injure reputation of). 2. hitei suru 否定する (reject).

discreet, adj. 1. kenmei (na) 賢明 (な) (wise). 2. shiryobukai 思慮深い (careful).

discrepancy, n. 1. kuichigai 食い違い (difference). 2. mujun 矛盾 (inconsistency).

discrimination, n. sabetsu 差別.

discuss, vb. giron suru 議論する (debate); hanashiau 話し合う (talk about).

disease, n. byōki 病気.

disfavor, n. 1. fukō 不興 (displeasure). 2. ken'o 嫌悪 (dislike).

disfigure, vb. sokonau 損う (mar); minikuku suru 醜くする (make ugly).

disgrace, 1. n. haji 恥 (shame); fumeiyo 不名誉 (infamy). 2. vb. meiyo o kegasu 名誉を汚す (dishonor); haji o kakaseru 恥をかかせる (humiliate).

disguise, 1. n. hensō 変装 (costume); misekake 見せかけ (pretense); **in disguise** hensō shite. 2. vb. hensō suru 変装する (conceal by costume); kakusu 隠す

(hide).

dish, n. 1. sara 皿 (plate). 2. ryōri 料理 (particular food).

dishearten, vb. rakutan saseru 落胆させる.

dishonest, adj. fushōjiki (na) 不正直 (な).

dishonor, 1. n. fumeiyo 不名誉. 2. vb. meiyo o kegasu 名誉を汚す.

dishwasher, n. sara'araiki 皿洗い機 (machine); sara'arai 皿洗い (person).

disillusion, vb. genmetsu saseru 幻滅させる.

disinfect, vb. shōdoku suru 消毒する.

disintegrate, vb. bunkai suru 分解する.

disjointed, adj. bara-bara (na) ばらばら (な) (in pieces); shirimetsuretsu (na) 支離滅裂 (na) (disorganized).

dislike, 1. n. ken'o 嫌悪. 2. vb. kirau 嫌う.

dislodge, vb. oidasu 追い出す (chase out); dokeru どける (move out from original place).

dismay, 1. n. gyōten 仰天; shokku ショック (astonishment); rakutan 落胆 (discouragement). 2. vb. rakutan saseru 落胆させる (discourage).

dismiss, vb. 1. kaiko suru 解雇する (from employment). 2. kaisan saseru 解散させる (from meeting, class, etc.). 3. shirizokeru 退ける (reject).

dismount, vb. oriru 降りる.

disobedient, adj. hankō-teki (na) 反抗的 (な).

disobey, vb. shitagawanai 従わない (not obey); hankō suru 反抗する (rebel).

disorder, n. 1. byōki 病気

(illness or disease). 2. konran 混乱 (confusion); ranzatsu 乱雑 (untidiness). 3. sōdō 騒動 (riot).

disorganized, adj. mechakucha (na) 滅茶苦茶 (な) (chaotic); shirimetsuretsu (na) 支離滅裂 (な) (disjointed).

disown, vb. 1. kobamu 拒む (refuse). 2. kandō suru 勘当する (disinherit).

disparity, n. chigai 違い (difference).

dispel, vb. shizumeru 静める (allay); chirasu 散らす (cause to dissipate).

dispense, vb. 1. kubaru 配る (distribute). 2. jisshi suru 実施する (administer). 3. **dispense with** nashi de sumasu 無しで済ます (do without).

disperse, vb. chirabaru/chirasu 散らば／散らす (scatter/cause to scatter).

displace, vb. 1. ... ni tottekawaru ... に取って代わる (take the place of). 2. oidasu 追い出す (force out of place); **displaced person** nanmin 難民.

display, 1. n. tenji 展示 (at a show or exhibition); chinretsu 陳列 (store display); hyōgen 表現 (expression). 2. vb. tenji suru 展示する (exhibit); chinretsu suru 陳列する (lay out goods); miseru 見せる (show).

displease, vb. okoraseru 怒らせる; **be displeased with** ... ni okoru.

dispose, vb. 1. haichi suru 配置する (place in good order). 2. **dispose of** ... o shobun suru ... を処分する

(get rid of); ... o suteru ... を捨てる (discard).

disposition, n. 1. seishitsu 性質 (personality). 2. keikōsei 傾向性 (tendency).

disproportionate, adj. 1. ōsugiru 多過ぎる (too much); sukunasugiru 少な過ぎる (too little). 2. futsuriai (na, no) 不釣り合い (な、の) (unbalanced).

disprove, vb. hanshō suru 反証する.

dispute, 1. n. giron 議論 (argument); kōron 口論 (quarrel). 2. vb. giron suru 議論する (argue); iiarasou 言い争う (quarrel); gimonshi suru 疑問視する (doubt).

disqualify, vb. shikkaku saseru 失格させる; shikaku o toriageru 資格を取り上げる (make ineligible); **be disqualified** shikaku o nakusu (lose eligibility).

disregard, 1. n. mushi 無視 (neglect). 2. vb. mushi suru 無視する (ignore).

disrepair, n. **fall into disrepair** areru 荒れる.

disrespect, n. burei 無礼; shitsurei 失礼 (rudeness, insolence).

disrupt, vb. 1. samatageru 妨げる (interrupt, disturb). 2. konran saseru 混乱させる (cause disorder in).

dissatisfaction, n. fuman 不満.

dissect, vb. kaibō suru 解剖する.

disseminate, vb. hiromeru 広める (spread).

dissent, 1. n. hantai 反対 (objection). 2. vb. hantai suru 反対する (disagree).

dissertation, n. ronbun 論文 (treatise); hakushironbun

博士論文 (treatise for a doctoral degree).

disservice gai o oyobosu.

dissipate, vb. 1. chiru/chirasu 散る／散らす (scatter/cause to scatter). 2. muda ni suru 無駄にする (waste). 3. tsukaihatasu 使い果たす (use up).

dissolve, vb. 1. tokeru/tokasu 溶ける／溶かす (become/make liquid). 2. kaisan suru/saseru 解散する／させる (break up/cause to break up).

distance, n. 1. kyori 距離 (space between); hedatari 隔り (time in between; remoteness in any respect, as in a relationship). 2. tōsa 遠さ (remoteness); **in the distance** tōku de/ni 遠くで／に (far away). 3. yoso-yososhisa よそよそしさ (aloofness, unfriendliness); **keep one's distance** yoso-yososhiku suru よそよそしくする.

distant, adj. 1. tōi 遠い; haruka (na) 遥か（な）(remote). 2. yoso-yososhii よそよそしい (unfriendly).

distill, vb. jōryū suru 蒸留する.

distinct, adj. 1. meihaku (na) 明白（な）(clear). 2. kotonaru 異なる (different, separate).

distinctive, adj. dokutoku (no) 独特（の）(characteristic).

distinguish, vb. 1. kubetsu suru 区別する (identify as different). 2. wakaru 分かる (identify, perceive). 3. **distinguish oneself** meisei o eru 名声を得る (make oneself eminent).

distortion, n. 1. yugami 歪

み (twist). 2. waikyoku 歪曲 (falsification).

distract, vb. 1. ki o chiraseru 気を散らせる (divert attention of); **be distracted by** ... de ki ga chiru. 2. nayamaseru 悩ませる (worry).

distress, 1. n. kurushimi 苦しみ (agony, pain); nayami 悩み (anxiety, trouble); kiki 危機 (crisis); **be in distress** kiki ni ochi'itte. 2. vb. kurushimeru 苦しめる (afflict with agony or pain); nayamaseru 悩ませる (worry).

distribute, vb. 1. wakeru 分ける (divide in shares). 2. maku 撒く (spread out). 3. kubaru 配る (circulate, disperse).

district, n. chiku 地区; chi'iki 地域.

distrust, 1. n. fushin 不信. 2. vb. utagau 疑う.

disturb, vb. 1. jama suru 邪魔する (interrupt). 2. iradataseru 苛立たせる (irritate). 3. midasu 乱す (unsettle).

ditch, n. mizo 溝.

dive, 1. n. tobikomi 飛び込み (act of jumping into water, etc.); sensui 潜水 (submergence); kyūkōka 急降下 (sharp descent of airplane). 2. vb. tobikomu 飛び込む (jump into); moguru 潜る (plunge deeply); kyūkōka suru 急降下する (plunge through the air).

diverge, vb. 1. wakareru 別れる (separate, split). 2. soreru それる (deviate).

diversion, n. 1. ii kibarashi 良い気晴らし (amusing distraction, pastime); goraku 娯楽

娯楽 (amusement, entertainment). 2. ukairo 迂回路 (detour). 3. mondai kaihi 問題回避 (intentional digression).

divert, vb. 1. tanoshimaseru 楽しませる (entertain). 2. ukai saseru 迂回させる (road). 3. sorasu そらす (turn aside).

divide, vb. wakeru 分ける (apportion, share, separate into parts); wakareru 別れる (be separated into parts); **divide into two** futatsu ni wakeru.

divine, 1. adj. kami (no) 神 (の) (of God or a god); shinsei (na) 神聖 (な) (sacred); kōgōshii 神々しい (glorious). 2. vb. yogen suru 予言する (prophesy).

diving board, n. tobikomidai 飛び込み台.

division, n. 1. bunpai 分配 (distribution). 2. bunkatsu 分割 (separation); bunkatsuten 分割点 (point that separates). 3. bubun 部分 (section). 4. shibu 支部 (branch); bumon 部門 (department). 5. bunretsu 分裂 (disagreement). 6. warizan 割り算 (math).

divorce, 1. n. rikon 離婚. 2. vb. rikon suru 離婚する.

dizziness, n. memai めまい.

dizzy, adj. **feel dizzy** memai ga suru めまいがする.

do, vb. 1. suru する (perform, execute, behave). 2. oeru 終える (finish). 3. taru 足る (be enough). 4. au 合う (be suitable). 5. maniau 間に合う (suffice). 6. **do away with** ... ... o korosu ... を殺す (kill); haishi suru 廃止する (abolish); **do without** ...

nashi de sumasu ... なしで済ます; **have something to do with** ... to kankei ga aru ... と関係がある; **have nothing to do with** ... to nan no kankei mo nai.

docile, adj. sunao (na) 素直 (な).

dock, n. 1. hatoba 波止場 (wharf).

doctor, n. 1. isha 医者 (medical doctor). 2. hakushi 博士 (holder of highest degree).

doctorate, n. hakushigō 博士号.

doctrinaire, adj. kyōjōshugi (no) 教条主義 (の).

doctrine, n. 1. kyōgi 教義 (teachings). 2. shugi 主義 (principle).

document, 1. n. shorui 書類 (paper); kiroku 記録 (record). 2. vb. shōmei suru 証明する (prove); kiroku suru 記録する (record).

dodge, vb. 1. mi o kawasu 身をかわす (elude). 2. kaihi 回避する (avoid).

doe, n. mejika 雌鹿.

dog, n. inu 犬.

dogma, n. kyōgi 教義 (doctrine); shinjō 信条 (belief).

dogmatic, adj. dokudan-teki (na) 独断的 (な).

dole, vb. **dole out** wakeataeru 分け与える (distribute).

doll, n. ningyō 人形.

dollar, n. doru ドル.

dolphin, n. iruka いるか.

domain, n. 1. shihaichi 支配地 (land under the control of a ruler); shoyūchi 所有地 (private estate); ryōdo 領土 (territory). 2. senmonbun'ya 専門分野 (specialty).

dome, *n.* maruyane 丸屋根 (roof).

domestic, *adj.* 1. kokunai (no) 国内 (の) (of a country); **domestic flight** kokunaisen. 2. kokusan (no) 国産 (の) (produced locally); **domestic car** kokusansha. 3. katei (no) 家庭 (の) (of the home or family). 4. hitonare shiteiru 人慣れしている (domesticated, tame); kachiku (no) 家畜 (の) (of cattle).

dominate, *vb.* 1. shihai suru 支配する (control, rule). 2. sobietatsu そびえ立つ (tower above). 3. attō suru 圧倒する (overpower).

donate, *vb.* kifu suru 寄付する.

done, *adj.* 1. owatta 終わった (finished). 2. **be done for** oshimai de aru お仕舞いである; **be done in** kutakuta ni tsukarete iru くたくたに疲れている.

donkey, *n.* roba ろば.

doom, 1. *n.* fu'un 不運. 2. *vb.* **be doomed to do** ... suru sadame de aru ... する定めである.

door, *n.* to 戸.

doorway, *n.* iriguchi 入口.

dope, *n.* 1. mayaku 麻薬 (narcotic). 2. baka 馬鹿 (idiot).

dormant, *adj.* 1. nemutteiru 眠っている (asleep). 2. kyūshi shite-iru 休止している (temporarily inactive). 3. mukiryoku (na) 無気力 (な) (lethargic).

dormitory, *n.* ryō 寮.

dot, 1. *n.* ten 点; **on the dot** jikandōri 時間通り. 2. *vb.* ten o utsu 点を打つ (mark with dot or dots); ten-ten to

saseru 点々とさせる (stud with dots); **be dotted with** ... ga ten-ten to shiteiru ... が点々としている.

dotted line, *n.* tensen 点線.

double-cross, *vb.* uragiru 裏切る.

doubt, 1. *n.* gimon 疑問 (uncertainty); kenen 懸念 (apprehension); **without doubt** machigainaku 間違いなく. 2. *vb.* gimonshi suru 疑問視する (be uncertain); **doubt that** ... to omowanai ... と思わない (consider unlikely).

doubtful, *adj.* 1. ayafuya (na) あやふや (な) (uncertain). 2. utagawashii 疑わしい; shinjirarenai 信じられない (unlikely).

doubtlessly, *adv.* machigainaku 間違いなく (without doubt).

dough, *n.* neriko 練り粉.

douse, *vb.* 1. mizu o kakeru 水をかける (throw water over). 2. kesu 消す (extinguish).

dove, *n.* hato 鳩.

down, 1. *n.* umō 羽毛 (feather[s]). 2. *adv.* shita de/ni 下で/に (at, in/to a lower place); kami ni 紙に (on paper). 3. *prep.* (... no) shita de/ni (... の) 下で/に (in/to a descent).

downcast, *adj.* unadareteiru うなだれている.

downhearted, *adj.* gakkari shite-iru がっかりしている.

downhill, *adv.* kudatte 下って; shita ni 下に (in downward direction); **go downhill** akka suru 悪化する (deteriorate).

downright, *adj.* mattaku (no) 全く (の).

downstairs, *adv.* shita de/ni

下で/に.

downstream, *adv.* karyū de/ni 下流で/に.

downward, 1. *adj.* shita (no) 下 (の). 2. *adv.* shita de/ni 下で/に.

doze, *n.* inemuri 居眠り. 2. *vb.* inemuri suru 居眠りする.

dozen, *n.* dāsu ダース; jūni 十二; **one dozen** ichidāsu 一ダース.

drab, *adj.* tsumaranai つまらない (dull).

draft, 1. *n.* zuan 図案 (sketch); sōan 草案 (preliminary version); kawase 為替 (money order); sukimakaze すき間風 (current of air); tegata 手形 (commercial bill); chōhei 徴兵 (military). 2. *vb.* keikaku suru 計画する (plan); sōan o kaku 草案を書く (write a draft); chōhei suru 徴兵する (military).

draftsman, *n.* 1. ritsuansha 立案者 (planner). 2. seizuka 製図家 (person who draws a draft).

drag, 1. *n.* hikizuru koto 引きずること (act of dragging); jama 邪魔 (hindrance); taikutsu 退屈 (boredom); josō 女装 (female impersonation). 2. *vb.* hikizuru 引きずる (trail on ground, pull heavily); guzu-guzu suru ぐずぐずする (lag behind).

dragon, *n.* ryū 竜.

dragonfly, *n.* tonbo とんぼ.

drain, 1. *n.* haisui setsubi 排水設備 (drain pipe, ditch, etc.). 2. *vb.* haisui suru 排水する (draw off liquid); hirōkonbai suru 疲労困ぱいする (be exhausted); tsukaihatasu 使い果たす

(use up).

drama, *n.* geki 劇 (play).

dramatic, *adj.* geki-teki (na) 劇的 (な).

dramatist, *n.* geki sakka 劇作家.

dramatize, *vb.* gekika suru 劇化する.

drastic, *adj.* 1. kyokutan (na) 極端 (な) (extreme). 2. kageki (na) 過激 (な) (radical).

draw, 1. *n.* kujibiki くじ引き (lottery); hikiwake 引き分け (sports); yobimono 呼び物 (attraction). 2. *vb.* hiku 引く (pull, attract); hipparu 引っ張る (pull strongly); hikidasu 引き出す (take out); hikitsukeru 引きつける (attract); e o kaku 絵を描く; suketchi o suru スケッチをする (sketch); hikiwake ni naru 引き分けになる (sports); **draw up** sakusei suru 作成する (prepare).

drawer, *n.* hikidashi 引き出し.

drawing, *n.* e 絵 (picture); suketchi スケッチ (sketch).

dread, 1. *n.* kyōfu 恐怖. 2. *vb.* osoreru 恐れる.

dreadful, *adj.* 1. osoroshii 恐ろしい (horrifying). 2. hidoi ひどい (very bad).

dream, 1. *n.* yume 夢. 2. *vb.* yumemiru 夢見る; **dream of ...** o yumemiru.

drench, *vb.* **be drenched** zubunure ni naru ずぶ濡れになる.

dress, 1. *n.* wanpīsu ワンピース (woman's outer garment); fuku 服 (attire). 2. *vb.* fuku o kiru/kiseru 服を着る／着せる (clothe oneself/someone); seisō suru 正装する (dress oneself up); ...no fukusō o suru ...の 服装をする (be dressed in); teate o suru 手当てをする (wound).

dresser, n. kagamidansu 鏡だんす (chest of drawers with mirror).

dressing, n. 1. hōtai 包帯 (wound). 2. fuku o kiru koto 服を着ること (act of putting on clothing).

dressing table, n. keshōdai 化粧台.

drift, 1. n. keikō 傾向 (tendency); fukidamari 吹き溜まり (snow, sand, ash); imi 意味 (meaning). 2. vb. hyōryū suru 漂流する (be carried by currents); samayou 彷徨う (wander); fukidamari ni naru 吹き溜まりになる (pile up); **drift apart** hanarebanare ni naru 離れ離れになる.

drifter, n. nagaremono 流れ者.

drill, 1. n. kunren 訓練 (training); doriru ドリル (tool). 2. vb. kunren suru 訓練する (train); **drill a hole** doriru de ana o akeru ドリルで穴を開ける.

drink, 1. n. nomimono 飲み物 (liquid); sake 酒 (liquor). 2. vb. nomu 飲む (swallow); sake o nomu 酒を飲む (drink liquor).

drip, 1. n. shitatari 滴り (act of dripping); shitataru oto 滴る音 (sound of dripping). 2. vb. shitataru 滴る.

drive, 1. n. yaruki やる気 (motivation, enthusiasm); undō 運動 (campaign); shadō 車道 (roadway). 2. vb. unten suru 運転する (car); kuruma ni noseru 車に乗せる (give a ride); oiyaru 追いやる (chase away); ugokasu 動かす

(move); karitateru 駆り立てる (force to work); uchikomu 打ち込む (nail).

driver, n. untensha 運転者 (car); untenshu 運転手 (bus, taxi, etc.); **driver's license** untenmenkyo 運転免許.

driveway, n. kojin no shadō 個人の車道.

drone, 1. n. unaru oto 唸る音 (sound). 2. vb. bun-bun unaru ぶんぶん唸る (make humming sound); en-en to shaberu えんえんとしゃべる (babble).

drool, vb. yodare o tarasu 涎を垂らす (salivate).

droop, vb. 1. shioreru しおれる (wilt, wither); tareru 垂れる (sag, hang down). 2. ikishōchin suru 意気消沈する (lose spirit).

drop, 1. n. shizuku しずく (droplet); shōryō 少量 (small quantity); rakka 落下 (fall). 2. vb. ochiru/otosu 落ちる／落とす (fall/let fall); sagaru/sageru 下がる／下げる (decrease/cause to decrease in price, etc.); yameru 止める (cease); otosu/nukasu 落とす／抜かす (leave out); **drop in** ... ni tachiyoru ... に立ち寄る; **drop off** orosu 降ろす (someone from vehicle); **drop out** yameru 止める (leave).

dropper, n. supoito スポイト.

drown, vb. 1. oboreshinu 溺れ死ぬ (death); oboreru 溺れる (be drowned). 2. oboresaseru 溺れさせる (drown someone). 3. **drown out** attō suru 圧倒する (overpower).

drowsy, adj. nemui 眠い (sleepy).

drug, *n.* 1. kusuri 薬 (medicine). 2. mayaku 麻薬 (narcotic).

druggist, *n.* yakuzaishi 薬剤師.

drugstore, *n.* yakkyoku 薬局 (pharmacy).

drum, *n.* taiko 太鼓.

drunk, 1. *n.* yopparai 酔払い. 2. *adj.* yopparatteiru 酔っ払っている; **get drunk** yopparau 酔払う.

dry, 1. *adj.* kawaiteiru 乾いている (not wet); ame ga furanai 雨が降らない (rainless); nodo ga kawaku 喉が乾く (thirsty); karakuchi (no) 辛口 (の) (not sweet); taikutsu (na) 退屈 (な) (boring). 2. *vb.* kawaku/kawakasu 乾く／乾かす (become/make dry); fuku 拭く (wipe dry).

dryer, *n.* kansōki 乾燥機 (for clothes). **dryness,** *n.* kansō 乾燥.

dual, *adj.* nijū (no) 二重 (の).

dub, *vb.* 1. fukikaeru 吹き替える (film). 2. adana o tsukeru あだ名をつける (give nickname).

dubious, *adj.* 1. mayotteiru 迷っている (uncertain). 2. ayashii 怪しい (doubtful).

duck, 1. *n.* ahiru あひる (domestic duck); kamo 鴨 (wild duck). 2. *vb.* moguru 潜る (plunge under water); mi o kagameru 身をかがめる (stoop, bend); kaihi suru 回避する (avoid).

due, *adj.* 1. shiharau beki (no) 支払うべき (の) (payable). 2. tekitō (na) 適当 (な) (suitable); seitō (na) 正当 (な) (just). 3. yotei (no) 予定 (の) (scheduled). 4. **due to** ... ga gen'in de ...

ga gen'in de (caused by); ... no okage de ... のおかげで (owing to); **in due time** yagate やがて.

dues, *n.* kaihi 会費 (membership).

dull, 1. *adj.* kusundeiru くすんでいる (not bright in color); taikutsu (na) 退屈 (な) (tedious); nibui 鈍い (not sharp, blunt). 2. *vb.* nibuku naru/suru 鈍くなる／する (become/make blunt).

dumb, *adj.* 1. kuchi ga kikenai 口がきけない (unable to speak). 2. baka (na) 馬鹿 (な) (stupid).

dummy, *n.* 1. manekin'ningyō マネキン人形 (mannequin). 2. mokei 模型 (copy, model). 3. baka 馬鹿 (idiot).

dump, 1. *n.* gomisuteba ごみ捨場 (dumping site); gomitame ごみ溜め (dirty place). 2. *vb.* suteru 捨てる (discard).

dune, *n.* sakyū 砂丘.

dungeon, *n.* chikarō 地下牢.

dunk, *vb.* hitasu 浸す (immerse).

duplicate, 1. *n.* kopī コピー; fukusei 複製 (copy). 2. *vb.* fukusei o tsukuru 複製を作る (copy a key, etc.); kopī o suru コピーをする (copy using copy machine).

durable, *adj.* 1. nagamochi suru 長持ちする (long-wearing, sturdy). 2. nagatsuzuki suru 長続きする (long-lasting).

duration, *n.* aida 間; kikan 期間.

during, *prep.* (... no) aida ni (... の) 間に.

dusk, *n.* yūgure 夕暮れ.

dust, 1. *n.* hokori 埃 (fine

particles). 2. vb. hokori o toru 埃をとる (clean); maku 撒く (sprinkle).

Dutch, 1. n. orandajin オランダ人 (person); orandago オランダ語 (language). 2. adj. oranda (no) オランダ (の) (of Holland); orandajin (no) オランダ人 (の) (of the Dutch).

duty, n. 1. gimu 義務 (obligation); sekinin 責任 (responsibility); shigoto 仕事 (function); **on duty** shigotochū 仕事中; **off duty**

yasumi 休み. 2. zeikin 税金 (tax).

dwell, vb. 1. ... ni sumu ... に住む (live). 2. **dwell on** ... ni tsuite kangaeru ... について考える.

dwelling, n. jūkyo 住居.

dwindle, vb. yowamaru 弱まる (weaken); heru 減る (decrease).

dye, 1. n. senryō 染料. 2. vb. someru 染める.

dying, adj. shinikaketeiru 死にかけている.

dysentery, n. sekiri 赤痢.

E

each, 1. pron. sorezore それぞれ; **each other** otagai (o, ni) お互い(を、に). 2. adj. sorezore no それぞれの.

eager, adj. nesshin (na) 熱心 (な); **be eager to do ...** nesshin ni ... o shitagatteiru.

eagle, n. washi 鷲.

ear, n. 1. mimi 耳. 2. ho 穂 (of corn).

early, 1. adj. hayai 早い (early in time; premature); shoki (no) 初期 (の) (of an initial stage); wakai koro (no) 若い頃 (の) (of a person's youth). 2. adv. hayaku 早く.

earn, vb. eru 得る (acquire). 2. kasegu 稼ぐ (earn money).

earnest, adj. 1. nesshin (na) 熱心 (な) (zealous). 2. seijitsu (na) 誠実 (な) (sincere).

earth, n. 1. chikyū 地球 (planet). 2. tsuchi 土 (soil). 3. tochi 土地 (land); jimen 地面 (ground).

earthquake, n. jishin 地震.

earthworm, n. mimizu みみず.

ease, 1. n. anraku 安楽 (comfort); raku 楽 (coziness, relief); kantan 簡単 (absence of difficulty); **be at ease** ochitsuite-iru 落着いている; **be ill at ease** ochitsukanai 落ち着かない. 2. vb. yawarageru 和らげる (mitigate); raku ni suru 楽にする (make comfortable); **ease (someone's) mind** anshin saseru 安心させる.

east, n. higashi 東; **the East** tōyō 東洋 (the Orient).

eastern, adj. 1. higashi no 東の (of the east); higashi kara no 東からの (from the east). 2. tōbu (no) 東部 (の) (of the eastern part). 3. tōyō (no) 東洋 (の) (of the Orient); higashi yōroppa (no) 東ヨーロッパ (の) (of Eastern Europe).

easy, adj. 1. yasashii 易しい (not difficult). 2. raku (na) 楽 (な) (relieved, comfortable).

easygoing, adj. kiraku (na)

気楽 (な).

eat, vb. taberu 食べる.

eaves, n. noki 軒.

ebb, 1. n. hikishio 引き潮 (ebb tide); suitai 衰退 (decline). 2. vb. hiku 引く (flow away); otoroeru 衰え る (decline).

eccentric, adj. fūgawari (na) 風変わり (な).

echo, 1. n. kodama こだま; hibiki 響き. 2. vb. kodama suru こだまする; hibiku 響 く.

economy, n. 1. keizai 経済 (system). 2. ken'yaku 倹約 (thrifty management).

edge, n. 1. hashi 端; fuchi 縁 (border). 2. ha/yaiba 刃 (cutting edge).

edict, n. meirei 命令 (command); seirei 政令 (official order).

edit, vb. henshū suru 編集す る.

editorial, 1. n. shasetsu 社説 (of newspaper). 2. adj. henshūjō (no) 編集上 (の) (related to editing).

educate, vb. kyōiku suru 教 育する; oshieru 教える.

eel, n. unagi うなぎ (freshwater eel); anago 穴子 (marine eel).

effect, 1. n. kōka 効果 (result); kekka 結果 (outcome); jisshi 実施 (operation); in effect jisshitsu-teki ni 実質的に (virtually); yōsuru ni 要するに (essentially); take effect jisshi sareru. 2. vb. ... no kōka o motarasu ... の効果 をもたらす.

effective, adj. 1. kōka-teki (na) 効果的 (な) (producing results). 2. jisshi sareru 実 施される (operative).

efficient, adj. kōritsu-teki (na) 効率的 (な); nōritsu-teki (na) 能率的 (な).

effort, n. doryoku 努力; **make an effort** doryoku suru.

egg, 1. n. tamago 卵; **egg shell** tamago no kara; **egg white** shiromi 白身; **egg yolk** kimi 黄身; **fried egg** medamayaki 目玉焼; **lay eggs** tamago o umu. 2. vb. **egg on** susumeru 勧める.

eggplant, n. nasu(bi) なす (び).

egocentric, adj. jikochūshin-teki (na) 自己中 心的 (な).

egotism, n. 1. jiko chūshin shugi 自己中心主義 (self-centeredness). 2. unubore うぬぼれ (self-conceit).

eight, n. hachi 八; yattsu 八 つ.

eighteen, n. jūhachi 十八.

eighteenth, adj. jūhachibanme (no) 十八番 目 (の).

eighth, adj. hachibanme (no) 八番目 (の).

eight hundred, n. happyaku 八百.

eightieth, adj. hachijūbanme (no) 八十番 目 (の).

eighty, n. hachijū 八十.

either, 1. pron., adj. dochiraka (no) どちらか (の) (one or the other); sōhō (no) 双方 (の) (each of two). 2. adv. ... mo (mata) ... も (また). 3. conj. **either ... or** ... ka ... ka ... か... か.

eject, vb. hōridasu 放り出す.

elaborate, 1. adj. kotta 凝っ た (painstaking, ornate); tan'nen (na) 丹念 (な) (precise, meticulous). 2. vb. tema o kakeru 手間をかける

(take pains to do);
kuwashiku setsumei suru 詳しく説明する (expand on).

elastic, adj. shinshukusei (no) 伸縮性 (の); nobiru 伸びる.

elbow, 1. n. hiji 肘. **2.** vb. hiji de tsuku 肘で突く.

elder, 1. n. toshiue no hito 年上の人. **2.** adj. toshiue (no) 年上 (の).

elderly, adj. toshiyori (no) 年寄り (の).

election, n. senkyo 選挙.

electricity, n. denki 電気.

electrocute, vb. **be electrocuted** kandenshi suru 感電死する.

electronic, adj. denshi (no) 電子 (の).

electronics, n. denshi-kōgaku 電子工学.

elegant, adj. yūga (na) 優雅 (な).

element, n. **1.** yōso 要素 (component part). **2.** kiso 基礎 (rudiment). **3.** genso 元素 (chemical).

elementary, adj. **1.** shoho no shoteki 初歩の (rudimentary); **elementary school** shōgakkō 小学校. **2.** kihon-teki (na) 基本的 (な) (fundamental).

elephant, n. zō 象.

eleven, n. jūichi 十一.

eleventh, adj. jūichibanme (no) 十一番目 (の).

elicit, vb. hikidasu 引き出す (draw out).

eligible, adj. **1.** shikaku ga aru 資格がある; atehamaru 当てはまる (qualified). **2.** nozomashii 望ましい (desirable).

eliminate, vb. **1.** nozoku 除く (remove, omit). **2.** korosu 殺す (kill).

elongate, vb. nagaku suru 長くする.

elope, vb. kakeochi suru 駆け落ちする.

else, adj. hoka (no) 他 (の); **someone else** hoka no hito; **something else** hoka no mono; **anything else** hoka ni nanika; **no one else** hoka ni daremo ... nai; **nothing else** hoka ni nanimo ... nai. **2.** adv. **or else** sōdenakereba そうでなければ (if not).

elsewhere, adv. yoso ni よそに.

elude, vb. **1.** sakeru 避ける (evade); ... kara nigeru ...から逃げる (escape from ...). **2.** wakaranai わからない (be incomprehen-sible); **elude one's memory** omoidasenai 思い出せない.

emaciated, adj. yaseotoroete iru やせ衰えている.

emanate, vb. (... kara) hassuru (...から) 発する; (... kara) detekuru (...から) 出て来る.

emancipate, vb. kaihō suru 解放する.

embankment, n. teibō 堤防; tsutsumi 堤.

embargo, n. **1.** teishi meirei 停止命令 (ban). **2.** seigen 制限 (restriction). **3.** kinshi 禁止 (prohibition).

embark, vb. **1.** (... ni) noru (...に) 乗る (board a ship, etc.). **2. embark on** ... o hajimeru ...を始める.

embarrass, vb. **1.** haji'iraseru 恥じ入らせる (make ashamed); tomadowaseru 戸惑わせる (fluster). **2.** komaraseru 困らせる (disconcert, complicate). **3. be embarrassed** hazukashii 恥

ずかしい (feel ashamed); tomadou 戸惑う (feel flustered); komaru 困る (feel disconcerted or helpless).

embassy, n. taishikan 大使館 (building).

ember, n. moenokori 燃え残り.

embitter, vb. be embittered nigai omoi o suru 苦い思いをする.

emblem, n. shinboru シンボル; shirushi 微; shōchō 象徴.

embody, vb. 1. taigen suru 体現する (personify, exemplify). 2. arawasu 表わす (express).

embrace, 1. n. hōyō 包容 (hugging). 2. vb. daku 抱く (hug); ukeireru 受け入れる (accept); fukumu 含む (contain).

embroider, vb. shishū o suru 刺繍をする.

embroidery, n. shishū 刺繍.

emerge, vb. arawareru 現れる (appear); dete kuru 出て来る (come forth).

emergency, n. hijōjitai 非常事態; **emergency exit** hijōguchi.

eminent, adj. 1. nadakai 名高い (distinguished). 2. saidai (no) 最大 (の) (utmost). 3. kōi no 高位の (highly ranked).

emotion, n. kanjō 感情.

emotional, adj. 1. kanjō no 感情の (of the emotions). 2. kanjō-teki (na) 感情的 (な) (high strung, stirring).

emperor, n. 1. kōtei 皇帝. 2. ten'nō 天皇 (Japanese emperor).

emphasize, vb. kyōchō suru 強調する.

empire, n. teikoku 帝国.

employ, vb. yatou 雇う

(hire); tsukau 使う (use).

empower, vb. kengen o ataeru 権限を与える.

empress, n. kōgō 皇后.

empty, 1. adj. kara (no) 空 (の) (containing nothing); aiteiru 空いている (unoccupied); munashii 空しい (meaningless). 2. vb. kara ni suru 空にする (make empty); akeru 空ける (discharge contents); kara ni naru 空になる (become empty).

empty-headed, adj. baka (na, no) 馬鹿 (な、の).

enable, vb. (... o) kanō ni suru (...を) 可能にする; (... ga) dekiru yōni suru (...が) 出来るようにする.

enact, vb. hō(ritsu) ni sadameru 法(律) に定める (make into law).

enactment, n. hōritsu(ka) 法律(化) (law).

enamored, adj. daisuki 大好き.

enchant, vb. 1. miwaku suru 魅惑する (captivate). 2. mahō o kakeru 魔法をかける (bewitch).

enchantment, n. 1. miwaku 魅惑 (fascination). 2. mahō 魔法 (magic).

encircle, vb. kakomu 囲む.

enclose, vb. 1. kakomu 囲む. 2. dōfū suru 同封する (letter).

encounter, 1. n. deai 出会い (meeting). 2. vb. (... ni) deau (...に) 出会う (meet); (... to) tatakau (...と) 戦う (combat).

encourage, vb. 1. hagemasu 励ます (inspire, cheer up). 2. susumeru 勧める (promote, stimulate).

encyclopedia, n. hyakkajiten 百科辞典.

end, 1. *n.* owari 終り (close, conclusion); hashi 端; saki 先 (extremity); mokuteki 目 的 (purpose); kekka 結果 (result); **in the end** tsui ni 遂に (finally); **come to an end** owaru 終わる; **on end** tsuzukete 続けて. 2. *vb.* owaru 終わる; **end up (in)** ... ni itaru ...に至る.

endanger, *vb.* kiken ni sarasu 危険にさらす.

endless, *adj.* mugen (no) 無限 (の); saigen ga nai 際限が無い.

endorse, *vb.* 1. shiji suru 支持する (support). 2. shomei suru 署名する (authorize).

endure, *vb.* 1. taeru 耐える; shinbō suru 辛抱する (tolerate). 2. motsu もつ (last).

enemy, *n.* teki 敵.

energy, *n.* enerugī エネルギー; seiryoku 精力.

enfold, *vb.* tsutsumu 包む.

engagement, *n.* 1. yoyaku 予約 (appointment). 2. kon'yaku 婚約 (betrothal). 3. shigoto 仕事 (employment).

engine, *n.* 1. mōtā モーター (machine). 2. kikansha 機関車 (locomotive).

engineering, *n.* kōgaku 工学.

England, *n.* igirisu イギリス.

English, 1. *n.* igirisujin イギリス人(person); eigo 英語 (language). 2. *adj.* igirisu (no) イギリス (の) (of England); igirisujin (no) イギリス人(の) (of the English).

engrave, *vb.* horu 掘る (cut into something).

engross, *vb.* **be engrossed in** ... ni bottō shiteiru ...に没頭している.

enhance, *vb.* takameru 高める.

enjoy, *vb.* tanoshimu 楽しむ; **enjoy dinner** bangohan o tanoshimu; **enjoy oneself** tanoshimu.

enjoyment, *n.* yorokobi 喜び.

enlarge, *vb.* kakudai suru 拡大する.

enlist, *vb.* nyūtai suru 入隊する (in army, etc.).

enormous, *adj.* kyodai (na) 巨大 (な); bōdai (na) 膨大 (な).

enough, *adj., adv.* jūbun (na, ni) 十分 (な、に).

enrage, *vb.* okoraseru 怒らせる.

enrich, *vb.* 1. yutaka ni suru 豊かにする (make rich). 2. jūjitsu saseru 充実させる (add greater value); yoku suru 良くする (improve).

enroll, *vb.* 1. tōroku suru 登録する (register). 2. nyūgaku suru 入学する (enroll in school).

enslave, *vb.* dorei ni suru 奴隷にする.

entangle, *vb.* **be entangled in** ... ni karamaru ...に絡まる.

enter, *vb.* 1. hairu 入る (come or go in, be admitted into). 2. ireru 入れる (put into). 3. hajimeru 始める (begin). 4. kinyū suru 記入する (record). 5. shutsujō suru 出場する (enter a competition).

enterprise, *n.* 1. jigyō 事業 (project). 2. kigyō 企業 (business firm). 3. yaru ki やる気 (initiative).

entertain, *n.* 1. tanoshimaseru 楽しませる (amuse). 2. motenasu もてなす; kangei suru 歓迎する

(have as a guest). 3. idaku 抱く (have in mind).

entertainer, *n.* geinōjin 芸能人.

entice, *vb.* 1. hikitsukeru 引き付ける (attract). 2. yūwaku suru 誘惑する (seduce).

entire, *adj.* subete (no) 全て(の); zenbu (no) 全部 (の).

entitle, *vb.* 1. kenri o ataeru 権利を与える; **be entitled to do** ... suru kenri ga aru. 2. (... to) dai o tsukeru (... と) 題をつける (entitle a book, etc.).

entity, *n.* 1. sonzai 存在 (existence). 2. jittai 実態 (reality).

entrance, 1. *n.* nyūjō 入場 (act of entering); nyūgaku 入学 (entrance to school); iriguchi 入口 (doorway, etc.); nyūjōkyoka 入場許可 (permission to enter). 2. *vb.* miwaku suru 魅惑する (charm).

entreat, *vb.* kongan suru 懇願する.

entrepreneur, *n.* kigyōka 企業家.

entrust, *vb.* azukeru 預ける; yudaneru 委ねる (commit in trust).

entry, *n.* 1. nyūjō 入場 (act of entering a place). 2. kinyū 記入 (record). 3. sanka 参加 (participation); sankasha 参加者 (participant, competitor). 4. kōmoku 項目 (entry in dictionary, etc.).

enumerate, *vb.* rekkyo suru 列挙する.

envelop, *vb.* 1. tsutsumu 包む (wrap). 2. kakomu 囲む (surround).

envelope, *n.* fūtō 封筒.

envious, *adj.* urayamashii 羨ましい.

environment, *n.* kankyō 環境.

envy, 1. *n.* senbō 羨望; urayamashisa 羨ましさ. 2. *vb.* urayamu 羨む.

epidemic, *n.* densenbyō 伝染病.

epilepsy, *n.* tenkan てんかん.

episode, *n.* dekigoto 出来事 (incident).

epithet, *n.* 1. keiyōshi 形容詞 (adjective). 2. batō 罵倒 (abusive words).

epitome, *n.* kakkō no mihon 格好の見本 (typical specimen).

epoch, *n.* jidai 時代.

equal, 1. *n.* hittekisha 匹敵者 (person that is equal). *adj.* hitoshii 等しい; onaji 同じ (same, alike); byōdō 平等 (having the same right); jūbun dekiru 十分出来る (adequate in ability). 2. *vb.* ... ni hitoshii ...に等しい.

equation, *n.* 1. hōteishiki 方程式 (algebra). 2. hikaku 比較 (comparison).

equator, *n.* sekidō 赤道.

equilibrium, *n.* 1. baransu バランス; heikō 平衡 (balance). 2. ochitsuki 落ち着き (equanimity).

equip, *vb.* 1. sōbi suru 装備する (fit out). 2. sonaetsukeru 備え付ける (furnish). 3. **be equipped with** ... ga aru ...がある.

equitable, *adj.* kōhei (na) 公平 (な) (just and fair).

equivalent, 1. *n.* sōtō suru mono 相当するもの. 2. *adj.* (... ni) hitoshii (...に) 等しい (equal); (... ni) sōtō suru (...に) 相当する (corresponding).

era, n. jidai 時代.

erase, vb. kesu 消す.

eraser, n. kokubanfuki 黒板拭き (blackboard); keshigomu 消しゴム (rubber).

erect, 1. adj. tatte iru 立っている (upright). 2. vb. tateru 立てる (put upright); tateru 建てる (build).

erode, vb. fushoku suru 腐食する (of metal); shinshoku suru 侵食する (of land); surikireru 擦り切れる (wear away).

erotic, adj. sei-teki (na) 性的 (な); kōshoku (na) 好色 (な).

err, vb. machigau 間違う (be mistaken).

errand, n. yōji 用事; (o)tsukai (お)使い.

erroneous, adj. machigatta 間違った.

error, n. machigai 間違い.

erupt, vb. 1. funka suru 噴火する (volcano). 2. boppatsu suru 勃発する (incident).

escape, 1. n. tōbō 逃亡 (flight); genjitsu tōhi 現実逃避 (avoidance of reality); more 漏れ (leakage). 2. vb. nigeru 逃げる (get away); sakeru 避ける (avoid); moreru 漏れる (leak).

escort, 1. n. tsukisoi 付き添い (companion, attendant); goei 護衛 (guard). 2. vb. tsukisou 付き添う.

especially, adv. toku ni 特に.

espouse, vb. 1. saiyō suru 採用する (adopt). 2. shiji suru 支持する (advocate).

essay, n. 1. shōronbun 小論文 (short thesis); zuihitsu 随筆 (composition); kokoromi 試み (attempt). 2. vb. kokoromiru 試みる (attempt).

essence, n. 1. honshitsu 本質 (intrinsic nature). 2. shinzui 真髄 (gist).

essential, adj. 1. mottomo hitsuyō (na) 最も必要 (な) (most necessary). 2. honshitsu-teki (na) 本質的 (な) (central).

esteem, 1. n. sonkei 尊敬 (respect). 2. vb. sonkei suru 尊敬する (respect); ... to minasu ...と見なす (regard as ...).

estimate, 1. n. mitsumori 見積り (calculation); iken 意見; handan 判断 (opinion). 2. vb. mitsumoru 見積もる (calculate); handan suru 判断する (form an opinion).

etch, vb. horu 彫る.

eternal, adj. eien (no) 永遠 (の).

ethereal, adj. 1. konoyo naranu この世ならぬ (heavenly). 2. reimyō (na) 霊妙な (delicate).

ethic, n. 1. rinri 倫理. 2. **ethics** rinrigaku 倫理学 (philosophy).

etiquette, n. manā マナー; reigi 礼儀.

Europe, n. yōroppa ヨーロッパ.

evacuate, vb. 1. kara ni suru 空にする (vacate). 2. hinan saseru 避難させる (remove a person for safety).

evaluate, vb. hyōka suru 評価する.

evaporate, vb. jōhatsu suru 蒸発する.

eve, n. zen'ya 前夜 (evening before).

even, 1. adj. nameraka (na) 滑らか (な) (smooth); taira (na) 平ら (な) (level); ichiyō (na) 一様 (な) (unchanging); hitoshii 等しい; gokaku (no) 互角 (の)

(equal); gūsū no 偶数の (of a number); **break even** shūshi ga zero de aru 収支がゼロである; **get even** shikaeshi suru 仕返しする. 2. adv. ... sae mo ...さえも (unlikely or extreme case); sara ni さらに (still, yet); **even now** ima demo 今でも; **even so** sore demo それでも. 3. vb. **even up** hitoshiku suru.

evening, n. yūgata 夕方; ban 晩; **Good evening.** Konban wa. 今晩は.

event, n. 1. dekigoto 出来事 (something that happens). 2. kekka 結果 (result). 3. shiai 試合 (competition). 4. **in any event** tonikaku とにかく; **in the event of** ... no bāi niwa ...の場合には.

eventually, adv. saigo ni 最後に; kekkyoku 結局.

ever, adv. 1. itsuka いつか (at some time); itsumo いつも (always); moshimo もしも (at any time); mae ni 前に (at any time up to the present). 2. tsune ni 常に (always); man ga ichi 万が一 (by any chance). 3. **ever since** ... irai zutto ...以来ずっと; **ever so** ... taihen ... 大変; **than ever** mae yori 前より.

every, adj. 1. (dekiru kagiri) subete no (出来る限り) 全ての (all possible); 2. sorezore no それぞれの; mai- 毎; dono ... mo どの...も (each). 3. **every month** mai-tsuki; **every country** dono kuni mo; **every now and then** tokidoki 時々; **every other day** ichinichi oki ni 一日おきに.

everybody, everyone, pron. min'na 皆; subete no hito 全

ての人.

everyday, adj. 1. mainichi (no) 毎日 (の) (of every day). 2. fudan (no) 普段 (の) (of ordinary days).

everything, pron. subete (no koto/mono) 全て (のこと／もの).

everywhere, adv. itaru tokoro (de, ni) 至るところ (で、に); doko demo どこでも.

evidence, n. shōko 証拠.

evil, 1. n. aku 悪. 2. adj. warui 悪い (bad); ja'aku (na) 邪悪 (な) (wicked).

evolution, n. 1. hatten 発展 (development). 2. shinka 進化 (biological concept).

exact, 1. adj. seikaku 正確 (な) (accurate, precise). 2. vb. kyōyō suru 強要する (force).

exalt, vb. 1. shōshin saseru 昇進させる (elevate in rank). 2. tataeru 賛える (extol).

examination, n. 1. shiken 試験 (test); kensa 検査 (inspection, checking). 2. chōsa 調査 (investigation). 3. shinsatsu 診察 (medical).

example, n. rei 例; tatoe 例え; **for example** tatoeba 例えば.

excavation, n. hakkutsu 発掘.

exceed, vb. 1. koeru 越える (go beyond). 2. shinogu 凌ぐ (surpass).

excellent, adj. subarashii 素晴らしい; yūshū (na) 優秀 (な).

except, 1. vb. nozoku 除く (exclude). 2. prep. ... o nozoite ...を除いて.

exceptional, adj. 1. reigaiteki (na) 例外的 (な) (unusual). 2. kiwadatteiru

際立っている (outstanding).

excess, 1. *n.* chōka 超過; kajō 過剰 (surplus); ikisugi 行き過ぎ; yarisugi やり過ぎ (lack of moderation). 2. *adj.* chōka (no) 超過 (の) (superfluous).

exchange, 1. *n.* kōkan 交換 (reciprocal exchange); torikae 取り替え (act of replacing); ryōgae 両替 (currency exchange); torihikisho 取引所 (place for exchange); **exchange rate** ryōgaeritsu; kawase-rēto 為替レート; **in exchange for** ... to hikikae ni ...と引き替えに; **stock exchange** shōken-torihikisho 証券取引所; **telephone exchange** denwa-kōkankyoku 電話交換局. 2. *vb.* kōkan suru 交換する (give and receive); torikaeru 取り替える (replace); ryōgae suru 両替えする (exchange currencies).

excite, *vb.* 1. kōfun saseru 興奮させる (stir up the emotions), **be excited** kōfun shiteiru. 2. shigeki suru 刺激する (stimulate).

exclaim, *vb.* sakebu 叫ぶ.

exclusive, *adj.* 1. sen'yō (no) 専用 (の) (for private use). 2. yui'itsu (no) 唯一 (の) (sole). 3. haita-teki (na) 排他的 (な) (not admitting others). 4. kōkyū (na) 高級 (な) (expensive and chic). 4. **exclusive of** ... o nozoite ...を除いて.

excruciating, *adj.* kakoku (na) 苛酷 (な).

excuse, 1. *n.* benkai 弁解 (reasons for being excused). 2. *vb.* yurusu 許す (pardon); ayamaru 謝る (apologize for); benkai suru 弁解する

(justify); menjo suru 免除する (release from obligation). **Excuse me.** Sumimasen. すみません.

execute, *vb.* 1. jisshi suru 実施する (carry out, make effective). 2. okonau 行う (do, perform). 3. shokei suru 処刑する (put to death).

exempt, 1. *adj.* menjo sareta 免除された. 2. *vb.* menjo suru 免除する.

exercise, 1. *n.* undō 運動 (bodily exercise); kunren 訓練 (training); renshūmondai 練習問題 (set of practice questions); shiyō 使用 (putting to use). 2. *vb.* undō suru 運動する (do exercise); kunren suru 訓練する (train); tsukau 使う (use, activate).

exertion, *n.* doryoku 努力 (effort).

exhaust, 1. *n.* haiki-gasu 排気ガス (waste gases); haikikō 排気口 (pipe). 2. *vb.* tsukare saseru 疲れさせる (fatigue); tsukaihatasu 使い果たす (use up).

exhibit, 1. *n.* tenji 展示 (exhibition); tenjihin 展示品 (something exhibited). 2. *vb.* tenji suru 展示する (place on show); miseru 見せる (offer to view).

exhibition, *n.* 1. tenji 展示 (presenting to view). 2. tenrankai 展覧会 (public show).

exile, 1. *n.* ruzai 流罪 (expulsion); bōmei 亡命 (refuge abroad); bōmeisha 亡命者 (voluntary exile, refugee). 2. *vb.* ruzai ni suru 流罪にする (expel); **exile oneself** bōmei suru 亡命する.

exist, vb. 1. sonzai suru 存在する; aru/iru ある／いる (be). 2. ikite-iku 生きて行く (continue to live).

existentialism, n. jitsuzonshugi 実存主義.

exit, 1. n. deguchi 出口 (way out); taishutsu 退出 (departure). 2. vb. deru 出る.

exorbitant, adj. 1. takasugiru 高過ぎる (too expensive). 2. hōgai (na) 法外 (な) (outrageous).

expand, 1. hirogaru 広がる (grow larger, spread out); hirogeru 広げる (cause to grow large or spread out). 2. fueru 増える (increase in quantity); fuyasu 増やす (cause to increase). 3. hatten suru 発展する (develop); hatten saseru 発展させる (cause to develop).

expect, vb. 1. kitai suru 期待する (anticipate). 2. matsu 待つ (wait). 3. omou 思う (suppose). 4. shussan o matsu 出産を待つ (anticipate a baby); **be expecting** ninshinchū 妊娠中 (be pregnant).

expel, vb. tsuihō suru 追放する.

expend, vb. tsukaihatasu 使い果たす.

expense, n. 1. hiyō 費用 (cost). 2. shōhi 消費 (expenditure). 3. **at the expense of** ... o gisei ni shite ... を犠牲にして.

experience, 1. n. keiken 経験. 2. vb. keiken suru 経験する.

experiment, 1. n. jikken 実験. 2. vb. jikken suru 実験する; tamesu 試す.

experimental, adj. jikken-teki (na) 実験的 (な).

expert, 1. n. senmonka 専門家. 2. adj. senmonka (no) 専門家 (の) (of an expert); jukuren shita 熟練した (skillful).

expire, vb. owaru 終わる; kigen ga kireru 期限が切れる (come to an end).

explain, vb. setsumei suru 説明する.

explode, vb. bakuhatsu suru 爆発する (of an explosive or feeling).

explore, vb. 1. tanken suru 探検する (go on an expedition). 2. saguru 探る; shiraberu 調べる (investigate).

export, 1. n. yushutsu 輸出 (trade); yushutsuhin 輸出品 (things exported). 2. vb. yushutsu suru 輸出する.

express, 1. kyūkō(densha) 急行(電車) (train); sokutatsu 速達 (express mail). 2. noberu 述べる (put into words); arawasu 表わす; hyōgen suru 表現する (show); tsutaeru 伝える (communicate).

expulsion, n. tsuihō 追放.

extend, vb. 1. nobiru 伸びる (stretch); nobasu 伸ばす (cause to stretch). 2. hirogeru 広げる (stretch to limit). 3. sashinoberu 差し伸べる (offer).

extension, n. 1. enchō 延長 (act of extending). 2. tsuika 追加 (addition); zōchiku 増築 (additional construction). 3. naisen 内線 (telephone).

extent, n. 1. teido 程度 (degree of extension). 2. han'i 範囲 (range); hirosa 広さ (area); nagasa 長さ (length); ōkisa 大きさ (volume). 3. **to a certain**

extent aru teido made; **to the extent that** ... (suru) teido made.

exterior, 1. *n.* sotogawa 外側 (outside). 2. *adj.* sotogawa (no) 外側 (の) (of the outside).

external, *adj.* 1. soto (no) 外 (の); gaibu (no) 外部 (の) (of the outside). 2. gaiyō (no) 外用 (の) (for use on the outside of the body). 3. gaikoku (no) 外国 (の) (foreign).

extinction, *n.* 1. zetsumetsu 絶滅 (of a species). 2. shōmetsu 消滅 (dying out).

extinguisher, *n.* shōkaki 消火器.

extra, 1. *n.* yobun na mono 余分なもの (surplus); tokubetsu na mono 特別なもの (special thing); tsuikaryōkin 追加料金 (additional charge); ekisutora エキストラ (actor). 2. *adj.* yobun (na, no) 余分 (な、の) (spare, superfluous); tsuika ryōkin (no) 追加料金 (の) (added charge); tokubetsu (no) 特別 (の) (special, exceptional).

extract, 1. *n.* bassui 抜粋 (excerpt); ekisu エキス (extracted essence). 2. *vb.* nuku 抜く (draw out); hikidasu 引き出す (draw forth); eru 得る (obtain); bassui suru 抜粋する (copy out excerpts).

extraneous, *adj.* mukankei (na, no) 無関係 (な、の) (irrelevant).

extravagant, *adj.* 1. rōhi (no) 浪費 (の) (spending too much); zeitaku 贅沢 (costly). 2. hōgai (na) 法外 (な) (exorbitant, outrageous). 3. kabi (na) 華美 (な) (showy).

extricate, *vb.* kyūjo suru 救助する.

extrovert, *n.* gaikō-teki na hito 外向的な人.

exuberant, *adj.* 1. yorokobi ni michita 喜びに満ちた (enthusiastic). 2. sei'iku ga yutaka (na) 生育が豊か (な) (growing profusely).

exult, *vb.* yorokobu 喜ぶ.

eye, *n.* me 眼.

eyebrow, *n.* mayuge 眉毛.

eyeglasses, *n.* megane 眼鏡.

eyelash, *n.* matsuge 睫毛.

eyelid, *n.* mabuta 瞼.

eyesight, *n.* shiryoku 視力.

eyewitness, *n.* mokugekisha 目撃者.

F

fabric, *n.* nuno 布 (cloth).

fabricate, *vb.* 1. tsukuru 作る (make, construct). 2. detchiageru でっちあげる (forge).

fabulous, *adj.* 1. subarashii 素晴らしい (wonderful). 2. shinjirarenai 信じられない (incredible).

face, 1. *n.* kao 顔 (of a head); kaotsuki 顔付き (facial expression); omote 表 (surface); mikake 見かけ (appearance); menboku 面目 (dignity); **face to face** men to mukatte 面と向かって; **in the face of** ... nimo kakawarazu ...にもかかわらず (despite); **lose/save face** menboku o ushinau/hodokosu; **make faces** shikameru しかめる. 2. *vb.*

(... ni) men suru (...に) 面する (look toward); chokumen suru 直面する (confront); **face up to** ... ni tachimukau ...に立ち向かう。

facet, n. (soku)men (側)面.

facial, adj. kao (no) 顔 (の).

facilitate, vb. yōi ni suru 容易にする.

facility, n. 1. setsubi 設備 (in a building). 2. nōryoku 能力 (ability). 3. bengi 便宜 (convenience).

fact, n. 1. shinjitsu 真実 (truth). 2. jijitsu 事実 (real story); jissai 実際 (reality). 3. **in fact** hontō wa 本当は; jissai wa 実際は (really, actually).

factory, n. kōjō 工場.

fade, vb. 1. kieru 消える (disappear). 2. shioreru しおれる (wither). 3. aseru 焦る (discolor).

fail, 1. n. **without fail** kanarazu 必ず. 2. vb. shippai suru 失敗する (be unsuccessful); ochiru 落ちる (fail a test); otosu 落とす (fail a student); kinō shinai 機能しない (cease to function); yowaru 弱る (become weaker).

fair, 1. n. ichi 市 (market). 2. adj. kōsei (na) 公正 (な) (just); kōhei 公平 (unbiased); mā-mā (no) まあまあ (の) (so-so); irojiro (no) 色白 (の) (fair-skinned); kinpatsu (no) 金髪 (の) (blond); hare (no) 晴れ (の) (weather).

fairly, adv. 1. kanari かなり (rather). 2. kōhei ni 公平に (honestly, equally).

fairy, n. yōsei 妖精; **fairy tale** otogibanashi おとぎ話.

faith, n. 1. shinrai 信頼 (trust). 2. yakusoku 約束

(promise). 3. shinkō 信仰 (religious belief).

fake, 1. n. nisemono 贋物. 2. adj. nise (no) 贋 (の). 3. vb. detchiageru でっちあげる (counterfeit).

falcon, n. taka 鷹.

fall, 1. n. rakka 落下 (act of falling); kōka 降下 (decrease); taki 滝 (waterfall); aki 秋 (autumn); haiboku 敗北 (defeat). 2. vb. ochiru 落ちる (drop); taoreru 倒れる (fall down); sagaru 下がる (decline in degree); **fall back on** ... ni tayoru ...に頼る; **fall behind** okureru 遅れる; **fall due** kigen ga kuru 期限が来る; **fall flat** shippai suru 失敗する (fail); **fall for** damasareru 騙される (be deceived by); **fall ill** byōki ni naru 病気になる; **fall in love** koi o suru 恋をする; **fall off** heru 減る (decline).

false, adj. 1. machigatteiru 間違っている (incorrect); itsuwari (no) 偽り (の) (not truthful); nise (no) 偽せ (の) (spurious); **false teeth** ireba 入れ歯. 3. fujitsu (na) 不実 (な) (unfaithful).

falter, vb. 1. yoromeku よろめく (in walking). 2. motatsuku もたつく (in speaking).

fame, n. meisei 名声.

familiar, adj. 1. shitashii 親しい (intimate); yoku shitte iru よく知っている (well-known, versed in); **be familiar with** ... to shitashii (be intimate with); ... o yoku shitte iru ...をよく知っている (know well, be versed in). 2. (o)najimi (no) (お) 馴染み (の) (well-acquainted).

family, *n.* 1. kazoku 家族 (parent[s] and children). 2. shinseki 親戚 (relative[s]). 3. zoku 族; nakama 仲間 (group).

famine, *n.* kikin 飢饉.

famous, *adj.* yūmei (na) 有名 (な).

fan, 1. *n.* ōgi 扇 (folding fan); senpūki 扇風機 (electric fan). 2. *vb.* aogu 扇ぐ (send air); aoru 煽る (instigate).

fanciful, *adj.* 1. kūsō yutaka (na) 空想豊か (な) (full of imagination). 2. sōzōjō (no) 想像上 (の) (imaginary).

fancy, 1. *n.* kūsō 空想 (imagination); kūsōryoku 空想力 (imaginative power); musō 夢想 (daydream). **take a fancy to** ... ga ki ni iru ...が気に入る. 2. *adj.* kazari no ōi 飾りの多い (decorative). 3. *vb.* kūsō suru 空想する (imagine); hoshigaru 欲しがる (crave).

fang, *n.* kiba 牙.

fantastic, *adj.* 1. higenjitsu-teki (na) 非現実的 (な) (unrealistic). 2. kikai (na) 奇怪 (な) (bizarre). 3. subarashii 素晴らしい (wonderful).

fantasy, *n.* 1. yume 夢 (dream). 2. sōzō 想像 (imagination).

far, 1. *adj.* tōi 遠い (remote). 2. *adv.* tōku ni 遠くに (at or to a distant place); haruka ni 遥かに (very much); **as far as I know** watashi ga shitte iru kagiri 私が知っている限り; **how far** dono kurai どの位 (to what extent); **so far** kore made no tokoro これまでのところ (until now).

fare, 1. *n.* ryōkin 料金 (fee);

tabemono 食べ物 (food). 2. *vb.* yatte ikku やって行く (get along).

Far East, *n.* kyokutō 極東.

farewell, 1. *n.* wakare 別れ (leavetaking); **bid farewell to** wakare o tsugeru. 2. *interj.* Sayonara. さよなら.

farm, 1. *n.* nōjō 農場. 2. *vb.* tagayasu 耕す (cultivate).

farming, *n.* nōgyō 農業.

fascinate, *vb.* miwaku suru 魅惑する.

fashion, 1. *n.* ryūkō 流行 (prevailing style); yarikata やり方 (manner); **in fashion** ryūkōchū (no). 2. *vb.* tsukuru 作る (make).

fast, 1. *n.* danjiki 断食 (abstinence from food). 2. *adj.* hayai 速い (rapid); shikkari shiteiru しっかりしている (firm); susundeiru 進んでいる (ahead of correct time). 3. *vb.* danjiki suru 断食する (abstain from food). 4. *adv.* hayaku 速く (rapidly); shikkari しっかり (tightly).

fasten, *vb.* tomeru 留める; shimeru 閉める (fix); tomaru 留まる; shimaru 閉まる (become fixed).

fastener, *n.* chakku チャック.

fat, 1. *n.* shibō 脂肪 (grease). 2. *adj.* futotteiru 太っている (plump).

fatal, *adj.* chimei-teki (na) 致命的 (な) (causing death or ruin).

fate, *n.* 1. shukumei 宿命 (destiny). 2. shi 死 (death); hametsu 破滅 (ruin).

fateful, *adj.* jūdai (na) 重大 (な) (important).

father, *n.* chichi 父; otōsan お父さん; papa パパ.

father-in-law, *n.* gifu 義父.

fathom, vb. wakaru わかる (understand).

fatigue, 1. n. hirō 疲労. 2. vb. tsukaresaseru 疲れさせる.

fatten, vb. futoraseru 太らせる.

faucet, n. jaguchi 蛇口.

fault, 1. n. kashitsu 過失 (mistake); kekkan 欠陥 (defect); **at fault** warui 悪い; **be one's fault** ... no sekinin de aru ...の責任である. 2. vb. ... no arasagashi o suru ...の荒捜しをする.

favor, 1. n. kōi 好意 (good will, high regard); onegai お願い (a favor to ask); shinsetsu 親切 (kind act); ekohiiki えこひいき (partiality); **ask a favor** onegai suru; **be in favor** kōi o motarete-iru; **Can you do me a favor?** Onegai ga arimasu; **in favor of** ... no tame ni ...の為に (to the advantage of); ... ni sansei ...に賛成 (in support of). 2. vb. konomu 好む (prefer); ekohiiki suru えこひいきする (treat with partiality).

favorite, adj. oki ni iri (no) お気に入り (の); suki (na) 好き (な).

fear, 1. n. kyōfu 恐怖; **in fear of** ... o osorete ...を恐れて. 2. vb. osoreru 恐れる (be afraid of); shinpai suru 心配する (worry).

fearful, adj. osoroshii 恐ろしい (afraid, frightening).

feasible, adj. kanō (na) 可能 (な).

feast, 1. n. gochisō 御馳走 (meal); enkai 宴会 (party); saijitsu 祭日 (holiday). 2. vb. gochisō o taberu 御馳走を食べる (eat); **feast on** ...

o tanoshimu ...を楽しむ (relish).

feather, n. hane 羽.

feature, n. tokuchō 特徴 (characteristic); medatsu bubun 目立つ部分 (noticeable part); chōhen-eiga 長編映画 (full-length movie); tokubetsukiji 特別記事 (feature article).

February, n. nigatsu 二月.

fed, adj. **fed up** unzari shita うんざりした.

federal, adj. 1. renpō (no) 連邦 (の) (of a union of states). 2. kuni (no) 国 (の) (of the U.S. government).

federation, n. renpō 連邦; renmei 連盟.

fee, n. 1. ryōkin 料金 (charge). 2. jugyōryō 授業料 (tuition).

feeble, adj. yowai 弱い.

feed, 1. n. esa 餌 (for an animal). 2. vb. tabesaseru 食べさせる (give food to); taberu 食べる (eat); ataeru 与える (supply, provide); **feed on** ... o tabete ikiru ...を食べて生きる.

feel, 1. n. kanshoku 感触 (touch); kanji 感じ (sensation). 2. vb. sawaru 触る (touch); kanjiru 感じる (experience, perceive); tesaguri suru 手探りする (search for by touching); omou 思う (think); **feel as if** marude ... no yō da to omou まるで...のようだと思う. **feel like doing** ... shitai ...したい (want to do).

feeling, n. 1. ishiki 意識 (awareness). 2. kanjō 感情; kimochi 気持ち (emotion). 3. kanji 感じ (impression). 4. shokkaku 触覚; kankaku 感覚 (capacity to perceive by touching).

feline, adj. 1. nekoka (no) 猫科 (の) (of the cat family). 2. neko no yō (na) 猫のよう (な) (resembling a cat).

fell, vb. uchitaosu 打ち倒す (knock down).

fellowship, n. 1. kai 会 (society). 2. shinkō 親交 (companionship). 3. shōgakukin 奨学金 (money); kenkyūin 研究員 (academic position).

felony, n. jūzai 重罪.

female, n. josei 女性; on'na 女 (human); mesu 雌 (animal, plant).

feminine, adj. 1. josei (no) 女性 (の) (of a woman). 2. joseirashii 女性らしい (womanly). 3. josei-teki (na) 女性的 (な) (effeminate).

fence, n. 1. saku 柵; kakoi 囲い (barrier). 2. vb. kakomu 囲む (surround).

ferment, n. 1. kōbo 酵母 (yeast). 2. sōran 騒乱 (agitation).

fern, n. shida しだ.

ferocious, adj. kyōaku (na) 凶悪 (な); mugoi 惨い.

fertile, adj. 1. tasan (na) 多産 (な) (productive). 2. hiyoku (na) 肥沃 (な) (soil). 3. kodomo ga umeru 子供が産める (capable of bearing young).

fertility, n. 1. hanshokuryoku 繁殖力 (ability to reproduce). 2. yutakasa 豊かさ (profuseness).

fertilize, vb. 1. hiryō o yaru 肥料をやる (feed with fertilizer). 2. jusei saseru 受精させる (impregnate).

fervent, adj. jōnetsu-teki (na) 情熱的 (な).

festival, n. 1. (o)matsuri (お)祭り; saiten 祭典 (program of festive activities, gaiety). 2. saijitsu 祭日 (time of celebration).

fetch, vb. 1. tsurete kuru 連れて来る (person); totte kuru 取って来る (thing). 2. ... ni ureru ...に売れる (be sold for ...).

fetus, n. taiji 胎児.

feud, n. arasoi 争い.

fever, n. 1. netsu 熱 (high temperature). 2. nekkyō 熱狂 (craze).

few, 1. n. **a few** ikutsu ka 幾つか (things); ikunin ka 幾人か (people); **quite a few** tasū 多数. 2. adj. sukunai 少ない (not enough); shōsū (no) 少数 (not many); **no fewer than** sukunakutemo.

fiancé, -cée, n. kon'yakusha 婚約者.

fib, n. uso 嘘.

fiber, n. sen'i 繊維 (threadlike piece).

fiction, n. 1. shōsetsu 小説 (literature). 2. detchiage ででっちあげ (fabrication).

fictional, adj. kakū (no) 架空 (の) (imaginary).

fidelity, n. chūsei 忠誠 (faithfulness).

fidget, vb. sowa-sowa suru そわそわする.

field, n. 1. kyōgijō 競技場 (sports). 2. nohara 野原 (grassland); hatake 畑 (farmland). 3. bun'ya 分野 (area of interest).

fierce, adj. 1. kyōretsu (na) 強烈 (na) (intense). 2. dōmō (na) 獰猛 (な) (ferocious).

fiery, adj. 1. hi no yō (na) 火のよう (な) (resembling fire). 2. hageshii 激しい (fervent).

fifteen, n. jūgo 十五.

fifteenth, *adj.* jūgobanme (no) 十五番目 (の).

fifth, *adj.* gobanme (no) 五番目 (の).

fifty, *n.* gojū 五十.

fifty-fifty, *adj.* gobu-gobu (no) 五分五分 (の).

fig, *n.* ichijiku いちじく.

fight, 1. *n.* kenka 喧嘩 (quarrel); tatakai 戦い (battle, confrontation, war); tōshi 闘志 (fighting spirit). 2. *vb.* (... to) kenka suru (...と) 喧嘩する (quarrel); (... to) tatakau (...と) 戦う (do battle).

figurative, *adj.* hiyu-teki (na) 比喩的 (な).

figure, 1. *n.* sūji 数字 (numerical symbol, amount); jinbutsu 人物 (person); katachi 形 (shape); zu 図 (illustration, diagram); **figure of speech** hiyu 比喩. 2. *vb.* keisan suru 計算する (compute); omou 思う (consider); **figure on** ... o ate ni suru ...を当てにする (count on); **figure out** wakaru わかる (understand); mitsukedasu 見つけ出す (find out).

file, 1. *n.* shorui 書類 (documents); yasuri やすり (tool); retsu 列 (row); **file cabinet** fairu-kabinetto ファイル・キャビネット. 2. *vb.* teishutsu suru 提出する (submit); yasuri o kakeru やすりをかける (grind with a file).

fill, *vb.* 1. michiru 満ちる (become full); mitasu 満たす (make full). 2. michiru 満ちる (occupy to capacity). 3. tsumeru 詰める (stuff, pack). 4. shimeru 占める (position). 5. **fill in** kakikomu 書き込む (write in); daiyaku o suru 代役を

する (substitute for someone).

filling, *n.* tsumemono 詰め物.

fin, *n.* hire ひれ (fish).

final, 1. *n.* kimatsushiken 期末試験 (final exam); kesshōsen 決勝戦 (decisive match). 2. *adj.* saigo 最後; saishū 最終 (last).

finalist, *n.* kesshō shutsujōsha 決勝出場者.

finally, *adv.* 1. tsui ni 遂に (at last). 2. saishū-teki ni 最終的に (conclusively).

finance, 1. *n.* zaisei 財政 (money matters); zaigen 財源 (funds). 2. *vb.* yūshi suru 融資する (supply with money).

find, 1. *n.* mekkemono めっけもの (discovery). 2. *vb.* mitsukeru 見つける (discover, come across); **find out** mitsukedasu 見つけ出す.

fine, 1. *n.* bakkin 罰金 (penalty). 2. *adj.* rippa (na) 立派 (な) (excellent); hosoi 細い (thin); sensai (na) 繊細 (な) (delicate); komakai 細かい (minute); hare (no) 晴れ (の) (weather); genki 元気 (healthy). 3. *vb.* bakkin o kasu 罰金を課す. 4. *adv.* yoku 良く (well); komakaku 細かく (thinly).

finger, *n.* yubi 指; **fingertip** yubisaki 指先; **keep one's fingers crossed** kōun o inoru 幸運を祈る (pray for good luck).

fingernail, *n.* tsume 爪.

fingerprint, *n.* shimon 指紋.

finish, 1. *n.* owari 終わり (end); shiage 仕上げ (surface coating or treatment). 2. *vb.* owaru 終わる (end); oeru 終える

(bring to an end); shiageru
仕上げる (give a desired
coating to); sumaseru 済ま
せる (finish eating,
studying, etc.).

fir, n. momi no ki もみの木.

fire, 1. n. hi 火 (flame,
burning); kaji 火事 (burning
of a building, etc.); netsui 熱
意 (ardor); **on fire** moete 燃
えて; **catch fire** hi ga tsuku;
set on fire hi o tsukeru. 2.
vb. ... ni au ...に合う (be
suitable for, be the right size
for); ... ni awaseru ...に合わ
せる (make suitable for);
tsukeru 付ける (equip).

fire alarm kasai keihōki 火
災警報器; **fire engine**
shōbōsha 消防車; **fire
escape** hijōguchi 非常口;
fire extinguisher shōkaki
消火器. 2. vb. takitsukeru 焚
き付ける (ignite); happō
suru 発砲する (shoot);
kaiko suru 解雇する
(dismiss).

fireplace, n. danro 暖炉.

firewood, n. maki 薪.

fireworks, n. hanabi 花火.

firm, 1. n. kaisha 会社
(company). 2. adj. katai 硬
い (hard); tsuyoi 強い
(strong); kotei shiteiru 固定
している (fixed,
unchanging); ketsui ga katai
決意が固い (resolute).

first, adj. 1. saisho (no) 最初
(の); hajime (no) 初め (の)
(earliest, initial, primary).
2. ichiban (no) 一番 (の)
(leading, best, earliest,
initial). 3. first floor ikkai
一階; **first of all** mazu まず;
at first hajime wa 初めは;
for the first time hajimete.

first aid, n. ōkyū teate 応急
手当て.

first-class, adj. ittō (no) 一等
(の).

fish, 1. n. sakana 魚. 2. vb.
tsuru 釣る.

fishing, n. tsuri 釣り.

fishy, adj. 1. sakana kusai 魚

臭い (having a fishy smell or
taste). 2. ayashii 怪しい
(dubious).

fist, n. kobushi 拳.

fit, 1. n. hossa 発作 (spasm,
paroxysm); bakuhatsu 爆発
(emotional explosion);
have a fit bakuhatsu suru
(explode). 2. adj. fusawashii
ふさわしい (suitable);
kenkō (na) 健康 (な)
(healthy). 3. vb. ... ni au ...
に合う (be suitable for, be
the right size for); ... ni
awaseru ...に合わせる
(make suitable for); tsukeru
付ける (equip).

fitful, adj. ochitsukanai 落
ち着かない (disturbed). 2.
hossa-teki (na) 発作的 (な)
(spasmodic).

fitting, adj. fusawashii ふさ
わしい.

five, n. go 五; itsutsu 五つ.

five hundred, n. gohyaku
五百.

fix, 1. n. kyūchi 窮地
(predicament). 2. vb. kotei
suru 固定する (fasten, make
steady); naosu 直す (repair,
correct); tsukuru 作る
(cook); kimeru 決める
(determine).

fixture, n. setsubi 設備.

fizzle out, vb. shirisubomi ni
owaru 尻すぼみに終わる.

flag, n. hata 旗.

flagrant, adj. me ni amaru
目に余る (brazen);
hajishirazu (no) 恥知らず
(の) (shameless).

flair, n. sainō 才能 (talent).

flame, 1. n. hono'o 炎
(blaze). 2. vb. moeru 燃える.

flammable, adj. moeyasui
燃え易い.

flank, 1. n. wakibara 脇腹
(of a body); yoko 横 (side).

2. *vb.* (... no) yoko ni aru (... の) 横にある (be at the side of).

flap, *vb.* habatakaseru 羽ばたかせる (wings); hirugaeru 翻る (flag).

flare, 1. *n.* yureru hono'o 揺れる炎 (swaying flame); shōmeidan 照明弾 (signal). 2. *vb.* yura-yura moeru ゆらゆら燃える (burn); **flare up** moeagaru 燃え上がる.

flash, 1. *n.* senkō 閃光 (lightning); kirameki きらめき (spark); furasshu フラッシュ (camera); isshun 一瞬 (instant); nyūsu-furasshu ニュースフラッシュ (news); **in a flash** tachimachi たちまち. 2. *vb.* isshun hikaru 一瞬光る (sparkle); hikaraseru 光らせる (make sparkle).

flashy, *adj.* hade (na) 派手 (な).

flat, 1. *n.* panku パンク (flat tire). 2. *adj.* taira (na) 平ら (な) (level); hiratai 平たい (not thick); panku shita パンクした (of a tire); tsumaranai つまらない (dull).

flatten, *vb.* taira ni suru 平らにする (make flat); taira ni naru 平らになる (become flat).

flatter, *n.* 1. oseji o iu お世辞を言う (praise insincerely); hetsurau へつらう (be subservient). 2. **be flattered** ureshigaru 嬉しがる; **flatter oneself** unuboreru うぬぼれる.

flaunt, *vb.* misebirakasu 見せびらかす.

flavor, *n.* 1. aji 味 (taste). 2. *vb.* aji o tsukeru 味をつける.

flawless, *adj.* mukizu (no)

無傷 (の); kanpeki (na) 完璧 (な).

flea, *n.* nomi 蚤.

fledgling, *n.* hinadori ひな鳥 (bird); shinmai 新米; kakedashi 駆け出し (person).

flee, *vb.* nigeru 逃げる (escape).

fleece, 1. *n.* yōmō 羊毛 (wool). 2. *vb.* damashitoru 騙し取る (swindle).

fleet, *n.* sentai 船隊 (ships); kantai 艦隊 (navy).

fleeting, *adj.* 1. mijikai 短い (not lasting). 2. hayaku sugiru 速く過ぎる (quick).

flesh, *n.* 1. niku 肉 (muscle and fat). 2. nikutai 肉体 (human body). 3. **in the flesh** jitsubutsu (o, ni, wa) 実物 (を、に、は) (in person).

flexible, *adj.* jūnan (na) 柔軟 (な) (elastic, adaptable).

flicker, *vb.* chira-chira hikaru/moeru ちらちら光る/燃える (glow/burn unsteadily).

flier, *n.* chirashi 散らし; bira ビラ (handbill).

flight, *n.* 1. hikō 飛行 (flying); hikō 飛行 (flying by airplane); **flight attendant** jōkyakugakari 乗客係. 2. tōsō 逃走 (fleeing). 3. kaidan 階段 (steps).

flimsy, *adj.* 1. moroi 脆い (feeble). 2. konkyo no hakujaku (na) 根拠の薄弱 (な) (unconvincing).

flinch, *vb.* tajirogu たじろぐ; shirigomi suru 尻込みする (shrink).

fling, *vb.* nagetsukeru 投げつける.

flip, *vb.* 1. hajiku 弾く (toss by snapping finger). 2. hikkurikaesu ひっくり返す

(turn over).

flippant, *adj.* keisotsu (na) 軽卒 (な).

flirt, *vb.* ichatsuku いちゃつく (trifle in love).

float, *vb.* ukabu 浮かぶ (bob, hover); ukaberu 浮かべる (cause to float).

flood, 1. *n.* kōzui 洪水; hanran 氾濫 (inundation); sattō 殺到 (overflow). 2. *vb.* hanran suru 氾濫する (inundate); sattō suru 殺到する (surge).

floor, 1. *n.* yuka 床 (surface); kai 階 (story). 2. *vb.* yuka o haru 床を張る (cover); uchinomesu 打ちのめす (knock down).

flop, 1. *n.* daishippai 大失敗 (failure). 2. *vb.* daishippai suru 大失敗する (fail).

floppy, *adj.* funya-funya shiteiru ふにゃふにゃしている.

flounder, 1. *n.* hirame 平目 (fish). 2. *vb.* mogaku もがく (struggle clumsily); magotsuku まごつく (falter in speaking).

flour, *n.* komugiko 小麦粉 (wheat flour).

flow, 1. *n.* nagare 流れ (stream); ryūshutsu 流出 (outpouring). 2. *vb.* nagareru 流れる (move in stream); nagarederu 流れ出る (pour out).

flower, 1. *n.* hana 花. 2. *vb.* hana ga saku 花が咲く.

flowery, *adj.* 1. hana ippai (no) 花一杯 (の) (full of flowers). 2. hanagara (no) 花柄 (の) (flower-patterned). 3. hanayaka (na) 華やか (な) (florid).

fluctuate, *vb.* hendō suru 変動する (change); jōge suru 上下する (shift up and

down).

fluffy, *adj.* fuwa-fuwa shite iru ふわふわしている.

fluid, 1. *n.* ekitai 液体 (liquid); kitai 気体 (gas). 2. *adj.* ekijō (no) 液状 (の) (liquid); kitai (no) 気体 (の) (gaseous); ryūdō-teki (na) 流動的 (な) (changeable).

flunk, *vb.* ochiru 落ちる (fail examination); otosu 落とす (cause to fail).

fluorescent, *adj.* keikōsei (no) 蛍光性 (の);

fluorescent light keikōtō 蛍光灯.

flurry, *n.* 1. niwakayuki にわか雪 (snow); toppū 突風 (wind). 2. arashi 嵐; dōyō 動揺 (sudden excitement, commotion, etc.).

flush, 1. *n.* kōchō 紅潮 (rosy glow). 2. *adj.* suisen(shiki no) 水洗(式の) (toilet); onaji takasa (no) 同じ高さ (の) (even with surrounding surface); yutaka (na) 豊か (な) (rich). 3. *vb.* akaku naru 赤くなる (become red); mizu de oshinagasu 水で押し流す (wash out with water).

flutter, 1. *n.* kōfun 興奮 (agitation). 2. *vb.* habataku 羽ばたく (wave in the air).

fly, 1. *n.* hae 蝿 (insect); chakku チャック (of pants). 2. *vb.* tobu 飛ぶ (move or travel through the air); sōjū suru 操縦する (operate an airplane).

foam, 1. *n.* awa 泡. 2. *vb.* awa o tateru 泡を立てる.

focus, 1. *n.* shōten 焦点 (focal point); chūshin 中心 (center); **in/out of focus** shōten ga atte/hazurete. 2. *vb.* (... ni) shōten o awaseru (...に) 焦点を合わせる.

foe, n. teki 敵.

fog, n. kiri 霧.

foggy, adj. kiri ga ōi 霧が多い.

foil, 1. n. haku 箔 (metallic sheet); hikitate-yaku/-mono 引き立て役／〜もの (supporting role/thing). 2. vb. habamu 阻む (frustrate).

foist, vb. oshitsukeru 押し付ける (impinge).

fold, 1. n. orime 折り目 (crease); hida ひだ (pleat); shiwa しわ (wrinkle); kakoi 囲い (for sheep). 2. vb. oru 折る (paper, handkerchief, etc.); tsutsumu 包む (wrap); kumu 組む (limbs); oru 折る (collapse).

foliage, n. ha 葉.

folk, 1. n. hitobito 人々 (people); kokumin 国民 (nation); minzoku 民族 (race). 2. adj. minkan (no) 民間 (の) (of people).

folklore, n. minkandensetsu 民間伝説.

follow, vb. 1. ... ni tsuite kuru/iku ...について来る／行く (come/go after). 2. tsugi ni kuru 次に来る (come next). 3. bikō suru 尾行する (chase). 4. ... ni shitagau ...に従う (conform, observe). 5. ... ni sotte iku ...に沿って行く (move along over or beside). 6. chūmoku suru 注目する (pay attention to). 7. wakaru わかる (understand). 8. **as follows** tsugi no tōri 次の通り; **follow up** tsuikyū suru 追求する (pursue).

following, 1. n. tsugi no koto 次の事 (what follows). 2. adj. tsugi (no) 次 (の).

fond, adj. 1. suki 好き (having affection); ai ni afureta 愛に溢れた (full of love); **be fond of** ... ga suki de aru. 2. dekiai (no) 溺愛 (の) (doting).

food, n. tabemono 食べ物.

fool, 1. n. baka 馬鹿; **make a fool of** ... o baka ni suru. 2. vb. damasu 騙す (deceive); jōdan o iu 冗談を言う (joke); **fool around** fuzakemawaru ふざけ回る.

foolish, adj. baka (na) 馬鹿 (な); oroka (na) 愚か (な).

foot, n. 1. ashi 足 (part of body); **on foot** aruite 歩いて. 2. fīto フィート (unit of length). 3. moto もと (lowest part); fumoto 麓 (mountain foot).

foothold, n. ashiba 足場.

footprint, n. ashiato 足跡.

footstep, n. ashioto 足音.

for, 1. prep. ... no tame ni ... の為に (with the purpose of, in the interest of, in favor of); ... no kawari ni ... の代わりに (in place of); ... no aida ...の間; -kan -間 (during); ... ni mukatte ...に向かって (toward); ... to shite ...として (as being). 2. conj. naze nara 何故なら (because). **for five hours** gojikan 五時間; **as for** ... ni tsuite wa ...については; **for all** ... nimo kakawarazu にみかかわらず (despite); **for good** eikyū ni 永久に (forever); **for once** ichido dake 一度だけ; **if it were not for** ... ga (i)nakereba ...が（い）なければ.

forage, vb. sagasu 捜す.

forbearance, n. 1. nintai 忍耐 (patience). 2. kandaisa 寛大さ (tolerance, mercy).

forbid, vb. kinjiru 禁じる.

force, 1. n. chikara 力 (power, strength,

influence); bōryoku 暴力 (violence); kenryoku 権力 (political power); guntai 軍隊 (military units); **by force** bōryoku de (using violence); **force of arms** buryoku 武力; **in force** ōzei de 大勢で (in large numbers). 2. vb. kyōsei suru 強制する (impose upon a person); muri ni ... saseru 無理に...させる (compel to do...); oshiakeru 押し開ける (break open by force).

ford, n. asase 浅瀬.

fore, n. zenmen 前面; **to the fore** zenmen ni.

foreboding, n. warui yokan 悪い予感.

forecast, 1. n. yohō 予報. 2. vb. yosoku suru 予測する.

forefather, n. senzo 先祖.

forefinger, n. hitosashi yubi 人差し指.

forehead, n. hitai 額.

foreign, adj. 1. gaikoku (no) 外国 (の) (of or related to a foreign country). 2. ishitsu (no) 異質 (の) (incompatible). 3. soto kara (no) 外から (の) (from outside). 4. **foreign affairs** gaikōmondai 外交問題; **foreign exchange** gaikokukawase.

foreigner, n. gaikokujin 外国人.

foremost, adj. ichiban (no) 一番 (の).

forensic, adj. hōtei (no) 法廷 (の); **forensic medicine** hōigaku 法医学.

foresee, vb. yosoku suru 予測する.

forest, n. mori 森.

foretell, vb. yogen suru 予言する.

forever, adv. 1. itsu made mo いつまでも; eien ni 永遠

に (eternally). 2. itsumo いつも (always).

foreword, n. maegaki 前書き.

forge, 1. n. ro 炉 (furnace, smithy). 2. vb. gizō suru 偽造する (imitate fraudulently); tsukuru 作る (make).

forgery, n. gizō 偽造 (act of counterfeiting); gizōhin 偽造品 (counterfeit).

forgetful, adj. wasureppoi 忘れっぽい.

forgive, vb. yurusu 許す.

fork, n. 1. fōku フォーク (for eating). 2. kumade 熊手 (for farming). 3. wakaremichi 別れ道 (in a road); mata 股 (of a tree).

forlorn, adj. kodoku (na, no) 孤独 (な、の) (solitary); sabishii 寂しい (lonely).

form, 1. n. katachi 形 (shape, sort); kata 型 (mold); yōshi 用紙 (document); hōshiki 方式 (standard practice). 2. vb. katachizukuru 形作る (shape); tsukuru 作る (build, make).

formality, n. 1. keishiki 形式 (ceremony). 2. keishiki-teki tetsuzuki 形式的手続き (formal procedure). 3. keishikisonchō 形式尊重 (observance of convention).

format, n. teisai 体裁 (in printed matter).

former, adj. mae (no) 前 (の); **the former** zensha 前者.

formerly, adv. mae ni/wa 前に／は.

formulate, vb. junjoyoku noberu 順序良く述べる (state systematically).

forsake, vb. suteru 捨てる (give up something);

misuteru 見捨てる
(abandon someone).

forth, adv. saki ni 先に
(forward); soto ni 外に
(out); ato ni 後に (onward);
and so forth ... nado ... な
ど; **go forth** susumu 進む;
back and forth ittari kitari
行ったり来たり.

forthright, adj. sotchoku
(na) 卒直 (な).

fortieth, adj. yonjūbanme
(no) 四十番目 (の).

fortnight, n. nishūkan 二週
間.

fortune, n. **good fortune**
kōun 幸運.

fortuneteller, n. uranaishi
占い師.

forty, n. yonjū 四十.

forward, 1. adj. mae (no) 前
(の) (toward the front); ato
(no) 後 (の) (future);
susunde iru 進んでいる
(advanced). 2. vb. kaisō
suru 回送する(forward a
letter). 3. adv. mae ni 前に
(toward the front); ato ni 後
に (toward the future).

fossil, n. kaseki 化石.

foster, 1. adj. **foster parent**
sato-oya 里親. 2. vb.
sodateru 育てる (promote
growth).

foul, 1. adj. kitanai 汚い
(dirty); kusai 臭い (bad
smelling); areru 荒れる
(stormy); akushitsu (na) 悪
質 (な) (bad); iya (na) 嫌
(な) (abominable). 2. vb.
yogosu 汚す (make impure);
yogoreru 汚れる (become
impure).

found, vb. setsuritsu suru 設
立する (establish).

foundation, n. 1. kiso 基礎
(base). 2. zaidan 団団; kikin
基金 (organization).

fountain, n. izumi 泉

(spring); funsui 噴水
(mechanical jet).

four, n. yon 四; yottsu 四つ;
on all fours yotsunbai de
四つん這いで (crawling).

four hundred, n. yonhyaku
四百.

fourteen, n. jūyon 十四.

fourteenth, adj.
jūyonbanme 十四番目.

fourth, adj. yonbanme 四番
目.

fowl, n. tori 鳥 (bird);
niwatori 鶏 (chicken).

fox, n. kitsune 狐.

foyer, n. genkan 玄関
(entrance); robī ロビー
(lobby).

fraction, n. 1. ichibubun 一
部分 (small part). 2. bunsū
分数 (math).

fracture, 1. n. kossetsu 骨折
(breaking of bone). 2. vb.
oreru/oru 折れる／折る
(break/cause to break bone,
etc.).

fragile, adj. 1. moroi 脆い;
kowareyasui 壊れ易い
(easily damaged). 2.
hiyowa (na) ひ弱 (な)
(weak).

fragment, n. danpen 断片
(of a story, etc.); hahen 破片
(of glass, etc.).

fragrance, n. kaori 香り.

frame, 1. n. gaku 額 (for a
painting, etc); waku 枠
(enclosing frame); taikaku
体格 (bodily build);
kokkaku 骨格 (skeleton);
kōzō 構造 (structure);
frame of mind shinjō 心情.
2. vb. gaku ni ireru 額に入れ
る (painting).

framework, n. honegumi 骨
組み.

France, n. furansu フランス.

frank, adj. sotchoku (na) 卒
直 (な) (candid).

frantic, adj. kōfun shiteiru 興奮している.

fraternal, adj. 1. kyōdai (no) 兄弟 (の) (of brothers). 2. kyōdai no yō (na) 兄弟のよう (な) (like brothers).

fraud, n. sagi 詐欺.

fray, 1. n. kenka 喧嘩 (fight). 2. vb. suriheru 磨り減る (wear out by rubbing).

freak, n. 1. kikei 奇形 (unnatural form). 2. kichigai 気違い (enthusiast). 3. henjin 変人 (eccentric person).

freckle, n. sobakasu そばかす.

free, 1. adj. jiyū (na, no) 自由 (な、の) (liberated, emancipated); hima (na) 暇 (な) (not busy); tada (no) 只 (の) (without charge); aiteiru 空いている (not occupied); **for free** tada de, **free from** ... o manugarete ...を免れて. 2. vb. kaihō suru 解放する (emancipate, make free).

freedom, n. jiyū 自由.

free will, n. jiyūishi 自由意志.

freeze, vb. 1. kōru/kōraseru 凍る/凍らせる (harden/cause to harden into ice). 2. kogoeru 凍える (feel extremely cold). 3. reitō suru 冷凍する (freeze food). 4. tachitsukusu 立ち尽くす; ugokanai 動かない (stand still). 5. tōketsu suru 凍結する (freeze prices, wages, etc.).

freight, n. 1. yusō 輸送 (conveyance of goods). 2. kamotsu 貨物 (thing conveyed). 3. yusōryō 輸送料 (charges).

freighter, n. kamotsusen 貨物船.

frequency, n. 1. shūhasū 周波数 (radio). 2. hindo 頻度 (rate of recurrence).

frequent, 1. adj. hinpan (na) 頻繁 (な). 2. vb. hinpan ni otozureru 頻繁に訪れる.

fresh, adj. 1. shinsen (na) 新鮮 (な) (air, food, flower, etc.). 2. mamizu (no) 真水 (の) (fresh-water). 3. atarashii 新しい (new). betsu (no) 別 (の) (another). 5. namaiki (na) 生意気 (な) (cheeky).

fret, vb. 1. yakimoki suru やきもきする (worry). 2. iratsuku 苛つく (irritate).

friction, n. masatsu 摩擦.

Friday, n. kin'yōbi 金曜日.

friend, n. tomodachi 友達; **make friends with** ... to tomodachi ni naru.

friendly, adj. 1. shinsetsu (na) 親切 (な) (kind, helpful). 2. hito natsukkoi 人なつっこい (fond of people); aisō ga ii 愛想がいい (affable, sociable). 3. yūkō-teki (na) 友好的 (な) (amicable); **friendly nation** yūkōkoku 友好国.

fright, n. kyōfu 恐怖; obie 怯え (fear); **in a fright** obiete 怯えて.

frigid, adj. 1. tsumetai 冷たい (cold, unfriendly). 2. fukanshō 不感症 (の) (lacking sexual appetite).

fringe, n. 1. fuchidori 縁取り (border). 2. hashikko 端っこ; katsumi 片隅 (farthest end); **fringe of society** shakai no katasumi.

frivolous, adj. 1. fuzake hanbun (no) ふざけ半分 (の) (not serious). 2. keihaku (na) 軽薄 (な) (flippant).

frog, *n.* kaeru 蛙.

frolic, 1. *n.* ukaresawagi 浮かれ騒ぎ. 2. *vb.* asobimawaru 遊び回る.

from, *prep.* 1. ...kara ...から (out of, starting at, given by); **from America** amerika kara; **from nine o'clock** kuji kara. 2. ...de ...で (because of); **die from ...** de shinu ...で死ぬ.

front, 1. *n.* mae 前; zenmen 前面 (foremost part); shōmen 正面 (of a building); hyōmen 表面 (foremost surface); misekake 見せかけ (outward appearance); zensen 前線 (military, weather); **in front** mae de/ni; **in front of ...** no mae de/ni. 2. *adj.* mae (no) 前 (の) (of, situated in, or at the front); shōmen (no) 正面 (の) (of a building).

frontier, *n.* 1. kokkyō 国境 (border of a country). 2. henkyō 辺境 (outer edge of civilization).

frost, *n.* shimo 霜.

froth, *n.* awa 泡.

frown, 1. *n.* shikamettsura しかめっ面. 2. *vb.* kao o shikameru 顔をしかめる.

fruit, *n.* 1. kudamono 果物 (food). 2. seika 成果 (result).

fruitful, *adj.* minori yutaka (na) 実り豊かな.

fruitless, *adj.* muda (na) 無駄 (な) (useless).

frustrate, *vb.* 1. habamu 阻む (thwart). 2. yokkyūfuman ni ochi'iraseru 欲求不満に陥らせる (cause frustration).

fry, *vb.* ageru 揚げる (deep-fry); itameru 炒める (stir-fry); yaku 焼く (fry lightly).

fuel, *n.* nenryō 燃料.

fulfill, *vb.* 1. mitasu 満たす (satisfy desire, etc.). 2. hatasu 果たす (carry out, achieve, finish, succeed).

full, *adj.* 1. ippai haitteiru 一杯入っている (filled completely); man'in (no) 満員 (の) (filled with people). 2. takusan (no) たくさん (の) (abundant). 3. zenbu (no) 全部 (の) (entire); kanzen (na) 完全 (な) (complete). 4. onaka ga ippai (no) お腹が一杯 (の) (having a full stomach). 5. **full of ...** de ippai.

fumble, *vb.* 1. tesaguri suru 手探りする (grope). 2. hema o suru へまをする (bungle, botch).

fume, *vb.* gekido suru 激怒する.

fun, *n.* 1. yukai na koto 愉快なこと; tanoshii koto 楽しいこと (enjoyment, playfulness). 2. **have fun** tanoshimu 楽しむ; **make fun of ...** o karakau ...をからかう; **in fun** jōdan de 冗談で.

function, 1. *n.* kinō 機能; hataraki 働き (fitting or assigned activity); gyōji 行事 (formal social gathering). 2. *vb.* kinō suru 機能する (perform a function); ugoku 動く (work, operate).

fund, *n.* kikin 基金 (supply of money).

fundamental, *adj.* kihon-teki (na) 基本的 (な).

funeral, *n.* sōshiki 葬式.

funnel, *n.* 1. jōgo じょうご (utensil). 2. entotsu 煙突 (smokestack).

funny, *adj.* 1. okashii おかしい (amusing). 2. hen (na) 変 (な) (strange).

fur, *n.* kegawa 毛皮 (skin,

garment).

furious, *adj.* 1. ikarikuru'u 怒り狂う (angry). 2. arekuru'u 荒れ狂う (violent).

furlough, *n.* 1. kyūka 休暇 (leave of absence). 2. ichijikaiko 一時解雇 (temporary layoff).

furnish, *vb.* kagu o sonaetsukeru 家具を備え付ける (fit out with furniture). 2. kyōkyū suru 供給する (supply).

furniture, *n.* kagu 家具.

furrow, *n.* 1. unema 畝間 (trench made by plow). 2. shiwa しわ (wrinkle).

furry, *adj.* 1. kegawa (no) 毛皮 (の) (of fur). 2. kegawa de ōwareteiru 毛皮で覆われている (covered with fur).

further, 1. *adj.* sore ijō (no) それ以上 (の) (more); hoka (no) 他 (の) (other). 2. *adv.* sara ni 更に; motto もっと (more); motto tōku made も

つと遠くまで (to a greater distance). 3. *vb.* sokushin suru 促進する (promote).

furthermore, *adv.* sore ni それに.

fury, *n.* gekido 激怒 (anger).

fuse, *n.* 1. dōkasen 導火線 (for a bomb). 2. *vb.* tokeru 溶ける (melt); tokasu 溶かす (cause to melt); tokeau 溶け合う (blend).

fuss, 1. *n.* torikoshigurō 取り越し苦労 (needless concern); ōsawagi 大騒ぎ (overreaction); fuhei 不平 (complaint); **make a fuss** ōsawagi o suru. 2. *vb.* sawagi tateru 騒ぎ立てる (overreact).

futile, *adj.* muda (na) 無駄 (な).

future, *n.* mirai 未来; shōrai 将来.

fuzzy, *adj.* 1. kebadatteiru 毛ば立っている (fluffy). 2. hakkiri shinai はっきりしない (vague).

gag, *n.* 1. sarugutsuwa 猿轡 (restraint). 2. jōdan 冗談 (joke).

gain, 1. *n.* mōke 儲け; rieki 利益 (profit); zōka 増加 (increase). 2. *vb.* eru 得る (obtain); fueru 増える (increase); mōkeru 儲ける (gain profit); kachieru 勝ち得る (win); oiageru 追い上げる (in a race); susumu 進む (of a watch); **gain weight** taijū ga fueru 体重が増える.

gait, *n.* ashidori 足取り.

galaxy, *n.* 1. ginga 銀河; **Galaxy** amanogawa 天の川 (Milky Way). 2.

kagayakashii ichidan 輝かしい一団 (brilliant group).

gall bladder, *n.* tan'nō 胆のう.

gallery, *n.* 1. garō 画廊 (for art exhibition); bijutsukan 美術館 (art museum). 2. tenjishitsu 展示室 (exhibition room). 3. rōka 廊下 (hallway).

gallows, *n.* kōshudai 絞首台.

galore, *adv.* tappuri たっぷり; takusan たくさん.

galvanize, *vb.* 1. aenmekki o suru 亜鉛めっきをする (coat with zinc). 2. denki o nagasu 電気を流す (conduct electric current). 3.

karitateru 駆り立てる (startle into action).

gamble, 1. *n.* kake 賭け. 2. *vb.* kakeru 賭ける.

game, *n.* 1. asobi 遊び (pastime). 2. shiai 試合; kyōgi 競技; gēmu ゲーム (match, contest). 3. emono 獲物 (hunted animal).

gang, *n.* ichimi 一味; bōryokudan 暴力団 (group of gangsters).

gangster, *n.* bōryokudan'in 暴力団員.

gap, *n.* 1. mizo 溝 (disparity). 2. ana 穴; sukima 隙間 (opening). 3. kūhaku 空白 (blank space).

gape, *vb.* 1. kuchi o akeru 口を開ける (open one's mouth). 2. pokan to shite mitsumeru ぽかんとして見つめる (stare with open mouth).

garage, *n.* shako 車庫.

garbage, *n.* gomi ゴミ; kuzu 屑.

garden, *n.* niwa 庭 (private); teien 庭園 (public); **botanical garden** shokubutsuen 植物園.

gargle, 1. *n.* ugai うがい. 2. *vb.* ugai o suru うがいをする.

garland, *n.* hanawa 花輪.

garlic, *n.* nin'niku にんにく.

garnish, 1. *n.* kazari 飾り (decoration); ryōri no soemono 料理の添え物 (food). 2. *vb.* kazaru 飾る (decorate).

gasp, 1. *n.* iki o nomu koto 息を飲む事 (intake of breath); aegi あえぎ (convulsive effort to breathe). 2. *vb.* iki o nomu 息を飲む (catch one's breath); aegu あえぐ (struggle for breath); aeide iu あえいで言う (say while gasping).

gastronomy, *n.* bishokuhō 美食法.

gate, *n.* mon 門.

gather, *vb.* 1. atsumeru 集める (bring together); atsumaru 集まる (get together). 2. suisoku suru 推測する (infer). 3. tori'ireru 取り入れる (harvest).

gathering, *n.* tsudoi 集い; atsumari 集まり.

gauge, 1. *n.* hakari 計り (measurement); keiryōki 計量器 (measuring instrument); hyōka 評価 (appraisal); kijun 基準 (criterion). 2. *vb.* hakaru 計る (measure); hyōka suru 評価する (appraise).

gaunt, *adj.* yasekokete iru やせこけている.

gauze, *n.* 1. sha 紗 (fabric). 2. gāze ガーゼ (medical).

gay, 1. *n.* homo ホモ; dōseiaisha 同性愛者 (homosexual). 2. *adj.* yōki (na) 陽気 (な); hade (na) 派手 (な) (bright, showy); homo (no) ホモ (の).

gaze, 1. *n.* gyōshi 凝視. 2. *vb.* mitsumeru 見つめる.

gear, *n.* 1. haguruma 歯車 (cogwheel). 2. dōgu 道具 (tools).

gem, *n.* hōseki 宝石.

gender, *n.* sei 性; **gender discrimination** seisabetsu.

gene, *n.* idenshi 遺伝子.

general, 1. *n.* rikugunshōkan 陸軍将官 (military). 2. *adj.* ippan no 一般の (usual); zentai-teki (na) 全体的 (な) (of entirety); daitai no 大体の (approximate).

generate, *vb.* umidasu 生み

出す (produce).

generation, n. 1. sedai 世代 (of people); **generation gap** sedaisa. 2. seisan 生産 (production); hatsuden 発電 (generation of electricity).

generator, n. hatsudenki 発電機 (electrical).

generous, adj. 1. kandai (na) 寛大 (な) (magnanimous); kimae ga ii 気前が良い (giving freely). 2. tappuri (no) たっぷり (の) (abundant).

genesis, n. hajimari 始まり; hassei 発生 (beginning, origin).

genius, n. tensai 天才.

genocide, n. minzoku-bokumetsu 民族撲滅.

gentle, adj. 1. yasashii 優しい (kindly). 2. odayaka (na) 穏やかな (mild, moderate). 3. yuruyaka (na) 緩やか (な) (gradual). 4. shizuka (na) 静か (な) (quiet).

gentleman, n. shinshi 紳士.

genuine, adj. 1. honmono (no) 本物 (の) (authentic, real). 2. kokoro no komotta 心の込もった (sincere).

geography, n. chirigaku 地理学.

geology, n. chishitsugaku 地質学.

geometry, n. kikagaku 幾何学.

germ, n. saikin 細菌; baikin ばい菌.

Germany, n. doitsu ドイツ.

germinate, vb. mebaeru 芽生える.

gesture, n. dōsa 動作; miburi 身振り.

get, vb. 1. eru 得る; te ni ireru 手に入れる (obtain). 2. uketoru 受け取る (receive). 3. ... ni naru ...になる (become). 4. ... te

morau ...てもらう; ... saseru ...させる (cause to do); **get hair cut** kami o kitte morau. 5. kasegu 稼ぐ (earn). 6. mottekuru 持って来る (fetch). 7. kikoeru 聞こえる (hear clearly). 8. wakaru わかる (understand). 9. ... ni kakaru ...にかかる (suffer from an illness). 10. **get around** ugokimawaru 動き回る (move around); **get along** saru 去る (leave); yatteiku やっていく (go on); **get away** nigeru 逃げる; **get off** (... o) oriru (... を) 降りる; **get on** ... ni noru ... に乗る; **get over** kaifuku suru 回復する; **get to** ... ni tsuku ...に着く (arrive); **get together** atsumaru 集まる (congregate, meet); atsumeru 集める (gather); **get up** okiru 起きる; **have got to do** ... shinakereba-naranai ...しなければならない.

get-together, n. atsumari 集まり.

ghastly, adj. 1. osoroshii 恐ろしい (dreadful). 2. obake no yō (na) お化けのよう (な) (spectral).

ghost, n. obake お化け; yūrei 幽霊.

giant, 1. n. kyojin 巨人. 2. adj. kyodai (na) 巨大 (な).

giddy, adj. me no kuramu (yō na) 目の眩む (ような) (dizzy).

gift, n. 1. okurimono 贈り物 (present). 2. sainō 才能 (talent).

gifted, adj. sainō yutaka (na) 才能豊か (な).

gigantic, adj. kyodai (na) 巨大 (な).

giggle, 1. *n.* kusu-kusu warai くすくす笑い. 2. *vb.* kusu-kusu warau くすくす笑う.

gills, *n.* era えら.

ginger, *n.* shōga 生姜.

giraffe, *n.* kirin きりん.

gird, *vb.* beruto o shimeru ベルトを締める (bind with a belt).

girl, *n.* 1. on'na no ko 女の子; shōjo 少女 (female child). 2. wakai josei 若い女性 (young woman). 3. musume 娘 (one's daughter).

girlfriend, *n.* kanojo 彼女.

give, *vb.* 1. ataeru 与える; ageru 上げる. 2. **give back** kaesu 返す (return); **give in** makeru 負ける (yield); **give off** hanatsu 放つ (emanate); **give out** kubaru 配る (distribute); happyō suru 発表する (make public); **give up** akirameru あきらめる (abandon hope); yameru 止める (desist from, stop); hikiwatasu 引き渡す (surrender).

glacier, *n.* hyōga 氷河.

glad, *adj.* 1. ureshii 嬉しい (happy). 2. **be glad to do** yorokonde... suru 喜んで...する.

glamour, *n.* miryoku 魅力 (fascination).

glance, 1. *n.* ichibetsu 一べつ. 2. *vb.* chotto miru; ちょっと見る ichibetsu suru 一べつする (look briefly).

gland, *n.* sen 腺; **endocrine gland** naibunpisen 内分泌腺.

glare, 1. *n.* giratsuku hikari ぎらつく光り (dazzling light); nirami にらみ (stare). 2. *vb.* giratsuku ぎらつく (shine); niramitsukeru にら

miru みつける (stare).

glasses, *n.* megane 眼鏡.

glaze, 1. *n.* uwagusuri うわ薬 (pottery). 2. *vb.* garasu o hameru ガラスをはめる (insert glass); uwagusuri o kakeru うわ薬をかける (coat pottery); tsuya o kakeru つやをかける (gloss).

gleam, 1. *n.* hikari 光. 2. *vb.* hikaru 光る.

glee, *n.* yorokobi 喜び.

glide, *vb.* suberu 滑る; nameraka ni ugoku 滑らかに動く.

glimmer, 1. *n.* kasuka na hikari 微かな光. 2. *vb.* kasuka ni hikaru 微かに光る.

glimpse, 1. *n.* ichibetsu 一べつ. 2. *vb.* chirari to mieru ちらりと見える (catch a glimpse of); chirari to miru ちらりと見る (look briefly).

glisten, *vb.* matataku またたく; kirameku きらめく.

glitter, 1. *n.* kagayaki 輝き. 2. *vb.* kagayaku 輝く.

globe, *n.* chikyū 地球.

gloom, *n.* 1. usugurasa 薄暗さ (darkness). 2. yū'utsu 憂うつ (depression); kanashimi 悲しみ (sadness).

glory, *n.* kagayakashisa 輝かしさ; eikō 栄光; homare 誉れ.

glossary, *n.* shiyōgo-ichiranhyō 使用語一覧表; yōgojiten 用語辞典.

glove, *n.* tebukuro 手袋.

glow, 1. *vb.* moeru 燃える (burn). 2. hikaru 光る (shine). 3. hoteru 火照る (feel hot).

glue, 1. *n.* setchakuzai 接着剤; nori 糊. 2. *vb.* setchaku suru 接着する; tsukeru 付ける.

glum, *adj.* fukigen (na) 不機嫌 (な) (sullen); fusagikondeiru 塞ぎ込んでいる (silently gloomy).

glutton, *n.* ōgui 大食い; taishokukan 大食漢.

gnat, *n.* buyo 蚋.

gnaw, *vb.* kajiru かじる.

go, *vb.* 1. iku 行く (move from one place to another). 2. ugoku 動く (function). 3. ... ni naru ...になる (become). 4. **be going to do** ... suru tsumori ...するつもり (intend to do); ... suru tokoro ...するところ (be about to do); **go around** hiromaru 広まる (be pervasive); **go after** motomeru 求める (try to win); **go ahead** hajimeru 始める (begin); **go away** saru 去る (leave); **go back** kaeru 帰る (return); **go by** sugiru 過ぎる (pass); **go down** sagaru 下がる (decrease); kudaru 下る (descend); shizumu 沈む (sink); **go on** aru ある (take place); tsuzukeru 続ける (continue); **go out** dekakeru 出掛ける (leave); kieru 消える (burn out); **go over** shiraberu 調べる (examine); kurikaesu 繰り返す (repeat); **go through** keiken suru 経験する (experience); tsūka suru 通過する (pass through); **go up** agaru 上がる (rise); noboru 上る (ascend).

goat, *n.* yagi 山羊.

God, god, *n.* kami 神.

goddess, *n.* megami 女神.

going, *n.* shuppatsu 出発 (departure).

gold, *n.* 1. kin 金; ōgon 黄金 (metal). 2. kin'iro 金色 (color).

goldfish, *n.* kingyo 金魚.

good, 1. *n.* eki 益 (benefit); zen 善 (moral excellence); **goods** shōhin 商品 (merchandise); shoyūhin 所有品 (possession[s]); **for good** eikyū ni 永久に. 2. *adj.* ii/yoi いい／良い; zenryō na 善良 (na) (morally excellent); jōshitsu (no) 上質 (の) (of good quality); jōzu (na) 上手 (な) (skillful); shinsetsu (na) 親切 (な) (kind); **a good deal** takusan たくさん (abundant); **no good** muda 無駄 (be useless).

good afternoon, *interj.* kon'nichi wa 今日は.

good-bye, *interj.* sayōnara さようなら; bai-bai バイバイ.

good evening, *interj.* konban wa 今晩は.

good-hearted, *adj.* shinsetsu (na) 親切 (な).

good-humored, *adj.* akarui 明るい.

good morning, *interj.* ohayō gozaimasu おはようございます.

good-natured, *adj.* seikaku ga ii 性格が良い.

good night, *interj.* oyasuminasai お休みなさい.

good-looking, *adj.* 1. kao ga ii 顔が良い; kakko ii かっこ良い. 2. hansamu (na) ハンサム (な) (man); kirei (na) きれい (な) (woman).

goodness, *n.* 1. zenryō 善良 (state of being good). 2. bitoku 美徳 (virtue). 3. yasashisa 優しさ (kindly feeling). 4. **Thank goodness!** Yare-yare. やれやれ.

goodwill, *n.* zen'i 善意.

goose, *n.* gachō 鵞鳥.

gorge, 1. *n.* kyōkoku 峡谷 (canyon). 2. *vb.* musaboriku 貪り食う (stuff with food).

gorgeous, *adj.* 1. gōka (na) 豪華 (な) (luxurious). 2. subarashii 素晴らしい (splendid). 3. kirei (na) き れい (な) (very beautiful).

gosh, *interj.* oya mā おやま あ.

gossip, 1. *n.* uwasa 噂; oshaberiya おしゃべり屋 (person). 2. *vb.* uwasabanashi o suru 噂話し をする.

gourd, *n.* hyōtan ひょうた ん.

government, *n.* seiji 政治 (system of rule). 2. seifu 政 府 (governing body).

governor, *n.* 1. shūchiji 州知 事 (in the U.S.). 2. chiji 知 事 (province ruler).

grab, *vb.* tsukamu つかむ; toraeru 捕える (seize).

grace, 1. *n.* yūgasa 優雅さ; jōhinsa 上品さ (elegance). 2. biten 美点 (attractive quality). 3. megumi 恵み (favor, mercy); **in someone's good graces** (... no) okiniiri de (...の) お気に 入りの.

gracious, *adj.* 1. shinsetsu (na) 親切 (な) (kind). 2. michitarita 満ち足りた (pleasant).

grade, 1. *n.* tōkyū 等級 (degree of quality, rank); dankai 段階 (step); gakunen 学年 (scholastic division); seiseki 成績 (rating in school). 2. *vb.* tōkyū ni wakeru 等級に分ける (categorize); seiseki o tsukeru 成績をつける (assign a grade).

gradual, *adj.* sukoshi zutsu

(no) 少しずつ (の).

graduate school, *n.* daigakuin 大学院.

graduation, *n.* sotsugyō 卒 業.

graft, 1. *n.* tsugiki 接ぎ木 (of plant); ishoku 移植 (surgical); oshoku 汚職 (political). 2. *vb.* tsugiki suru 接ぎ木する; ishoku suru 移植する; oshoku o okosu 汚職を起こす

grain, *n.* 1. kokumotsu 穀物 (seed). 2. tsubu 粒 (hard particle); **a grain of** hitotsubu (no). 3. mokume 木目 (wood grain). 4. seishitsu 性質 (one's nature).

grammar, *n.* bunpō 文法.

grand, *adj.* 1. sōdai (na) 壮 大 (な) (impressive in size); dō-dōtaru 堂々たる (stately); subarashii 素晴ら しい (splendid). 2. ōkii 大き い (large, major).

granddaughter, *n.* magomusume 孫娘.

grandfather, *n.* sofu 祖父; ojiisan おじいさん.

grandmother, *n.* sobo 祖母; obāsan おばあさん.

grandparents, *n.* sofubo 祖 父母.

grandson, *n.* magomusuko 孫息子.

grandstand, *n.* sutando ス タンド; kankyakuseki 観客 席.

granite, *n.* mikageishi 御影 石.

grant, 1. *n.* joseikin 助成金 (subsidy); shōgakukin 奨学 金 (scholarship fund). 2. *vb.* ataeru 与える (confer, give); mitomeru 認める (admit). **take for granted** atarimae to kangaeru 当たり前と考え る (assume without question); keishi suru 軽視する (treat indifferently).

granular, *adj.* tsubujō (no) 粒状 (の).

granulate, *vb.* tsubu ni suru 粒にする.

grape, *n.* budō 葡萄.

graph, *n.* zuhyō 図表.

graphic, *adj.* 1. zushi sareta 図示された (pertaining to graphs or diagrams). 2. nama-namashii 生々しい (vivid).

grapple, *vb.* **grapple with** ... ni torikumu ...に取り組む (try to overcome); ... to momiau ...揉み合う (wrestle with).

grasp, 1. *n.* haaku 把握 (hold); rikai 理解 (comprehension). 2. *vb.* haaku suru 把握する; rikai suru 理解する (understand); tsukamu つかむ (seize).

grass, *n.* 1. kusa 草. 2. shibafu 芝生 (lawn).

grasshopper, *n.* batta ばった.

grate, *vb.* 1. kan ni sawaru 癇に触る (irritate). 2. kishiraseru きしらせる (make harsh sound). 3. suru 擦る (grind into small pieces).

grateful, *adj.* kansha shiteiru 感謝している; arigatai 有難い.

grating, *n.* 1. kōshi 格子 (latticework). 2. *adj.* iratsukaseru 苛つかせる (irritating).

gratitude, *n.* kansha 感謝.

grave, 1. *n.* haka 墓 (for burial). 2. *adj.* omo-omoshii 重々しい (weighty, solemn); jūyō (na) 重要 (な) (critical).

gravity, *n.* 1. jūryoku 重力 (terrestrial force). 2. omo-omoshisa 重々しさ

(solemnity).

gray, 1. *adj.* haiiro (no) 灰色 (の). 2. *n.* haiiro 灰色 (color).

graze, *vb.* 1. kasuru 擦る (scrape). 2. kusa o taberu 草を食べる (feed on grass).

greasy, *adj.* aburakkoi 油っこい; beto-beto shita べとべとした.

great, *adj.* 1. ōkii 大きい (large). 2. idai (na) 偉大 (な) (distinguished); yūmei (na) 有名 (な) (famous). 3. jūyō (na) 重要 (な) (important).

Great Britain, *n.* igirisu イギリス.

great-grandchild, *n.* himago ひ孫.

great-grandfather, *n.* hisofu ひ祖父.

great-grandmother, *n.* hisobo ひ祖母.

greatly, *adv.* taihen 大変.

Greece, *n.* girisha ギリシャ.

greed, *n.* don'yoku 貪欲.

green, 1. *adj.* midori(iro no) 緑(色の). 2. *n.* midori (color).

greet, *vb.* 1. aisatsu suru 挨拶する (salute). 2. kangei suru 歓迎する (welcome).

greeting, *n.* 1. aisatsu 挨拶. 2. **greetings** kangei 歓迎.

grief, *n.* kanashimi 悲しみ.

grievance, *n.* fufuku no moto 不服の元 (cause for complaint).

grim, *adj.* 1. kibishii 厳しい (stern); ganko (na) 頑固 (na) (unyielding). 2. zotto saseru yō (na) ぞっとさせるよう (na) (ghastly). 3. zankoku (na) 残酷 (な) (cruel).

grimace, 1. *n.* shikamettsura しかめっ面. 2. *vb.* kao o shikameru 顔をしかめる.

grime, *n.* yogore 汚れ.

grin, 1. *n.* usuwarai 薄笑い.
2. *vb.* usuwarai o suru 薄笑いをする.

grind, *vb.* 1. hiku 挽く
(grind flour). 2. togu 研ぐ
(grind a knife). 3. (ha o)
kishiraseru (歯を) きしらせる (grind teeth).

grip, 1. *n.* tsukamu koto つかむこと (grasp); shihai 支配 (control); totte 取っ手 (handle). 2. *vb.* nigiru 握る; tsukamu つかむ (grasp).

gripe, 1. *n.* guchi 愚痴
(complaint). 2. *vb.* guchi o iu 愚痴を言う (complain).

grit, *n.* 1. jari 砂利 (gravel).
2. yūki 勇気 (courage).

groan, 1. *n.* umeki 呻き. 2.
vb. umeku 呻く.

grocer, *n.* shokuryōhinten
食料品店 (dealer).

grocery, *n.* 1. shokuryōhin
食料品 (goods). 2.
shokuryōhinten 食料品店
(store).

groin, *n.* mata 股.

groom, *n.* shinrō 新郎
(bridegroom).

groove, *n.* mizo 溝.

grope, *vb.* 1. tesaguri suru 手
探りする (feel about with
hands). 2. mosaku suru 模
索する (search blindly).

gross, 1. *n.* sōshūnyū 総収入
(total income). 2. *adj.* zentai
(no) 全体 (の) (whole);
hanahadashii はなはだしい
(extreme); gehin (na) 下品
(な) (indecent); soya (na) 粗
野 (な) (coarse); futoi 太い
(thick); **gross national
product** kokumin-sōseisan
国民総生産.

ground, *n.* 1. jimen 地面
(earth); tsuchi 土 (soil). 2.
gurando グランド
(playground). 3. **grounds**

konkyo 根拠 (reason).

group, 1. *n.* dantai 団体. 2.
vb. atsumeru 集める.

grove, *n.* hayashi 林.

grovel, *vb.* 1. hige suru 卑下
する (humble oneself). 2.
hirefusu ひれ伏す (prostrate
oneself).

grow, *vb.* 1. sodatsu 育つ
(increase in size); fueru 増え
る (increase in quantity);
sodateru 育てる (raise
plants, etc.). 2. haeru 生え
る (sprout). 3. ... ni naru ...
になる (develop).

growl, 1. *n.* unarigoe 唸り
声. 2. *vb.* unaru 唸る.

grownup, *n.* otona 大人;
seijin 成人.

grudge, 1. *n.* urami 恨み
(resentment); **bear a
grudge** uramu 恨む. 2. *vb.* iya-
iya ataeru いやいや与える
(give unwillingly).

gruff, *adj.* 1. bukkirabō (na)
ぶっきらぼう (な) (surly).
2. damigoe (no) だみ声 (の)
(hoarse).

grumble, *vb.* guchi o iu 愚痴
を言う.

grumpy, *adj.* buaiso (na) 無
愛想 (な); fukigen (na) 不機
嫌 (な).

grunt, *vb.* 1. bū-bū naku ぶ
ーぶー鳴く (a hog). 2.
guchi o iu 愚痴を言う
(grumble).

guarantee, 1. *n.* hoshō 保証
(security); hoshōsho 保証書
(written assurance). 2. *vb.*
hoshō suru 保証する.

guard, 1. *n.* ban'nin 番人
(person); kanshi 監視 (close
watch); bōgyo 防御
(safeguard). 2. *vb.* hogo
suru 保護する; mamoru 守
る (protect); miharu 見張る
(keep watch); yōjin suru 用
心する (take precautions).

guess, 1. *n.* suisoku 推測 (conjecture). 2. *vb.* suisoku suru 推測する (conjecture); iiateru 言い当てる (guess right); ... to omou ...と思う (think).

guidance, *n.* 1. jogen 助言; adobaisu アドバイス (advice). 2. an'nai 案内 (information).

guide, 1. *n.* an'nainin 案内人 (person); hyōji 表示 (mark, tab, sign); tebiki 手引き (instruction). 2. *vb.* an'nai suru 案内する (show, introduce); michibiku 導く (direct, lead).

guided missile, *n.* yūdōdan 誘導弾.

guild, *n.* kumiai 組合.

guilt, *n.* 1. tsumi 罪 (blame). 2. hanzai 犯罪 (criminal conduct). 3. tsumi no ishiki 罪の意識 (guilty conscience).

guilty, *adj.* 1. ushirometai 後ろめたい (feeling culpable). 2. yūzai (no) 有罪 (の) (criminal).

guinea pig, *n.* jikkendōbutsu 実験動物 (subject of experiment). 2. morumotto モルモット (animal).

guise, *n.* 1. mikake 見かけ (appearance). 2. misekake 見せかけ (assumed appearance).

gulf, *n.* wan 湾 (water).

gull, *n.* kamome かもめ.

gullible, *adj.* damasareyasui だまされ易い.

gulp, *vb.* nomu 飲む (swallow); **gulp down** nomikomu 飲み込む (gobble).

gum, *n.* 1. gomu ゴム (material for rubber). 2. gamu ガム (chewing gum). 3. haguki 歯ぐき (of teeth).

gun, *n.* teppō 鉄砲; kenjū 拳銃; pisutoru ピストル (handgun); raifuru ライフル (rifle).

gurgle, 1. *n.* mizu no oto 水の音 (sound of water). 2. *vb.* goku-goku oto o tateru ごくごく音を立てる (drink noisily).

gush, 1. *n.* hotobashiri ほとばしり (sudden flow). 2. *vb.* hotobashiru ほとばしる (flow out).

gut, *n.* 1. chō 腸 (intestine, bowel). 2. **guts** harawata 腸 (intestines, bowels); yūki 勇気 (courage).

gutter, *n.* 1. mizo 溝 (along road). 2. amadoi 雨樋 (along roof).

guy, *n.* otoko 男; yatsu 奴.

gym, *n.* tai'ikukan 体育館.

gymnastics, *n.* taisō 体操.

gynecology, *n.* fujinka 婦人科.

---

habit, *n.* 1. shūkan 習慣 (customary practice). 2. kuse 癖 (acquired behavior).

habitable, *adj.* sumeru 住める.

habitat, *n.* seisokuchi 生息地.

habitual, *adj.* 1. shūkan-teki (na) 習慣的 (な) (resulting from habit). 2. itsumo (no) いつも (の) (customary).

hag, *n.* baba ばば.

haggard, *adj.* yatsurete iru やつれている.

hail, 1. *n.* arare あられ; hyō ひょう (ice); kansei 歓声

(shout); aisatsu 挨拶 (salutation). 2. *vb.* arare/hyō ga furu あられ／ひょうが降る (pour down hail); kangei suru 歓迎する (welcome); aisatsu suru 挨拶する (salute); yobu 呼ぶ (call out to); **hail from** ... shusshin de aru ...出身である.

hair, *n.* kami(noke) 髪(の毛) (head hair); ke 毛 (body hair, fur).

hairdo, *n.* kamigata 髪型.

hairdresser, *n.* biyōshi 美容師.

hair-raising, *adj.* zotto suru (yō na) ぞっとする (ような).

hairy, *adj.* kebukai 毛深い (covered with hair).

half, 1. *n.* han(bun) 半(分); nibun no ichi 二分の一; **in half** hanbun ni 半分に; **half a year** hantoshi 半年; **half an hour** hanjikan 半時間. 2. *adj.* hanbun (no) 半分 (の). 3. *adv.* hanbun ni 半分に.

half brother/sister, *n.* ibo(ifu) kyōdai/-shimai 異母(異父)兄弟／～姉妹.

half-cooked, *adj.* namanie (no) 生煮え (の).

half-hearted, *adj.* ki ga noranai 気が乗らない.

halfway, *adv.* 1. nakaba de/made 半ばで／まで (at/to the midway point); hotondo ほとんど (almost).

hall, *n.* rōka 廊下 (corridor). 3. genkan 玄関; robī ロビー (entrance, lobby).

hallucination, *n.* genkaku 幻覚.

halt, 1. *n.* teishi 停止 (stop). 2. *vb.* tomaru 止まる (stop); tomeru 止める (cause to stop); tsumazuku つまずく

(stumble). 3. *interj.* Tomare. 止まれ.

halve, *vb.* 1. hanbun ni wakeru 半分に分ける (divide, share). 2. hanbun ni suru 半分にする (reduce to half).

hamlet, *n.* chiisai mura 小さい村.

hammer, 1. *n.* kanazuchi 金槌. 2. *vb.* uchikomu 打ち込む; tataku 叩く (pound).

hand, 1. *n.* te 手 (physical); hatarakite 働き手 (worker); hari 針 (of clock); tasuke 助け (assistance); hisseki 筆跡 (handwriting); gawa 側 (side); kekkonseiyaku 結婚誓約 (pledge of marriage); **at hand** tejika ni 手近に; **by hand** te de 手で; **hands down** tayasuku たやすく; **in hand in hand** tomo ni 共に; **on the other hand** sono ippō その一方; **shake hands** akushu suru 握手する; **out of hand** te ni oenai 手に負えない. 2. *adj.* te (no) 手 (の) (of the hand); tesei (no) 手製 (の) (handmade); shudō (no) 手動 (の) (operated by hand). 3. *vb.* tewatasu 手渡す (pass); te o kasu 手を貸す (help, guide); **hand in** teishutsu suru 提出する; **hand out** kubaru 配る.

handbook, *n.* tebikisho 手引書.

handcuffs, *n.* tejō 手錠.

handful, *n.* 1. hitonigiri 一握り (amount). 2. shōsū 少数 (small number).

handicapped, *adj.* shintaishōgaisha (no) 身体障害者 (の) (person).

handle, 1. *n.* totte 取っ手. 2. *vb.* atsukau 扱う (feel, deal with, manipulate).

handlebar, *n.* handoru ハンドル.

handshake, *n.* akushu 握手.

handwriting, *n.* tegaki 手書き.

hang, *vb.* kakeru 掛ける; sageru 下げる (suspend); kubi o tsuru 首を吊る (die by hanging); **hang around** buratsuku ぶらつく; **hang on** shigamitsuku しがみつく (cling to); ganbaru 頑張る (persevere); matsu 待つ (telephone); **hang up** kakeru かける (suspend on hook); denwa o kiru 電話を切る (telephone).

hanger, *n.* emonkake 衣紋掛け.

hangover, *n.* futsukayoi 二日酔い.

haphazard, *adj.* detarame (na) でたらめ(な).

happen, *vb.* 1. okoru 起こる (take place). 2. gūzen ...suru 偶然...する (come by chance).

happening, *n.* dekigoto 出来事

happy, *adj.* shiawase (na) 幸せ(な); kōfuku (na) 幸福(な); ureshii 嬉しい.

happy-go-lucky, *adj.* rakuten-teki (na) 楽天的(な).

harassment, *n.* iyagarase 嫌がらせ; **sexual harassment** sei-teki iyagarase 性的嫌がらせ; sekuhara セクハラ.

harbor, 1. *n.* minato 港 (port); hinansho 避難所 (shelter). 2. *vb.* kakumau かくまう (give shelter).

hard, 1. *adj.* katai 固い (solid); muzukashii 難しい (difficult); nesshin na 熱心な (energetic, persistent); kibishii 厳しい (severe). 2.

adv. nesshin ni 熱心に (earnestly; with vigor); kataku 固く (firmly, solidly); tsuyoku 強く (violently); **be hard up** (o)kane ga nai (お)金がない; **be hard hit** itade o ukeru 痛手を受ける.

harden, *vb.* 1. kataku naru 固くなる (become hard); kataku suru 固くする (make hard). 2. mujihi ni naru 無慈悲になる (become pitiless); mujihi ni suru 無慈悲にする (make pitiless).

hard-headed, *adj.* 1. reitetsu (na) 冷徹 (な) (not easily moved). 2. ganko (na) 頑固 (な) (stubborn).

hard-hearted, *adj.* mujihi (na) 無慈悲(な).

hardly, *adv.* 1. hotondo ... nai ほとんど...ない (almost not). 2. mattaku ... nai 全く...ない (not at all).

hardship, *n.* kon'nan 困難; kurō 苦労.

hardy, *adj.* ganjō (na) 頑丈(な) (sturdy, strong).

hare, *n.* usagi うさぎ.

harm, 1. *n.* gai 害 (damage); kega 怪我 (injury). 2. *vb.* kizu tsukeru 傷つける (damage, injure).

harmful, *adj.* yūgai (na) 有害(な).

harmless, *adj.* mugai (na) 無害(な).

harness, 1. *n.* bagu 馬具 (horse). 2. *vb.* tsukaikonasu 使いこなす (control and use).

harp, *n.* tategoto 竪琴.

harry, *vb.* 1. sainamu 苛む (torment). 2. hakai suru 破壊する (devastate).

harsh, *adj.* 1. arai 荒い (rough). 2. fukai (na) 不快(な) (unpleasant). 3.

kibishii 厳しい (severe).

harvest, 1. *n.* shūkaku 収穫; tori'ire 取り入れ (gathering of crops); shūkakubutsu 収穫物 (crop). 2. *vb.* shūkaku suru 収穫する; tori'ireru 取り入れる (reap).

hassle, 1. *n.* kuchigenka 口喧嘩 (dispute). 2. mendō 面倒 (trouble).

hasten, *vb.* 1. isogu 急ぐ (hurry). 2. hayameru 早める (cause to hurry).

hasty, *adj.* 1. subayai 素早い (hurried, speedy). 2. seikyū (na) 性急 (な) (impetuous).

hat, *n.* bōshi 帽子.

hatch, *vb.* 1. (tamago o) kaesu (卵を) かえす (hatch an egg); (tamago ga) kaeru (卵が) かえる (egg hatches).

hatchet, *n.* teono 手斧.

hate, 1. *n.* nikushimi 憎しみ. 2. *vb.* nikumu 憎む (detest); kirau 嫌う (dislike).

haughty, *adj.* kōman (na) 高慢 (な).

haul, 1. *n.* yusōhin 輸送品 (transported load). 2. *vb.* hiku 引く (pull); yusō suru 輸送する (transport).

haunted, *adj.* toritsukarete iru 取りつかれている.

haunted house yūreiyashiki 幽霊屋敷.

have, 1. *vb.* aru ある; motteiru 持っている (possess); nomu 飲む (drink); taberu 食べる (eat); uketoru 受け取る (receive); idaku 抱く (hold in mind). 2. *aux. vb.* (used with past participle) ... shita koto ga aru ...したことがある (have experienced); mō ... shita mo ō ...した; ... shite shimatta ...してしまった (have finished doing). 3. **have been doing** zutto ... shite

iru ずっと ... している;

have (something) done ... shite morau ...してもらう;

have to do ... shinakereba-naranai ...しなければならない; **had better do** ... shita hō ga ii ...したほうがいい;

have on ... o kite iru ...を着ている (be clothed in);

have to do with ... to kankei ga aru ...と関係がある (have dealings with); **have had it** mō takusan もうたくさん.

hawk, *n.* taka 鷹.

hay, *n.* hoshikusa 干し草.

hay fever, *n.* kafunshō 花粉症.

hazard, 1. *n.* kiken 危険 (danger); kikenbutsu 危険物 (object causing hazard). 2. *vb.* kaketemiru 賭けてみる (risk).

haze, *n.* 1. kasumi 霞 (mistlike obscurity). 2. mōrō もうろう (vagueness of mind).

he, *pron.* kare (ga/wa) 彼 (が／は).

head, 1. *n.* atama 頭 (part of body, brain); chō 長 (chief); saki 先 (topmost part); **heads or tails** omote ka ura ka 表か裏か. 2. *vb.* hiki'iru 率いる (lead); mukau 向かう (move); **head for** ... ni mukau ...に向かう.

headache, *n.* zutsū 頭痛.

head-on, *adj.* shōmen (no) 正面 (の) (with head foremost); **head-on collision** shōmen-shōtotsu 正面衝突.

headquarters, *n.* 1. honbu 本部. 2. sōshireibu 総司令部 (military).

headstrong, *adj.* ganko (na) 頑固 (な).

headway, *n.* zenshin 前進

(movement forward).

heal, vb. naosu 治す (restore to health); naoru 治る (get well).

healthy, adj. 1. kenkō (na) 健康 (な) (vigorous). 2. kenkō ni ii 健康に良い (good for health).

heap, 1. n. yamazumi 山積み (pile); **a heap of** takusan (no) たくさん (の) (a lot of). 2. vb. tsumiageru 積み上げる (pile up); yama to ataeru 山と与える (give abundantly); yama to tsumekomu 山と詰め込む (fill).

hear, vb. kiku 聞く (listen, be informed); kikoeru 聞こえる (audible); **hear from** ... kara tayori/tegami ga aru ...から便り／手紙がある; **hear about/of** ... no koto o kiku ...のことを聞く.

hearing, n. 1. chōkaku 聴覚 (sense). 2. chōmonkai 聴聞会 (legal session).

heart, n. 1. shinzō 心臓 (organ); **heart attack** shinzō hossa 心臓発作; **heart disease** shinzōbyō 心臓病; 2. kokoro 心 (seat of emotion). 3. jō 情 (sympathy). 4. yūki 勇気 (courage); yaruki やる気 (enthusiasm). 5. chūshin 中心 (central part). 6. **at heart** kihon-teki ni 基本的に (fundamentally); **by heart** sora de そらで; **from the bottom of one's heart** kokoro kara 心から; **lose heart** yaruki o nakusu やる気を無くす; **set one's heart on** kesshin suru 決心する; **take to heart** meiki suru 銘記する (take seriously); kanji'iru 感じ入る (be deeply affected).

heartbroken, adj. shitsui (no) 失意 (の); hitsū (na) 悲痛 (na).

heartburn, n. muneyake 胸焼け.

hearty, adj. 1. kokoro no atatakai 心の暖かい (cordial). 2. shin (no) 真 (の) (genuine). 3. kokoro kara (no) 心から (の) (heartfelt). 4. genki (na) 元気 (な) (vigorous). 5. ōkii 大きい (substantial).

heat, 1. n. netsu 熱 (hot); nekkyō 熱狂 (ardor). 2. vb. atatameru 暖める (warm); atatamaru 暖まる (become warm); nekkyō suru 熱狂する (excite).

heating, n. danbō 暖房.

heatstroke, n. nesshabyō 熱射病.

heave, vb. 1. mochiageru 持ち上げる (raise). 2. nageru 投げる (throw). 3. (koe o) tateru (声を)たてる (utter). **heave a sigh** tameiki o tsuku ため息を吐く. 4. jōge suru 上下する (rise and fall).

heaven, n. 1. tengoku 天国. 2. **heavens** sora 空; ten 天 (sky).

heavy, adj. 1. omoi 重い (weighty, burdensome, oppressive); futotte-iru 太っている (overweight). 2. takusan (no) たくさん (の) (large amount); ōkii 大きい (of great size, substantial). 3. hageshii 激しい (intense, violent, crowded); **heavy rain** hageshii ame 激しい雨; **heavy traffic** hageshii kōtsū 激しい交通. 4. jūdai (na) 重大 (な) (serious). 5. kitsui きつい (trying). 6. dai (no) 大 (の) (excessive); **heavy drinker** dai no

sakenomi 大の酒飲み;
ōzakenomi 大酒飲み。 7.
futoi 太い (broad). 8. atsui
厚い (thick). 9. arai 粗い
(coarse). 10. fukai 深い
(deep); **heavy slumber**
fukai nemuri 深い眠り。 11.
heavy industry jūkōgyō 重
工業; **heavy metal**
jūkinzoku 重金属; **heavy
heart** omoi kokoro 重い心。

hectic, adj. awatadashii あわ
ただしい。

hedge, n. ikegaki 生け垣。

heed, 1. n. chūi 注意
(notice). 2. vb. ... ni chūi
suru ... に注意する (notice);
kiki'ireru 聞き入れる (pay
serious attention to).

heel, n. kakato 踵 (of foot or
shoe).

height, n. 1. takasa 高さ。 2.
shinchō 身長 (height of a
person). 3. kōdo 高度
(altitude). 4. chōten 頂点
(apex, peak). 5. **heights**
oka 丘、岡; takadai 高台。

hell, n. jigoku 地獄。

hello, interj. 1. konnichi wa
今日は (greeting). 2. moshi-
moshi もしもし (answering
telephone).

helmsman, n. kajitorinin 舵
取り人。

help, 1. n. tasuke 助け (aid,
assistance); tetsudai 手伝い
(helper). 2. vb. tetsudau 手
伝う; tasukeru 助ける (aid);
(... no) tasuke ni naru (...の)
助けになる (be of service
to); **Please help yourself!**
Gojiyū ni dōzo. 御自由にど
うぞ; **help oneself to** jiyū
ni ... o taberu/nomu 自由
に... を食べる/飲む
(eat/drink); ... o ōryō suru
...を横領する
(misappropriate, embezzle);
help out sukuu 救う。 3.

interj. Tasukete. 助けて。

helper, n. tetsudai 手伝い。

helpful, adj. yaku ni tatsu 役
に立つ (useful).

hem, 1. n. heri 縁 (hemmed
edge). 2. vb. heri o tsukeru
縁を付ける (sew down the
edge); kakomu 囲む
(enclose).

hemisphere, n. hankyū 半
球。

hemp, n. asa 麻。

hen, n. mendori 雌鳥。

hence, adv. 1. sore de それ
で; yue ni 故に (therefore).
2. ima kara 今から (from
this time).

henceforth, adv. kongo 今後
(from now on).

her, 1. adj. kanojo (no) 彼女
(の)。 2. pron. kanojo o/ni 彼
女を/に。

herb, n. yakusō 薬草。

herd, n. mure 群れ (flock,
mass).

here, adv. 1. koko de (e/ni)
ここで (へ/に)。

heredity, n. iden 遺伝。

heritage, n. isan 遺産
(inheritance, traditions).

hero, n. 1. eiyū 英雄 (man of
valor). 2. shujinkō 主人公
(main character).

heroine, n. 1. joketsu 女傑
(female hero). 2.
on'nashujinkō 女主人公
(main character).

hers, pron. kanojo no mono
彼女のもの。

herself, pron. kanojojishin
彼女自身; **by herself**
kanojojishin de 彼女自身で。

hesitate, vb. tamerau ためら
う。

heterosexual, 1. n. iseiaisha
異性愛者。 2. adj. iseiai (no)
異性愛 (の)。

heyday, n. sakari 盛り;
zenseiki 全盛期。

hibernate, *vb.* tōmin suru 冬眠する.

hiccup, 1. *n.* shakkuri しゃっくり. **2.** *vb.* shakkuri o suru しゃっくりをする.

hide, 1. *n.* kawa 皮 (animal skin). **2.** *vb.* kakusu 隠す (conceal); kakureru 隠れる (conceal oneself); himitsu ni suru 秘密にする (keep secret).

hideous, *adj.* osoroshii 恐ろしい; minikui 醜い.

hierarchy, *n.* kaisōsei 階層制 (system).

high, *adj.* **1.** takai 高い (tall, lofty, expensive). **2.** kōon (no) 高音 (の) (shrill). **3.** jōkyū (no) 上級 (の); jōryū (no) 上流 (の) (high in position or status); **high official** jōkyūkanryō 上級官僚; **high society** jōryūshakai 上流社会. **4.** **high speed** kōsoku 高速; **high living** zeitaku (na) seikatsu 贅沢 (な) 生活.

highbrow, *adj.* inteributteiru インテリぶっている.

high-class, *adj.* ikkyū (no) 一級 (の) (first rate).

high fidelity, *n.* kōseinō 高性能.

highly, *adv.* **1.** hijō ni 非常に (extremely). **2.** yoku よく (admiringly).

high school, *n.* kō(tōgak)kō 高(等学)校.

highway, *n.* kōsokudōro 高速道路.

hijack, *vb.* nottoru 乗っ取る.

hijacker, *n.* nottorihan 乗っ取り犯.

hilarious, *adj.* **1.** yukai (na) 愉快 (な) (merry). **2.** okashii おかしい (funny).

hill, *n.* oka 丘、岡; yama 山.

him, *pron.* kare o/ni 彼を/に.

に.

himself, *pron.* karejishin wa (o/ni) 彼自身は (を／に); **by himself** kare jishin de 彼自身で.

hinder, *vb.* samatageru 妨げる.

hinge, 1. *n.* chōtsugai 蝶番. **2.** *vb.* chōtsugai o tsukeru 蝶番を付ける (furnish with a hinge).

hip, *n.* koshi 腰 (haunch); (o)shiri (お) 尻 (buttock).

hippopotamus, *n.* kaba 河馬.

hire, 1. *n.* yatoichin 雇い賃 (price of hiring a person); kashichin 貸し賃 (price of hiring an item); chingashi 賃貸し (act of hiring an item). **2.** *vb.* yatou 雇う (employ a person); chingari suru 賃借りする (purchase services or use of); chingashi suru 賃貸しする (offer services or use of).

his, 1. *pron.* kare no mono 彼のもの. **2.** *adj.* kare no 彼の.

hiss, 1. *n.* shī/shū しーっ／しゅーっ. **2.** *vb.* shī to iu しーっと言う (make a sound); hantai suru 反対する (disapprove).

history, *n.* rekishi 歴史.

hit, 1. *n.* shōtotsu 衝突 (collision); dageki 打撃 (blow); seikō 成功 (success); **hit or miss** noru ka soru ka のるかそるか. **2.** *vb.* utsu 打つ (strike); shōtotsu suru 衝突する (collide with); ... ni dekuwasu ...に出くわす (come upon); omoitsuku 思い付く (get a good idea).

hitch, 1. *n.* musubime 結び目 (knot); shōgai 障害 (obstruction); hippari 引っ張り (pull). **2.** *vb.* tsunagu つなぐ (fasten); hikiageru 引

き上げる (raise).

hoard, 1. *n.* takuwae 貯え. 2. *vb.* tameru 溜める.

hoarse, *adj.* shagaregoe (no) しゃがれ声 (の) (voice).

hobby, *n.* shumi 趣味.

hoe, *n.* kuwa くわ.

hog, *n.* buta 豚 (pig).

hoist, *vb.* hikiageru 引き上げる.

hold, 1. *n.* tsukamu koto 摑む事 (grasp); **get a hold on** ... o tsukamu ...を摑む (grasp). 2. *vb.* motsu 持つ; nigiru 握る (have in hand); motteiru 持っている (possess); tamotsu 保つ (retain); hikitomeru 引き止める (detain); (... to) omou (...と) 思う (consider, think); shinjiru 信じる (believe); okonau 行う (hold a meeting, ceremony, etc.); shimeru 占める (occupy); **hold back** osaeru 抑える; **hold down** osaeru 抑える (keep under control); **hold on** tsukamu 摑む (grip); tsuzukeru 続ける (continue); **Hold on, please.** Chotto matte kudasai. ちょっと待って下さい (telephone); **hold out** sashidasu 差し出す (offer); motsu 持つ (last); **hold up** sasaeru 支える (support); okuraseru 遅らせる (delay); mochikotaeru 持ちこたえる (persevere).

hole, *n.* ana 穴.

holiday, *n.* 1. shukujitsu 祝日 (public holiday). 2. kyūjitsu 休日; yasumi 休み (exemption from work/school). 3. saijitsu 祭日 (religious holiday).

Holland, *n.* oranda オランダ.

hollow, 1. *n.* ana 穴 (hole);

tani 谷 (valley). 2. *adj.* utsuro (na) 虚ろ (な) (empty, sounding hollow); kubonde iru 窪んでいる (sunken); kudaranai 下らない (without worth); munashii 空しい (having an empty feeling). 3. *vb.* ana o akeru 穴を開ける.

holy, *adj.* 1. shinsei (na) 神聖 (な) (sacred); kiyoraka (na) 清らか (な) (pure). 2. kami ni sasagerareta 神に捧げられた (dedicated to God).

home, *n.* 1. ie 家 (residence); katei 家庭 (place of domestic affections). 2. furusato 故郷 (native area). 3. shisetsu 施設 (institution). 4. **be at home** uchi ni iru うちにいる (be in one's own house); kutsurogu くつろぐ (be at ease); yoku shitte iru よく知っている (be well-informed); **bring home** akiraka ni suru 明らかにする (clarify).

homeland, *n.* sokoku 祖国.

homely, *adj.* 1. heibon (na) 平凡 (な) (unattractive). 2. soboku (na) 素朴 (な) (simple).

homemaker, *n.* shufu 主婦 (housewife).

hometown, *n.* furusato 故郷; inaka 田舎.

homework, *n.* 1. shukudai 宿題 (school work). 2. junbi 準備 (preparation).

homicide, *n.* satsujin 殺人 (murder); satsujinhan 殺人犯 (murderer).

homosexual, 1. *n.* dōseiaisha 同性愛者 (homosexual person). 2. *adj.* dōseiai (no) 同性愛 (の).

honest, *adj.* 1. shōjiki (na)

正直 (な) (upright). 2. seijitsu (na) 誠実 (な) (sincere). 3. sotchoku (na) 率直 (な) (frank).

honk, 1. *n.* kurakushon no oto クラクションの音 (sound of car horn). 2. *vb.* kurakushon o narasu クラクションを鳴らす.

honor, 1. *n.* meisei 名声 (public esteem, reputation); meiyo 名誉 (high ethical character, source of distinction); sonkei 尊敬 (respect); **do honor to** ... ni keii o harau ...に敬意を払う. 2. *vb.* tataeru 讃える (revere); meiyo o ataeru 名誉を与える (confer honor); **I am honored.** Kōei desu 光栄です.

honorarium, *n.* sharei 謝礼.

hoodlum, *n.* chinpira ちんぴら; gorotsuki ごろつき.

hoof, *n.* hizume ひづめ.

hook, 1. *n.* kagi 鉤 (curved piece of metal); yōfukukake 洋服掛け (for clothing); tsuribari 釣り針 (fishhook). 2. *vb.* kakeru 掛ける (suspend); toraeru 捕える (catch); magaru 曲がる (curve); **hook up** tomeru 留める (fasten); **be off the hook** juwaki ga hazurete iru 受話器が外れている (telephone); kirinukeru 切り抜ける (be released from difficulty).

hoop, *n.* wa 輪.

hop, *vb.* tobu 跳ぶ (leap); kataashi de tobu 片足で跳ぶ (leap on one foot).

hope, 1. *n.* kibō 希望; nozomi 望み. 2. *vb.* kitai suru 期待する; nozomu 望む.

horizon, *n.* suiheisen 水平線 (sea); chiheisen 地平線

(land).

horizontal, *adj.* suihei (na) 水平 (な).

horn, *n.* 1. tsuno 角 (animal). 2. kurakushon クラクション (car).

horoscope, *n.* hoshiuranai 星占い.

horrible, *adj.* 1. osoroshii 恐ろしい (dreadful). 2. fuyukai (na) 不愉快 (な) (unpleasant); hidoi ひどい (disgusting).

horror, *n.* 1. kyōfu 恐怖 (fear). 2. ken'o 嫌悪 (repugnance).

horse, *n.* uma 馬; **ride a horse** uma ni noru 馬に乗る.

horsepower, *n.* bariki 馬力.

horseradish, *n.* wasabi わさび.

hose, *n.* 1. hōsu ホース. 2. sutokkingu ストッキング (stockings); kutsushita 靴下 (socks).

hospital, *n.* byōin 病院.

hospitality, *n.* kantai 歓待; kokoro kara no motenashi 心からのもてなし.

host, *n.* 1. shujin 主人 (person who receives guests). 2. shikaisha 司会者 (master of ceremonies). 3. **a host of** takusan (no) たくさん (の).

hostile, *adj.* 1. tekii ga aru 敵意がある (unfriendly). 2. teki (no) 敵 (の) (of an enemy).

hot, *adj.* 1. atsui 熱い (high temperature); **hot water** (o)yu (お)湯. 2. atsui 熱い (feeling great heat). 3. karai 辛い (peppery). 4. hageshii 激しい (violent). 5. nesshin (na) 熱心 (な) (earnest).

hot-headed, *adj.* 1. tanki (na) 短気 (な) (short-tempered). 2. sekkachi (na) せっかち (な) (hasty).

hothouse, *n.* onshitsu 温室.

hound, 1. *n.* ryōken 猟犬 (hunting dog). 2. *vb.* ou 追う (track); semesainamu 責め苛む (harass).

hour, *n.* 1. jikan 時間 (any specific time or period of day). 2. ichijikan 一時間 (sixty minutes).

house, 1. *n.* ie 家; uchi うち (home); gekijō 劇場 (theater). 2. *vb.* jūkyo o ataeru 住居を与える (provide with a dwelling); shūyō suru 収容する (receive into a shelter); motteiru 持っている (contain).

housewife, *n.* shufu 主婦.

housing, *n.* 1. jūkyo 住居 (dwelling place, houses). 2. jūtakukyōkyū 住宅供給 (providing houses).

hover, *vb.* 1. ukabu 浮かぶ (hover in the air). 2. urotsuku うろつく (linger about). 3. samayou さまよう (stay uncertain).

how, 1. *adv.* dōyatte どうやって (by what means); dono gurai どの位 (to what extent); dō どう (in what condition); dōshite どうして (why); nanto 何と (used as an intensifier); **how about** ... wa dō/ikaga desu ka ...はどう/いかがですか; **How are you?** Genki desu ka 元気ですか; **how come** dōshite どうして; **how far** dono gurai tōi desu ka どの位遠いですか; **how long** dono gurai どの位; **how much** ikura いくら (what is the cost); dono gurai どの位 (in what quantity); **how many** nan'nin 何人 (how many people); ikutsu いくつ (how many things); **How old (are you)?** Nansai desu ka. 何歳ですか; **How pretty!** Nanto kawaii. 何とかわいい. 2. *conj.* shikata 仕方; dōyatte どうやって (way in which); **how to drive** unten no shikata 運転の仕方.

however, 1. *adv.* don'na ni ... temo/demo どんなに...ても/でも. 2. *conj.* shikashi しかし.

huddle, 1. *n.* ranzatsu 乱雑 (confused pile). 2. *vb.* (people) mi o yoseau 身を寄せ合う (gather together); (objects) tsumekomu 詰め込む (cause to crowd together).

hue, *n.* shikichō 色調 (color).

huff, *n.* ikari 怒り (anger); **in a huff** okotte 怒って.

hug, 1. *n.* dakishime 抱き締め. 2. *vb.* dakishimeru 抱き締める.

huge, *adj.* kyodai (na) 巨大 (な).

hull, *n.* 1. kawa 皮 (grain, seeds). 2. sentai 船体 (ship).

human, 1. *adj.* ningen (no) 人間 (の) (of human beings); ningen-teki (na) 人間的 (な) (sympathetic). 2. *n.* ningen 人間.

humanitarian, *adj.* jindō-teki (na) 人道的 (な).

humble, 1. *adj.* kenkyo (na) 謙虚 (な) (not arrogant); hige shite iru 卑下している (feeling inferior); hikui 低い (low). 2. *vb.* hige suru 卑下する (abase oneself); otoshimeru おとしめる (humble someone).

humbug, *n.* 1. inchiki いんちき (fraud). 2. ikasamashi いかさまし

いかさま師 (impostor).

humidity, n. shikke 湿気.

humiliation, n. haji 恥.

humility, n. kenkyo 謙虚.

humor, 1. n. jōdan 冗談 (funniness); kishitsu 気質 (mental disposition); kimagure 気紛れ (whim). 2. vb. kigen o toru 機嫌を取る.

humorous, adj. okashii おかしい; kokkei (na) 滑稽 (な) (funny).

hump, n. 1. kobu こぶ (of a camel). 2. koyama 小山 (small hill).

humpback, hunchback, n. semushi せむし.

hunch, n. 1. kobu こぶ (hump). 2. yokan 予感 (premonition).

hundred, 1. n. hyaku 百. 2. adj. hyaku (no) 百 (の).

Hungary, n. hangarī ハンガリー.

hunger, 1. n. ue 飢え (starvation); kūfuku 空腹 (empty stomach). 2. vb. ueru 飢える (starve); onaka ga suku お腹が空く (become hungry); **hunger for** ... ni ueru ...に飢える.

hunt, 1. n. kari 狩り (hunting game); sagashi 捜し (search). 2. vb. kari o suru 狩りをする (chase game), sagasu 捜す (search for); **hunt down** oitsumeru 追い詰める; **hunt out** sagashidasu 捜し出す; **hunt for a house** ie o sagasu 家を捜す.

hunter, -tress, n. ryōshi 猟師.

hunting, n. 1. kari 狩り (hunting game). 2. sagashi 捜し (search); **job-hunting** shokusagashi 職捜し.

hurl, vb. nagetsukeru 投げつ

ける (throw, utter).

hurried, adj. ōisogi (no) 大急ぎ (の).

hurry, 1. n. isogi 急ぎ (haste); **(be) in a hurry** isoide (iru) 急いで (いる). 2. vb. isogu 急ぐ (act with speed); isogasu 急がす (hasten); **hurry up** isogu 急ぐ (do faster); isogaseru 急がせる (make someone act faster).

hurt, 1. n. kizu 傷 (wound); kutsū 苦痛 (pain). 2. vb. kizutsukeru 傷つける (cause bodily or mental pain); kibun o gaisuru 気分を害する (offend); itamu 痛む (suffer from pain).

husband, n. otto 夫; shujin 主人.

hustle, 1. n. kakki 活気 (energetic activity); oshinoke 押しのけ (jostling); **hustle and bustle** zattō 雑踏. 2. vb. seiryoku-teki ni hataraku 精力的に働く (work energetically); oshinokeru 押しのける (push one's way); ... ni oshikomu ...に押し込む (force someone into).

hut, n. koya 小屋.

hydrangea, n. ajisai あじさい.

hydrant, n. shōkasen 消火栓.

hydrogen, n. suiso 水素.

hygiene, n. eisei 衛生.

hymn, n. 1. sanbika 賛美歌 (religious). 2. sanka 賛歌 (song of praise).

hyperbole, n. kochō 誇張.

hypertension, n. kōketsuatsu 高血圧 (elevation of blood pressure).

hypertensive, n. kōketsuatsu kanja 高血圧患

者.

hypnotism, *n.* saiminjutsu
催眠術 (practice of inducing
sleep).

hypochondriac, *n.*
shinkishō kanja 心気症患者.

hypocritical, *adj.* gizen-teki
偽善的

(na) 偽善的 (na).

hypodermic, *adj.* hika (no)
皮下 (の).

hypothesis, *n.* 1. katei 仮定
(proposition, guess). 2.
kasetsu 仮説 (provisional
theory).

I

I, *pron.* watashi (ga, wa) 私
(が、は).

ice, 1. *n.* kōri 氷. 2. *vb.*
kōraseru 凍らせる (freeze);
kōri de hiyasu 氷で冷やす
(cool with ice).

iceberg, *n.* hyōzan 氷山.

icicle, *n.* tsurara つらら.

icon, *n.* 1. shirushi 印
(symbol). 2. zō 像 (image).
3. seizō 聖像 (sacred image).

icy, *adj.* 1. kōri ga hatteiru 氷
が張っている (covered with
ice). 2. tsumetai 冷たい
(cold).

idea, *n.* 1. kangae 考え
(concept in mind, thought);
good idea ii kangae 良い考
え. 2. chishiki 知識
(knowledge). 3. inshō 印象
(impression). 4. iken 意見
(opinion). 5. keikaku 計画
(plan). 6. rikai 理解
(understanding); **have no
idea** sappari wakaranai さ
っぱりわからない.

ideal, *adj.* risō-teki (na) 理想
的 (な).

idealism, *n.* risōshugi 理想
主義.

identical, *adj.* 1. onaji (no)
同じ (の) (same). 2. niteiru
似ている (resembling).

identify, *vb.* 1. mitomeru 認
める (recognize). 2. onaji to
shōmei suru 同じと証明す
る (prove to be identical).
3. dōitsushi suru 同一視する

(consider as same).

identity, *n.* 1. dōitsu 同一
(state of being the same). 2.
hontō no jibun 本当の自分
(true self); mimoto 身元
(origin, background).

idiosyncrasy, *n.* tokuchō 特
長 (individual trait).

idiot, *n.* baka 馬鹿.

idle, 1. *adj.* hima (na) 暇
(な) (not active, not busy);
bushō (na) 無精 (な) (lazy);
kudaranai 下らない (of no
worth); **idle talk** kudaranai
hanashi 下らない話;
oshaberi おしゃべり. 2. *vb.*
nani mo shinai 何もしない
(do nothing); bura-bura
suru ぶらぶらする (saunter
aimlessly, idle away).

idleness, *n.* bushō 無精.

if, *conj.* 1. moshi(mo) ...
naraba もし(も) ...ならば (in
case that). 2. tatoe ... demo
たとえ...でも (even
though). 3. ... ka dōka ...か
どうか (whether). 4. **if
only** ... nara ii noni ...なら
いいのに; **even if** tatoe ...
demo/temo たとえ...でも／
ても; **as if** marude ... no yō
ni まるで...のように; **if you
like** moshi yokereba もしよ
ければ.

ignorance, *n.* 1. muchi 無知
(lack of knowledge). 2.
mugaku 無学 (lack of
learning).

ignorant, *adj.* 1. shiranai 知らない (lacking knowledge). 2. ki ga tsukanai 気がつかない (unaware).

ignore, *vb.* mushi suru 無視する.

ill, 1. *adj.* byōki (no) 病気(の) (sick); warui 悪い (evil, faulty, unfavorable); **ill at ease** igokochi ga warui 居心地が悪い. 2. *n.* byōki 病気 (ailment); aku 悪 (evil). 3. *adv.* waruku 悪く (badly, unfavorably); **speak ill of** ... o waruku iu ...を悪く言う.

illegal, *adj.* fuhō (na) 不法(な).

illegible, *adj.* yomenai 読めない.

illegitimate, *adj.* 1. shoshi (no) 庶子 (の) (born out of wedlock). 2. fuhō (na) 不法(な) (unlawful).

ill-mannered, *adj.* gyōgi ga warui 行儀が悪い.

illness, *n.* byōki 病気.

illogical, *adj.* fugōri (na) 不合理な).

illuminate, *vb.* terasu 照らす; akari o tsukeru 明りをつける (supply with light).

illumination, *n.* shōmei 照明 (lighting).

illusion, *n.* 1. genkaku 幻覚 (false optical impression). 2. sakkaku 錯覚 (confusion, false impression). 3. giman 欺瞞 (deception).

illustrate, *vb.* 1. rei o ageru 例を挙げる (give example); zushi suru 図示する (provide charts, etc.). 2. sashie o tsukeru 挿絵を付ける (furnish with pictures).

illustrious, *adj.* chomei (na) 著名(な) (famous).

ill will, *n.* tekii 敵意 (enmity); ken'o 嫌悪

(hatred).

image, *n.* 1. shinzō 心像 (idea, mental representation, impression). 2. zō 像; sugata 姿 (physical representation or likeness, image in mirror).

imagination, *n.* 1. sōzō 想像 (creation of the mind). 2. sōzōryoku 想像力 (creative talent); hassōryoku 発想力 (resourcefulness).

imagine, *vb.* 1. sōzō suru 想像する (form mental images). 2. omou 思う (think, guess).

imitate, *vb.* mane suru 真似する.

immaculate, *adj.* 1. shimihitotsu nai shiraga-hitotsu nai 染み一つない (spotlessly clean). 2. kiyoraka (na) 清らか(な) (morally pure). 3. kanpeki (na) 完璧(な) (flawless).

immature, *adj.* mijuku (na) 未熟(な) (unripe, childish).

immediate, *adj.* 1. sokuji (no) 即時 (の) (instant). 2. ichiban chikai 一番近い (nearest). 3. mokka (no) 目下 (の) (present).

immense, *adj.* bōdai (na) 膨大(な) (vast).

immigrant, *n.* imin 移民.

immobile, *adj.* fudō (no) 不動 (の).

immoral, *adj.* fudōtoku-teki (na) 不道徳的(な).

immortal, *adj.* 1. fushi (no) 不死 (の) (not mortal). 2. eien 永遠 (の) (everlasting).

impact, *n.* 1. shōgeki 衝撃 (force, collision). 2. eikyō 影響 (influence).

impart, *vb.* 1. uchiakeru 打ち明ける (disclose). 2. ataeru 与える (bestow); wakeataeru 分け与える

(give a share of).

impartial, *adj.* kōhei (na) 公平 (な).

impassioned, *adj.* nesshin (na) 熱心 (な).

impatient, *adj.* 1. **be impatient (to do)** (... suru koto ga) matenai (...することが) 待てない (be unable to wait, be eager). 2. gaman dekinai 我慢出来ない (intolerant).

impeach, *vb.* hihan suru 批判する (criticize); dangai suru 弾劾する (accuse official).

impeccable, *adj.* kanpeki (na) 完璧 (な) (flawless).

impede, *vb.* jama o suru 邪魔をする.

impel, *vb.* unagasu 促す.

impending, *adj.* sashisematte-iru 差し迫っている.

imperative, 1. *n.* meireikei 命令形 (grammar). 2. *adj.* hitsuyō (na) 必要 (な) (necessary); meirei (no) 命令 (の) (expressing a command).

imperceptible, *adj.* 1. kanjirarenai 感じられない (not perceived by the senses). 2. komakai 細かい (slight).

imperial, *adj.* 1. teikoku (no) 帝国 (の) (empire). 2. ōshitsu (no) 王室 (の) (king); kōshitsu (no) 皇室 (の) (emperor).

impersonal, *adj.* 1. kyakkan-teki (na) 客観的 (な) (objective). 2. ippan-teki (na) 一般的 (な) (general).

impertinent, *adj.* burei (na) 無礼 (な).

impetuous, *adj.* seikyū (na) 性急 (な).

implant, *vb.* 1. uetsukeru 植え付ける (instill, plant). 2. ishoku suru 移植する (graft).

implement, 1. *n.* dōgu 道具. 2. *vb.* jikkō ni utsusu 実行に移す (carry out).

implore, *vb.* kongan suru 懇願する.

imply, *vb.* 1. honomekasu 仄めかす (suggest). 2. imi suru 意味する (signify).

impolite, *adj.* shitsurei (na) 失礼 (な).

import, 1. *n.* yunyū 輸入 (act of importing); yunyūhin 輸入品 (something imported); imi 意味 (meaning). 2. *vb.* yunyū suru 輸入する (ship); imi suru 意味する (signify).

important, *adj.* jūyō (na) 重要 (な); daiji (na) 大事 (な) (of great significance).

impose, *vb.* 1. kasu 課す (as an obligation). 2. oshitsukeru 押し付ける (force oneself on others). 3. **impose on** tsukekomu 付け込む (take advantage of); damasu だます (deceive).

imposition, *n.* 1. futan 負担 (burden); gimu 義務 (obligation). 2. kyōsei 強制 (act of imposing).

impossible, *adj.* 1. fukanō (na) 不可能 (な) (cannot be done or effected). 2. arienai あり得ない (cannot exist or happen).

impress, *vb.* 1. kanshin saseru 感心させる (cause respect). 2. inshōzukeru 印象付ける (fix in mind). 3. osu 押す (press).

impression, *n.* 1. inshō 印象 (effect on the mind). 2. kanji 感じ (vague awareness). 3. shirushi 印

(stamped mark).

impressive, *adj.* migoto (na) 見事 (な) (admirable).

imprison, *vb.* keimusho ni ireru 刑務所に入れる.

imprisonment, *n.* tōgoku 投獄.

improbable, *adj.* arisō ni nai ありそうにない.

impromptu, *adj.* sokkyō (no) 即興 (の).

improper, *adj.* futekitō (na) 不適当 (な) (not suitable).

improve, *vb.* 1. kaizen suru 改善する; yoku suru 良くする (make better). 2. yoku naru 良くなる (become better).

impulse, *n.* 1. shigeki 刺激; shōgeki 衝撃 (stimulus). 2. shōdō 衝動 (sudden inclination).

impure, *adj.* 1. fujun (na) 不純 (な) (not pure). 2. 2. fudōtoku (na) 不道徳 (な) (immoral).

in, 1. *prep.* ... no naka de/ni ...の中で／に (inside, within, among); ... no aida ni ...の間に (while, during); ... de ...で (by way of, within a space of time); ... no tame ni ...のために (for the purpose of). 2. *adv.* naka de/ni 中で／に (inside, within); iru いる ([be] in) one's house, office, etc.).

inaccessible, *adj.* chikazukenai 近づけない (unapproachable).

inaccurate, *adj.* fuseikaku (na) 不正確 (な).

inasmuch as, *conj.* ... node ...ので; ... kara ...から.

inborn, *adj.* umaretsuki (no) 生まれつき (の).

incantation, *n.* jumon 呪文.

incapable, *adj.* **be incapable of** ... ga dekinai

...ができない.

incapacitate, *vb.* dekinaku suru できなくする (make unable).

incense, 1. *n.* senkō 線香. 2. *vb.* gekido saseru 激怒させる (infuriate).

incentive, *n.* 1. dōki 動機 (motive). 2. shigeki 刺激 (stimulus).

incessant, *adj.* hikkirinashi (no) ひっきりなし (の).

incident, *n.* 1. jiken 事件; jihen 事変 (riotous incident). 2. dekigoto 出来事 (happening, event).

incinerate, *vb.* yaku 焼く; hai ni suru 灰にする.

incision, *n.* kirikomi 切り込み (cut); sekkai 切開 (surgery).

incite, *vb.* karitateru 駆り立てる (stir up); sosonokasu そそのかす (instigate).

incline, 1. *n.* shamen 斜面 (inclined surface); sakamichi 坂道 (of a road). 2. *vb.* katamuku 傾く (slope, tilt); katamukeru 傾ける (cause to slope or tilt); mageru 曲げる (bend or bow one's head, etc.); **be inclined to** ... shitai ki ga suru ...したい気がする (feel like doing); ... shigachi de aru ...しがちである (have a tendency to do).

include, *vb.* fukumu 含む.

income, *n.* shotoku 所得; shūnyū 収入; **income tax** shotokuzei 所得税.

inconvenience, *n.* fuben 不便; mendō 面倒.

incorporate, *vb.* kumikomu 組み込む (form as a part).

increase, 1. *n.* zōka 増加; jōshō 上昇. 2. *vb.* fuyasu 増やす (make more numerous or greater); fueru 増える

incredible, *adj.* shinjirarenai 信じられない.

incubator, *n.* hoikuki 保育機 (for baby).

incur, *vb.* 1. maneku 招く; hikiokosu 引き起こす (bring upon oneself). 2. seoikomu 背負い込む (become liable for).

indebted, *adj.* be indebted to ... ni kari ga aru ...に借りがある (owing money to); ... ni on ga aru ...に恩がある (owing gratitude to).

indeed, *adv.* hontō ni 本当に; jitsu ni 実に; mattaku 全く.

indefinite, *adj.* 1. futei (no) 不定 (の) (without fixed limit, not clearly determined). 2. fumeiryō (na) 不明瞭 (な) (uncertain).

indelible, *adj.* kesu koto ga dekinai 消すことができない.

indent, *vb.* 1. hekomi o tsukeru 凹みを付ける (form recess). 2. kakidashi o zurasu 書き出しをずらす (set back from margin).

independence, *n.* 1. dokuritsu 独立 (not dependent on others); dokuritsudoppo 独立独歩 (self-reliance). 2. jiyū 自由 (freedom).

index, 1. *n.* sakuin 索引 (list); shihyō 指標 (indication); **index card** sakuin-kādo 索引カード; **index finger** hitosashiyubi 人差し指. 2. *vb.* sakuin o tsukeru 索引を付ける (provide with index).

India, *n.* indo インド.

indicate, *vb.* 1. imi suru 意味する (mean); shisa suru 示唆する (be a sign of). 2. sashishimesu 指し示す (point to).

indict, *vb.* kiso suru 起訴する.

indifferent, *adj.* 1. mukanshin (na) 無関心 (な) (without interest). 2. nami (no) 並 (の) (not particularly good).

indigestion, *n.* shōkafuryō 消化不良.

indignant, *adj.* rippuku shiteiru 立腹している.

indignity, *n.* kutsujoku 屈辱.

indigo, *n.* ai 藍 (dye).

indirect, *adj.* kansetsu-teki (na) 間接的 (な).

indiscreet, *adj.* keisotsu (na) 軽率 (な) (not prudent).

indiscriminate, *adj.* 1. teatari-battari (no) 手当たりばったり (の) (haphazard). 2. musabetsu (no) 無差別 (の) (lacking in selectivity).

indispensable, *adj.* fukaketsu (na, no) 不可欠 (な、の).

individual, 1. *n.* kojin 個人; hito人 (person). 2. *adj.* kojin (no) 個人 (の) (of person); ko-ko (no) 個々 (の) (of item).

indivisible, *adj.* fukabun (no) 不可分 (の).

indoor, 1. *adj.* okunai (no) 屋内 (の). 2. *adv.* **indoors** okunai de/ni 屋内で／に.

induce, *vb.* 1. sono ki ni suru その気にする (persuade). 2. motarasu もたらす (bring about, produce).

indulge, *vb.* 1. amayakasu 甘やかす (spoil); mankitsu saseru 満喫させる (gratify). 2. **indulge in** ... ni fukeru ...

に耽る; ... o omou zonbun ni suru ...を思う存分にする.

industry, n. 1. kōgyō 工業; sangyō 産業 (trade or manufacture). 2. kinben 勤勉 (diligence).

inertia, n. 1. fukappatsu 不活発 (inactivity). 2. bushō 無精 (laziness).

inevitable, adj. sakerarenai 避けられない.

inexperienced, adj. keikenbusoku (no) 経験不足 (の).

inexplicable, adj. setsumei dekinai 説明できない.

infamous, adj. 1. akumyōdakai 悪名高い (having a bad reputation). 2. hidoi ひどい (detestable).

infancy, n. nyūjiki 乳児期 (babyhood); yōjiki 幼児期 (early childhood).

infant, n. akachan 赤ちゃん; nyūji 乳児.

infect, vb. 1. kansen saseru 感染させる (afflict with disease). 2. eikyō o ataeru 影響を与える (affect). 3. **be infected with** ... ni kansen suru ...に感染する (be afflicted with disease); ... ni eikyō sareru ...に影響させる (be affected).

inferior, adj. 1. ototteiru 劣っている (lower in quality). 2. shita (no) 下 (の) (lower in rank).

infest, vb. habikoru はびこる (overrun).

infidelity, n. fujitsu 不実; uwaki 浮気 (extramarital affair).

infinite, adj. 1. mugen (no) 無限(の) (endless). 2. bakudai (na) 莫大 (な) (immeasurably great).

infinitive, n. futeishi 不定詞.

infinity, n. mugen 無限 (infinite space or quantity); eien 永遠 (infinite time).

infirmity, n. kyojaku 虚弱 (weakness); byōki 病気 (ailment).

inflame, vb. 1. moyasu 燃やす (set afire). 2. okoraseru 怒らせる (anger). 3. **be inflamed** enshō o okosu 炎症をおこす (be affected with inflammation).

inflammation, n. enshō 炎症 (redness and swelling).

inflation, n. infure インフレ (economic).

inflection, n. gobihenka 語尾変化; gokeihenka 語形変化 (grammar).

inflict, vb. 1. ataeru 与える (impose harmfully). 2. oshitsukeru 押し付ける (force).

influence, 1. n. eikyō 影響 (influential power). 2. vb. eikyō o ataeru 影響を与える.

influx, n. nagarekomi 流れ込み.

inform, vb. shiraseru 知らせる; tsugeru 告げる.

informal, adj. 1. hikōshiki (na) 非公式 (な) (unofficial); gishiki nuki (no) 儀式抜き (の) (without ceremony). 2. katakurushiku nai 堅苦しくない (relaxed).

informant, n. 1. tsūkokusha 通告者 (informer). 2. jōhōteikyōsha 情報提供者 (person who supplies cultural or social data).

information, n. jōhō 情報.

informative, adj. tame ni naru 為になる.

infraction, n. ihan 違反.

infuriate, vb. kan-kan ni okoraseru かんかんに怒らせる.

ingenious, *adj.* 1. hassō yutaka (na) 発想豊か (な) (characterized by originality). 2. rikō (na) 利口 (な) (cleverly inventive); kōmyō (na) 巧妙 (な) (cleverly skillful).

ingenuous, *adj.* 1. seijitsu (na) 誠実 (な) (sincere). 2. junshin (na) 純心 (な) (artless, naive).

ingrained, *adj.* nebukai 根深い (deep-rooted).

ingratitude, *n.* onshirazu 恩知らず.

ingredient, *n.* 1. zairyō 材料 (element of a mixture). 2. seibun 成分 (constituent).

inhabit, *vb.* sumu 住む.

inhale, *vb.* su'u 吸う; suikomu 吸い込む.

inherent, *adj.* 1. naizai-teki (na) 内在的 (な) (innate). 2. kirihanasenai 切り離せない (inseparable).

inherit, *vb.* 1. sōzoku suru 相続する (be an heir to). 2. uketsugu 受け継ぐ (receive).

inhibit, *vb.* osaeru 抑える (restrain).

inhuman, *adj.* hiningen-teki (na) 非人間的 (な).

iniquity, *n.* aku 悪.

initiate, *vb.* 1. hajimeru 始める (begin). 2. michibiku 導く; tehodoki o suru 手ほどきをする (introduce some knowledge). 3. nyūkai saseru 入会させる (admit into a group).

initiative, *n.* 1. sossen 率先 (leading action); **take the initiative** sossen suru 率先する. 2. sossenryoku 率先力 (ability to initiate action). 3. ishi 意志 (one's decision); **on one's own initiative** jibun no ishi de 自分の意志で.

inject, *vb.* 1. chūsha suru 注射する (inject with syringe). 2. ireru 入れる (add).

injure, *vb.* 1. kizutsukeru 傷付ける (hurt); sokonau 損なう (impair). 2. gai suru 害する (offend, do wrong).

inkling, *n.* 1. honomekashi 仄めかし (suggestion). 2. nantonaku kanzuku koto 何となく感付くこと (vague idea).

inland, *adj.* nairiku (no) 内陸 (の).

inmate, *n.* nyūinkanja 入院患者 (in hospital); shūjin 囚人 (in prison).

innate, *adj.* umaretsuki (no) 生まれつき (の).

inner, 1. naka (no) 中 (の) (interior). 2. seishin-teki (na) 精神的 (な); kokoro (no) 心 (の) (emotional).

innocence, *n.* 1. mujaki 無邪気; junshin 純心 (naive quality). 2. mujitsu 無実 (freedom from guilt).

innocent, *adj.* 1. mujaki (na) 無邪気 (な); junshin 純真 (na) (naive). 2. mujitsu (no) 無実 (の) (free from guilt).

innovate, *vb.* kaikaku suru 改革する (bring in something new).

innumerable, *adj.* musū (no) 無数 (の) (cannot be counted); takusan (no) たくさん (の) (numerous).

inoculate, *vb.* yobōsesshu o suru 予防接種をする (immunization).

input, *n.* 1. nyūryoku 入力 (power, energy). 2. dēta データ (data, information).

inquire, *vb.* 1. chōsa suru 調査する (conduct

investigation). 2. tazuneru 尋ねる (ask). 3. toiawaseru 問い合わせる (seek information).

inquisitive, adj. kōkishin ga tsuyoi 好奇心が強い (very curious); sensakuzuki (na, no) 詮索好き (な、の) (prying).

inroads, n. 1. dageki 打撃 (damaging encroachment). 2. shūgeki 襲撃 (raid).

insane, adj. kurutteiru 狂っている; kichigai (no) 気違い (の); **insane asylum** seishin byōin 精神病院.

inscribe, vb. 1. kakikomu 書き込む (write); horikomu 彫り込む (engrave). 2. sasageru 捧げる (dedicate).

insect, n. konchū 昆虫; mushi 虫.

insecticide, n. satchūzai 殺虫剤.

insensitive, adj. nibui 鈍い; mushinkei (no) 無神経 (の).

insert, vb. ireru 入れる.

inside, 1. n. naka 中; uchigawa 内側 (inner side, interior). 2. adj. naka (no) 中 (の) (internal, interior); naibu (no) 内部 (の) (confidential). 3. adv. naka de/e/ni/o 中で／に／を (within, indoors); **inside out** uragaeshi ni 裏返しに (with the inner side turned out). 4. prep. ...no naka de/e/ni ...の中で／へ／に.

insight, n. dōsatsuryoku 洞察力.

insignificant, adj. tsumaranai つまらない; toru ni tarinai 取るに足りない.

insist, vb. iiharu 言い張る; shuchō suru 主張する (declare firmly, be persistent).

insistent, adj. shitsukoi しつ

koi.

insomnia, n. fuminshō 不眠症.

inspect, vb. kensa suru 検査する; shiraberu 調べる.

inspector, n. 1. kensakan 検査官 (person who inspects). 2. keibu 警部 (police official).

instability, n. fuantei 不安定.

install, vb. 1. sonaetsukeru 備え付ける (set up apparatus). 2. shūnin saseru 就任させる (establish in office).

instant, 1. n. shunkan 瞬間 (moment). 2. adj. shunkan (no) 瞬間 (の) (immediate); sokuseki (no) 即席 (の) (short preparation time); kinkyū (no) 緊急 (の) (urgent).

instead, adv. sono kawari ni その代わりに; **instead of ...** no kawari ni ...の代わりに.

instinct, n. hon'nō 本能.

institute, 1. n. kyōkai 協会 (society); senmongakkō 専門学校 (specialized school). 2. vb. setsuritsu suru 設立する (establish); hajimeru 始める (start).

instruct, vb. 1. oshieru 教える (teach). 2. meijiru 命じる (order).

instrument, n. 1. dōgu 道具 (tool). 2. shudan 手段 (means). 3. **musical instrument** gakki 楽器.

insulation, n. bōon 防音 (act of insulating for sound); dan'netsu 断熱 (heat); zetsuen 絶縁 (electricity).

insulator, n. zetsuenbutsu 絶縁物 (material of low conductivity).

insult, 1. n. bujoku 侮辱. 2. vb. bujoku suru 侮辱する.

insurance, n. hoken 保険; **insurance policy** hoken-keiyakusho 保険契約書; **life insurance** seimeihoken 生命保険.

intact, adj. kawaranai 変わらない; moto no mama (no) 元のまま (の) (not altered).

integrate, vb. 1. kumikomu 組み込む (incorporate into whole). 2. tokekomu 溶け込む (become part of a group); tokekomaseru 溶け込ませる (make part of a group).

integrity, n. seijitsusa 誠実さ (sincerity).

intellect, n. chisei 知性.

intend, vb. 1. **intend to do** ... suru tsumori ...するつもり (plan to do). 2. **be intended for** ... no tame (no) ...のため (の) (be designed for).

intense, adj. kyōryoku (na) 強力 (な) (strong).

intent, 1. n. mokuteki 目的; ito 意図 (purpose). 2. adj. **intent on** ... ni muchū (no) ...に夢中 (の) (firmly concentrated on).

intentional, adj. ishiki-teki (na) 意識的 (な); koi (no) 故意 (の).

interchangeable, adj. gokansei (no) 互換性 (の); kōkan dekiru 交換できる.

intercourse, n. 1. kōsai 交際 (dealings between people, etc.) 2. seikō 性交 (sexual intercourse).

interest, 1. n. kyōmi 興味; kanshin 関心 (concern, curiosity); kabu 株 (shares); rieki 利益 (profit); rishi 利子 (payment for use of money). 2. vb. kyōmi o motaseru 興味を持たせる; **be interested in** ... ni

kyōmi ga aru ...に興味があ る.

interesting, adj. omoshiroi おもしろい.

interfere, vb. 1. bōgai suru 妨害する (obstruct). 2. kanshō suru 干渉する (meddle).

interim, 1. n. aida 間; **in the interim** sono aida ni そ の間に. 2. adj. ima no tokoro (no) 今のところ (の).

interior, 1. n. naibu 内部; naka 中 (the internal or inner part, inside); naisō 内 装 (interior decoration). 2. adj. naibu (no) 内部 (の); naka (no) 中 (の); naisō (no) 内装 (の).

interlude, n. 1. aima 合間 (intervening time). 2. makuaikyōgen 幕間狂言 (performance).

intermediate, adj. chūkan (no) 中間 (の) (being between two points).

intermission, n. kyūkei 休 憩 (break, interval).

intermittent, adj. danzoku-teki (na) 断続的 (な).

intern, 1. n. kenshūsei 研修 生 (trainee). 2. vb. kōsoku suru 拘束する (keep as hostage).

internal, adj. 1. naibu (no) 内部 (の) (interior, inner); **internal medicine** naika 内科. 2. kokunai (no) 国内 (の) (domestic).

international, adj. kokusai-teki (na) 国際的 (な).

interpret, vb. 1. kaishaku suru 解釈する (construe). 2. tsūyaku suru 通訳する (translate).

interrogate, vb. shitsumon suru 質問する.

interrupt, vb. 1. saegiru 遮

る; jama suru 邪魔する (break in). 2. chūdan suru 中断する (stop).

intersect, vb. kōsa suru 交差する.

intersperse, vb. baramaku ばらまく.

interval, n. aima 合間 (of time); kankaku 間隔 (of space); **at intervals** tokidoki 時々 (now and then).

interview, 1. n. mensetsu 面接 (meeting for evaluation); kaiken 会見 (journalism). 2. vb. mensetsu o suru 面接をする (meet to evaluate); kaiken o suru 会見をする (journalism).

intestine, n. chō 腸.

intimate, 1. n. shin'yū 親友 (intimate friend). 2. adj. shitashii 親しい (close); shitashimi afureru 親しみ溢れる (friendly); kojin-teki (na) 個人的 (な) (private). 3. vb. honomekasu 仄めかす.

intimidate, vb. 1. odosu 脅す (scare). 2. ojike-zukaseru 怖じけづかせる (make timid).

into, prep. ... no naka e/ni ... の中へ／に (to the inside of).

intoxicate, vb. yowaseru 酔わせる; **be intoxicated by** ... ni you ...に酔う.

intransitive verb, n. jidōshi 自動詞.

intricate, adj. fukuzatsu (na) 複雑 (な).

intrigue, 1. n. keiryaku 計略 (plot). 2. vb. takuramu 企む (plot); kyōmi o sosoru 興味をそそる (interest by puzzling).

introduce, vb. 1. shōkai suru 紹介する (present a person to another; bring in something for the first time). 2. tehodoki o suru 手ほどきをする (give a person first experience of). 3. hajimeru 始める (begin, preface).

introvert, n. 1. uchiki na hito 内気な人 (shy person). 2. naisei-teki na hito 内省的な人 (introspective person).

intrude, vb. 1. warikomu 割り込む (thrust in without welcome). 2. jama suru 邪魔する (come in without welcome).

intuition, n. chokkan 直感.

invade, vb. shinryaku suru 侵略する.

invalid, 1. n. byōnin 病人 (sick person). 2. adj. byōjaku (na) 病弱 (な) (infirm); byōnin (no) 病人 (の) (of invalids); mukō (no) 無効 (の) (void of legal force).

invariable, adj. kawaranai 変わらない.

invasion, n. shinryaku 侵略.

invent, vb. 1. hatsumei suru 発明する (originate). 2. kangaedasu 考え出す (create with imagination). 3. detchiageru でっち上げる (fabricate).

inventory, n. mokuroku 目録 (list); tanaoroshi 棚卸し (yearly check).

invert, vb. gyaku ni suru 逆にする (reverse); sakasama ni suru 逆さまにする (turn upside down).

invertebrate, n. musekitsui-dōbutsu 無脊椎動物.

invest, vb. 1. tōshi suru 投資する (spend money for future return). 2. tsugikomu 注ぎ込む (make effort for future return). 3.

kiseru 着せる (clothe).

investigate, *vb.* 1. shiraberu 調べる (examine). 2. torishirabe o suru 取り調べをする (search).

investment, *n.* tōshi 投資 (investing of money or effort).

invigorate, *vb.* genkizukeru 元気付ける; yūkizukeru 勇気付ける.

invincible, *adj.* muteki (no) 無敵 (の).

invisible, *adj.* mienai 見えない.

invite, *vb.* 1. shōtai suru 招待する (invite to dinner, etc.). 2. maneku 招く (cause; ask for participation). 3. onegai suru お願いする (ask politely).

invoice, *n.* seikyūsho 請求書.

involve, *vb.* 1. tomonau 伴う (include as necessary). 2. makikomu 巻き込む (cause others to become concerned; implicate). 3. ... ni kan'yo shiteiru ...に関与している (be related to). 4. **be involved in** ... de isogashii ...で忙しい (be busy with).

inward, *adj.* 1. naka (no) 中 (の); uchi (no) 内 (の). 2. *adv.* naka e/ni 中へ/に.

I.O.U., *n.* shakuyōsho 借用書.

I.Q., *n.* chinōshisū 知能指数.

Iran, *n.* iran イラン.

Iraq, *n.* iraku イラク.

irate, *adj.* okotte iru 怒っている.

ire, *n.* ikari 怒り.

Ireland, *n.* airurando アイルランド.

iris, *n.* 1. ayame あやめ (plant). 2. kōsai 虹彩 (eye).

irk, *vb.* komaraseru 困らせる (annoy); iradataseru 苛立たせる (irritate).

iron, 1. *n.* tetsu 鉄 (metallic element). 2. *vb.* airon o kakeru アイロンをかける (press clothes).

ironic, *adj.* hiniku (na) 皮肉 (な).

irony, *n.* hiniku 皮肉.

irrational, *adj.* fugōri 不合理 (な).

irreconcilable, *adj.* oriawanai 折り合わない.

irregular, *adj.* 1. fukisoku (na) 不規則 (な) (not conforming to rule). 2. fuzoroi (no) 不揃い (の) (not symmetrical).

irresistible, *adj.* teikō dekinai 抵抗できない.

irresponsible, *adj.* musekinin (na) 無責任 (な).

Islam, *n.* isuramu-kyō イスラム教 (religion).

island, *n.* shima 島.

isolate, *vb.* 1. koritsu saseru 孤立させる (cause to be separated from others). 2. kakuri suru 隔離する (quarantine).

Israel, *n.* isuraeru イスラエル.

issue, 1. *n.* hakkō 発行 (act of issuing); mondaiten 問題点 (point in question); shison 子孫 (offspring); gō 号 (one of a series of periodicals); kekka 結果 (result); **at issue** giron no mato 議論の的 (being disputed). 2. *vb.* hakkō suru 発行する (publish); haikyū suru 配給する (distribute); dasu 出す (send out, emit); deru 出る (emerge, go); **issue from** ... ni yurai suru ...に由来する (result from).

it, *pron.* (often omitted in

Japanese) sore (ga, wa, o, ni) それ(が、は、を、に).

Italy, *n.* itaria イタリア.

itch, 1. *n.* kayumi 痒み (skin irritation); yokkyū 欲求 (desire). 2. *vb.* kayui 痒い (feel skin irritation); muzu-muzu suru むずむずする (desire).

item, *n.* 1. kōmoku 項目; mokuroku 目録 (separate

article). 2. kiji 記事 (news). 3. mono 物(thing).

itinerary, *n.* ryokōnittei 旅行日程.

its, *adj.* sono その; sore no その.

itself, *pron.* sono mono そのもの.

ivory, *n.* zōge 象牙 (elephant tusk); **ivory tower** zōge no tō 象牙の塔.

J

jab, 1. *n.* tsuki 突き. 2. *vb.* tsuku 突く; tsukisasu 突き刺す.

jabber, 1. *n.* hayakuchi 早口. 2. *vb.* hayakuchi de shaberu 早口でしゃべる.

jagged, *adj.* giza-giza (no) ぎざぎざ(の).

jail, 1. *n.* rōya 牢屋; kangoku 監獄; keimusho 刑務所. 2. *vb.* rō/keimusho ni ireru 牢／刑務所に入れる.

janitor, *n* kanrinin 管理人.

January, *n.* ichigatsu 一月.

Japan. *n.* nihon/nippon 日本／日本.

Japanese, 1. *n.* nihonjin 日本人 (person); nihongo 日本語 (language). 2. *adj.* nihon (no) 日本 (の) (of Japan); nihonjin (no) 日本人 (の) (of the Japanese).

jar, 1. *n.* bin 瓶; tsubo壷 (container); hageshii shindō 激しい震動 (jolt). 2. *vb.* hageshiku shindō saseru 激しく震動させる (jolt).

jargon, *n.* nakamakotoba 仲間言葉 (informal); senmon'yōgo 専門用語 (specialized vocabulary).

jaundice, *n.* ōdan 黄疸.

jaunt, *n.* ryokō 旅行 (trip); ensoku 遠足 (day

excursion).

javelin, *n.* nageyari 投げ槍.

jaw, *n.* ago あご.

jealous, *adj.* 1. shittobukai 嫉妬深い (fearful of losing love). 2. netamibukai 妬み深い (resentful and envious); urayamashigaru 羨ましがる (envious).

jealousy, *n.* 1. shitto 嫉妬. 2. netami 妬み.

jeer, 1. *n.* azakeri 嘲けり; karakai からかい. 2 *vb* azakeru 嘲ける; karakau からかう.

jellyfish, *n.* kurage くらげ.

jest, 1. *n.* jōdan 冗談 (joke). 2. *vb.* jōdan o iu 冗談を言う.

jester, *n.* fuzake/odoke mono ふざけ／おどけ者.

jet, *n.* funsha 噴射 (gas stream).

jet-black, *adj.* makkura (na, no) 真っ暗 (な、の).

jetty, *n.* 1. bōhatei 防波堤 (harbor protection). 2. sanbashi 桟橋 (pier).

jewel, *n.* hōseki 宝石.

jewelry, *n.* hōseki 宝石 (precious stones); sōshingu 装身具(adornments).

Jewish, *adj.* yudayajin (no) ユダヤ人 (の).

jingle, 1. *n.* rin-rin りんりん.

2. *vb.* rin-rin to naru りんり
んと鳴る。

job, *n.* shigoto 仕事。

jog, *vb.* 1. chotto tsuku ちょ
っと突く (nudge); chotto
yusuru ちょっと揺する
(shake). 2. hashiru 走る;
jogingu suru ジョギングす
る (run).

join, *vb.* 1. musubu 結ぶ
(put together). 2. hitotsu ni
naru 一つになる (unite). 3.
kuwawaru 加わる (become
member of).

joint, 1. *n.* setsugō-ten/-bu
接合点/〜部 (connection);
kansetsu 関節 (movable
joint). 2. *adj.* kyōdō (no) 共
同 (の)。

joke, 1. *n.* jōdan 冗談。 2. *vb.*
jōdan o iu 冗談を言う。

jolly, *adj.* tanoshii 楽しい;
yukai (na) 愉快 (な)。

jolt, 1. *n.* yure 揺れ
(shaking). 2. *vb.*
yurigokasu 揺り動かす
(shake).

journal, *n.* 1. shinbun 新聞
(newspaper). 2. nisshi 日誌
(daily record). 3. zasshi 雑
誌 (periodical).

journey, 1. *n.* tabi 旅; ryokō
旅行。 2. *vb.* tabi/ryokō suru
旅/旅行する。

joy, *n.* kōfuku 幸福;
yorokobi 喜び。

Judaism, *n.* yudaya-kyō ユ
ダヤ教。

judge, 1. *n.* saibankan 裁判
官 (law); shinpan 審判
(sports); shinsain 審査員
(competition). 2. *vb.* sabaku
裁く (pass legal judgment);
handan suru 判断する (form
judgment); shinsa suru 審査
する (in competition).

judgment, *n.* 1. hanketsu 判

決 (official decision). 2.
handan 判断 (opinion). 3.
handanryoku 判断力
(judging ability).

judicial, *adj.* shihō/saiban
(no) 司法/裁判 (の)。

judicious, *adj.* rikō (na) 利
口 (な); handanryoku ga aru
判断力がある。

judo, *n.* jūdō 柔道。

jug, *n.* mizusashi 水差し。

juice, *n.* shiru 汁 (liquid).

juicy, *adj.* shiruke ga ōi 汁気
が多い。

July, *n.* shichigatsu 七月。

jump, *vb.* tobu 飛ぶ。

jumpy, *adj.* ochitsukanai 落
ち着かない (nervous).

junction, *n.* 1. setsuzokuten
接続点 (connection); 2.
kōsaten 交差点 (crossroads).

June, *n.* rokugatsu 六月。

junior, *n.* 1. san'nensei 三年
生 (college student);
toshishita 年下 (younger
person). 2. *adj.* toshishita
(no) 年下 (の)。

junk, *n.* garakuta がらくた
(rubbish); jankusen ジャン
ク船 (ship).

just, 1. *adj.* kōsei (na) 公正
(な) (fair); tadashii 正しい
(right); datō (na) 妥当 (な)
(proper); seikaku (na) 正確
(な) (exact). 2. *adv.* chōdo
丁度 (exactly); tatta たった
(only); **just now** tatta ima
たった今。

justice, *n.* 1. seigi 正義; kōsei
公正 (fairness). 2. saiban 裁
判 (administration of law).
3. saibankan 裁判官 (judge).

juvenile, *adj.* seishōnen (no)
青少年 (の) (youth); jidō
(no) 児童 (の) (child);
shōnen (no) 少年 (の) (boy);
shōjo (no) 少女 (の) (girl).

K

keen, *adj.* 1. surudoi 鋭い (sharp). 2. kibishii 厳しい (biting). 3. eibin (na) 鋭敏 (な) (sensitive). 4. hageshii 激しい (fierce). 5. nesshin (na) 熱心 (な) (eager).

keep, *vb.* 1. tsuzukeru 続ける (continue to do). 2. tamotsu 保つ (maintain). 3. motsu 持つ (have). 4. yashinau 養う (support). 5. mamoru 守る (observe, guard). 6. **keep on** tsuzukeru 続ける; **keep up with** ... ni tsuite iku ... について行く.

keepsake, *n.* kinenhin 記念品; katami 形見.

keg, *n.* chiisai taru 小さい樽.

kennel, *n.* inugoya 犬小屋.

kerchief, *n.* nekkachifu ネッカチーフ (for head, neck); hankachi ハンカチ (handkerchief).

kernel, *n.* tsubu 粒 (grain); kaku 核 (center).

kerosene, *n.* tōyu 灯油.

kettle, *n.* yakan やかん.

key, 1. *n.* kagi 鍵 (for a lock, clue); chō 調 (principal music key); ken 鍵 (piano). 2. *adj.* jūyō (na) 重要 (な) (important).

keyboard, *n.* kenban 鍵盤.

kick, *vb.* keru 蹴る.

kid, *n.* 1. koyagi 子山羊 (young goat); kodomo 子供 (child). 2. *vb.* karakau からかう (fool); jōdan o iu 冗談を言う (jest).

kidnapping, *n.* yūkai 誘拐.

kidney, *n.* jinzō 腎臓.

kill, *vb.* 1. korosu 殺す (end life, murder). 2. hakai suru 破壊する (destroy). 3. **kill time** jikan o tsubusu 時間をつぶす.

kiln, *n.* kama 釜; ro 炉.

kin, *n.* shinseki 親戚; ketsuen(sha) 血縁(者) (relatives).

kind, 1. *adj.* shinsetsu (na) 親切 (な) (gentle, kind-hearted); ii 良い (good); yasashii 優しい (tender). *n.* shurui 種類 (type); tokushitsu 特質 (nature); **a kind of** isshu (no) 一種 (の); **kind of** chotto ちょっと; yaya やや.

kindergarten, *n.* yōchien 幼稚園.

kindle, *vb.* 1. hi o tsukeru 火を点ける (set afire). 2. kakitateru 掻き立てる (rouse feelings).

king, *n.* ō(sama) 王(様); kokuō 国王.

kingdom, *n.* ōkoku 王国.

kit, *n.* 1. dōguisshiki 道具一式 (set of tools). 2. zairyōisshiki 材料一式 (set of materials).

kitchen, *n.* daidokoro 台所.

kite, *n.* tako 凧.

kitten, *n.* koneko 子猫.

knead, *vb.* neru 練る; koneru こねる.

knee, *n.* hiza 膝.

kneel, *vb.* hizamazuku 膝跪く.

knife, *n.* hōchō 包丁 (for cutting); kogatana 小刀 (dagger).

knit, *vb.* amu 編む.

knob, *n.* totte 取っ手 (handle).

knot, 1. *n.* musubime 結び目. 2. *vb.* musubu 結ぶ (tie); motsureru もつれる (become entangled).

know, *vb.* 1. shiru 知る (get knowledge); shitteiru 知っている (have knowledge, be

acquainted). 2. wakaru わかる (understand).
know-it-all, *n.* shittakaburi 知ったかぶり.

knowledge, *n.* chishiki 知識.
Korea, *n.* kitachōsen 北朝鮮 (North Korea); kankoku 韓国 (South Korea).

L

labor, 1. *n.* shigoto 仕事; rōdō 労働 (work); osan お産 (childbirth). 2. *vb.* hataraku 働く.
laboratory, *n.* kenkyūjo 研究所 (place for scientific work); jikkenshitsu 実験室 (room for experiments).
laborious, *adj.* tema ga kakaru 手間がかかる.
labyrinth, *n.* meikyū 迷宮; meiro 迷路.
lacerate, *vb.* hikisaku 引き裂く (tear).
lack, 1. *n.* fusoku 不足; ketsubō 欠乏. 2. *vb.* kaku 欠く; (... ga) nai (...が) 無い.
lacquer, *n.* 1. wanisu ワニス. 2. urushi 漆 (Japanese lacquer); shikki 漆器 (Japanese lacquerware).
lad, *n.* shōnen 少年; wakamono 若者.
ladder, *n.* hashigo 梯子.
laden, *adj.* mansai shita 満載した.
ladle, *n.* hishaku 柄杓 (for dipping water); shakushi 杓子 (soup).
lady, *n.* 1. shukujo 淑女 (woman of refinement). 2. fujin 婦人 (woman).
ladybug, *n.* tentōmushi 天道虫.
lag, 1. *n.* okure 遅れ. 2. *vb.* okureru 遅れる (delay, fail to maintain speed).
lake, *n.* mizuumi 湖; -ko -湖; **Lake Biwa** biwako 琵琶湖.
lamb, *n.* 1. kohitsuji 小羊 (young sheep).

ramuniku ラム肉 (meat).
lame, *adj.* 1. bikko (no) びっこ (の) (crippled); heta (na) 下手 (な) (inadequate).
lament, 1. *n.* nageki 嘆き. 2. *vb.* nageki-kanashimu 嘆き悲しむ.
lamp, *n.* akari 明り.
land, *n.* 1. riku 陸 (dry part of earth's surface); tochi 土地 (a portion of land); kuni 国 (country); tsuchi 土 (soil); **native land** sokoku 祖国. 2. *vb.* chakuriku suru 着陸する (plane); jōriku suru 上陸する (ship).
landlord, *n.* yanushi 家主 (house, apartment, etc.).
landmark, *n.* 1. mejirushi 目印 (prominent object serving as guide). 2. kakkiteki na koto 画期的なこと (landmark event).
landscape, *n.* 1. keshiki 景色 (scenery). 2. fūkeiga 風景画 (picture).
landslide, *n.* 1. jisuberi 地滑り (fall of earth or rock). 2. asshō 圧勝 (victory).
lane, *n.* 1. komichi 小道; yokochō 横丁 (narrow road). 2. shasen 車線 (car lane).
language, *n.* kotoba 言葉; -go -語.
lantern, *n.* chōchin 提灯.
lap, 1. *n.* hiza 膝 (body); kasanari 重なり (overlapping part); isshū 一周 (racecourse). 2. *vb.* tsutsumu 包む (wrap);

uchiyoseru 打ち寄せる (wash against); nameru なめる (lick).

lapse, 1. *n.* chiisana machigai 小さな間違い (small error); kashitsu 過失 (failure); keika 経過 (slow passing). 2. *vb.* ochiiru 陥る (fall); keika suru 経過する (pass).

large, *adj.* ōkii 大きい (great in number or size); hiroi 広い (spacious).

largely, *adv.* omo ni 主に; shutoshite 主として (in great part).

largeness, *n.* ōkisa 大きさ; hirosa 広さ.

large-scale, *adj.* daikibo (na, no) 大規模 (な、の).

lark, *n.* hibari ひばり (bird).

larva, *n.* yōchū 幼虫.

larynx, *n.* kōtō 喉頭.

lash, 1. *n.* muchihimo 鞭紐 (part of whip); muchiuchi 鞭打ち (whipping); matsuge まつげ (eyelash). 2. *vb.* muchiutsu むち打つ (whip); shibaru 縛る (bind); **lash out** kōgeki suru 攻撃する (attack).

last, 1. *n.* saigo 最後; **at last** tsui ni 遂に. 2. *adj.* saigo no 最後の (final); saikin no 最近の (most recent); mae no 前の (latest); sen- 先-; saku- 昨-; **last month** sengetsu 先月; **last week** senshu 先週; **last year** sakunen 昨年. 3. *adv.* saikin 最近 (most recently); saigo ni 最後に (in the end). 4. *vb.* tsuzuku 続く (continue); motsu 持つ (remain useful).

lasting, *adj.* 1. nagaku tsuzuku 長く続く (continuing). 2. nagamochi suru 長持ちする (durable).

last name, *n.* myōji 名字; sei 姓.

latch, *n.* kakegane 掛け金; kan'nuki 閂.

late, 1. *adj.* osoi 遅い; okureteiru 遅れている (after the usual time); (... no) owarigoro (no) (...の) 終わり頃 (の) (at the end of a day, season, etc.); **late April** shigatsu no owarigoro 四月の終わり頃; saikin no 最近の (recent); ko 故 (deceased). 2. *adv.* osoku 遅く; okurete 遅れて (occurring after the proper time); osoku made 遅くまで (until a late hour).

latent, *adj.* senzai-teki (na) 潜在的 (な).

later, *adj.* 1. ato no hō (no) 後の方 (の). 2. *adv.* ato de 後で; **See you later.** Ato de aimashō. 後で会いましょう.

lather, *n.* sekken no awa 石けんの泡 (detergent foam).

Latin, 1. *n.* ratengo ラテン語 (language). 2. *adj.* ratengo (no) ラテン語 (の) (of the language).

latitude, *n.* ido 緯度.

latter, *adj.* kōsha no 後者 (の) (second); **the latter** kōsha 後者.

lattice, *n.* kōshi 格子.

laugh, 1. *n.* warai 笑い. 2. *vb.* warau 笑う; **laugh at** azakeri-warau 嘲り笑う; baka ni suru 馬鹿にする.

launch, 1. *n.* shinsui 進水 (floating a boat). 2. *vb.* hajimeru 始める (start); shinsui saseru 進水させる (float); hassha saseru 発車させる (send forth a spacecraft).

launder, *vb.* sentaku suru 洗濯する (wash).

laundromat, *n.* koinrandorī コインランドリー.

laundry, *n.* 1. sentakumono 洗濯物 (clothes, etc.). 2. sentakuba 洗濯場 (place for doing the family wash). 3. sentakuya 洗濯屋 (commercial establishment).

laurel, *n.* gekkeiju 月桂樹 (tree); gekkeikan 月桂冠 (wreath).

lavish, 1. *adj.* takusan (no) たくさん (の) (abundant); kimae ga ii 気前が良い (giving). 2. *vb.* kimaeyoku ataeru (tsukau) 気前良く与える (使う) (give or spend lavishly).

law, *n.* 1. hō 法 (rule); hōritsu 法律 (legal rules). 2. hō(ritsu)gaku 法(律)学 (study). 3. soshō 訴訟 (legal action). 4. hōsoku 法則 (principle).

lawn, *n.* shibafu 芝生; **lawn mower** shibakariki 芝刈り機.

lawyer, *n.* bengoshi 弁護士.

lay, 1. *adj.* zokujin (no) 俗人 (の) (of the laity); shirōto (no) 素人 (の) (not professional). 2. *vb.* oku 置く (put down, place); taosu 倒す (knock down); tateru 立てる (devise, as a plan); (tamago o) umu (卵を) 産む (produce eggs); **lay aside** totteoku とっておく (save for future use); **lay off** ichijikaiko suru 一時解雇する; **lay out** hirogeru 広げる (spread out); haichi suru 配置する (arrange well).

layer, *n.* sō 層 (one thickness). 2. nuri 塗り (of paint, lacquer, etc.).

layman, *n.* 1. zokujin 俗人 (member of the laity). 2. shirōto 素人 (non-professional).

layout, *n.* haichi 配置 (arrangement). 2. sekkei 設計; keikaku 計画 (plan).

lazy, *adj.* 1. taiman (na) 怠慢 (な); namakemono (no) 怠け者 (の) (disliking effort). 2. noroi のろい (slow moving).

lead, *n.* namari 鉛 (metal).

lead, 1. *n.* sentō 先頭 (foremost place); sendō 先導 (act of leading); tegakari 手掛かり (clue); rīdāshippu リーダーシップ (leadership); shuensha 主演者 (principal performer). 2. *vb.* sentō o iku 先頭を行く (be ahead); michibiku 導く (guide); ... yō ni naru ...ようになる (induce); **lead to** ... ni itaru ...に至る (result in).

leaden, *adj.* 1. namari (no) 鉛 (の) (of lead). 2. namari'iro (no) 鉛色 (の) (of a leaden color). 3. omoi 重い (heavy); omogurushii 重苦しい (gloomy).

leader, *n.* shidōsha 指導者 (person who guides). 2. sentō 先頭 (person who is ahead of others).

leadership, *n.* shidōryoku 指導力.

leaf, *n.* 1. ha 葉 (plant). 2. pēji ページ (book).

leaflet, *n.* chirashi 散らし.

leak, 1. *n.* ana 穴 (hole); more 漏れ (leaking gas, etc.). 2. *vb.* moreru 漏れる (pass through leak); morasu 漏らす (make known, let pass through leak).

lean, 1. *adj.* yaseteiru やせている (not fat); shibō ga sukunai 脂肪が少ない (meat). 2. *vb.* katamuku 傾く (incline); katamukeru 傾ける (cause to lean); (... ni) motareru (...に) もたれる

(rest against); **lean on** tayoru 頼る (rely on).

leap, 1. *n.* chōyaku 跳躍 (jump); yakushin 躍進 (advancement); jōshō 上昇 (increase). 2. *vb.* tobiagaru 飛び上がる (spring through the air); tobu 飛ぶ (jump); **leap at** ... ni tobitsuku ...に飛びつく.

learn, 1. *n.* narau 習う; manabu 学ぶ (learn skill). 2. oboeru 覚える (memorize). 3. shiru 知る (be informed).

learning, *n.* gakumon 学問.

lease, 1. *n.* shakuyō-shōsho 借用証書 (lease contract). 2. *vb.* kasu 貸す (grant lease); kariru 借りる (hold by lease).

leash, *n.* himo 紐 (cord).

least, 1. *n.* **at least** sukunakutomo 少くとも. 2. *adj.* ichiban chiisai 一番小さい (smallest in size); ichiban sukunai 一番少ない (smallest in amount).

leather, *n.* kawa 皮.

leave, 1. *n.* kyoka 許可 (permission), wakare 別れ (farewell); kyūka 休暇 (furlough). 2. *vb.* saru 去る (depart); deru 出る (go out); itomagoi o suru 暇乞いをする (say good-bye); yameru 止める (stop); nokosu 残す (leave behind, bequeath); (... no mama ni) shiteoku (...のままに) しておく (leave unchanged); wasureru 忘れる (forget); **leave for** ... e tabidatsu ...へ旅立つ; **leave off** yameru 止める; **leave out** habuku 省く.

leaven, *n.* kōbo 酵母 (leavening substance).

lecture, 1. *n.* kōgi 講義

(discourse); sekkyō 説教 (reprimand). 2. *vb.* kōgi o suru 講義をする; sekkyō suru 説教する.

leech, *n.* hiru 蛭.

leek, *n.* nira にら.

leery, *adj.* keikai shiteiru 警戒している.

leeway, *n.* yochi 余地.

left, 1. *n.* hidari 左 (direction); sayoku 左翼 (political). 2. *adj.* hidari (no) 左 (の). 3. *adv.* hidari ni/e 左に／へ.

left-handed, *adj.* hidarikiki (no) 左利き (の).

leftovers, *n.* nokorimono 残り物.

leg, *n.* ashi 足.

legacy, *n.* isan 遺産.

legal, *adj.* 1. gōhō (na) 合法 (な) (lawful). 2. hōritsu (no) 法律 (の) (of law).

legend, *n.* densetsu 伝説 (story).

legible, *adj.* wakariyasui 分かり易い (easy to understand); yomiyasui 読み易い (easy to read).

legislation, *n.* hōteika 法定化; rippō 立法.

legitimate, *adj.* 1. gōhō (na) 合法 (な); seitō (na) 正当 (な) (lawful). 2. mottomo (na) 最も (な) (valid, logical). 3. chakushutsu (no) 嫡出 (の) (born to a married couple).

legume, *n.* mame 豆 (peas or beans).

leisure, *n.* hima 暇; **at one's leisure** hima na toki ni 暇な時に.

leisurely, *adj.* yukkuri shita ゆっくりした.

lend, *vb.* kasu 貸す.

length, *n.* nagasa 長さ (size or extent from end to end); **at length** sukkari すっかり

(fully); tsui ni 遂に (at last).

lengthen, vb. nagaku suru 長くする (make longer); nagaku naru 長くなる (become longer).

lengthwise, adv. tate ni 縦に.

lengthy, adj. naga-nagashii 長々しい.

lenient, adj. kan'yō (na) 寛容 (な); amai 甘い.

leopard, n. hyō ひょう.

lesbian, n. rezu(bian) レズ (ビアン); dōseiaisha 同性愛者.

less, 1. adj. ... yori sukunai ... より少ない (less in amount); ... yori chiisai ...より小さい (smaller); **less expensive than this** kore yori yasui. **2.** adv. ... yori sukunaku ...より少なく; ... yori chiisaku ...より小さく; **less and less** dan-dan sukunaku だんだん少なく.

lesson, n. **1.** kurasu クラス; jugyō 授業 (session). **2.** ka 課 (unit of a book). **3.** benkyō 勉強 (something to be learned, useful experience). **4.** imashime 戒め (reproof).

lest, conj. ... (shi)nai tame/yō ni ... (し)ないため/ように.

let, vb. **1.** yurusu 許す (permit). **2.** tōsu 通す (allow to pass). **3.** saseru さ せる (make). **4.** kasu 貸す (rent out). **5. let down** gakkari saseru がっかりさせる (disappoint); **let on** morasu 漏らす (tell a secret); **let up** owaru 終わる (cease); **let's** ... -mashō ...-ましょう; **let us do** sasete kudasai ...させてください (allow us to).

letdown, n. kiochi 気落ち; gakkari suru koto がっかり

すること (disappointment).

lethal, adj. chimei-teki (na) 致命的 (な).

letter, n. **1.** tegami 手紙 (written communication). **2.** moji 文字 (alphabet).

leukemia, n. hakketsubyō 白血病.

level, 1. n. takasa 高さ (height); heimen 平面 (flat surface). **2.** adj. taira (na) 平ら (な) (even and flat); suihei (na) 水平 (な) (horizontal); ichiyō (no) 一様 (の) (uniform).

levy, 1. n. zeikin 税金 (tax); chōhei 徴兵 (conscription); chōshū 徴収 (collection). **2.** vb. kazei suru 課税する (tax); chōhei suru 徴兵する (conscript); sensō o hajimeru 戦争を始める (start war).

liability, n. **1. liabilities** shakkin 借金; fusai 負債 (debt). **2.** furi 不利 (disadvantage). **3.** sekinin 責任 (state of being liable).

liable, adj. **1.** sekinin ga aru 責任がある (responsible); harau beki 払うべき (responsible for payment). **2.** ... shigachi (na) ...しがち (な) (likely to do).

liar, n. usotsuki 嘘吐き.

liberal, adj. **1.** jiyūshugi (no) 自由主義 (の) (political). **2.** kan'yō (na) 寛容 (な); kandai (na) 寛大 (な) (tolerant). **3.** kimae ga ii 気前がいい (generous).

liberate, vb. kaihō suru 解放する.

liberty, n. jiyū 自由.

library, n. **1.** toshokan 図書館 (communal library); dokushobeya 読書部屋 (home library). **2.** zōsho 蔵書 (collection).

license, *n.* 1. kyoka 許可
(permission). 2. menkyo 免
許 (certificate); **driver's
license** unten menkyo 運転
免許.

lick, *vb.* 1. nameru なめる
(pass the tongue over). 2.
katsu 勝つ (overcome,
defeat).

lid, *n.* 1. futa 蓋 (cover). 2.
mabuta まぶた (eyelid).

lie, 1. *n.* uso 嘘 (false
statement). 2. *vb.* uso o
tsuku 嘘を吐く (tell a lie);
yokotawaru 横たわる (be in
a flat position); (... ni) aru
(... に) ある (be placed).

life, *n.* 1. inochi 命
(animation). 2. jinsei 人生;
shōgai 生涯 (period of one's
being alive); jumyō 寿命
(lifespan). 3. seikatsu 生活
(mode of existence). 4.
seibutsu 生物 (living things).

lifeboat, *n.* kyūmei-bōto 救
命ボート.

life expectancy, *n.*
heikinjumyō 平均寿命.

lifeguard, *n.* kyūmei'in 救命
員.

life insurance, *n.*
seimeihoken 生命保険.

lifelong, *adj.* isshō no 一生
の.

life preserver, *n.* kyūmeigu
救命具.

lifestyle, *n.* ikikata 生き方.

lift, 1. *n.* **give a lift** nosete
iku 乗せて行く. 2. *vb.* ageru
上げる (raise, bring
upward); haishi suru 廃止す
る (end).

light, 1. *n.* akari 明り
(illumination); hikari 光
(natural light); **bring to
light** shiraseru 知らせる;
come to light shirareru yō
ni naru 知られるようにな
る. 2. *adj.* akarui 明るい

(bright); karui 軽い (not
heavy, not serious, easy);
usui 薄い (color). 3. *vb.*
akari o tsukeru 明りを点け
る (illuminate); hi o tsukeru
火を点ける (ignite).

light bulb, *n.* denkyū 電球.

lightheaded, *adj.* 1.
furatsuite-iru ふらついてい
る (giddy). 2. asahaka (na)
浅はか (な) (silly,
thoughtless).

lighthouse, *n.* tōdai 灯台.

lighting, *n.* shōmei 照明
(theater, etc.).

lightning, *n.* inazuma 稲妻.

light-year, *n.* kōnen 光年.

likable, *adj.* sukareru 好かれ
る.

like, 1. *adj.* (... ni) niteiru (...
に) 似ている (similar); onaji
yō na 同じような (alike). 2.
conj. ... no yō ni ... のように (just
as, as if). 3. *prep.* (... no) yō
ni (...の) ように (similar to);
(... no) yō na (...の) ような
(such as); ... rashii ...らしい
(characteristic of). 4. *vb.*
konomu 好む; (... ga) suki
(de aru) (...が) 好き (であ
る); **would like to** ...
(shi)tai ... (し)たい.

likely, *adj.* arisō (na) あり
そう (な) (probable,
believable). 2. mikomi ga
aru 見込みがある
(promising).

lily, *n.* yuri 百合.

limb, *n.* 1. teashi 手足
(body). 2. eda 枝 (branch).

lime, *n.* sekkai 石灰
(quicklime).

limelight, *n.* chūmoku no
mato 注目の的 (center of
interest).

limit, 1. *n.* genkai 限界
(farthest extent); kyōkai 境
界 (boundary); **off limits**
tachi'iri kinshi 立入禁止. 2.

vb. kagiru 限る.

limitation, *n.* genkai 限界.

limp, 1. *n.* bikko びっこ. **2.** *adj.* gunya-gunya shiteiru ぐにゃぐにゃしている (not firm). **3.** *vb.* bikko o hiku びっこを引く (walk with a limp).

line, 1. *n.* sen 線 (thin mark, string, cord); denwa 電話 (telephone); shiwa しわ (wrinkle); retsu 列 (row). **2.** *vb.* sen o hiku 線を引く (mark with a line); uraji o tsukeru 裏地を付ける (cover inner side of); **line up** narabu 並ぶ (form a row).

lineage, *n.* kakei 家系; kettō 血統 (ancestry).

linear, *adj.* **1.** sen (no) 線 (の) (lines). **2.** tate (no) 縦 (の) (length).

linger, *vb.* **1.** inokoru 居残る (stay on). **2.** kangaekomu 考え込む (dwell in thought). **3.** nagabiku 長引く (persist).

linguistics, *n.* gengogaku 言語学.

lining, *n.* uraji 裏地.

link, 1. *n.* wa 輪 (section of a chain); tsunagari つながり (bond). **2.** *vb.* tsunagu つなぐ (unite).

lint, *n.* itokuzu 糸屑.

lip, *n.* kuchibiru 唇.

lipstick, *n.* kuchibeni 口紅.

liquid, *n.* ekitai 液体.

liquidate, *vb.* **1.** hensai suru 返済する (pay a debt). **2.** heiten/heisa suru 閉店/閉鎖する (dissolve a business). **3.** genkinka suru 現金化する (convert into cash).

liquor, *n.* sake 酒.

lisp, 1. *n.* shitatarazu 舌足らず. **2.** *vb.* shitatarazu ni hanasu 舌足らずに話す.

list, 1. *n.* ichiranhyō 一覧表; meibo 名簿. **2.** *vb.* risuto ni ageru リストに挙げる.

listen (to), *vb.* (... o) kiku (...を) 聞く.

listless, *adj.* mukanshin (na) 無関心 (な); monoui 物憂い.

literacy, *n.* shikiji 識字.

literal, *adj.* mojidōri (no) 文字通り (の); chikugo-teki (na) 逐語的 (な) (following the original words).

literally, *adv.* **1.** genmitsu ni 厳密に (strictly). **2.** mojidōri ni 文字通りに (word for word).

literature, *n.* **1.** bungaku 文学 (prose, poetry, etc.). **2.** bunken 文献 (entire body of writings on a specific subject).

litter, 1. *n.* gomi ごみ (rubbish). **2.** chirakasu 散らかす (strew, scatter).

little, 1. *n.* **a little** sukoshi 少し. **2.** *adj.* chiisai 小さい (size, mind); sukunai 少ない (quantity); mijikai 短い (time). **3.** *adv.* sukoshi 少し (slightly); **little by little** sukoshi zutsu 少しずつ.

live, 1. *adj.* ikiteiru 生きている (alive); kakki ga aru 活気がある (energetic); jitsuen (no) 実演 (の) (performance). **2.** *vb.* ikiru 生きる (have life); sumu 住む (reside); ikiteiru 生きている (be alive); seikatsu suru 生活する (maintain a lifestyle); nokoru 残る (endure in reputation).

lively, *adj.* **1.** kappatsu (na) 活発 (な); nigiyaka (na) にぎやか (な) (active). **2.** kakki ni michita 活気に満ちた (spirited). **3.** waku-waku suru わくわくする (exciting).

livestock, *n.* kachiku 家畜 (domestic farm animals).

living, 1. *n.* seikatsu 生活 (lifestyle); seikatsuhi 生活費 (livelihood); **earn a living** seikatsuhi o eru 生活費を得る. **2.** *adj.* ikiteiru 生きている (alive); tsukawarete-iru 使われている (in active use).

living room, *n.* ima 居間.

lizard, *n.* tokage とかげ.

load, 1. *n.* ni(motsu) 荷(物) (cargo, anything carried). **2.** *vb.* ni o tsumu 荷を積む (put a load in or on); tama o tsumeru 弾を詰める (charge a gun).

loan, 1. *n.* rōn ローン; kashitsuke 貸し付け. **2.** *vb.* kasu 貸す.

lobe, *n.* mimitabu 耳たぶ (earlobe).

lobster, *n.* iseebi 伊勢えび.

local, 1. *n.* kakuekiteisha 各駅停車 (local train). **2.** *adj.* chihō (no) 地方 (の); tōchi (no) 当地 (の); **local color** chihōshoku 地方色.

locale, *n.* basho 場所 (place, setting).

locality, *n.* tokoro 所; basho 場所 (place, area).

locate, *vb.* **1.** mitsukeru 見つける (find). **2.** **be located at** ... ni aru/iru ...にある／いる.

location, *n.* basho 場所.

lock, 1. *n.* jō 錠 (security device); makige 巻毛 (curl); **locks** kami 髪 (hair). **2.** *vb.* kagi o kakeru 鍵を掛ける (secure with a lock); **lock in** tojikomeru 閉じ込める (confine); **lock out** heisa suru 閉鎖する.

locomotive, *n.* kikansha 機関車.

locust, *n.* inago 蝗.

lodge, 1. *n.* koya 小屋 (hut); rojji ロッジ (inn); (himitsu)kessha (秘密)結社 (secret society). **2.** *vb.* tomaru 泊まる (stay at an inn); geshuku suru 下宿する (live in rented quarters); tsukaeru つかえる (clog at a particular position); umaru 埋まる (be implanted); mōshitateru 申し立てる (lodge a complaint).

lodging, *n.* **1.** yado 宿 (temporary house). **2.** **lodgings** geshukubeya 下宿部屋 (rooms).

lofty, *adj.* **1.** kōshō (na) 高尚 (な) (exalted in dignity). **2.** takai 高い (high). **3.** kōman (na) 高慢 (な) (arrogant).

log, *n.* **1.** maruta 丸太 (tree). **2.** nisshi 日誌 (nautical).

logic, *n.* ronri 論理.

logistics, *n.* keikaku 計画 (planning).

loin, *n.* **1.** koshi 腰 (hips and groin); seiki 性器 (genitalia). **2.** koshiniku 腰肉 (of meat).

loincloth, *n.* fundoshi ふんどし.

loiter, *vb.* buratsuku ぶらつく (linger).

lollipop, *n.* pero-pero kyandē ぺろぺろキャンデー.

lonely, lonesome, *adj.* **1.** kodoku (na, no) 孤独 (な、の) (alone). **2.** sabishii 寂しい (wishing for company). **3.** koritsu shita 孤立した (isolated).

long, 1. *adj.* nagai 長い. **2.** *adv.* nagaku 長く. **3.** *vb.* **long for** ... o koimotomeru ...をこい求める. **4.** **long ago** zutto mae ni ずっと前に; **long live!** banzai 万歳; **a long time** nagai aida 長い

間; **as long as** ... (suru)
kagiri ... (する) 限り
(provided that); ... node ...
ので (since); ... no aida ...の
間 (while); **before long**
sugu ni すぐに; mamonaku
間もなく; **How long?**
Dono gurai. どの位; **no
longer** mohaya ... (dewa)
nai もはや... (では) ない; **so
long** dewa mata ではまた;
sayōnara さようなら.

long-distance, adj. chōkyori
(no) 長距離 (の).

longevity, n. 1. shihaisha 長寿
(long life). 2. jumyō 寿命
(length of life).

longing, n. setsubō 切望.

look, 1. n. miru koto 見るこ
と (act of looking); mikake
見かけ (appearance); **take a
look** miru 見る; **looks** yōbō
容貌. 2. vb. miru 見る
(direct the eyes); (...no yō
ni) mieru (...のように) 見え
る (seem); **look after** sewa
o suru 世話をする; **look at**
... o miru ...を見る; **look
for** ... o sagasu ...を捜す;
look forward to ... o
tanoshimi ni suru ...を楽し
みにする; **look into** ... o
shiraberu ...を調べる; **look
like** ... ni niteiru ...に似てい
る; ... no yō da ...
のようだ (seem); **look out**
(... ni) ki o tsukeru (...に) 気
をつける; **look up** miageru
見上げる (see upward);
shiraberu 調べる (check);
look up to ... o sonkei suru
...を尊敬する.

loom, 1. n. hataoriki 機織機.
2. vb. hata o oru 機を織る
(weave); ōkiku ukabiagaru
大きく浮かび上がる
(appear).

loop, n. wa 輪 (circle).

loose, adj. 1. jiyū (na) 自由

(na) (free). 2. tokareta 解か
れた (released from
binding). 3. yurui 緩い (not
tight). 4. ōmaka (na) 大ま
か (na) (not exact, broad).
5. fushidara (na) ふしだら
(na) (promiscuous).

loot, 1. n. ryakudatsu-hin 略
奪品 (spoils). 2. vb.
ryakudatsu suru 略奪する
(plunder).

lopsided, adj. katamuita 傾
いた.

lord, n. 1. shihaisha 支配者
(ruler). 2. kunshu 君主
(monarch, master, etc.). 3.
kizoku 貴族 (nobleman); -
kyō -卿 (British title); 4.
Lord shu 主 (Christ).

lose, vb. 1. nakusu 無くす;
ushinau 失う (fail to keep,
fail to find, cease to have, be
bereaved of). 2. wasureru
忘れる (misplace). 3. heru
減る; hikuku naru 低くなる
(become less or smaller).
lose weight taijū ga heru 体重が
減る. 4. makeru 負ける (fail
to win). 5. okureru 遅れる
(become slower by). 6. **lose
oneself** (... de) ware o
wasureru (...で) 我を忘れる
(become engrossed in); **lose
one's way** michi ni mayou
道に迷う.

loss, n. 1. nakusu koto 無く
すこと (deprivation);
sonshitsu 損失
(disadvantage); sōshitsu 喪
失 (deprivation through
death). 2. funshitsu 紛失
(act of losing something);
funshitsubutsu 紛失物
(something lost). 3. make
負け (losing by defeat). 4.
be at a loss tohō ni kureru
途方に暮れる (be
bewildered).

lost, adj. 1. nakushita 無くし

た (no longer possessed or found). 2. maigo (no) 迷子 (の) (having gone astray); **lost dog** maigo no inu 迷子の犬.

lot, n. 1. kuji くじ (object drawn to decide); **draw lots** kuji o hiku くじを引く. 2. wariate 割当て (allocation). 3. sadame 定め (fortune). 4. basho 場所, -jō -場 (piece of land); **parking lot** chūshajō 駐車場. 5. **a lot (of)**, **lots (of)** takusan (no) たくさん (の).

lottery, n. takarakuji 宝くじ.

loud, 1. adj. ōgoe (no) 大声 (の) (strong voice); oto ga ōkii 音が大きい (making loud sound); urusai うるさい (clamorous); hade (na) 派手 (な) (loud color). 2. adv. ōgoe de 大声で (in a loud voice).

lounge, 1. n. raunji ラウンジ; robī ロビー. 2. vb. motareru もたれる (recline); buratsuku ぶらつく (saunter).

love, 1. n. koi 恋 (romantic attachment); ai 愛 (passionate attachment, affection); seiai 性愛 (sexual love); koibito 恋人 (sweetheart); **fall in love** ai/koi suru 愛/恋する; **be in love** ren'aichū (no) 恋愛中 (の); **make love** neru 寝る. 2. vb. ai suru 愛する (have love or affection, have a strong liking).

lovely, adj. 1. kawaii 可愛い (charming); kirei (na) きれい (な) (beautiful). 2. tanoshii 楽しい (delightful).

lover, n. 1. koibito 恋人 (girlfriend, boyfriend, sweetheart). 2. aijin 愛人 (mistress). 3. aikōka 愛好家

(devotee).

low, adj. 1. hikui 低い (not high or tall, humble in status, not loud). 2. ototta 劣った (inferior); warui 悪い (bad). 3. shizunda 沈んだ (depressed).

lower, adj. chūjitsu (na) 忠実 (な); seijitsu (na) 誠実 (な).

lower, vb. sageru 下げる (reduce, diminish, make lower).

loyal, adj. chūjitsu (na) 忠実 (な); seijitsu (na) 誠実 (な).

lubricate, vb. abura o sasu 油をさす (oil).

luck, n. un 運; **bad luck** aku'un 悪運; **good luck** kōun 幸運; **Good luck!** Ganbatte. がんばって.

lucky, adj. un ga ii 運が良い; kōun (na, no) 幸運 (な, の).

lucrative, adj. (okane ga) mōkaru (お金が) 儲かる.

luggage, n. ryokōkaban 旅行鞄 (traveling bag); sūtsukēsu スーツケース (suitcase); toranku トランク (trunk).

lukewarm, adj. 1. namanurui 生ぬるい (tepid); ? ozanari (na, no) おざなり (な, の) (having little zeal).

lull, 1. n. kyūshi 休止 (temporary calm). 2. vb. nekasetsukeru 寝かせつける (soothe to sleep).

lullaby, n. komoriuta 子守り歌.

lumber, n. zaimoku 材木.

luminous, adj. 1. kagayaku 輝く (giving light). 2. meikai (na) 明解 (な) (easily understood).

lump, n. 1. katamari 塊 (mass); **a lump of sugar** kakuzatō hitotsu 角砂糖一つ. 2. hare 腫れ (swelling).

lunatic, 1. n. kichigai 気違い (insane or foolish person).

2. *adj.* kichigai (no) 気違い
(の).

lunch, 1. *n.* hirugohan 昼御
飯. 2. *vb.* hirugohan o
taberu 昼御飯を食べる.
lung, *n.* hai 肺.
lunge, 1. *n.* hitotsuki 一突き
(thrust). 2. *vb.* tobikakaru 飛
びかかる.
lure, 1. *n.* yūwaku 誘惑
(enticement); otori おとり
(decoy, bait). 2. *vb.* yūwaku
suru 誘惑する (entice);

obikiyoseru 誘き寄せる
(bait).
lurk, *vb.* hisomu 潜む (lie
hidden, exist unperceived).
lust, *n.* yokubō 欲望 (desire).
luster, *n.* kōtaku 光沢; tsuya
艶.
luxury, *n.* zeitaku 贅沢;
zeitakuhin 贅沢品
(indulgence).
lyre, *n.* tategoto 竪琴.
lyric, *n.* jojōshi 叙情詩;
lyrics kashi 歌詞.

M

macabre, *adj.* 1. shi (no) 死
(の) (of death). 2. kimi ga
warui 気味が悪い
(gruesome).
machination, *n.* keiryaku
計略 (crafty plot).
machine, *n.* kikai 機械
(apparatus, instrument).
machine gun, *n.* kikanjū 機
関銃.
machinery, *n.* 1. kikai 機械
(machines). 2. kikō 機構
(system).
mackerel, *n.* saba 鯖.
mad, *adj.* 1. kichigai (no) 気
違い (の) (lunatic). 2.
okotteiru 怒っている
(furious).
madam, *n.* okusama 奥様.
madden, *vb.* okoru 怒る
(become angry); okoraseru
怒らせる (make angry).
madman, -woman, *n.*
kichigai 気違い.
madness, *n.* kyōki 狂気
(lunacy).
magazine, *n.* zasshi 雑誌.
maggot, *n.* ujimushi 蛆虫.
magic, *n.* mahō 魔法
(mystical charm or power).
2. tejina 手品 (art of causing
illusions).

magical, *adj.* mahō (no) 魔
法 (の) (mystical power).
magician, *n.* 1. mahōtsukai
魔法使い; majutsushi 魔術師
(enchanter, sorcerer). 2.
tejinashi 手品師 (illusionist,
conjuror).
magnet, *n.* jishaku 磁石.
magnificent, *adj.* subarashii
素晴らしい (splendid).
maiden, 1. *n.* otome 乙女
(young girl). 2. *adj.* mikon
(no) 未婚 (の) (unmarried).
maiden name kyūsei 旧姓.
mail, 1. *n.* yūbin 郵便
(postal system); yūbinbutsu
郵便物 (things sent by mail);
tegami 手紙
(correspondence). 2. *vb.*
yūsō suru 郵送する (post).
mail order, *n.*
tsūshinhanbai 通信販売.
maim, *vb.* fugu ni suru 不具
にする.
main, 1. *n.* honkan 本管
(principal pipe); 2. *adj.*
shuyō (na) 主要 (な) (chief).
mainland, *n.* hondo 本土.
mainstay, *n.* daikokubashira 大黒柱 (person).
maintain, *vb.* 1. tamotsu 保
つ (keep in existence, keep

unimpaired); iji suru 維持する (keep in good condition). 2. shuchō suru 主張する (assert, insist). 3. sasaeru 支える (support).

maintenance, n. 1. iji 維持 (act of maintaining). 2. seikatsuhi 生活費 (livelihood).

majestic, adj. igen ga aru 威厳がある; dōdōtaru 堂々たる.

majority, n. 1. daitasū 大多数 (greater number). 2. kahansū 過半数 (more than half). 3. seinen 青年 (adulthood).

make, vb. 1. tsukuru 作る (produce, prepare). 2. saseru させる (force). 3. kasegu 稼ぐ (earn). 4. naru なる (become, add up). 5. **make believe** ... no furi o suru ...のふりをする; **make it** yaritogeru やり遂げる (achieve); ma ni au 間に合う (be in time); **make out** wakaru 分かる (comprehend); umaku yaru うまくやる (succeed); **make over** kaeru 変える (alter); **make up** tsukuriageru 作り上げる (concoct); keshō suru 化粧する (put on cosmetics); **make up for** ... no umeawase o suru ...の埋め合わせをする; **make up one's mind** kesshin suru 決心する.

makeshift, n. maniawase 間に合わせ.

malady, n. 1. byōki 病気 (disease). 2. byōgai 病害 (social malady).

male, n., adj. dansei (no) 男性 (の); otoko (no) 男 (の) (human); osu (no) 雄 (の) (animal).

malice, n. akui 悪意 (desire to harm others).

malign, vb. chūshō suru 中傷する.

malignant, adj. 1. akui ni michiteiru 悪意に満ちている (disposed to hurt others). 2. akusei (no) 悪性 (の) (tumor).

mallet, n. kizuchi 木槌.

malnutrition, n. eiyōfuryō 栄養不良.

mammal, n. honyūdōbutsu 哺乳動物.

mammoth, adj. kyodai (na) 巨大 (な) (gigantic).

man, n. 1. hito 人 (person, human being); jinrui 人類 (human race). 2. otoko 男 (adult male).

manage, vb. 1. nantoka ... suru 何とか...する (succeed in accomplishing). 2. kontorōru suru コントロールする (control); atsukau 扱う (handle). 3. kantoku suru 監督する (supervise). 4. kanri suru 管理する (administer).

management, n. 1. keiei 経営; kanri 管理 (business administration). 2. kanrishoku 管理職 (executives).

manager, n. 1. shihainin 支配人 (person who manages an enterprise). 2. kantoku 監督 (sports).

mandarin orange, n. mikan みかん.

mandatory, adj. kyōsei-teki (na) 強制的 (な); gimu-teki (na) 義務的 (な).

maneuver, 1. n. sakusen 作戦 (stratagem); **maneuvers** enshū 演習 (military). 2. vb. ugokasu 動かす (move); enshū o okonau 演習を行う (military).

mangle, *vb.* 1. zuta-zuta ni suru ずたずたにする (disfigure). 2. sokonau 損う (spoil).

mangy, *adj.* misuborashii みすぼらしい (shabby).

manhandle, *vb.* tearaku atsukau 手荒く扱う.

manhood, *n.* 1. seijin 成人 (state of being an adult). 2. otokorashisa 男らしさ (manly qualities). 3. dansei 男性 (men collectively).

mania, *n.* 1. nekkyō 熱狂 (excessive enthusiasm). 2. sōbyō 躁病 (psychological disorder).

-mania, -kyō 〜狂; -kichigai 〜気違い; **bibliomania** honkichigai 本気違い.

maniac, *n.* kichigai 気違い.

manipulate, *vb.* 1. sōsa suru 操作する (handle with skill). 2. ayatsuru 操る (influence by devious skill).

mankind, *n.* jinrui 人類.

manliness, *n.* otokorashisa 男らしさ (masculine qualities).

manly, *adj.* otokorashii 男らしい (having masculine qualities).

manner, *n.* 1. hōhō 方法 (way of doing). 2. taido 態度 (bearing).

manners, *n.* 1. reigi(sahō) 礼儀 (作法) (polite behavior); shūzoku 習俗 (prevailing customs).

manpower, *n.* rōdōryoku 労働力.

mantelpiece, *n.* danro no ue no tana 暖炉の上の棚.

manual, 1. *n.* tebikisho 手引き書 (guidebook). 2. *adj.* shudō (no) 手動 (の) (operated by hand); teshigoto (no) 手仕事 (の) (involving work with the hands).

manufacture, 1. *n.* seizō 製造 (act of manufacturing); seihin 製品 (product). 2. *vb.* seizō suru 製造する (make with machinery); detchiageru でっち上げる (fabricate).

many, *pron., adj.* takusan (no) たくさん (の); tasū (no) 多数 (の).

map, *n.* chizu 地図.

maple, *n.* momiji もみじ.

mar, *vb.* sokonau 損う (impair, spoil).

maraud, *vb.* ryakudatsu suru 略奪する.

marble, *n.* 1. dairiseki 大理石 (stone); bīdama ビー玉 (glass sphere).

march, 1. *n.* kōshinkyoku 行進曲 (music); kōshin 行進 (act of marching). 2. *vb.* kōshin suru 行進する (walk with measured tread); susumu 進む (advance).

margin, *n.* 1. yohaku 余白 (of a page). 2. hashi 端; fuchi 縁 (edge). 3. yoyū 余裕 (amount above what is necessary). 4. sa 差 (difference).

marginal, *adj.* toru ni tarinai 取るに足りない (insignificant).

marine, 1. *adj.* umi (no) 海 (の) (sea); senpaku (no) 船舶 (の) (ships); kaiheitai (no) 海兵隊 (の) (Marines). 2. *n.* kaiheitai'in 海兵隊員 (member of the Marine Corps).

marionette, *n.* ayatsuriningyō 操り人形.

maritime, *adj.* 1. senpaku (no) 船舶 (の) (ships). 2. umi (no) 海 (の) (sea).

mark, 1. *n.* shimi 染み (stain); kizu 傷 (blemish);

shirushi 印 (sign, symbol); ten 点 (score); mato 的 (target); maruku マルク (German money); **hit/miss the mark** mato ni ataru/o hazusu 的に当たる/を外す. 2. vb. shirushi o tsukeru 印を付ける (put a mark on); ... no shirushi de aru ...の印である (indicate); chūmoku suru 注目する (give heed to); ten o tsukeru 点を付ける (rate); **mark down/up** nesage/neage suru 値下げ/値上げする (price).

market, n. 1. ichiba 市場 (physical location). 2. shijō 市場 (potential buyers); **stock market** kabushiki shijō 株式市場.

maroon, n. kuri'iro 栗色 (color).

marriage, n. 1. kekkon 結婚 (state of being married). 2. kekkonshiki 結婚式 (ceremony).

marry, vb. 1. kekkon suru 結婚する (take in marriage); kekkon saseru 結婚させる (cause to take in marriage). 2. **marry off** kekkon saseru 結婚させる.

Mars, n. kasei 火星.

marsh, n. shitchi 湿地.

martial, adj. 1. kōsen-teki (na) 好戦的 (な) (inclined to war). 2. sensō (no) 戦争 (の) (war). 3. **martial arts** bugei 武芸; **martial law** kaigenrei 戒厳令.

marvelous, adj. kyōi-teki (na) 驚異的 (な); subarashii 素晴らしい (fabulous).

masculine, adj. 1. otokorashii 男らしい (having qualities characteristic of men). 2. dansei (no) 男性 (の) (men).

mash, vb. suritsubusu 磨り

つぶす.

mask, 1. n. (ka)men (仮)面. 2. vb. kamen o kaburu 仮面を被る (wear a mask); ōu 覆う (cover).

mason, n. ishidaiku 石大工 (stone mason).

masquerade, 1. n. kamenbutōkai 仮面舞踏会 (masked ball); hensō 変装 (false outward show). 2. vb. hensō suru 変装する (go about under false pretenses).

mass, n. 1. tasū 多数 (great number of); tairyō 大量 (large amount of); **mass production** tairyōseisan; ryōsan 量産. 2. misa ミサ (religion). 3. **masses** taishū 大衆.

massacre, 1. n. tairyōgyakusatsu 大量虐殺. 2. vb. minagoroshi ni suru 皆殺しにする.

massive, adj. 1. bōdai (na) 膨大 (な) (large in scale, amount, or degree). 2. kasabaru かさばる (bulky).

master, n. 1. meijin 名人 (skilled person); goshujin 御主人 (employer of servants or workers); kachō 家長 (master of household); shūshi 修士 (degree holder); **master of ceremonies** shikai 司会. 2. vb. shihai suru 支配する (conquer).

masterpiece, n. kessaku 傑作.

master's degree, n. shūshigō 修士号.

mastery, n. shihai 支配 (control).

masturbate, vb. jii ni fukeru 自慰に耽る.

mat, 1. n. tatami 畳 (Japanese straw mat). 2. vb. matto o shiku マットを敷く

(cover floor, etc., with a mat).

match, 1. *n.* shiai 試合 (game, competition); gokaku no aite 互角の相手 (equal opponent); kekkon'aite 結婚相手 (partner in marriage). **2.** *vb.* dōtō de aru 同等である (be equal to); ... ni hitteki suru ...に匹敵する (be the counterpart of, correspond to); ... to au ...と合う (fit together); kekkon saseru 結婚させる (unite in marriage).

mate, 1. *n.* haigūsha 配偶者 (spouse); katahō 片方 (one of a pair); nakama 仲間 (companion). **2.** *vb.* majiwaru 交わる (join as mates, copulate).

material, 1. *n.* zairyō 材料 (substance); nuno 布 (fabric); shiryō 資料 (material for research); **raw material** genryō 原料. **2.** *adj.* busshitsu-teki (na) 物質的 (な) (corporeal).

materialize, *vb.* jitsugen suru 実現する (realize).

mathematics, *n.* sūgaku 数学.

matrimony, *n.* kekkon 結婚.

matron, *n.* **1.** fujin 婦人 (married woman). **2.** joseikanrinin 女性管理人 (female supervisor).

matter, 1. *n.* busshitsu 物質 (material); kotogara 事柄 (affair); mondai 問題 (trouble); kakimono 書き物 (printed matter); **as a matter of course** tōzen 当然; **as a matter of fact** jissai 実際; **What's the matter?** Dō shita no. どうしたの. **no matter (how,**

what, etc.) tatoe ... demo/temo たとえ...でも／ても. **2.** *vb.* jūyō de aru 重要である (be important); **it doesn't matter** jūyō ja nai 重要じゃない.

mature, 1. *adj.* seijuku shita 成熟した (fully developed); ōkiku natta 大きくなった (fully grown); ureta 熟れた (ripe). **2.** *vb.* seijuku suru 成熟する (bring to full development); seiiku suru 成育する (grow); jukusuru 熟する (become ripe).

maturity, *n.* seijuku 成熟 (state of being mature).

maul, *vb.* **1.** tearaku atsukau 手荒く扱う (manhandle). **2.** kega o saseru 怪我をさせる (bruise).

maximize, *vb.* **1.** saidaigen made fuyasu 最大限まで増やす (increase to a maximum). **2.** ōi ni katsuyō suru 大いに活用する (make fullest use of).

maximum, *n., adj.* **1.** saidai (no) 最大 (の) (highest amount). **2.** saidaigen (no) 最大限 (の) (upper limit).

may, *aux. vb.* **1.** ...kamoshirenai ...かもしれない (to express contingency or possibility). **2.** ... temo ii ...ても良い (permission). **3.** ... yō ni ... ように (wish); **May you live long!** Nagaiki suru yō ni. 長生きするように. **4. may as well do** ... shita hō ga ii ...した方が良い.

May, *n.* gogatsu 五月.

maybe, *adv.* osoraku おそらく.

mayor, *n.* shichō 市長 (city); chōchō 町長 (town); sonchō 村長 (village).

maze, *n.* meiro 迷路.

me, *pron.* watashi (o/ni) 私 (を/に); **with me** watashi to 私と.

meadow, *n.* kusahara 草原.

meager, *adj.* 1. yaseteiru やせている (thin). 2. sukunai 少ない (scanty). 3. mazushii 貧しい (poor).

meal, *n.* gohan 御飯; shokuji 食事.

mean, 1. *n.* chūkan 中間 (midway between extremes); heikin 平均 (average). 2. *adj.* ijiwaru (na) 意地悪 (な) (malicious); iyashii 卑しい (ignoble); kechi (na) けち (な) (stingy); ototteiru 劣っている (inferior). 2. *vb.* (... suru) tsumori de aru (...する) つもりである (intend); imi suru 意味する (signify).

meaning, *n.* imi 意味 (purport, significance).

means, *n.* 1. hōhō 方法; shudan 手段 (method, agency). 2. (o)kane (お)金 (money); tomi 富 (wealth). 3. **by all means** zehi 是非; **by means of** ... ni yotte ... によって; **by no means** kesshite ... nai 決して...ない.

meantime, *adv.* aida 間; **in the meantime** sono aida ni その間に.

measles, *n.* hashika はしか.

measly, *adj.* hon no wazuka (no) ほんのわずか (の).

measure, 1. *n.* monosashi 物差し (yardstick); hakari 秤 (scale); sunpō 寸法; ōkisa 大きさ (dimensions); omosa 重さ (weight); nagasa 長さ (length); shochi 処置 (action); hyōshi 拍子 (rhythm). 2. *vb.* hakaru はかる (ascertain size or extent).

meat, *n.* niku 肉.

mechanic, *n.* 1. jukurenkō 熟練工 (skilled worker with tools, etc.). 2. seibishi 整備士 (repairer).

mechanical, *adj.* 1. kikai (no) 機械 (の) (pertaining to machinery). 2. kikai-teki (na) 機械的 (な) (going through the motions).

mechanism, *n.* mekanizumu メカニズム; shikumi 仕組み; naritachi 成り立ち.

mechanize, *vb.* kikaika suru 機械化する (adapt to machinery).

media, *n.* masukomi マスコミ (mass media).

mediate, *vb.* chōtei suru 調停する (settle dispute).

medical, *adj.* igaku (no) 医学 (の) (of the science of medicine).

medicine, *n.* 1. kusuri 薬 (medical substance). 2. igaku 医学 (science of restoring health).

medieval, *adj.* chūsei (no) 中世 (の).

mediocre, *adj.* nami (no) 並 (の).

meditation, *n.* meisō 瞑想.

Mediterranean, *n., adj.* chichūkai (no) 地中海 (の).

medium, 1. *n.* chūkan 中間 (mean, something intermediate); baitai 媒体 (intervening substance); hōhō 方法 (means of doing); kankyō 環境 (environment); reibai 霊媒 (spiritualist). 2. *adj.* chūkan (no) 中間 (の) (intermediate).

meet, 1. *n.* kyōgikai 競技会; taikai 大会 (athletic meet). 2. *vb.* (... ni) deau (...に) 出会う (encounter); au 会う (join at an agreed time or place); shiriau 知り合う (be introduced to); mukaeru 迎える (be present at the arrival of); atsumaru 集まる (assemble for action); mitasu 満たす (satisfy).

meeting, n. 1. kaigi 会議 (conference, business meeting). 2. deai 出会い (encounter). 3. shūkai 集会 (tsudoi 集い (gathering for a purpose).

megaphone, n. kakuseiki 拡声器.

melancholy, n., adj. yūutsu (na) 憂うつ (な).

mellow, adj. 1. jukushiteiru 熟している (ripe). 2. yutaka (na) 豊か (な) (rich). 3. yawarakai 柔らかい (soft).

melt, vb. tokeru 溶ける (become liquified, dissolve); tokasu 溶かす (reduce to a liquid state).

member, n. 1. kai'in 会員 (person belonging to an organization). 2. karada no ichibu 体の一部 (part of body).

membrane, n. usumaku 薄膜.

memento, n. katami 形見; kinenhin 記念品.

memorable, adj. omoidebukai 思い出深い (worth remembering).

memorial, 1. n. kinenhi 記念碑 (monument honoring memory). 2. adj. kinen (no) 記念 (の) (serving to preserve the memory).

memorize, vb. anki suru 暗記する.

memory, n. 1. kioku 記憶 (faculty of remembering). 2. omoide 思い出 (recollection). 3. kinen 記念 (commemoration); **in**

memory of ... o kinen shite ...を記念して.

menace, 1. n. kyōi 脅威 (something that threatens). 2. vb. obiyakasu 脅かす (threaten).

mend, vb. shūri suru 修理する (repair a machine); tsukurou 繕う (repair something by sewing).

menstruation, n. gekkei 月経; mensu メンス; seiri 生理.

mental, adj. 1. kokoro (no) 心 (の); seishin (no) 精神 (の) (of the mind). 2. seishinbyō (no) 精神病 (の) (of mental disorder). 3. atama no naka (no) 頭の中 (の) (performed in the mind). 4. chiteki (na) 知的 (な) (intellectual).

mentality, n. 1. chinō 知能 (mental capacity). 2. kangaekata 考え方 (outlook).

mention, 1. n. genkyū 言及 (reference). 2. vb. noberu 述べる (speak of); genkyū suru 言及する (refer to, cite); **not to mention** sono ue ni その上に.

mentor, n. onshi 恩師.

merchandise, n. shōhin 商品 (goods).

merchant, n. shōnin 商人.

merciful, adj. jihibukai 慈悲深い.

mercury, n. 1. suigin 水銀. 2. **Mercury** suisei 水星.

mercy, n. jihi 慈悲 (benevolence); dōjō 同情 (compassion); awaremi 哀れみ (pity); **at the mercy of** ... no nasu ga mama de ...のなすがままで.

mere, adj. tatta no たったの; hon no ほんの.

merge, vb. 1. hitotsu ni

naru/suru 一つになる／する (become united/cause to unite or blend). 2. gappei suru 合併する (business).

merit, 1. n. kachi 価値 (worth); riten 利点 (something that deserves praise); **merits** kōseki 功績 (state of deserving). 2. vb. atai suru 値する (deserve).

mermaid, n. ningyo 人魚.

merry, adj. yukai (na) 愉快 (な); tanoshii 楽しい.

merry-go-round, n. kaiten-mokuba 回転木馬.

mesh, 1. n. ami 網 (net). 2. vb. ami de toru 網で捕る (catch in mesh).

mess, 1. n. yogore 汚れ (dirty jumble or condition); konzatsu 混雑 (confusion); yakkai 厄介 (difficult situation); **in a mess** chirakkate 散らかって (in disorder); **make a mess of** ... o dainashi ni suru ... を台無しにする (ruin). 2. vb. chirakasu 散らかす (disorder); yogosu 汚す (make dirty); **mess up** mecha-mecha ni suru めちゃめちゃにする (disorder, ruin).

message, n. dengon 伝言.

messenger, n. tsukai 使い.

messy, adj. chirakatteiru 散らかっている (disorderly); yogoreteiru 汚れている (dirty).

metabolism, n. shinchintaisha 新陳代謝.

metal, n. kinzoku 金属.

metamorphosis, n. henshin 変身 (of a person); henka 変化; hensei 変性 (of a thing or animal).

meteor, n. nagareboshi 流れ星.

method, n. hōhō 方法

(manner).

meticulous, adj. saishin (na, no) 細心 (な、の).

metric, adj. mētoru (no) メートル (の) (pertaining to the meter); **metric system** mētoru-hō メートル法.

metropolis, n. daitokai 大都会.

metropolitan, adj. daitokai (no) 大都会 (の).

Mexico, n. mekishiko メキシコ

mezzanine, n. nikai-shōmenseki 二階正面席 (theater); chūnikai 中二階 (architecture).

microbe, n. 1. biseibutsu 微生物 (microorganism). 2. baikin ばい菌; saikin 細菌 (disease-causing bacteria).

microphone, n. maiku マイク.

microscope, n. kenbikyō 顕微鏡.

microwave oven, n. denshi-renji 電子レンジ.

middle, 1. n. chūkan 中間 (intermediate); man'naka 真中 (central point); chūō 中央 (center); **in the middle of** ... no saichū ni ... の最中に (engaged in). 2. adj. chūkan (no) 中間 (の); man'naka (no) 真中 (の) (intermediate); chūō (no) 中央 (の) (central).

middle-aged, adj. chūnen (no) 中年 (の).

Middle Ages, n. chūsei 中世.

Middle East, n. chūtō 中東.

middle school, n. chūgakkō 中学校.

midnight, n. mayonaka 真夜中.

might, n. chikara 力 (strength).

mighty, adj. 1. kyōryoku

(na) 強力 (な) (powerful).
2. kyodai (na) 巨大 (な)
(huge).

mild, adj. 1. odayaka (na) 穏
やか (な) (gentle). 2. karui
軽い (light, not severe). 3.
atatakai 暖かい (not cold);
kaiteki (na) 快適 (な)
(comfortable); **mild
winter** ondan na fuyu 温暖
な冬. 4. mairudo (na) マイ
ルド (な) (not bitter or
pungent). 5. yowai 弱い
(moderate in force).

mildew, n. kabi かび.

milestone, n. kakki-teki na
koto 画期的なこと (epoch-
making thing or event).

military, n., adj. gun (no) 軍
(の); guntai (no) 軍隊 (の);
military man gunjin 軍人.

milk, 1. n. gyūnyū 牛乳. 2.
vb. chichi o shiboru 乳を搾
る (draw milk); shiboritoru
搾り取る (exploit).

Milky Way, n. amanogawa
天の川.

mill, 1. n. kōjō 工場
(factory); konahikiki 粉碾き
機 (machine for grinding
beans or grain); kōhī-hiki コ
ーヒー碾き (coffee mill). 2.
vb. hiku 碾く (grind).

miller, n. konaya 粉屋.

million, n., adj. hyakuman
(no) 百万 (の); **two million**
nihyakuman (no) 二百万
(の).

millionaire, n. ōganemochi
大金持ち; chōja 長者.

mimic, 1. n. monomaneshi
物真似師 (performer); 2. vb.
mane suru 真似する
(imitate).

mince, vb. hiku 挽く (chop
meat); komagire ni suru 細
切れにする (chop foods).

mind, 1. n. kokoro 心
(center of thoughts and

emotions); chisei 知性
(intellect); ikō 意向
(intention); shōki 正気
(sound mental condition);
kangae 考え (opinion);
bear/keep in mind
oboeteoku 覚えておく **be
on one's mind** ki ni kakaru
気にかかる; **be out of
one's mind** ki ga kuruu 気
が狂う; **call to mind**
omoidasu 思い出す; **make
up one's mind** kesshin
suru 決心する. 2. vb. ki ni
suru 気にする (heed); chūi
suru 注意する (pay
attention to; be careful);
sen'nen suru 専念する
(apply oneself to); shinpai
suru 心配する (care about).

mine, 1. n. kōzan 鉱山
(excavation). 2. pron.
watashi no mono 私のもの.
3. vb. horidasu 掘り出す
(dig).

mingle, vb. majiwaru 交わ
る; mazaru 混ざる (become
mixed or blended); mazeru
混ぜる (mix, blend).

minimal, adj. saishō(gendo
no) 最小(限度の).

minimum, n. 1.
saishōgendo 最小限度 (least
amount possible). 2. saitei
最低 (lowest amount, value,
etc.); **minimum wage**
saiteichingin 最低賃金.

minister, 1. n. daijin 大臣
(government); bokushi 牧師
(religion). 2. vb. tsukaeru 仕
える.

minor, 1. n. miseinen 未成
年 (youth). 2. adj. (yori)
chiisai (より) 小さい (lesser
in seriousness, importance,
etc.); (yori) sukunai (より)
少ない (lesser in amount);
miseinen (no) 未成年 (の)
(youth); tanchō (no) 短調

(の) (music).

mint, 1. n. hakka 薄荷 (herb); zōheikyoku 造幣局 (place where money is coined). 2. vb. chūzō suru 鋳造する (make by stamping metal); tsukuridasu 作り出す (invent).

minus, prep. hiku 引く (less by subtraction of).

minute, 1 n. fun 分 (sixty seconds); chotto ちょっと (short space of time); **Wait a minute!** Chotto matte kudasai. ちょっと待って下さい; **up to the minute** saishin (no) 最新 (の) (up-to-date). 2. adj. komakai 細かい (extremely small).

minutes, n. kaigiroku 会議録 (record of meeting).

miracle, n. kiseki 奇蹟.

mire, 1. n. doronuma 泥沼 (bog). 2. vb. doronuma ni hamarikomu 泥沼にはまり込む (be stuck in bog or difficulty).

mirror, n. kagami 鏡.

misbehave, vb. gyōgi waruku suru 行儀悪くする.

miscarriage, n. 1. ryūzan 流産 (miscarriage of a baby). 2. shippai 失敗 (failure).

miscellaneous, adj. samazama (na, no) 様々 (な、の).

mischief, n. 1. kigai 危害 (harm, evil); yakkai 厄介 (trouble). 2. itazura いたずら (petty annoyance). 3. chame 茶目 (harmless teasing).

mischievous, adj. 1. ijiwaru (na) 意地悪 (na) (malicious). 2. itazura (na) いたずら (な) (playfully annoying).

miserable, adj. 1. aware (na) 哀れ (な); mijime (na)

miserable (na) (pitiable, wretched). 2. hidoi ひどい (despicable). 3. fukō (na) 不幸 (な) (unfortunate).

misery, n. 1. awaresa 哀れさ; mijimesa 惨めさ (wretchedness).

misfit, n. futekiōsha 不適応者.

misfortune, n. fu'un 不運 (bad luck).

misgiving, n. 1. kenen 懸念 (apprehension). 2. utagai 疑い (doubt).

mishap, n. sainan 災難.

mishmash, n. gotamaze ごたまぜ.

misinformation, n. gohō 誤報.

misinterpret, vb. gokai suru 誤解する.

mislead, vb. 1. machigawaseru 間違わせる (lead in the wrong direction). 2. damasu だます (deceive).

misplace, vb. 1. oki machigaeru 置き間違える (put in wrong place). 2. oki-wasureru 置き忘れる (mislay, lose).

misrepresent, vb. tadashiku tsutaenai 正しく伝えない (inform incorrectly).

miss, 1. n. atesokonai 当て損ない (failure to hit); dokushinjosei 独身女性 (unmarried woman); **Miss -san** -さん; -様 (title); **Miss Oda** odasan 小田さん. 2. vb. atesokonau 当て損なう (fail to hit); nogasu 逃す (fail to catch, take advantage of, etc.); nakusu 無くす (lose); nogareru 逃れる (escape); samishigaru 淋しがる (regret the absence of); yasumu 休む (be absent from); **be missing** ... ga nai

... が無い.

missing, *adj.* yukuefumei (no) 行方不明 (の) (person, dog, etc.).

mission, *n.* 1. shimei 使命 (duty). 2. dendō 伝道; senkyō 宣教 (religious).

mist, *n.* kiri 霧; moya もや.

mistake, 1. *n.* ayamari 誤り; machigai 間違い; **by mistake** ayamatte 誤って; **make a mistake** machigaeru 間違える. 2. *vb.* machigaeru 間違える.

Mister, see **Mr.**

mistreat, *vb.* kokushi suru 酷使する (treat abusively); gyakutai suru 虐待する (treat cruelly).

mistress, *n.* 1. aijin 愛人; mekake 妾 (extramarital partner). 2. on'nashujin 女主人 (female head, female owner).

mistrust, *vb.* utagau 疑う.

misunderstand, *vb.* gokai suru 誤解する.

mite, *n.* dani だに (insect).

mitigate, *vb.* yawarageru 和らげる.

mitten, *n.* tebukuro 手袋.

mix, 1. *n.* kongō 混合 (mixture). 2. *vb.* mazeru 混ぜる (combine into one inseparable mass); hitotsu ni suru 一つにする (unite); ireru 入れる (add as an ingredient); **mix up** kondō suru 混同する (confuse).

mix-up, *n.* konran 混乱 (state of confusion).

moan, 1. *n.* umeki 呻き. 2. *vb.* umeku 呻く.

moat, *n.* hori 堀.

mob, *n.* 1. bōto 暴徒 (riotous crowd of people). gunshū 群衆 (any large group of people).

mobility, *n.* idōsei 移動性

(quality of being mobile).

mock, *vb.* 1. azawarau 嘲笑う; karakau からかう (deride). 2. mohō suru 模倣する (imitate).

mode, *n.* 1. yōshiki 様式 (manner). 2. hōhō 方法 (method). 3. sutairu スタイル (style).

model, 1. *n.* mihon 見本 (standard for imitation); kata 型 (typical form). 2. *vb.* tsukuru 作る (shape, form).

moderation, *n.* setsudo 節度; tekido 適度 (temperance); **in moderation** tekido ni 適度に.

moderator, *n.* shikaisha 司会者 (at meeting).

modern, *adj.* modan (na) モダン (な); gendai-teki (na) 現代的 (の).

modernize, *vb.* gendaika suru 現代化する.

modify, *vb.* 1. shūsei suru 修正する (alter partially). 2. kagen suru 加減する (reduce in degree).

moist, *adj.* shimetteiru 湿っている (damp).

moisture, *n.* shikke 湿気; suibun 水分.

mold, 1. *n.* kabi かび (fungus growth); kata 型 (cast). 2. *vb.* kata ni ireru 型に入れる (put into a mold); katachizukuru 形作る (shape).

mole, *n.* 1. hokuro ほくろ (spot on skin). 2. mogura もぐら (animal).

molest, *vb.* 1. komaraseru 困らせる (annoy). 2. bōkō suru 暴行する (assault sexually).

moment, *n.* 1. shunkan 瞬間 (instant). 2. ima 今 (present time). 3. toki 時

(definite period, as in a course of events; occasion). 4. jūyōsa 重要さ (importance). 5. **at the last moment** giri-giri no toki ni ぎりぎりの時に; **at the moment** tadaima 只今; **in a moment** sugu ni すぐに.

momentum, n. suishinryoku 推進力; hazumi 弾み.

monarchy, n. ōkoku 王国 (country governed by monarch).

Monday, n. getsuyōbi 月曜日.

monetary, adj. (o)kane (no) (お)金 (の).

money, n. (o)kane (お)金 (coin and paper money).

money order, n. kawase 為替.

mongrel, n., adj. zasshu (no) 雑種 (の).

monitor, 1. n. kyūchō 級長 (student). 2. vb. miharu 見張る.

monkey, n. saru 猿.

monologue, n. hitorigoto 独り言; dokuhaku 独白.

monopolize, vb. dokusen suru 独占する (obtain exclusive possession of).

monotone, n. tanchō 単調.

monotonous, adj. 1. tanchō (na) 単調 (な) (sounded in one unvarying tone). 2. taikutsu (na) 退屈 (な) (boring).

monster, n. kaibutsu 怪物 (creature of abnormal form, wicked creature).

month, n. tsuki 月 (calendar month).

monthly, 1. n. gekkanzasshi 月刊雑誌 (monthly magazine). 2. adj. hitotsuki (no) ひと月 (の); ikkagetsu (no) 一か月 (の) (month,

computed by the month); tsuki'ikkai (no) 月一回 (の) (once a month); maitsuki (no) 毎月 (の) (every month).

monument, n. kinenhi 記念碑 (memorial pillar).

moo, n. mō モー.

mood, n. 1. fun'iki 雰囲気 (prevailing emotional tone, general attitude). 2. kibun 気分 (person's emotional state). 3. johō 叙法 (grammar).

moody, adj. fukigen (na) 不機嫌 (な) (sullen); inki (na) 陰気 (な) (gloomy).

moon, n. tsuki 月.

moonlight, n. gekkō 月光.

mope, vb. fukureru 膨れる (pout).

moral, 1. n. kyōkun 教訓 (moral teaching); (pl.) dōtoku 道徳 (principles of right conduct). 2. adj. dōtoku-teki na 道徳的 (な) (right conduct); **moral support** seishin-tekl na sasae 精神的な支え.

morale, n. shiki 士気.

morality, n. 1. dōtoku-teki okonai 道徳的行い (moral conduct). 2. dōtokusei 道徳性 (moral quality).

moralize, vb. sekkyō suru 説教する.

moratorium, n. yūyo 猶予 (temporary cessation).

morbid, adj. 1. inki (na) 陰気 (な) (gloomy). 2. kimi ga warui 気味が悪い (gruesome). 3. byō-teki (na) 病的 (な) (sick).

more, adj., adv. 1. yori ōi より多い; motto もっと; sara ni 更に. 2. **all the more** naosara 尚更; **what is more** sono ue ni その上に; **more and more** masu-

masu ますます; **more or less** hobo ほぼ; **more than ever** yori issō より一層; **no more** mohaya ... nai もはや...ない (no longer); **no more than** seizei せいぜい; **once more** mō ichido もう一度; **the more the better** ōkereba ōi hodo ii 多ければ多い程良い.

moreover, adv. sono ue ni その上に.

morgue, n. shitaihokansho 死体保管所.

morning, n., adj. 1. asa (no) 朝 (の); gozen (no) 午前 (の). 2. **in the morning** gozenchū ni 午前中に; **Good morning!** Ohayō gozaimasu. おはようございます.

moron, n. baka 馬鹿.

morose, adj. fukigen (na) 不機嫌 (な).

morsel, n. 1. kakera かけら (small piece). 2. hitokuchi 一口 (small piece of food).

mortal, 1. n. ningen 人間 (human being). 2. adj. ningen no 人間 (の) (of human beings); shinu sadame (no) 死ぬ定め (の) (subject to death); chimei-teki (na) 致命的 (な) (causing death); **mortal wound** chimeishō 致命傷.

mortar, n. shikkui 漆喰 (mixture of lime and cement).

mortify, vb. kuyashigara-seru 悔しがらせる (humiliate, anger).

Moslem, n., adj. isuramu-kyō (no) イスラム教 (の); kaikyō 回教 (の).

mosque, n. kaikyō-jiin 回教寺院.

mosquito, n. ka 蚊.

moss, n. koke 苔.

most, 1. adj. ichiban ōi 一番多い (greatest in amount); daibubun (no) 大部分 (の) (the majority of). 2. adv. ichiban 一番; mottomo 最も (to the greatest extent). 3. **at most** seizei せいぜい; **for the most part** daibubun wa 大部分は; **make the most of ...** o katsuyō suru ...を活用する.

moth, n. ga 蛾.

mothball, n. bōchūzai 防虫剤.

mother, n. haha 母; okāsan お母さん.

mother-in-law, n. gibo 義母; shūtome 姑.

mother-of-pearl, n. shinjugai 真珠貝.

motif, n. moyō 模様 (pattern).

motion, 1. n. ugoki 動き (action, movement); aizu 合図 (signal); teian 提案 (suggestion). 2. vb. aizu suru 合図する (signal).

motion picture, n. eiga 映画.

motivate, vb. suruki ni saseru する気にさせる.

motive, n. dōki 動機.

motorist, n. untensha 運転者.

mottled, adj. madara (no) まだら (の).

mount, 1. n. yama 山 (mountain). 2. vb. noru 乗る (get on); noboru 登る (climb); agaru 上がる (rise); fueru 増える (increase); suetsukeru 据え付ける (install); hiraku 開く (launch).

mountain, n. yama 山.

mourn, n. 1. itamu 悼む (mourn for someone's death). 2. kanashimu 悲しむ (lament).

mouse, *n.* nezumi ねずみ.

mousetrap, *n.* nezumitori ねずみ取り.

mouth, *n.* 1. kuchi 口 (of an animal, anything resembling a mouth); **mouth of a bottle** bin no kuchi 瓶の口. 2. kakō 河口 (of a river). 3. ana 穴 (opening). 4. iriguchi 入口 (entrance). 5. **by word of mouth** kuchi-komi de 口コミで.

move, 1. *n.* ugoki 動き (movement, purposeful action); iten 移転 (act of going to a new apartment, office, etc.); te 手 (in chess); **get a move on** isogu 急ぐ; **on the move** kappatsu (na) 活発 (な) (active); hattenchū (no) 発展中 (の) (progressing). 2. *vb.* ugoku 動く (change place or position, go, run); ugokasu 動かす (cause to change); hikkosu 引越す (change one's abode); shinten suru 進展する (advance); kandō saseru 感動させる (affect emotionally); teian suru 提案する (propose); **move along** susumu 進む (move further); saru 去る (go away); **move around** ugokimawaru 動き回る; **move in** nyūkyo suru 入居する; **move on** utsuru 移る (change).

movie, *n.* eiga 映画; **movie theater** eigakan 映画館.

moving, *adj.* 1. kandō-teki (na) 感動的 (な) (touching). 2. ugoku 動く (that can move).

mow, *vb.* karu 刈る (grass).

Mr., -san -さん; -様 **Mr. Abe** abe-san 阿部さん.

Mrs., -san -さん; -様 **Mrs. Taki** taki-san 滝さん.

much, 1. *adj.* takusan (no) たくさん (の) (in great quantity). 2. *adv.* taihen 大変 (greatly); hobo ほぼ (nearly). 3. **as much as ...** to onaji hodo ...と同じ程; **How much?** Ikura. いくら; **make much of** omonjiru 重んじる; **much more** motto takusan もっとたくさん; **too much for (a person)** (... no) te ni oenai (...の) 手に負えない.

mud, *n.* doro 泥.

muffle, *vb.* osaeru 抑える (suppress).

muggy, *adj.* mushiatsui 蒸し暑い.

mugging, *n.* gōtō 強盗.

mull, *vb.* **mull over** kangaeru 考える.

multiple, *adj.* tayō (na) 多様 (な); samazama (no) 様々 (の) (consisting of many).

multiplication, *n.* kakezan 掛け算 (math).

multiply, *vb.* 1. kakeru 掛ける (math). 2. fuyasu 増やす (increase).

multitude, *n.* tasū 多数.

mumble, *vb.* mogu-mogu iu もぐもぐ言う.

mumps, *n.* otafukukaze おたふく風邪.

munch, *vb.* kamu 噛む.

mundane, *adj.* arifureteiru ありふれている (commonplace).

municipal, *adj.* machi (no) 町 (の) (town); shi (no) 市 (の) (city).

mural painting, *n.* hekiga 壁画.

murder, 1. *n.* satsujin 殺人. 2. *vb.* korosu 殺す.

murky, *adj.* 1. inki (na) 陰気 (な) (gloomily dark). 2. bon'yari shiteiru ぼんやりている (obscured with haze).

murmur, 1. *n.* sasayaki ささ
やき (soft speech); fuhei 不
平 (complaint). 2. *vb.*
sasayaku ささやく (speak
softly); fuhei o iu 不平を言
う (complain).

muscle, *n.* kin'niku 筋肉.

muse, *vb.* kangaekomu 考え
込む; hansū suru 反すうす
る (meditate).

museum, *n.* hakubutsukan
博物館 (any museum);
bijutsukan 美術館 (art
museum).

mushroom, *n.* kinoko きの
こ.

music, *n.* ongaku 音楽 (art,
score).

musical, *adj.* ongaku (no) 音
楽 (の) (pertaining to
music); ongaku-teki (na) 音
楽的 (な) (melodious).

musical instrument, *n.*
gakki 楽器.

must, 1. *n.* hitsujuhin 必需
品 (anything necessary). 2.
aux. vb. ... nakereba-naranai
...なければならない (be
obliged to); ... ni chigainai
...に違いない (be reasonably
expected to); **must not do**
... subeki dewa nai ...すべき
ではない.

mustache, *n.* kuchihige 口髭.

mustard, *n.* karashi 辛子、
芥子.

mutation, *n.* 1. totsuzenhen'i
突然変異 (sudden change in
offspring). 2. henka 変化

(change).

mute, 1. *n.* rōasha ろうあ者
(deaf person without
speech). 2. *adj.* mugon (no)
無言 (の) (without speech).

mutilate, *vb.* sonshō suru 損
傷する.

mutt, *n.* zasshu 雑種 (mixed
breed).

mutter, *vb.* 1. tsubuyaku 呟
く (utter in low tone). 2.
fuhei o iu 不平を言う
(grumble).

mutual, *adj.* 1. tagai (no) 互
い (の) (reciprocal). 2. kyōtsū
(no) 共通 (の) (common).

my, *adj.* watashi no 私の.

myopia, *n.* kinshi 近視;
kingan 近眼.

myriad, *n.* musū 無数.

myself, *pron.* watashijishin
私自身.

mysterious, *adj.* 1. nazo
(no) 謎 (の); fushigi (na) 不
思議 (な) (enigmatic). 2.
shinpi-teki (na) 神秘的 (な)
(supernatural).

mystery, *n.* 1. nazo 謎
(enigma). 2. shinpi 神秘
(supernatural event).

mystify, *vb.* tōwaku saseru
当惑させる.

myth, *n.* 1. shinwa 神話
(legendary story). 2.
meishin 迷信 (false popular
belief).

mythology, *n.* 1. shinwa 神
話 (body of myths). 2.
shinwagaku 神話学 (study
of myth).

N

nab, *vb.* tsukamaeru 捕まえ
る; toraeru 捕える.

nag, *vb.* gami-gami iu がみが
み言う (pester); shitsukoku
kogoto o iu しつこく小言を

言う (scold constantly).

nail, 1. *n.* kugi 釘 (metal);
tsume 爪 (fingernail). 2. *vb.*
kugi o utsu 釘を打つ
(fasten); **nail down** kotei

suru 固定する (fasten down); kakujitsu ni suru 確実にする (make definite).

naïve, *adj.* ubu (na) うぶ (な); soboku (na) 素朴 (な).

naked, *adj.* hadaka (no) 裸 (の).

name, 1. *n.* namae 名前; meishō 名称 (designating object or person); meisei 名声 (reputation). **2.** *vb.* nazukeru 名付ける (give name to); na o ageru 名をあげる (identify); shimei/ninmei suru 指名／任命する (appoint); shitei suru 指定する (specify).

namely, *adv.* sunawachi 即ち; tsumari つまり.

nap, 1. *n.* hirune 昼寝 (daytime sleep); inemuri 居眠り (doze). **2.** *vb.* hirune o suru 昼寝をする; inemuri o suru 居眠りをする.

narcissus, *n.* suisen 水仙.

narcotic, *n.* **1.** kakuseizai 覚醒剤; mayaku 麻薬 (drug). **2.** masuizai 麻酔剤 (anesthetic).

narrate, *vb.* kataru 語る; hanasu 話す.

narrator, *n.* katarite 語り手.

narrow, 1. *adj.* semai 狭い (of little breadth or width); kagirareta 限られた (limited); yatto (no) やっと (の) (barely adequate or successful). **2.** *vb.* sebameru 狭める (make narrow); kagiru 限る (limit).

narrowly, *adv.* nantoka 何とか; karōjite 辛うじて (barely).

narrow-minded, *adj.* kokoro no semai 心の狭い.

nasty, *adj.* **1.** kitanai 汚い (unclean). **2.** iya (na) 嫌 (な); fukai (na) 不快 (な) (unpleasant). **3.** ijiwaru (na) 意地悪 (な); hiretsu (na) 卑劣 (な) (vicious,

mean-spirited).

nation, *n.* **1.** kokka 国家; kuni 国 (country). **2.** kokumin 国民 (people).

nationality, *n.* kokuseki 国籍.

native, 1. *adj.* bokoku/jikoku (no) 母国／自国 (の) (of one's nation); umaretsuki (no) 生まれつき (の) (by birth); jimoto (no) 地元 (の) (of local area); genjūmin (no) 現住民 (の) (of original inhabitants); **native language** bokokugo/ jikokugo. **2.** *n.* jimoto no hito 地元の人 (local people); genjūmin 原住民 (original inhabitants); ... umare no hito ...生まれの人 (person born in a particular place).

naturally, *adv.* **1.** mochiron もちろん; tōzen 当然 (as would be expected). **2.** umaretsuki 生まれつき; seirai 生来 (inherent in character). **3.** shizen ni/to 自然に／と (according to nature).

nature, *n.* **1.** shizen 自然 (Nature). **2.** seikaku 性格 (character of person); seishitsu/tokushitsu 性質／特質 (characteristic of animal or object). **3.** shurui 種類 (sort).

navel, *n.* (o)heso (お)へそ.

navy, *n.* kaigun 海軍.

near, 1. *adj.* chikai 近い. **2.** *adv.* chikaku de/ni 近くで／に. **3.** *prep.* (... no) chikaku de/ni (...の) 近くで／に.

nearby, 1. *adj.* chikaku/soba (no) 近く／側 (の). **2.** *adv.* chikaku/soba ni 近く／側に.

nearly, *adv.* hotondo ほとんど.

near-sighted, *adj.*

kinshi/kingan (no) 近視／近眼 (の).

neat, *adj.* 1. kichin to shita きちんとした (tidy). 2. kireizuki (na) きれい好き (な) (habitually orderly). 3. kirei (na) きれい (な) (good-looking); kimochi ga ii 気持がいい (pleasant); ii 良い (good). 4. ki ga kiita 気が利いた (cleverly effective).

necessary, *adj.* hitsuyō (na) 必要 (な).

neck, *n.* kubi 首.

necklace, *n.* kubikazari 首飾り.

need, 1. *n.* hitsuyō 必要 (necessity); hinkon 貧困 (poverty). 2. *vb.* hitsuyō to suru 必要とする; iru 要る (require). **need to ...** (shi)-nakerebanaranai ...(し)なければならない (be obliged).

needle, *n.* hari 針.

negative, 1. *adj.* hitei (no) 否定 (の); hitei-teki (na) 否定的 (な) (expressing negation, denying); shōkyoku-teki (na) 消極的 (な) (lacking positive attitude); hantai (no) 反対 (の) (contrary); mainasu (no) マイナス (の) (negative number, detracting quality). 2. *n.* hitei 否定 (negation, denial); hiteikei 否定形 (negative word); nega ネガ (photographic image).

neglect, 1. *vb.* mushi suru 無視する (disregard); orosoka ni suru おろそかにする; okotaru 怠る (be remiss). 2. *n.* mushi 無視 (disregard); hōchi 放置; taiman 怠慢 (negligence).

negotiate, *vb.* kōshō suru 交渉する.

neigh, 1. *n.* inanaki いなな

き. 2. *vb.* inanaku いななく.

neighbor, *n.* kinjo no hito 近所の人; rinjin 隣人.

neighborhood, *n.* kinjo 近所; fukin 付近.

neighboring, *adj.* tonari (no) 隣り (の); sessuru 接する.

neither, 1. *pron., adj.* dochira (no ...) mo ... nai どちら (の...) も...ない; 2. *conj.* **neither ... nor ...** mo ... mo ... nai; ... mo (... nai). **Neither can I.** Watashi mo dekinai 私も出来ない.

nephew, *n.* oi 甥.

nerve, *n.* 1. shinkei 神経 (physical). 2. yūki 勇気 (courage). 3. atsukamashisa 厚かましさ (impudence).

nervous, *adj.* 1. shinkeishitsu (na, no) 神経質 (な、の) (easily upset, fearful). 2. shinkei (no) 神経 (の) (pertaining to nerves). 3. shinpai (na) 心配 (na) (worried).

nest, *n.* su 巣.

net, 1. *adj.* shōmi (no) 正味 (の) (amount). 2. *n.* ami 網. 3. *vb.* ami de kakomu 網で囲む (enclose); ami de toraeru 網で捕える (catch).

Netherlands, 1. *n.* oranda オランダ. 2. *adj.* oranda (no) オランダ (の) (of the Netherlands).

neutral, *adj.* chūritsu (no) 中立 (の) (impartial); chūsei (no) 中性 (の) (chemical).

never, *adv.* kesshite/zettai ... nai 決して／絶対...ない.

nevertheless, *adv.* sore nimo kakawarazu それにもかかわらず; sore demo それでも.

new, *adj.* atarashii 新しい.

new- 1. shin 新; **new theory** shinsetsu 新説. 2.

(... ta) bakari (no) (...た) ば
かり (の); **newborn**
umareta bakari (no) 生まれ
たばかり (の).

newlywed, n. shinkon(san)
新婚(さん).

newsboy, n.
shinbunhaitatsu 新聞配達
(deliverer); shinbun'uri 新聞
売り (seller).

newsletter, n. kaihō 会報.

newspaper, n. shinbun 新
聞.

New Year, n. shin'nen 新年.

New Year's Day, n. ganjitsu
元日; gantan 元旦.

New Year's Eve, n. ōmisoka
大晦日.

next, 1. adj. tsugi (no) 次
(の) (immediately
following); tonari (no) 隣り
(の) (adjacent). **2.** adv. tsugi
ni 次に (nearest in space).
3. next-door tonari no ie
隣りの家 (next-door
neighbor); **next to** (... no)
tonari (...の) 隣り (adjacent);
hotondo ほとんど (almost);
next day yokujitsu 翌日;
next week raishū 来週;
next month raigetsu 来月;
next year rainen 来年.

nibble, vb. sukoshizutsu
taberu 少しずつ食べる;
kajiru かじる.

nice, adj. **1.** ii ii 良い (good,
fine, pleasant). **2.** yasashii
優しい (kind).

nickname, n. adana あだ名.

niece, n. mei 姪.

night, n. yoru 夜; ban 晩;
good night oyasuminasai
おやすみなさい; **last night**
sakuban 昨晩; kinō no
ban/yoru 昨日の晩／夜.

nightfall, n. yūgure 夕暮れ,
tasogare たそがれ.

nightgown, n. nemaki 寝巻.

nightmare, n. akumu 悪夢.

nimble, adj. **1.** keikai (na) 軽
快 (な); kibin (na) 機敏 (な)
(quick and light in
movement). **2.**
monowakari ga hayai 物わ
かりが早い (quick to
understand).

nine, n. kyū 九; kokonotsu
九つ.

nine hundred, n. kyūhyaku
九百.

nineteen, n. jūkyū 十九.

ninety, n. kyūjū 九十.

ninth, adj. daikyū (no) 第九
(の); kyūbanme (no) 九番目
(の).

nip, vb. **1.** hasamu 挟む
(pinch). **2.** kamu 噛む
(bite).

no, 1. adj. ... nai ...ない. **2.**
adv. iie いいえ.

nobody. 1. n. mumei no
hito 無名の人. **2.** pron.
daremo ... nai だれも...ない.

nod, 1. n. unazuki 頷き
(inclination of head). **2.** vb.
unazuku 頷く (incline
head); inemuri suru 居眠り
する (become sleepy).

noise, n. sōon 騒音; zatsuon
雑音.

noisy, adj. urusai うるさい.

nominal, adj. **1.** namae dake
(no) 名前だけ (の) (in name
only). **2.** wazuka (no) わず
か (の) (small).

nominate, vb. **1.** shimei
suru 指名する; ageru あげる
(name a candidate). **2.**
ninmei suru 任命する
(appoint).

non- hi-, mu- 非-, 無-; **non-
profit** hieiri (no) 非営利
(の).

none, pron. nani/dore mo(...
nai) 何／どれも(...ない)
(not any); dare mo (... nai)
誰も(...ない) (nobody).

nonetheless, adv. sore nimo

kakawarazu それにもかかわらず; soredemo それでも.

nonsense, *n.* tawagoto たわ言; kudaranai koto 下らない事.

nonsmoking, *adj.* kin'en (no) 禁煙 (の);
nonsmoking seat kin'enseki 禁煙席.

nonstop, *adj.* chokkō (no) 直行 (の).

noodle, *n.* men めん; udon うどん (wheat); soba そば (buckwheat).

noon, *n.* shōgo 正午; gogo jūniji 午後十二時.

no one, *pron.* dare mo ... nai 誰も...ない.

nor, *conj.* (...) mo ... nai (...)も...ない; **neither ... nor ...** mo ... mo ... nai ...も...も...ない.

normal, *adj.* futsū (no) 普通 (の); nōmaru (na) ノーマル (な).

north, *n., adj.* kita (no) 北 (の).

North America, *n.* kita-amerika 北アメリカ; hokubei 北米.

northeast, *n., adj.* hokutō (no) 北東 (の).

northern, *adj.* kita (no) 北 (の).

North Pole, *n.* hokkyoku 北極.

northwest, *n., adj.* hokusei (no) 北西 (の).

nose, *n.* hana 鼻.

nosebleed, *n.* hanaji 鼻血.

nostril, *n.* hana no ana 鼻の穴.

nosy, *adj.* sensakuzuki (na) 詮索好き (な).

not, *adv.* (de) nai (で) ない; **not at all** zen'zen/mattaku ... nai 全然/全く...ない.

notable, *adj.* chūmoku subeki 注目すべき.

note, 1. *n.* **1.** memo メモ (record); oboegaki 覚え書き (reminder); hashirigaki 走り書き (quick letter); jūyō 重要 (importance); chūmoku 注目 (notice); yakusoku-tegata 約束手形 (paper promising payment); onpu 音符 (music); **notes** shuki 手記; kiroku 記録 (written summary). **2.** *vb.* memo o toru メモを取る (write); kiroku suru 記録する; chūmoku suru 注目する (pay attention); kizuku 気付く (recognize); genkyū suru 言及する (mention).

notebook, *n.* nōto ノート; chōmen 帳面.

noted, *adj.* yūmei (na) 有名 (な).

nothing, *n.* nani mo ... nai 何も...ない; **for nothing** tada de 只で (free of charge); muda ni 無駄に (in vain); **nothing but** ... nomi ...のみ; **have nothing to do with** ... towa kankei ga nai ...とは関係がない.

notice, 1. *n.* tsūchi 通知; shirase 知らせ (information); keikoku 警告 (warning); kaikotsūkoku 解雇通告 (termination of employment); chūi/chūmoku 注意/注目 (attention); **on short notice** kyū ni 急に; **take notice of** ... ni chūi/chūmoku suru ...に注目する (pay attention to); ... ni ki ga tsuku ...に気が付く (perceive); noberu 述べる (mention).

notify, *vb.* (... ni) ... o shiraseru (...に) ... を知らせる; (... ni) ... o tsūchi suru (...に) ... を通知する.

notion, *n.* 1. gainen 概念 (general idea). 2. iken 意見; kangae 考え (opinion, view).

notwithstanding, *adv.* sore demo nao それでもなお; sore nimo kakawarazu それにもかかわらず.

noun, *n.* meishi 名詞.

novel, 1. *adj.* atarashii 新しい (new). 2. *n.* shōsetsu 小説 (book).

novelist, *n.* shōsetsuka 小説家; sakka 作家.

November, *n.* jūichigatsu 十一月.

now, *adv.* ima 今; **now and then** tokidoki 時々; **by now** imagoro wa (mō) 今ごろは (もう); **from now on** korekara これから; **just now** tatta ima たった今 (a moment ago); mokka 目下 (at this moment); **right now** imasugu ni 今すぐに (right away).

nowadays, *adv.* kon'nichi 今日; chikagoro 近頃.

nowhere, *adv.* doko nimo ... nai どこにも...ない.

nuclear, *adj.* 1. kaku (no) 核 (の) (of nucleus). 2. genshiryoku (no) 原子力 (の) (of atomic energy); **nuclear power** genshiryoku 原子力.

nude, *adj.* hadaka (no) 裸 (の).

nudge, *vb.* 1. hiji de tsuku 肘で突く (push with one's elbow). 2. wakeiru 分け入る (push into).

nuisance, *n.* 1. meiwakumono 迷惑者 (person). 2. meiwaku na koto 迷惑な事 (thing). 3. meiwaku 迷惑; yakkai 厄介

(annoyance, trouble).

null, *adj.* 1. mukō (na, no) 無効 (な、の) (of no effect). 2. zero (no) ゼロ (の); mu (no) 無 (の) (nil).

numb, *adj.* mukankaku (no) 無感覚 (の); shibireta しびれた.

number, 1. *n.* kazu 数; sūji 数字 (figure, amount); bangō 番号 (assigned number); **telephone number** denwabangō; **a large number of** tasū (no) 多数 (の). 2. *vb.* kazoeru 数える (count); ... ni tassuru ...に達する (amount to); bangō o tsukeru 番号を付ける (give a number to).

nun, *n.* shūdōjo 修道女; shisutā シスター.

nurse, 1. *n.* kangofu 看護婦 (person who cares for the sick); uba 乳母 (wet nurse); hobo 保母 (dry nurse). 2. *vb.* kango suru 看護する (tend in sickness); junyū suru 授乳する (suckle); sodateru 育てる (feed and tend).

nursery, *n.* 1. kodomobeya 子供部屋 (room). 2. hoikuen 保育園 (nursery school). 3. shubyōen 種苗園 (plants).

nursing home, *n.* 1. yōrōin 養老院; rōjin-hōmu 老人ホーム (for aged people). 2. ryōyōsho 療養所 (for the infirm).

nurture, *vb.* sodateru 育てる.

nut, *n.* ki/ko no mi 木の実; nattsu ナッツ (seed). 2. natto ナット (for bolt).

nutrition, *n.* eiyō 栄養.

nymph, *n.* yōsei 妖精.

O

oak, *n.* kashi (no ki) 樫 (の木).

oat, *n.* karasumugi 烏麦.

oath, *n.* 1. chikai 誓い (vow). 2. fukei na kotoba 不敬な言葉 (blasphemous words).

obedient, *adj.* jūjun (na) 従順 (な); otonashii おとなしい.

obese, *adj.* futtoteiru 太っている; himan (no) 肥満 (の).

obey, *vb.* ... ni fukujū suru ...に服従する; ... ni shitagau ...に従う.

object, 1. *n.* buttai 物体; mono 物 (thing); taishō 対象 (focus of attention); mokuteki 目的 (end); mokutekigo 目的語 (grammatical). 2. *vb.* hantai suru 反対する.

objective, 1. *adj.* kyakkan-teki (na) 客観的 (な). 2. *n.* mokuteki 目的 (end).

obligate, *vb.* gimuzukeru 義務づける.

oblige, *vb.* 1. ... sezaru o enaku suru ...せざるを得なくする (require or constrain to do). 2. on ni kiseru 恩に着せる (place under debt of gratitude). 3. on o hodokosu 恩を施す (do favor for). 4. **be obliged** kansha suru 感謝する (feel grateful); **be obliged to do** ... shinakutewa-naranai ...しなくてはならない (must do).

obliterate, *vb.* keshisaru 消し去る (erase).

obnoxious, *adj.* hatameiwaku (na) はた迷惑 (な) (bothersome); fukai (na) 不快 (な) (unpleasant).

obscene, *adj.* hiwai (na) 卑

猥 (な); midara (na) 淫ら (な).

obscure, 1. *adj.* aimai (na) あいまい (な); hakkirishinai はっきりしない (not clear); mumei (no) 無名 (の) (unknown); kurai 暗い (dark). 2. *vb.* kakusu 隠す (conceal, cover); kuraku suru 暗くする (make dark).

observance, *n.* 1. junshu 遵守; jikkō 実行 (obeying, following). 2. iwai 祝い (due celebration); shikiten 式典 (ceremony).

observant, *adj.* chūibukai 注意深い; surudoi 鋭い (alert).

observe, *vb.* 1. kansatsu suru 観察する (watch closely). 2. chūi suru 注意する (pay attention). 3. mamoru 守る (obey). 4. iwau 祝う (celebrate). 5. noberu 述べる (comment).

observer, *n.* kansatsusha 観察者.

obsess, *vb.* toritsuku 取り憑く; **be obsessed with** ... ni toritsukarete iru ...に取り憑かれている.

obstinate, *adj.* ganko (na) 頑固 (な).

obstruct, *vb.* jama suru 邪魔する; bōgai suru 妨害する.

obtain, *vb.* te ni ireru 手に入れる; eru 得る (get, acquire).

obvious, *adj.* akiraka (na) 明らか (な); meihaku (na) 明白 (な).

occasion, 1. *n.* toki 時 (particular time); taisetsu na toki 大切な時 (important time); moyo'oshi 催し (event); kikai 機会 (opportunity); riyū 理由 (reason). 2. *vb.* hikiokosu

引き起こす.

occasionally, *adv.* tokiori 時折; tokidoki 時々.

occupation, *n.* 1. shokugyō 職業; shigoto 仕事 (work). 2. senryō 占領 (military takeover).

occupy, *vb.* 1. (... o) shimeru (...を) 占める (fill, hold attention of). 2. (... ni) sumu (...に) 住む (inhabit); (... ni) iru (...に) いる (be in). 3. senryō suru 占領する (by military invasion).

occur, *vb.* 1. okoru 起こる (happen, present itself). 2. (kokoro ni) ukabu (心に) 浮かぶ (come to mind).

ocean, *n.* umi 海; -yō -洋; **Pacific Ocean** taiheiyō 太平洋; **Atlantic Ocean** taiseiyō 大西洋.

o'clock, *adv.* -ji -時; **It is one o'clock.** Ichiji desu 一時です. **at two o'clock** niji ni 二時に.

October, *n.* jūgatsu 十月.

octopus, *n.* tako 蛸.

odd, *adj.* 1. kimyō (na) 奇妙 (な); kawatta 変わった (strange). 2. kisū (no) 奇数 (の) (number). 3. hanpa (no) 半端 (の) (not part of set).

odds, *n.* 1. kachime 勝ち目; kanōsei 可能性 (probability to win). 2. handikyappu ハンディキャップ (handicap). **3. be at odds with** ... to (iken ga) awanai ...と (意見が) 合わない; **odds and ends** yoseatsume 寄せ集め; hanpamono 半端物.

odor, *n.* nioi 匂い.

of, *prep.* 1. ...no ...の (belonging to, by, possessed or ruled by). 2. ...kara ...から (from, so as to be rid of). 3. ...de ...で (owing to, made

with). 4. ... no aru ...のある (having particular qualities). 5. ... ni tsuite no ...についての (concerning).

off, 1. *adj.* machigatteiru 間違っている (in error); torikesareta 取り消された (no longer in effect); hima (na) 暇 (な) (free from duty). 2. *adv.* hanarete 離れて (up, away); torete 取れて (coming off); mukō ni 向こうに (at a distance); tomatte 止まって (not in operation); yasunde 休んで (in absence); **be off** ... o yasumu ...を休む (be absent); hanareru 離れる (leave); iku 行く (leave); **come off** toreru 取れる; **get off** oriru 降りる; **take off** nugu 脱ぐ (undress); **turn off** tomeru 止める; kesu 消す; **off and on** tokiori 時折 (with intervals between); **be well off** yutaka de aru 豊かである (be rich); **20 percent off** niwaribiki de 二割引で. 3. *prep.* ...kara ...から (away from); ... kara hanarete ...から離れて (apart from); ... yori shita de/ni ...より下で／に (below the standard); ... nashi de ...なしで (without).

offend, *vb.* okoraseru 怒らせる (anger); kizutsukeru 傷つける (hurt); **be offended** okoru 怒る.

offense, *n.* 1. hanzai 犯罪 (crime); ihan 違反 (violation). 2. kōgeki 攻撃 (attack). 3. rippuku 立腹 (anger); hankan 反感 (resentment); **take offense at** ... ni rippuku suru ...に立腹する.

offer, 1. *n.* mōshide 申し出

(something offered);
mōshikomi 申し込み
(proposal). 2. vb. teikyō
suru 提供する (hold out);
teian suru 提案する
(propose); hikiukeru 引き受
ける (volunteer).

office, n. 1. jimusho 事務所;
shigotoba 仕事場; kaisha 会
社 (place of business). 2.
shinsatsushitsu 診察室
(doctor's office); kurinikku
クリニック (clinic). 3.
yakusho 役所 (public
office); **take office** shūnin
suru 就任する.

office hours, n. 1.
eigyōjikan 営業時間
(business). 2.
shinsatsujikan 診察時間
(clinic). 3. mensetsu-jikan
面接時間 (school).

official, 1. adj. kōshiki (no)
公式 (の) (formal); kōnin
(no) 公認 (の) (authorized);
ōyake (no) 公 (の) (public).
2. n. yakunin 役人; kōmuin
公務員 (public official).

offspring, n. shison 子孫.

often, adv. shiba-shiba しば
しば; yoku よく.

off-the-record, adj. hikōkai
(no) 非公開 (の).

oil, 1. n. abura 油 (liquid);
sekiyu 石油 (petroleum); **oil
painting** aburae; **oil well**
yuden 油田. 2. vb. abura o
sasu 油を注す.

ointment, n. nankō 軟膏.

okay, O.K., adj., adv., interj.
1. ii 良い; daijōbu 大丈夫
(good, right, adequate,
feeling well; fine, all right).
2. wakarimashita 分かりま
した (in agreement).

old, adj. 1. furui 古い
(objects and concepts); toshi
totta 年取った; toshiyori
(no) 年寄り (の) (people,

animals); **old man/woman**
toshiyori 年寄り; rōjin 老人.
2. ... sai (no) ...歳 (の) (of
one's age); **... years old** ...
sai desu ...歳です; **How old
is ...?** ... wa nansai desu ka
...は何歳ですか. 3. mae
前 (no) 前 (の) (former).

older, adj. toshiue (no) 年上
(の) (senior); **older than**
...yori toshiue (no) ...より年
上 (の) (older than); **older
brother** ani 兄; oniisan お
兄さん.

old-fashioned, adj.
jidaiokure (no) 時代遅れ
(の); kyūshiki (na) 旧式
(な).

omen, n. maebure 前触れ;
kizashi 兆し.

ominous, adj. fukitsu (na)
不吉 (な).

omit, vb. 1. shōryaku suru
省略する (leave out on
purpose); nukasu 抜かす
(leave out by mistake). 2.
wasureru 忘れる (forget).

omnipotent, adj. ban'nō
(no) 万能 (の).

on, 1. prep. ... no ue de/ni
...の上で／に (on top of); ...ni
...に (at the time of); **on
Sunday** nichiyōbi ni 日曜日
に; ... ni tsuite ...について
(concerning); ... no soba
de/ni ...の側で／に (near);
... de ...で (by means of); ...
no hō ni ...の方に (toward).
2. adv. ue de/ni/e 上で／
に／へ (above); **and so on**
... nado などと; sonota その他.

once, 1. adv. katsute かつて;
mukashi 昔 (formerly);
ichido/ikkai 一度／一回
(one time); **at once** dōji ni
同時に (at the same time);
sugu ni すぐに
(immediately); **once and
for all** kore o kagiri ni これ

を限りに; **once in a while** tokidoki 時々; **once upon a time** mukashi-mukashi 昔々; **all at once** totsuzen 突然; **once more** mō ichido もう一度; **once a month** hitotsuki ni ichido 一月に一度. 2. *conj.* moshi ... shitara もし...したら (if ever); ... shitara sugi ni ...したらすぐに (as soon as).

one, 1. *n., pron.* ichi 一; hitotsu 一つ (single item); hitori 一人 (single person); **one after another** tsugi-tsugi ni 次々に; **one another** otagai (o, ni) お互い (を、に); **no one** dare mo ... nai 誰も...ない; **that one** are あれ; sore それ; **this one** kore これ; **one by one** jun ni 順に. 2. *adj.* ichi (no) 一 (の); hitotsu (no) 一つ (の); hitori (no) 一人 (の) (single); onaji (no) 同じ (の) (the same); aru (no) ある (の) (some); **one day** aru hi あ る日.

one-way, *adj.* 1. ippōtsūkō (no) 一方通行 (の) (street). 2. katamichi (no) 片道 (の) (ticket).

onion, *n.* tamanegi 玉ねぎ.

only, 1. *adj.* yuiitsu (no) 唯一 (の) (sole); tada hitotsu (no) 只一つ (の) (item); tada hitori (no) 只一人 (の) (person). 2. *adv* ...dake ...だけ (merely); ... dake ...だけ (solely); **only you** anata dake.

onward, *adv.* saki ni/e/wa 先に/へ/は.

ooze, *vb.* nijimu 滲む.

open, 1. *adj.* hiraita/hiraiteiru 開いた/開いている; aita/aiteiru 開いた/開いている (not shut, enclosed, covered, filled);

hirobiro to shita 広々とした (wide space); sotchoku (na) 率直 (な) (frank); kaihō sareteiru 解放されている (accessible); eigyōchū (no) 営業中 (の) (business); kaikanchū (no) 開館中 (の) (museum, library); **open the market** (... ni) shijō o kaihō suru (...に) 市場を開放する. 2. *vb.* hiraku 開く; akeru 開ける (make open); hajimaru 始まる (begin); hajimeru 始める (cause to begin); kaihō suru 解放する (make accessible).

opening, *n.* aki 空き (vacancy); ketsuin 欠員 (job).

operate, *vb.* 1. sōsa suru 操作する; ugokasu 動かす (operate machine). 2. un'ei suru 運営する (manage). 3. sayō suru 作用する (have effect). 4. shujutsu o suru 手術をする (perform surgery).

operation, *n.* 1. shujutsu 手術 (surgery); **have an operation** shujutsu o ukeru 手術を受ける. 2. sōsa 操作; unten 運転 (machine). 3. gunjikōdō 軍事行動 (military operation).

operator, *n.* denwakōkanshu 電話交換手 (telephone).

opinion, *n.* iken 意見.

opponent, *n.* 1. aite 相手; taikōsha 対抗者 (person on opposite side). 2. hantaisha 反対者 (person who opposes).

opportune, *adj.* 1. tekisetsu (na) 適切 (な) (suitable). 2. ii taimingu (no) 良いタイミング (の) (well-timed).

opportunity, *n.* kōki 好機; kikai 機会.

oppose, vb. 1. (... ni) hantai suru (...ni) 反対する (resist). 2. saegiru 遮る (obstruct).

opposite, 1. adj. hantai (no) 反対 (の) (reverse of); taisuru 対する (face to face). 2. prep. ... ni taishite ...に対して; ... ni mukai ni ...の向かいに (across from).

oppress, vb. appaku suru 圧迫する.

optics, n. kōgaku 光学.

optimal, adj. saiteki (no) 最適 (の).

optimistic, adj. rakkan-/rakuten-teki (na) 楽観／楽天的 (な).

optimum, adj. saiteki (no) 最適 (の).

opulent, adj. yutaka (na) 豊か (な); hōfu (na) 豊富 (な).

or, conj. 1. matawa 又は; soretomo それとも (used to represent alternatives). 2. tsumari つまり (that is). 3. samonaito さもないと (otherwise).

oral, adj. kōtō (no) 口頭 (の) (uttered in words); hanashikotoba (no) 話し言葉 (の) (of spoken language); **oral exam** kōtōshiken 口頭試験.

orbit, n. 1. kidō 軌道 (path).

orchard, n. kajuen 果樹園.

orchestra, n. kangengakudan 管弦楽団; **symphony orchestra** kōkyō-gakudan 交響楽団.

orchid, n. ran 蘭.

ordain, vb. 1. ninmei suru 任命する (religion). 2. meijiru 命じる (order).

ordeal, n. shiren 試練.

order, 1. n. meirei 命令 (command); junban 順番 (systematic arrangement); chitsujo 秩序 (neatness); chūmon 注文 (request); **in**

order that, in order to ... suru tame ni ...するために; **out of order** koshōchū 故障中. 2. vb. meijiru 命じる (command); chūmon suru 注文する (place an order); seiri suru 整理する (put things in order).

orderly, adj. seiton sareta 整頓された; kichin to shita きちんとした (neatly arranged); kiritsu tadashii 規律正しい (calm, organized).

ordinary, adj. futsū (no) 普通 (の); arifureta ありふれた.

ore, n. kōseki 鉱石.

organic, adj. 1. kikan (no) 器官 (の) (of bodily organs). 2. yūki (no) 有機 (の) (organic compound). 3. yūkisaibai (no) 有機栽培 (の) (grown without chemicals).

organization, n. soshiki 組織; dantai 団体.

organize, vb. 1. soshiki suru 組織する (form). 2. taikeidateru 体系だてる (systematize); totonoeru 整える (order).

orient, 1. n. **the Orient** tōyō 東洋. 2. vb. tehodoki suru 手ほどきする (introduce).

Oriental, 1. n. tōyōjin 東洋人. 2. adj. tōyō (no) 東洋 (の).

orientation, n. 1. tehodoki 手ほどき (introductory program). 2. hōkō 方向 (direction).

origin, n. 1. kigen 起源; hajimari 始まり (beginning, source). 2. umare 生まれ (birth, parentage).

original, 1. n. genkei 原型 (primary type, form); gensho 原書 (book in the

original language);
gensakuhin 原作品 (original
work as opposed to a copy).
2. *adj.* dokusō-teki (na) 独創
的 (な) (creative); hajime
(no) 始め (の) (first);
atarashii 新しい (new);
moto (no) 元 (の) (not
copied).

ornament, 1. *n.* kazari 飾り;
sōshoku 装飾. 2. *vb.* kazaru
飾る.

ornate, *adj.* 1. hade (na) 派
手 (な) (pompous). 2.
kazaritateta 飾りたてた
(decorative).

orphan, *n.* koji 孤児
(without parents);
minashigo みなし児
(without protective
affiliation).

orphanage, *n.* koji'in 孤児
院.

oscillate, *vb.* 1. fureru 振れ
る (sway). 2. mayou 迷う
(fluctuate).

ostracism, *n.* murahachibu
村八分; nakama hazure 仲間
外れ.

ostrich, *n.* dachō 駝鳥.

other, 1. *adj.* hoka (no) 他
(の); ta (no) 他 (の)
(additional, different); mō
hitotsu (no) もう一つ (の)
(remaining one); **the other
day** senjitsu 先日; **every
other day** ichinichi oki ni
一日おきに; **on the other
hand** sono ippō その一方;
in other words tsumari つ
まり. 2. *pron.* **the others**
hoka no hito 他の人 (other
people); hoka no mono 他の
物 (other things); **each
other** otagai ni/o お互い
に／を.

otherwise, *adv.* 1. sō de
nakereba そうでなければ (if
not). 2. sore o nozokeba そ

れを除けば (apart from
that). 3. chigatta fū niwa 違
ったふうには (differently).

otter, *n.* rakko らっこ (sea
otter); kawauso 川うそ
(river otter).

ought, *aux. vb.* 1. ... beki ...
べき (should); **ought to
know** shiru beki 知るべき.
2. kitto (... ni) chigainai き
っと (...に) 違いない (used to
express probability).

our, *adj., pron.* watashitachi
(no) 私達 (の); ware-ware
(no) 我々 (の).

oust, *vb.* tsuihō suru 追放す
る.

out, 1. *adv.* soto de/ni/e 外
で／に／へ (outside);
hanarete/hazurete 離れて／
外れて (away from); sukkari
すっかり (completely);
nakunatte/kirete 無くなっ
て／切れて (none left); **go
out of a room** heya kara
deru 部屋から出る; **out of
pity** dōjō kara 同情から;
out of money okane ga
nakunatte お金が無くなっ
て; **out of breath** iki ga
kirete 息が切れて; **out of
reach** te ga todokanai 手が
届かない. 2. *prep.* ... kara ...
から (out from).

outbreak, *n.* 1. hassei 発生;
boppatsu 勃発 (sudden
occurrence). 2. hōdō 暴動
(insurrection).

outburst, *n.* bakuhatsu 爆発
(outpouring, sudden spell of
activity).

outcome, *n.* kekka 結果.

outdated, *adj.* jidaiokure
(no) 時代遅れ (の) (old-
fashioned).

outdo, *vb.* (... ni) masaru (...
に) 勝る; (...o) shinogu (...
を) 凌ぐ.

outdoor, 1. *adj.* kogai (no)

戸外 (の); soto (no) 外 (の).
2. adv. **outdoors** kogai de/ni 戸外で／に; soto de/ni 外で／に.

outfit, n. 1. sōbi 装備 (equipment). 2. fuku 服 (clothing).

outgoing, adj. 1. deteiku 出て行く (leaving). 2. gaikō-teki (na) 外交的 (な) (sociable).

outgrow, vb. 1. (... ga) hairanaku-naru (...が) 入らなくなる (grow too large for); **outgrow one's clothes** fuku ga hairanaku-naru 服が入らなくなる. 2. (... yori) ōkiku naru (...より) 大きくなる (grow more than).

outing, n. ensoku 遠足 (excursion); pikunikku ピクニック (picnic).

outlaw, 1. n. muhōmono 無法者; narazumono ならず者. 2. vb. kinshi suru 禁止する.

outlet, n. 1. deguchi 出口 (exit). 2. hakeguchi はけ口 (outlet for expression). 3. hanbaiten 販売店 (retailer); hanbairo 販売路 (market for goods). 4. konsento コンセント (electrical).

outline, n. 1. rinkaku 輪郭 (line); gairyaku 概略 (general account). 2. vb. rinkaku o egaku 輪郭を描く (draw outline); gairyaku o noberu 概略を述べる (give an account).

outlook, n. 1. nagame 眺め (view). 2. mitōshi 見通し; yosō 予想 (speculation). 3. kangaekata 考え方 (mental view).

out-of-date, adj. 1. kigengire (no) 期限切れ (の) (no longer valid). 2.

jidaiokure (no) 時代遅れ (の) (old-fashioned).

outpatient, n. gairaikanja 外来患者.

output, n. 1. shutsuryoku 出力 (electrical or computer). 2. seisandaka 生産高 (quantity produced).

outrage, 1. n. bōryoku 暴力 (violence); gekido 激怒; ikari 怒り (fury); tondemonai koto とんでもないこと (unthinkable). 2. vb. gekido saseru 激怒させる (anger); okasu 犯す (violate).

outright, adj. 1. mattaku no 全くの (complete). 2. akiraka (na) 明らか (な) (obvious).

outset, n. hajime/hajimari 始め／始まり; **from the outset** hajime kara 始めから.

outside, 1. adj. soto (no) 外 (の); gaibu (no) 外部 (の). 2. n. soto 外; sotogawa 外側. 3. adv. soto de/ni/e 外で／に／へ. 4. prep. ... no soto de/ni/e ...の外で／に／へ.

outsmart, vb. (... yori) uwate ni deru (...より) 上手に出る.

outspoken, adj. sotchoku (na) 率直な (unreserved).

outstanding, adj. 1. namihazureta 並外れた; subarashii 素晴らしい (prominent). 2. mikaiketsu (no) 未解決 (の) (unsettled); miharai (no) 未払い (の) (unpaid).

outward, adv. sotogawa de/ni/e 外側で／に／へ (toward the outside).

oval, n., adj. daenkei (no) 楕円形 (の).

ovary, n. ransō 卵巣.

ovation, n. hakushu kassai

拍手喝采.

oven, *n.* tenpi 天火.

over, 1. *adv.* ue de/ni 上で/に (above); ue no 上の (so as to cover); koete 超えて (across, beyond); mata また (again); sukkari すっかり (throughout); **over and over** kurikaeshite 繰り返して; **over here** koko de/ni ここで/に; **over there** mukō de/ni 向こうで/に; **all over** achikochi de/ni あちこちで/に (here and there); zentai ni 全体に (over entirety). 2. *prep.* ... no ue de/ni/e/o ...の上で/に/へ/を (above in place, authority, etc.); ... no mukō ni ...の向こうに (to the other side of); ... o koete ...を超えて (across); ... o tōtte ...を通って (through); ... ni wattate ...に渡って (throughout).

overboard, *adv.* **go overboard** ikisugiru 行き過ぎる; kyokutan ni hashiru 極端に走る.

overcast, *adj.* 1. kumotta 曇った (cloudy). 2. inki (na) 陰気 (な) (gloomy).

overcoat, *n.* ōbā オーバー; gaitō 外套.

overcome, *vb.* 1. makasu 負かす (defeat). 2. (... ni) uchikatsu (...に) 打ち勝つ (prevail over). 3. kokufuku suru 克服する (conquer). 4. **be overcome by** ... ni uchinomesareru ...に打ちのめされる.

overdue, *adj.* 1. kigengire (no) 期限切れ (の) (past due). 2. minō (no) 未納 (の) (unpaid). 3. okureteiru 遅れている (delayed).

overflow, *vb.* afureru 溢れる.

overhaul, *vb.* 1. zentai no kensa o suru 全体の検査をする (examine thoroughly). 2. sukkari shūri suru すっかり修理する (repair thoroughly).

overlap, *vb.* chōfuku suru 重複する (; kasanaru 重なる.

overnight, *adv.* hitobanjū 一晩中 (all night); **stay overnight** ippaku suru 一泊する.

overpower, *vb.* 1. atto suru 圧倒する (subdue). 2. (... ni) uchikatsu (...に) 打ち勝つ (overcome).

overrule, *vb.* kyakka suru 却下する.

overseas, 1. *adj.* kaigai (no) 海外 (の); gaikoku (no) 外国 (の). 2. *adv.* kaigai de/ni 海外で/に.

oversee, *vb.* kantoku suru 監督する (supervise).

overtake, *vb.* (... ni) oitsuku (...に) 追い付く (catch up with).

overthrow, *vb.* 1. taosu 倒す (depose, put an end to). 2. hikkurikaesu ひっくり返す (topple).

overturn, *vb.* 1. hikkurikaesu ひっくり返す (turn over). 2. taosu 倒す (depose).

overweight, *adj.* 1. jūryōchōka (no) 重量超過 (の) (load). 2. himan (no) 肥満 (の); futorisugi (no) 太り過ぎ (の) (person).

overwork, 1. *n.* karō 過労. 2. *vb.* hataraki-sugiru 働き過ぎる.

owe, *vb.* 1. kari ga aru 借りがある (owe money); harawa-nakereba-naranai 払わなければならない (need to pay). 2. ... no okage de aru ...のおかげで

ある; ... ni on ga aru ...に恩
がある (indebted to); **owing
to** ... no okage de ...のおか
げで.

owl, *n.* fukurō ふくろう.

own, 1. *adj.* jishin no 自身
の; hon'nin no 本人の. 2.

vb. motsu 持つ; shoyū suru
所有する.

owner, *n.* mochinushi 持
主; ōnā オーナー.

ox, *n.* oushi 雄牛.

oxygen, *n.* sanso 酸素.

oyster, *n.* kaki 牡蠣.

P

pace, *n.* 1. sokudo 速度 (rate
of movement); shinpo no
doai 進歩の度合い (rate of
progress). 2. ippo 一歩
(single step).

Pacific Ocean, *n.* taiheiyō
太平洋.

pacifier, *n.* oshaburi おしゃ
ぶり (baby).

pacify, *vb.* 1. nadameru なだ
める (calm). 2. heiwa o
motarasu 平和をもたらす
(bring peace).

pack, 1. *n.* tsutsumi 包み
(bundle); mure 群れ (dogs,
crooks); hako 箱
(cigarettes); **a pack of
cigarettes** tabako hito hako
タバコ一箱. 2. *vb.* nimotsu
o matomeru 荷物をまとめ
る (prepare for traveling,
etc.); mitasu 満たす (fill
with objects); tsumekomu
詰め込む (cram).

package, *n.* tsutsumi 包み.

pact, *n.* kyōtei 協定.

paddle, 1. *n.* raketto ラケッ
ト (table tennis); kai 櫂
(oar). 2. *vb.* kogu 漕ぐ
(propel with a paddle).

paid-up, *adj.* shiharaizumi
(no) 支払い済み (の).

pail, *n.* baketsu バケツ.

pain, 1. *n.* itami 痛み (bodily
or mental suffering);
kurushimi 苦しみ (pang,
woe). 2. **pains** doryoku 努
力 (effort). 3. **be in pain**

kurushindeiru 苦しんでい
る; **pain in the neck**
yakkaimono 厄介もの
(nuisance); **take pains**
doryoku suru 努力する.

painkiller, *n.* chintsūzai 鎮
痛剤.

paint, 1. *n.* penki ペンキ
(house paint); enogu 絵の具
(oil or watercolor paint);
Wet Paint. Penki nuritate
ペンキ塗り立て. 2. *vb.*
penki o nuru ペンキを塗る
(house, wall, etc.); e o kaku
絵を描く (picture).

paintbrush, *n.* fude 筆;
burashi ブラシ.

painting, *n.* e 絵; kaiga 絵画
(picture).

pair, *n.* pea ペア; futari 二人
(two people); ittsui 一対 (set
of two).

palace, *n.* kyūden 宮殿.

pale, 1. *adj.* aojiroi 青白い
(near-white); usui 薄い
(dim). 2. *vb.* ao-zameru/
zamesaseru 青ざめる/～ざ
めさせる (become/make
pale).

pall, 1. *n.* tobari 帳 (cover of
darkness). 2. *vb.* otoroeru
衰える (fade); taikutsu ni
naru 退屈になる (become
uninterested).

palm, 1. *n.* tenohira 掌
(hand); yashi no ki 椰子の
木 (tree). 2. *vb.* **palm off**
damashite uritsukeru だま

して売りつける.

palpable, adj. 1. kanjirareru 感じられる (tangible). 2. akiraka (na) 明らか (な) (obvious).

palpitate, vb. doki-doki suru どきどきする.

pamper, vb. amayakasu 甘やかす.

pan, n. nabe 鍋.

pane, n. mado-garasu 窓ガラス (windowpane).

panel, n. 1. hameita 羽目板 (of a door). 2. i'inkai 委員会 (committee).

pang, n. kurushimi 苦しみ (pain).

pant, vb. aegu あえぐ.

panther, n. hyō ひょう.

pantry, n. shokuhin chozōshitsu 食品貯蔵室.

pants, n. 1. zubon ズボン (trousers). 2. pantī パンティー (panties).

pantyhose, n. pantī-sutokkingu パンティーストッキング.

paper, n. 1. kami 紙 (fibrous sheet). 2. shinbun 新聞 (newspaper) 3 kenkyū ronbun 研究論文 (research paper); ronbun 論文 (essay, thesis). 4. shorui 書類 (document).

paperback, n. bunkobon 文庫本.

paperweight, n. bunchin 文鎮.

par, n. 1. dōtō 同等; onaji 同じ (parity); **on a par (with)** (... to) onaji (...と) 同じ. 2. pā パー (golf, etc.) 3. **below par** suijun ika 水準以下.

paradise, n. tengoku 天国 (Heaven).

paragon, n. tenkei 典型 (model).

paragraph, n. danraku 段落.

parallel, 1. n. heikōsen 平行線 (parallel line); hitteki-butsu/-sha 匹敵物/〜者 (a comparable thing/person). 2. adj. heikō (no) 平行 (の) (not converging or diverging); 3. vb. heikō suru 平行する (be parallel to); ... ni hitteki suru ...に匹敵する (be comparable to).

paralysis, n. mahi 麻痺.

paramedic, n. ishi no joshu 医師の助手 (assistant to a doctor).

paranoid, adj. higai mōsō (no) 被害妄想 (の).

paraphernalia, n. 1. kodōgu 小道具 (equipment). 2. shojihin 所持品 (belongings).

paraphrase, 1. n. iikae 言い換え. 2. vb. iikaeru 言い換える.

parasite, n. kiseichū 寄生虫 (animal, useless person).

parcel, n. kozutsumi 小包み (package); **parcel post** kozutsumi-yūbin 小包み郵便.

parch, vb. hiagaraseru 干上がらせる (make dry); **be parched** nodo ga kawaita 喉が乾いた (be thirsty).

pardon, 1. n. yurushi 許し (forgiveness); onsha 恩謝 (legal); **I beg your pardon?** Sumimasen, mō ichido itte kudasai. すみません、もう一度言って下さい. (Please repeat what you said.). 2. vb. yurusu 許す (excuse, forgive); onsha or ataeru 恩謝を与える (legal); **Pardon me.** Sumimasen すみません (Excuse me).

parent, n. kataoya 片親 (mother or father); chichi 父 (father); haha 母 (mother); **parents** ryōshin 両親.

parenthesis, n. kakko 括弧.

park, 1. n. kōen 公園 (public space). 2. vb. chūsha suru 駐車する (a vehicle).

parking lot/place, n. chūshajō 駐車場.

parliament, n. gikai 議会; kokkai 国会.

parole, n. karishakuhō 仮釈放.

parrot, n. ōmu おうむ.

part, 1. n. bubun 部分 (portion or division of a whole); buntan 分担 (share of duty); buhin 部品 (mechanical); yaku 役 (theatrical); **for my part** watashi to shite wa 私としては; **for the most part** taitei 大抵; **in part** bubun-teki ni 部分的に; **on the part of** ... no hō de ...の方で; **take part in** ... ni sanka suru ...に参加する. 2. vb. wakeru 分ける (divide, separate); wakareru 分かれる (be divided, be separated); **part company with** ... to wakareru ...と別れる; **part with** ... o tebanasu ...を手放す (relinquish).

partial, adj. 1. bubun-teki (na) 部分的 (な) (incomplete). 2. ekohi'iki (no) えこひいき (の) (unfair, biased). 3. **partial to** ... ga toku ni suki ...が特に好き (especially fond of).

participate, vb. sanka suru 参加する (take part in an event); **participate in** ... ni sanka suru ...に参加する.

participle, n. bunshi 分詞.

particle, n. ryūshi 粒子 (extremely minute piece, elementary particle); kakera 欠けら (small portion, fragment).

particular, adj. 1. tokubetsu (na) 特別 (な) (noteworthy). 2. tokutei (no) 特定 (の) (pertaining to some one person, thing, etc.). 3. (... ni) urusai (...に) うるさい (fastidious). 4. **in particular** toku ni 特に.

parting, n. wakare 別れ (departure, separation).

partly, adv. bubun-teki ni 部分的に.

partridge, n. uzura うずら.

pass, 1. n. kyoka 許可 (permit); tōge 峠 (mountain pass); gōkaku 合格 (success in an exam). 2. vb. tōru 通る (go forward); tsūka suru 通過する (go through); watasu 渡す (hand over); sugosu 過ごす (spend, as time); ... ni gōkaku suru ...に合格する (succeed in an examination); **pass away** shinu 死ぬ (die); **pass by** mushi suru 無視する (ignore); **pass out** kubaru 配る (distribute).

passable, adj. 1. māmā (no) まあまあ (の) (marginally adequate). 2. tsūyō suru 通用する (valid, acceptable). 3. tsūkō dekiru 通行出来る (capable of being passed).

passage, n. 1. michi 道 (road, way); rōka 廊下 (corridor). 2. nagare 流れ (flow or lapse, as of time). 3. issetsu 一節 (section of a written work, etc.). 4. tsūka 通過 (act of passing). 5. funatabi 船旅 (journey by ship).

passenger, n. jōkyaku 乗客.

passionate, adj. jōnetsu-teki (na) 情熱的 (な).

passive, adj. 1. shōkyoku-teki (na) 消極的 (な). 2. ukemikei (no) 受身形 (の)

(grammar).

password, n. aikotoba 合い言葉.

past, 1. n. kako 過去 (time gone by); kakokei 過去形 (grammar). **2.** adj. kako (no) 過去 (の) (gone by, as in time); konomae no この前の (of an earlier time, former); owatta 終わった (over); kakokei (no) 過去形 (の) (grammar); **in the past few years** kono sūnenkan この数年間. **3.** prep. ... sugi ...過ぎ (beyond, as in time or age); ... no mukō ni ...の向こうに; ... o sugite ...を過ぎて (beyond); **ten past one** ichiji juppun sugi 一時十分過ぎ.

pasta, n. menrui めん類.

paste, n. nori 糊 (glue).

pasteurize, vb. teionsakkin suru 低温殺菌する.

pastime, n. goraku 娯楽; tanoshimi 楽しみ.

pastry, n. kēki ケーキ; yōgashi 洋菓子 (pie, tart, etc.).

pasture, n. bokusōchi 牧草地.

pat, 1. n. hitonade 一撫で (light touch). **2.** vb. karuku tataku 軽くたたく (strike gently).

patch, 1. n. tsugi 継ぎ (material used to mend or protect); bubun 部分 (any small piece). **2.** vb. tsugi o ateru 継ぎを当てる (mend); **patch up** tsukurou 繕う (mend, fix); toriosameru 取り治める (smooth over, as a quarrel, etc.).

patent, 1. n. tokkyo 特許 (copyright, etc.). **2.** adj. akiraka (na) 明らか (な) (obvious). **3.** vb. (... no) tokkyo o toru (... の) 特許を取る (secure a patent on).

path, n. **1.** komichi 小道 (narrow way); tōrimichi 通り道 (passage). **2.** kidō 軌道 (route).

pathetic, adj. **1.** itamashii 痛ましい (arousing pity). **2.** aware (na) 哀れ (な) (pitiful).

patience, n. nintai 忍耐; gaman 我慢 (endurance).

patient, 1. n. kanja 患者. **2.** adj. 我慢強い gamanzuyoi.

patio, n. nakaniwa 中庭 (inner open court).

patriot, n. aikokusha 愛国者.

patriotism, n. aikokushin 愛国心.

patron, n. **1.** shiensha 支援者 (supporter). **2.** otokuikyaku お得意客 (regular customer).

patronize, vb. **1.** shien suru 支援する (support). **2.** hi'iki ni suru ひいきにする (buy from regularly). **3.** mottai buru 勿体ぶる (behave haughtily).

pattern, n. **1.** moyō 模様 (surface design). **2.** kata 型 (characteristic mode). **3.** mihon 見本 (excellent example, sample). **4.** katagami 型紙 (sewing, stencil, etc.).

paunch, n. taikobara 太鼓腹.

pauper, n. binbōnin 貧乏人.

pause, 1. n. kyūshi 休止 (temporary stop). **2.** vb. kyūshi suru 休止する (make a pause); tamerau ためらう (hesitate).

pave, vb. hosō suru 舗装する (cover with concrete, etc.); **pave the way for** ... e no michi o hiraku ...への道を開く.

pavement, n. hosōdōro 舗

装道路 (paved road).

paw, *n.* te 手 (foreleg); ashi 足 (hind leg).

pawn, *vb.* shichi ni ireru 質に入れる.

pay 1. *n.* kyūryō 給料 (wages, salary). 2. *vb.* harau 払う (give money to, give as compensation); rieki o ageru 利益を上げる (yield profit); **pay attention to** ... ni chūi suru ...に注意する; **pay back** haraikaesu 払い返す; **pay for** ... no daikin o harau ...の代金を払う (pay money for); ... no mukui o ukeru ...の報いを受ける (be retaliated against); **pay off** zenbu harau 全部払う; **pay a visit** tazuneru 訪ねる.

payment, *n.* 1. shiharai 支払い (act of paying). 2. shiharaikin 支払い金 (sum of money to be paid).

payroll, *n.* 1. jūgyōinkyūryō-ichiranhyō 従業員給料一覧表 (list). 2. kyūryōsōgaku 給料総額 (sum total to be paid).

pea, *n.* endōmame えんどう豆.

peace, *n.* 1. heiwa 平和 (freedom from wars); anshin 安心 (freedom from troubles); heion 平穏 (calmness); shizukesa 静けさ (quietness). 3. **make peace with** ... to nakayoku suru ...と仲良くする.

peach, *n.* momo 桃.

peacock, *n.* kujaku 孔雀.

peak, *n.* 1. itadaki 頂 (mountain peak). 2. chōten 頂点 (highest point, culmination).

peal, 1. *n.* hibiki 響き (ringing of bells); todoroki とどろき (loud sound, as of thunder). 2. *vb.* hibiku 響く

(ring out); todoroku とどろく (sound loudly).

pear, *n.* nashi 梨.

pearl, *n.* shinju 真珠.

peasant, *n.* hyakushō 百姓; nōfu 農夫.

pebble, *n.* koishi 小石.

peck, *vb.* tsutsuku 突く (pick at, strike with beak).

peculiar, *adj.* 1. fūgawari (na) 風変わり (な) (strange). 2. **peculiar to** ... ni dokutoku (na, no) ...に独特 (な、の) (characteristic of).

pedestal, *n.* dai 台.

pedestrian, *n.* hokōsha 歩行者.

pediatrician, *n.* shōnikai 小児科医.

pedigree, *n.* 1. kettō 血統 (of a dog or cat); kettōsho 血統書 (certificate of ancestry). 2. kakei 家系 (lineage).

peek, 1. *n.* ichibetsu 一瞥; **have a peek** satto miru さっと見る. 2. *vb.* nozoku 覗く.

peel, 1. *n.* kawa 皮 (skin of fruit, etc.). 2. *vb.* kawa o muku 皮を剥く (remove the skin); kawa ga mukeru 皮が剥ける (lose the skin); hageru 剥げる (paint: come off).

peep, 1. *n.* ichibetsu 一瞥 (quick look). 2. *vb.* nozoku 覗く (look secretly).

peer, 1. *n.* dōhai 同輩 (equal); kizoku 貴族 (nobleman). 2. *vb.* yoku miru よく見る (look closely).

peg, *n.* kakekugi 掛け釘 (pin of wood, metal, etc.)

pejorative, *adj.* keibetsu-teki (na) 軽蔑的 (な).

Peking, *n.* pekin 北京.

pellet, *n.* chiisai tama 小さい

玉 (little ball).

pelt, 1. *n.* kegawa 毛皮 (skin of a beast). 2. *vb.* nagetsukeru 投げつける (throw); hageshiku furu 激しく降る (rain).

pelvis, *n.* kotsuban 骨盤.

penalty, *n.* 1. keibatsu 刑罰 (punishment). 2. bakkin 罰金 (money).

penance, *n.* tsumihoroboshi 罪滅ぼし.

pencil, *n.* enpitsu 鉛筆.

pending, *adj.* mikettei (no) 未決定 (の).

penetrate, *vb.* 1. tsuranuku 貫く (pierce); hairikomu 入り込む (enter). 2. minuku 見抜く (understand).

peninsula, *n.* hantō 半島.

penis, *n.* inkei 陰茎.

penniless, *adj.* ichimon nashi (no) 一文なし (の).

pension, *n.* nenkin 年金 (money).

pensive, *adj.* mono'omoi ni fuketteiru 物思いに耽っている.

pent-up, *adj.* tojikome-rarete-iru 閉じ込められている (shut up).

people, *n.* 1. hitobito 人々 (persons). 2. kokumin 国民 (nation); minzoku 民族 (race). 3. ichizoku 一族 (relatives).

pep, *n.* katsuryoku 活力.

pepper, *n.* 1. koshō 胡椒 (condiment). 2. pīman ピーマン (vegetable).

peppermint, *n.* hakka 薄荷 (herb).

per, *prep.* ... ni tsuki ... につき (for each ...).

perceive, *vb.* 1. satchi suru 察知する (discern, sense). 2. wakaru 分かる (understand). 3. mitomeru 認める (recognize).

percentage, *n.* wari(ai) 割 (合).

perception, *n.* 1. rikairyoku 理解力 (ability to understand). 2. ninshiki 認識 (recognition).

perceptive, *adj.* rikairyoku ni tomu 理解力に富む (keen).

perch, *vb.* 1. tomaru 止まる (of a bird). 2. suwaru 座る (of a person).

perfect, *adj.* 1. kanpeki (na) 完璧 (な) (faultless). 2. kanzen (na) 完全 (な) (complete). 3. mattaku (no) 全く (の) (utter).

perfect tense, *n.* kanryōkei 完了形.

perforate, *vb.* ana o akeru 穴を開ける (make a hole or holes).

perform, *vb.* 1. okonau 行う (execute). 2. ensō suru 演奏する (play an instrument). 3. enjiru 演じる (act). 4. ugoku 動く (move, function).

perfume, *n.* kōsui 香水.

perhaps, *adv.* tabun 多分.

peril, *n.* kiken 危険; **at one's peril** kiken o okashite 危険を冒して.

perimeter, *n.* shūhen 周辺.

period, *n.* 1. kikan 期間 (portion of time). 2. jidai 時代 (epoch). 3. shūshifu 終止符 (punctuation).

periodic, *adj.* shūki-teki (na) 周期的 (な) (recurring regularly).

periphery, *n.* shūhen 周辺.

perish, *vb.* 1. shinu 死ぬ (die). 2. horobiru 滅びる (be ruined or destroyed).

perishable, *adj.* kusareyasui 腐れ易い (of food).

permanence, *n.* eien 永遠.

permanent, *adj.* 1. eien

(no) 永遠 (の) (lasting). 2. eijū (no) 永住 (の) (of an address). 3. teishoku (no) 定職 (の) (of a job).

permission, n. kyoka 許可.

permit, 1. n. kyokashō 許可書 (written statement, license). 2. vb. kyoka suru 許可する (allow, license); yurusu 許す (afford opportunity, allow).

perpendicular, adj. suichoku (na, no) 垂直 (な, の) (vertical, meeting at right angle).

perpetrate, vb. okasu 犯す.

perpetual, adj. 1. eien (no) 永遠 (の) (lasting forever). 2. taemanai 絶え間ない (constant).

perplex, vb. tomadowaseru 戸惑わせる.

persecution, n. hakugai 迫害.

perseverance, n. nintai 忍耐.

persimmon, n. kaki 柿.

persist, vb. 1. shitsukoku tsuzukeru しつこく続ける (continue stubbornly). 2. tsuzuku 続く (continue).

person, n. hito 人; **in person** hon'ninmizukara 本人自ら.

personal, adj. 1. kojin (no) 個人 (の); kojin-teki (na) 個人的 (な) (of, by, or relating to a particular person). 2. shiteki (na) 私的 (な) (private).

personality, n. 1. kosei 個性 (personal character). 2. chomeijin 著名人 (famous person).

perspective, n. 1. enkinhō 遠近法 (spatial relationship). 2. kenchi 見地 (viewpoint). 3. tenbō 展望 (vista, view).

perspiration, n. ase 汗.

persuade, vb. 1. settoku suru 説得する (prevail on). 2. nattoku saseru 納得させる (convince).

persuasion, n. 1. settoku 説得 (act of persuading). 2. settokuryoku 説得力 (power of persuading). 3. shin'nen 信念 (conviction).

perverse, adj. 1. tsumujimagari (no) つむじ曲がり (の) (stubbornly contrary). 2. ijō (na) 異常 (な) (abnormal).

pervert, 1. n. hentaisha 変態者 (perverted person). 2. vb. akuyō suru 悪用する (turn something to a wrong use); daraku saseru 堕落させる (turn someone away from the moral course).

pessimistic, adj. hikan-teki (na) 悲観的 (な).

pest, n. 1. gaichū 害虫 (insect). 2. iya na yatsu 嫌な奴 (person).

pesticide, n. satchūzai 殺虫剤.

petal, n. hanabira 花びら.

petrify, vb. 1. kasekika suru 化石化する (fossilize). 2. **be petrified** kyōfu de tachisukumu 恐怖で立ちすくむ (be paralyzed with fear).

petroleum, n. sekiyu 石油.

phantom, n. obake お化け.

pharmacy, n. yakkyoku 薬局.

phase, 1. kyokumen 局面; dankai 段階 (stage of change). 2. men 面 (aspect).

pheasant, n. kiji 雉子.

phenomenon, n. 1. genshō 現象 (something observable). 2. kyōi 驚異 (marvel).

philanthropy, n. 1. jinruiai

人類愛 (concern for human beings). 2. jizen 慈善 (benevolent act).

Philippines, *n.* firipin フィリピン.

philosophy, *n.* tetsugaku 哲学.

phlegm, *n.* tan 痰 (mucus secretion).

phobia, *n.* kyōfu 恐怖.

phoenix, *n.* fushichō 不死鳥.

phone, 1. *n.* denwa 電話. 2. *vb.* denwa suru 電話する.

phony, *adj.* nisemono (no) 偽物 (の) (fake).

phosphorus, *n.* rin 燐.

photo, *n.* shashin 写真.

photocopy, 1. *n.* kopī コピー. 2. *vb.* ...no kopī o suru ...のコピーをする.

photograph, *n.* shashin 写真; **take a photograph** shashin o toru 写真を撮る.

phrase, 1. *n.* ku 句 (unit of words). 2. *vb.* hyōgen suru 表現する.

physical, *adj.* 1. nikutai (no) 肉体 (の) (of the body). 2. busshitsu-teki (na) 物質的 (な) (of matter). 3. butsurigaku (no) 物理学 (の) (of physics).

physics, *n.* butsurigaku 物理学.

physique, *n.* taikaku 体格.

pick, 1. *n.* sentaku 選択 (choice); pikku ピック (plectrum, pointed tool); **take one's pick** erabu 選ぶ. 2. *vb.* tsumiatsumeru 摘み集める (gather, as fruit, etc); tsumamiageru 摘まみ上げる (take up with fingers); erabu 選ぶ (choose); tsuku 突く (dig, break into); hiku 弾く (guitar); hojikuru ほじくる (teeth, nose); suru 掘る

(pocket); **pick up** tori ni iku 取りに行く (go and get a thing); mukae ni iku 迎えに行く (go and get a person); atsumeru 集める (collect); yoku naru 良くなる (improve); oboeru 覚える (learn); kiku 聞く (hear).

pickle, *n.* tsukemono 漬物 (pickled vegetable).

pickpocket, *n.* suri すり.

picture, 1. *n.* e 絵 (drawing, painting); shashin 写真 (photograph); eiga 映画 (motion picture). 2. *vb.* egaku 描く (draw, paint); omoiegaku 思い描く (imagine).

piece, *n.* 1. bubun 部分 (part). 2. danpen 断片 (broken piece). 3. sakuhin 作品 (artistic work). 4. **a piece of** hitotsu (no) 一つ (の); **a piece of paper** kami ichimai 紙一枚.

pierce, *vb.* tsuranuku 貫く.

pig, *n.* buta 豚 (animal, person).

pigeon, *n.* hato 鳩.

pigment, *n.* shikiso 色素.

pigpen, *n.* butagoya 豚小屋.

pile, 1. *n.* yama 山 (heap); takusan 沢山 (large quantity). 2. *vb.* tsumikasaneru 積み重ねる (make a pile); tamaru 溜まる (accumulate).

pilgrimage, *n.* junrei 巡礼.

pill, *n.* 1. jōzai 錠剤 (medicine). 2. hinin'yaku 避妊薬 (for birth control).

pillar, *n.* hashira 柱.

pillow, *n.* makura 枕 (for sleeping); **pillow case** makura-kabā 枕カバー.

pilot, *vb.* sōjū suru 操縦する (airplane); michibiku 導く (guide, lead).

pimento, *n.* pīman ピーマ

ン.

pimple, *n.* nikibi にきび.

pincers, *n.* yattoko やっとこ (tool); hasami 鋏 (crab).

pinch, 1. *n.* hitotsumami 一 摘み (tiny amount); **in a pinch** hitsuyō naraba 必要 ならば (if necessary). 2. *vb.* tsumamu 摘む (squeeze); tsuneru つねる (squeeze painfully); nusumu 盗む (steal); **be pinched** komatteiru 困っている (be in trouble).

pine, 1. *n.* matsu 松 (tree); **pine cone** matsukasa 松か さ. 2. *vb.* omoi kogareru 思 い焦がれる (long painfully).

pink, *n.,* *adj.* momoiro (no) 桃色 (の).

pinnacle, *n.* 1. itadaki 頂 (mountaintop). 2. chōten 頂点 (culmination).

pioneer, *n.* 1. senkusha 先駆 者 (art, thought, etc.). 2. kaitakusha 開拓者 (first settler, explorer).

pipe, *n.* 1. kuda 管 (tube). 2. paipu パイプ (smoking). 3. kangakki 管楽器 (musical instrument).

pirate, *n.* kaizoku 海賊 (robber at sea).

pit, *n.* ana 穴 (hole); kubomi 凹み (hollow); naraku 奈落 (stage).

pitch, 1. *n.* pitchi ピッチ (musical tone, baseball); kōbaido 勾配度 (slope); teido 程度 (degree). 2. *vb.* nageru 投げる (throw); setchi suru 設置する (set up); taoreru 倒れる (fall); yureru 揺れる (drop and rise).

pitfall, *n.* otoshiana 落とし 穴 (trap).

pith, *n.* 1. zui 髄 (spongy tissue). 2. seizui 精髄 (essence).

pitiful, *adj.* 1. aware (na) 哀 れ (な) (lamentable). 2. nasakenai 情けない (contemptible).

pittance, *n.* namidakin 涙 金.

pity, 1. *n.* awaremi 哀れみ (sympathetic sorrow); zan'nen 残念 (regret); **it is a pity that** ... to wa zan'nen da ... とは残念だ; **What a pity!** Zan'nen. 残念. 2. *vb.* awaremu 哀れむ (feel pity for); dōjō suru 同情する (sympathize with).

pivot, *n.* kaitenjiku 回転軸 (shaft on which something turns).

place, 1. *n.* basho 場所; tokoro 所 (particular portion of space); chii 地位 (social standing); -i -位 (at a competition); **first place** ichii 一位; **in place** tekisetsu (na) 適切 (な) (proper); **out of place** bachigai (na) 場違い (な) (awkward); futekisetsu (na) 不適切 (な) (improper); **take the place of** ... ni totte kawaru ... に取って代 わる; **take place** okoru 起 こる. 2. *vb.* oku 置く (put in place); omoidasu 思い出す (remember); **place an order** chūmon o suru 注文 をする.

placid, *adj.* odayaka (na) 穏 やか (な).

plain, 1. *n.* heichi 平地 (level area). 2. *adj.* meikai (na) 明 快 (な) (clear); shisso (na) 質素 (な) (simple); muji (no) 無地 (の) (without pattern); bukiryō (na) 不器 量 (な) (unattractive); sotchoku (na) 率直 (な) (candid).

plan, 1. *n.* keikaku 計画 (project); sekkeizu 設計図 (drawing). 2. *vb.* keikaku suru 計画する (make a plan); sekkei suru 設計する (design).

plane, *n.* 1. heimen 平面 (flat surface). 2. reberu レベル (level). 3. kan'na 鉋 (tool). 4. hikōki 飛行機 (airplane).

planet, *n.* wakusei 惑星.

plank, *n.* ita 板 (lumber).

planner, *n.* keikakusha 計画者.

plant, 1. *n.* shokubutsu 植物 (organism); kōjō 工場 (factory); setsubi 設備 (apparatus). 2. *vb.* ueru 植える (set in ground for growth).

plaque, *n.* 1. shikō 歯こう (on teeth). 2. meiban 銘板 (monumental tablet).

plasma, *n.* kesshō 血しょう (blood).

plaster, *n.* 1. shikkui 漆喰 (for construction). 2. bansōkō ばんそうこう (adhesive plaster).

plastic bag, *n.* binīrubukuro ビニール袋.

plastic surgery, *n.* biyōseikei 美容整形; seikeishujutsu 整形手術.

plate, *n.* 1. sara 皿 (dish). 2. ginshokki 銀食器 (silver plate). 3. kinzokuban 金属板 (metal sheet). 4. ireba 入れ歯 (denture).

platter, *n.* moritsukezara 盛りつけ皿.

play, 1. *n.* asobi 遊び (recreation, fun); geki 劇 (theater). 2. *vb.* asobu 遊ぶ (amuse oneself); suru する (engage in, as a game); ensō suru 演奏する (perform on a musical instrument);

enzuru 演ずる (play a part).

playful, *adj.* 1. tanoshii 楽しい (full of fun). 2. jōdan (no) 冗談 (の) (not serious).

playground, *n.* gakkō no asobiba 学校の遊び場 (at a school).

playmate, *n.* asobinakama 遊び仲間.

playwright, *n.* gekisakka 劇作家.

plea, *n.* 1. kongan 懇願 (entreaty); kōjitsu 口実 (excuse); **on the plea that** ... to iu kōjitsu de ... という口実で. 2. tōben 答弁 (defendant's answer).

pleasant, *adj.* 1. kokoroyoi 快い (pleasing). 2. aisō ga ii 愛想がいい (friendly).

please, 1. *vb.* yorokobaseru 喜ばせる (give pleasure); **if you please** yokereba 良ければ (if you like); **Please yourself!** Sukikatte ni shiro. 好き勝手にしろ. 2. *adv.* onegai shimasu お願いします (used when making a request).

pleasure, *n.* 1. yorokobi 喜び (joy). 2. manzoku 満足 (satisfaction).

pleat, *n.* hida ひだ.

pledge, 1. *n.* shirushi 印 (sign); seiyaku 誓約 (solemn promise). 2. *vb.* seiyaku suru 誓約する (promise).

plentiful, *adj.* jūbun (na) 十分 (な).

plenty, *n.* jūbun 十分 (abundant quantity); **plenty of** jūbun na 十分な; **in plenty** jūbun ni 十分に.

pliable, *adj.* 1. shinayaka (na) しなやか (な) (supple). 2. sayū sareyasui 左右され易い (easily influenced).

plight, *n.* kyūchi 窮地; gyakkyō 逆境.

plod, vb. 1. tobo-tobo aruku とぼとぼ歩く (manner of walking). 2. kotsu-kotsu hataraku こつこつ働く (manner of working).

plot, 1. n. kukaku 区画 (piece of ground); inbō 陰謀 (secret scheme); arasuji 荒筋 (main story). 2. vb. zushi suru 図示する (mark on a map, etc.); takuramu 企む (conspire).

plow, 1. n. suki 鋤 (farming tool). 2. vb. suki de tagayasu 鋤で耕す (cultivate with a plow); oshisusumu 押し進む (move forcefully through).

plug, 1. n. sen 栓 (for stopping a hole); 2. vb. sen o suru 栓をする (stop with a plug); **plug in** ... no puragu o soketto ni ireru ... のプラグをソケットに入れる (electrical).

plumage, n. hane 羽.

plumb, 1. n. omori おもり (piece of lead). 2. vb. hakaru 測る、計る (measure depth of); saguru 探る (try to get to the root of).

plume, n. hane 羽.

plummet, vb. kyūgeki ni ochiru 急激に落ちる.

plump, adj. maru-maru to shiteiru 丸々としている.

plunge, 1. n. tobikomi 飛び込み (dive). 2. vb. tsukkomu 突っ込む (put into); tobikomu 飛び込む (dive into); tosshin suru 突進する (move forward quickly); kyū ni sagaru 急に下がる (become low suddenly).

plural, n., adj. fukusūkei (no) 複数形（の）.

plush, adj. gōka (na) 豪華

(na) (luxurious).

ply, 1. n. sō 層 (layer). 2. vb. ōfuku suru 往復する (travel regularly); **ply a trade** shōbai ni hagemu 商売に励む.

plywood, n. beniyaita ベニヤ板.

p.m., gogo 午後; **5:00 p.m.** gogo goji 午後五時.

pneumonia, n. haien 肺炎.

poach, vb. 1. yuderu ゆでる (boil); otoshitamago ni suru 落し卵にする (poach an egg). 2. mitsuryō suru 密猟する (catch animals illegally).

pocketbook, n. handobaggu ハンドバッグ.

pod, n. saya さや.

podium, n. dai 台.

poem, n. shi 詩.

point, 1. n. ten 点 (dot, score in game, decimal point, detail in conversation or writing); saki 先 (projecting part, tip); chiten 地点 (definite place); jiten 時点 (definite time); yōten 要点 (issue, central topic); **at the point of** ... no magiwa ni ...の間際に; **be beside the point** yōten o hazureteiru 要点を外れている; **make a point of doing** kanarazu ...suru 必ず...する (do without fail); **miss the point** mato o hazusu 的を外す; **on the point of doing** ... shiyō to suru tokoro ...しようとするところ; **point of view** kenkai 見解; **to the point of** hotondo ほとんど (almost). 2. vb. sasu 指す (indicate); yubisasu 指差す (indicate with a finger); mukeru 向ける (direct); **point out** shiteki suru 指摘する.

pointed, adj. togatteiru 尖っている (sharp).

poise, n. 1. ochitsuki 落ち着き (composure). 2. mi no tsuriai 身の釣り合い (balance).

poison, 1. n. doku 毒. 2. adj. yūdoku (na) 有毒 (な). 3. vb. ... ni doku o moru ...に毒を盛る.

poke, vb. tsutsuku 突く.

polar, adj. kyokuchi (no) 極地 (の).

pole, n. bō 棒 (long slender piece of wood, etc.). 2. kyoku 極 (geographical).

police, n. keisatsu 警察.

police officer, n. kei(satsu)kan 警(察)官.

policy, n. 1.hōshin 方針 (course of action). 2. hoken shōsho 保険証書 (insurance contract).

polio, n. porio ポリオ; shōnimahi 小児麻痺.

polish, 1. n. kenmazai 研磨剤 (polishing substance); kōtaku 光沢 (luster); senren 洗練 (refinement); **shoe polish** kutsuzumi 靴墨. 2. vb. migaku 磨く (make glossy, refine).

polite, adj. 1. reigi tadashii 礼儀正しい (showing good manners). 2. jōhin (na) 上品 (な) (refined).

politics, n. 1. seiji 政治 (administration of government). 2. seijigaku 政治学 (political science).

pollen, n. kafun 花粉.

pollution, n. osen 汚染; kankyō osen 環境汚染.

pond, n. ike 池.

pony, n. kouma 子馬.

pool, n. 1. mizutamari 水溜まり (of water); **swimming pool** pūru プール. 2. tamatsuki 玉突き (game).

poor, adj. 1. mazushii 貧しい (destitute). 2. hinjaku (na) 貧弱 (な) (inferior). 3. kawaisō (na) 可哀そう (な) (unfortunate).

pop, 1. n. pon to iu oto ぽんと言う音 (short, quick sound); poppusu ポップス (music); tansan inryō 炭酸飲料 (soft drink). 2. vb. pon to hajikeru ぽんとはじける (burst with a short, quick sound); tobideru 飛び出る (spring).

poppy, n. keshi けし.

popular, adj. 1. ninki ga aru 人気がある (liked). 2. taishū (no) 大衆 (の) (of the general public); taishūmuke (no) 大衆向け (の) (aimed at the general public). 3. hayari (no) はやり (の) (prevalent, current).

population, n. jinkō 人口.

porcupine, n. yama'arashi 山荒し.

pore, n. keana 毛穴 (in the skin).

pork, n. butaniku 豚肉.

porpoise, n. iruka いるか.

port, n. 1. minato 港 (harbor). 2. pōto-wain ポートワイン (type of wine).

portable, adj. keitaiyō (no) 携帯用 (の).

portfolio, n. kamibasami 紙挟み (case).

portion, n. 1. bubun 部分 (part). 2. wakemae 分け前 (share).

portly, adj. futotteiru 太っている.

portrait, n. shōzōga 肖像画.

portray, vb. egaku 描く (depict).

portrayal, n. byōsha 描写 (depiction).

position, n. 1. ichi 位置; basho 場所 (location). 2.

chi'i 地位 (social standing).
3. tachiba 立場 (condition,
state). 4. shoku 職 (job).
positive, *adj.* 1. tashika (na)
確か (な) (certain). 2. kōtei-
teki (na) 肯定的 (な)
(affirmative). 3. zettai (no)
絶対 (の) (definite). 4.
kensetsu-teki (na) 建設的
(な) (constructive). 5. yōsei
(no) 陽性 (の) (medical
test).
possess, *vb.* 1. shoyū suru 所
有する (own). 3. toritsuku
取り憑く (obsess).
possible, *adj.* kanō (na) 可能
(な); **if possible** dekireba 出
来れば; **as much as
possible** dekirudake
takusan 出来るだけ沢山.
post, 1. *n.* hashira 柱 (pole);
shoku 職 (job); mochiba 持
ち場 (place of duty); yūbin
郵便 (mail). 2. *vb.* keiji suru
掲示する (display, as a
notice); haichi suru 配置す
る (station); tōkan suru 投函
する (mail).
postbox, *n.* posuto ポスト
(mailbox).
postcard, *n.* hagaki 葉書.
postman, *n.* yūbinhaitatsu
郵便配達.
post office, *n.* yūbinkyoku
郵便局.
postscript, *n.* tsuishin 追伸.
posture, *n.* shisei 姿勢
(position of the body).
potable, *adj.* nomeru 飲め
る.
potato, *n.* jagaimo じゃが芋.
potbelly, *n.* taikobara 太鼓
腹.
potential, 1. *n.*
senzainōryoku 潜在能力. 2.
adj. senzainōryoku ga aru 潜
在能力がある.
potion, *n.* mizugusuri 水薬
(liquid medicine).

pouch, *n.* fukuro 袋.
poultry, *n.* 1. kakin 家禽
(domestic fowl). 2. toriniku
鳥肉 (meat).
pounce on, *vb.* ... ni
tobikakaru ...に飛びかかる.
pound, *vb.* kudaku 砕く
(crush by pounding); utsu
打つ (strike).
pour, *vb.* 1. sosogu 注ぐ
(send a liquid flowing out);
nagareru 流れる (flow out
or along). 2. tsugu 注ぐ
(tea).
poverty, *n.* binbō 貧乏.
powder, *n.* kona 粉.
power, *n.* 1. chikara 力
(strength). 2. nōryoku 能力
(ability, faculty). 3.
denryoku 電力 (electricity).
4. kenryoku 権力
(authority, control,
domination).
practice, 1. *n.* renshū 練習
(repeated performance);
jikkō 実行 (actual
performance); genjitsu 現実
(actuality); shūkan 習慣
(customary action); kaigyō
開業 (pursuit, as of a
profession); **in practice**
genjitsu niwa 現実には; **put
into practice** jikkō suru 実
行する. 2. *vb.* renshū suru
練習する (perform
repeatedly); kaigyō suru 開
業する (pursue as
profession); okonau 行う
(do habitually).
pragmatic, *adj.* genjitsu-teki
(na) 現実的 (な).
prairie, *n.* sōgen 草原.
praise, 1. *n.* shōsan 賞讃, 称
讃. 2. *vb.* shōsan suru 賞
讃/称讃する.
prank, *n.* itazura いたずら.
prawn, *n.* kuruma ebi 車え
び.
prayer, *n.* inori 祈り (devout

petition).

preach, vb. sekkyō suru 説教する (deliver a sermon, moralize).

preacher, n. bokushi 牧師.

precarious, adj. 1. abunakkashii 危なっかしい (dangerous). 2. fuantei (na) 不安定 (な) (unsteady).

precaution, n. yōjin 用心; **take precautions** yōjin suru 用心する.

precede, vb. mae ni kuru/okoru 前に来る／起こる (come/happen before).

precious, adj. 1. kichō (na) 貴重 (な) (beloved, important). 2. kōka (na) 高価 (な) (valuable).

preclude, vb. fusegu 防ぐ.

predecessor, n. zen'ninsha 前任者.

predict, vb. yogen suru 予言する.

predisposition, n. keikōsei 傾向性 (tendency).

predominant, adj. kencho (na) 顕著 (な) (most conspicuous); shuyō (na) 主要 (な) (chief).

preface, n. jo 序.

prefer, vb. ... no hō o konomu ...の方を好む.

pregnancy, n. ninshin 妊娠.

prejudice, 1. n. henken 偏見 (bigotry); sen'nyūken 先入観 (preconception). 2. vb. **be prejudiced against** ... ni taishite henken ga aru ...に対して偏見がある.

preliminary, adj. yobi (no) 予備 (の).

prelude, n. 1. maebure 前触れ (preliminary to a major event). 2. zensōkyoku 前奏曲 (music).

premeditated, adj. keikaku-teki (na) 計画的 (な).

premier, n. shushō 首相.

premise, n. zentei 前提.

preoccupied, vb. **preoccupied by/with ...** de atama ga ippai ...で頭が一杯.

prepare, vb. 1. junbi suru 準備する (get ready). 2. ryōri suru 料理する (cook). 3. kokorogamae o saseru 心構えをさせる (make someone ready to accept something new).

preposition, n. zenchishi 前置詞.

prescribe, vb. 1. meijiru 命じる (order). 2. shohō suru 処方する (medical).

presence, n. 1. shusseki 出席 (attendance). 2. sonzai 存在 (existence, fact of being present); **presence of mind** ochitsuki 落ち着き (composure); **in my presence** watashi no me no mae de 私の目の前で. 3. sonzaikan 存在感 (perceived personal quality).

present, 1. n. okurimono 贈り物 (gift); ima 今 (present time); **at present** ima 今; **for the present** ima no tokoro 今のところ. 2. adj. ima (no) 今 (の) (being or occurring now); kiteiru 来ている (being at particular place). 3. vb. ataeru 与える (offer); motarasu もたらす (bring, pose); teishutsu suru 提出する (offer for consideration); miseru 見せる (exhibit); shōkai suru 紹介する (introduce).

preserve, vb. hozon suru 保存する (keep from decay);

hogo suru 保護する (keep safe); iji suru 維持する (maintain).

preside, vb. **preside over ...** no gijichō o tsutomeru ...の議事長を務める (committee, etc.).

president, n. daitōryō 大統領 (chief of state of a republic); shachō 社長 (company); gakuchō 学長 (college or university).

presume, vb. katei suru 仮定する (suppose).

presumptuous, adj. atsukamashii 厚かしい.

presupposition, n. zentei 前提.

pretend, vb. furi o suru 振りをする.

pretext, n. kōjitsu 口実.

pretty, 1. adj. kirei (na) きれい (な) (beautiful); kawaii 可愛い (cute). 2. adv. kanari かなり.

prevail, vb. 1. katsu 勝つ (gain victory). 2. ikiwatatte-iru 行き渡っている (be widespread).

prevent, vb. fusegu 防ぐ.

preventive, preventative, adj. yobō (no) 予防 (の).

preview, n. shisha 試写 (advance showing of film); shien 試演 (advance performance of play).

previous, adj. mae (no) 前 (の); **previous to ...** no mae (no) ...の前 (の).

prey, 1. n. ejiki えじき (animal, victim). 2. vb. **prey on ...** no ejiki ni suru ...をえじきにする.

price, 1. n. nedan 値段 (sum of money); **at any price** dōshitemo どうしても (by all means); **at the price of ...** o gisei ni shite ...を犠牲にして. 2. vb. nedan o tsukeru

nedan o tsukeru 値段を付ける (set the price of).

priceless, adj. 1. totemo kōka (na) とても高価 (な) (very expensive). 2. kakegae ga nai 掛け替えがない (very important).

pride, n. 1. hokori 誇り (high opinion of oneself, something that causes one to be proud); **take pride in ...** o hokori ni suru ...を誇りにする. 2. jisonshin 自尊心 (self-respect).

primary, adj. omo (na) 主 (な) (chief).

prime, 1. n. saiseiki 最盛期 (best stage of one's life). 2. adj. ichiban (no) 一番 (の) (first, best).

prime minister, n. sōridaijin 総理大臣.

primitive, adj. genshi-teki na 原始的な (early, unrefined).

prince, n. ōji(sama) 王子 (様); **crown prince** kōtaishi 皇太子.

princess, n. ohimesama お姫様; ōjo(sama) 王女(様).

principal, 1. n. kōchō 校長 (elementary or secondary school); gankin 元金 (capital sum); shuyaku 主役 (leading performer). 2. adj. shuyō (na) 主要 (な) (main).

principle, n. 1. gensoku 原則 (general rule); **in principle** gensoku to shite 原則として. 2. shin'nen 信念 (faith, belief); **on principle** shin'nen kara 信念から.

print, 1. n. insatsu 印刷 (printed lettering); ato 跡 (mark, indentation); hanga 版画 (woodblock, etc.); shashin 写真

(photographic); **out of print** zeppan (no) 絶版 (の). 2. *vb.* insatsu suru 印刷する (reproduce from inked type); katsujitai de kaku 活字体で書く (write with printed-style letters); yakitsukeru 焼き付ける (photo).

prior, *adj.* mae (no) 前 (の) (earlier); mae kara (no) 前から (の) (planned before); **prior to** ... no mae ni ...の前に.

prison, *n.* keimusho 刑務所.

private, 1. *adj.* shi-teki (na) 私的 (な) (personal, secret); kojin-teki (na) 個人的 (な) (individual); hikōshiki (na, no) 非公式 (な、の) (unofficial); minkan (no) 民間 (の) (of the general population); shiritsu (no) 私立 (の) (of a private institution). 2. *n.* hohei 歩兵 (military); **in private** naimitsu ni 内密に (secretly)

privilege, *n.* tokken 特権.

prize, 1. *n.* shō 賞. 2. *vb.* taisetsu ni suru 大切にする.

probable, *adj.* arisō (na) ありそう (な) (likely).

probably, *adv.* tabun 多分.

probation, *n.* 1. minarai 見習い (test of ability). 2. shikkōyūyo 執行猶予 (legal).

problem, *n.* mondai 問題 (trouble, question).

proceed, *vb.* 1. tsuzukeru 続ける (continue); susumu 進む (advance).

proceedings, *n.* **bring legal proceedings against** ... o uttaeru ...を訴える.

process, 1. *n.* katei 過程 (course); **in the process of** ... no katei de ...の過程で.

2. *vb.* kakō suru 加工する (food).

procession, *n.* gyōretsu 行列.

proclaim, *vb.* sengen suru 宣言する.

procrastinate, *vb.* guzuguzu suru 愚図愚図する.

procreate, *vb.* ko o umu 子を産む.

procure, *vb.* 1. nyūshu suru 入手する (obtain). 2. ponbiki o suru ぽん引きをする (hire a prostitute).

prod, *vb.* tsutsuku 突く.

prodigal, *adj.* rōhiteki (na) 浪費的 (な).

prodigy, *n.* tensai 天才.

produce, 1. *n.* seihin 製品 (product); nōsanbutsu 農産物 (agricultural products). 2. *vb.* umu 産む (bear young); ... no mi ga naru ...の実がなる (bear fruit); sanshutsu suru 産出する (grow and supply); tsukuru 作る (make, create); shimesu 示す (show).

product, *n.* seihin 製品 (manufactured article).

profanity, *n.* bōtoku 冒瀆.

profess, *vb.* genmei suru 言明する.

profession, *n.* 1. shokugyō 職業 (vocation). 2. genmei 言明 (declaration).

professional, 1. *n.* puro プロ (professional person). 2. *adj.* puro (no) プロ (の) (working for money)

professor, *n.* kyōju 教授.

proficient, *adj.* jukuren shiteiru 熟練している.

profile, *n.* yokogao 横顔 (side view).

profit, 1. *n.* rieki 利益 (gain). 2. *vb.* rieki o ageru 利益を上げる (make profit); **profit from** ... kara manabu ...から学ぶ (learn from).

profound, *adj.* fukai 深い (deep, thinking deeply).

program, *n.* keikaku 計画 (plan); dashimono 出し物 (schedule of entertainments); bangumi 番組 (TV or radio program).

progress, 1. *n.* shinkō 進行 (act of moving forward); kaizen 改善 (improvement); hatten 発展 (growth); **in progress** shinkōchū 進行中; **make progress** hakadoru 捗る (get better, develop). 2. *vb.* shinkō suru 進行する (move forward); yoku naru 良くなる (improve); hatten suru 発展する (develop).

prohibit, *vb.* kinjiru 禁じる.

project, 1. *n.* purojekuto プロジェクト (enterprise, aim); keikaku 計画 (plan). 2. *vb.* keikaku suru 計画する (plan); tsukideru 突き出る (protrude); hassha suru 発射する (hurl); tōsha suru 投射する (display upon surface, attribute unconsciously).

projectile, *n.* dangan 弾丸 (gun).

projector, *n.* eishaki 映写機 (apparatus).

prolific, *adj.* tasan (na) 多産 (な).

prolong, *vb.* nobasu 延ばす.

prominent, *adj.* 1. tsukideta 突き出た (projecting). 2. medatsu 目立つ (conspicuous). 3. chomei (na) 著名 (な) (well-known).

promiscuous, *adj.* sei-teki ni hōshō (na) 性的に放縦 (な) (sexually).

promise, 1. *n.* yakusoku 約束 (assurance); yūbōsei 有望

性 (potentiality); **make/keep/break a promise** yakusoku o suru/mamoru/yaburu 約束をする／守る／破る. 2. *vb.* yakusoku suru 約束する (assure by promise); kitai saseru 期待させる (afford ground for expecting).

promote, *vb.* 1. shōshin saseru 昇進させる (cause to advance in position). 2. sokushin suru 促進する (further the progress of). 3. senden suru 宣伝する (advertise). 4. kikaku suru 企画する (organize).

prompt, 1. *adj.* jinsoku (na) 迅速 (な) (swift); jikandōri (no) 時間通り (の) (punctual). 2. *vb.* hikiokosu 引き起こす (cause).

prone, *adj.* 1. utsubuse (no) うつぶせ (の) (lying flat). 2. **prone to** ... e no keikō ga aru ...への傾向がある (have a tendency toward).

pronoun, *n.* daimeishi 代名詞.

pronounce, *vb.* 1. hatsuon suru 発音する (enunciate or articulate). 2. genmei suru 言明する (declare as one's opinion). 3. senkoku suru 宣告する (announce).

proof, *n.* 1. shōko 証拠 (evidence). 2. do 度 (alcohol).

prop, 1. *n.* sasae 支え (support). 2. *vb.* sasaeru 支える.

propel, *vb.* susumeru 進める (drive forward).

proper, *adj.* 1. fusawashii ふさわしい (suitable). 2. tadashii 正しい (right).

property, *n.* 1. bukken 物件 (assets, holdings, real estate). 2. tochi 土地 (land).

3. tokushitsu 特質 (attribute).

prophecy, *n.* yogen 予言.

proponent, *n.* shijisha 支持者.

proportional, proportionate, *adj.*

proportional to ... ni hirei shite ...に比例して.

proposal, *n.* 1. teian 提案 (proposition). 2. kekkon-mōshikomi 結婚申し込み (offer of marriage).

propriety, *n.* 1. datōsei 妥当性 (appropriateness). 2. reigi-tadashisa 礼儀正しさ (moral correctness).

proscribe, *vb.* kinjiru 禁じる.

prospect, *n.* 1. kanōsei 可能性 (likelihood of success). 2. miharashi 見晴らし (view). 3. mitōshi 見通し (outlook).

prosper, *vb.* sakaeru 栄える.

prostitute, 1. *n.* baishunfu 売春婦. 2. *vb.* baishun o suru 売春をする (sell one's body); uriwatasu 売り渡す (sell, degrade).

prostrate, 1. *adj.* hirefushiteiru ひれ伏している. 2. *vb.* heifuku suru 平伏する.

protect, *vb.* mamoru 守る (defend).

protection, *n.* hogo 保護 (act of defending, thing that defends).

protein, *n.* tanpakushitsu 蛋白質.

protest, 1. *n.* kōgi 抗議. 2. *vb.* kōgi suru 抗議する.

protract, *vb.* nagabikaseru 長引かせる.

protrude, *vb.* tsuki-deru/-dasu 突き出る／〜出す (project/cause to project).

proud, *adj.* 1. hokoritakai 誇り高い (having pride). 2. kōman (na) 高慢 (な) (arrogant).

prove, *vb.* 1. shōmei suru 証明する (establish as fact). 2. ... to hanmei suru ...と判明する (be or become ultimately).

proverb, *n.* kotowaza 諺.

provide, *vb.* 1. ataeru 与える (supply). 2. sadameru 定める (stipulate). 3. **provide for** yashinau 養う (raise, feed).

province, *n.* shū 州.

provision, *n.* 1. yōi 用意 (preparation). 2. kitei 規定 (condition). 3. kyōkyū 供給 (supply). 4. **provisions** shokuryō 食料 (food).

provoke, *vb.* chōhatsu suru 挑発する.

prowl, *vb.* urotsuku うろつく.

proximity, *n.* **in the proximity of** ... no chikaku ni ...の近くに.

prudent, *adj.* 1. funbetsu ga aru 分別がある (discreet). 2. shinchō (na) 慎重 (な) (cautious).

prune, 1. *n.* hoshi sumomo 干し李 (food). 2. *vb.* sentei suru 剪定する (tree).

pry, *vb.* sensaku suru 詮索する (investigate).

psychology, *n.* 1. shinri 心理 (mind). 2. shinrigaku 心理学 (science).

puberty, *n.* shishunki 思春期.

public, 1. *n.* hitobito 人々 (people in general); **in public** ōyake no ba de 公の場で. 2. *adj.* kōkyō (no) 公共 (の) (for use of the public); ōyake (no) 公 (の) (open to view or knowledge of all); hitobito (no) 人々

(の) (of people).

publicity, n. 1. chūmoku 注目 (attention). 2. senden 宣伝 (promotion).

publish, vb. 1. shuppan suru 出版する (in printed form). 2. happyō suru 発表する (bring to public notice).

puddle, n. mizutamari 水溜まり.

puff, 1. n. ippuku 一服 (cigarette). 2. vb. fukasu ふかす (cigarette); aegu あえぐ (breathe hard and fast); fukuramaseru 膨らませる (inflate); **puff up** fukureru 膨れる (swell).

pull, vb. 1. hiku 引く (draw); hipparu 引張る (draw with force). 2. saku 裂く (tear). 3. **pull apart** bara-bara ni suru ばらばらにする; **pull out** saru 去る (leave); nuku 抜く (extract); **pull through** kirinukeru 切り抜ける (manage); **pull up** tomaru 止まる (come to a stop).

pulley, n. kassha 滑車.

pulpit, n. sekkyōdan 説教壇.

pulsate, vb. myaku utsu 脈打つ.

pulse, 1. n. kodō 鼓動; myaku 脈 (beat of arteries). 2. vb. myaku utsu 脈打つ (throb).

pumpkin, n. kabocha かぼちゃ.

pun, n. share しゃれ.

punctual, adj. jikandōri (no) 時間通り (の).

puncture, 1. n. ana 穴 (hole); panku パンク (hole in a tire). 2. vb. ... ni ana o akeru ...に穴を開ける (make a hole in); panku suru パンクする (get a flat tire); kujiku 挫く (discourage).

punishment, n. 1. batsu 罰 (act of punishing). 2. keibatsu 刑罰 (judicial punishment).

puny, adj. hinjaku (na) 貧弱 (な).

pupil, n. 1. seito 生徒 (student). 2. hitomi 瞳 (eye).

puppet, n. ayatsuriningyō 操り人形 (stringed, etc.); yubiningyō 指人形 (hand).

puppy, n. koinu 小犬.

purchase, n. 1. kōbai 購買 (act of buying); kōbaihin 購買品 (thing bought). 2. vb. kau 買う (buy).

pure, adj. 1. junsui (na, no) 純粋 (な、の) (unmixed, innocent). 2. junketsu (na) 純潔 (な) (chaste). 3. junshin (na) 純心 (な) (innocent). 4. mattaku (no) 全く (の) (utter).

purify, vb. 1. junka suru 純化する (make pure, as sugar, etc.). 2. kiyomeru 清める (purge, cleanse).

purity, n. 1. kiyorakasa 清らかさ (clearness, chastity). 2. junsuisa 純粋さ (innocence).

purple, adj. murasaki (no) 紫 (の).

purpose, n. 1. mokuteki 目的 (aim); **for the purpose of** ... no mokuteki de ...の目的で; **on purpose** wazato わざと.

purr, vb. nodo o narasu 喉を鳴らす (cat).

purse, n. 1. saifu 財布 (wallet). 2. handobaggu ハンドバッグ (handbag).

pursue, vb. 1. oikakeru 追いかける (chase). 2. tsuzukeru 続ける (carry on). 3. tsuikyū suru 追求する (search for, commit oneself to).

pus, *n.* umi 膿.

push, 1. *n.* oshi 押し. 2. *vb.* osu 押す (put pressure on, thrust, elbow, shoulder, urge); oshiwakeru 押し分ける (make one's way by pushing); ... ni chikara o ireru ...に力を入れる (promote).

put, *vb.* 1. oku 置く (lay, place). 2. ireru 入れる (put into). 3. hyōgen suru 表現する (express). 4. **put aside/by** takuwaeru 貯える (store up); totteoku 取って置く (save); **put away** shimau 仕舞う; **put down** kaku 書く (write); osaetsukeru 抑え付ける (suppress); **put an end to** ... o oeru ...を終える; **put in** kakeru かける (spend time);

teishutsu suru 提出する (vb.); **put in for** mōshikomu 申し込む (request, apply for); **put off** enki suru 延期する; sakeru 避ける (get rid of by evasion); **put on** kiru 着る (dress); haku 履く (footwear); kaburu 被る (hat); ... no furi o suru ...の振りをする (adopt, as an affectation); tsukeru 点ける (turn on); **put out** kesu 消す (light, fire); komaraseru 困らせる (annoy); **put up** tateru 建てる (construct, erect); **put up with** ... o gaman suru ...を我慢する.

puzzle, 1. *n.* nazo 謎 (enigma). 2. *vb.* tomadowaseru 戸惑わせる (perplex); komaraseru 困らせる (trouble).

Q

quack, 1. *n.* yabuisha やぶ医者 (pretender to medical skill); gā-gā ガーガー (duck). 2. *vb.* gā-gā to naku がーがーと鳴く.

quadruple, *vb.* yonbai suru 四倍する.

quail, *n.* uzura うずら.

quaint, *adj.* fūgawari (na) 風変わり (な).

quake, 1. *n.* jishin 地震 (earthquake); furue 震え (trembling). 2. *vb.* furueru 震える.

qualification, *n.* 1. shikaku 資格 (skill). 2. gentei 限定; seigen 制限 (restriction).

qualify, *vb.* 1. shikaku o ataeru 資格を与える; atehamaraseru 当てはまらせる (make fit); shikaku ga aru 資格がある; atehamaru

当てはまる (fit). 2. shikaku o toru 資格を取る (get a license). 3. gentei/ seigen suru 限定/制限する (limit).

quality, *n.* 1. shitsu 質 (grade of excellence). 2. ryōshitsu 良質 (excellence). 3. tokushoku 特色; seishitsu 性質 (characteristic).

qualm, *n.* 1. ryōshin no kashaku 良心の呵責 (pang of conscience). 2. fuan 不安 (apprehension).

quantity, *n.* ryō 量 (qty); **a large quantity** takusan (no) 沢山 (の).

quarrel, 1. *n.* kenka 喧嘩 (fight); kōron 口論 (dispute). 2. *vb.* kenka suru 喧嘩する; kōron suru 口論する.

quarter, *n.* 1. yonbun no ichi 四分の一 (one-fourth). 2. nijūgo sento 二十五セント (25 cents). 3. jūgofun 十五分 (15 minutes). 4. chiku 地区 (part of a town).

quarterly, *adj.* 1. nen ni yonkai (no) 年に四回 (の). 2. kikan no 季刊の (periodical).

quartet, *n.* shijūsō 四重奏.

quartz, *n.* suishō 水晶 (uncomfortable).

queen, *n.* jo'ō(sama) 女王 (様).

queer, *adj.* hen (na) 変 (な); kimyō (na) 奇妙 (な).

quench, *vb.* 1. kesu 消す (extinguish). 2. iyasu 癒す (satisfy).

quest, *n.* tankyū 探求.

question, 1. *n.* shitsumon 質問 (query); mondai 問題 (problem); gimon 疑問 (doubt). 2. *vb.* shitsumon suru 質問する; kiku 聞く (ask question); gimonshi suru 疑問視する (doubt).

questionnaire, *n.* an'kēto アンケート; shitsumon(hyo) 質問(表).

quick, *adj.* 1. hayai 速い (prompt, fast). 2. rikō (na) 利口 (な) (alert).

quiet, 1. *n.* shizukesa 静けさ (noiselessness); heion 平穏 (calmness). 2. *adj.* shizuka (na) 静か (な) (free from noise); heion (na) 平穏 (な) (calm). 3. *vb.* shizumeru 静める.

quintet, *n.* gojūsō 五重奏.

quit, *vb.* 1. yameru やめる (stop, resign). 2. deru 出る (depart from).

quite, *adv.* 1. mattaku 全く; sukkari すっかり (completely). 2. hontō ni 本当に (really).

quiz, 1. *n.* shiken 試験; tesuto テスト. 2. *vb.* shiken/tesuto o suru 試験／テストをする.

quota, *n.* wariate 割当て.

quotation, *n.* 1. in'yō 引用; **quotation marks** in'yōfu 引用符. 2. kakaku 価格 (quoted price).

quote, *vb.* in'yō suru 引用する; hiku 引く (cite); nedan o tsukeru 値段を付ける (give price).

R

rabbit, *n.* usagi 兎; **rabbit hutch** usagigoya 兎小屋.

race, 1. *n.* jinshu 人種; minzoku 民族 (group of persons of common origin); -rui 〜類; -shu 〜種 (class); rēsu レース (competition). 2. *vb.* kyōgikai ni deru 競技会に出る (participate in a race); kisou 競う (compete); isogu 急ぐ (move swiftly).

race track, *n.* keibajō 競馬場 (course for horse racing).

racial, *adj.* jinshu (no) 人種

(の); minzoku (no) 民族 (の).

rack, 1. *n.* amidana 網棚 (luggage rack); tana 棚 (storage unit). 2. *vb.* kurushimeru 苦しめる (afflict).

racket, *n.* 1. sōon 騒音 (noise). 2. fusei 不正; inchiki いんちき (deception).

radiate, *vb.* 1. hikaru 光る; kagayaku 輝く (emit light). 2. hōsha suru 放射する

radical, 1. *n.* kagekiha 過激派 (extremist). 2. *adj.* kageki (na) 過激 (な) (militant); bappon-teki (na) 抜本的 (な) (complete, thorough).

radio, *n.* 1. musen 無線 (communication system). 2. rajio ラジオ (apparatus); **on the radio** rajio de ラジオで.

radioactive, *adj.* hōshasei (no) 放射性 (の).

radio station, *n.* hōsōkyoku 放送局.

radish, *n.* radisshu ラディッシュ (small); daikon 大根 (long Japanese radish).

radius, *n.* hankei 半径.

raffle, *n.* takarakuji 宝くじ (lottery).

raft, *n.* ikada 筏 (floating platform).

rafter, *n.* hari 梁.

rag, *n.* borogire ぼろぎれ (old cloth); boro ぼろ (worn-out clothes).

rage, 1. *n.* gekido 激怒 (fury); ryūkō 流行 (fad). 2. *vb.* ikari kuru'u 怒り狂う (be in a fury).

ragged, *adj.* 1. boro-boro (no) ぼろぼろ (の) (worn-out). 2. zatsu na 雑な (uneven).

raid, 1. *n.* shūgeki 襲撃 (attack); teire 手入れ (police); **air raid** kūshū 空襲. 2. *vb.* shūgeki suru 襲撃する; teire suru 手入れする.

railroad, *n.* senro 線路; tetsudō 鉄道.

rain, 1. *n.* ame 雨. 2. *vb.* ame ga furu 雨が降る.

rainbow, *n.* niji 虹.

raise, (1. *n.* shōkyū 昇給 (increase in pay). 2. *vb.*

ageru 上げる (lift up, increase); atsumeru 集める (collect); sodateru 育てる (bring up); hikiokosu 引き起こす (cause).

rake, *n.* kumade 熊手 (tool).

rally, 1. *n.* shūkai 集会 (meeting); rarī ラリー (car race, recovery in tennis). 2. *vb.* atsumaru 集まる (come together); atsumeru 集める (call together); kaifuku suru 回復する (recover).

ram, 1. *n.* ohitsuji 雄羊 (sheep). 2. *vb.* gekitotsu suru 撃突する (collide violently).

ramble, *vb.* sansaku suru 散策する (stroll idly).

rampant, *adj.* man'en shite iru 蔓延している (widespread).

ramshackle, *adj.* onboro (no) おんぼろ (の).

ranch, *n.* bokujō 牧場 (farm for raising stock).

rancid, *adj.* furui 古い (old); kusai 臭い (odorous).

random, *adj.* teatarishidai (no) 手当たり次第 (の); **at random** teatari-shidai ni 手当り次第に.

range, *n.* sanmyaku 山脈 (mountain range); retsu 列 (row); shatekijō 射的場 (place for target shooting); shatei 射程 (distance between gun and target); bokujō 牧場 (pasture); han'i 範囲 (extent); genkai 限界 (limit); renji レンジ (cooking range). 2. *vb.* arukimawaru 歩き回る (wander); naraberu 並べる (arrange); mōra suru 網羅する (vary within specified limits); **range over** oyobu 及ぶ; wataru 渡る.

rank, 1. *n.* chi'i 地位 (official

position); mibun 身分;
kaikyū 階級 (social standing
or class); kurai 位 (class in
any scale of comparison);
retsu 列 (row); **rank and
file** ippanjin 一般人
(ordinary people). 2. *adj.*
habikotteiru はびこってい
る (growing excessively);
kusai 臭い (smelly). 3. *vb.*
kurai suru 位する (be in a
particular rank); kurai ni
ireru 位に入れる (put in a
particular rank).

ransom, *n.* minoshirokin 身
代金.

rap, *vb.* tataku 叩く (strike).

rape, 1. *n.* bōkō 暴行; gōkan
強姦. 2. *vb.* gōkan suru 強姦
する.

rapid, *adj.* subayai 素早い;
jinsoku (na) 迅速 (な).

rapture, *n.* kyōki 狂喜;
uchōten 有頂天.

rare, *adj.* mare (na) 稀れ
(な); mezurashii 珍しい
(unusual). 2. namayake
(no) 生焼け (の) (meat).

rascal, *n.* narazumono なら
ず者.

rash, 1. *n.* hasshin 発疹. 2.
adj. seikyū (na) 性急 (な)
(thoughtlessly hasty);
keisotsu (na) 軽率 (な)
(imprudent).

rat, *n.* ōnezumi 大ねずみ.

rate, 1. *n.* ritsu 率; wariai 割
合 (percentage); sokudo 速
度 (degree of speed); ryōkin
料金 (charge); tōkyū 等級
(rating); **at any rate**
tonikaku とにかく; **at the
rate of** ... no wariai de ...の
割合で. 2. *vb.* hyōka suru 評
価する (estimate).

rather, *adv.* 1. ikubun ka 幾
分か (somewhat). 2. kanari
かなり (quite). 3. mushiro
むしろ (in preference).

rather than ... yori
mushiro ...よりむしろ; **I
would rather** mushiro ...
no hō ga ii むしろ...の方が
いい. 4. gyaku ni 逆に (on
the contrary).

ratio, *n.* ritsu 率; wariai 割
合.

rational, *adj.* 1. risei-teki
(na) 理性的 (な) (able to
reason). 2. suji ga tōtteiru
筋が通っている (sensible).

rattle, 1. *n.* gara-gara がらが
ら (toy). 2. *vb.* gara-gara
naru がらがら鳴る; gara-
gara narasu がらがら鳴らす
(make something rattle).

rattlesnake, *n.* gara-gara
hebi がらがら蛇.

ravage, *vb.* 1. hakai suru 破
壊する (destroy). 2.
ryakudatsu suru 略奪する
(loot).

rave, *vb.* 1. wameku 喚く
(talk wildly). 2.
homechigiru 褒めちぎる
(praise).

raven, *n.* karasu 烏.

raw, *adj.* 1. nama (no) 生
(の) (uncooked). 2. mikakō
(no) 未加工 (の)
(unprocessed); gen- 原～
(basic); **raw material**
genzairyō 原材料. 3.
mikeiken (no) 未経験 (の)
(inexperienced). 4. kawa ga
muketa 皮が剥けた (peeled
skin).

ray, *n.* 1. kōsen 光線 (beam).
2. **a ray of** ichimatsu no 一
抹の; hitosuji no 一筋の (a
trace of). 3. ei えい (fish).

razor, *n.* kamisori 剃刀 (for
shaving); **razor blade**
kamisori no ha 剃刀の刃.

re-, *pref.* sai- 再- (repetition);
rearmament saigunbi 再軍
備.

reach, 1. *n.* todoku han'i 届

く範囲 (distance that one can touch or attain); ikeru han'i 行ける範囲 (distance that one can go); **within/beyond one's reach** (te no) todoku/todokanai han'i ni (手の)届く/届かない範囲に. 2. *vb.* tsuku 着く (arrive at); todoku 届く (be able to touch); nobasu 伸ばす (extend); renraku o toru 連絡を取る (contact).

reaction, *n.* han'nō 反応 (response).

read, *vb.* yomu 読む.

readily, *adv.* 1. yorokonde 喜んで (willingly). 2. kantan ni 簡単に (easily).

ready, 1. *adj.* yōi (ga) dekiteiru (用意が) 出来ている (fully prepared); jinsoku (na) 迅速 (な) (prompt); **be ready to do** yorokonde suru 喜んでする (willing to do). 2. *vb.* junbi suru 準備する.

real, *adj.* 1. jissai (no) 実際 (の); genjitsu (no) 現実 (の) (actual). 2. hontō (no) 本当 (の) (true). 3. honmono (no) 本物 (の) (genuine).

realism, *n.* 1. genjitsusei 現実性 (actuality). 2. shajitsushugi 写実主義 (in art).

reality, *n.* 1. genjitsu 現実; jijitsu 事実; jissai 実際 (real fact or thing); **in reality** jissai wa 実際は. 2. jitsuzai 実在 (real existence).

realize, *vb.* 1. satoru 悟る; wakaru 分かる (understand clearly). 2. jitsugen suru 実現する (happen). 3. rieki o eru 利益を得る (acquire profit).

realm, *n.* 1. ōkoku 王国 (kingdom). 2. bun'ya 分野

(area of activity).

reap, *vb.* shūkaku suru 収穫する (harvest).

rear, 1. *n.* ushiro 後ろ (back); (o)shiri (お)尻 (buttocks). 2. *vb.* sodateru 育てる (care for to maturity); ageru 上げる (lift up); tateru 立てる (raise, erect).

rear-view mirror, *n.* bakku-mirā バックミラー.

reason, 1. *n.* riyū 理由 (cause); risei 理性 (mental powers); shōki 正気 (sanity). 2. *vb.* handan suru 判断する (judge); suitei suru 推定する (infer); **reason with** settoku suru 説得する (persuade).

reasonable, *adj.* 1. mottomo (na) もっとも (な); funbetsu ni kanau 分別に適う (sensible). 2. datō (na) 妥当 (な) (fair).

reassure, *vb.* anshin saseru 安心させる.

rebellion, *n.* hangyaku 反逆 (against government); hankō 反抗 (against authority).

rebound, 1. *n.* hanekaeri 跳ね返り (act of rebounding); handō 反動 (reaction). 2. *vb.* hanekaeru 跳ね返る.

rebuke, *vb.* tashinameru たしなめる.

recall, 1. *n.* omoidasu 思い出す (remember). 2. yobimodosu 呼び戻す (call back). 3. kaishū suru 回収する (take off market). 4. torikesu 取り消す (withdraw).

recede, *vb.* 1. shirizoku 退く (move back). 2. hageagaru 禿げ上がる (hair).

receipt, *n.* 1. ryōshūsho 領収書 (written statement).

uketori 受け取り (act of receiving).

receive, vb. 1. ukeru 受ける; uketoru 受け取る (get). 2. mukaeru 迎える (welcome). 3. ukeireru 受け入れる (accept).

recent, adj. saikin (no) 最近 (の).

receptacle, n. yōki 容器.

receptionist, n. uketsuke(-gakari) 受け付け(係).

recess, n. 1. yasumi 休み (pause). 2. kubomi 凹み (alcove). 3. **recesses** oku 奥.

recession, n. fukeiki 不景気; keiki-kōtai 景気後退 (economic).

recipe, n. ryōrihō 料理法; tsukurikata 作り方 (cooking).

recital, n. ensōkai 演奏会.

recite, vb. 1. anshō suru 暗誦する (repeat from memory). 2. kataru 語る (narrate).

reckless, adj. 1. mubō (na) 無謀 (な) (heedless). 2. seikyū (na) 性急 (な) (hasty).

recline, vb. motareru もたれる; yorikakaru 寄り掛かる (lean).

recognize, vb. 1. wakaru 分かる (identify, see clearly, understand). 2. mitomeru 認める (admit, acknowledge). 3. shōnin suru 証認する (approve). 4. aisatsu suru 挨拶する (greet).

recollect, vb. omoidasu 思い出す.

recommend, vb. 1. suisen suru 推薦する (commend as worthy). 2. susumeru 勧める (advise).

recommendation, n. 1.

susume 勧め (advice). 2. suisenjō 推薦状 (letter of recommendation).

reconcile, vb. wakai suru 和解する.

record, 1. n. kiroku 記録 (account, documentation); keireki 経歴 (one's past history); shinkiroku 新記録 (sports); rekōdo レコード (phonograph); **keep a record** kiroku suru 記録する; **off the record** hikōshiki ni 非公式に; **on the record** kōshiki ni 公式に (officially). 2. vb. kiroku suru 記録する (register, write down); rokuon suru 録音する (tape); shimesu 示す (indicate).

recount, vb. 1. kataru 語る (narrate). 2. kazoenaosu 数えなおす (count again).

recourse, n. **have recourse to** ... ni tayoru ...に頼る.

recover, vb. kaifuku suru 回復する; torimodosu 取り戻す (regain, restore).

re-create, vb. saigen suru 再現する (create anew).

recreation, n. goraku 娯楽.

recruit, 1. n. shin-menbā 新メンバー (new member); shin'nyūshain 新入社員 (new company worker). 2. vb. boshū suru 募集する (enlist).

rectangle, n. chōhōkei 長方形.

recuperate, vb. genki ni naru 元気になる; kaifuku suru 回復する.

red, 1. adj. akai 赤い (color); **turn red** akaku naru 赤くなる. 2. n. aka(iro) 赤(色) (color); **be in the red** akaji de aru 赤字である.

Red Cross, n. sekijūji 赤十字.

redeem, vb. 1. kaimodosu 買い戻す (buy back). 2. kaifuku suru 回復する (recover). 3. hatasu 果たす (fulfill). 4. sukuu 救う (deliver from sin).

red pepper, n. tōgarashi 唐辛子.

redress, 1. n. baishō 賠償 (recompense). 2. vb. tadasu 正す (set right); tsugunau 償う (recompense).

reduce, vb. 1. herasu 減らす (make less in amount, weight, etc.). 2. sageru 下げる (lower in degree, rank, intensity, etc.); nesage suru 値下げする (lower price). 3. taijū ga heru 体重が減る (lose weight). 4. **reduce something/someone to** o ... ni shite shimau を... にしてしまう (change something/someone to); **be reduced to** ... ni natte shimau ...になってしまう (be changed into).

reed, n ashi 葦 (plant).

reek, vb. akushū ga suru 悪臭がする (smell strongly).

refer (to), vb. 1. ... ni tsuite noberu ...について述べる; ... ni genkyū suru ...に言及する (mention). 2. ... o sankō ni suru ...を参考にする (draw information from). 3. makaseru 任せる (hand over for decision).

referee, n. shinpan 審判 (judge).

refill, 1. n. okawari お代わり (food); tsumekaehin 詰め替え品 (object). 2. vb. okawari o suru お代わりをする (food); futatabi mitasu 再び満たす (object, liquid, etc.).

refine, vb. seiren suru 精練する (object); senren suru 洗練する (person).

reflect, vb. hansha suru 反射する (cast image/light back). 2. han'ei suru 反映する (mirror, express). 3. yoku kangaeru よく考える (meditate); **reflect on** ... ni tsuite yoku kangaeru ...について よく考える (think carefully).

reform, 1. n. kaisei 改正 (object); kaishin 改心 (person). 2. vb. kaisei suru 改正する (condition or object); kaishin suru 改心する (person).

reformation, n. 1. kaikaku 改革. 2. **Reformation** shūkyōkaikaku 宗教改革.

refrain, 1. n. kurikaeshi 繰り返し (music). 2. vb. **refrain from** ... o hikaeru ...を控える (abstain).

refresh, vb. 1. genkizukeru 元気づける (reinvigorate). 2. arata ni suru 新たにする (renew).

refrigerator, n. reizōko 冷蔵庫.

refuge, n. hinan(sho) 避難(所); **take refuge** hinan suru 避難する.

refugee, n. nanmin 難民.

refund, 1. n. haraimodoshi 払い戻し. 2. vb. haraimodosu 払い戻す.

refuse, 1. n. gomi ごみ (garbage); haikibutsu 廃棄物 (any waste material). 2. vb. kyohi suru 拒否する; kotowaru 断る (decline).

regain, vb. torimodosu 取り戻す.

regard, 1. n. sonkei 尊敬 (respect); kanshin 関心 (concern); **with regard to** ... ni kanshite ...に関して. 2. vb. miru 見る (look); sonkei suru 尊敬する (respect); **regard as** ... to

minasu ...と見なす
(consider to be); **regard
highly** takaku hyōka suru
高く評価する (consider
highly).

regardless, *adv.* 1. tonikaku
とにかく (despite
everything, anyway). 2.
regardless of ... ni
kakawarazu ...にかかわらず
(in spite of); ... o mushi
shite ...を無視して
(ignoring).

region, *n.* chi'iki 地域 (area);
chiku 地区 (district).

register, 1. *n.* tōrokubo 登録
簿 (written list); sei'iki 声域
(voice); reji レジ (cash
register). 2. *vb.* tōroku suru
登録する (enter in a
register); namae o kaku 名
前を書く (sign up); inshō ga
nokoru 印象が残る (make
some impression); shimesu
示す (show); kakitome de
dasu 書留で出す (mail).

registry, *n.* tōkisho 登記所
(place); tōrokubo 登録簿
(registration list).

regret, 1. *n.* kanashimi 悲し
み (grief); kōkai 後悔
(repentance). 2. *vb.*
kuyamu 悔む (feel sorry
about); kōkai suru 後悔する
(repent).

regular, 1. *n.* jōren 常連
(regular visitor); otokuisama
お得意様 (regular
customer). 2. *adj.* itsumo no
いつもの (usual); heijō (no) 平常
(の) (usual); futsū (no) 普通
(の) (ordinary); teiki-teki
(na) 定期的 (な) (recurring
at fixed intervals); kisoku-
teki (na) 規則的 (な)
(orderly); ittei (no) 一定
(の) (constant).

regulate, *vb.* 1. kisei suru 規
制する (control by rules,

method, etc.). 2. chōsei
suru 調整する (adjust).

rehabilitate, *vb.* 1. kaifuku
suru 回復する (health,
honor, etc.). 2. shakaifukki
suru 社会復帰する (return
to society).

rehearsal, *n.* keiko 稽古.

reign, 1. *n.* chisei 治世 (royal
rule). 2. *vb.* osameru 治める
(have sovereign power);
shihai suru 支配する
(dominate).

reimburse, *vb.* haraimodosu
払い戻す.

reinforce, *vb.* hokyō suru 補
強する (strengthen with support);
tsuyomeru 強める
(strengthen with support).

reject, *vb.* 1. kyohi suru 拒否
する (decline). 2. suteru 捨
てる (throw away).

rejoice, *vb.* yorokobu 喜ぶ.

relapse, 1. *n.* atomodori
suru 後戻りする (revert). 2.
saihatsu suru 再発する (fall
back into illness).

relate, *vb.* 1. hanasu 話す
(tell). 2. kankeizukeru 関係
づける (connect in thought
or meaning). 3. kankei ga
aru 関係がある (have
relation). 4. shitashimu 親
しむ (establish a friendly or
meaningful relationship).

relationship, *n.* 1. kankei 関
係 (connection). 2. kankei
関係 (personal connection);
shinseki kankei 親戚関係
(family connection).

relative, 1. *n.* shinseki 親戚
(family). 2. *adj.* sōtai-teki
(na) 相対的 (な); hikaku-
teki (na) 比較的 (な)
(comparative).

relax, *vb.* 1. kutsurogu くつ
ろぐ (rest). 2. yurumu 緩む
(become slack); yurumeru
緩める (loosen).

relaxation, *n.* 1. ikinuki 息

抜き (diversion). 2. kanwa 緩和 (relief from tension or restriction).

relay, 1. *n.* kōtai 交代 (new shift); chūkeihōsō 中継放送 (TV). 2. *vb.* toritsugu 取り次ぐ (send message); kōtai saseru 交代させる (replace with fresh relays); chūkeihōsō suru 中継放送する (TV).

release, 1. *n.* fūkiri 封切り (movie); shakuhō 釈放 (prisoner); hōmen 放免 (setting free from an obligation). 2. *vb.* fūkiru 封切る (movie); shakuhō suru 釈放する (prisoner); hōmen suru 放免する (set free from an obligation).

relevant, *adj.* 1. tekisetsu (na) 適切 (な) (appropriate). 2. kankei ga aru 関係がある (pertinent).

reliable, *adj.* ate ni dekiru 当てに出来る; tayori ni naru 頼りになる (dependable, trustworthy). 2. shinjirareru 信じられる (credible).

relic, *n.* 1. sei'i 聖遺 (religious object). 2. ibutsu 遺物 (object surviving from the past).

relief, *n.* 1. anshin 安心 (from anxiety); keigen 軽減 (from pain). 2. kyūenbusshi 救援物資 (help, such as money, food, etc.). 3. kōtai 交代 (new shift).

relieve, *vb.* 1. anshin saseru 安心させる (anxiety); keigen suru 軽減する (pain); sukuu 救う (trouble). 2. kōtai suru 交代する (shift). 3. **relieve (someone) of (something)** ... o motte ageru ...を持ってあげる

(carry).

religion, *n.* shūkyō 宗教.

reluctant, *adj.* ki ga susumanai 気が進まない (hesitant).

rely on, *vb.* ... o ate ni suru ...を当てにする; shin'yō suru 信用する (put trust in).

remain, 1. *n.* **remains** nokori 残り (that which remains); itai 遺体 (corpse). 2. *vb.* nokoru 残る (stay); ... no mama de iru ...のままでいる (continue to be).

remark, 1. *n.* iken 意見 (comment); chūmoku 注目 (attention); **make remarks** iken o noberu 意見を述べる. 2. *vb.* noberu 述べる (say); kizuku 気付く (notice).

remedy, 1. *n.* chiryō 治療. 2. *vb.* tadasu 正す (correct); naosu 治す (cure).

remember, *vb.* 1. omoidasu 思い出す (recall). 2. oboeteoku 覚えておく (keep in mind). 3. okurimono o suru 贈り物をする (give a present).

remind, *vb.* omoidasaseru 思い出させる.

remnant, *n.* 1. nokori 残り (remaining part). 2. nokorimono 残り物 (leftover).

remorse, *n.* kōkai 後悔.

remote, *adj.* 1. tōi 遠い (distant). 2. kasuka (na) 微か (な) (faint).

remote control, *n.* rimokon リモコン.

remove, *vb.* 1. torinozoku 取り除く (get rid of). 2. nugu 脱ぐ (take off). 3. korosu 殺す (murder). 4. utsusu 移す (move to another place). 5. kaiko suru 解雇する (dismiss).

rend, vb. hikisaku 引き裂く
(tear).

rendezvous, n. 1.
machiawase 待ち合わせ
(appointment to meet). 2.
machiawase-basho 待ち合わ
せ場所 (meeting place).

renew, vb. 1. saikai suru 再
開する (begin again). 2.
arata ni suru 新たにする
(make new). 3. kōshin suru
更新する (extend contract,
etc.).

renounce, vb. hōki suru 放
棄する (give up).

renovate, vb. kaizō/shūri
suru 改造／修理する
(remodel/repair).

rent, 1. n. karichin 借り賃
(payment); yachin 家賃
(house rent); yabure 破れ
(tear). **house for rent**
kashiya 貸家. 2. vb. kariru
借りる (pay for lease); kasu
貸す (grant a lease).

repair, 1. n. shūri 修理. 2.
vb. shūri suru 修理する.

repay, n. hensai suru 返済す
る (pay back money).

repeat, 1. n. saihōsō 再放送
(TV). 2. vb. kurikaesu 繰り
返す (do or say again);
saihōsō suru 再放送する
(TV).

repent, vb. kōkai suru 後悔
する.

repercussion, n. eikyō 影響
(effect).

repetition, n. kurikaeshi 繰
り返し.

replace, vb. 1. modosu 戻す
(return). 2. kawaru する
(take place of). 3. **replace
(with)** (... to) torikaeru (...
と) 取り替える (change one
thing for another).

replete, adj. 1. ippai (no) 一
杯 (の) (filled). 2. manpuku
(no) 満腹 (の) (full

stomach).

replica, n. fukusei 複製.

reply, 1. n. henji 返事
(response); **in reply to** ...
no henji ni ...の返事に. 2.
vb. kotaeru 答える (answer).

report, 1. n. hōkoku 報告
(account); uwasa 噂
(rumor); jūsei 銃声
(gunfire). 2. vb. hōkoku
suru 報告する (give an
account of); shiraseru 知ら
せる (make known).

report card, n. tsūchihyō 通
知表.

reporter, n. shinbunkisha 新
聞記者 (newspaper
reporter); terebi-kisha テレ
ビ記者 (TV reporter).

repose, 1. n. yasumi 休み
(rest); nemuri 眠り (sleep).
2. vb. yasumu 休む (rest);
nemuru 眠る (sleep).

represent, vb. 1. arawasu 現
わす (signify). 2. daihyō
suru 代表する (act for). 3.
egaku 描く (portray).

representation, n. 1.
daihyō 代表 (being a
representative). 2. hyōgen
表現; byōsha 描写
(depiction).

repress, vb. 1. osaeru 抑える
(control). 2. yokuatsu suru
抑圧する (suppress by
force).

reproach, 1. n. hinan 非難.
2. vb. hinan suru 非難する.

reproduce, vb. 1. ko o umu
子を産む (procreate). 2.
fukusei o tsukuru 複製を作
る (copy). 3. saisei suru 再
生する (produce anew or
again).

reptile, n. hachūrui は虫類.

republic, n. kyōwakoku 共
和国.

reputation, n. hyōban 評判.

request, 1. n. rikuesuto リク

エスト; (o)negai (お)願い; yōbō 要望; **at the request of** ... no yōbō ni ōjite ...の要望に応じて; **on request** yōbō ga ari shidai 要望があり次第. 2. vb. tanomu 頼む (ask for).

require, vb. 1. hitsuyō to suru ...を必要とする (need); **be required to do** ... suru hitsuyō ga aru ...する必要がある. 2. yōkyū suru 要求する (demand).

rescue, 1. n. kyūjo 救助. 2. vb. kyūjo suru 救助する.

research, 1. n. chōsa 調査 (investigation); kenkyū 研究 (advanced study). 2. vb. chōsa suru 調査する (investigate); kenkyū suru 研究する (study).

resemble, vb. niteiru 似ている.

reservation, n. 1. utagai 疑い (doubt). 2. yoyaku 予約 (booking).

reside, vb. sumu 住む.

residential, adj. jūtakuchi (no) 住宅地 (の).

resign, vb. 1. yameru 辞める; jinin suru 辞任する (give up job, office, etc.). 2. **resign oneself to** akiramete ... o suru 諦めて...をする.

resin, n. jushi 樹脂.

resist, vb. 1. teikō suru 抵抗する (offer opposition to, remain unaffected). 2. gaman suru 我慢する (withstand).

resolution, n. 1. katai ketsui 固い決意 (firmness). 2. kaiketsu 解決 (solution). 3. kettei 決定 (decision).

resolve, vb. 1. kaiketsu suru 解決する (solve). 2. kimeru 決める (decide).

resort, 1. n. shudan 手段

(recourse); **as a last resort** saigo no shudan ni 最後の手段に. 2. vb. **resort to** ... ni tayoru ...に頼る (rely on).

resound, vb. hibiku 響く (echo).

resources, n. 1. shigen 資源; **natural resources** ten'nenshigen 天然資源. 2. shiryoku 資力 (money).

respect, 1. n. sonkei 尊敬 (esteem); ten ten 点 (point); kanshin 関心 (attention); **in all respects** subete no ten de 全ての点で; **with respect to** ... ni kanshite ...に関して. 2. vb. sonkei suru 尊敬する.

respectful, adj. reigi tadashii 礼儀正しい.

respiration, n. kokyū 呼吸.

respite, n. kyūshi 休止 (temporary pause).

respond, vb. 1. henji suru 返事する (answer). 2. ōjiru 応じる (react).

responsibility, n. sekinin 責任.

responsive, adj. han'nō ga tsuyoi 反応が強い.

rest, 1. n. yasumi 休み (refreshing quiet; cessation from motion, work, etc.); sasae 支え (support); nokori 残り (remainder, others); **at rest** yasunde 休んで; **come to rest** tomaru 止まる. 2. vb. yasumu 休む (be quiet or at ease); yameru 止める (stop); tomaru 止まる (cease motion); yokotawaru 横たわる (lay); yokotaru 横たえる (lay); **rest against** ... ni motasekakeru ...にもたせかける; **rest on** ... ni motozuku ...に基づく (be based on).

restless, adj. ochitsukanai 落ち着かない.

restore, *vb.* 1. kaifuku suru 回復する (bring back). 2. shūfuku suru 修復する (repair).

restrict, *vb.* seigen suru 制限する (limit).

restriction, *n.* seigen 制限.

restroom, *n.* (o)tearai (お)手洗; toire トイレ.

result, 1. *n.* kekka 結果 (outcome, consequence); **as a result** ... no kekka ... の結果. 2. *vb.* **result in** ... ni owaru ... に終わる.

resume, *vb.* 1. saikai suru 再開する (begin again).

résumé, *n.* rirekisho 履歴書 (curriculum vitae).

resuscitate, *vb.* sosei saseru 蘇生させる.

retail, *n., adv.* kouri (de) 小売り (で).

retard, *vb.* okuraseru 遅らせる (delay).

retarded, *adj.* chieokure (no) 知恵遅れ (の) (person).

retire, *vb.* 1. taishoku suru 退職する (from profession). 2. sagaru 下がる (go).

retort, *vb.* 1. iikaesu 言い返す (answer in anger). 2. ōsen suru 応戦する (answer smartly).

retreat, 1. *n.* taikyaku 退却 (military); kakurega 隠れ家 (private place). 2. *vb.* taikyaku suru 退却する (military).

retrieve, *vb.* 1. torimodosu 取り戻す (regain, restore, recover). 2. tsugunau 償う (make amends for).

return, 1. *n.* kaeri 帰り (act of coming or going back); kitaku 帰宅 (act of returning to one's home); henkyaku 返却 (act of giving back something); shinkoku 申告 (report); *(pl.)* rieki 利益

(profit); **by return mail** orikaeshi-yūbin de 折り返し郵便で; **in return (for)** (... no) okaeshi ni (...の) お返しに. 2. *vb.* kaeru 帰る (go or come back); kaesu 返す; modosu 戻す (give, put, or bring back); kotaeru 答える (reply).

reveal, *vb.* arawasu 現わす; shimesu 示す (disclose).

revelation, *n.* 1. keiji 啓示 (religious). 2. bakuro 暴露 (act of revealing). 3. omoigakenai nyūsu 思いがけないニュース (surprising information).

revenge, *n.* 1. fukushū 復讐 (vengeance). 2. hōfuku 報復 (retaliation); **in revenge for** ... no hōfuku ni ...の報復に.

revenue, *n.* shūnyū 収入 (income); sainyū 歳入 (income of government).

revere, *vb.* keiai suru 敬愛する (respect).

reverse, 1. *n.* hantai 反対; gyaku 逆 (reverse part, position, etc.); ura 裏 (back); fu'un 不運 (misfortune). 2. *adj.* hantai (no) 反対 (の); gyaku (no) 逆 (の) (opposite); ura (no) 裏 (の) (back); ribāsu (no) リバース (の) (in car). 3. *vb.* gyaku ni suru 逆にする (invert); uragaeshi ni suru 裏返しにする (turn inside out); bakku suru/saseru バックする／させる (go/cause to go backward in car).

review, 1. *n.* bunseki 分析 (analysis); kentō 検討 (consideration); fukushū 復習 (repeated study of something); hihyō 批評 (critical article); hyōronzasshi 評論雑誌

(magazine); **under review** kentōchū 検討中. 2. *vb.* bunseki suru 分析する (analyze); kentō suru 検討する (examine, consider); hihyō suru 批評する (give criticism); fukushū suru 復習する (study again).

revise, *vb.* 1. kaeru 変える (change). 2. kaitei suru 改訂する (amend).

revive, *vb.* yomigaeru/ yomigaeraseru 蘇る／蘇らせる (return/restore to life); fukkō suru/saseru 復興する／させる (come/bring back into use); kaifuku suru/saseru 回復する／させる (return/restore to consciousness, vigor, etc.).

revolt, 1. *n.* hankō 反抗; hangyaku 反逆 (rebellion). 2. *vb.* hankō suru 反抗する; hangyaku suru 反逆する (rebel); ken'o suru/saseru 嫌悪する／させる (feel/cause to feel disgust).

revolution, *n.* 1. kakumei 革命 (overthrow of an old political system; fundamental change). 2. kaiten 回転 (rotation).

revolve, *vb.* 1. mawaru 回る; kaiten suru 回転する. 2. **revolve around** ... o chūshin ni mawaru ...を中心に回る.

reward, 1. *n.* hōshū 報酬; hōbi 褒美; **in reward** hōbi ni 褒美に. 2. *vb.* hōshū o ataeru 報酬を与える; mukuiru 報いる.

rheumatism, *n.* ryūmachi リューマチ.

rhinoceros, *n.* sai さい.

rhyme, 1. *n.* inbun 韻文 (verse); in 韻 (similar terminal sounds). 2. *vb.* in o fumu 韻を踏む.

rib, *n.* rokkotsu 肋骨 (bone).

rice, *n.* gohan 御飯 (cooked); kome 米 (uncooked).

rich, *adj.* 1. kanemochi (no) 金持ち (の) (of a wealthy person); **get rich** kanemochi ni naru 金持ちになる. 2. kotteri shiteiru こってりしている (containing butter, cream, etc.). 3. yutaka na 豊か (な) (affluent, abundant, fertile, sumptuous).

rid, *vb.* 1. **rid oneself of, get rid of** ... o torinozoku ...を取り除く (free oneself from, eliminate); ... o oiharau ...を追い払う (drive away). 2. **be rid of** ... ga nai ...がない (be without a thing); ... ga inai ...がいない (be without a person).

riddle, *n.* nazo 謎.

ride, 1. *n.* jōsha 乗車 (in a vehicle); jōba 乗馬 (on a horse); **go for a ride** doraibu suru ドライブする (in a car); **take for a ride** damasu だます (deceive). 2. *vb.* (...ni) noru (...に) 乗る (ride a bicycle, horse, etc.; rest on something); notteiku 乗って行く (be carried in a vehicle); susumu 進む (move along).

ridiculous, *adj.* bakarashii 馬鹿らしい.

rife, *adj.* 1. michiteiru 満ちている (full of); **rife with** ... ni michite-iru ... に満ちている. 2. man'en shiteiru 蔓延している (widespread).

right, 1. *adj.* migi (no) 右 (の) (side or direction); tadashii 正しい (correct, just, morally good); ii 良い (good); hontō (no) 本当の (true); massugu (na) 真っ直ぐ (な) (straight). 2. *n.* migi

右 (side or direction); hoshuha 保守派 (conservative political group); tadashii koto 正しいこと (what is morally good); kenri 権利 (something justly due to a person); **turn to the right** migi ni magaru 右に曲がる. 3. *adv.* migi ni 右に (on/to the right); tadashiku 正しく (correctly); chōdo 丁度 (exactly); sugu すぐ (directly); sō そう (yes); **right away** sugu すぐ; **right now** tada ima 只今.

righthanded, *adj.* migikiki (no) 右利き (の).

rightist, *n., adj.* uyoku (no) 右翼 (の).

rigid, *adj.* 1. katai 硬い; 固い (stiff, inflexible). 2. genkaku (na) 厳格 (な) (rigorous).

rim, *n.* fuchi 縁; heri へり.

rind, *n.* kawa 皮.

ring, 1. *n.* wa 輪 (circular band, line, etc.); yubiwa 指輪 (for finger); ringu リング (boxing ring); ichimi 一味 (group)/beru/denwa no oto ベル/電話の音 (sound of a bell/telephone); **give someone a ring** denwa o suru 電話をする (telephone). 2. *vb.* kakomu 囲む (encircle, surround); narasu 鳴らす (cause to sound); naru 鳴る (sound); beru o narasu ベルを鳴らす (signal by a bell); **ring true** hontōrashiku kikoeru 本当らしく聞こえる.

rinse, *vb.* yusugu ゆすぐ.

riot, *n.* 1. bōdō 暴動 (violent disturbance by mob); sōdō 騒動 (tumult). 2. yukai na koto 愉快なこと (fun).

rip, *vb.* 1. yaburu 破る

(tear); yabureru 破れる (be torn). 2. **rip off** ne o fukikakeru 値を吹き掛ける (charge too much); nusumu 盗む (steal); **rip up** yaburu 破る.

ripe, *adj.* 1. ureteiru 熟れている (of a fruit). 2. ki ga jukushiteiru 期が熟している (ready).

ripple, 1. *n.* sazanami 小波 (wave); seseragi せせらぎ (sound of small waves). 2. *vb.* sazanami o tateru 小波を立てる (make ripples).

rise, 1. *n.* jōshō 上昇 (increase, upward motion); neage 値上げ (increase in price); kōryū 興隆 (ascendance to prosperity); noborizaka 上り坂 (slope); **give rise to** ... o hikiokosu ...を引き起こす (get up); noboru 昇る (sun); agaru 上がる (move upward); hanran o okosu 反乱を起こす (revolt); arawareru 現われる (appear); **rise from** ... yori shōjiru ...より生じる (originate from).

risk, 1. *n.* kiken 危険 (danger); **at risk** kiken ni sarasarete 危険に晒されて; **run a risk** kiken o okasu 危険を冒す. 2. *vb.* kakeru 賭ける (take the risk of); kiken ni sarasu 危険に晒す (expose to a risk).

ritual, *n.* gishiki 儀式. 2. *adj.* gishiki-teki (na) 儀式的 (な).

rival, 1. *n.* kyōsōaite 競争相手. 2. *vb.* (... to) kisou (...と) 競う (compete with); hitteki suru 匹敵する (match).

rivalry, *n.* 1. kyōsō 競争 (competition).

river, *n.* kawa 川.

roach, n. gokiburi ごきぶり.

road, n. michi 道; dōro 道路; **on the road** ryokōchū 旅行中 (traveling); jungyōchū 巡業中 (touring with a show).

roam, vb. samayou さまよう (wander).

roar, 1. n. hoegoe 吠え声 (animal); bakushō 爆笑 (laughter); unari 唸り (machine). 2. vb. hoeru 吠える (animal); bakushō suru 爆笑する (laugh); unaru 唸る (machine).

roast, vb. yaku 焼く; aburu あぶる.

rob, vb. nusumu 盗む; **rob someone of something** ... kara ... o nusumu ...から...を盗む.

robber, n. dorobō 泥棒.

robbery, n. settō 窃盗; nusumi 盗み.

robust, adj. kenkō (na) 健康 (な).

rock, 1. n. iwa 岩 (stone); rokku ロック (music); **on the rocks** on za rokku オンザ ロック (drink); kiki ni hinshite 危機に瀕して (in difficulty). 2. vb. yusuru 揺する (child); yureru 揺れる (move back and forth); yusaburu 揺さぶる (shock).

rocking chair, n. yuri'isu 揺り椅子.

rocky, adj. iwa ga ōi 岩が多い.

rod, n. 1. tsue 杖 (for walking). 2. sao 竿 (for fishing).

role, n. 1. yaku(wari) 役(割) (part). 2. **play the role of** ... no yakuwari o ... の役割をする; ... no yaku o enjiru ...の役を演じる (theater).

roll, 1. n. maki 巻 (anything rolled); rōru-pan ロールパ

ン (bread); todoroki とどろき (sound); meibo 名簿 (register); **call the roll** shusseki o toru 出席をとる. 2. vb. mawaru 回る (revolve); susumu 進む (move forward); maku 巻く (form into a roll); marumeru 丸める (form into a ball); yusaburu 揺さぶる (rock); todoroku とどろく (have a deep, loud sound); **roll back** nedan o modosu 値段を戻す (reduce price); **roll in** takusan haitteku 沢山入って来る (come in abundantly); **roll up** makiageru 巻き上げる (tuck up).

romance, n. 1. ren'ai 恋愛 (love). 2. monogatari 物語 (story). 3. yume 夢 (fantasy).

Rome, n. rōma ローマ.

roof, n. yane 屋根; **hit the roof** kan-kan ni okoru かんかんに怒る (be angry).

room, n. 1. heya 部屋 (compartment). 2. basho 場所 (space); **make room for** ... no tame ni basho o akeru ... のために場所を空ける. 3. yochi 余地 (opportunity or scope for something); **room for improvement** kaizen no yochi 改善の余地.

roomy, adj. hiroi 広い.

rooster, n. ondori 雄鶏.

root, 1. n. ne 根 (of a plant, tooth, etc.); konpon 根本 (origin); rūto ルート (math); **take root** ne o haru 根を張る (begin to grow). 2. vb. nezuku 根付く (grow roots); **root for** ... ōen suru ...を応援する (lend support to); **root out** nekosogi ni suru 根こそぎにする.

rope, n. tsuna 綱; nawa 縄.

rose, n. bara ばら (flower).

rosy, adj. bairo (no) ばら色 (の) (rosy color, promising).

rot, 1. n. fuhai 腐敗 (decay). 2. vb. kusaru/kusaraseru 腐る/腐らせる (become/cause to spoil).

rotate, vb. 1. mawaru 回る (turn around) mawasu 回す (cause to turn around). 2. kōtai suru/saseru 交代する/させる (take or cause to take turns).

rotten, adj. kusatteiru 腐っている (decayed, dishonest).

rough, adj. 1. arai 粗い (not smooth). 2. arai 荒い (violent, tempestuous). 3. soya (na) 粗野 (な) (crude). 4. ōmaka (na) 大まか (な) (preliminary). 5. kurushii 苦しい (painful). 6. shagaregoe (no) しゃがれ声 (の) (voice).

round, 1. n. kai 回 (number of events); renzoku 連続 (complete series); junkai 巡回 (regular visit); marui mono 丸い物 (something round-shaped). 2. adj. marui 丸い (circular, globular); maru-maru shita 丸々した (fat); **round trip** ōfukuryokō 往復旅行. 3. adv. mawari ni 周りに (in circumference); mawatte 回って (moving in a circle) **all year round** ichinenjū 一年中. 4. vb. mawaru 回る (go around); marumeru 丸める (make round); **round up** atsumeru 集める.

roundup, n. 1. matome まとめ (summary). 2. yobiatsume 呼び集め (bringing together).

rouse, vb. 1. okosu 起こす

(waken). 2. yobiokosu 呼び起こす (stir up).

route, n. rūto ルート; michi 道.

routine, 1. n. itsumo no koto いつものこと (customary course of procedure); okimari no koto お決まりのこと (unimaginative procedure); **daily routine** nikka 日課. 2. adj. itsumo (no) いつも (の) (regular); kimarikitta 決まりきった (regular and dull).

rove, vb. samayou さまよう.

row, 1. n. narabi 並び; retsu 列 (line); sawagi 騒ぎ (noise); kenka 喧嘩 (quarrel). 2. vb. kogu 漕ぐ (propel by oars); sawagu 騒ぐ (make noise); kenka suru 喧嘩する (quarrel).

rowdy, adj. ranbō (na) 乱暴 (な) (rough and noisy).

royalty, n. 1. kōzoku 皇族 (royal persons). 2. ōken 王権 (royal power). 3. inzei 印税 (share).

rub, vb. kosuru 擦る (apply friction or pressure).

rubber, n. gomu ゴム (substance); **rubber band** wa-gomu 輪ゴム; **rubber plant** gomu no ki ゴムの木.

rubbish, n. 1. gomi ごみ (waste). 2. tawagoto たわ言 (nonsense).

rude, adj. burei (na) 無礼 (な) (impolite).

ruffle, 1. n. hida ひだ (band of cloth); midare 乱れ (break in evenness). 2. vb. midasu 乱す (destroy the smoothness of); okoraseru 怒らせる (anger); shiwa ni naru しわになる (become wrinkled).

rug, n. kāpetto カーペット;

jūtan じゅうたん (floor covering).

rugged, adj. gotsu-gotsu shita ごつごつした.

ruin, 1. n. hametsu 破滅 (destruction); shittsui 失墜 (downfall); haikyo 廃墟; iseki 遺跡 (remains). **2.** vb. hakai suru 破壊する (demolish); dainashi ni suru 台無しにする (spoil); hasan suru 破産する (bankrupt).

rule, 1. n. kisoku 規則 (regulation); shihai 支配 (reign); jōgi 定規 (for measurement); **as a rule** ippan ni 一般に (generally). **2.** vb. shihai suru 支配する (reign); kettei suru 決定する (decide); jōgi de sen o hiku 定規で線を引く (mark with a ruler); **rule out** jogai suru 除外する.

ruler, n. **1.** jōgi 定規 (for measurement). **2.** shihaisha 支配者 (one who rules).

ruling, 1. n. kettei 決定 (decision). **2.** adj. omo na 主な (predominant); shihai (no) 支配 (の) (governing).

rumble, vb. goro-goro naru ごろごろ鳴る (make rumbling sound).

rumor, n. uwasa 噂 (gossip, hearsay).

run, vb. **1.** hashiru 走る (move quickly); hashiraseru 走らせる (cause to move quickly). **2.** keiei suru 経営する (run a business). **3.** rikkōho suru 立候補する (be a candidate). **4.** nagareru 流れる (flow). **5.**

tokeru 溶ける (melt). **6.** nobiru 伸びる (extend). **7.** ugoku 動く (be in operation). **8.** jōen suru 上演する (be performed). **9. run across** dekuwasu 出くわす; **run after** oikakeru 追いかける; **run away** nigeru 逃げる; **run into** butsukeru ぶつける (cause to hit); **run out of** ... ga kireru ...が切れる; **run over** hiku ひく (knock down with a car).

runway, n. kassōro 滑走路 (airplane).

rural, adj. inaka (no) 田舎 (の).

rush, 1. n. ōisogi 大急ぎ (hurried activity or state); sattō 殺到 (eager rushing of people to one place); tosshin 突進 (sudden and hasty movement). **2.** vb. isogu 急ぐ (hurry); isogaseru 急がせる (cause to hurry); tobikakaru 飛びかかる (attack).

Russian, 1. n. roshiajin ロシア人 (person); roshiago ロシア語 (language). **2.** adj. roshia (no) ロシア (の) (of Russia); roshiajin (no) ロシア人 (の) (of the Russians); roshiago (no) ロシア語 (の) (language).

rust, 1. n. sabi 錆. **2.** vb. sabiru 錆びる.

rut, n. **1.** wadachi 轍; mizo 溝 (furrow). **2. get into a rut** kata ni hamaru 型にはまる.

ruthless, adj. zan'nin (na) 残忍 (な) (cruel).

rye, n. rai-mugi ライ麦.

S

sabotage, n. bōgai kōsaku 妨害工作 (obstructive activities).

sack, n. **1.** fukuro 袋 (bag).

2. ryakudatsu 略奪 (pillage).

sacred, *adj.* 1. shinsei 神聖 (な) (holy). 2. shūkyō (no) 宗教 (の) (religious).

sad, *adj.* 1. kanashii 悲しい (sorrowful). 2. nagekawashii 嘆かわしい (deplorable).

safe, 1. *n.* kinko 金庫. 2. *adj.* anzen (na) 安全 (な) (secure, free from danger); kakujitsu (na) 確実 (な) (dependable).

safety belt, *n.* anzen-beruto 安全ベルト.

safety pin, *n.* anzen-pin 安全ピン.

sag, *vb.* 1. tawamu たわむ (bend). 2. tareru 垂れる (hang loose).

saga, *n.* buyūdan 武勇談 (heroic tale).

sail, 1. *n.* ho 帆 (sheet); kōkō 航行 (trip on sailing vessel). 2. *vb.* kōkai suru 航海する (travel over the sea); funatabi o suru 船旅をする (voyage).

sailboat, *n.* kogata hosen 小型帆船 (small boat).

sake, *n.* 1. **for the sake of** ... no tame ni ... の為に (for the good of). 2. **for the sake of doing** ... suru tame ni ... する為に (for the purpose of doing).

salad, *n.* sarada サラダ; **salad bowl** sarada-bōru サラダボウル.

sale, *n.* 1. hanbai 販売 (act of selling). 2. sēru セール (bargain sale). 3. **for sale** urimono 売り物; **on sale** waribiki (de) 割り引き (で) (able to be bought at reduced prices).

sales tax, *n.* shōhizei 消費税.

saliva, *n.* daeki 唾液.

salmon, *n.* sake 鮭.

salt, 1. *n.* shio 塩 (sodium chloride). 2. *vb.* shioaji o tsukeru 塩味を付ける (season with salt); shiozuke ni suru 塩漬けにする (preserve).

salt shaker, *n.* shioire 塩入れ.

salty, *adj.* shiokarai 塩辛い.

salute, *vb.* 1. ... ni aisatsu suru ... に挨拶する (greet). 2. ... keirei suru 敬礼する (make a gesture of respect to a superior).

salvation, *n.* kyūsai 救済.

same, *adj.* onaji 同じ; **same as** ... to onaji ... と同じ; **all the same** sore demo それでも (even so); **Same to you!** Anata mo. あなたも。

sample, 1. *n.* mihon 見本. 2. *vb.* tamesu 試す (experiment, test).

sanatorium, *n.* ryōyōsho 療養所.

sanction, 1. *n.* ninka 認可 (permission); seisai 制裁 (international law). 2. *vb.* mitomeru 認める (approve).

sand, 1. *n.* suna 砂. 2. *vb.* kamiyasuri o kakeru 紙やすりをかける (smooth with sandpaper).

sandy, *adj.* 1. suna darake (no) 砂だらけ (の) (full of sand). 2. suna ga majitteiru 砂が混じっている (containing sand).

sane, *adj.* 1. shōki (no) 正気 (の) (not deranged). 2. funbetsu ga aru 分別がある (showing good sense).

sanitarium, *n.* see sanatorium.

sanitary, *adj.* 1. eisei (no) 衛生 (の) (hygienic). 2. seiketsu (na) 清潔 (な) (free from dirt, germs, etc.).

sanitary napkin, *n.* seiriyōnapukin 生理用ナプキン.

sanity, *n.* 1. shōki 正気 (soundness of mind). 2. funbetsu 分別 (soundness of judgment).

sap, *vb.* yowaraseru 弱らせる (weaken).

sarcastic, *adj.* iyami tappuri (na, no) 嫌味たっぷり（な、の).

sardine, *n.* iwashi いわし.

Satan, *n.* akuma 悪魔 (devil).

satellite, *n.* jinkōeisei 人工衛星.

satisfaction, *n.* 1. manzoku 満足 (contentment). 2. manzoku saseru koto 満足させること (act of satisfying).

satisfy, *vb.* 1. manzoku saseru 満足させる (make contented). 2. mitasu 満たす (fulfill).

Saturday, *n.* doyōbi 土曜日.

saucer, *n.* ukezara 受け皿.

saucy, *adj.* burei (na) 無礼 (な) (insolent).

savage, 1. *n.* yabanjin 野蛮人. *adj.* yaban (na) 野蛮 (な) (uncivilized); dōmō (na) どうもう (な) (fierce).

save, 1. *vb.* tasukeru 助ける (rescue); setsuyaku suru 節約する (economize); takuwaeru 貯える、蓄える (store up). 2. *prep.* ... o nozoite ...を除いて (except).

savings, *n.* chokin 貯金 (money).

savor, *vb.* tanoshimu 楽しむ (enjoy); ajiwau 味わう (taste).

saw, 1. *n.* nokogiri 鋸 (tool). 2. *vb.* nokogiri de kiru 鋸で切る (cut).

sawmill, *n.* seizaisho 製材所.

say, 1. *vb.* iu 言う (speak,

state, utter); **that is to say** sunawachi 即ち; **it goes without saying** mochiron もちろん; **You don't say!** Masaka. まさか. 2. *adv.* daitai 大体い (approximately); tatoeba 例えば (for example).

saying, *n.* kotowaza ことわざ (proverb).

scale, 1. *n.* uroko うろこ (fish); hakari 秤 (tool for weighing); tenbin 天秤 (balance); shakudo 尺度 (standard, relative measure); sukēru スケール; kibo 規模 (size, magnitude); onkai 音階 (music). 2. *vb.* noboru 登る (climb up); jōge suru 上下する (increase or decrease); **scale down** kibo o chiisaku suru 規模を小さくする.

scallop, *n.* hotategai 帆立て貝.

scalp, *n.* tōhi 頭皮 (skin).

scamper, *vb.* satto hashiru さっと走る.

scan, 1. *vb.* shiraberu 調べる (examine). 2. zatto me o tōsu ざっと目を通す (skim).

scant, *adj.* saishōgen (no) 最小限 (の) (barely adequate).

scapegoat, *n.* migawari 身代わり.

scar, *n.* kizuato 傷跡.

scarce, *adj.* sukunai 少ない (insufficient, sparse).

scarcity, *n.* fusoku 不足.

scare, 1. *n.* kyōfu 恐怖 (fear). 2. *vb.* kowagaraseru 恐がらせる (frighten).

scarecrow, *n.* kakashi かかし.

scared, *adj.* **be scared** kowai 恐い.

scary, *adj.* osoroshii 恐ろしい.

scatter, *vb.* 1. makichirasu

撒き散らす (strew loosely about). 2. chirabaraseru 散らばらせる (cause to disperse); chirabaru 散らばる (disperse).

scene, n. 1. bamen 場面 (film, play). 2. ba 場 (location of action). 3. kōkei 光景 (view). 4. **behind the scenes** kossori (to)こっそり (と) (secretly).

scenery, n. 1. fūkei 風景; keshiki 景色 (landscape). 2. butaihaikei 舞台背景 (theater).

scenic, adj. keshiki ga ii 景色が良い.

scent, 1. n. nioi 匂い (smell); kaori 香り (fragrance). 2. vb. kagu 嗅ぐ (smell).

schedule, n. 1. keikakuhyō 計画表 (list of plans, events, etc.); jikokuhyō 時刻表 (timetable of buses, planes, etc.); **ahead of/behind schedule** yotei yori hayaku/yori okurete 予定より早く/より遅れて; **on schedule** yoteidōri ni 予定通りに. 2. vb. yotei suru 予定する (plan).

scheme, 1. n. keikaku 計画 (plan); takurami 企み (plot). 2. vb. takuramu 企む (plot).

scholar, n. 1. gakusha 学者 (learned person). 2. gakusei 学生 (pupil).

school, n. 1. gakkō 学校 (place for instruction); gakubu 学部 (university department); **elementary school** shōgakkō 小学校; **middle school** chūgakkō 中学校; **high school** kōtōgakkō 高等学校. 2. ha 派 (group). 3. mure 群れ (fish).

schoolroom, n. kyōshitsu 教室.

school year, n. gakunen 学年.

science, n. kagaku 科学; **science fiction** kūsōkagaku shōsetsu 空想科学小説.

scissors, n. hasami 鋏.

scoff, vb. scoff at ... o azawarau ... を嘲笑う.

scold, vb. shikaru 叱る.

scoop, 1. n. sukūpu スクープ (news report); sukoppu スコップ (small shovel); sukui 掬い (quantity taken up). 2. vb. **scoop up** sukuiageru 掬い上げる (take up); **scoop out** sukuitoru 掬い取る.

scope, n. 1. han'i 範囲 (extent). 2. genkai 限界 (limit). 3. kikai 機会 (opportunity).

scorch, vb. kogasu 焦がす.

score, 1. n. tokuten 得点 (points made in a game, examination, etc.); riyū 理由 (reason); gakufu 楽譜 (written music); ongaku 音楽 (music used in a film, etc.); nijū 二十 (twenty); **on that score** sono ten dewa その点では; **settle a score** fukushū suru 復習する (retaliate). 2. vb. tokuten o ageru 得点を上げる (game, examination); ten o tsukeru 点を付ける (keep a record); kizamime o tsukeru 刻み目を付ける (notch); kachieru 勝ち得る (gain, win).

scorn, 1. n. keibetsu 軽蔑. 2. vb. keibetsu suru 軽蔑する.

scorpion, n. sasori さそり.

Scotch tape, n. serotēpu セロテープ.

scout, 1. n. teisatsu 偵察 (person sent ahead); bōisukauto ボーイスカウト (Boy Scout). 2. vb. shirabemawaru 調べ回る

(explore); sagashimawaru 捜し回る (seek).

scowl, 1. *n.* shikamettsura しかめつ面. 2. *vb.* okotte kao o shikameru 怒って顔をしかめる (frown with anger).

scramble, 1. *n.* yojinoboru koto よじ登ること (act of climbing); arasoi 争い (struggle). 2. *vb.* yojinoboru よじ登る (climb); aiarasou 相争う (struggle).

scrap, 1. *n.* kakera 欠けら (fragment); kozeriai 小競り合い (fight); **scraps** tabenokoshi 食べ残し (leftover food). 2. *vb.* suteru 捨てる (discard); kenka suru 喧嘩する (fight).

scrape, 1. *n.* kosuru koto 擦ること (act of rubbing); kukyō 苦境 (predicament); surikizu 擦り傷 (wound). 2. *vb.* kosuru 擦る (rub harshly); kosuriotosu 擦り落とす (remove by scraping).

scratch, 1. *n.* kakikizu 掻き傷 (mark from scratching); hikkaku oto 引っ掻く音 (sound); **from scratch** mattaku no hajime kara 全くの初めから. 2. *vb.* hikkaku 引っ掻く (mark, tear, rub); kaku 掻く (rub slightly with the fingernails); **scratch off/out** kakikesu 掻き消す.

scream, 1. *n.* sakebigoe 叫び声. 2. *vb.* sakebu 叫ぶ.

screen, 1. *n.* tsuitate つい立て (partition); amido 網戸 (window screen); gamen men 画面 (TV or movie screen). 2. *vb.* kakusu 隠す (hide); furui ni kakeru ふるいにかける (sift through a screen); shiraberu 調べる (examine).

screw, 1. *n.* neji ねじ (fastener); sukuryū スクリュー (propeller). 2. *vb.* neji de tomeru ねじで留める (fasten).

screwdriver, *n.* nejimawashi ねじ回し (tool).

scribble, 1. *n.* hashirigaki 走り書き (something written hastily). 2. *vb.* hashirigaki suru 走り書きする (write hastily).

script, *n.* 1. kyakuhon 脚本 (play, film, etc.). 2. tegaki 手書き (handwriting).

scroll, *n.* 1. makimono 巻き物 (roll of inscribed paper). 2. kakejiku 掛け軸 (hanging scroll).

scrub, *vb.* 1. goshi-goshi arau ごしごし洗う (wash roughly). 2. toriyameru 取り止める (cancel).

scuffle, *n.* rantō 乱闘 (fight).

sculpture, *n.* chōkoku 彫刻.

scum, *n.* 1. kasu かす (film). 2. kuzu 屑 (person).

scythe, *n.* ōgama 大鎌.

sea, *n.* umi 海 (body of salty water, ocean); -kai 海; **Japan Sea** Nihonkai 日本海; **by sea** fune de 船で (by ship); **at sea** tohō ni kurete 途方に暮れて (at a loss).

seafood, *n.* gyokairui 魚貝類.

sea gull, *n.* kamome かもめ.

seal, 1. *n.* in 印; han 判 (mark); fūin 封印 (means of closing); azarashi あざらし (mammal). 2. *vb.* ... ni in o osu ...に印を押す (affix seal to); fūin o suru 封印をする (close with a seal); fūjiru 封じる (close); **seal in** tojikomeru 閉じ込める.

sea level, *n.* kaibatsu 海抜.

seam, *n.* nuime 縫い目 (line formed in sewing).

search, 1. *n.* sōsaku 捜索 (act of searching for someone or something missing); chōsa 調査 (investigation); **in search of** ... o motomete ... を求めて. 2. *vb.* sagasu 捜す (look for); chōsa suru 調査する (investigate); **search for** ... o sagasu ... を捜す.

seashore, *n.* kaigan 海岸.

seasickness, *n.* funayoi 船酔い.

season, 1. *n.* kisetsu 季節 (any of the four periods of the year; best or usual time); **in season** shun (no) 旬 (の); **out of season** jikihazure (no) 時季外れ (の). 2. *vb.* ... ni aji o tsukeru ... に味を付ける (flavor).

seat, 1. *n.* seki 席 (place for sitting); giseki 議席 (right to sit, as in Congress); tokoro 所 (site); **take a seat** suwaru 座る. 2. *vb.* suwaraseru 座らせる (place someone on a seat); **seat oneself** suwaru 座る; **be seated** suwaru 座る.

sea urchin, *n.* uni うに.

seaweed, *n.* kaisō 海草.

second, 1. *n.* byō 秒 (sixtieth part of a minute); **seconds** nikyūhin 二級品 (imperfect goods); okawari お代わり (second helping). 2. *adj.* nibanme (no) 二番目 (の); daini (no) 第二 (の) (next after the first); **second to none** saijō 最上 (の) (best). 3. *vb.* shiji suru 支持する (support).

secondary, *adj.* 1. chūtō (no) 中等 (の) (of the second stage, as education).

2. niji-teki (na) 二次的 (な) (deriving from the original, of lesser importance).

second-class, *adj.* ototteiru 劣っている (inferior); niryū (no) 二流 (の) (inferior).

second-hand, *adj.* 1. chūko (no) 中古 (の) (used). 2. matagiki (no) 又聞き (の) (indirect).

secret, *n.* 1. himitsu 秘密. 2. *adj.* himitsu (no) 秘密 (の).

secretary, *n.* 1. hisho 秘書 (clerical worker). 2. chōkan 長官 (head of department of government). 3. shoki 書記 (official in an organization).

secrete, *vb.* bunpitsu suru 分泌する.

section, *n.* 1. bubun 部分 (separate part). 2. bu 部; ka 課 (part of an organization or company). 3. chi'iki 地域 (part of a town).

sector, *n.* 1. hōmen 方面 (area). 2. bumon 部門 (part of a business activity).

secure, 1. *adj.* anzen (na) 安全 (な) (safe); kakujitsu (na) 確実 (な) (assured); shikkari shiteiru しっかりしている (firm, reliable). 2. *vb.* kakuho suru 確保する (get); kakujitsu ni suru 確実にする (make certain); tomeru 留める (fasten).

security, *n.* 1. anzen 安全 (safety). 2. bōei 防衛 (protection). 3. tanpo 担保 (security for a loan).

seduce, *vb.* yūwaku suru 誘惑する.

see, *vb.* miru 見る; **see off** ... o miokuru ... を見送る; **see to** ... o kakujitsu ni suru ... を確実にする.

seed, 1. *n.* tane 種 (plant, cause of anything). 2. *vb.* tane o maku 種を蒔く

(plant seeds); tane o toru 種を取る (remove seeds).

seek, *vb.* 1. sagasu 捜す (search). 2. motomeru 求める (request). 3. **seek to do** ... shiyō to suru ... しようとする (try to do). 4. **be sought after** juyō ga ōi 需要が多い.

seem, *vb.* ... yō ni mieru ... ように見える (appear).

seemly, *adj.* fusawashii ふさわしい.

seep, *vb.* shintō suru 浸透する; **seep into** ... ni shimikomu ... に染み込む.

seer, *n.* yogensha 予言者.

seethe, *vb.* wakitatsu 沸き立つ (surge or foam as if boiling).

segment, *n.* bubun 部分 (part).

seismic, *adj.* jishin (no) 地震 (の).

seize, *vb.* 1. tsukamu 摑む (grab). 2. bosshū suru 没収する (confiscate). 3. **be seized with** ... ni toritsukareru ... に取り憑かれる.

seldom, *adv.* mettani ... nai めったに ... ない; **seldom come** mettani konai めったに来ない.

select, 1. *adj.* yorinuki (no) 選り抜き (の) (carefully chosen). 2. *vb.* erabu 選ぶ (choose).

self, *n.* 1. jibun 自分; jiko 自己 (person's own nature); **by oneself** jibun de 自分で; hitori de 一人で. 2. rikoshin 利己心 (personal interest).

self-centered, *adj.* jikochūshin-teki (na) 自己中心的 (な).

self-confident, *adj.* jishin ga aru 自信がある.

self-control, *n.* jisei 自制.

Self-Defence Forces, *n.* jieitai 自衛隊 (Japanese armed services).

self-denial, *n.* jikohitei 自己否定.

self-esteem, *n.* jikosonchō 自己尊重.

self-indulgent, *adj.* wagamama (na) 我がまま (な).

selfish, *adj.* riko-teki (na) 利己的 (な).

self-made, *adj.* dokuryoku (no) 独力 (の).

self-portrait, *n.* jigazō 自画像.

self-respect, *n.* jisonshin 自尊心.

self-righteous, *adj.* hitoriyogari (no) 一人よがり (の).

self-satisfaction, *n.* jikomanzoku 自己満足.

sell, *vb.* 1. uru 売る (part with in exchange for money). 2. ureru 売れる (find a buyer). 3. **sell out** uritsukusu 売り尽くす; **be sold out** urikire 売り切れ.

seller, *n.* urite 売り手.

semen, *n.* seieki 精液.

semester, *n.* gakki 学期.

semi-, han- 半- (half); **semicircle** han'en 半円.

semimonthly, *adj.* hantsukigoto (no) 半月毎 (の).

send, *vb.* 1. okuru 送る (cause to go or be conveyed). 2. **send out** hanatsu 放つ (emit); **send back** okurikaesu 送り返す; **send for** ... o yobu ... を呼ぶ (summon).

send-off, *n.* sōbetsu 送別 (a farewell).

senior, 1. *n.* nenchōsha 年長者 (older person); jōshi 上司 (company worker of higher

rank); senpai 先輩 (older
colleague); yonensei 四年生
(fourth year college
student). 2. adj. nenchō
(no) 年長 (の) (older); jōkyū
(no) 上級 (の) (higher in
rank); yonensei (no) 四年生
(の) (of a fourth year
student).

senior citizen, n. rōjin 老人;
(o)toshiyori (お)年寄り.

seniority, n. nenchō 年長
(condition of being senior);
sen'nin 先任 (precedence by
length of service).

sensation, n. 1. kankaku 感
覚 (ability to feel or sense).
2. kimochi 気持ち
(impression, perception). 3.
kōfun 興奮 (excitement).

sense, 1. n. imi 意味
(meaning); kankaku 感覚
(faculty for perceiving
physical things); kanji 感じ
(feeling so produced);
funbetsu 分別 (rationality);
senses gokan 五感 (five
senses); ishiki 意識
(consciousness); **in a sense**
aru imi de wa ある意味では;
make sense suji ga tōru 筋
が通る. 2. vb. kanjiru 感じ
る (perceive).

sensible, adj. 1. funbetsu ga
aru 分別がある (wise or
practical). 2. ishiki shiteiru
意識している (aware).

sensitive, adj. 1. binkan (na)
敏感 (な) (easily affected).
2. omoiyari ga aru 思い遣り
がある (compassionate). 3.
okoriyasui 怒り易い (easily
offended). 4. shinchō o
yōsuru 慎重を要する
(requiring prudence).

sensual, adj. 1. kan'nō-teki
(na) 官能的 (な) (gratifying
to the senses). 2.
nikuwaku-teki (na) 肉感的

(な) (carnal).

sentence, 1. n. bun 文
(group of words); hanketsu
判決 (assignment of
punishment). 2. vb.
hanketsu o iiwatasu 判決を
言い渡す.

sentiment, n. 1. kanjō 感情
(emotion). 2. iken 意見
(opinion).

sentry, n. hoshō 歩哨.

separate, 1. adj. betsu (no)
別 (の) (not connected);
sorezore (no) それぞれ (の)
(individual). 2. vb.
wakareru 分かれる (come
apart); wakareru 別れる
(part company); wakeru 分
ける (keep or put apart).

September, n. kugatsu 九
月.

sequel, n. 1. tsuzuki 続き
(film, story). 2. kekka 結果
(consequence).

sequence, n. renzoku 連続
(series).

serene, adj. odayaka (na) 穏
やか (な) (calm).

sergeant, n. gunsō 軍曹
(military); keibu 警部
(police).

serial, 1. n. tsuzukimono 続
き物. 2. adj. renzoku (no)
連続 (の).

series, n. renzoku 連続
(things in succession); **a
series of** ichiren no 一連の.

serious, adj. 1. shinken (na)
真剣 (な) (of deep thought,
earnest). 2. jūdai (na) 重大
(な) (significant). 3.
shinkoku (na) 深刻 (な)
(giving cause for
apprehension).

sermon, n. sekkyō 説教
(religious discourse,
lecture).

serpent, n. hebi 蛇 (snake).

servant, n. meshitsukai 召し

serve, *vb.* tsukaeru 仕える (work for someone); kyūji suru 給仕する (wait on table); sashiageru 差し上げる (provide, as with food or drink); hōshi suru 奉仕する (render assistance free); yō o nasu 用をなす (have definite use); yaku ni tatsu 役に立つ (be useful); tsutomeru 務める (perform the duties of; serve as a juror, senator, etc.); kei ni fukusuru 刑に服する (submit to a criminal sentence).

service, *n.* 1. taiō 対応 (treatment in a hotel, restaurant, etc.). 2. **services** joryoku 助力 (assistance). 3. heieki 兵役 (military service). 4. shokumu 職務 (duty or work). 5. shiki 式 (ritual). 6. shisetsu 施設 (supplier of gas, water, etc.). 7. kōtsū no ben 交通の便 (transportation system). 8. seibi 整備 (maintenance and repair).

service station, *n.* gasorin-sutando ガソリンスタンド.

sesame, *n.* goma 胡麻.

session, *n.* 1. kai 会 (assembly, sitting); **in session** kaiteichū (no) 開廷中 (の) (court); kaikaichū (no) 開会中 (の) (legislature). 2. kōza 講座 (class).

set, 1. *n.* soroi 揃い (group); butai sōchi 舞台装置 (theater); terebi テレビ (TV set); **a set of** hitosoroi no 一揃いの. 2. *adj.* kimatteiru 決まっている (fixed); junbibantan (no) 準備万端 (の) (ready); **set phrase**

kimarimonku 決まり文句. 3. *vb.* oku 置く (place); setto suru セットする (arrange, as hair, clock, etc.); kimeru 決める (determine); uchitateru 打ち立てる (establish); shizumu 沈む (pass below horizon); **set a record** kiroku o uchitateru 記録を打ち立てる; **set the table** shokutaku no junbi o suru 食卓の準備をする; **set free** jiyū ni suru 自由にする; **set aside** betsu ni totte oku 別に取って置く (reserve); **set back** okuraseru 遅らせる (make late); **set forth** noberu 述べる (state); **set off/out** hajimeru 始める (start); tabidatsu 旅立つ (begin a journey); **set up** sōsetsu suru 創設する (establish).

settle, *vb.* 1. kimeru 決める (decide). 2. kaiketsu suru 解決する (resolve). 3. wakai suru 和解する (reconcile in a dispute). 4. sumitsuku 住みつく (take up residence). 5. shizumeru 静める (quiet). 6. shiharau 支払う (pay).

setup, *n.* shikumi 仕組み (arrangement).

seven, *n.* nana/nanatsu/shichi 七/七つ/七.

seventeen, *n.* jūnana 十七.

seventeenth, *adj.* jūnanabanme (no) 十七番目 (な); daijūnana (no) 第十七 (の).

seventy, *n.* nanajū/shichijū 七十.

several, *adj.* 1. ikutsuka (no) 幾つか (の) (things); sūnin (no) 数人 (の) (people). 2. sū- 数-; **several thousand** sūsen (no) 数千 (の).

severe, *adj.* 1. genkaku (na)

厳格 (な) (strict). 2. hageshii 激しい (violent, hard). 3. kibishii 厳しい (harsh, as weather). 4. kanso (na) 簡素 (な) (plain).

sew, vb. nuu 縫う.

sexism, n. seisabetsu 性差別.

sexual, adj. sei-teki (na) 性的 (な) (of sex); **sexual harassment** sekuhara セクハラ; **sexual intercourse** sekkusu セックス.

shabby, adj. 1. boro-boro (no) ぼろぼろ (の) (worn-out); misuborashii みすぼらしい (meager). 2. kudaranai 下らない (contemptible, inferior).

shade, 1. n. kage 陰 (dimness); hikage 日陰 (shady place under the sun); yūrei 幽霊 (ghost); iroai 色合い (degree of color); hiyoke 日除け (window shade); kasa 傘 (of a lamp); sukoshi 少し (slight amount). 2. vb. saegiru 遮る (protect from light).

shadow, n. 1. kage 影 (dark image); atokata 跡形 (trace).

shaft, n. 1. e 柄 (long slender rod); yagara 矢柄 (arrow shaft). 2. shinbō 心棒 (revolving bar in engine). 3. kōsen 光線 (beam of light).

shake, vb. 1. furu 振る (agitate, as container, bottle, etc.). 2. yureru 揺れる (move with short movements); yusuburu 揺すぶる (cause to move with short movements). 3. furueru 震える (tremble); furuwaseru 震わせる (cause to tremble). 4. furiharau 振り払う (remove by shaking). 5. **shake hands**

akushu suru 握手する; **shake one's head** kubi o yoko ni furu 首を横に振る.

shaky, adj. 1. fuantei (na) 不安定 (な) (insecure). 2. furueru 震える (tending to tremble).

shall, aux. vb. **Shall I (we)...?** ... mashō ka. ... ましょうか.

shallow, adj. asai 浅い (not deep).

shame, 1. n. haji 恥 (painful feeling); fumeiyo 不名誉 (disgrace); **What a shame!** Nasakenai. 情けない (It is deplorable); **Shame on you!** Haji o shire. 恥を知れ. 2. vb. haji o kakaseru 恥をかかせる (cause to feel shame, disgrace).

shameful, adj. hazubeki (no) 恥ずべき (の).

shameless, adj. hajishirazu (na, no) 恥知らず (な、の) (brazen, unashamed).

shape, 1. n. katachi 形 (form); jōtai 状態 (condition); **take shape** katachi o toru 形をとる. 2. vb. katachizukuru 形作る (form).

shapely, adj. katachi ga ii 形が良い.

share, 1. n. wakemae 分け前 (portion); buntan 分担 (allotment, assignment); kabu 株 (corporate stock). 2. vb. wakeru 分ける; buntan suru 分担する.

shark, n. same 鮫.

sharp, 1. adj. surudoi 鋭い (acute, insightful); eibin (na) 鋭敏 (な) (keen, sensitive); kyū (na) 急 (な) (abrupt); meikaku (na) 明確 (な) (distinct); piritto suru ぴりっとする (in taste). 2. adv. chōdo 丁度 (of time).

sharpener, n. enpitsukezuri 鉛筆削り (pencil).

shatter, vb. 1. kudakeru 砕ける (break); kudaku 砕く (cause to be broken).

shave, vb. 1. soru 剃る (hair); **shave one's beard** hige o soru 髭を剃る. 2. kezuru 削る (cut or scrape in thin slices).

she, pron. kanojo 彼女.

sheaf, n. taba 束.

shear, vb. karitoru 刈り取る.

shears, n. ōbasami 大鋏.

sheath, n. saya さや.

shed, 1. n. koya 小屋 (hut). 2. vb. nagasu 流す (pour forth); otosu 落とす (throw off); dappi suru 脱皮する (of a snake or insect); **shed light on** ... o akiraka ni suru ... を明らかにする.

sheep, n. hitsuji 羊.

sheepish, adj. hanikami (no) はにかみ (の).

sheer, adj. mattaku (no) 全く (の) (utter, absolute).

shelf, n. tana 棚 (furniture).

shell, 1. n. kara 殻 (hard outer covering); kaigara 貝殻 (sea shell); dan'yaku 弾薬 (shotgun cartridge). 2. vb. ... no kara o toru ... の殻を取る (remove the shell of); bakugeki suru 爆撃する (bombard); **shell out** harau 払う (pay).

shelter, 1. n. hinansho 避難所 (place for protection); bōkūgō 防空壕 (from air-raid); ichiji-shukuhakusho 一時宿泊所 (temporary residence). 2. vb. hogo suru 保護する (protect); hinan suru 避難する (take shelter).

shield, 1. n. tate 盾 (armor); hogo sōchi 保護装置 (device for protection). 2. vb.

mamoru 守る (protect).

shift, 1. n. henka 変化 (change); kōtai 交代 (work). 2. vb. utsusu 移す (transfer something); utsuru 移る (be transferred); kawaru 変わる (change); kaeru 変える (cause to change).

shimmer, vb. matataku 瞬く.

shine, 1. n. kagayaki 輝き (radiance); kōtaku 光沢 (sheen); migaki 磨き (act of polishing); **rain or shine** nani ga attemo 何があっても (whatever happens). 2. vb. hikaru 光る (give forth light); migaku 磨く (polish).

ship, 1. n. fune 船 (boat). 2. vb. okuru 送る (send).

shiver, vb. miburui suru 身震いする.

shock, 1. n. shōgeki 衝撃 (emotional disturbance, blow, impact); seishin-teki dageki 精神的打撃 (emotional disturbance); dengeki 電撃 (electric). 2. vb. **be shocked (by)** ... ni gakuzen to suru ... に愕然とする (become emotionally devastated).

shoddy, adj. hinjaku (na) 貧弱 (な).

shoe, n. kutsu 靴.

shoe polish, n. kutsuzumi 靴墨.

shoestring, n. wazuka no okane わずかのお金 (small amount of money).

shoot, 1. n. me 芽 (new growth). 2. vb. utsu 撃つ (hit with bullet, discharge firearm); iru 射る (discharge, as bow).

shop, 1. n. mise 店 (store); kōjō 工場 (factory); shigotoba 仕事場

(workshop). 2. *vb.* kau 買う (purchase); **shop around** kurabemawaru 比べ回る (compare); **shop for** ... o sagasu ... を捜す (hunt for).

shoplifting, *n.* manbiki 万引き.

shopper, *n.* kaimonokyaku 買い物客.

shopping, *n.* kaimono 買い物.

shore, 1. *n.* kishibe 岸辺 (land beside water); riku 陸 (land). 2. *vb.* **shore up** sasaeru 支える (support).

short, 1. *adj.* mijikai 短い (not long); hikui 低い (not tall); tarinai 足りない (not enough); bukkirabō (na) ぶっきらぼう (な) (rudely brief). 2. *adv.* kyū ni 急に (abruptly). 3. **fall short of** ... ni tasshinai ... に達しない (fail to reach); **for short** chijimete 縮めて (as a shorter form); **in short** yōsuru ni 要するに; **run short of** ... ga fusoku suru ... が不足する.

shortage, *n.* fusoku 不足.

shortcut, *n.* chikamichi 近道 (way or method).

shorten, *vb.* mijikaku suru 短くする.

shorthand, *n.* sokki 速記.

shortly, *adv.* 1. sugu ni すぐに (soon). 2. bukkirabō ni ぶっきらぼうに (impatiently).

shorts, *n.* 1. han-zubon 半ズボン (pants). 2. pantsu パンツ (underwear).

shortsighted, *adj.* 1. kingan (no) 近眼 (の) (nearsighted). 2. chōki-tenbō ni kakeru 長期展望に欠ける (lacking foresight).

short story, *n.* tanpenshōsetsu 短編小説.

shortwave, *n.* tanpa 短波.

shot, *n.* 1. happō 発砲 (discharge of firearm); shashu 射手 (marksman); dangan 弾丸 (lead pellet). 2. chūsha 注射 (injection). 3. shūto シュート (sports). 4. **big shot** ōmono 大物; **long shot** mikominashi 見込み無し; **have a shot** yattemiru やってみる.

should, *aux. vb.* ... beki ... べき.

shoulder, 1. *n.* kata 肩 (body). 2. *vb.* ninau 担う (carry); kata de osu 肩で押す (push).

shoulder blade, *n.* kenkōkotsu 肩甲骨.

shout, 1. *n.* sakebi 叫び (cry); kansei 歓声 (hurrah). 2. *vb.* sakebu 叫ぶ (yell).

shove, 1. *n.* hitooshi 一押し. 2. *vb.* tsuyoku osu 強く押す.

show, 1. *n.* tenjikai 展示会 (exhibition); misekake 見せ掛け (appearance); **on show** tenjichū 展示中 (on display). 2. *vb.* tenji suru 展示する (display at a show); miseru 見せる (allow to be seen); shimesu 示す (demonstrate); mieru 見える (be visible); jōen suru 上演する (theater); an'nai suru 案内する (guide); **show off** misebirakasu 見せびらかす; **show up** kuru 来る (arrive).

show-off, *n.* misebirakashi-ya 見せびらかし屋.

shrew, *n.* gami-gami on'na がみがみ女 (woman).

shriek, 1. *n.* kanakirigoe 金切り声 (loud shrill cry). 2. *vb.* kanakirigoe o ageru 金切り声を上げる (cry).

shrimp, *n.* koebi 小海老.

shrink, *vb.* 1. chijimu 縮む

(contract in size). 2.
hikisagaru 引き下がる
(draw back). 3. heru 減る
(reduce).

shrivel, vb. shioreru しおれ
る (wrinkle and fade).

shroud, n. 1. kyōkatabira 経
帷子 (burial). 2. ōi 覆い
(cover).

shrub, n. yabu やぶ.

shrug, vb. kata o sukumeru
肩をすくめる; **shrug off**
karuku inasu 軽くいなす
(dismiss).

shuffle, vb. ashi o hikizuru
足を引きずる (drag feet);
kiru 切る (cards).

shut, vb. 1. tojiru 閉じる
(make closed). 2.
tojikomeru 閉じ込める
(confine). 3. shimeru 閉め
る (cause to cease
operations). 4. shimaru 閉
まる (become shut). 5.
shut down kyūgyō suru 休
業する (close temporarily).
Shut up! Shizuka ni. 静か
に (Be quiet!); Damare. だま
れ (Don't say anything!).

shuttle, n. shuttle bus
kinkyori-ōfuku-basu 近距離
往復バス; **free shuttle
service** sōgeisha 送迎車.

shy, 1. adj. uchiki (na) 内気
(な) (bashful); okubyō (na)
臆病 (な) (timid). 2. vb. **shy
away** sakeru 避ける
(avoid).

sibling, n. kyōdai 兄弟
(male); shimai 姉妹
(female).

sick, adj. 1. byōki (no) 病気
(の) (ill, of sickness). 2.
hakike ga suru 吐き気がす
る (nauseated). 3. byō teki
(na) 病的 (な) (morbid). 4.
be sick of ... ni unzari
shiteiru ... にうんざりして
いる (be fed up with).

side, 1. n. bubun 部分 (part);
gawa 側 (part or group);
yoko(gawa) 横(側) (part
other than front, back, top
or bottom); men 面 (surface
or aspect); fuchi 縁 (edge);
soba 側 (nearby area);
chi'iki 地域 (region); **side
by side** narande 並んで;
take sides mikata suru 味
方する (be partial). 2. vb.
side with ... o shien suru ...
を支援する; ... no mikata o
suru ... の味方をする
(support).

sidewalk, n. hodō 歩道.

sieve, n. furui ふるい.

sift, vb. 1. furui ni kakeru ふ
るいに掛ける (separate with
a sieve). 2. yoku shiraberu
よく調べる (scrutinize).

sigh, 1. n. tameiki 溜め息. 2.
vb. tameiki o tsuku 溜め息を
吐く.

sight, 1. n. kōkei 光景
(vista); shiryoku 視力
(eyesight); shikai 視界
(range of vision); meisho 名
所 (interesting place); **at
first sight** hitome de 一目
で; **on sight** sugu ni すぐに
(immediately); **catch/ lose
sight of** ... o mikakeru/
miushinau ... を見掛ける／
見失う; **in sight** chikaku ni
近くに (nearby). 2. vb. miru
見る (see); mokugeki suru
目撃する (witness).

sign, 1. n. shirushi 印
(symbol); kigō 記号
(conventional mark, figure,
etc.); kanban 看板
(advertising board); chōkō
兆候 (portent); aizu 合図
(signal through gesture);
keiseki 形跡 (trace). 2. vb.
shomei suru 署名する (put
signature to); aizu suru 合図
する (signal); **sign up** ōbo

suru 応募する (enlist).

signal, 1. *n.* aizu 合図 (symbolic communication); shingō 信号 (traffic light). **2.** *vb.* aizu suru 合図する (communicate).

signature, *n.* shomei 署名.

significance, *n.* **1.** imi 意味 (meaning). **2.** jūdaisa 重大 さ (importance).

silent, *adj.* **1.** shizuka (na) 静 か (な) (quiet). **2.** mugon (no) 無言 (の) (speechless).

silk, *n.* kinu 絹.

silky, *adj.* kinu no yō (na) 絹 のよう (な).

sill, *n.* shikii 敷居 (of a door or window).

silly, *adj.* baka (na) 馬鹿 (な).

silver, 1. *n.* gin 銀 (metal); ginshokki 銀食器 (silverware). **2.** *adj.* gin (no) 銀 (の) (of silver); ginsei (no) 銀製 (の) (made of silver).

similar, *adj.* dōyō (na, no) 同様 (な、の) (same); niteiru 似ている (resembling).

simile, *n.* chokuyu 直喩.

simmer, *vb.* gutsu-gutsu nieru ぐつぐつ煮える.

simple, *adj.* **1.** kantan (na) 簡単 (な) (easy); tanjun (na) 単純 (な) (uncomplicated). **2.** soboku (na) 素朴 (な) (unpretentious). **3.** shisso (na) 質素 (な) (plain, undecorated). **4.** tonma (na, no) 頓馬 (な、の) (foolish).

simultaneous, *adj.* dōji ni okoru 同時に起こる.

sin, 1. *n.* tsumi 罪. **2.** *vb.* tsumi o okasu 罪を犯す.

since, 1. *adv.* sore kara それ から. **2.** *prep.* ... kara ... か ら. **3.** *conj.* kara から.

sincerity, *n.* seijitsusa 誠実 さ.

sing, *vb.* utau 歌う.

singer, *n.* kashu 歌手.

single, 1. *n.* dokushinsha 独 身者 (unmarried person); shinguru シングル (record). **2.** *adj.* hitotsu (no) 一つ (の) (one); yui'itsu (no) 唯一 (の) (only); dokushin (no) 独身 (の) (unmarried); koko (no) 個々 (の) (individual); hitoe (no) 一重 (の) (not multiple). **3.** *vb.* **single out** erabidasu 選び出す.

singular, *adj.* **1.** tansū (no) 単数 (の) (grammar). **2.** namihazurete-iru 並外れて いる (extraordinary). **3.** hen (na) 変 (な) (strange).

sinister, *adj.* bukimi (na) 無 気味 (な).

sink, 1. *n.* nagashi 流し (kitchen). **2.** *vb.* shizumu 沈 む (submerge); shizumaseru 沈ませる (cause to submerge); heru 減る (decrease); taoreru 倒れる (fall); yowaru 弱る (deteriorate).

sinuous, *adj.* magarikunette- iru 曲がりくねっている.

sip, 1. *n.* hitosusuri 一すす り. **2.** *vb.* susuru すする.

sister, *n.* **1.** shimai 姉妹 (female family member); ane 姉; onēsan お姉さん (older sister); imōto 妹 (younger sister); **sister city** shimaitoshi 姉妹都市. **2.** shūdōjo 修道女 (Catholic).

sister-in-law, *n.* giri no shimai 義理の姉妹.

sit, *vb.* **1.** suwaru 座る (take a seat); suwaraseru 座らせ る (cause to take seat). **2.** soboku (na) 素朴 (な)... **sit back** kutsurogu 寛ぐ (rest); **sit down** suwaru 座 る; **sit up** mi o okosu 身を

起こす (rise); osoku made okiteiru 遅くまで起きている (stay up late).

site, n. basho 場所 (place).

sitting, n. 1. kai 会 (session). 2. suwatteiru jikan 座っている時間 (period of being seated).

situation, n. 1. jōkyō 状況 (state of affairs). 2. ichi 位置 (position). 3. shoku 職 (employment).

six, n. roku/muttsu 六／六つ.

six hundred, n. roppyaku 六百.

sixteen, n. jūroku 十六.

sixty, n. rokujū 六十.

size, n. 1. ōkisa 大きさ (dimensions or extent). 2. kibo 規模 (scale).

sizzle, vb. jū-jū yakeru じゅーじゅー焼ける (cooking).

skeleton, n. 1. gaikotsu 骸骨 (bones). 2. kokkaku 骨格 (framework).

sketchy, adj. 1. fukanzen (na) 不完全 (な) (incomplete). 2. ayafuya (na) あやふや (な) (vague).

skid, vb. yoko ni suberu 横に滑る.

skill, n. gijutsu 技術; udemae 腕前 (dexterity).

skillful, adj. takumi (na) 巧み (な) (skill).

skim, vb. 1. sukuitoru 掬い取る (remove). 2. kasumeru 掠める (move lightly over).

skin, n. 1. hada 肌 (animal, human being); kawa 皮 (plant, fruit); **get under one's skin** iradataseru 苛立たせる (irritate one). 2. vb. kawa o muku 皮を剥く (remove skin).

skinny, adj. (gari-gari ni) yaseteiru (がりがりに) やせ

ている.

skip, vb. tobu 飛ぶ (jump, disregard order); **skip over** tobasu 飛ばす (leave out).

skull, n. zugaikotsu 頭骸骨.

sky, n. sora 空.

skylark, n. hibari ひばり.

skyscraper, n. chōkōsō-biru 超高層ビル.

slab, n. atsuita 厚板 (flat piece); atsugiri 厚切り (food).

slack, 1. adj. yurui 緩い (loose, lenient); hima (na) 暇 (な) (not busy, slow); taiman (na) 怠慢 (な) (inattentive). 2. vb. **slack off** yurumeru 緩める; namakeru 怠ける (be lazy).

slam, vb. 1. batan to shimeru ばたんと閉める (shut noisily). 2. hihan suru 批判する (criticize).

slander, 1. n. chūshō 中傷. 2. vb. chūshō suru 中傷する.

slant, 1. n. keisha 傾斜 (slope); kenkai 見解 (view). 2. vb. keisha suru 傾斜する (slope); henkō suru 偏向する (be biased).

slap, 1. n. hirateuchi 平手打ち. 2. vb. hirate de tataku 平手で叩く.

slapstick, n. dotabata-kigeki どたばた喜劇.

slash, 1. n. kirikizu 切り傷 (wound); shasen 斜線 (symbol). 2. vb. kiritsukeru 切りつける (cut); nesage suru 値下げする (price).

slaughter, 1. n. gyakusatsu 虐殺 (massacre); tosatsu 屠殺 (killing of animals). 2. vb. gyakusatsu suru 虐殺する (massacre); tosatsu suru 屠殺する (kill animals).

slave, 1. n. dorei 奴隷. 2. vb. akuseku hataraku あくせく働く.

sleek, *adj.* 1. kakkoii かっこ良い (stylish); iki (na) 粋 (な) (smooth in manners). 2. namaraka (na) 滑らか (な) (smooth, as hair).

sleep, 1. *n.* nemuri 眠り. 2. *vb.* nemuru 眠る; neru 寝る **sleep off** nemutte naosu 眠って治す (get rid of by sleeping); **sleep with** ... to sekkusu o suru ... とセックスをする (have sex with).

sleepy, *adj.* 1. nemui 眠い (drowsy). 2. kakki ga nai 活気が無い (inactive).

sleeve, *n.* sode 袖 (garment); **keep something up one's sleeve** hisoka ni junbi suru 密かに準備する.

sleigh, *n.* sori そり.

slice, 1. *n.* **a slice of** hitokire no 一切れの. 2. *vb.* kiru 切る (cut through with a knife).

slick, *adj.* 1. josai ga nai 如才がない (shrewdly adroit). 2. mottomorashii もっともらしい (sleek but shallow).

slide, 1. *n.* suberidai 滑り台 (playground); suberi 滑り (act of sliding); geraku 下落 (fall). 2. *vb.* suberu 滑る (move); suberaseru 滑らせる (cause to move).

slight, 1. *n.* bujoku 侮辱 (insult). 2. *adj.* kasuka (na) 微か (な) (small in amount or degree); sasai (na) 些細 (な) (trivial); yaseteiru やせている (slender). 3. *vb.* keishi suru 軽視する (treat as unimportant); bujoku suru 侮辱する (insult).

slim, *adj.* 1. hossori-shiteiru ほっそりしている (slender). 2. wazuka (na, no) わずか (な、の) (slight).

slink, *vb.* koso-koso iku こそこそ行く.

slip, 1. *n.* suberi 滑り (act of slipping); machigai 間違い (mistake); hitokire 一切れ (piece). 2. *vb.* suberu 滑る (glide); suberaseru 滑らせる (cause to glide); akka suru 悪化する (deteriorate); machigaeru 間違える (make a mistake); **slip into (a place)** ... ni kossori hairu ... にこっそり入る (enter); **slip out of (a place)** ... o kossori deru ... をこっそり出る; **slip into/out of (a garment)** ... o sururi to kiru/nugu ... をするりと着る／脱ぐ.

slit, 1. *n.* kireme 切れ目 (narrow opening). 2. *vb.* kirihiraku 切り開く (cut open).

slob, *n.* darashinai ningen だらしない人間 (slovenly person); bukotsumono 武骨者 (boorish person).

slope, 1. *n.* shamen 斜面 (surface, road); kōbai 勾配 (angle); keisha shiteiru/saseru 傾斜している／させる (incline/cause to incline).

sloppy, *adj.* 1. iikagen (na) 好い加減 (な) (careless). 2. darashi ga nai だらしがない (unkempt).

slot, *n.* ana 穴 (opening).

sloth, *n.* taida 怠惰 (laziness).

slouch, 1. *n.* noroma のろま (lazy, inept person). 2. *vb.* darashinaku suwaru だらしなく座る (sit with a slovenly posture).

slow, 1. *adj.* osoi 遅い (not fast); okureteiru 遅れている (delayed, as clock); taikutsu (na) 退屈 (な) (boring); hima (na) 暇 (な) (not busy, slack); atama ga warui 頭が悪い (unintelligent). 2. *vb.*

osoku naru/suru 遅くなる／する (become/make slower); **slow down** sokudo o otosu 速度を落とす (reduce speed); hima ni naru 暇になる (business).

slowly, adv. yukkuri ゆっくり.

slug, n. namekuji なめくじ (mollusk).

sluggish, adj. 1. taida (na) 怠惰 (な) (lazy). 2. noroi のろい (slow).

slumber, 1. n. madoromi まどろみ (nap). 2. vb. madoromu まどろむ (doze).

slump, 1. n. fukeiki 不景気 (economic depression); gekigen 激減 (decline in number); bōraku 暴落 (decline in value). 2. vb. kuzureochiru 崩れ落ちる (drop heavily); kyūraku suru 急落する (drop suddenly).

slur, 1. n. wakarinikui hatsuon 分かりにくい発音 (indistinct speech); chūshō 中傷 (disparagement). 2. vb. mogo-mogo hanasu もごもご話す (pronounce indistinctly); chūshō suru 中傷する (disparage).

slush, n. handoke no yuki 半溶けの雪 (partly melted snow).

sly, adj. zurugashikoi ずる賢い (cunning).

small, adj. 1. chiisai 小さい (small in size, importance, degree, voice, etc.). 2. sukunai 少ない (small in amount).

smart, 1. adj. atama ga ii 頭が良い (intelligent); ereganto (na) エレガント (な) (elegant); surudoi 鋭い (sharp). 2. vb. hiri-hiri suru ひりひりする (be a source of sharp pain); zuki-zuki itamu ずきずき痛む (feel a stinging pain); kutsujoku ni kurushimu 屈辱に苦しむ (suffer from shame).

smash, 1. n. ichigeki 一撃 (blow); wareru oto 割れる音 (noise); ōatari 大当り (smash hit). 2. vb. konagona ni kudakeru/kudaku 粉々に砕ける／砕く (break/cause to break into pieces).

smattering, n. **a smattering of** sukoshi no 少しの.

smear, 1. n. yogore 汚れ (stain); chūshō 中傷 (defamation). 2. vb. nuru 塗る (spread); kegasu 汚す (stain); chūshō suru 中傷する (defame).

smell, 1. n. nioi 匂い (odor); kyūkaku 嗅覚 (sense). 2. vb. nioi ga suru 匂いがする (emit smell); kagu 嗅ぐ (perceive with nose); akushū ga suru 悪臭がする (stink); **smell of** ... no nioi ga suru ... の匂いがする.

smile, 1. n. hohoemi 微笑み. 2. vb. hohoemu 微笑む.

smite, vb. uchinomesu 打ちのめす (strike); **be smitten by** ... ni karareru ... に駆られる (be carried away by).

smith, n. kajiya 鍛冶屋 (blacksmith); kinzaikushi 金細工師 (goldsmith).

smoke, 1. n. kemuri 煙 (visible vapor); kitsuen 喫煙 (act of smoking). 2. vb. tabako o su'u 煙草を吸う (smoke a cigarette); kemuri o dasu 煙を出す (emit smoke); kunsei ni suru 薫製にする (food). 3. **No Smoking** Kin'en 禁煙; **smoking section**

kitsuenseki 喫煙席;
nonsmoking section
kin'eneseki 禁煙席.

smooth, 1. *adj.* nameraka (na) 滑らか (な) (even in surface or movement); junchō (na) 順調 (な) (free from difficulties); maroyaka (na) 円やか (な) (tasting smooth); odayaka (na) 穏やか (な) (tranquil). 2. *vb.* nameraka ni suru 滑らかにする (make smooth of surface); enkatsu ni suru 円滑にする (free from difficulties); **smooth away** torinozoku 取り除く (remove, as obstacles); **smooth out** nobasu 伸ばす (stretch or remove, as wrinkles); **smooth over** yawarageru 和らげる (mitigate).

smug, *adj.* dokuzen-teki (na) 独善的 (な).

smuggler, *n.* mitsuyusha 密輸者.

snack, *n.* keishoku 軽食.

snag, *n.* 1. tosshutsubutsu 突出物 (sharp projection). 2. omoigakenai mondai 思いがけない問題 (obstacle).

snail, *n.* katatsumuri かたつむり.

snake, *n.* hebi 蛇.

snap, 1. *n.* pokiri to iu oto ポキリという音 (sound of breaking); pachiri to iu oto ぱちりという音 (sound of snapping fingers). 2. *vb.* oreru 折れる (break); oru 折る (cause to break); kamu 噛む (bite); shashin o toru 写真を撮る (photograph); **snap up** hittakuru ひったくる (grab).

snatch, *vb.* hittakuru ひったくる (grab); **snatch at** ... o tsukamō to suru ... を掴もう

とする (try to get).

sneak, *vb.* 1. kossori iku/suru こっそり行く／する (go/act furtively). 2.

sneak into ... ni shinobikomu ... に忍び込む (enter); **sneak something into** ... o kossori mochikomu ... をこっそり持ち込む (bring something into).

sneer, 1. *n.* azawarai 嘲笑い. 2. *vb.* azawarau 嘲笑う.

sneeze, 1. *n.* kushami くしゃみ. 2. *vb.* kushami o suru くしゃみをする.

sniff, *vb.* 1. su'u 吸う (inhale). 2. kagu 嗅ぐ (smell).

snip, *vb.* hasami de kiru 鋏で切る (cut with scissors).

snoop, *vb.* nozokimawaru 覗き回る.

snore, 1. *n.* ibiki いびき. 2. *vb.* ibiki o kaku いびきをかく.

snow, 1. *n.* yuki 雪. 2. *vb.* yuki ga furu 雪が降る.

snowstorm, *n.* fubuki 吹雪.

snub, *vb.* mushi suru 無視する (ignore).

snug, *adj.* kaiteki (na) 快適 (な) (comfortable).

so, 1. *adv.* sō そう (in the manner indicated); kono/sono yō ni この／その ように (in this/that way); totemo とても (very); sore hodo それほど (to such a degree); ... mo mata ... もまた (also); sorede それで (therefore). **... or so** ... hodo ... ほど (approximately); **so as to** ... tame ni ... ために (for the purpose of); **so far** kore made wa これまでは; **so far as I am concerned** ... watashi ni kansuru kagiri wa 私に関する限りは; **so**

much son'na ni takusan そんなにたくさん; **so that** ... yō ni ... ように (with the effect that); **and so on** ... nado ... など. 2. *conj.* ... yō ni ... ように (in order that).

soak, *vb.* 1. tsukaru 浸かる (lie in liquid); tsukeru 浸ける (place something in liquid). 2. zubunure ni naru/suru ずぶ濡れになる/する (become/cause to become thoroughly wet). 3. shīmikomu 染み込む (pass through something). 4. **soak up** ... o kyūshū suru ... を吸収する (absorb).

soap, *n.* sekken 石けん (bar).

soar, *vb.* maiagaru 舞い上がる.

sober, *adj.* 1. shirafu (no) 素面 (の) (not drunk). 2. omo-omoshii 重々しい (grave). 3. jimi (na) 地味 (な) (subdued).

social, *adj.* 1. shakai (no) 社会 (の); shakai-teki (na) 社会的 (な) (of human society). 2. shakō (no) 社交 (の) (relating to companionship).

society, *n.* 1. shakai 社会 (human beings generally). 2. kyōkai 協会 (association). 3. jōryūshakai 上流社会 (fashionable people).

sock, *n.* kutsushita 靴下.

sod, *n.* shibatsuchi 芝土 (turf).

soda, *n.* tansan'inryō 炭酸飲料 (drink made with soda water).

soft, *adj.* 1. yawarakai 柔らかい (not strong; fluffy, pleasant, supple). 2. amai 甘い (too kind). 3. hi-arukōru (no) 非アルコール (の) (without alcohol). 4.

soft water nansui 軟水.

soggy, *adj.* becha-becha (no) べちゃべちゃ (の) (soaked).

soil, 1. *n.* tsuchi 土. 2. *vb.* yogosu 汚す.

solace, 1. *n.* nagusame 慰め. 2. *vb.* nagusameru 慰める.

solar, *adj.* taiyō (no) 太陽 (の) (of the sun); **solar system** taiyōkei 太陽系.

soldier, *n.* heishi 兵士.

sole, 1. *n.* ashi no ura 足の裏 (foot); kutsuzoko 靴底 (shoe); karei かれい (fish). 2. *adj.* yui'itsu (no) 唯一 (の) (only).

solemn, *adj.* 1. shinken (na) 真剣 (な) (earnest or serious). 2. ogosoka (na) 厳か (な) (characterized by dignity, awe, or formality).

solid, *adj.* 1. rittai (no) 立体 (の) (three-dimensional). 2. kotai (no) 固体 (の) (having definite shape and size). 3. naka ga tsumatteiru 中が詰まっている (not hollow). 4. ganjō (na) 頑丈 (な) (sturdy). 5. junsui (na, no) 純粋 (な、の) (unmixed).

solitary, *adj.* 1. kodoku (na) 孤独 (な) (lonely). 2. hitori dake (no) 一人だけ (の) (done alone).

soloist, *n.* dokusōsha 独奏者 (of a musical instrument); dokushōsha 独唱者 (singer).

soluble, *adj.* **be soluble** tokeru 溶ける.

solution, *n.* 1. kaiketsu 解決 (settlement or answer). 2. yōkaieki 溶解液 (liquid).

solve, *vb.* kaiketsu suru 解決する.

some, 1. *pron.* aru hitobito/mono ある人々／物 (unspecified people/things); sūnin 数人 (several people); ikutsuka 幾つか (unspecified number of things); ikuraka 幾らか (unspecified in number, several); ikutsuka (no) 幾つか（の）(referring to things); **sū-** 数-(unspecified in number, several); ikuraka (no) 幾らか（の）(unspecified in amount); aru ある (unspecified); nanika (no) 何か（の）(unknown); **to some extent** aru teido ある程度; **some weeks** sūshūkan 数週間. 3. *adv.* yaku 約 (approximately).

somebody, someone, *pron.* dareka 誰か; **someone else** dareka hoka no hito 誰か他の人.

someday, *adv.* itsuka いつか.

somehow, *adv.* 1. nantokashite 何とかして (in some way or other). 2. dōshiteka どうしてか (for an unknown reason).

something, *pron.* nanika 何か.

sometime, *adv.* itsuka いつか.

sometimes, *adv.* tokidoki 時々.

somewhere, *adv.* dokoka どこか.

son, *n.* musuko 息子.

song, *n.* uta 歌.

son-in-law, *n.* giri no musuko 義理の息子.

soon, *adv.* sugu すぐ (in a short time); (... no) sugu ato de (... の) すぐ後で; **sooner or later** osokare-hayakare 遅かれ早かれ; **as soon as** ... (suru) to sugu ni ... (する) とすぐに; **as soon as possible** dekirudake hayaku 出来るだけ早く.

soot, *n.* susu 煤.

soothing, *adj.* 1. kokoronagomu 心和む (for the mind). 2. yawarageru 和らげる (for pain).

sophisticated, *adj.* 1. senren sareteiru 洗練されている (refined). 2. fukuzatsu (na) 複雑（な）(complicated). 3. yonareteiru 世慣れている (worldly).

sophomore, *n.* ninensei 二年生.

sore, *adj.* itai 痛い (painful); **be sore** itamu 痛む.

sorry, *adj.* 1. zan'nen (na) 残念（な）(feeling sad). 2. sumanaku omou すまなく思う (feeling regret); **I am sorry.** Sumimasen. すみません. 3. kinodoku (na) 気の毒（な）(feeling pity); **feel sorry for** ... o kinodoku ni omou ... を気の毒に思う.

sort, 1. *n.* shurui 種類 (type); ningen 人間 (person); **sort of** ikubun ka 幾分か. 2. *vb.* bunrui suru 分類する (classify); **sort out** yoriwakeru 選り分ける.

soul, *n.* 1. tamashii 魂 (spirit, essence, heart). 2. hito 人 (person).

sound, 1. *n.* oto 音 (tone or noise); kaikyō 海峡 (strait). 2. *adj.* sukoyaka (na) 健やか（な）(untroubled); kenkō (na) 健康（な）(healthy); kenjitsu (na) 堅実（な）(firm or reliable); ii jōtai (no) 良い状態（の）(being in a good condition). 3. *vb.* ... yō ni kikoeru ... ように聞こえる (seem); naru 鳴る (make sound); narasu 鳴らす (cause to make sound); hakaru 測る (measure); **sound out** dashin suru 打診する.

sound effects, *n.* onkyōkōka 音響効果.

sour, *adj.* 1. suppai 酸っぱい (taste). 2. fukigen (na) 不機嫌 (な) (cross).

source, *n.* 1. minamoto 源 (origin or beginning). 2. kongen 根源 (basis or root). 3. dedokoro 出所 (source of information).

south, *n.* minami 南.

South Africa, *n.* minami-afurika 南アフリカ.

South America, *n.* minami-amerika 南アメリカ.

southeast, *n.* nantō 南東.

Southeast Asia, *n.* tōnan-ajia 東南アジア.

South Pole, *n.* nankyoku 南極.

southwest, *n.* nansei 南西.

souvenir, *n.* (o)miyage (お)土産.

Soviet Union, *n.* sobieto(-renpō) ソビエト(-連邦); soren ソ連.

soy, *n.* daizu 大豆 (soybean).

soy sauce, *n.* shōyu しょう油.

space, 1. *n.* kūkan 空間 (expanse); basho 場所 (place); aida 間 (interval or distance); kikan 期間 (time); yochi 余地 (room); uchū 宇宙 (outer space). 2. *vb.* aida o oku 間を置く (set some distance apart).

Spain, *n.* supein スペイン.

span, 1. *n.* kikan 期間 (length of time); kyori 距離 (distance). 2. *vb.* ... ni oyobu ... に及ぶ (extend over ...); ... no ue ni kakaru ... の上にかかる (make bridge over ...).

spare, 1. *adj.* yobi (no) 予備 (の) (kept in reserve); yobun (no) 余分 (の) (extra); hima (na) 暇 (な)

(free). 2. *vb.* yōsha suru 容赦する (refrain from hurting or destroying; deal leniently with); kureru くれる (give); habuku 省く (omit); oshimu 惜しむ (use grudgingly).

spark, *n.* hibana 火花.

sparkle, *vb.* 1. kirameku きらめく (shine). 2. awadatsu 泡立つ (effervesce).

sparrow, *n.* suzume 雀.

sparse, *adj.* mabara (na) 疎ら (な).

spat, *n.* karui kenka 軽い喧嘩 (quarrel).

spatter, *vb.* hanetobasu 跳ね飛ばす (splash).

spatula, *n.* hera へら.

speak, *vb.* hanasu 話す (talk, say); **so to speak** iwaba いわば; **speak about** ... ni tsuite hanasu ... について話す; **speak for** ... no daiben o suru ... の代弁をする (represent).

speaker, *n.* 1. hanashite 話し手 (person). 2. supīkā スピーカー (appliance).

spear, *n.* yari 槍.

special, *adj.* tokubetsu (na, no) 特別 (な、の) (particular, extraordinary).

specialty, *n.* 1. senmon 専門 (field of special interest). 2. senmonhin 専門品 (specialty product); jimanryōri 自慢料理 (at a restaurant).

specific, *adj.* 1. tokutei (no) 特定 (の) (definite or particular). 2. komakai 細かい (detailed). 3. seikaku (na) 正確 (な) (precise).

specify, *vb.* shitei suru 指定する.

specimen, *n.* mihon 見本; sanpuru サンプル (sample).

speck, *n.* 1. hanten 斑点 (dot). 2. shimi 染み (stain).

spectacular, *adj.* 1. daikibo (no) 大規模 (の) (grand in scale). 2. migoto (na) 見事 (な) (impressive). 2. waku-waku suru わくわくする (thrilling).

speculate, *vb.* 1. shisaku suru 思索する (meditate). 2. yosō suru 予想する (conjecture). 3. tōki suru 投機する (invest).

speech, *n.* 1. hanashikotoba 話し言葉 (spoken language). 2. gengo-nōryoku 言語能力 (faculty of speaking). 3. enzetsu 演説 (talk before an audience).

speed, 1. *n.* hayasa 速さ (rapidity); sokudo 速度 (rate of motion). **at full speed** zensokuryoku de 全速力で. 2. *vb.* isogu 急ぐ (hurry); shissō suru 疾走する (run with speed); **speed up** hayameru 速める.

speed limit, *n.* seigensokudo 制限速度 (speed of motion).

spell, 1. *n.* jumon 呪文 (incantation); **under a spell** mahō ni kakatte 魔法にかかつて. 2. *vb.* tsuzuru 綴る (words); **spell out** wakariyasuku iu 分かり易く言う (explain plainly).

spelling, *n.* tsuzuri 綴り.

spend, *vb.* 1. tsukau 使う (pay out). 2. sugosu 過ごす (pass time).

sperm, *n.* seishi 精子.

spew, *vb.* haku 吐く (vomit).

sphere, *n.* 1. kyū 球 (round ball). 2. tentai 天体 (heavenly body). 3. bun'ya 分野 (field). 4. han'i 範囲 (range).

spicy. *adj.* piri-piri suru ぴりぴりする (hot or piquant).

spider, *n.* kumo 蜘蛛;

spider web kumo no su 蜘蛛の巣.

spill, *vb.* koboreru こぼれる (run over); kobosu こぼす (let run over).

spin, 1. *n.* kaiten 回転 (spinning motion). 2. *vb.* tsumugu 紡ぐ (make yarn); mawasu 回す (cause to rotate); mawaru 回る (revolve).

spinach, *n.* hōrensō ほうれん草.

spiny, *adj.* 1. toge ga ōi とげが多い (thorny). 2. muzukashii 難しい (difficult).

spirit, *n.* 1. kokoro 心; tamashii 魂 (soul). 2. seishin 精神 (mind, soul). 3. rei 霊 (supernatural being); bōrei 亡霊 (ghost). 4. **spirits** sake 酒 (liquor). 5. **spirits** kibun 気分 (feelings). 6. genki 元気 (vigor).

spiritual, *adj.* 1. seishin-teki (na) 精神的 (な) (pertaining to the mind or soul). 2. rei-teki (na) 霊的 (な) (supernatural). 3. shūkyō-teki (na) 宗教的 (な) (religious).

spit, 1. *n.* tsuba 唾. 2. *vb.* tsuba o haku 唾を吐く.

spite, *n.* 1. akui 悪意 (malice). 2. urami 恨み (grudge). 3. **in spite of** ... nimo kakawarazu ... にもかかわらず.

splendid, *adj.* subarashii 素晴らしい (magnificent).

split, 1. *n.* sakeme 裂け目 (rent); bunretsu 分裂 (separation). 2. *vb.* waru 割る (break); wareru 割れる (become broken); wakeru 分ける (divide, separate, share); wakareru 別れる (be separated, end marriage or friendship).

spoil, 1. *n.* ryakudatsuhin 略奪品 (loot). 2. *vb.* dame ni suru だめにする (damage or ruin, cause to lose good quality); dame ni naru だめになる (be damaged or ruined, lose good quality); amayakasu 甘やかす (spoil someone by indulgence).

spoilsport, *n.* kyōzame na ningen 興醒めな人間.

spontaneous, *adj.* jihatsuteki (na) 自発的 (な) (unpremeditated).

spoon, *n.* supūn スプーン; saji さじ.

spoonful, *n.* hitosajibun 一さじ分; **a spoonful of sugar** hitosaji no satō 一さじの砂糖.

spore, *n.* hōshi 胞子.

spot, 1. *n.* ten 点 (dot); shimi 染み (stain); basho 場所 (place); bubun 部分 (part); **on the spot** sono ba de その場で (at the very place). 2. *vb.* ten o tsukeru 点を付ける (dot); mitsukeru 見つける (notice, find).

spouse, *n.* haigūsha 配偶者.

spout, 1. *n.* sosogiguchi 注ぎ口 (on a container). 2. *vb.* fukidasu 吹き出す (discharge).

spread, *vb.* hirogaru 広がる (extend over); hirogeru 広げる (cause to stretch out); hiromaru 広まる (become known); nuru 塗る (apply a thin layer).

spring, 1. *n.* bane ばね (metal); haru 春 (season); izumi 泉 (water). 2. *vb.* tobiagaru 飛び上がる (jump); **spring over** ... o tobikosu ... を飛び越す; **spring up** shōjiru 生じる

(arise).

sprinkle, *vb.* furikakeru 振り掛ける.

sprout, 1. *n.* me 芽 (shoot). 2. *vb.* mebaeru 芽生える (bud).

spry, *adj.* kakushakutaru かくしゃくたる.

spur, 1. *n.* shigeki 刺激 (incentive). 2. *vb.* hakusha o kakeru 拍車をかける (drive, urge).

spurn, *vb.* hanetsukeru はねつける.

spurt, 1. *n.* funshutsu 噴出 (forceful gush); funpatsu 奮発 (brief increase of effort). 2. *vb.* funshutsu suru 噴出する (gush or eject).

spy, 1. *n.* nusumimiru 盗み見る (watch secretly); hisoka ni shiraberu 密かに調べる (search for); supai o suru スパイをする (act as a spy).

squabble, *n.* kozeriai 小競り合い.

square, 1. *n.* seihōkei 正方形 (geometry); hiroba 広場 (public space); heihō 平方 (math). 2. *adj.* seihōkei (no) 正方形 (の) (being a square); shikakubatte-iru 四角張っている (formed with a right angle); suihei (na) 水平 (な) (level); heihō (no) 平方 (の) (math).

square root, *n.* heihōkon 平方根.

squash, 1. *n.* kabocha かぼちゃ (plant). 2. *vb.* oshitsubusu 押し潰す (crush).

squeeze, *vb.* 1. shiboru 絞る (press together). **squeeze (into)** (... ni) oshikomu (... に) 押し込む (cram); **squeeze out of** ... kara oshidasu ... から押し出す (push out).

squid, *n.* ika いか.

squire, *n.* daijinushi 大地主 (landowner).

squirm, *vb.* mi o yojiru 身をよじる.

squirrel, *n.* risu りす.

squirt, 1. *vb.* fukideru 吹き出る (gush out); fukidasu 吹き出す (cause to gush out).

stab, 1. *n.* sashikizu 刺し傷 (wound). 2. *vb.* tsukisasu 突き刺す.

stable, 1. *n.* umaya 馬屋 (for horses). 2. *adj.* antei shiteiru 安定している (firm, balanced).

stack, 1. *n.* yama 山 (heap); **stacks** shoka 書架 (books). 2. *vb.* tsumikasaneru 積み重ねる (pile in a stack); saiku suru 細工する (arrange unfairly).

staff, *n.* shokuin 職員 (group of workers); kanbu 幹部 (administrators).

stage, 1. *n.* sutēji ステージ; butai 舞台 (in a theater); haiyūgyō 俳優業 (theatrical profession); dankai 段階 (single period or phase). 2. *vb.* jōen suru 上演する (present, as a play); kōdō ni utsusu 行動に移す (plan and carry out).

stagecoach, *n.* ekibasha 駅馬車.

stagger, *vb.* yoromeku よろめく.

stagnant, *adj.* 1. yodondeiru 淀んでいる (not flowing). 2. teitai shiteiru 停滞している (inactive).

stain, 1. *n.* shimi 染み (blotch, blemish); chakushokuzai 着色剤 (coloring agent). 2. *vb.* shimi o tsukeru 染みを付ける (mark with stains); chakushoku suru 着色する

(color).

stairs, staircase, *n.* kaidan 階段.

stake, 1. *n.* kui 杭 (pointed post); kakekin 掛け金 (money wagered); **stakes** shōkin 賞金 (prize money); **at stake** kiki ni hinshite 危機に瀕して (in danger). 2. *vb.* kakeru 賭ける (risk or bet); **stake off** kui de kugiru 杭で区切る.

stalk, 1. *n.* kuki 茎 (plant stem). 2. *vb.* kossori ou こっそり追う (pursue stealthily); noshiaruku のし歩く (march haughtily).

stall, 1. *n.* shikiri 仕切り (compartment); yatai 屋台 (sales booth). 2. *vb.* tomaru 止まる (stop functioning); iinogare o suru 言い逃れをする (delay by evasion); hikinobasu 引き延ばす (delay, put off).

stalwart, *adj.* 1. ganjō (na) 頑丈 (な) (sturdy and robust). 2. yūkan (na) 勇敢 (な) (brave). 3. yuruginai 揺るぎない (firm and steadfast).

stammer, *vb.* domoru 吃る.

stamp, 1. *n.* kitte 切手 (postage); shirushi 印 (mark). 2. *vb.* kitte o haru 切手を貼る (put a paper stamp on); ashi o fuminarasu 足を踏みならす (trample).

stampede, 1. *n.* panikku パニック (panic flight). 2. *vb.* awate-futameku あわてふためく (flee in a stampede); sattō suru 殺到する (rush).

stance, *n.* shisei 姿勢 (position, attitude).

stand, 1. *n.* kiritsu 起立 (act of standing); tachiba 立場 (position taken); baiten 売店

(stall); noriba 乗り場 (taxi); dai 台 (platform). 2. vb. tatsu 立つ (be upright); tateru 立てる (make upright); aru ある (be located); (... de) aru (... で) ある (be in a certain condition); taeru 耐える (endure or bear); **stand by** tasukeru 助ける (help); taiki suru 待機する (be ready); **stand for** arawasu 表わす (represent); **stand out** medatsu 目立つ (be conspicuous); tsukideru 突き出る (protrude); **stand up** tachiagaru 立ち上がる (rise to one's feet); nagamochi suru 長持ちする (be durable).

standard, 1. n. mohan 模範 (approved model); kijun 基準 (basis for comparison); suijun 水準 (norm); hata 旗 (banner); **standard of living** seikatsu-suijun 生活水準. 2. adj. hyōjun 標準 (の) (customary); hyōjun-teki (na) 標準的 (な) (being a model).

stand-in, n. daiyōin 代用員.

standing, 1. n. chi'i 地位 (rank); kikan 期間 (length of continuance); **of long standing** nagai aida no 長い間の. 2. adj. keizoku-teki (na) 継続的 (な) (lasting).

standpoint, n. kenchi 見地.

standstill, n. teishi 停止 (stop).

staple, 1. n. shuyōsanbutsu 主要産物 (principal product); shushoku 主食 (basic food); hotchikisu no hari ホッチキスの針 (for a stapler). 2. vb. hotchikisu de tomeru ホッチキスで留める.

star, n. 1. hoshi 星 (heavenly body, asterisk).

starch, 1. n. denpun でんぷん (food); nori 糊 (stiffening agent). 2. vb. nori o tsukeru 糊を付ける (stiffen).

stare, 1. n. gyōshi 凝視. 2. vb. **stare (at)** (... o) mitsumeru (... を) 見つめる.

starfish, n. hitode ひとで.

start, 1. n. hajime 初め (beginning); kaishiten 開始点 (place or time of beginning); **from the start** hajime kara 初めから. 2. vb. hajimaru 始まる (begin on a course of action); hajimeru 始める (set something moving); shuppatsu suru 出発する (leave); **start doing/to do** ... shidasu ...しだす; **start all over again** hajime kara yarinaosu 初めからやり直す; **to start with** somo-somo そもそも.

startle, vb. bikkuri saseru びっくりさせる; **be startled** bikkuri suru びっくりする.

starve, vb. ueru 飢える (suffer from hunger); uejini suru 飢え死にする (die from hunger).

state, 1. n. jōtai 状態 (condition); kuni 国 (nation); shū 州 (commonwealth of a federal union). 2. vb. noberu 述べる; shitei suru 指定する (express).

stately, adj. dōdō to shiteiru 堂々としている (majestic).

static, adj. ittei (no) 一定 (の) (fixed).

station, 1. n. hōsōkyoku 放送局 (radio or TV); kyoku 局 (headquarters for public services, police, fire); eki 駅 (bus, train, etc.); chūtonchi 駐屯地 (military); **police**

station keisatsusho 警察署. 2. *vb.* haichi suru 配置する (assign place to).

stationery, *n.* binsen 便せん (writing paper); bunbōgu 文房具 (writing materials);

stationery store bunbōguten 文房具店.

station wagon, *n.* wagon-sha ワゴン車.

statistics, *n.* tōkei 統計.

statue, *n.* zō 像.

stature, *n.* 1. shinchō 身長 (person's height). 2. gyōseki 業績 (level of achievement).

status, *n.* 1. mibun 身分 (social standing); chii 地位 (professional standing). 2. jōkyō 状況 (present condition).

statute, *n.* hōki 法規.

staunch, *adj.* yuruginai 揺るぎない (firm).

stay, 1. *n.* taizai 滞在 (temporary residence). 2. *vb.* taizai suru 滞在する (reside temporarily); tomaru 泊まる (be an overnight guest); nokoru 残る (remain at a place); ... mama de iru ... ままでいる (remain through time); tsuzukeru 続ける (continue); **stay away** chikayoranai 近寄らない (keep a distance); **stay up** osoku made okiteiru 遅くまで起きている.

steady, *adj.* 1. chakujitsu (na) 着実 (な) (regular or habitual). 2. antei shiteiru 安定している (stable).

steal, 1. *n.* okaidoku お買得 (bargain). 2. *vb.* nusumu 盗む (commit theft); kossori ugoku こっそり動く (move secretly); **steal away** kossori deru こっそり出る.

stealth, *n.* **by stealth** kossori (to) こっそり (と).

stealthy, *adj.* hisoka (na) 密か (な).

steam, 1. *n.* suchīmu スチーム; yuge 湯気 (vapor). 2. *vb.* musu 蒸す (cook).

steamboat, steamship, steamer, *n.* jōkisen 蒸気船.

steed, *n.* jōyōba 乗用馬.

steel, *n.* tekkō 鉄鋼 (metal);

steel mill tekkōsho 鉄工所.

steep, *adj.* 1. kyū (na) 急 (な) (sloping or rising sharply). 2. hōgai (na) 法外 (な) (unreasonably high).

steer, *vb.* 1. michibiku 導く (lead). 2. mukeru 向ける (direct).

stem, 1. *n.* kuki 茎 (of a plant); gokan 語幹 (of a word). 2. *vb.* tomeru 止める (stop); **stem from** ... ni yurai suru ... に由来する (originate from).

stencil, *n.* kirinuki-katagami 切り抜き型紙.

step, 1. *n.* ayumi 歩み (movement of the foot); ippo 一歩 (distance of such movement); ashioto 足音 (sound); dankai 段階 (stage in a process); **steps** kaidan 階段 (stairs); **take steps** kōdō o okosu 行動を起こす; **step by step** jojo ni 徐々に; **Watch your step!** Ashimoto ni chūi. 足元に注意. 2. *vb.* **step aside** yoko ni noku 横に退く; **step back** hikisagaru 引き下がる; **step in** ... ni hairu ... に入る (enter); naka ni hairu 中に入る (intervene); **step on** ... o fumu ... を踏む; **step out** hamidasu はみ出す.

stepladder, *n.* kyatatsu 脚立.

sterile, adj. 1. fumō (no) 不毛 (の) (barren or fruitless). 2. funin (no) 不妊 (の) (incapable of producing offspring). 3. sakkin sareteiru 殺菌されている (free of germs).

stern, 1. adj. kibishii 厳しい (rigid or severe). 2. n. senbi 船尾 (boat).

stethoscope, n. chōshinki 聴診器.

stew, 1. n. shichū シチュー (dish). 2. vb. torobi de niru とろ火で煮る (cook).

stick, 1. n. eda 枝 (twig); bō 棒 (drumstick or club). 2. vb. tsukisasu 突き刺す (pierce or thrust); tsukisasaru 突き刺さる (have the point embedded); haru はる (glue); tsukeru 付ける (cause to adhere); kuttsuku くっつく (adhere); **stick by** ... ni chūjitsu o tsukusu ... に忠実を尽くす (be faithful to); **stick out** tsukideru 突き出る (protrude); **stick to** ... ni shigamitsuku ... にしがみつく (cling to); **stick up for** mamoru 守る (defend).

sticky, adj. **be sticky** nebaneba suru ねばねばする.

stiff, n. 1. katai 固い (difficult to bend). 2. katakurushii 堅苦しい (formal).

still, n. 1. seijaku 静寂 (calmness or silence). 2. adj. shizuka (na) 静か (な) (quiet); ugokanai ugokanai 動かない (motionless). 3. vb. shizumeru 静める (make calm). 4. adv. mada 未だ (as previously); sore demo それでも (in spite of that); sara ni 更に (further).

still life, n. seibutsuga 静物

画 (painting).

stilts, n. takeuma 竹馬.

stimulate, vb. shigeki suru 刺激する (incite).

sting, 1. n. hari 針 (insect); sashikizu 刺し傷 (wound). 2. vb. sasu 刺す (wound, as a bee); chiku-chiku suru/saseru ちくちくする／させる (feel/cause to feel pain).

stingy, adj. kechi (na) けち (な).

stinking, adj. 1. kusai 臭い (foul-smelling). 2. gesu (na) 下司 (な) (despicable).

stipulate, vb. jōken o tsukeru 条件をつける.

stir, 1. n. kakuhan かくはん (act of mixing); kōfun 興奮 (excitement). 2. vb. kakimazeru 掻き混ぜる (mix); ugoku 動く (move); ugokasu 動かす (cause to move).

stitch, 1. n. hitohari 一針 (complete movement of a needle); nuime 縫い目 (loop of thread); yokobara no gekitsū 横腹の激痛 (sharp pain in the side). 2. vb. nuu 縫う (sew).

stock, n. 1. zaiko 在庫 (goods on hand); **in stock** zaikoari 在庫あり; **out of stock** zaikogire 在庫切れ. 2. takuwae 貯え; 蓄え (supply). 3. kabu 株 (capital or share of a company, stem or trunk). 4. kachiku 家畜 (livestock). 5. iegara 家柄 (line of descent).

stockpile, vb. bichiku suru 備蓄する.

stocky, adj. zunguri shiteiru ずんぐりしている.

stoke, vb. kuberu くべる (tend a fire).

stomach, n. i 胃.

stone, 1. *n.* ishi 石 (small rock); tane 種 (of fruit). 2. *vb.* ... ni ishi o nageru ... に石を投げる (throw stones at).

stool, *n.* koshikake 腰掛け (seat).

stop, 1. *n.* teishi 停止 (act of stopping); owari 終わり (end); tachiyori 立ち寄り (act of stopping at); teiryūsho 停留所 (bus stop); **put a stop to** ... o yamesaseru ... を止めさせる. 2. *vb.* owaru 終わる (come to an end); owaraseru 終わらせる (cause to end); tomaru 止まる (cease moving); tomeru 止める (prevent, cause to halt); saegiru 遮る (block); yamu 止む (of rain); **stop by** (tachi)yoru (立ち)寄る; **stop doing** ... suru no o yameru ... するのを止める; **stop over** tachiyoru 立ち寄る.

stop light, *n.* akashingō 赤信号 (red light).

stopover, *n.* tachiyori 立ち寄り.

storage, *n.* sōko 倉庫 (place).

store, 1. *n.* mise 店 (shop); takuwae 貯え (supply); **in store for** ... o machiukete ... を待ち受けて. 2. *vb.* takuwaeru 貯える; tsumeru 蓄える (accumulate).

stork, *n.* kōnotori こうのとり.

storm, *n.* arashi 嵐.

story, *n.* 1. hanashi 話; monogatari 物語 (tale); uso 嘘 (lie). 2. kiji 記事 (newspaper report). 3. kai 階 (floor).

stout, *adj.* 1. ganjō 頑丈 (na) (strong). 2. futotteiru

(na) (weighty).

stow, *vb.* shimau 仕舞う (put away).

straight, 1. *adj.* massugu (na) 真っ直ぐ (な) (without a bend); tate (no) 縦 (の) (vertical); tadashii 正しい (correct); shōjiki 正直 (na) (honest); sutorēto (na, no) ストレート (な、の) (without water added). 2. *adv.* massugu ni 真っ直ぐに (in a straight line, directly); **straight off** tadachi ni 直ちに (immediately).

straightforward, *adj.* shōjiki (na) 正直 (な) (honest).

strain, 1. *n.* futan 負担 (severe pressure); kinchō 緊張 (tension); nenza 捻挫 (sprain). 2. *vb.* hipparu 引っ張る (pull); sei ippai tsutomeru 精一杯努める (exert to utmost); kujiku 挫く (sprain); kosu 濾す (filter).

straits, *n.* 1. kaikyō 海峡 (water). 2. kukyō 苦境 (a plight).

strange, *adj.* 1. hen (na) 変 (な) (odd). 2. shiranai 知らない (unfamiliar).

stranger, *n.* shiranai hito 知らない人 (unfamiliar person); **be a stranger** hajimete de aru 初めてである (be a first-timer).

strangle, *vb.* shimekorosu 絞め殺す (kill).

straw, *n.* 1. wara わら (dried stalks). 2. sutorō ストロー (for drinking).

strawberry, *n.* ichigo 苺.

stray, 1. *adj.* maigo no 迷子 (の) (lost). 2. *vb.* samayou さまよう (wander); soreru 逸れる (digress).

streak, 1. *n.* suji 筋 (line); **a streak of** ichijō no 一条の. 2. *vb.* suji o tsukeru 筋をつける (mark with streaks); mōshin suru 猛進する (run headlong).

stream, *n.* kawa 川 (river); nagare 流れ (current, flow, river).

street, *n.* tōri 通り.

strength, *n.* 1. tsuyosa 強さ; chikara 力 (power). 2. tsuyomi 強み (strong point).

stretch, 1. *n.* hirogari 広がり (unbroken space); kikan 期間 (period of time). 2. *vb.* nobiru 伸びる (expand or extend); nobasu 伸ばす (cause to expand or extend); hirogaru 広がる (spread); hirogeru 広げる (cause to spread); ganbaru 頑張る (exert oneself to the limit).

stretcher, *n.* tanka 担架.

strict, *adj.* 1. kibishii 厳しい (stern). 2. genmitsu (na) 厳密 (な) (exact).

stride, 1. *n.* ōmata 大股 (long step). 2. *vb.* ōmata de aruku 大股で歩く (walk).

strife, *n.* arasoi 争い.

strike, 1. *n.* utsu koto 打つこと (act of hitting); sutoraiku ストライク (sports); sutoraiki ストライキ (walkout); **be on strike** suto-kekkōchū de aru スト決行中である. 2. *vb.* tataku 叩く (deal a blow); utsu 打つ (hit); suru 擦る (of a match); kōgeki suru 攻撃する (attack); inshō-zukeru 印象付ける (impress); mitsukeru 見つける (discover); **strike a bargain** gōi ni tassuru 合意に達する; **strike down** uchinomesu 打ちのめす (knock down;

beat up); **strike up** hajimeru 始める.

striking, *adj.* 1. subarashii 素晴らしい (outstanding). 2. kirei (na) きれい (な) (attractive).

string, *n.* 1. himo 紐 (cord). 2. gengakki 弦楽器 (musical instrument); gen 弦 (cord for an instrument).

strip, *vb.* 1. hagitoru 剥ぎ取る (remove). 2. nugu 脱ぐ (undress).

strive, *vb.* doryoku suru 努力する.

stroke, *n.* tokei no utsu oto 時計の打つ音 (sound of a striking clock); ichigeki 一撃 (blow); nōsotchū 脳卒中 (cerebral); kaku 画 (single movement of a pen). 2. *vb.* naderu 撫でる (pet).

stroll, *vb.* sansaku 散策.

strong, *adj.* 1. tsuyoi 強い (powerful, sturdy). 2. koi 濃い (tea, coffee, etc.).

strongbox, *n.* kinko 金庫.

structure, *n.* 1. kōzō 構造 (formation). 2. kenchikubutsu 建築物 (building).

struggle, 1. *n.* tatakai 戦い (combat, strong effort). 2. *vb.* tatakau 戦う (combat, strive).

stub, 1. *n.* suisashi 吸いさし (cigarette); hanken 半券 (ticket). 2. *vb.* butsukeru ぶつける (toe).

stubborn, *adj.* ganko (na) 頑固 (な).

stuck-up, *adj.* kidotteiru 気取っている.

stud, *n.* taneuma 種馬 (horse).

student, *n.* gakusei 学生 (college student); seito 生徒 (elementary or secondary school student).

study, 1. *n.* kenkyū 研究; benkyō 勉強; shosai 書斎 (room). 2. *vb.* kenkyū suru 研究する; benkyō suru 勉強する.

stuff, 1. *n.* mono 物 (material, things); bakageta koto 馬鹿げたこと (nonsense); soshitsu 素質 (character, qualities). 2. *vb.* ... ni tsumeru ... に詰める (fill); ... ni tsumemono o suru ... に詰め物をする (cooking).

stuffing, *n.* tsumemono 詰め物.

stuffy, *adj.* kūki ga yodondeiru 空気が淀んでいる (lacking fresh air).

stumble, *vb.* 1. tsumazuku つまずく (trip while walking). 2. shikujiru しくじる (blunder). 3. **stumble across** ... ni dekuwasu ... に出くわす.

stump, *n.* 1. kirikabu 切り株 (tree). 2. nokorihashi 残り端 (part remaining).

stun, *vb.* akke ni toraseru あっけにとらせる (surprise); **be stunned** akke ni torareru あっけにとられる.

stunt, 1. *n.* sakuryaku 策略 (trick). 2. *vb.* samatageru 妨げる (prevent growth of).

stupid, *adj.* baka (na) 馬鹿 (な).

sturdy, *adj.* ganjō (na) 頑丈 (な) (strong).

subconscious, *n.* senzai'ishiki 潜在意識.

subdue, *vb.* 1. seifuku suru 征服する (conquer). 2. osaeru 抑える (control).

subject, 1. *n.* wadai 話題 (conversational topic); shudai 主題 (theme); kamoku 科目 (field of study); shugo 主語

(grammar); shinmin 臣民 (person). 2. *adj.* **be subject to** ... no kanōsei ga aru ... の可能性がある (have the possibility of); ... no shihai o ukeru ... の支配を受ける (be under the domination of); ... no taishō ni nariyasui ... の対象になり易い (be vulnerable to); ... shidai de aru ... 次第である (be dependent on).

subjunctive, *n.* kateihō 仮定法.

sublet, *vb.* matagashi suru suru 又貸しする.

submarine, 1. *n.* sensuikan 潜水艦 (boat). 2. *adj.* kaichū (no) 海中 (の) (being under the sea).

submissive, *adj.* jūjun (na) 従順 (な).

submit, *vb.* 1. teishutsu suru 提出する (present). 2. shitagau 従う (obey).

subordinate, *n.* buka 部下.

subscribe, *vb.* **subscribe to** 1. ... o teiki-kōdoku suru ... を定期購読する (periodical). 2. ... ni kifukin o ataeru ... に寄付金を与える (donate money to). 3. ... ni shomei suru ... に署名する (sign).

subsequent, *adj.* sono go (no) その後 (の).

subside, *vb.* 1. shizumaru 静まる (abate). 2. shizumu 沈む (sink).

substance, *n.* 1. busshitsu 物質 (matter or material). 2. jisshitsu 実質 (substantial quality, content); igi 意義 (significance).

substantial, *adj.* 1. kanari no かなりの (fairly large). 2. ganjō (na) 頑丈 (な) (strong). 3. jisshitsu-teki (na) 実質的 (な) (actual).

substitute, 1. *n.* kawari 代わ

り. 2. *vb.* dairi o suru 代理
をする (person); daiyō suru
代用する (thing).

subtle, *adj.* 1. bimyō (na) 微
妙 (な) (delicate). 2. kōmyō
(na) 巧妙 (な) (crafty).

subtract, *vb.* hiku 引く.

suburb, *n.* kōgai 郊外.

subway, *n.* chikatetsu 地下
鉄.

succeed, *vb.* 1. **succeed (in)**
(... ni) seikō suru (... に) 成
功する (accomplish). 2. ...
ni tsuzuku ... に続く
(follow). 3. **succeed (to)**
(... o) keishō suru (... を) 継
承する (inherit).

success, *n.* seikō 成功.

succession, *n.* 1. renzoku 連
続 (series); **in succession**
tsuzukete 続けて. 2. keishō
継承 (act of inheriting).

successor, *n.* kōkeisha 後継
者.

such, 1. *pron.* sono yō na
mono/hito そのような物／
人 (such a thing/person). 2.
adj. sono yō na そのような
(of the kind indicated). 3.
adv. sore hodo ni mo それほ
どにも (to so large an
extent); taihen 大変 (very).
4. **as such** sono yō na koto
de そのようなことで; **such
as** ... no yō (na) ... のよう
(な); tatoeba 例えば (for
example).

suck, *vb.* 1. su'u 吸う (draw
in). 2. shaburu しゃぶる
(put in the mouth and draw
upon).

sudden, *adj.* totsuzen (no)
突然 (の); **all of a sudden**
totsuzen (ni) 突然 (に).

suds, *n.* awa 泡 (foam).

suffer, *n.* 1. kurushimu 苦し
む (undergo pain). 2.
kōmuru 被る (experience
an unpleasant condition).

3. teika suru 低下する
(deteriorate).

suffix, *n.* setsubiji 接尾辞.

suffocate, *vb.* chissoku
suru/saseru 窒息する／させ
る (die/cause to die).

sugar, *n.* satō 砂糖.

sugary, *adj.* amai 甘い
(sweet tasting).

suggest, *vb.* 1. teian suru 提
案する (offer for
consideration). 2. anji suru
暗示する (imply).

suicide, *n.* jisatsu 自殺;
commit suicide jisatsu
suru 自殺する.

suit, *n.* 1. soshō 訴訟
(lawsuit); **follow suit** ta ni
narau 他に倣う. 2. *vb.* (...
ni) au (... に) 合う; (... ni)
teki suru (... に) 適する (be
fitting or appropriate); (... ni
totte) tsugō ga ii (... にとっ
て) 都合が良い (be
convenient); (... ni) niau (...
に) 似合う (be becoming
to).

suitable, *adj.* fusawashii ふ
さわしい.

suitor, *n.* kyūkonsha 求婚者.

sulfur, *n.* iō 硫黄.

sulk, *vb.* fukureru ふくれる.

sullen, *adj.* 1. fukigen (na)
不機嫌 (な) (bad-tempered).
2. inki (na) 陰気 (な)
(gloomy).

sum, 1. *n.* gōkei 合計 (total);
gōkeikin 合計金 (money);
keisan 計算 (calculation); **in
sum** yō suru ni 要するに
(namely). 2. *vb.* **sum up**
gōkei suru 合計する (total);
yōyaku suru 要約する
(summarize).

summary, *n.* yōyaku 要約.

summer, *n.* natsu 夏.

summit, *n.* chōjō 頂上.

sun, *n.* 1. taiyō 太陽 (the
star). 2. nikkō 日光

(sunshine).

Sunday, *n.* nichiyōbi 日曜日.

sunflower, *n.* himawari ひまわり.

sunlight, *n.* nikkō 日光.

sunny, *adj.* 1. hare (no) 晴れ(の) (weather). 2. hiatari ga ii 日当たりが良い (bright with sunlight). 3. hogaraka (na) 朗らか(な) (cheerful).

sunrise, *n.* hinode 日の出.

sunset, *n.* nichibotsu 日没.

super-, chō- 超-;
superhuman chōningen-teki (na) 超人間的(な).

superficial, *adj.* hyōmen-teki (na) 表面的(な).

superintendent, *n.* 1. kantokusha 監督者 (manager). 2. kanrinin 管理人 (building superintendent).

superior, 1. *n.* jōshi 上司 (person of higher rank in a job). 2. *adj.* ue (no) 上(の) (upper); jōshitsu (no) 上質(の) (of high quality);
superior to ... yori yoi ... より良い (better than).

superlative, *adj.* 1. saijō (no) 最上(の) (best). 2. saijōkyūkei (no) 最上級型(の) (grammar).

supernatural, *adj.* chōshizen (no) 超自然(の).

supersede, *vb.* ... ni totte kawaru ... に取って代わる.

supersonic, *adj.* chō'onsoku (no) 超音速(の).

superstition, *n.* meishin 迷信.

supervise, *vb.* kantoku suru 監督する.

supper, *n.* yūshoku 夕食; bangohan 晩御飯 (evening meal).

supplement, 1. *n.* hosoku 補足. 2. *vb.* hosoku suru 補足する.

supply, 1. *n.* kyōkyū 供給 (act of supplying); kyōkyūhin 供給品 (things supplied); **supplies** zaiko 在庫 (stores); **supplies** hitsujuhin 必需品 (necessities); **supply and demand** jukyū 需給. 2. *vb.* kyōkyū suru 供給する (provide); ataeru 与える (give).

support, 1. *n.* sasae 支え (prop); shiji 支持 (help, patronage); seikatsuhi 生活費 (money to live). 2. *vb.* sasaeru 支える (hold up, bear); shiji suru 支持する (advocate, encourage); fuyō suru 扶養する (provide with money to live).

supporter, *n.* shijisha 支持者 (person).

suppose, *vb.* 1. ... to omou ... と思う (think). 2. ... to katei suru ... と仮定する (assume). 3. **be supposed to** ... to kimerareteiru ... と決められている (be required to); ... to omowareteiru ... と思われている (be considered to).

suppress, *vb.* 1. dan'atsu suru 弾圧する (put down by force). 2. yokusei suru 抑制する (restrain). 3. sashitomeru 差し止める (prevent from appearing).

supreme, *adj.* ichiban (no) 一番(の); saikō (no) 最高(の) (greatest).

sure, *adj.* 1. tashika (na) 確か(な) (certain or reliable). 2. **be sure to** kitto ... suru きっと...する; **make sure** tashikameru 確かめる (confirm).

surface, 1. *n.* omote 表; hyōmen 表面 (outside); **on**

the surface hyōmenjō wa 表面上は. 2. vb. fujō suru 浮上する (come to the surface).

surgeon, n. gekai 外科医.

surgical, adj. gekashujutsu (no) 外科手術 (の).

surly, adj. 1. burei (na) 無礼 (な) (rude). 2. buaisō (na) 無愛想 (な) (unfriendly).

surmise, vb. suisoku suru 推測する.

surname, n. myōji 名字; sei 姓.

surplus, n. yojō 余剰; yobun 余分.

surprise, 1. n. odoroki 驚き. 2. vb. odorokaseru 驚かせる.

surprising, adj. odorokubeki 驚くべき.

surrender, 1. n. kōfuku 降伏 (act of yielding). 2. vb. kōfuku suru 降伏する (yield); hōki suru 放棄する (give up).

surrogate, n. dairinin 代理人 (substitute, judge).

surround, vb. kakomu 囲む.

surroundings, n. kankyō 環境.

survey, 1. n. gaikan 概観 (general view); chōsa 調査 (investigation); sokuryō 測量 (measurement). 2. vb. nagameru 眺める (view); shiraberu 調べる (investigate); sokuryō suru 測量する (measure).

survive, vb. 1. ikinokoru 生き残る (live after a disaster); ... yori nagaiki suru ... より長生きする (outlive). 2. sonzoku suru 存続する (continue to exist).

suspect, 1. n. yōgisha 容疑者. 2. vb. kengi o kakeru 嫌疑をかける (imagine to be guilty); ... to omou ... と思う (imagine); utagau 疑う

(distrust).

suspend, vb. 1. tsurusu 吊す (hang). 2. horyū suru 保留する (keep temporarily inactive).

suspense, n. 1. kinchō 緊張 (tension). 2. fuan 不安 (anxiety).

suspicious, adj. 1. utagaibukai 疑い深い (distrustful). 2. ayashii 怪しい (causing suspicion).

sustain, vb. 1. sasaeru 支える (support). 2. jizoku suru 持続する (maintain).

swallow, 1. n. tsubame つばめ (bird). 2. vb. nomikomu 飲み込む (gulp).

swan, n. hakuchō 白鳥.

swap, 1. n. kōkan 交換. 2. vb. kōkan suru 交換する.

swarm, 1. n. mure 群れ. 2. vb. muragaru 群がる (throng).

swear, vb. chikau 誓う (vow).

sweat, 1. n. ase 汗. 2. vb. ase o kaku 汗をかく.

sweep, 1. n. sōji 掃除 (cleaning of a room); hitofuri 一振り (sweeping movement of the arm). 2. vb. haku 掃く (clean with a broom); kasumeru 掠める (pass over a surface); oshiyoseru 押し寄せる (rush).

sweet, 1. n. (o)kashi (お)菓子 (food). 2. adj. amai 甘い (having the taste of sugar, honey, etc.); kokochiyoi 心地良い (pleasing); yasashii 優しい (gentle).

sweetheart, n. koibito 恋人.

sweet potato, n. satsuma Imo さつま芋.

swell, vb. 1. hareru 腫れる (swell from injury). 2. fukureru 膨れる (puff up).

3. fueru 増える (increase).

swift, *adj.* hayai 速い (quick).

swim, *vb.* oyogu 泳ぐ.

swimming, *n.* oyogi 泳ぎ; suiei 水泳.

swimming trunks, *n.* kaisui-pantsu 海水パンツ.

swimsuit, *n.* mizugi 水着.

swindle, 1. *n.* sagi 詐欺. 2. *vb.* damashitoru 騙し取る.

swing, 1. *n.* buranko ブランコ (suspended seat). 2. *vb.* yureru 揺れる (move to and fro); yuriugokasu 揺り動かす (cause to move to and fro); furimawasu 振り回す (cause to move in a circular movement).

switch, 1. *n.* henka 変化 (change). 2. *vb.* kawaru 変わる (change); kaeru 変える (cause to change); **switch off** kesu 消す; **switch on** tsukeru 点ける.

sword, *n.* katana 刀; ken 剣.

syllable, *n.* onsetsu 音節.

symbol, *n.* 1. shōchō 象徴 (representation). 2. kigō 記号 (sign).

sympathetic, *adj.* 1. dōjō-teki (na) 同情的 (な) (compassionate); **be sympathetic towards ...** ni dōjō suru ... に同情する. 2. dōchō-teki (na) 同調的 (な) (supportive).

sympathy, *n.* 1. dōjō 同情 (compassion). 2. dōi 同意 (agreement).

symphony, *n.* 1. kōkyōkyoku 交響曲 (music). 2. kōkyōgakudan 交響楽団 (orchestra).

symposium, *n.* tōronkai 討論会.

synchronize, *vb.* dōji ni okoru 同時に起こる (occur at the same time); awaseru 合わせる (clocks, etc.).

syndrome, *n.* shōkōgun 症候群.

synonym, *n.* dōgigo 同義語.

synthesize, *vb.* gōsei suru 合成する.

syringe, *n.* chūshaki 注射器 (for injection).

system, *n.* 1. seido 制度 (structure). 2. hōhō 方法 (method).

T

tab, *n.* himo 紐 (flap, strip); sakuin'hyō 索引表 (file tab).

table, *n.* 1. tēburu テーブル (furniture); **at table** shokujichū ni 食事中に (during a meal); **under the table** kossori こっそり (covertly). 2. tabemono 食べ物 (food). 3. hyō 表 (columns of data); **table of contents** mokuji 目次.

tablespoon, *n.* ōsaji 大さじ.

tablet, *n.* 1. jōzai 錠剤 (pill). 2. nōto-paddo ノートパッド (note pad). 3. ita 板 (slab, plaque).

tack, *n.* 1. byō 鋲 (nail). 2. *vb.* byō de tomeru 鋲で留める (fasten with a nail) byō 鋲.

tackle, *vb.* 1. torikumu 取り組む (undertake).

tact, *n.* josainasa 如才なさ (social skill).

tadpole, *n.* otamajakushi おたまじゃくし.

tag, *n.* fuda 札 (label).

tail, *n.* 1. shippo 尻尾 (of an animal). 2. kōbu 後部 (back part).

taint, 1. *n.* oten 汚点

(unfavorable trace). 2. *vb.* kegasu 汚す (tarnish, corrupt morally); sokonau 損なう (spoil, contaminate).
take, *vb.* 1. toru 取る (get into one's possession, react in a specified manner, get, win, steal, occupy or fill time or space, study, swallow medicine, write down); **take a math course** sūgaku o toru 数学を取る. 2. tsukamu 摑む (grasp); nigiru 握る (grip). 3. toraeru 捕える (catch a thief, etc.). 4. erabu 選ぶ (select). 5. uketoru 受け取る (receive and accept willingly, be the recipient of); **take someone's advice** adobaisu o ukeru アドバイスを受ける. 6. eru 得る (obtain). 7. mukaeru 迎える (receive into some relation); **take a wife** tsuma o mukaeru 妻を迎える. 8. kōdoku suru 購読する (subscribe). 9. hiku 引く (subtract). 10. motteiku 持って行く (carry with one). 11. atsukau 扱う (deal with, handle). 12. kakaru かかる (require a certain time). 13. ... ni noru ...に乗る (travel by). 14. shimeru 占める (occupy). 15. kau 買う (buy). 16. nomu 飲む (swallow); taberu 食べる (eat). 17. **take after** ... ni niru ...に似る (resemble); **take apart** bunkai suru 分解する (disassemble); **take away** torisaru 取り去る (remove); **take back** torimodosu 取り戻す (regain possession of); **take care of** ... no mendō o miru ...の面倒を見る (look after); **take for** ... to minasu ...と

見なす (regard as); **take long** jikan ga kakaru 時間がかかる (take time); **take off** ririku suru 離陸する (plane); nugu 脱ぐ (clothing); **take out** toridasu 取り出す (remove); **take over** hikitsugu 引き継ぐ (assume responsibility for); **take part in** ... ni kuwawaru ...に加わる; **take up** toriageru 取り上げる (pick up, choose as a topic); shimeru 占める (occupy space or time); tsuzukeru 続ける (continue); **take a walk** sanpo o suru 散歩をする.
takeoff, *n.* 1. ririku 離陸 (plane). 2. monomane 物真似 (mimicry).
takeout, *n.* mochikaeri 持ち帰り (food).
tale, *n.* hanashi 話; monogatari 物語.
talented, *adj.* sainō ga aru 才能ある.
talisman, *n.* omamori お守り.
talk, 1. *n.* hanashi 話 (speech); kaiwa 会話 (conversation); kaidan 会談 (negotiation session); uwasa 噂 (rumor). 2. *vb.* hanasu 話す (speak, deliver a speech, discuss); sōdan suru 相談する (consult); uwasa suru 噂する (spread a rumor); shaberu しゃべる (chatter); kaiwa suru 会話する (converse). 3. **talk about** ... ni tsuite hanasu ...について話す; **talk big** hora o fuku ほらを吹く; **talk back** kuchigotae o suru 口答えをする; **talk over** hanashiau 話し合う (discuss); **talk to** ... ni hanashikakeru ...に話し掛け

る; **talk with ...** to hanasu
...と話す.

talkative, *adj.* oshaberi (no)
おしゃべり (の).

tall, *adj.* (se ga) takai (背が)
高い.

talon, *n.* tsume 爪.

tame, 1. *adj.* otonashii 大人
しい (gentle); tsumaranai つ
まらない (uninteresting). 2.
vb. narasu 慣らす
(domesticate).

tamper, *vb.* **tamper with ...**
o ijiru ...をいじる (meddle
with); kaizan suru 改ざんす
る (alter, falsify).

tan, 1. *adj.* shakudōshoku
(no) 赤銅色 (の) (of bronze
color). 2. *vb.* kawa o
namesu 皮をなめす
(convert into leather); hi ni
yakeru 日に焼ける (be
tanned by the sun).

tang, *n.* tokuyū no nioi/aji
特有の匂い／味 (special
smell/taste).

tangerine, *n.* mikan みかん.

tangible, *adj.* 1. yūkei (no)
有形 (の) (material); te ni
kanjirareru 手に感じられる
(discernible by touch). 3.
jissai (no) 実際 (の) (real).

tangle, 1. *n.* motsure もつれ
(tangled mass). 2. *vb.*
motsureru もつれる;
kongarakaru こんがらかる
(become confused);
motsuresaseru (snarl) もつ
れさせる.

tap, 1. *n.* karuku utsu koto
軽く打つこと (light blow);
jaguchi 蛇口 (faucet); sen 栓
(plug, stopper). 2. *vb.*
karuku utsu 軽く打つ
(strike lightly); sen o hineru
栓を捻る (open a plug);
jaguchi o hineru 蛇口を捻る
(open a faucet).

taper, *vb.* hosoku/chiisaku

naru 細く／小さくなる
(become thinner/smaller).

tardy, *adj.* 1. osoi 遅い
(late). 2. noroi のろい
(slow).

target, *n.* 1. mato 的 (aim,
mark). 2. mokuhyō 目標
(purpose).

tarnish, *vb.* 1. kumoru 曇る
(lose luster); kumoraseru
(cause to lose luster) 曇らせ
る. 2. kegasu 汚す
(disgrace).

tart, *adj.* suppai 酸っぱい
(sour); shinratsu (na) 辛辣
(な) (sarcastic).

task, *n.* shigoto 仕事 (work).

taste, 1. *n.* mikaku 味覚
(sense); aji 味 (flavor);
hitokuchi 一口 (small
portion of food); shumi 趣味
(sensitivity to beauty, etc.);
be in good/bad taste
shumi ga ii/warui 趣味が良
い／悪い. 2. *vb.* ajiwau 味わ
う (enjoy eating/ drinking;
experience); hitokuchi
taberu 一口食べる (eat a
little bit); shishoku suru 試
食する (sample food); **taste
like ...** no yō na aji ga suru
...のような味がする.

tasty, *adj.* oishii おいしい.

tattered, *adj.* boro-boro
(no) ぼろぼろ (の) (ragged).

tattoo, *n.* irezumi 入れ墨
(design on the skin).

taut, *adj.* 1. (of a rope) pin
to hatta ぴんと張った
(tightly drawn). 2. kinchō
shiteiru 緊張している
(emotionally tense).

tavern, *n.* sakaba 酒場 (bar).

tax, 1. *n.* zeikin 税金 (money
levied). 2. *vb.* zeikin o
kakeru 税金をかける
(impose tax).

tea, *n.* (o)cha (お)茶 (any
tea); kōcha 紅茶 (black tea);

ryokucha 緑茶 (green tea).

teach, vb. 1. oshieru 教える (impart knowledge). 2. sensei o shiteiru 先生をしている (be employed as a teacher).

teacher, n. sensei 先生; kyōshi 教師.

teacup, n. yunomi 湯飲み (for green tea); chawan 茶碗 (for tea ceremony).

teahouse, n. kissaten 喫茶店 (cafe).

teakettle, n. yakan やかん; chagama 茶釜.

teapot, n. kyūsu 急須.

tear, 1. n. yabure 破れ (rip, hole); namida 涙 (teardrop); **in tears** naiteiru 泣いている; **burst into tears** nakidasu 泣き出す; **tear gas** sairui-gasu 催涙ガス. 2. vb. saku 裂く; yaburu 破る (pull apart); yabureru 破れる (become torn); **tear down** torikowasu 取り壊す (pull down).

tease, vb. 1. karakau からかう (make fun of). 2. komaraseru 困らせる (annoy).

teaspoon, n. chasaji 茶さじ.

technical, adj. 1. gijutsujō (no) 技術上 (の); gijutsu-teki (na) 技術的 (な) (pertaining to skilled activity). 2. senmon (no) 専門の (pertaining to a particular art, science, etc.). 3. genmitsu (na) 厳密 (な) (considered in the strict sense).

tedious, adj. taikutsu (na) 退屈 (な).

teenage, adj. jūdai (no) 十代 (の).

teeter, vb. 1. jōge ni yureru 上下に揺れる (seesaw). 2. fura-fura aruku ふらふら歩

く (walk unsteadily).

telegram, n. denpō 電報 (message).

telephone, 1. n. denwa 電話. 2. adj. denwa (no) 電話 (の). 3. vb. (... ni) denwa o suru/kakeru (... に) 電話をする/かける.

telephone directory, n. denwachō 電話帳.

telephone number, n. denwa-bangō 電話番号.

telescope, n. bōenkyō 望遠鏡.

televise, vb. hōei suru 放映する.

tell, vb. 1. iu 言う (say positively, communicate); hanasu 話す (relate). 2. kubetsu suru 区別する (distinguish). 3. oshieru 教える (inform). 4. meijiru 命じる (order). 5. **tell off** hinan suru 非難する (rebuke); **tell on** himitsu o barasu 秘密をばらす (tattle on).

telltale, n. oshaberi おしゃべり (tattler).

temper, 1. n. kigen 機嫌 (particular state of mind); kishitsu 気質 (disposition); kanshaku 癇癪 (outburst of anger); **keep one's temper** gaman suru 我慢する; **lose one's temper** okoridasu 怒り出す; **out of temper** okotte (-iru) 怒っている). 2. vb. yawarageru 和らげる (moderate, soften).

temperate, adj. 1. odayaka (na) 穏やか (な) (not extreme in opinion, statement, etc.). 2. ondan (na) 温暖 (な) (moderate in respect to temperature). 3. hikaeme (na, no) 控え目 (な、の) (moderate in any indulgence).

temperature, *n.* 1. ondo 温度 (degree of warmth or coldness). 2. taion 体温 (body temperature).

temple, *n.* 1. shinden 神殿 (house of worship); (o)tera (お)寺 (Buddhism). 2. komekami こめかみ (side of head).

temporary, *adj.* ichiji-teki (na) 一時的 (な).

tempt, *vb.* 1. yūwaku suru 誘惑する (entice). 2. hikitsukeru 引きつける (appeal).

ten, *n.* jū 十; tō 十.

tenacious, *adj.* 1. tsuyoi 強い (firm). 2. shitsu(k)koi しつ(っ)こい (persistent). 3. **having a tenacious memory** kiokuryoku ga ii 記憶力が良い.

tenacity, *n.* ganbari 頑張り; konki 根気 (perseverance).

tenant, *n.* karite 借手; karinushi 借主 (person or group that rents).

tend, *vb.* 1. sewa o suru 世話をする (take care of); miharu 見張る (watch over). 2. keikō ga aru 傾向がある (be disposed in action or operation); mukau 向かう (lead in a particular direction).

tender, 1. *adj.* yawarakai 柔らかい (soft); yowai 弱い (weak); derikēto (na) デリケート (な) (delicate); osanai 幼い (young or immature); yasashii 優しい (gentle). 2. *vb.* teishutsu suru 提出する (present); teikyō suru 提供する (offer).

tense, 1. *n.* jisei 時制 (grammar). 2. *adj.* kataku hatta 固く張った (stretched tight); katai 硬い、固い (stiff); kinchō shiteiru 緊張

している (emotionally strained).

tension, *n.* 1. chōryoku 張力 (degree of tightness, as of a rope). 2. kinchō 緊張 (emotional strain, strained relationship between parties).

term, 1. *n.* kikan 期間 (period); gakki 学期 (division of a school year); na(mae) 名(前) (name); yōgo 用語 (word, group of words); **terms** jōken 条件 (stipulations); **in terms of** ... ni kanshite ...に関して; **on good terms with** ... to naka ga ii ...と仲が良い; **come to terms** dōi suru 同意する. 2. *vb.* nazukeru 名付ける (name); yobu 呼ぶ (call).

terminate, *vb.* owaraseru 終わらせる (bring to an end); owaru 終わる (end).

terminology, *n.* senmon'yōgo 専門用語 (nomenclature).

terrace, *n.* 1. beranda ベランダ (veranda). 2. niwa 庭 (garden); nakaniwa 中庭 (patio). 3. daichi 大地 (plateau).

terrain, *n.* chi'iki 地域 (stretch of land); chikei 地形 (topography).

terrible, *adj.* 1. kowai 恐い (scary). 2. hidoi ひどい (very bad, distressing).

terrific, *adj.* subarashii 素晴らしい (wonderful).

territory, *n.* 1. ryōdo 領土 (land belonging to a state, etc.). 2. ryōiki 領域 (field of action or thought). 3. nawabari 縄張り (domain, sphere of influence).

terror, *n.* kyōfu 恐怖.

terrorize, *vb.* kowagaraseru

恐がらせる (intimidate, scare).

test, 1. *n.* shiken 試験. 2. *vb.* shiken o ukeru 試験を受ける (undergo a test); shiken o suru 試験をする (conduct a test, subject to a test).

testament, *n.* isho 遺書; yuigon 遺言 (will).

testicle, *n.* kōgan 睾丸.

testify, *vb.* 1. shōgen suru suru 証言する (in court). 2. shōmei suru 証明する (give evidence).

textbook, *n.* kyōkasho 教科書.

texture, *n.* 1. kime きめ (degree of smoothness); tezawari 手触り (tactile quality of a surface). 2. ori 織り (structure of the fibers that make up a textile fabric).

Thailand, *n.* tai タイ.

than, *conj.* ... yori ... より; **more than** ... ijō ... 以上.

thank, *vb.* kansha suru 感謝する; **Thank you.** Arigatō. 有難う; **No, thank you** Kekkō desu. 結構です.

thanks, 1. *n.* kansha no kotoba 感謝の言葉 (words expressing thankfulness); **thanks to** ... no okage de ... のおかげで. 2. *interj.* Arigatō. 有難う.

Thanksgiving Day, *n.* kanshasai 感謝祭.

that, 1. *pron.* are あれ; sore それ; **that is to say** tsumari つまり. 2. *adj.* ano あの; sono その. 3. *adv.* son'na ni そんなに; an'na ni あんなに; **that many, that much** son'na ni takusan そんなに沢山; an'na ni takusan あんなに沢山.

thaw, 1. *n.* yukidoke 雪解け (of snow). 2. *vb.* tokeru 溶

ける (melt); tokasu 溶かす (cause to thaw); yawaragu 和らぐ (become less hostile).

the, *art.* ano あの; sono その (often not translated into Japanese).

theater, *n.* 1. gekijō 劇場 (building). 2. butai 舞台 (place of performance). 3. **the theater** engeki 演劇 (drama).

theft, *n.* nusumi 盗み; dorobō 泥棒.

their, *adj.* karera no 彼らの.

them, *pron.* karera o/ni 彼らを/に.

theme, *n.* tēma テーマ; shudai 主題.

then, *adv.* 1. sono toki その時 (at that time). 2. soshite sugu ni そしてすぐに (immediately after). 3. soshite そして; sore kara それから (next in order). 4. sore ni それに (in addition).

theology, *n.* shingaku 神学.

theory, *n.* 1. riron 理論; gensoku 原則 (principle). 2. gakusetsu 学説 (proposed explanation). 3. iken 意見 (view, guess).

therapy, *n.* chiryō 治療.

there, *adv.* (a)soko de/ni (あ)そこで/に.

thereafter, *adv.* sore igo それ以後.

therefore, *adv., conj.* dakara だから; sorede それで.

thermometer, *n.* 1. ondokei 温度計. 2. **clinical thermometer** taionkei 体温計.

thermos, *n.* mahōbin 魔法瓶.

these, 1. *pron.* korera これら. 2. *adj.* korera (no) これら (の).

they, *pron.* karera 彼ら.

thick, *adj.* 1. futoi 太い (fat, as a cylindrical object or line); atsui 厚い (thick in depth, as a layer). 2. koi 濃い (dense, not watery). 3. tsumatta 詰まった (compact). 4. **thick fog** fukai kiri 深い霧.

thief, *n.* dorobō 泥棒.

thigh, *n.* futomomo 太股.

thin, 1. *adj.* hosoi 細い (slender); usui 薄い (small in extent between two surfaces, as a layer; of relatively slight consistency; lacking volume); yaseta や せた (skinny); mabara (na) 疎ら (な) (sparse). 2. *vb.* hosoku suru 細くする (make slender); usumeru 薄める (make less thick or dense); mabara ni suru 疎ら にする (make sparse).

thing, *n.* 1. mono 物 (material object, substance). 2. koto こと, 事 (intangible object, object of thought). 3. jitai 事態; jōkyō 状況 (things, general state of affairs). 4. jijitsu 事実 (fact). 5. okonai 行い (deed); dekigoto 出来事 (event). 6. **things** yōgu 用具 (utensils). 7. **things** shoyūhin 所有品 (personal possessions).

think, *vb.* 1. omou 思う (believe, regard). 2. kangaeru 考える (reason, meditate). 3. **think about** ... ni tsuite kangaeru ... につ いて考える; **think of** (people, things) ... no koto o omou ...のことを思う; **think of doing** ... shiyō to omou ...しようと思う; **think over** ... ni tsuite yoku kangaeru ... について よく考える.

third person, *n.* san'ninshō

三人称 (grammar).

thirsty, *adj.* 1. **be thirsty** nodo ga kawaiteiru 喉が渇 いている (need to drink). 2. ueteiru 餓えている (eager to obtain something).

thirteen, *n.* jūsan 十三.

thirty, *n.* sanjū 三十.

this, 1. *pron.* kore これ (thing); kochira こちら (person). 2. *adj.* kono この; ko(n)- こ(ん)-; **this country** kono kuni この国; **this week** konshū 今週; **this year** kotoshi 今年.

thistle, *n.* azami あざみ.

thorn, *n.* toge とげ.

thorough, *adj.* 1. tettei-teki (na) 徹底的 (な); kanzen (na) 完全 (な) (complete). 2. kichōmen (na) 几帳面 (な) (meticulous).

those, *pron., adj.* sorera (no) それら (の); arera (no) あれ ら (の).

though, 1. *adv.* dakedo だけ ど; sore demo それでも (however). 2. *conj.* dakedo だけど; sore nimo kakawarazu それにもかかわ らず (notwithstanding that); **as though** ... marude ... ka no yō ni まるで...かのよう に.

thought, *n.* 1. kangae 考え (product of mental activity, idea, opinion). 2. shikō 思 考 (mental activity). 3. shikōryoku 思考力 (capacity of reasoning). 4. omoi 思い (meditation). 5. ito 意図 (intention). 6. kōryo 考慮 (consideration). 7. shisō 思 想 (ideas characteristic of a place or time); **Greek thought** girisha-shisō ギリ シャ思想.

thousand, *n.* 1. sen 千. 2. **thousands (of)** sūsen (no)

数千 (の) (thousands of); takusan (no) 沢山 (の) (great number or amount). 3. **two thousand** nisen 二千; **three thousand** sanzen 三千; **ten thousand** ichiman 一万; **one hundred thousand** jūman 十万.

thread, n. 1. ito 糸 (for sewing). 2. sujimichi 筋道 (line of reasoning).

threat, n. 1. odoshi 脅し (declaration to hurt). 2. kiken 危険 (danger).

three, n. san 三; mittsu 三つ.

three hundred, n. sanbyaku 三百.

thrift, n. ken'yaku 倹約 (economical management).

thrill, vb. waku-waku saseru わくわくさせる (cause to feel excited); waku-waku suru わくわくする (feel excited).

thrilling, adj. waku-waku suru わくわくする (exciting).

thrive, vb. 1. sakaeru 栄える (prosper). 2. yoku sodatsu よく育つ (grow well).

throat, n. nodo 喉.

throne, n. 1. ōza 王座 (chair). 2. ōi 王位 (office of a sovereign).

through, prep. 1. ... o tōtte ...を通って (in at one end and out at the other, by way of, across). 2. ... no aida zutto ...の間ずっと (throughout). 3. ... no kekka ... の結果 (as a result of). 4. ... ni yotte ... によって (by means of). 5. ... made ...まで (to and including). 6. **be through** owaru 終わる (be over with).

throughout, 1. prep. ... no

itaru tokoro ni ... の至る所に (in all parts of); ... no aida zutto ...の間ずっと (from beginning to end). 2. adv. itaru tokoro de/ni 至る所で/に (in every part).

throw, 1. n. nageru koto 投げること (act of throwing). 2. vb. nageru 投げる (cast, hurl, send forth); nagetaosu 投げ倒す (cause to fall on the ground). 3. **throw away** rōhi suru 浪費する (waste); nogasu 逃す (miss); suteru 捨てる (discard). **throw in** omake suru おまけする (add as a bonus); **throw over** misuteru 見捨てる (forsake); **throw up** haku 吐く (vomit).

thumb, n. oyayubi 親指 (of the hand).

thunder, 1. n. raimei 雷鳴 (noise accompanying lightning). 2. vb. kaminari ga naru 雷が鳴る (give forth thunder).

Thursday, n. mokuyōbi 木曜日.

thus, adv. 1. kono yō ni (shite) このように (して) (in this way). 2. sore de それで (consequently). 3. **thus far** kore made no tokoro これまでのところ (to this extent).

ticket, n. 1. kippu 切符; ken 券. 2. jōshaken 乗車券 (for vehicular travel); nyūjōken 入場券 (admission); chūshaihanken 駐車違反券 (for parking violation); **ticket office** kippu'uriba 切符売り場; **ticket window** kippuhanbai-madoguchi 切符販売窓口.

tickle, vb. 1. kusuguru くすぐる (touch with the fingers). 2. manzoku saseru 満足させる (gratify).

tide, *n.* 1. shio no michihi 潮
の満ち干 (periodic rise and
fall of the waters). 2.
chōryū 潮流 (current of
water). 3. nagare 流れ
(trend). 4. ugoki 動き
(movement).

tie, 1. *n.* himo 紐 (string);
nekutai ネクタイ (necktie);
tai タイ (sports). 2. *vb.*
musubu 結ぶ (bind); tai ni
naru タイになる (sports);
tie down shibaritsukeru 縛
りつける (confine); **tie up**
tomeru 留める (secure by
tying); **be tied up** isogashii
忙しい (be busy).

tiger, *n.* taiga タイガー; tora
虎.

tight, *adj.* 1. kitsui きつい
(firmly fixed in place, fitting
closely, scarce, as money).
2. katai 固い (firmly
knotted). 3. kataku hatta 固
く張った (taut, as a rope).
4. bōsui (no) 防水 (の)
(waterproof); kimitsusei
(no) 気密性 (の) (air-tight).
5. tsumatta 詰まった (fully
packed). 6. muzukashii 難
しい (difficult). 7. kibishii
厳しい (rigid).

tile, *n.* tairu タイル (any
tile); kawara 瓦 (roof tile).

tilt, 1. *n.* katamuki 傾き;
naname 斜め (slope). 2. *vb.*
katamukeru 傾ける (cause
to incline); katamuku
(incline) 傾く.

time, *n.* 1. jikan 時間
(duration, definite point in
time, hour, particular period
in a day, appointed time).
2. kikan 期間 (period). 3.
jidai 時代 (era, period).
4. -do/-kai -度／-回 (each
occasion of a recurring
action or event); **do
something five times** ... o

go-do/-kai suru ... を五度／
～回する. 5. **times** -bai
-倍 (multiplication); **five
times faster** gobai hayai 五
倍早い. 6. **ahead of time**
hayaku 早く; **ahead of
one's time** jisei ni sakinjite
時勢に先んじて; **all the
time** zutto ずっと; **a long
time** nagai aida 長い間; **a
long time ago** mukashi 昔;
at the same time dōji ni 同
時に (simultaneously); **at
times** tokidoki 時々;
behind the times
jidaiokure (no) 時代遅れ
(の); **for a time** shibaraku
暫く (for a while); **for the
time being** ichiji-teki (ni)
一時的 (に) (temporarily);
sashiatatte 差し当たって
(for the present); **from
time to time** tokidoki 時々;
to have a good time
tanoshimu 楽しむ; **in time**
jikan'nai ni 時間内に (early
enough); chikai uchi ni 近い
うちに (in the future); **it's
time to do** ... suru jikan
da/desu ...する時間だ／で
す; **kill time** jikan o
tsubusu 時間を潰す; **on
time** teikoku ni 定刻に
(punctually); **once upon a
time** mukashi-mukashi
昔々; **What time is it?** Ima
nanji desu ka. 今何時です
か.

times, *prep.* kakeru 掛ける
(multiplied by); **five times
six** go kakeru roku 五掛け
る六.

timid, *adj.* okubyō (na) 臆病
(な).

tin, *n.* 1. buriki ブリキ
(tinplate). 2. suzu 錫
(element). 3. **tin can** kan
缶; **tinfoil** gingami 銀紙.

tinker, *vb.* **tinker with**

ijikuru いじくる (try to repair clumsily).

tint, 1. *n.* iro(ai) 色(合い) (hue). 2. *vb.* iro o tsukeru 色をつける (give a tint to).

tiny, *adj.* chiisai 小さい.

tip, 1. *n.* hashi 端; saki 先 (end). 2. *vb.* katamukeru 傾ける (cause to tilt); taosu 倒す (cause to overturn).

tiptoe, on tiptoe tsumasakidatte 爪先立って.

tire, *vb.* tsukareru 疲れる (become weary); tsukare saseru 疲れさせる (make weary).

tired, *adj.* 1. tsukareteiru／tsukareta 疲れている／疲れた (exhausted). 2. akiteiru 飽きている (bored). 3. chinpu (na) 陳腐 (な) (hackneyed).

tissue, *n.* 1. soshiki 組織 (body). 2. tisshū ティッシュー (tissue paper; facial tissue).

to, *prep.* 1. ... e/ni ...へ／に (so as to reach, toward, on). 2. ... made ...まで (until). 3. **in order to do** ... suru tame ni ...するために; **to and fro** achikochi ni あちこちに.

toad, *n.* kaeru 蛙; hikigaeru ひき蛙.

toast, 1. *n.* kanpai 乾杯 (ceremonial drink). 2. *vb.* yaku 焼く (brown bread, cheese, etc.); kanpai suru 乾杯する (drink to).

today, *n., adv.* 1. kyō 今日 (this present day). 2. kon'nichi 今日 (the present age, nowadays).

toe, *n.* 1. ashi no yubi 足の指 (of the foot). 2. tsumasaki 爪先 (forepart of a shoe).

together, *adv.* 1. issho ni 一

緒に; tomo ni 共に (in a single mass, in cooperation).

together with ... to issho ni ... と一緒に. 2. dōji ni 同時に (at the same time).

toil, 1. *n.* kurō 苦労; nangi 難儀 (laborious task). 2. *vb.* nangi suru 難儀する (move with great effort); akuseku suru あくせくする (labor arduously).

toilet, *n.* 1. benki 便器 (toilet fixture). 2. (o)tearai (お)手洗い (bathroom); keshōshitsu 化粧室 (powder room). 3. mizukuroi 身繕い (dressing oneself).

token, *n.* 1. shirushi 印; shōchō 象徴 (representation). 2. shōko 証拠 (evidence). 3. kinenhin 記念品 (memento). 4. jōshayōkoin 乗用車コイン (metal disk for riding a bus, etc.). 5. **by the same token** dōyō ni 同様に (in the same manner); **in token of** ... no shirushi ni ...の印に (as a sign of).

tolerant, *adj.* kan'yō (na) 寛容 (な) (lenient).

toll, *n.* 1. tsūkōryōkin 通行料金 (fee for passage). 2. tsūwaryōkin 通話料金 (fee for telephone call); **toll call** chōkyoridenwa 長距離電話 (long distance call).

tomorrow, *n., adv.* ashita 明日; **tomorrow morning/night** ashita no asa/ban 明日の朝／晩; **the day after tomorrow** asatte あさって.

tone, *n.* 1. oto 音 (sound). 2. onshitsu 音質 (quality of sound); seishitsu 声質 (quality of voice); gochō 語調 (expressive quality of

voice). 3. shikichō 色調
(hue). 4. yōsu 様子
(appearance, manner).

tongue, n. 1. shita 舌
(organ). 2. kotoba 言葉
(language); kokugo 国語
(national language);
mother tongue bokokugo
母国語.

tonight, n., adv. kon'ya 今
夜; konban 今晩.

too, adv. 1. ... mo (mata) ...
も (又); sono ue ni その上に
(also, in addition). 2. amari
ni 余りに; ... sugiru ... 過ぎ
る (excessively); **Too bad!**
Zan'nen da. 残念だ; **too
many** ōsugiru 多過ぎる.

tool, n. dōgu 道具.

tooth, n. ha 歯.

toothpaste, n. nerihamigaki
練り歯磨き.

toothpick, n. tsumayōji 爪
楊枝.

top, 1. n. chōten 頂点
(highest point); ichiban 一番
(highest rank or quality);
futa 蓋 (lid); koma こま
(toy). 2. adj. ichiban ue
(no) 一番上 (の) (situated at
the highest point, highest in
degree). 2. vb. kabuseru 被
せる (put something on top
of); shinogu 凌ぐ (surpass).

topic, n. 1. tēma テーマ
(theme of a discourse). 2.
wadai 話題 (subject of
conversation).

topping, n. 1. sōsu ソース
(sauce). 2. kazari 飾り;
soemono 添え物 (garnish).

torch, n. taimatsu 松明
(flaming stick).

torment, 1. n. kurushimi 苦
しみ (agony). 2. vb.
kurushimeru 苦しめる
(inflict agony on).

tornado, n. tatsumaki 竜巻.

tortoise, n. kame 亀.

torture, 1. n. kutsū 苦痛
(anguish); gōmon 拷問 (act
of inflicting severe pain). 2.
vb. kurushimeru 苦しめる
(inflict with anguish);
gōmon ni kakeru 拷問にか
ける (subject to torture).

toss, vb. 1. nageru 投げる
(throw). 2. korogemawaru
転げ回る (writhe about);
yureru 揺れる (rock). 3.
karuku mazeru 軽く混ぜる
(mix lightly).

total, 1. n. gōkei 合計; zenbu
全部 (sum, full amount); **in
total** zenbu de 全部で. 2.
adj. zenbu (no) 全部 (の);
gōkei (no) 合計 (の)
(comprising the whole);
mattaku (no) 全く (の)
(complete). 3. vb. gōkei
suru 合計する (bring to a
total).

totality, n. zentaisei 全体性
(state of being total).

touch, 1. n. fureru koto 触れ
ること (act of touching);
shokkaku 触覚 (sense);
tezawari 手触り (feel);
sesshoku 接触 (coming or
being in contact with);
renraku 連絡
(communication); udemae
腕前 (skill); kimi 気味 (slight
addition or change, trace); **a
touch of** sukoshi no 少し
の; **keep in touch with** ...
to renraku shiau ...と連絡し
合う; **be out of touch**
tōzakatteiru 遠ざかってい
る. 2. vb. (... ni) fureru (...
に) 触れる (put the hand
on, be adjacent to, strike
lightly, deal with as a topic);
...to narabu ...と並ぶ (be
equal with); ... ni kankei
suru ... に関係する
(concern); kandō saseru 感
動させる (cause to feel

sympathy); **touch on** ... ni fureru ...に触れる (refer to).

tough, *adj.* 1. katai 固い (not easily broken, hard to chew). 2. ganjō (na) 頑丈 (な) (sturdy). 3. muzukashii 難しい (difficult). 4. ganko (na) 頑固 (な) (stubborn).

tour, 1. *n.* ryokō 旅行 (trip); kengaku 見学 (trip through a place to view or inspect it). 2. *vb.* ryokō suru 旅行する (make a tour); kengaku suru 見学する (travel through a place for viewing or inspection).

tourism, *n.* kankō 観光.

tourist, *n.* kankōkyaku 観光客.

toward, *prep.* 1. ... no hō e/ni ...の方へ／に (in the direction of). 2. ... no tame ni ...のために (for, as a contribution to). 3. ... ni taishite ...に対して (turned to). 4. ... goro/koro ...頃 (shortly before in time).

tower, *n.* tō 塔.

town, *n.* 1. machi 町 (populated area smaller than city); **town hall** yakuba 役場; yakusho 役所. 2. machi no chūshin 町の中心 (center of a city).

toy, *n.* omocha おもちゃ; gangu 玩具.

track, 1. *n.* atokata 跡形 (mark); michi 道 (path); senro 線路 (train). 2. *vb.* ato o ou 後を追う (follow the track of); **track down** tsukitomeru 突き止める.

trade, 1. *n.* shōgyō 商業; torihiki 取り引き (commerce); bōeki 貿易 (foreign trade); kōkan 交換 (exchange of things); shokugyō 職業 (occupation). 2. *vb.* kōkan

suru 交換する (exchange); **trade in** akinau 商う; torihiki o suru 取り引きをする (buy and sell).

trademark, *n.* shōhyō 商標.

traditional, *adj.* dentō-teki (na) 伝統的 (な).

traffic, 1. *n.* kōtsū 交通 (traveling persons and things); **traffic jam** kōtsūjūtai 交通渋滞; **traffic light, signal** kōtsūshingō 交通信号; baibai 売買 (buying and selling). 2. *vb.* baibai suru 売買する (buy and sell).

tragedy, *n.* higeki 悲劇 (drama, sad event).

trail, 1. *n.* ato 跡 (tracks, traces); michi 道 (path). 2. *vb.* hikizuru 引きずる (drag along the ground); ato ni hiku 後に引く (draw behind); ou 追う (follow).

train, 1. *n.* ressha 列車 (railway train); gyōretsu 行列 (moving line of people, vehicles, etc.). 2. *vb.* kyōiku suru 教育する (instruct); kyōiku o ukeru 教育を受ける (undergo instruction); kunren suru 訓練する (make fit or proficient by exercise or practice).

training, *n.* kunren 訓練 (exercise, practice).

trait, *n.* tokuchō 特徴 (characteristic).

trample, *vb.* fumitsukeru 踏みつける.

tranquil, *adj.* shizuka (na) 静か (な) (quiet); heiwa (na) 平和 (な) (peaceful).

tranquilizer, *n.* chinseizai 鎮静剤.

transcend, *vb.* 1. chōetsu suru 超越する (rise above ordinary limits). 2. masaru 勝る (excel).

transcribe, *vb.* 1. utsusu 写す (copy). 2. kiroku suru 記録する (make record of).

transcript, *n.* 1. utsushi 写し (copy). 2. seisekihyō 成績表 (copy of one's academic record).

transfer, 1. *n.* idō 移動 (moving from one place to another); norikaeken 乗り換え券 (ticket for passenger). 2. *vb.* utsusu/utsusu 移る／移す; idō suru/saseru 移動する／させる (move/cause to move from one place to another); jōto suru 譲渡する (make over the legal title of).

transfuse, *vb.* yuketsu suru 輸血する (perform a blood transfusion).

transitive verb, *n.* tadōshi 他動詞.

translate, *vb.* hon'yaku suru 翻訳する (change from one language to another).

transmission, *n.* 1. dentatsu 伝達 (act of sending out, communication). 2. hōsō 放送 (broadcasting).

transparent, *adj.* tōmei (na) 透明 (な).

transplant, *vb.* 1. utsusu 移す (remove from one place to another). 2. ishoku suru 移植する (plant, body organ).

transport, 1. *n.* yusō 輸送 (conveyance). 2. *vb.* hakobu 運ぶ (convey).

trap, 1. *n.* wana 罠 (snare). 2. *vb.* wana ni kakeru 罠に掛ける (ensnare); tojikomeru 閉じ込める (confine).

trash, *n.* 1. garakuta がらくた; kuzu 屑 (worthless thing, garbage). 2. tawagoto 戯言 (nonsense).

travel, 1. *n.* tabi 旅; ryokō 旅行 (journey); ugoki 動き (movement); **travel agency** ryokō-dairiten/-gaisha 旅行代理店／〜会社. 2. *vb.* ryokō suru 旅行する (journey); susumu 進む (move).

tray, *n.* bon 盆 (flat, shallow container).

tread, 1. *n.* arukiburi 歩き振り (manner of walking); ashioto 足音 (walking sound). 2. *vb.* aruku 歩く (walk); fumu 踏む (trample).

treasure, 1. *n.* zaisan 財産 (accumulated wealth); takara 宝 (valuable thing, jewel). 2. *vb.* taisetsu ni suru 大切にする (retain carefully, cherish); shimau 仕舞う (put away for future use).

treat, 1. *n.* ogori 奢り (food, etc., paid for by another). 2. *vb.* atsukau 扱う (deal with); motenasu もてなす (entertain); ogoru 奢る (provide food at one's own expense); chiryō suru 治療する (give medical care to).

treatment, *n.* 1. atsukai 扱い (act, manner, or process of dealing with). 2. chiryō 治療 (medical).

treaty, *n.* jōyaku 条約 (formal agreement between states).

tree, *n.* ki 木.

tremble, *vb.* furueru 震える (shake, as from cold, etc.); yureru 揺れる (quake).

trench, *n.* mizo 溝 (ditch).

trend, *n.* 1. ryūkō 流行 (vogue). 2. nagare 流れ (general course); keikō 傾向 (tendency).

trial, n. 1. saiban 裁判 (judicial). 2. shiken 試験 (test). 3. kokoromi 試み (attempt). 4. shiren 試練 (act of being tested, hardship). 5. kurō no tane 苦労の種 (source of distress). 6. **on trial** tameshi ni 試しに (in order to test); **stand trial** saiban ni kakerareru 裁判にかけられる (be tried in a court); **trial and error** shikō sakugo 試行錯誤.

triangle, n. sankakkei 三角形.

tribe, n. buzoku 部族; shuzoku 種族 (people united by common descent).

tribute, n. 1. kansha no okurimono 感謝の贈り物 (gift given as an expression of gratitude). 2. sanji 賛辞 (praise); **pay tribute to ...** ni sanji o okuru ...に賛辞を送る.

trick, 1. n. keiryaku 計略 (stratagem); warufuzake 悪ふざけ (prank); kotsu こつ (knack); tejina 手品 (feat of magic). 2. vb. damasu だます (deceive).

trifle, 1. n. kudaranai mono/koto 下らない物/事 (useless or trivial thing or matter); **a trifle** chotto ちょっと (a little bit, somewhat). 2. vb. **trifle away** rōhi suru 浪費する; **trifle with** moteasobu 弄ぶ (play with); zonzai ni atsukau ぞんざいに扱う (deal with without respect).

trigger, 1. n. hikigane 引き金 (of a gun). 2. vb. hikiokosu 引き起こす (provoke).

trim, 1. adj. kichin to shita きちんとした (neat). 2. vb.

kichin to suru きちんとする (make tidy); kichin to karu きちんと刈る (make neat by cutting); kazaru 飾る (ornament).

trip, 1. n. ryokō 旅行 (journey); tsumazuki つまずき (stumble). 2. vb. tsumazuku つまずく (stumble); tsumazukaseru つまずかせる (cause to stumble); shikujiru しくじる (make a mistake).

triple, adj. sanbai (no) 三倍 (の) (three times as great); sanjū (no) 三重 (の) (threefold).

triplets, n. mitsugo 三つ子 (three offspring born at one birth).

tripod, n. sankyaku 三脚.

triumph, 1. n. shōri 勝利 (victory or success). 2. vb. shōri suru 勝利する; uchikatsu 打ち勝つ (be victorious).

trivia, n. kudaranai mono/koto 下らない物/事 (inconsequential things or matters).

troop, n. 1. ichidan 一団 (group). 2. **troops** guntai 軍隊.

tropics, n. nettai 熱帯.

trouble, 1. n. kon'nan 困難 (difficulty); kurō 苦労 (distress); mondai 問題 (annoyance, problem); mendō 面倒 (inconvenience); shinpai 心配 (worry); kiken 危険 (danger); **be in trouble** komatteiru 困っている. 2. vb. shinpai saseru 心配させる (cause to be worried); mendō o kakeru 面倒をかける (cause inconvenience to); kurushimeru 苦しめる (cause pain to).

troublesome, *adj.* yakkai (na) 厄介 (な); muzukashii 難しい.

trout, *n.* masu ます.

trowel, *n.* kote こて.

true, *adj.* 1. hontō (no) 本当 (の) (actual, sincere, genuine). 2. jissai (no) 実際 (の) (actual). 3. honmono (no) 本物 (の) (real, genuine). 4. seijitsu (na) 誠実 (な) (sincere). 5. seikaku (na) 正確 (な) (exact). 6. **come true** jitsugen suru 実現する; **be true to** ...ni chūjitsu de aru ...に忠実である.

true-life, *adj.* jijitsu ni motozuku 事実に基づく.

truly, *adv.* hontō ni 本当に (sincerely, really); **yours truly** keigu 敬具 (in complimentary close of letter).

trunk, *n.* miki 幹 (of a tree); dō(tai) 胴(体) (of a human body); hana 鼻 (of an elephant).

trust, 1. *n.* shinrai 信頼; shin'yō 信用 (belief); sekinin 責任 (responsibility); sewa 世話 (care). 2. *vb.* shinrai suru 信頼する; shin'yō suru 信用する (believe, have faith in); ate ni suru 当てにする (rely on); makaseru 任せる (entrust); tayoru 頼る.

truth, 1. *n.* shinjitsu 真実 (true fact). 2. shinjitsusei 真実性 (quality of being true). 3. seijitsusa 誠実さ (sincerity). 4. shinri 真理 (principle, concept). 5. **in truth** hontō ni 本当に; **to tell the truth** jitsu wa 実は.

truthful, *adj.* 1. shinjitsu (no) 真実 (の) (conforming to truth). 2. shōjiki (na) 正直 (na) (telling the truth).

try, 1. *n.* kokoromi 試み (attempt); doryoku 努力 (effort). 2. *vb.* tamesu 試す (test); kokoromiru 試みる (attempt); doryoku suru 努力する (make an effort); saiban ni kakeru 裁判にかける (examine judicially); **try on** ... o kite miru ...を着てみる (try on a garment); **try to do** ... shiyō to suru ... しようとする.

tryout, *n.* shien 試演 (theater).

T-shirt, *n.* tī-shatsu ティーシャツ.

tub, *n.* 1. oke 桶 (wide, round container). 2. furo'oke 風呂桶 (bathtub).

tuck, *vb.* oshikomu 押し込む (thrust); tsumekomu 詰め込む (cram).

Tuesday, *n.* kayōbi 火曜日.

tug, *vb.* 1. hipparu 引っ張る (pull hard). 2. hikizuru 引きずる (move by pulling).

tuition, *n.* jugyōryō 授業料 (fee).

tumble, *vb.* 1. korogaru 転がる (roll). 2. ochiru 落ちる (fall). 3. tsumazuku つまずく (stumble).

tuna, *n.* maguro 鮪.

tune, 1. *n.* kyoku 曲 (melody); tadashii chōshi 正しい調子 (proper condition); **in/out of tune** oto ga atte/hazurete 音が合って／外れて (music); **in/out of tune with** ... ni au/awanai に合う／合わない (compatible/incompatible with). 2. *vb.* chōritsu suru 調律する (adjust musical instrument); chōsetsu suru 調節する (adjust a motor, etc.); **tune in** chan'neru o

awaseru チャンネルを合わせる (TV).

turf, n. shibafu 芝生 (grassy earth).

turkey, n. shichimenchō 七面鳥.

turn, 1. n. kaiten 回転 (revolution, rotation, twirl); henka 変化 (change); ban 番 (shift); keikō 傾向 (inclination); **at every turn** itsumo いつも (at every moment); **in turn** junban ni 順番に (in due order); **take turns** kōtai de suru 交代でする. 2. vb. mawaru 回る (move around); mawasu 回す (cause to move around, as a faucet); magaru 曲がる (at corner); kawaru 変わる (change). 3. **turn around** furimuku 振り向く; **turn back** kaeru/kaesu 返る／返す (return/cause to return); **turn down** kotowaru 断る (reject); **turn in** teishutsu suru 提出する (submit); **turn into** ... ni naru ...になる (become); **turn off** kesu 消す (gas, light, etc.); shimeru 閉める (faucet); **turn on** tsukeru 点ける (gas, light, etc.); **turn out to be** ... kekkyoku ... to naru 結局...となる (become ultimately); **turn to the right** migi ni magaru 右に曲がる; **turn up** tsuku 着く (arrive).

turnip, n. kabu かぶ.

turnover, n. 1. kaiten 回転 (act of turning over). 2. uriagedaka 売り上げ高 (total amount of business done in a given time). 3. rōdōsha-idōritsu 労働者移動率 (rate of replacement of employees); shōhin-

kaitenritsu 商品回転率 (rate of replacement of goods).

turquoise, n. toruko-ishi トルコ石 (gemstone).

turtle, n. kame 亀.

turtledove, n. kijibato 雉子鳩.

tutor, 1. n. kateikyōshi 家庭教師 (private tutor). 2. vb. oshieru 教える.

tuxedo, n. takishīdo タキシード.

twelve, n. jūni 十二.

twenty, n. nijū 二十.

twice, adv. 1. nido 二度; nikai 二回 (two times). 2. nibai ni 二倍に (in twofold quantity).

twin, n. futago 双子 (one of two offspring born at the same time).

twin bed, n. tsuin(-beddo) ツイン(ベッド).

twine, 1. n. himo 紐 (cord). 2. vb. makitsuku 巻き付く (wind around); yoru よる (twist together).

twinkle, 1. n. kirameki きらめき; matataki 瞬き (brightness). 2. vb. kirameku きらめく; matataku 瞬く (shine).

twist, 1. n. magari 曲がり (curve); kaiten 回転 (spin); waikyoku 歪曲 (distortion, as of meaning); igai na tenkai 以外な展開 (unexpected development). 2. vb. yoriawaseru より合わせる (combine by winding); yugameru 歪める (distort); makitsukeru 巻き付ける (wind around something); magaru 曲がる (bend, wind about); mageru 曲げる (cause to bend); mawasu 回す (turn).

two, n. ni 二; futatsu 二つ.

two hundred, n. nihyaku

二百.

tycoon, *n.* ōdatemono 大立て者.

type, *n.* 1. katsuji 活字; taipu タイプ (printing). 2. shurui

種類 (kind, class). 3. mihon 見本; tenkei 典型 (representative specimen).

typical, *adj.* tenkei-teki (na) 典型的 (な).

U

udder, *n.* chichi 乳; chibusa 乳房.

ugly, *adj.* minikui 醜い (ugly to the sight).

ulcer, *n.* kaiyō 潰瘍.

ultimate, *adj.* 1. saigo (no) 最後 (の) (final). 2. kyūkyoku (no) 究極 (の) (highest). 3. konpon-teki (na) 根本的 (な) (basic).

umbrella, *n.* kasa 傘.

umpire, *n.* shinpan 審判.

unable, *adj.* (... koto ga) dekinai (...ことが) 出来ない.

unabridged, *adj.* kanzen (na) 完全 (な).

unanimous, *adj.* manjōitchi (no) 満場一致 (の); kanzengōi (no) 完全合意 (の).

unavoidable, *adj.* sakerarenai 避けられない; yamu o enai やむを得ない.

unaware, *adj.* kizukanai 気付かない.

unbalanced, *adj.* fukinkō (na) 不均衡 (な); fuantei (na) 不安定 (な); katayotta 片寄った.

uncertain, *adj.* 1. futashika (na) 不確か (な); hakkiri shinai はっきりしない (unclear, changeable). 2. ate ni dekinai 当てに出来ない (unreliable).

uncle, *n.* oji(san) 伯父(さん).

uncomfortable, *adj.* fukai (na) 不快 (な); iya (na) 嫌 (な).

uncommon, *adj.* 1. mezurashii 珍しい (unusual). 2. hibon (na) 非凡 (な) (outstanding).

unconditional, *adj.* 1. mujōken (no) 無条件 (の) (without conditions). 2. museigen (no) 無制限 (の) (without reservations).

unconscious, 1. *n.* muishiki 無意識 (the unconscious). 2. *adj.* muishiki (no) 無意識 (の).

uncontrollable, *adj.* te ni oenai 手に負えない.

uncover, *vb.* 1. futa o toru 蓋を取る (remove lid). 2. arawasu 現わす (reveal).

undamaged, *adj.* mukizu (no) 無傷 (の); buji (na) 無事 (な).

under, *prep.* ... no shita de/ni ...の下で／に (beneath, below); ... yori ika/shita (no) ...より以下／下 (の) (less than, lower than); ... no moto de/ni ...のもとで／に (subject to condition, influence, etc., of; protected or watched by; during the rule of); ... chū de ...中で (in the process of).

undercut, *vb.* 1. ... yori yasuku uru ...より安く売る (sell cheaper than...); ... yori yasuku hataraku ...より安く働く (work cheaper than...). 2. sokonau 損なう (injure).

underdog, *n.* 1. makeinu 負

け犬 (loser). 2. giseisha 犠牲者 (victim).

undergo, *vb.* 1. taeru 耐える (endure). 2. keiken suru 経験する (experience).

undergraduate, *n.* daigakusei 大学生; gakubusei 学部生.

underground, 1. *n.* chika 地下 (place); chikasoshiki 地下組織 (resistance group); chikatetsu 地下鉄 (subway system). 2. *adj.* chika (no) 地下 (の) (under the ground, hidden); himitsu (no) 秘密 (の) (secret); zen'ei (no) 前衛 (の) (avant-garde).

underline, *vb.* 1. kasen o hiku 下線を引く (mark). 2. kyōchō suru 強調する (stress).

underlying, *adj.* 1. shita ni yokotawatte-iru 下に横たわっている (lying beneath). 2. kihon-teki (na) 基本的 (な) (basic).

undermine, *vb.* sokonau 損なう; kizutsukeru 傷つける (injure).

underneath, 1. *adv.* shita ni 下に. 2. *prep.* ... no shita ni/de ...の下に/で.

underpants, *n.* pantsu パンツ.

undersea, *adj.* kaitei (no) 海底 (の); kaichū (no) 海中 (の).

undershirt, *n.* hadagi 肌着.

understand, *vb.* 1. wakaru 分かる; rikai suru 理解する (know meaning, sympathize). 2. shōchi suru 承知する (accept).

understandable, *adj.* nattoku/ rikai dekiru 納得／理解出来る.

undertake, *vb.* 1. kokoromiru 試みる

(attempt). 2. hikiukeru 引き受ける (take upon oneself, take in charge). 3. ukeau 請け合う (warrant). 4. yakusoku suru 約束する (promise).

underwrite, *vb.* hoshō suru 保証する (guarantee).

undo, *vb.* 1. moto ni modosu 元に戻す (return to original state). 2. hodoku 解く; hazusu 外す (unfasten, untie); akeru 開ける (open). 3. hametsu saseru 破滅させる (bring to ruin).

undoubtedly, *adv.* machigainaku 間違いなく.

undress, *vb.* kimono o nugu 着物を脱ぐ (remove one's clothing); kimono o nugaseru 着物を脱がせる (remove clothing of).

uneasy, *adj.* fuan (na) 不安 (な); ochitsukanai 落ち着かない.

unemployed, *adj.* mushoku (no) 無職 (の); shitsugyō (no) 失業 (の).

unessential, *adj.* dodemo ii どうでも良い; honshitsu-teki ja nai 本質的じゃない.

unexpected, *adj.* omoigakenai 思いがけない; yosōgai (no) 予想外 (の) (unforeseen).

unfair, *adj.* fukōhei (na) 不公平 (な) (not just).

unfavorable, *adj.* 1. furi (na) 不利 (な) (disadvantageous). 2. konomashikunai 好ましくない (undesirable).

unfold, *vb.* akeru 開ける; hiraku 開く.

unfortunate, *adj.* fu'un (na) 不運 (な); zan'nen (na) 残念 (な).

unfortunately, *adv.* ainiku あいにく; unwaruku 運悪

く.

unfriendly, adj. aisō ga warui 愛想が悪い; tsumetai 冷たい.

ungrateful, adj. onshirazu (no) 恩知らず (の).

unhappy, adj. fushiawase (na) 不幸せ (な); fukō (na) 不幸 (な).

unharmed, adj. buji (na) 無事 (な).

uniform, 1. n. seifuku 制服. 2. adj. kin'itsu (no) 均一 (の); kakuitsu-teki (na) 画一的 (な).

unify, vb. hitotsu ni suru 一つにする (make a single unit); hitotsu ni naru 一つになる (become a single unit).

unilateral, adj. katagawa dake (no) 片側だけ (の); ippō dake (no) 一方だけ (の).

unimportant, adj. dōdemo ii どうでも良い; jūyō de nai 重要でない.

uninteresting, adj. omoshirokunai 面白くない; tsumaranai つまらない.

union, n. 1. rōdō-kumiai 労働組合 (labor). 2. ketsugō 結合 (uniting).

unique, adj. dokutoku (na/no) 独特 (な／の).

unisex, adj. danjoryōyō (no) 男女両用 (の).

unison, n. 1. seishō 斉唱 (chorus). 2. chōwa 調和 (harmony).

unit, n. tan'i 単位.

unite, vb. hitotsu ni suru 一つにする (make into one); hitotsu ni naru 一つになる (become one).

United Nations, n. koku(sai)ren(gō) 国(際)連(合).

United States, n. amerika-gasshūkoku アメリカ合衆

国; beikoku 米国.

universal, adj. 1. zenbu (no) 全部 (の) (of all). 2. ippan (no) 一般 (の) (general). 3. fuhen-teki (na) 普遍的 (な) (existing everywhere). 4. uchū (no) 宇宙 (の) (of the universe); sekai (no) 世界 (の) (of the world).

universe, n. 1. uchū 宇宙 (cosmos). 2. zensekai 全世界 (whole world).

university, n. daigaku 大学.

unkempt, adj. 1. moja-moja (no) もじゃもじゃ (の) (disheveled). 2. midareta 乱れた (messy).

unkind, adj. tsumetai 冷たい; fushinsetsu (na) 不親切 (な).

unknown, adj. 1. michi (no) 未知 (の) (not known, not explored). 2. mumei (no) 無名 (の) (obscure).

unleash, vb. 1. toku 解く (let loose). 2. kaihō suru 解放する (release).

unless, conj. ... de nakereba ... でなければ; ... (shi)nakereba ... (し)なければ.

unlike, 1. adj. chigau 違う; kotonaru 異なる (different). 2. prep. ... to chigau/kotonaru ...と違う／異なる (different from); ... rashikunai ...らしくない (not typical of).

unlikely, adj. arisō ni nai ありそうにない; muri (na) 無理 (な).

unload, vb. ni o orosu 荷を下ろす (remove cargo).

unlock, vb. 1. kagi o akeru 鍵を開ける (undo lock). 2. akeru 開ける; hiraku 開く (open).

unmanageable, adj. te ni oenai 手に負えない.

unpack, vb. ni o toku 荷を解く; nakami o toridasu 中身を取り出す.

unpleasant, adj. fukai (na) 不快 (な).

unpretentious, adj. shizen (na) 自然 (な); sunao (na) 素直 (な).

unrealistic, adj. higenjitsu-teki (na) 非現実的 (な).

unreasonable, adj. 1. fugōri (na) 不合理 (な) (irrational). 2. hōgai (na) 法外 (な) (exorbitant).

unrest, n. fuan 不安.

unsafe, adj. abunai 危ない; kiken (na) 危険 (な).

unscrupulous, adj. sessō ga nai 節操のない; iikagen (na) 好い加減 (な).

untie, vb. toku 解く; hodoku 解く.

until, 1. prep. ... made ... まで. 2. conj. ... suru made ... するまで.

untrue, adj. uso (no) 嘘 (の).

unusual, adj. kawatta 変わった; mezurashii 珍しい (uncommon).

unwilling, adj. ki ga susumanai 気が進まない; iya-iyanagara (no) 嫌々ながら (の); **unwilling to do** ... suru no/koto ga iya ... するの／ことが嫌.

up, 1. adv. ue de/e/ni 上で／へ／に (to or in a higher place); agatte 上がって (high); okite 起きて (out of bed); nobotte 昇って (above the horizon); **come up** nobottekuru 昇って来る; **Get up.** Okite kudasai. 起きて下さい. **Stand up.** Tachiagatte kudasai. 立ち上がって下さい. 2. prep. ... no ue de/e/ni ...の上で／へ／に (up onto or into); ue no hō

ni 上の方に (upward). 3. **be up** okiteiru 起きている (out of bed); **be up to (someone)** ... shidai de aru ...次第である; **What's up?** Dōshitano. どうしたの.

upbringing, n. sodachi 育ち.

update, vb. saishin no mono ni suru 最新の物にする (update something).

uphold, vb. 1. mamoru 守る (defend). 2. shiji suru 支持する; sasaeru 支える (support).

upon, prep. ... no ue de/e/ni ...の上で／へ／に.

upper, adj. (... yori) ue no (...より) 上の; motto takai もっと高い.

upper hand, n. yūri 有利; yūsei 優勢.

upright, adj. 1. tate (no) 縦 (の); suichoku (no) 垂直 (の) (erect). 2. shōjiki (na) 正直 (な) (righteous).

uproar, n. ōsawagi 大騒ぎ.

upset, 1. n. tentō 転倒 (overturning); igai na haiboku 意外な敗北 (defeat). 2. adj. kōfun shiteiru 興奮している (disturbed); chōshi ga warui 調子が悪い (slightly ill). **have an upset stomach** i no chōshi ga warui 胃の調子が悪い. 3. vb. kutsugaesu 覆す; hikkurikaesu ひっくり返す (overturn); kōfun saseru 興奮させる (disturb someone); makasu 負かす (defeat).

upside down, adv. sakasama ni 逆さまに.

upstairs, adv. nikai (de/e/ni) 二階 (で／へ／に) (on or to the second floor); ue no kai (de/e/ni) 上の階 (で／へ／に) (on or to an upper floor).

up-to-date, adj. saishin (no) 最新 (の).

upward, adv. ue ni 上に; ue ni mukatte 上に向かって.

urban, adj. tokai (no) 都会 (の); machi (no) 町 (の).

urge, 1. n. shōdō 衝動 (impulse). 2. vb. segamu せがむ (persuade); sekitateru 急き立てる (force); iiharu 言い張る (insist).

urgent, adj. kinkyū (no) 緊急 (の).

urinal, n. 1. danseiyō'otearai 男性用お手洗 (men's room). 2. shōbenki 小便器 (urinal).

urine, n. nyō 尿; shōben 小便; oshikko おしっこ.

us, pron. watashitachi (o/ni) 私達 (を/に); ware-ware (o/ni) 我々 (を/に); **with us** watashitachi to issho ni 私達と一緒に.

usage, n. 1. shūkan 習慣 (custom). 2. atsukai 扱い; yōhō 用法 (treatment). 3. kan'yōgohō 慣用語法 (customary usage of words).

use, 1. n. shiyō 使用 (act of using); shiyōhō 使用法 (way of using); shiyōmokuteki 使用目的 (purpose for which something is used); riyōkachi 利用価値 (usefulness); **it's no use** muda (desu/da) 無駄 (です／だ); **in use**

tsukawarete-iru 使われている; **out of use** tsukawarete-inai 使われていない; sutareta 廃れた. 2. vb. tsukau 使う; riyō suru 利用する (utilize); **use up** tsukaihatasu 使い果たす; **used to do** ... mukashi yoku ... shita mono datta/deshita 昔よく...したものだった/でした.

used, adj. 1. chūko (no) 中古 (の) (secondhand); **used car** chūkosha 中古車. 2. nareta 慣れた (accustomed); **be used to** ... ni narete iru ... に慣れている; **get used to** ... ni nareru ... に慣れる.

useful, adj. yaku ni tatsu 役に立つ (beneficial); benri (na) 便利 (な).

user, n. shiyōsha 使用者.

usher, 1. n. an'naigakari 案内係. 2. vb. **usher in** michibiku 導く.

usual, adj. 1. itsumo (no) いつも (の) (customary); **as usual** itsumo no yō ni いつものように. 2. futsū (no) 普通 (の) (ordinary).

utensil, n. dōgu 道具; yōgu 用具.

uterus, n. shikyū 子宮.

utmost, adj. ichiban (no) 一番 (の); saidai (no) 最大 (の).

utter, 1. adj. mattaku (no) 全く (の). 2. vb. iu 言う.

V

vacancy, n. 1. akibeya 空き部屋 (vacant room); akichi 空き地 (vacant place). 2. ketsuin 欠員 (vacant position). 3. kūkyo 空虚 (emptiness).

vacant, adj. 1. aiteiru 空いている (not occupied or filled). 2. kara (no) 空 (の)

(empty). 3. nai 無い (devoid). 4. bon'yari shita ぼんやりした (lacking in thought).

vacation, n. yasumi 休み; kyūka 休暇.

vaccine, n. yobōsesshu 予防接種; wakuchin ワクチン.

vacuum, n. shinkū 真空;

kūhaku 空白.

vacuum cleaner, n. denkisōjiki 電気掃除機.

vagina, n. chitsu 膣.

vagrant, n. furōsha 浮浪者 (homeless person).

vague, adj. 1. aimai (na) あいまい (な); bon'yari shita ぼんやりした; hakkiri shinai はっきりしない.

vain, adj. 1. unobore ga tsuyoi うぬぼれが強い (conceited). 2. muda (na) 無駄 (な); munashii 空しい (futile); **in vain** munashiku 空しく; muda ni 無駄に.

valet, n. bōi ボーイ (hotel).

valiant, adj. yūkan (na) 勇敢 (な).

valid, adj. 1. seitō (na) 正当 (な) (logical, sound). 2. yūkō (na) 有効 (な); tsūyō suru 通用する (effective).

valley, n. tani 谷.

valor, n. yūki 勇気.

valuable, adj. kichō (na) 貴重 (な); kachi ga aru 価値がある.

value, 1. n. kachi 価値 (worth, importance); kakaku 価格 (price); hyōka 評価 (estimation); hyōka suru 評価する; ne o tsukeru 値を付ける (estimate); sonchō suru 尊重する (respect).

valve, n. ben 弁.

vampire, n. kyūketsuki 吸血鬼.

van, n. unsōsha 運送車 (moving van); ban バン (vehicle).

vanish, vb. kieru 消える.

vapor, n. moya もや (haze); yuge 湯気; jōki 蒸気 (steam); kiri 霧 (mist).

variety, n. 1. tayōsei 多様性; henka 変化 (diversity). 2. iro-iro na koto 色々な事

(number of different things). 3. shurui 種類 (kind).

various, adj. 1. iro-iro (na, no) 色々 (な、の) (many, of different sorts). 2. ikutsuka (no) 幾つか (の) (several).

varnish, 1. n. (wa)nisu (ワ)ニス. 2. vb. nisu o nuru ニスを塗る.

vary, vb. 1. kawaru 変わる; henka suru 変化する (change). 2. kaeru 変える (cause to change). 3. chigau 違う (differ).

vase, n. 1. kabin 花瓶 (for flowers).

vast, adj. 1. kōdai (na) 広大 (な) (large and wide). 2. bōdai (na) 膨大 (な) (immense).

vat, n. taru 樽.

veal, n. koushi (no) niku 子牛 (の) 肉.

vegetable, n. yasai 野菜 (food); shokubutsu 植物 (plant).

vehicle, n. 1. norimono 乗り物 (for transport) ? shudan 手段 (means).

veil, 1. n. ōi 覆い (covering). 2. vb. bēru o kakeru ベールをかける; ōu 覆う.

vein, n. 1. jōmyaku 静脈 (blood vessel). 2. mokume 木目 (wood grain).

velvet, n. birōdo ビロード.

vendor, n. 1. urite 売り手. 2. rotenshō 露店商 (street vendor).

venereal, adj. seibyō (no) 性病 (の).

vengeance, n. fukushū 復讐.

venom, n. 1. dokueki 毒液 (liquid). 2. akui 悪意 (malice).

vent, 1. n. tsūkikō 通気孔; kanki-mado 換気窓

(opening for air, etc.); hakeguchi はけ口 (outlet for anger, etc.). 2. *vb.* hakidasu 吐き出す (express); dasu 出す (release).

ventilation, *n.* kanki 換気; tsūki 通気.

venture, 1. *n.* bōken 冒険 (undertaking); tōki 投機 (business venture). 2. *vb.* kakeru 賭ける (risk).

veracity, *n.* shinjitsusei 真実性.

verb, *n.* dōshi 動詞.

verbal, *adj.* 1. kotoba (no) 言葉 (の) (of words). 2. kōtō (no) 口頭 (の) (oral). 3. dōshi (no) 動詞 (の) (of verbs).

verge, 1. *n.* fuchi 縁; hashi 端; **on the verge of** ... sunzen (no) ... 寸前 (の); ... setogiwa ... 瀬戸際 (の). 2. *vb.* (...ni/to) sessuru (... に／と) 接する; (...ni) chikazuku (...に) 近づく.

verify, *vb.* 1. shōmei suru 証明する (prove). 2. tashikameru 確める (ascertain).

versatile, *adj.* 1. tasai (na) 多才 (な) (multi-talented). 2. tamokuteki (no) 多目的 (の) (of many uses).

verse, *n.* shi 詩; inbun 韻文.

version, *n.* 1. hon'yaku 翻訳 (translation). 2. hanashi 話; kaishaku 解釈 (account, interpretation). 3. -ban -版 (different form, copy).

versus, *prep.* tai 対.

vertical, *adj.* suichoku (na, no) 垂直 (な、の); tate (no) 縦 (の).

very, 1. *adj.* onaji (no) 同じ (の) (same); hon (no) ほん (の) (mere); mattaku (no) 全く (の) (utter); shin (no) 真 (の) (true); jissai (no) 実

際 (の) (actual). 2. *adv.* totemo とても; taihen 大変; hijō ni 非常に (in a high degree); chōdo 丁度; masani 正に (exactly).

vessel, *n.* 1. fune 船 (boat). 2. yōki 容器 (container). 3. kekkan 血管 (blood vessel).

vest, *n.* besuto ベスト; chokki チョッキ.

veteran, 1. *n.* taiekigunjin 退役軍人 (soldier); beteran ベテラン (experienced person). 2. *adj.* jukuren shita 熟練した (experienced).

veterinarian, *n.* jūi 獣医.

veto, 1. *n.* kyohiken 拒否権 (official right); kinshi 禁止 (prohibition). 2. *vb.* kyohi suru 拒否する; kinshi suru 禁止する.

via, *prep.* 1. -keiyu de -経由で (by way of); **via Hawaii** hawai-keiyu de ハワイ経由で. 2. (...o) tōshite (...を) 通して; (...ni) yotte (...に) よって (by means of).

vice, *n.* 1. aku(toku) 悪(徳) (wickedness). 2. fuhinkō 不品行; fudōtoku 不道徳 (immoral conduct or habit). 3. ketten 欠点 (fault).

vice-, fuku- 副-; **vice-chairman** fuku-gichō 副議長; **vice president** fuku-daitōryō 副大統領.

vicinity, *n.* fukin 付近; kinjo 近所.

vicious, *adj.* 1. iji ga warui 意地が悪い; akui ni michita 悪意に満ちた (malicious). 2. daraku shita 堕落した (depraved). 3. dōmō (na) どうもう (な) (ferocious).

victim, *n.* giseisha 犠牲者; higaisha 被害者.

victory, *n.* shōri 勝利.

Vietnam, *n.* betonamu ベト

ナム.

view, 1. *n.* nagame 眺め (scene); keshiki 景色 (landscape); shikai 視界 (range of vision); iken 意見 (opinion). 2. *vb.* miru 見る (see); shiraberu 調べる (survey); ...to minasu ...と見なす (consider to be).

viewer, *n.* 1. kenbutsunin 見物人 (bystander); shichōsha 視聴者 (TV viewer).

viewpoint, *n.* mikata 見方; kenchi 見地.

vigil, *n.* nezu/tetsuya no ban 寝ず/徹夜の番.

vigorous, *adj.* 1. kakki ga aru 活気がある (energetic). 2. kyōryoku (na) 強力 (な) (strong).

village, *n.* mura 村.

villain, *n.* warumono 悪者; akunin 悪人.

vine, *n.* 1. tsurukusa つる草; tsuta 蔦 (ivy, etc.). 2. budō no ki 葡萄の木 (grapevine).

vinegar, *n.* su 酢.

vineyard, *n.* budōen 葡萄園.

vinyl, *n.* bīniru ビニール.

violation, *n.* 1. ihan 違反 (infringement). 2. bōgai 妨害 (disturbance). 3. gōkan 強姦 (rape).

violence, *n.* 1. hageshisa 激しさ (great force); bōryoku 暴力 (harm).

violet, *n.* sumire 菫.

virgin, *n.* 1. shojo 処女 (woman); dōtei 童貞 (chaste man).

virtue, *n.* 1. (bi)toku (美)徳 (moral excellence). 2. biten 美点; chōsho 長所 (merit). 3. teisetsu 貞節 (chastity).

virus, *n.* uirusu ウイルス; saikin 細菌.

visible, *adj.* 1. mieru 見える (can be seen). 2. meihaku

vision, *n.* 1. shikaku 視覚 (sense of sight). 2. shiryoku 視力 (power of sight). 3. senken 先見 (foresight). 4. sōzōryoku 想像力 (mental image). 5. maboroshi 幻 (supernatural appearance).

visit, 1. *n.* hōmon 訪問. 2. *vb.* hōmon suru 訪問する; tazuneru 訪ねる.

visitor, *n.* 1. hōmonsha 訪問者; (o)kyaku(san) (お)客(さん).

visual, *adj.* shikaku (no) 視覚 (の); mieru 見える.

vital, *adj.* 1. seimei (no) 生命 (の) (of life). 2. iki-iki shita 生き生きした (lively). 3. jūyō (na) 重要 (な) (important). 4. fukaketsu (na) 不可欠 (な) (essential).

vitamin, *n.* bitamin ビタミン.

vivid, *adj.* 1. senmei (na) 鮮明 (な); azayaka (na) 鮮やか (な) (bright, perceptible). 2. iki-iki shita 生き生きした (lively).

vocal, *adj.* 1. koe (no) 声 (の) (voice). 2. yakamashiku shuchō suru やかましく主張する (adamant on issue).

vocalist, *n.* seigakuka 声楽家; kashu 歌手.

vocation, *n.* shokugyō 職業; shigoto 仕事.

vogue, *n.* 1. ryūkō 流行 (fashion). 2. ninki 人気 (popularity).

voice, 1. *n.* koe 声 (sound); tai 態 (grammar). 2. *vb.* iu 言う.

void, 1. *n.* kūkan 空間 (empty space). 2. *adj.* mukō (no) 無効 (の) (without legal force); kara (no) 空 (の) (empty). 3. *vb.* mukō ni suru 無効にする (invalidate).

volcano, *n.* kazan 火山; **active volcano** kakkazan 活火山.

volition, *n.* 1. ishi 意志 (will). 2. ketsudan 決断 (choice).

volleyball, *n.* barē(bōru) バレー (ボール).

volume, *n.* 1. ryō 量 (quantity, amount). 2. hon 本 (book); -kan -巻 -satsu -冊 (counter for books). 3. yōseki 容積 (size in three dimensions).

voluntary, *adj.* jihatsu-teki (na) 自発的 (な); shigan (no) 志願 (の) (willing).

vomit, 1. *n.* ōto 嘔吐. 2. *vb.* haku 吐く.

vote, 1. *n.* tōhyō 投票 (expression of choice); tōhyōken 投票権 (right). 2. *vb.* tōhyō suru 投票する.

vow, 1. *n.* chikai 誓い. 2. *vb.* chikau 誓う.

vowel, *n.* boin 母音.

voyage, 1. *n.* nagatabi 長旅. 2. *vb.* tabi suru 旅する; ryokō suru 旅行する.

vulgar, *adj.* zokuaku (na) 俗悪 (な); gehin (na) 下品 (な); chinpu (na) 陳腐 (な).

vulnerable, *adj.* kizutsuki-yasui 傷つき易い.

vulture, *n.* hagetaka 禿鷹.

W

wade, *vb.* 1. wataru 渡る. 2. kurōshite susumu 苦労して進む (proceed laboriously).

wag, *vb.* furu 振る.

wage, *n.* chingin 賃金; kyūryō 給料; kyūyo 給与; sararī サラリー (salary).

wager, 1. *n.* kake 賭け. 2. *vb.* kakeru 賭ける.

wagon, *n.* nibasha 荷馬車 (horse drawn).

wail, 1. *n.* nageki 嘆き (lament). 2. *vb.* nageki-kanashimu 嘆き悲しむ (cry).

wait, *vb.* 1. matsu 待つ; **wait for** ... o matsu ... を待つ. 2. kyūji suru 給仕する (serve food); **wait on (a person)** (... ni) tsukaeru (...に) 仕える

wake, 1. *n.* tsuya 通夜 (vigil beside corpse); ato 跡 (track). 2. *vb.* mezameru 目覚める (become awake); mezame saseru 目覚めさせる; okosu 起こす (cause to wake).

walk, 1. *n.* aruki 歩き (act of walking); hodō 歩道 (sidewalk); **take a walk** sanpo suru 散歩する. 2. *vb.* aruku 歩く.

wall, *n.* kabe 壁; hei 塀.

wallet, *n.* saifu 財布.

walnut, *n.* kurumi 胡桃.

walrus, *n.* seiuchi せいうち.

waltz, *n.* warutsu ワルツ; enbukyoku 円舞曲.

wand, *n.* mahō no tsue 魔法の杖 (magic wand).

wander, *vb.* 1. arukimawaru 歩きまわる (walk about). 2. mayou 迷う (go astray). 3. soreru 逸れる (deviate).

want, 1. *n.* hitsuyō 必要 (need); ketsubō 欠乏 (lack); mazushisa 貧しさ (poverty); **be in want of** ... ga iru ...が要る; **for want of** ... ga nai node ...が無いので. 2. *vb.* ... ga iru ...が要る (need); ... ga hoshii ... が欲しい (desire); ... ga kakete-iru ...が欠けて

いる (lack).

war, n. sensō 戦争; tatakai 戦い; **be at war (with)** (... to) sensō shite-iru (... と) 戦争している; **wage war against** ... to tatakau ... と戦う.

ware, n. 1. shōhin 商品 (merchandise). 2. seihin 製品 (manufactured article).

warehouse, n. sōko 倉庫.

warm, 1. adj. atatakai 暖かい (having moderate heat); kokoro ga komotta 心がこもった (cordial); nesshin (na) 熱心 (な) (lively); shinsetsu (na) 親切 (な) (kind). 2. vb. atatameru 暖める (make warm); atatakaku naru 暖かくなる (become warm).

warmth, n. atatakasa 暖かさ.

warn, vb. keikoku suru 警告する; chūkoku suru 忠告する.

warning, n. keikoku 警告; chūkoku 忠告.

warranty, n. hoshō 保証.

wart, n. ibo いぼ.

wash, vb. arau 洗う (cleanse in water); sentaku suru 洗濯する (wash clothes).

wasp, n. suzumebachi 雀蜂.

waste, 1. n. rōhi 浪費 (useless expenditure); arechi 荒れ地 (uncultivated land); haikibutsu 廃棄物 (leftovers from manufacturing). 2. vb. rōhi suru 浪費する (spend uselessly); muda ni suru 無駄にする (fail to use); suijaku suru 衰弱する (decay in health); shōmō saseru 消耗させる (wear away).

wastebasket, n. gomibako ごみ箱; kuzuire 屑入れ.

watch, 1. n. udedokei 腕時計 (wristwatch); mihari 見張り; ban 番 (guard, watchman); yōjin 用心 (caution). 2. vb. miru 見る (look); (... ni) ki o tsukeru (...に) 気をつける; (... ni) yōjin suru (...に) 用心する (be watchful); miharu 見張る (keep under surveillance); **watch out** ki o tsukeru 気をつける.

watchdog, n. banken 番犬 (dog).

water, 1. n. mizu 水 (cold water); oyu お湯 (hot water). 2. vb. mizu o yaru 水をやる (give water).

watercolor, n. 1. suisaienogu 水彩絵の具 (paint). 2. suisaiga 水彩画 (painting).

waterfall, n. taki 滝.

water lily, n. suiren 水蓮.

watermelon, n. suika 西瓜.

waterproof, adj. bōsui (no) 防水 (の); **waterproof watch** bōsuidokei 防水時計.

wave, 1. n. nami 波 (undulation, rush, mass movement); yure 揺れ (vibration); kābu カーブ (curve); **short wave** tanpa 短波. 2. vb. yureru 揺れる (move back and forth); furu 振る (flag, hand, etc.).

waver, vb. 1. yuragu 揺らぐ (sway). 2. tamerau ためらう (hesitate). 3. yureugoku 揺れ動く (fluctuate).

wavy, adj. namiutteiru 波打っている; namijō (no) 波状 (の).

way, n. 1. hōhō 方法; yarikata やり方 (manner, mode, method). 2. michi 道 (passage, road). 3. hōkō 方向 (direction). 4. michinori 道程 (distance). 5. **a long way** nagai michinori 長い道

程; **by the way** tokoro de ところで; **by way of ...** keiyu de ... 経由で; **in a way** aru teido ある程度 (to some extent); **on the way to ...** ni iku tochū de ...に行く途中で; **that way** achira あちら; **this way** kochira こちら; **which way** dochira どちら.

we, *pron.* watashitachi 私達; ware-ware 我々.

weak, *adj.* 1. yowai 弱い (feeble, fragile). 2. heta na 下手 (な) (deficient). 3. usui 薄い (tea, coffee, etc.).

wealth, *n.* tomi 富; yutakasa 豊かさ.

wealthy, *adj.* 1. yutaka (na) 豊か (な) (abundant, affluent). 2. kanemochi (no) 金持ち (の) (possessing riches).

weapon, *n.* buki 武器.

wear, 1. *n.* fuku 服 (clothing); shōmō 消耗 (deterioration, exhaustion). 2. *vb.* kiru 着る (waist up: shirt, jacket, etc.); haku はく (waist down: pants, shoes, socks); kaburu 被る (hat); kakeru かける (glasses); hameru はめる (gloves); mi ni tsukeru 身に着ける (accessories); suriherasu 擦り減らす (diminish, impair); tsukaifurusu 使い古す (damage, cause to deteriorate by use); kutabireru くたびれる (get exhausted); **wear out** shōmō suru 消耗する.

weather, *n.* tenki 天気; kishō 気象; **weather forecast** tenkiyohō 天気予報.

weave, *n.* oru 織る (fabric); 編む (basket).

web, *n.* kumo no su 蜘蛛の巣 (cobweb).

wedding, *n.* kekkonshiki 結婚式; **wedding ring** kekkon'yubiwa 結婚指輪.

Wednesday, *n.* suiyōbi 水曜日.

weed, 1. *n.* zassō 雑草. 2. *vb.* zassō o toru 雑草を取る (weed grass); **weed out** nozoku 除く.

week, *n.* shū(kan) 週(間); **once a week** shū ni ichido; 週に一度 **last week** senshū 先週; **this week** konshū 今週; **next week** raishū 来週.

weekday, *n.* heijitsu 平日.

weekend, *n.* shūmatsu 週末.

weekly, 1. *n.* shūkanshi 週刊誌 (weekly magazine). 2. *adj.* shū ni ichido (no) 週に一度 (の) (done once a week); isshūkan (no) 一週間 (の) (computed by the week).

weep, *vb.* naku 泣く.

weigh, *vb.* 1. omosa o hakaru 重さを計る／量る (measure heaviness). 2. ... no omosa ga aru ... の重さがある (have the stated weight). 3. yoku kangaeru よく考える (consider).

welcome, 1. *n.* kangei 歓迎. 2. *adj.* kangei subeki 歓迎すべき yorokobashii 喜ばしい; **you're welcome** dō itashimashite どういたしまして (response to "thank you"). 3. *vb.* kangei suru 歓迎する. 4. *interj.* yōkoso ようこそ; irrasshai(mase) いっらっしゃい(ませ).

welfare, *n.* 1. seikatsuhogo 生活保護 (public relief); fukushi 福祉 (social welfare). 2. kōfuku 幸福 (well-being).

well, 1. *n.* ido 井戸 (for water). **2.** *adj.* genki (na) 元気 (な) (healthy). **3.** *adv.* yoku よく (excellently, properly, thoroughly); **as well** ... mo (mata) ...も (又) ; **as well as** ... sono ue ni ... その上に...; sore kara それから (in addition); **be doing well** junchō de aru 順調である; **get well** genki ni naru 元気になる; **Well done!** Yoku yatta. よくやった. **4.** *interj.* sate さて; jā じゃあ.

west, 1. *n.* nishi 西; **the West** seiō 西欧 (Europe and America); seiyō 西洋 (western part of the world); seibu 西部 (western part of a country). **2.** *adj.* see **western.**

western, 1. *adj.* nishi (no) 西 (の); seiō (no) 西欧 (の); seiyō (no) 西洋 (の); seibu (no) 西部 (の). **2.** *n.* seibugeki 西部劇 (cowboy movie).

wet, 1. *adj.* nureta 濡れた (soaked with water); shimetta 湿った (moist, damp); **get wet** nureru 濡れる. **2.** *vb.* nurasu 濡らす.

whale, *n.* kujira 鯨.

what, 1. *adj.* nan no 何の; don'na どんな; **what time** nanji 何時. **2.** *pron.* nani/nan 何; **What for?** Dōshite どうして. **what about** ... wa dō desuka ...はどうですか; **What do you think?** Dō omou. どう思う. **what I like** watashi no sukina mono 私の好きなもの. **3.** *interj.* nan to ... 何と... (what a ...).

whatever, 1. *adj.* don'na ... demo どんな...でも (no matter what); **whatever reason** don'na riyū demo どんな理由でも. **2.** *pron.* ... koto o nan demo ... ことを何でも ... (... anything that ...); **Do whatever you like.** Sukina koto o nan demo shinasai. 好きなことを何でもしなさい. nani ga/o ... temo 何が/を...ても (no matter what...); **whatever happens** nani ga okottemo 何が起こっても; **whatever I say** nani o ittemo 何を言っても.

wheat, *n.* komugi 小麦.

wheel, *n.* kuruma 車; sharin 車輪; **wheel chair** kurumaisu 車椅子; **steering wheel** handoru ハンドル.

when, 1. *adv.* itsu いつ. **2.** *conj.* ... toki ...時 (at or during the time that); **when I feel sad** kanashii toki 悲しい時; ... -nara/-kereba ...-なら/-ければ (if ...); ... kara ...から (as, since ...); ... hazu no toki ni ...はずの時に (whereas ...); sono toki ni の時 (upon which).

whenever, 1. *adv.* (when ever, emphatic form of **when**) ittai-zentai itsu 一体全体いつ. **2.** *conj.* ... toki wa itsumo ...時はいつも (every time ...); itsu demo いつでも (at any time).

where, 1. *adv.* doko de/ni どこで/に (in or at what place); **Where is he?** Kare wa doko ni imasu ka. 彼はどこにいますか. **Where do you live?** Doko ni sunde imasu ka. どこに住んでいますか. doko e/ni どこへ/に (to what place); doko kara/de どこから/で (from what source or place). **2.** *conj.* tokoro 所; **Find where he is.** Kare no iru tokoro o sagase. 彼のいる所を探せ.

wherever, *conj.* ... tokoro wa doko demo ...所はどこで も (at whatever place ...).

whether, *conj.* ... ka dōka ... かどうか (if... or not); **do not know whether he has come or not** kita ka dōka wakaranai 来たかどう か分からない.

which, 1. *adj.* dono どの; dochira no どちらの. 2. *pron.* dore どれ; dochira ど ちら.

whichever, 1. *adj.* dono ... demo どの...でも. 2. *pron.* dore demo どれでも (any one that); dochira ga/o temo どちらが/を...ても (no matter which one is .../no matter which one you ...).

while, 1. *n.* aida 間 (interval); **after a while** shibaraku shite kara 暫くし てから; **all the while** zutto ずっと; **a while ago** sukoshi mae ni 少し前に; **once in a while** tokidoki 時々; **for a while** shibaraku 暫く; **worth one's while** kai ga aru 甲斐がある. 2. *conj.* ... aida ni ...間に (during the time that ...); ... kagiri wa ...限りは (as long as ...); keredomo けれども (even though).

whip, 1. *n.* muchi 鞭 (instrument). 2. *vb.* muchiutsu 鞭打つ (strike); awadateru 泡立てる (beat into a foam).

whiskers, *n.* hoohige 頬髭 (man); hige 髭 (cat).

whiskey, *n.* uisukī ウイスキ ー.

whisper, 1. *n.* sasayaki 囁き. 2. *vb.* sasayaku 囁く.

whistle, *n.* kuchibue 口笛

(from human mouth); fue no yō na oto 笛のような音 (any whistling sound).

white, 1. *adj.* shiroi 白い (lacking color); aojiroi 青白 い (pale); hakujin (no) 白人 (の) (race). 2. *n.* shiro(iro) 白(色) (color); hakujin 白人 (race or person).

who, *pron.* dare ga 誰が; donata ga どなたが.

whoever, *pron.* 1. dare demo 誰でも (whatever person). 2. dare ga ... temo 誰が...ても (whoever does ...).

whole, 1. *adj.* zenbu no 全部 の; subete no 全ての. 2. *n.* zenbu 全部; subete 全て; **as a whole** zentai-teki ni mite 全体的に見て; **on the whole** gaishite 概して.

wholesome, *adj.* 1. kenzen (na) 健全 (な) (morally good). 2. kenkō ni ii 健康に 良い (good for the health).

whose, *pron.* dare no 誰の; donata no どなたの.

why, *adv., conj.* naze 何故; dōshite どうして.

wicked, *adj.* 1. ja'aku (na) 邪悪 (な); ijiwarui 意地悪い (evil). 2. tsumibukai 罪深い (sinful).

wide, 1. *adj.* hiroi 広い; ōkii 大きい. 2. *adv.* hiroku 広く; ōkiku 大きく.

widen, *vb.* 1. hiroku suru 広 くする; ōkiku suru 大きくす る (make wide). 2. hirogaru 広がる (become wide).

widespread, *adj.* hiromatteiru 広まっている.

widow, *n.* mibōjin 未亡人.

wife, *n.* tsuma 妻; kanai 家 内 (one's own wife); okusan 奥さん (someone's wife).

wig, *n.* katsura かつら.

wild, *adj.* 1. yasei (no) 野性

(の) (living or growing in nature). 2. yaban (na) 野蛮 (な) (uncivilized). 3. arekuru'u 荒れ狂う (violent). 4. te ni oenai 手に負えない (unruly). 5. mugamuchū (no) 無我夢中 (の) (unrestrained).

wilderness, n. kōya 荒野.

will, 1. n. ishi 意志 (power of the mind, intention); yuigon 遺言 (testament). 2. vb. nozomu 望む (wish); yuigon ni nokosu 遺言に残す (bequeath). 3. aux. vb. ... deshō ...でしょう; ... darō ... だろう (probability); ... shitai ...したい (willingness); ... suru tsumori ...するつもり (intention).

willful, adj. 1. gōjō (na) 強情 (な) (obstinate). 2. waza to (no) わざと (の); koi (no) 故意 (の) (intentional).

willing, adj. **be willing to ...** yorokonde ... suru 喜んで...する.

willow, n. yanagi 柳.

willpower, n. ishiryoku 意志力.

win, 1. n. shōri 勝利; kachi 勝ち (victory). 2. vb. shōri suru 勝利する; katsu 勝つ (gain victory); kachieru 勝ち得る (get by effort); ateru 当てる (win lottery).

wind, 1. n. kaze 風 (air in motion). 2. vb. kaze ni ateru 風に当てる (expose to the air); maku 巻く (coil, roll); magarikuneru 曲がりくねる (move in a curving course).

window, n. 1. mado 窓. 2. madoguchi 窓口 (ticket, teller's). 3. uindō ウインドー (display).

windy, adj. kaze ga tsuyoi 風

が強い.

wing, n. hane 羽; tsubasa 翼.

winter, n. fuyu 冬.

wipe, vb. fuku 拭く; nugu'u 拭う; **wipe out** hakai suru 破壊する (destroy); korosu 殺す (kill).

wisdom, n. chie 知恵.

wise, adj. kashikoi 賢い.

wish, 1. n. kibō 希望; negai 願い (desire, hope, something desired or hoped); **My best wishes to your father.** Otōsan ni yoroshiku. お父さんによろしく. 2. vb. kibō suru 希望する; negau 願う (desire, hope).

with, prep. 1. ... to issho ni ...と一緒に (accompanied by). 2. ... de ...で (by means of, because of); **cut with a knife** naifu de kiru ナイフで切る. 3. ... ga aru ...がある (having); **a woman with ambition** yashin ga aru josei 野心がある女性. 4. ... to tomo ni ...と共に (in proportion to). 5. ... to ...と (against, separate from); **fight with the enemy** teki to tatakau 敵と戦う.

within, 1. adv. naka de/ni/e 中で/に/へ (inside). 2. prep. ... no naka de/ni ...の中で/に (in, inside of, in the scope of); ... inai ni ...以内に (within a certain distance or time); ... jū ni ...中に (within a certain time).

without, 1. adv. soto de/ni 外で/に (outside). 2. prep. ... nashi de ...無しで (not having); **do without ...** nashi de sumasu ... 無しで済ます.

witness, 1. n. mokugekisha 目撃者 (person who witnesses); shōnin 証人

(person who gives testimony, who attests by signature); shōgen 証言 (testimony); shōko 証拠 (evidence). 2. vb. mokugeki suru 目撃する (see); shōnin ni naru 証人になる (be present at as formal witness); shōgen suru 証言する (testify); hoshōnin no shomei o suru 保証人の署名をする (attest by signature).

wobble, vb. guratsuku ぐらつく (move); guratsukaseru ぐらつかせる (cause to move); furueru 震える (tremble).

wolf, n. ōkami 狼.

woman, n. josei 女性; on'na (no hito) 女 (の人).

womb, n. shikyū 子宮.

wonder, 1. n. odoroki 驚き (surprise); kyōi 驚異 (marvel); fushigi 不思議 (puzzlement); **no wonder** tōzen 当然. 2. vb. kangaeru 考える (speculate); (... ni) odoroku (...に) 驚く (be surprised, marvel); fushigi ni omou 不思議に思う (be puzzled); shiritai 知りたい (want to know).

wonderful, adj. subarashii 素晴らしい.

wood, n. 1. ki 木. 2. zaimoku 材木 (lumber); maki 薪 (firewood). 3. mori 森 (grove).

wooden, adj. mokusei (no) 木製 (の).

woodpecker, n. kitsutsuki きつつき.

word, n. 1. tango 単語; kotoba 言葉 (unit of language). 2. kotoba 言葉 (something said or written). 3. hitokoto 一言; hanashi 話 (short talk). 4. yakusoku 約束 (promise). 5. nyūsu ニュー

ス (news). 6. **words** kashi 歌詞 (lyrics); kenka 喧嘩 (angry speech).

work, 1. n. shigoto 仕事 (employment, task); rōdō 労働 (labor); sakuhin 作品 (result of work, writing, painting, etc.); doryoku 努力 (exertion); **at work** shigotochū 仕事中 (at one's job); **out of work** shitsugyōchū 失業中. 2. vb. shigoto suru 仕事する; hataraku 働く (do work, employed); isoshimu いそしむ (engage oneself in); benkyō suru 勉強する (work on an academic subject); ugoku 動く (operate, function); kiku 効く (function effectively).

worker, n. rōdōsha 労働者.

world, n. 1. sekai 世界 (globe, universe, part of the earth, group of living things). 2. jinrui 人類 (human race). 3. seken 世間; shakai 社会 (public). 4. bun'ya 分野 (area of interest).

worm, n. mimizu みみず.

worry, 1. n. shinpai 心配. 2. vb. shinpai saseru 心配させる (make anxious); shinpai suru 心配する (feel anxious).

worship, 1. n. sūhai 崇拝 (admiration); reihai 礼拝 (religious service, worship). 2. vb. sūhai suru 崇拝する; reihai suru 礼拝する.

worst, adj., adv. saiaku (no) 最悪 (の); ichiban warui 一番悪い; **at worst** warukute mo 一番悪くても.

worth, 1. n. kachi 価値 (value, importance). 2. prep. ... (no) kachi ga aru (...の) 価値がある (having

value of ..., deserving of ...).
worthy, adj. 1. **be worthy (of)** (... ni) atai suru (...に)値する. 2. rippa (na) 立派 (な) (having great merit).
would, aux. vb. 1. ... shita mono datta ...したものだった (used to do ...). 2. **Would you please ...?** ... kudasaimasen ka ...下さいませんか.
wound, 1. n. kizu 傷; kega 怪我. 2. vb. kizutsukeru 傷つける.
wrap, vb. tsutsumu 包む.
wreath, n. hanawa 花輪.
wreck, 1. n. zangai 残骸 (ruin); nanpasen 難破船 (ship); haijin 廃人 (person); hakai 破壊 (destruction). 2. vb. nanpa suru 難破する (shipwreck); hakai suru 破壊する (destroy).
wrench, 1. n. スパナー (tool); hineri 捻り (twist); nenza 捻挫 (injury). 2. vb. mogitoru もぎ取る (pull away); hineru 捻る (twist).
wring, vb. 1. hineru 捻る; nejiru ねじる (twist). 2.

shiboru しぼる (squeeze).
wrinkle, 1. n. shiwa しわ. 2. vb. shiwa o yoseru しわを寄せる (form wrinkles in); shiwa ga yoru しわが寄る (become wrinkled).
wrist, n. tekubi 手首.
write, vb. 1. kaku 書く. 2. **write down** kakitomeru 書き留める.
writer, n. sakka 作家; chosha 著者.
wrong, 1. n. fusei 不正 (injustice); aku 悪 (evil); gai 害 (damage); **do wrong to others** tanin ni gai o ataeru 他人に害を与える; **in the wrong** machigatteiru 間違っている. 2. adj. machigai (no) 間違い (の); ayamari (no) 誤り (の) (erroneous, deviating from the truth); warui 悪い (evil, erroneous, unjust, not suitable); fusei (na) 不正 (な) (unjust); **something wrong with ...** ga kowareteiru ...が壊れている (out of order). 3. vb. gai o ataeru 害を与える (harm).

X

x-ray, 1. n. rentogen レントゲン; ekkusu-sen エックス線. 2. vb. rentogen o toru レントゲンを撮る.
xylophone, n. mokkin 木琴.

Y

yarn, n. ito 糸 (thread); keito 毛糸 (woolen yarn).
yawn, 1. n. akubi あくび. 2. vb. akubi o suru あくびをする.
year, n. toshi 年; nen 年 (12 months); **all year round** ichinenjū 一年中.

yearly, adj. maitoshi (no) 毎年 (の); nen ni ichido (no) 年に一度 (の).
yearn, vb. netsubō suru 熱望する; akogareru 憧れる.
yeast, n. isuto イースト; kōbo 酵母.
yell, 1. n. sakebigoe 叫び声

(scream). 2. *vb.* sakebu 叫ぶ (scream); donaru どなる (shout).

yellow, 1. *adj.* kiiroi 黄色い. 2. *n.* ki(iro) 黄(色) (color).

yen, *n.* 1. en 円 (currency). 2. yokkyū 欲求; akogare 憧れ (desire).

yes, *adv.* hai はい; ee ええ; sō desu そうです; sono tōri desu その通りです.

yesterday, *adv.* kinō 昨日; sakujitsu 昨日.

yet, 1. *adv.* mada まだ (still); mō もう; sude ni すでに (already); **not yet** mada (...nai) まだ (...ない). 2. *conj.* soredemo それでも.

yield, 1. *n.* shūkaku 収穫 (crop); rieki 利益 (profit); seisandaka 生産高 (quantity produced). 2. *vb.* umu 産む; motarasu もたらす (produce); kuppuku suru 屈服する (surrender).

yin and yang, *n.* in/on (to) yō 陰 (と)陽.

yoga, *n.* yoga ヨガ.

yogurt, *n.* yōguruto ヨーグルト.

yolk, *n.* kimi 黄身.

you, *pron.* 1. anata あなた; (pl.) anata-tachi あなた達, anatagata あなた方; **with you** anata to (issho ni) あな

たと(一緒に). 2. kimi 君; (pl.) kimi-tachi 君達 (familiar form used by men).

young, *adj.* wakai 若い (youthful); atarashii 新しい (new); mijuku (na) 未熟 (な) (inexperienced).

youngster, *n.* 1. wakamono 若者 (young person). 2. kodomo 子供 (child).

your, *adj.* 1. anata no あなたの; (pl.) anata-tachi no あなた達の. 2. kimi no 君の; (pl.) kimi-tachi no 君達の (familiar form used by men).

yours, *pron.* 1. anata no mono あなたの物; (pl.) anata-tachi no mono あなた達の物. 2. kimi no mono 君の物; (pl.) kimi-tachi no mono 君達の mono (familiar form used by men).

yourself, -selves, *pron.* jibun 自分; anata jishin あなた自身; (pl.) anata-tachi jishin あなた達自身.

youth, *n.* 1. wakasa 若さ (age). 2. seishunjidai 青春時代 (early life). 3. wakamono 若者 (young person).

youthful, *adj.* 1. wakawakashii 若々しい (vigorous). 2. wakai 若い (young).

Z

zebra, *n.* shimauma 縞馬.

Zen, *n.* zen 禅 (Buddhist sect).

zero, *n.* zero ゼロ; rei 零.

zinc, *n.* aen 亜鉛; totan トタン.

zip code, *n.* yūbinbangō 郵

便番号.

zipper, *n.* chakku チャック.

zone, *n.* chiku 地区 (district); chitai 地帯 (area).

zoo, *n.* dōbutsuen 動物園.

zoology, *n.* dōbutsugaku 動物学.